Missionary of Reconciliation

The Role of the Doctrine of Reconciliation in the Preaching of Bishop Festo Kivengere of Uganda between 1971–1988

Alfred Olwa

ACADEMIC

© 2013 by Alfred Olwa

Published 2013 by Langham Academic (Previously Langham Monographs)
An imprint of Langham Publishing
www.langhampublishing.org

Langham Publishing and its imprints are a ministry of Langham Partnership

Langham Partnership
PO Box 296, Carlisle, Cumbria, CA3 9WZ, UK
www.langham.org

ISBNs:
978-1-783689-93-4 Print
978-1-783689-92-7 ePub
978-1-783680-34-4 PDF

Alfred Olwa has asserted his right under the Copyright, Designs and Patents Act, 1988 to be identified as the Author of this work.

All rights reserved. No part of this publication may be reproduced, stored in a retrieval system or transmitted, in any form or by any means, electronic, mechanical, photocopying, recording or otherwise, without the prior written permission of the publisher or the Copyright Licensing Agency.

Scriptures taken from the Holy Bible, New International Version®, NIV®. Copyright © 1973, 1978, 1984, 2011 by Biblica, Inc.™

British Library Cataloguing in Publication Data
Olwa, Alfred, author.
  Missionary of reconciliation : the role of the doctrine of
  reconciliation in the preaching of Bishop Festo Kivengere
  of Uganda between 1971-1988.
  1. Kivengere, Festo--Sermons. 2. Reconciliation--
  Religious aspects--Christianity--Sermons. 3. Anglican
  Communion--Uganda--Doctrines--History--20th century.
  I. Title
  234.5-dc23

ISBN-13: 9781783689934

Cover & Book Design: projectluz.com

Langham Partnership actively supports theological dialogue and a scholars right to publish but does not necessarily endorse the views and opinions set forth, and works referenced within this publication or guarantee its technical and grammatical correctness. Langham Partnership does not accept any responsibility or liability to persons or property as a consequence of the reading, use or interpretation of its published content.

To our children, Mercy, Mark, and Hope, who, share my life in the role of being 'ambassador for Christ' (2 Corinthians 5:20); and most of all to my beloved wife, Susan, who is my best friend and partner in proclaiming 'the message of reconciliation' (2 Corinthians 5:19).

Contents

Acknowledgements xiii

Note on the Catalogue of Kivengere's Sermons xv

Abbreviations xvii

Maps xxi

Abstract xxiii

Chapter One 1
   Orientation to this Study
   1.1 Thesis 1
   1.2 Reconciliation and Kivengere's Sermons 2
      1.2.1 Deep Wounds Created by Ethnic Conflicts 5
      1.2.2 Brain Drain out of Uganda 10
      1.2.3 Campaign for Ugandan Refugees and Coffee Farmers 11
      1.2.4 A Second Wave of Christian Persecution 15
      1.2.5 International Community Watches Uganda 16
      1.2.6 A Christ-centred Leadership 20
   1.3 The Need For This Study 21
      1.3.1 The Unstudied Kivengere: Preacher of Reconciliation 21
      1.3.2 Sermons at the Periphery 23
      1.3.3 Some Sermons in Focus 24
   1.4 The Present Study 29
      1.4.1 The Collection 30
      1.4.2 Rationale for the Selection 32
      1.4.3 The Shape of the Study 33
      1.4.4 Research Methodology 34
      1.4.5 The Influence of Kivengere's Reconciliation Preaching 36

Chapter Two 39
   Historical and Biographical Context of Kivengere's Preaching
   2.1 A Synopsis 39
   2.2 Historical Context (I): Uganda the Nation 39
      2.2.1 From 1894–1962: The Origin of Divisions and Tensions 40
      2.2.2 From 1962–1988: Deep Wounds Created in the Country 42
   2.3 Historical Context (II): Ugandan Christianity 44
      2.3.1 Missionary Origins 44

  2.3.2 Mwanga's Martyrdoms 48
  2.3.3 Religious Wars in Buganda 52
  2.3.4 Baganda Evangelists Spread the Gospel 54
 2.4 The East African Revival Movement 57
  2.4.1 Spread in Uganda 58
  2.4.2 The Church of Uganda: The 'Sick' Spiritual State 58
  2.4.3 The Search for Renewal and Holiness 60
  2.4.4 Uganda Synod: The Call to Zukuka 'Awake!' 62
  2.4.5 The Mukono Crisis 66
 2.5 Kivengere the Revival Preacher: A Homiletical Biographical
 Sketch 68
  2.5.1 Family Background 69
  2.5.2 Kivengere's Conversion: From Agnostic to Preacher 73
  2.5.3 Kivengere's Teacher Education 78
  2.5.4 Pittsburgh Seminary: From 1964–1967 80
 2.6 Summary of Chapter Two 86

Chapter Three 87
Potential Influences on Kivengere's Preaching
 3.1 A Trajectory of Influences: Synopsis 87
 3.2 The Keswick Movement and the East African Revival:
 The Approach and Context of Preaching 88
  3.2.1 Early Keswick Convention (1875–1920) 88
  3.2.2 Modern Keswick Convention (1950s–) 101
 3.3 Karl Barth's Influence: 'Theological Exegesis' and Reconciliation ... 104
  3.3.1 Kivengere's Reference to the Influence of Karl Barth 104
  3.3.2 Karl Barth's 'Theological Exegesis' 106
  3.3.3 Barth's Hermeneutics 109
  3.3.4 Barth: the Sache—The Subject-matter, God 111
 3.4 Markus Barth's Link to Kivengere 124
 3.5 Reconciliation in the New Testament 128
  3.5.1 Paul's Experience of Reconciliation 132
  3.5.2 2 Corinthian 5:11–20 133
  3.5.3 Romans 5:1–11 137
  3.5.4 Ephesians 2:14–18 141
  3.5.5 Colossians 1:19–22 144
 3.6 Summary of Chapter Three 147

Chapter Four 149
Kivengere's Preaching Reconciliation: A Reconciliation Time-Line
 4.1 A Synopsis 149

4.2 Before Exile (September 1971–February 1977) 150
4.3 The Exile (February 1977– May 1979) 161
4.4 After the Exile (May 1979 to May 1988) 166
4.5 Summary of Reconciliation Time-line 184

Chapter Five 185
Explicit Reconciliation Passages
    5.1 A Synopsis 185
    5.2 Kivengere's Framework for Explaining Reconciliation 186
    5.3 Reconciliation According to Kivengere 187
    5.4 Explicit Reconciliation Sermons (I): 2 Corinthians 5:18–20
        in Context 189
        5.4.1 'Ambassadors For Christ': AO: 19771016 189
        5.4.2 In Christ: AO: 19790429, [#2] 197
        5.4.3 The Cross Today and Divine Outreach:
            AO: 19800404 205
        5.4.4 'The Reconciling Love of Christ':
            AO: 198110[--], [#1] 212
        5.4.5 'Jesus Came as a Missionary of Reconciliation':
            AO: 19820221 220
        5.4.6 'Reconciliation': AO: 198204[--], [#1] 225
        5.4.7 Conclusions on the First Set of Six Sermons 229
    5.5 Explicit Reconciliation Sermons (II): Romans 5:1–11
        in Context 231
        5.5.1 Surprised by Joy: AO: 197109[--] 231
        5.5.2 God's Intervening Love: AO: 19750729, [#1] 241
        5.5.3 'The Love of Christ' AO: [197707--] 248
        5.5.4 'Life in Jesus': AO: 1978 [02--?], [#1] 257
        5.5.5 Conclusion 260
    5.6 Explicit Reconciliation Sermons (III): Ephesians 2:14–18
        in Context 261
        5.6.1 His Flooding Love: AO: 19750729, [#2] 261
        5.6.2 'Broken Relationships Restored': AO: 1977[0314?] 267
        5.6.3 The Whole Gospel for the Whole Church:
            AO: 197805[--], [#2] 279
        5.6.4 'No More Distance in the Love of Christ':
            AO: 19801014, [#1] 284
    5.7 Explicit Reconciliation Sermons (IV): Colossians 1:19–22
        in Context 289
        5.7.1 Christ Puts All Things Together: AO: 1972[----] 289

  5.7.2 The Unshakable Identity of the Church of Jesus Christ:
    AO: 19771029, [#1] 296
  5.7.3 'Christ has Reconciled the Universe to Himself':
    AO: [estimated after May 1979], [#2] 302
 5.8 Conclusion of Chapter Five 306

Chapter Six 313
 Non-Explicit Reconciliation Passages
 6.1 A Synopsis 313
 6.2 Four Sermons on Non-Explicit Passages...................................314
  6.2.1 The Cross: AO: 19740725 314
  6.2.2 The Triumph of God's Glory: AO: 19761231 328
  6.2.3 'A New Way of Seeing Jesus': AO: 19821012, [#1] 339
  6.2.4 The Pastor's Joy: AO: 19770120 347
 6.3 Four Thematic Addresses...353
  6.3.1 Revival Begins at the Cross 353
  6.3.2 Remove the Masks...357
  6.3.3 Peace and Victory for the Christian..................................361
  6.3.4 The Covenant of Love...363
 6.4 Kivengere's Theological Reflection...365
  6.4.1 The Evangelist's Ministry of Reconciliation:
    We Are Christ's Ambassadors: AO: 19830715.......................365
 6.5 Conclusion on Non-Explicit Reconciliation Passages 378

Chapter Seven 383
 Analysis and Conclusions—The Role of the Doctrine of Reconciliation
 in Kivengere's Preaching
 7.1 Collection of Kivengere's Sermons 383
 7.2 Evaluation of Method 384
 7.3 Towards Kivengere's Homiletics 385
  7.3.1 Content Determines Style..385
  7.3.2 Kivengere the Preacher of Reconciliation 386
  7.3.3 Kivengere the Preacher of Revival 388
 7.4 Five Angles of Influences..389
  7.4.1 Early English Keswick Influence 389
  7.4.2 Revival Influence 392
  7.4.3 Influences from Karl Barth 394
  7.4.4 Influences from Markus Barth 398
  7.4.5 Influences from Pauline Theology.....................................398
 7.5 Towards Kivengere's Doctrine of Reconciliation 400
 7.6 Impact of Kivengere's Preaching...402

  7.6.1 Influence Through his Publications and Recognitions
    of his Leadership 402
  7.6.2 A Forerunner of the South African Truth and
    Reconciliation Commission 403
  7.6.3 Influence on World Leaders 403
  7.6.4 Influence on Evangelical leaders and Preachers..................404
  7.6.5 Hope for Uganda and the World 405
7.7 Summary 407
7.8 Further Research 408
7.9 Conclusion 409

Bibliography.. 411
  1. Primary Sources 411
    1.1 Works by Festo Kivengere 411
    1.2 Other Primary Sources...418
  2. Secondary Sources..420
    2.1 Books and Articles About Festo Kivengere 420
    2.2 Theses About Festo Kivengere 421
    2.3 Other Secondary Sources 421

Appendix 1... 465
 Illustrations

Appendix 2... 467
 Letters

Appendix 3... 485
 Kivengere's Sermons Analyzed By Previous Scholars

Appendix 4... 491
 Some of Kivengere's Sermons Preached in Tandem with Cassidy

Appendix 5... 493
 Catalogue of Kivengere's Sermons

Acknowledgements

This book is a revision of my PhD thesis, which was accepted by the University of Western Sydney/Moore College, Sydney in 2012. I would like to express my gratitude to many who assisted me in various ways during the writing of my thesis: my University of Western supervisors, Dr. Christopher J Fleming, Associate Professor Judith M Snodgrass; Dr. Peter G Bolt, my Moore College supervisor—a model supervisor and scholar, Dr. Colin R Bale, my other Moore College supervisor; the Moore College Faculty, Dr. Constantine Campbell, Dr. George Athas, Dr. Bill Salier, Dr. Brian Rosner and Dr. Mark Thompson for feedback on parts of my argument, during both the writing of the thesis and the preparation of this book.

Many thanks go to the participants of the Moore College Advanced Research Seminar, Biblical Studies Seminar and the University of Western Sydney Postgraduate Seminars. Comments made by my two examiners, Dr. Colin Reed and Dr. Peter Davis, President of the Australasian Academy of Homeletics, and Lecturer in Homiletics, have been greatly appreciated. Last but by no means least special thanks must go to Charity Kivengere (one of the four daughters of Kivengere, living in Uganda) who introduced me to Keith Jession (long time ministry co-worker of Bishop Festo Kivengere, living in the United States of America) who gave me key primary materials that enabled me to write this book. Special thanks are due to Julie and Alan Hohne, Joan and Peter Tasker, and Valery and Peter Johns whose invaluable support has been beyond their interest.

I am indebted to the Moore College Library Staff, University of Sydney Fisher Library, Library of New South Wales Staff, and the National Library of Australia (Canberra), and friends in Uganda for their support that enabled me to access the materials I needed. I am immeasurably indebted to James Brennan who graciously inducted me to the use of Zotero Software that I used for all my Bibliography and footnotes in this thesis. Finally, I am thankful for the financial assistance of the Sydney Diocese, Langham UK and Ireland, Langham Australia, Australia—Federal CMS, Moore College, Uganda Christian University, and friends from Anglican Churches in Sydney Diocese (Panania Anglican, Christ Church Gladesville, and the Moore College Community).

Note on the Catalogue of Kivengere's Sermons

Since no catalogue of Kivengere's sermons is yet in existence one was developed as part of the preparation for my thesis. Because it is my own catalogue, each sermon is identified firstly by my initials: AO. This is then followed by the date the sermon was preached, as recorded on the transcript (year, month and day). Thus a sermon preached on the 29th January 1964 is assigned the catalogue number AO:19640129. If the sermon was preached in multiple services, an additional number indicates the repetition (#1—first time preached, #2—second time preached, etc.). Thus the full title: AO:19640129, #1. If the year is known but the month or day is unknown, we use square brackets with dashes to indicate the missing data (for example, AO:196401[--]; AO:1964[--]29; AO:1964[----]). If two sermons still have duplicate codes (e.g. multiple sermons on the same day, but the order in which they were preached is not known), we add an asterisk and an ascending sequence number to ensure each sermon has a unique identifying code.

Sermons with their title in **bold** are mentioned in the body of this book.

Abbreviations

AACC	All Africa Conference of Churches
AC	*African Communist*
AE	African Enterprise
AEE	African Evangelistic Enterprise
AFS	*Armed Forces and Society*
AIBEPM	*Africa: An International Business, Economic, and Political Monthly*
AQ	*Africa Quarterly*
ASR	*African Studies Review*
AT	*Africa Today*
ATR	*Anglican Theological Review*
AU	African Union
AV	*African Voice*
BAGD	Bauer, Danker, Arndt and Gingrich, *A Greek-English Lexicon of the New Testament and Other Early Christian Literature*. 3rd edition.
BBR	*Bulletin for Biblical Research*
Bib. Sac.	*Bibliotheca Sacra*
CBQ	*Catholic Biblical Quarterly*
CD	*Church Dogmatics*
cf.	*confer*, compare
Cf.	Compare with
CICCU	Cambridge Inter Collegiate Christian Union
CMS	Church Missionary Society

COU	Church of Uganda
CSDG	Conflict, Security and development Group
CT	*Christianity Today*
CT	*Christianity Today*
CTM	*Concordia Theological Monthly*
CV	*Communio Viatorum*
DP	Democratic Party
e.g.	*exampli gratia*, for example
ed(s).	edition, edited by, editor(s)
EJT	*European Journal of Theology*
ER	*Ecumenical review*
ERT	*Evangelical Review of Theology*
ET	*Expository Times*
f.	following verse
ff.	following verses
FJHP	*Flinders Journal of History*
FM	*Faith and Mission*
GCGB	*Global Church Growth Bulletin*
HBT	*Horizons in Biblical Theology*
IBEAC	Imperial British East Africa Company
IBMR	*International Bulletin of Missionary Research*
IBS	*Irish Biblical Studies*
IJWP	*International Journal of World Peace*
JAS	*Journal of African Studies*
JC	*Journal Champion*
JCPS	*Journal of Commonwealth Political Studies*
JCPS	*Journal of Commonwealth Political Studies*
JCS	*Journal of Church and State*
JETS	*Journal of the Evangelical Theological Society*
JIA	*Journal of International Affairs*
JILE	*Journal of International Law and Economics*
JIMMA	*Journal of the Institute of Muslim Minority Affairs*

JMAS	*Journal of Modern African Studies*
JMAS	*Journal of Modern African Studies*
JRA	*Journal of Religion in Africa*
JSNT	*Journal for the Study of the New Testament*
JSOT	*Journal for the Study of the Old Testament*
JSRI	*Journal for the Study of Religion and Ideologies*
JTS	*Journal of Theological Studies*
JTSA	*Journal of Theology for South Africa*
KW	The Keswick Week
LSI	*Law and Social Inquiry*
MJIS	*Millennium: Journal of International Studies*
MS	*Mission Studies*
MT	*Modern Theology*
n.d	no date
NA	*New African*
NAC	Native Anglican Church
NIR	National Initiative for Reconciliation
NKJV	New King James Version
NovT	*Novum Testamentum*
NRA	National Resistance Movement
OAU	Organization of African Union
PACLA	Pan African Christian Leaders Assembly
PEGLMBS	*Proceedings, Eastern Great Lakes and Midwest Biblical studies*
PS	*Political Studies*
PTA	Parents and Teacher's Association
RAPE	*Review of African Political Economy*
RAPS	*Review of African Political Studies*
REE	*Religion in Eastern Europe*
RETURN	Relief, Education for Uganda Refugees Now
Rev. Exp.	*Review & Expositor*
RTCWJIA	*Round Table: Commonwealth Journal of International Affairs*

RTR	*Reformed Theological Review*
SAJAA	*South African Journal of African Affairs*
SB	*Studia Biblica*
SJDA	*Scandinavian Journal of Development Alternative*
SJR	*Social Justice Research*
SLJT	*Saint Luke's Journal of Theology*
TESM	Trinity Episcopal School of Ministry
TPDF	Tanzania People's Defence Forces
TWQ	*Third World Quarterly*
UJCC	Uganda Joint Christian Council
ULF	*Uganda Law Focus*
UNLA	Uganda National Liberation Army
UNLF	Uganda National Liberation Front
UPC	Uganda People's Congress
vol.	Volume
WAJSPS	*West African Journal of Sociology and Political Science*
WCC	World Council of Churches
WNANT	*Wissenschaftliche Monographien zum AT & NT*
WT	*World Today*
WTJ	*Westminster Theological Journal*

Bible Quotations are taken from *The Holy Bible: New International Version* (Hodder and Stoughton: London, 1978), unless otherwise noted.

Maps

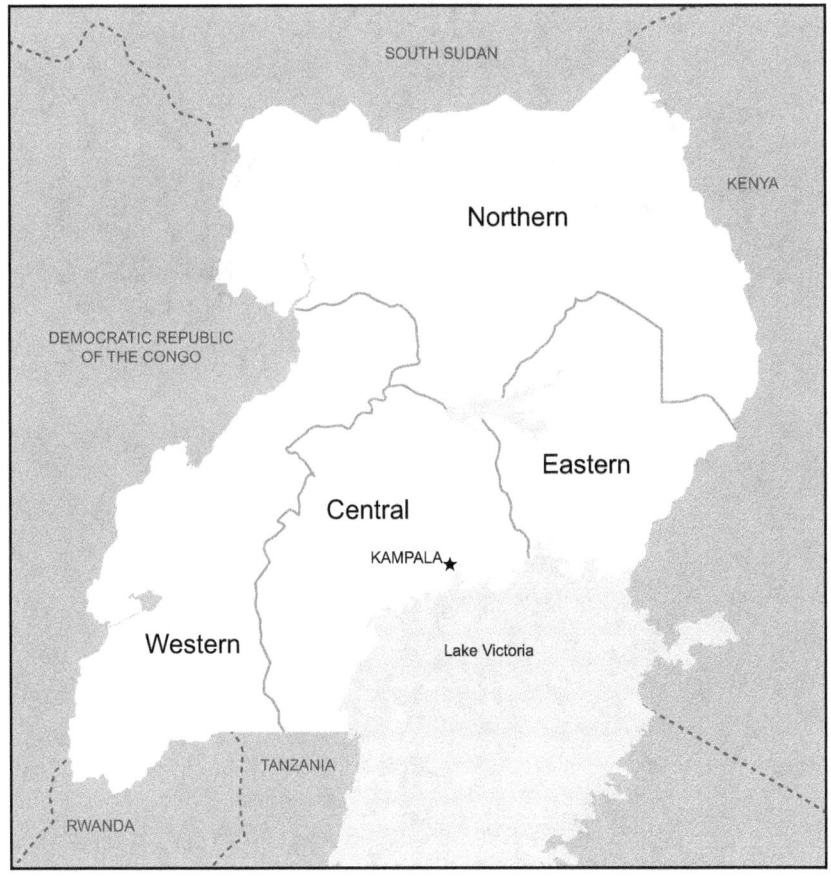

1. Map of Uganda

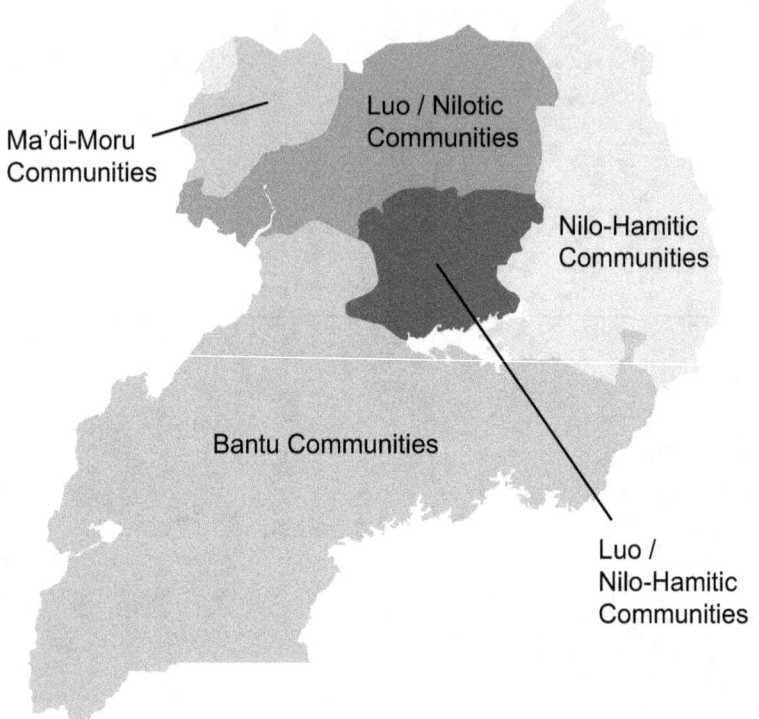

2. Ethnographic Map of Uganda

Abstract

This book attempts to understand the role of the doctrine of reconciliation in the preaching of Bishop Festo Kivengere (c. 1919–1988) of Uganda between the years 1971–1988, a most significant period in the recent history of Uganda.

It focuses upon an examination of a selection of twenty-six sermons including (1) all extant Kivengere sermons (17) preached from the Pauline passages explicitly mentioning reconciliation (2 Cor 5:18–20, Rom 5:9–11, Eph 2:16–18, Col 1:20–22), and (2) eight sermons touching upon the theme of reconciliation consisting of (i) four sermons from non-explicit reconciliation passages (Rom 1:16, John 17:22, Rev 3:1–21, John 20:19–20), and (ii) four thematic addresses: *Revival Begins at the Cross, Remove the Masks, Peace and Victory for the Christian,* and *the Covenant of Love.* The understanding of reconciliation that is derived from this sermonic material is then supplemented with that derived from (3) a theological reflection on this doctrine from Kivengere's own pen. Other writings will also be utilized where relevant.

The sermons are analyzed from a biblical-theological perspective. Attention is paid to issues of context and composition of the audience of the original biblical texts and the contemporary audiences of Kivengere's preaching. However, the book will focus particularly on the biblical-theological language and connections revealed in these sermons. Analyzed from a biblical-theological perspective, the book will argue, firstly, that for Kivengere reconciliation is 'the centre' of the Christian gospel. Secondly, that the sermons exhorted the different audiences to be reconciled with God and then to be reconciled with their fellow human beings as part of God's remedy for a broken world.

As well as analyzing the sermons from a biblical-theological perspective, the book attempts to appreciate the potential impact of Kivengere's preaching of reconciliation on his audiences, both from Uganda and further afield. In order to do so it pays attention to the relevant aspects of the influences over him by (1) the teaching and preaching of the English Keswick Movement, (2) the East African Revival Movement, (3) Karl Barth's 'Theological Exegesis' and doctrine of reconciliation, (4) his New Testament teacher, the son of Karl Barth, Markus Barth, and (5) the Pauline theology of reconciliation itself. These influences inform his thought and theology, in particular, the biblical theology of reconciliation that he preached. Appreciating the sermons from this perspective therefore shows that Kivengere, a child of the Revival and an African who preached the good news of reconciliation during turbulent times from the late 1950s to 1988, drew from these five sources to explain the reconciling work of Jesus Christ as the only antidote to the problems of the world.

Depicting Jesus as a missionary of reconciliation, the sermons present him as bringing a fresh and alternative life, characterized by the reconciling love and peace from God, into Uganda, where Christians (and some Muslims) lived under torture, murder, and persecution from Amin and his hit men. The same is true of Jesus' coming into the situation further afield (South Africa, Ethiopia, Burundi, Rhodesia, Vietnam, America, Northern Ireland, Israel, Australia) where there are also brokenness, misery and deep wounds. The reconciliation Jesus brings into the human situation therefore provides the only hope for the world.

Because of this hope, Kivengere's preaching of reconciliation had great potential to mobilize and rally the nation of Uganda, for healing deep wounds incurred by Amin's rule, reconstruction and rehabilitation. The book analyzes the sermons especially noting Kivengere's grasp of God's grand purpose for the world from creation to new creation, centring on the reconciling work of Jesus Christ. The book also attempts to unfold the potential impact of Kivengere's message about reconciliation. According to Kivengere the world changes because of preaching the Christian doctrine of reconciliation. It is the vehicle by which Jesus brings reconciliation.

I trust that this small offering towards a greater understanding of Kivengere's message might help others better appreciate a fuller extent of the content and impact of Kivengere's message of reconciliation.

CHAPTER ONE

Orientation to this Study

1.1 Thesis

This thesis argues that the Christian doctrine of reconciliation was central to Festo Kivengere's preaching. It examines twenty-six sermons preached by Kivengere between 1971–1988 to arrive at a clearer picture of the place and function of the Christian doctrine of reconciliation in his preaching.[1] The sermons show that this doctrine so gripped Kivengere that it shaped his attitude to life, to others, and even to his enemies, and that he exhorted his audiences to be reconciled with God and then with their fellow human beings, as part of God's remedy for a broken world.

The sermons are of two kinds: (1) those preached from the New Testament texts which explicitly refer to reconciliation: 2 Cor 5:11–20; Rom 5:1–11; Eph 2:12–22; Col 1:19–22;[2] and (2) those preached from biblical texts that do not explicitly mention reconciliation, but in which Kivengere nevertheless draws out teaching on reconciliation.[3] The second group comprise: (i) four sermons from non-explicit reconciliation passages (Rom 1:16, John 17:22, Rev 3:1–21, John 20:19–20); (ii) four thematic addresses that are not based upon a specific text: *Revival Begins at the Cross*,

---

1. For a fuller introduction to Bishop Festo Kivengere, see Chapter Two, 5. 'Kivengere the Revival Preacher'. The names 'Festo' and 'Kivengere' will be used interchangeably. For the most part we will use 'Kivengere', while 'Festo' will be in citations from other authors, including Kivengere himself.
2. See Chapter Five, 'Explicit Reconciliation Passages'.
3. See Chapter Six, 'Non-Explicit Reconciliation passages'.

Remove the Masks, Peace and Victory for the Christian, and the *Covenant of Love*. The understanding of reconciliation that is derived from this sermonic material is supplemented with an examination of (3) a theological reflection on this doctrine from Kivengere's own pen. The analysis of the sermons is from a stance that seeks to be alert to the concerns of Biblical Theology,[4] such as the issue of the 'centre' of Biblical teaching. On this question, Kivengere is clear. To use his own words, 'reconciliation is the centre of the Christian gospel';[5] and elsewhere he writes: 'Reconciliation is the central message of the New Testament'.[6] In his preaching, Kivengere depicts Jesus as a missionary of reconciliation who brings a fresh and alternative life, characterized by the reconciling love and peace from God. The study attempts to appreciate the potential impact and influence of this message in Uganda and further afield. He preached it into a Uganda where Christians lived under the horrors of Amin's rule and its aftermath. But Kivengere also preached it in other parts of the world, where people also lived in brokenness and misery, and with deep wounds. According to Kivengere, the world changes through the preaching of the reconciliation centred in Jesus Christ.

Having stated the thesis, we will now discuss the reason for choosing the period 1971–1988.

1.2 Reconciliation and Kivengere's Sermons

Bishop Festo Kivengere of Uganda (1919–1988) is described variously as 'the most widely known and influential African evangelical leader of the twentieth century',[7] 'the greatest evangelist to come out of [black] Africa

---

4. See below section 4.4.4 'Elements of Biblical Theology'.
5. Festo Kivengere, 'Ambassadors For Christ in a Miserable World', Sermon Transcript, October 16, 1977, p. 3, #5, AO:19771016.
6. Festo Kivengere, *Hope for Uganda and the World: The Secret of Rehabilitation* (ed. Dorothy Smoker; Nairobi: African Evangelistic Enterprise, 1980), 29.
7. P. Prigodich Raymond, 'A Review of Festo Kivengere: A Biography', *Missiology: An International Review* XXII/2 (April 1994).

in the twentieth century',[8] 'the Billy Graham of Africa',[9] 'Africa's Apostle of Love',[10] 'the man who would not hate',[11] 'a true apostle of reconciliation',[12] and 'a great man of reconciliation'.[13] He became a minister of reconciliation[14] who preached the good news of reconciliation to a broken world and especially to his own country of Uganda in the period 1971–1988.

Before discussing the reasons for selecting the period 1971–1988, it is helpful to state the reason why we chose 1971 as the start of the period of our inquiry and 1988 as its end. *First*, in 1971 his vision and message of reconciliation was still fresh in Kivengere's heart, because the previous year (1970), together with Michael Cassidy, they toured the United States of America preaching with the theme: 'God has reconciled us to himself and given us a ministry of reconciliation' (2 Cor 5:18).[15]

---

8. Richard H Schmidt, *Glorious Companions: Five Centuries of Anglican Spirituality* (Grand Rapids, Mich.: W.B. Eerdmans, 2002), 314.

9. Hughes Oliphant Old, *The Reading and Preaching of the Scriptures in the Worship of the Christian Church* (vol. 7; Grand Rapids, Mich.: W.B. Eerdmans, 2010), 200. Many people refer to Kivengere being the 'Billy Graham of Africa', but I have been unable to discover who first said this. For example, Marcus Loane writes: 'He was the real Billy Graham of black Africa'. See Marcus Loane, 'Memoirs', Unpublished Manuscript (Sydney, Australia), 104, Library of Moore Theological College.

10. Dave Jackson and Neta Jackson, *Heroes in Black History: True Stories from the Lives of Christian Heroes* (Reprinted.; Minneapolis: Bethany House, 2008), 149.

11. Jill Briscoe, *The Man Who Would Not Hate: Festo Kivengere* (Dallas, Texas: Word Publishing, 1991).

12. Episcopal Church, 'African Evangelist Dies in Nairobi', Press Release, Episcopal News Service, May 26, 1988, Cited 30 Jan 2012, Online: http://www.episcopalarchives.org/cgi-bin/ENS/ENSpress_release.pl?pr_number=88115.

13. Antoine Rutayisire, 'Forgiveness and Reconciliation', Unpublished Paper, delivered at the Bishop Festo Kivengere Memorial Lecture (Kampala, Uganda, 2001), 1; Andrew Watson, *Confidence in the Living God: David and Goliath Revisited* (Abingdon: The Bible Reading Fellowship, 2009), 9.

14. Mark Shaw, *Global Awakening: How 20th-Century Revivals Triggered a Christian Revolution* (Downers Grove, Ill.: IVP Academic, 2010), 107; John R. W Stott, *People My Teachers* (London: Candle Books, 2002), 53; Frederick Quinn, 'Kivengere, Festo', in *African Saints: Saints, Martyrs, and Holy People from the Continent of Africa* (New York: Crossroads Publishing, 2002), Cited 15 Mar 2012, Online: http://www.dacb.org/stories/uganda/kivengere_festo.html; Jay Russell, 'A Ministry of Reconciliation: Festo Kivengere: 1920-1988', in *Ambassadors for Christ* (ed. John D Woodbridge; Chicago, Ill.: Moody Press, 1994), 304–07.

15. Festo Kivengere, '25 Years of Ministry: 1962–1987', *Africa Enterprise (Special Centre Opening Edition)* (September 1987): 2.

Second, with the message of reconciliation still fresh in his heart, in 1971 Kivengere formed his African Evangelistic Enterprise (AEE) with the aim of preaching the biblical message of reconciliation to African cities and universities.[16] From that year onwards, his sermons became more accessible—because AEE kept them. Previous sermons are rarely available, such as a 1961 sermon he preached on 'Personal Revival', which only became available online in 2010.[17] The selection of 1971 is warranted, therefore, because after that date more sermons are available to be examined for the theme of reconciliation.

Third, from 1971 his mature Christian leadership emerged. For instance, in September 1971 Archbishop Erica Sabiti asked him to preach to bitter and divided delegates of the Anglican church to bring his audience to repent, forgive each other and realize healing and unity.[18] His Christian leadership emerged as he had come into contact with Amin's murderous rule in 1971, and his sermons begin to make constant reference to Amin's rule, which started that year. The reason to chose the period with 1988 is simple, for in May 1988 Kivengere died from malignant leukaemia, marking the end of his preaching of reconciliation.[19]

The years 1971 to 1988 can be described in terms of six main features. It was a period that experienced increasing ethnic divisions. It was a period when Uganda experienced a serious brain drain. This period saw Kivengere campaign relentlessly to the international community, especially to Christian churches, to help educate Ugandans in exile and give them a living, and against the exploitation of Ugandan coffee farmers by Amin's soldiers, asking the Washington administration to place a coffee trade embargo on Uganda. In this period Amin persecuted Christians in Uganda culminating in the murder of Archbishop Janani Luwum. During this period the international community monitored closely the events happening

---

16. Charlotte Inkelaar-de Mos, 'African Evangelistic Enterprise: Its History, Organization, Context, Message and Activities' (Unpublished PhD thesis, Netherlands: Utrecht University, 1988), 29–30.
17. Old, *Reading and Preaching*, 200–203.
18. Festo Kivengere, 'Surprised by Joy', Sermon Transcript, September 1971, AO: 197109[--].
19. M. Louise Pirouet, *Historical Dictionary of Uganda* (African Historical Dictionaries; Metuchen, N.J.: Scarecrow Press, 1995), 208.

in Uganda. Most importantly, it was a period when Kivengere offered a visionary, spiritual, and selfless leadership, himself being committed to the preaching of reconciliation to bring healing and hope to Ugandans and to others.

Taken together, these six features of the period 1971–1988 constitute the context of Kivengere's preaching of reconciliation and because the features show the level of brokenness, deep wounds, misery, hopelessness, and dire need for peace in Uganda, the features have a direct link with his sermons.

1.2.1 Deep Wounds Created by Ethnic Conflicts

1971–1988 was one of the most significant periods in Ugandan history. It is a period characterized by religious, social, and political changes that have shaped and defined a range of issues in the present-day nation.[20] At the centre of these changes was the ascendancy of President Idi Amin to power through a military coup,[21] which 'at first seem[ed] bloodless',[22]

---

20. See the excellent articles dealing with significant events and changes in Uganda from colonial times, especially the period under our inquiry compiled in Holger Bernt Hansen and Michael Twaddle, *Changing Uganda: Dilemmas Of Structural Adjustment* (1st ed.; Kampala: Fountain Publishers, 1991); and, Holger Bernt Hansen and Michael Twaddle, *Developing Uganda* (1st ed.; Kampala: Fountain Publishers, 1998). For major political changes in Uganda, see Phares Mutibwa, *Uganda Since Independence: A Story of Unfulfilled Hopes* (First Ugandan Edition.; Kampala: Fountain Publishers, 1991). For a recent (2008) in-depth analysis of the turbulent political story of Uganda, see F. Golooba-Mutebi, 'Collapse, War and Reconstruction in Uganda: An Analytical Narrative on State-Making', *Crisis Studies Research Centre Working Paper* 2/27 (2008): 1–27.
21. Ali Al'Amin Mazrui, 'The Lumpen Proletariat and the Lumpen Militariat: African Soldiers as a New Political Class', *Political Studies* 21/1 (1973): 1–12; James H. Mittelman, 'The Anatomy of a Coup: Uganda, 1971', *AQ* 11/3 (1971): 184–202; Henry Maya, 'The Imperialist Threat to Africa, 1: Uganda', *African Communist*/45 (1971): 37–44; Samuel Decalo, 'Military Coups and Military Regimes in Africa', *JMAS* 11/1: 105–207; Michael Lofchie, 'The Political Origins of the Uganda Coup', *JAS* 1/4 (Winter 1974): 464–96; Michael Lofchie, 'The Uganda Coup - Class Action by the Military', *JMAS* 10/1 (May 1972): 19–35(an bridged form appears in Amos Perlmutter and Valerie Plave Bennett, *The Political Influence of the Military: A Comparative Reader* (New Haven, Connecticut: Yale University Press, 1980), 337–84); John D. Chick, 'Class Conflict and Military Intervention in Uganda', *JMAS* 10/4 (December 1, 1972): 637–37; Amadu Sesay, 'The OAU and Regime Recognition: Politics of Discord and Collaboration in Africa', *Scandinavian Journal of Development Alternatives* 4/1 (March 1985): 25–41; Michael Twaddle, 'The Amin Coup', *JCPS* 10/2 (July 1972): 99–112. For a defence of Britain— that it did not assist Amin in his military coup, see Frederick John Ravenhill, 'Military Intervention in the Domestic Political Systems of Black Africa: The Case of Uganda' (Masters Thesis, Halifax, Nova Scotia, Canada: Dalhousie University, 1973).
22. Mittelman, 'Anatomy of a Coup', 184–202.

but soon became a bloody regime (1971–1979)[23] leading to 'a decaying Uganda'.[24]

Amin was a staunch Muslim from the remote Nilotic Kakwa tribe, found along the border of New Sudan and northern Uganda.[25] His ascendency to power in Uganda epitomises the ethnic conflict that has shaped and defined Uganda's long-standing problems, going as far back to the 1890s when Western colonial masters bundled together Uganda with no regard for ethnic boundaries.[26] The ethnic conflicts of the Amin years form a significant background to Kivengere's preaching of reconciliation.

Ethnic conflicts within the military were a significant factor in Amin's military coup of 25 January 1971.[27] Studies point to such things as the

---

23. William P. Wood, 'A Murder in Uganda', *America* 136/10 (March 12, 1977): 216–19; William P. Wood, 'The Bishop and Idi Amin', *America* 136/2 (January 15, 1977): 26–28; William P. Wood, 'The Trial of Idi Amin: It Is a Great Enigma That Something as Universally Abhorrent as Mass Murder Is Not Universally a Crime', *Christian Century* 97/18 (My 1980): 549–52; Arthur H. Matthews, 'Terror and death in Uganda', *CT* 21/12 (1977): 49–51; Margaret Ford, *Janani: The Making of Martyr* (London: Marshall, Morgan and Scott, 1978); Dan Wooding and Ray Barnett, *Uganda Holocaust* (Grand Rapids, Mich.: Zondervan, 1980). For the bloody atrocities of Amin, see U.S. Congress, 'Public Law 95-435', *United States Statues at Large* 92/1 (95th Congress, 2nd Session 1978): 1051–53.

24. The expression, 'Decaying Uganda', became a popular description of the appalling state of Uganda after Idi Amin's rule, following Ali Al'Amin Mazrui, 'Is Africa Decaying? The View from Uganda', in *Uganda Now: Between Decay & Development* (ed. Holger Bernt Hansen and Michael Twaddle; 1st ed.; London: James Curry, 1988), 261-78; Cf. Ali Al'Amin Mazrui, 'Between Development and Decay: Anarchy, Tyranny and Progress under Idi Amin', *Third World Quarterly* 2/1 (January 1980): 44–58.

25. For discussion on the ethnic origin of Amin, see Ade Adefuye, 'The Kakwa of Uganda and the Sudan: The Ethnic factor in National and International Politics', in *Partitioned Africans: Ethnic Relations across Africa's International Boundaries, 1884-1984* (ed. A. I. Asiwaju; London: C. Hurst and co., 1985), 51–69. Omari H. Kokole, 'The "Nubians" of East Africa: Muslim Club or African "Tribe"? The View From Within', *Journal of the Institute of Muslim Minority Affairs* 6/2 (July 1985): 420–48.

26. For an insightful analysis of the problem of ethnic conflict in the military and how it affects society, see Holger Bernt Hansen, *Ethnicity and Military Rule in Uganda: A Study of Ethnicity as a Political Factor in Uganda, Based on a Discussion of Political Anthropology and the Application of Its Results* (Research report (Nordiska Afrikainstitutet); no. 43., Uppsala: Scandinavian Inst. of African Studies, 1977).

27. Michel L. Martin, 'The Uganda Military Coup of 1971: A Study of Protest', *Ufahamu* 2/3 (Winter 1972): 80–121. Norman N. Millar, 'Military Coup in Uganda: The Rise of the Second Republic', *Fieldstaff Reports: East Africa Series* 10/3 (1971): 1–18. Paul Nursey-Bray, 'Uganda: The Resistible Rise of Idi Amin?', *Flinders Journal of History and Politics* 4 (1974): 95–116. Mazrui, 'Lumpen Proletariat', 1–12. Besides the problem of ethnicity, Edward Muhima speculates other reasons why Amin overthrew Obote's government. His

'northernisation' in the army, the discontent within the military, and the ideological threat within the army by Obote's 'Move to the Left' campaign, the dismantling of Obote's socialist programme in favour of new ties with the capitalist west, and tribal class conflict.[28]

This period also saw Amin's swift expulsion of 30-50,000 Ugandan Asians (August 1972),[29] which the international community watched with horror. They left with little more than the clothes they were wearing. Their shops, factories, and businesses were plundered and seized by Amin's soldiers, who were predominantly from the same northern tribe as Amin. Not only did the Ugandan Asians suffer under discrimination and abuse of human rights, they also bore the pain of becoming refugees after enjoying the status of citizens.[30] Because Asians dominated the Ugandan economy,

---

reasons include, fears of Obote's plan to implement 'Ugandan Socialism' which Obote had named in his document: 'Common Man's Charter', Obote's growing close relations with the Soviet Union, an agenda that Israeli military attachés in Uganda at the time disliked, Obote's headlong clash with the British Conservative Party over its intention to sell arms to South Africa and the fate of 'British Asians' in Uganda, and Obote's deteriorated relationship within Buganda, which led to his ending the 500-year long Buganda kingdom, turning Uganda into a Republic. Edward Bakaitwako Muhima, 'The Fellowship of Christian Suffering: A Theological Interpretation of Christian Suffering under Idi Amin' (PhD thesis, Evanston, Ill.: Northwestern University, 1981), 16–18.

28. Historians who discuss the problem of ethnic conflict and the split in the army, include: Nelson Kasfir, 'Civilian Participation Under Military Rule in Uganda and Sudan', *Armed Forces and Society* 1/3 (1975): 344–63; Nelson Kasfir, *The Shrinking Political Arena: Participation & Ethnicity in African Politics, With a Case Study of Uganda* (Berkeley: Univ of California Pr, 1976); Chick, 'Class Conflict', 634–37; Martin, 'Uganda Military Coup', 80–121; Ruth First, 'Uganda: The Latest Coup d'etat in Africa', *World Today* 27/3 (March 1971): 131–38; Irving Gershenberg, 'A Further Comment on the 1971 Coup', *JMAS* 10/4 (December 1972): 638–39; Maya, 'Imperialist Threat', 37–44; Claude E. Welch Jr., 'The OAU and the International Recognition: Lessons From Uganda', in *The ization of African Unity After Ten Years: Comparative Perspectives* (ed. Yassin El-Ayouty; Praeger Special Studies in International Politics and Government; New York: Praeger, 1975), 103–17; Aidan Southall, 'General Amin and the Coup: Great Man or Historical Inevitability?', *JMAS* 13/1 (March 1975): 85–105; Mahmood Mamdani, 'Class Struggles in Uganda', *Review of African Political Economy* 4 (November 1975): 26–61; Mahmood Mamdani, *Politics and Class Formation in Uganda* (New York: Monthly Review Press, 1978); Ali Al'Amin Mazrui, *Is the Nile Valley Emerging as a New Political System? the View from Lake Victoria* (Kampala: Makerere University, 1971), 1–53.

29. Bert N Adams, 'A Look at Uganda and Expulsion Through Ex-Ugandan Asian Eyes', *Kroniek van Afrika* 3/6 (1975): 237–94.

30. Among historians who discuss these problems, see Don Nanjira and D. C. Daniel, *Status of Aliens in East Africa: Asians and Europeans in Tanzania, Uganda and Kenya* (Praeger Special Studies in International Politics and Government; New York: Praeger Publishers Inc, 1976); Harrison, 'Uganda: The Expulsion of the Asians', in *Case Studies*

the expulsion limited its opportunity to expand, and so more than just the Asian community suffered by Amin's action.[31] Deep wounds were opening in Uganda. Although there is no direct reference to the pain of the Asian community in the sermons studied here, in an address to the press (10 May 1979) organized by World Vision, Nairobi, Kenya,[32] Kivengere publicly acknowledged the deep wounds Amin caused for Asians of Ugandan origin, as he explained what his reconciliatory role would be in the new Uganda.

The period of Amin's rule continued to inflict ethnically motivated atrocities on Ugandans, such as public executions by firing squads perpetrated by Amin's army. In his sermons, Kivengere frequently refers to the 1973 firing squad that he witnessed in Kabale, Kigezi.[33] Such public executions continued to leave deep wounds in Ugandans, causing the hatred of Amin's tribe by other tribes and a negative perception of the army. The period also witnessed the murder of foreigners living in or visiting Uganda,[34] and the torture and murder of prominent Ugandans in both church and

---

on Human Rights And Fundamental Freedoms: A World Survey (ed. Ruut Veenhoven; vol. 4, 1st ed.; The Hague: Martinus Nijhoff, 1976), 287–315; Winston E Langley and Julius Emeka Okolo, 'Uganda: Expulsion of Aliens, and Human Rights', *Current Bibliography on African Affairs* 7/4 (Fall 1974): 345–59; Mahmood Mamdani, *From Citizen to Refugee: Uganda Asians Come to Britain* (London: Frances Printer, 1973); Ali Al'Amin Mazrui, 'Casualties of an Underdeveloped Class Structure: The Expulsion of Luo Workers and Asian Bourgeoisie from Uganda', in *Strangers in African Societies* (ed. William A. Shack and Elliott P. Skinner; Berkeley: University of California Press, 1979), 261–78; Peter Nanyenya, 'A Case Study of the Law Relating to the Expulsion of Aliens and Nationalization of Alien Property: The Case of Uganda', *Uganda Law Focus* 2/2 (September 1974): 100–26.

31. M. A. Tribe, 'Economic Aspects of the Expulsion of Asians From Uganda', in *Expulsion of a Minority: Essays on Ugandan Asians* (ed. Michael Twaddle; First Edition.; London: Continuum International Publishing Group - Athlone, 1975), 140–76; E. A. Brett, 'Relations of Production, the State and the Uganda Crisis', *West African Journal of Sociology and Political Science* 1/3 (1978): 249–84; Timothy M. Shaw, 'Uganda Under Amin: The Cost of Confronting Independence', *Africa Today* 20/2 (Spring 1973): 32–45.

32. Festo Kivengere, 'World Vision: with Festo Kivengere', Sermon Transcript, May 10, 1979, AO:19790510.

33. Festo Kivengere, 'The Resurrection or Burning Hearts', Sermon Transcript, May 10, 1980, p. 9, #21, AO:19800510*2; Festo Kivengere, *I Love Idi Amin: The Story of Triumph Under Fire in the Midst of Suffering and Persecution in Uganda* (ed. Dorothy Smoker; Old Tapan, N.J.: Revell, 1973).

34. E.g., Denis Hills, 'The Jailer as Seen by His Ex-Prisoner', *New York Times Magazine* (September 7, 1975): 42–3, 45, 47, 49, 51, 53; Denis Hills, *The White Pumpkin* (New York: Grove Press, 1975); Denis Hills, *Rebel People* (New York: Africana Publishing, 1978).

civic leadership.³⁵ Even the 1977 murder of Luwum (1922–1977)³⁶ was probably motivated by ethnic hatred.³⁷ The ethnic atrocities of Amin and his hit men left many bitter widows and orphans.³⁸ Kivengere's sermons are littered with powerful stories of a personal nature revealing the impact of the ethnic hatred of Amin's rule on Ugandans.³⁹

---

35. E.g., Ford, *Janani*, 49–51; Wood, 'A Murder in Uganda', 216–19; Kevin Ward, 'Archbishop Janani Luwum', in *Christianity and the African Imagination: Essays in Honour of Adrian Hastings* (ed. David Maxwell, Ingrid Lawrie, and Adrian Hastings; Studies on Religion in Africa; Leiden: Brill, 2002), 199–224; Henry Kyemba, *A State of Blood: The Inside Story of Idi Amin* (New York: Grosset and Dunlap, 1977); Robert H. Jackson and Carl G. Rosberg, *Personal Rule in Black Africa: Prince, Autocrat, Prophet, Tyrant* (Berkeley: University of California Press, 1982). An anonymous article written in Uganda, reviewing the state of economic problems arising from Amin's rule, reviews the massacres of soldiers, citing various murders including that of Chief Justice Benedicto Kiwanuka for his involvement in the politics of Uganda. See Edwin S. Munger and Anon, *Inside Amin's Uganda: More Africans Murdered* (vol. 18; Munger Africana Library Notes; Pasadena, Ca.: California Institute of Technology, 1973), 11–22.

36. See in this Chapter, 2.4 'A Second Wave of Christian Persecutions'.

37. Ward, 'Archbishop Janani Luwum', 199–224.

38. He frequently spoke about the suffering widows and orphans in Uganda, especially in the Church. The list of sermons where he makes reference to widows and orphans include, Festo Kivengere, 'A New Way of Seeing Jesus', Sermon Transcript (Preached at Holy Trinity Church, Cambridge, October 12, 1982), p,. 2, #2, AO: 19821012, [#1]. Festo Kivengere, 'In Christ', Sermon Transcript, April 29, 1979, p. 4, #8–#9, AO: 19790429, [#2]. Festo Kivengere, 'The Reconciling Love of Christ', Sermon Transcript, October 1981, pp. 1–2, #2, AO: 198110[--], [#1]. Festo Kivengere, 'Jesus Came as a Missionary of Reconciliation', Sermon Transcript, February 21, 1982, p. 3, #4, AO: 19820221. Festo Kivengere, 'His Flooding Love', Sermon Transcript, July 29, 1975, p. 7, #10, AO: 19750729, [#2]. Festo Kivengere, 'Christ Has Reconciled the Universe to Himself', Sermon Transcript (Garden Grove, California., 1979), pp. 1–2, #2, AO: 1979[est. after May], [#2]. Festo Kivengere, 'Costly Breakthrough', Sermon Transcript (Preached at First United Methodist Church, Carollton, TX, January 12, 1980), p. 6, #19, AO:19800112. Festo Kivengere, 'The Master Came Down', Sermon Transcript (Preached at St. Andrew's Presbyterian Church, Newport Beach, CA, October 5, 1980), p. 2, #3, AO:19801005*1. Festo Kivengere, 'Compassion Harvest', Sermon Transcript, October 7, 1980, p. 3, #4, AO: 19801007. Festo Kivengere, 'How a Person Can Be Sure of His Right Relationship With God', Sermon Transcript, October 26, 1980, p. 2, #7, AO: 19801026.

39. E.g., Kivengere, 'In Christ', pp. 3–4, #8–#9. For personal stories revealing the impact of ethnic hatred of Amin's rule see Kivengere, *I Love Idi Amin*; Emmanuel Katongole, *The Sacrifice of Africa: A Political Theology for Africa* (Eerdmans Ekklesia Series; Grand Rapids, Mich.: W.B. Eerdmans Pub., 2011); H. Falke, *From Uganda with Love: An Inside Look by Means of Students' Essays and Paintings* (1st ed.; New York: Vantage Press, 1980); Peter Allen, *Days of Judgment: A Judge in Idi Amin's Uganda* (England: Kimber, 1987); G. H Barker, *A Circle of Trees* (Braunton: Merlin, 1989).

1.2.2 Brain Drain out of Uganda

The second reason why this period is important for understanding Kivengere's preaching is because it saw a serious brain-drain from the country: 'the country is undergoing a tremendous drain of brain power. I feel deeply for them [Ugandans who fled into exile] because I too escaped narrowly', he said.[40] Amin's reign was characterized by violence, murder, fear and revenge as a daily way of life.[41] As Amin continue to murder, Ugandans fled for safety and as the economic and cultural life of the nation nearly collapsed during his reign, they left to find 'greener pastures'.[42] The brain drain continued with his expulsion of the entire Indian [Asian] population: professors, doctors, dentists, and veterinarians left the country hoping to find asylum in Britain.[43] It was tragic for the nation of Uganda that an illiterate military leader like Amin exercised unchecked power with ruthless force causing many intelligent and professional people to flee.

His murderous rule mostly targeted Christians, since many educated Christians were (as now) working in his government and he felt threatened by the elites.[44] Another big wave of exiles followed the murder of Janani Luwum at the peak of Amin's persecution of Christians. Because the African Enterprise office in Nairobi acted as the point where refugees from Uganda first reported for help in finding a location elsewhere in the world, Kivengere was one of the first to become aware of this brain drain: '300 doctors have crossed the border of Uganda into Kenya, escaping. 200 lawyers have crossed, 300 businessmen, 1500 university students have escaped,

---

40. See, 'Help for Uganda Refugees', *Courier Mail* (Brisbane, February 6, 1978).
41. Four excellent studies that look at increasing violence in Uganda, especially due to Amin's army are: D. A. Low, 'Uganda Unhinged', *International Affairs* 49/2 (April 1973): 219–28; Jackson and Rosberg, *Personal Rule in Black Africa*; Kyemba, *State of Blood*; and, W. Senteza-Kajubi, 'Background to War and Violence in Uganda', in *War, Violence, and Children in Uganda* (ed. Cole P. Dodge and Magne Raundalen; Oslo: Norwegian University Press, 1987), 15–52.
42. Tribe, 'Economic Aspects', 140–76; Brett, 'Relations of Production', 249–84; Frederick John Ravenhill, 'The Military and Politics in Uganda', *AQ* 19/2 (September 1979): 122–47; G. K. Hellenier, 'Economic Collapse and Rehabilitation in Uganda', *Rural Africana* 11 (1981): 27–35.
43. Tribe, 'Economic Aspects', 140–76; Thomas P. Melady and Margaret Melady, *Uganda: The Asian Exiles* (Maryknoll, N.Y.: Orbis Books, 1978).
44. Muhima, 'The Fellowship of Christian Suffering: A Theological Interpretation of Christian Suffering under Idi Amin', 53.

200 professors from a young country of 11.5 million people'.[45] His preaching showed he was determined to counteract the waste of leadership, in Uganda in particular, but also in Africa more generally. While himself a refugee in Kenya, in May 1977 he founded the Relief, Education and Training for Uganda Refugees Now (RETURN).[46] This feature of Ugandan life in this period is a significant background to his preaching of reconciliation.[47]

1.2.3 Campaign for Ugandan Refugees and Coffee Farmers

The third feature of this period was Kivengere's rigorous campaign, conducted while he was in exile, for the suffering Ugandans in exile and for the Ugandan farmers who were exploited by Amin's soldiers. When he was a missionary teacher at Alliance Anglican School, Dodoma, Tanzania (1945–1958), Kivengere had established a connection with the American Mennonites. While living in exile in America this connection was re-established and the Mennonites assisted him in his appeal to the Washington Administration to help with the pressing problem of Ugandan refugees and to place an embargo on the U.S. import of Ugandan coffee. His appeal received serious attention.

> At the time, a bill that would give thirty million dollars for African assistance was before Congress. Kivengere sought to call Washington's attention to the fifty thousand refugees who had fled the increasingly brutal rule of President Idi Amin.
> [The Director of the Mennonite Central Committee, Franz Delton[48]] scheduled seventeen appointments over a two-day

---

45. Festo Kivengere, 'Glorified in Them', Sermon Transcript, May 22, 1977, p. 10, #4, AO:19770522*1; Inkelaar-de Mos, 'Evangelistic Enterprise', 83–85.
46. Kivengere, 'Glorified in Them', p. 10, #4. For a detailed account of the role of RETURN in Kivengere's preaching of reconciliation, see African Evangelistic Enterprise, *Return, Relief, Reconstruction and Reconciliation* (Pasadena, Calif.: African Evangelistic Enterprise, n.d.).
47. Kivengere, 'Glorified in Them', p. 10, #4.
48. Franz Delton has been the directed of the Mennonite Central Committee for twenty-three years (1971–1994). For an appreciation of the Mennonite perspective on Christian Activism, which he has been the director, see Franz Delton, 'A Biblical Context for Political Advocacy', in *Christian Political Activism at the Crossroads* (ed. William R. Stevenson; University Press of America, 1994), 51–56.

period for Kivengere, including meetings with six career Foreign Service officers on East Africa at the State Department, representatives of the State Department Bureau of Human Rights, staffers from the House and Senate subcommittee on Africa and key members of the House of Senate. Representative Donald Pease (D-Ohio) already had introduced a bill with twenty-three sponsors that placed an embargo on the U.S. importation of Ugandan coffee. Pease said he found helpful the information provided by Kivengere's documentation on Amin's atrocities and his armed troops' confiscation of most of the coffee crop for the dictator's treasury.[49]

Thus during his exile, Kivengere took serious action to secure the interest of the international community in what is happening in Uganda.[50] Regarding Amin's soldiers who were taking the bagged coffee from the Ugandan farmers at a meagre amount of its real market value, he argued with the U.S. Senators that coffee exports to the U.S. were providing two-thirds of Uganda's hard currency.[51] Thus, in his view, practically all of the funds from the U.S. importation of Ugandan coffee were being used recklessly by Amin to pursue his genocidal killings, to purchase expensive automobiles, and to import Scotch whisky to motivate his army officers to obey his orders. Kivengere's campaign for a U.S. trade embargo on Ugandan coffee was successful and after just a year of this sanction, Amin's regime fell.[52]

---

49. Keith Graber Miller, *Wise As Serpents, Innocent As Doves: American Mennonites Engage Washington* (1st ed.; Knoxville: University of Tennessee Press, 1996), 147–48; Cf. Cal Thomas, 'Uganda's New Day gets Big Boost from Christian Leaders', *Journal Champion* 1/25 (April 20, 1979): 6.

50. E.g., Kivengere addressed the Australian National Press Club on what is happening in Uganda with the aim of bringing international awareness and ask countries with a fair democracy to help Uganda's situation. See Festo Kivengere, *Address to the National Press Club*, Audio Recording from National Library of Australia (Canberra, 1978).

51. Helpful discussions on U.S. embargo on Uganda Coffee include, Ralph D. Nurnburger, 'The United States and Amin: Congress to the Rescue', *African Studies Review* 25/1 (March 1982): 49–65; Judith Miller, 'When Sanctions Worked', *Foreign Policy* 39 (Summer 1980): 118–29; Sally C. Andrews, 'The Legitimacy of the United States Embargo of Uganda', *JILE* 13/3 (1979): 651–73; U.S. Congress, 'Public Law 95-435', 1051–3.

52. For a discussion of how the United States Trade Embargo prepared the way for the

Not only was Kivengere actively involved in political action on behalf of suffering Ugandans, but he also expressed bitter disgust with others who did nothing. He strongly criticised the African Unity (AU), formerly the Organization of African Unity (OAU), for sitting back and doing nothing to help the Ugandans oppressed and suffering under Amin.[53] When Idi Amin continued to kill Ugandans at the rate of 150 people a day, Kivengere was irritated with the OAU's decision to meet in Kampala and make Amin its Chairman:

> The OAU's silence has encouraged and indirectly contributed to the bloodshed in Africa. I mean, the OAU even went as far as to go to Kampala [for its 1975 summit] and make Amin its chairman. And at the very moment the heads of state were meeting in the conference hall, talking about the lack of human rights in southern Africa, three blocks away, in Amin's torture chambers, my countrymen's heads were being smashed with sledgehammers and their legs were being chopped off with axes.[54]

This condemnation of the OAU shows how deeply Kivengere felt for the suffering Ugandans. His expression of disgust at their decision reveals his deep dislike of their politics of conciliation, and his crisis of confidence about the OAU to hold the meeting in Kampala,[55] as Amin's rule reduced

---

fall of Amin's government, see Nurnburger, 'United States and Amin', 49–65; Miller, 'Sanctions', 118–29.

53. For discussion of the OAU, see Welch Jr., 'The OAU and the International Recognition', 103–17; Sesay, 'OAU and Regime Recognition', 25–41.

54. As cited by David Lamb, *The Africans* (New York: Random House, 1984), 106; Cf., George B. N. Ayittey, *Africa Betrayed* (New York: St Martin's Press, 1992), 120. For a description of the suffering, in particular a systematic smashing of heads of Ugandans in Amin's torture chambers, See David Martin, *General Amin* (London: Sphere, 1978), 226.

55. For Amin's position as Chairman of the OAU detailing his rocky relations with the Soviet Union over policy toward Angola, his worsening relations with Kenya; and for the official Tanzanian statement on its boycott of the OAU's Kampala summit to the point that Tanzania's attendance would legitimise a criminal regime, see Colin Legum and Elizabeth Clements, *Africa Contemporary Record: Annual Survey and Documents, 1975–76, Vol. 8* (New York: Africana Publishing Co., 1976), 66–67. For the politics of conciliation at the OAU, see Godfrey P. Okoth, 'The OAU and the Uganda-Tanzania War, 1978-

Uganda to a broken, bleeding country. In his view, bleeding Africa[56] could be healed by the wounded Christ and Christ's reconciliation led to very different political outcomes.

In this period, Kivengere's reconciliatory role figured prominently in the quest for a solution to Ugandan and wider African problems.[57] His commitment to reconciliation even played a major role in bringing about the end of Amin's reign of terror.

> [K]ivengere played a major part in building bridges between rival Ugandan politicians to create a united front to be presented to Tanzanian President Julius Nyerere. Without that unity, Nyerere would never have committed his forces to the first invasion of one African country by another since colonial times.[58]

'Building bridges' towards a solution to the suffering of the African people, especially his nation of Uganda, was a direct outworking of Kivengere's understanding of reconciliation. At the Moshi Unity Conference in Tanzania (23–26 March 1979),[59] he had asserted: 'I am committed in my ministry as a bishop in the church to the job of bringing reconciliation to the government and building bridges over which the Ugandans can cross'.[60]

1979', *JAS* 14/3 (Fall 1987): 152–62.

56. Festo Kivengere, 'Bleeding Africa', in *Proclaiming Christ to His World* (ed. Hanne-Grete Brommeland and Knud Jørgensen; Oslo: Luther Forlag, 1984), 19–29.

57. For a discussion of the magnitude of the suffering and horror of the Ugandans people presented and discussed at the U.S Senate, see Nurnburger, 'United States and Amin', 49–65.

58. Thomas, 'Uganda's New Day', 6.

59. As the name suggests, the Moshi Unity Conference brought together twenty-two fighting groups of Ugandans opposed to Idi Amin who were in exile scattered around the globe. For a description of the lack of unity among them, see Pirouet, *Historical Dictionary of Uganda*, 255–56.

60. Episcopal Church, 'Bishop Kivengere Returns To Uganda', Press Release, Episcopal News Service, May 3, 1979, Cited 22 Nov 2011, Online: http://www.episcopalarchives.org/cgi-bin/ENS/ENSpress_release.pl?pr_number=79146.

1.2.4 A Second Wave of Christian Persecution

As the fourth feature, this period was marked by a second wave of Christian persecution, the first occurring within the first decade of planting Christianity in Uganda (1885–87).[61] The persecution of Christians during Amin's reign included him banning Christian radio programmes, shutting down religious organizations, and arresting and murdering Christian people.[62] In a 1982 interview, Kivengere tells of persecutions under Amin: 'Pressures were on. Harassments were on. Many arrests took place. Here and there people began to die. But the church grew. People realized their only hope was in the preaching of the gospel'.[63] As Amin's persecution of Christians increased, it culminated in him murdering Luwum in February 1977.[64] Amin's persecution pushed church activities underground,[65] and confronted Ugandan clerics like Kivengere with the dilemma 'either to speak out and die or not to speak and live'.[66] Despite Amin's murderous actions, Kivengere refused to hate or to rebel against him. He continued to preach the reconciling love of God centred in Jesus Christ.[67]

Because Kivengere had boldly spoken against atrocities in Uganda,[68] after Luwum was murdered this second wave of persecution pushed Kivengere into exile in the United States of America. From this base he continued to travel widely and to speak publically about the conditions in

---

61. Emmanuel K. Twesigye, *Religion, Politics, and Cults in East Africa* (First printing.; New York: Peter Lang Publishing, 2010), 92; William A Dyrness, Veli-Matti Kärkkäinen, and Juan Francisco Martinez, eds., *Global Dictionary of Theology: A Resource for the Worldwide Church* (Downers Grove, Ill.: IVP Academic, 2008).
62. Kefa F. Sempangi, 'Uganda's Reign of Terror', *Worldview (New York)* 18/5 (May 1975): 16–21; Kivengere, *I Love Idi Amin*, 28. For other articles on Amin's mounting opposition to Christians, see Akiiki B. Mujaju, 'The Political Crisis of Church Institutions in Uganda', *African Affairs* 75/298 (1976): 67–85.
63. Festo Kivengere, 'Awesome Growth in Troubled Uganda', *GCGB* 19/5 (1982): 218.
64. Wood, 'A Murder in Uganda', 216–19; Matthews, 'Terror and death in Uganda', 49–51; Ford, *Janani*; Muhima, 'The Fellowship of Christian Suffering: A Theological Interpretation of Christian Suffering under Idi Amin', 42–48.
65. Wooding and Barnett, *Uganda Holocaust*. Wooding and Barnett narrate numerous stories of atrocities that Christian individuals suffered at the hands of Amin's men.
66. Wood, 'The Bishop and Idi Amin', 26–28; Muhima, 'The Fellowship of Christian Suffering: A Theological Interpretation of Christian Suffering under Idi Amin', 46–48.
67. Kivengere, *I Love Idi Amin*; Briscoe, *The Man Who Would Not Hate*.
68. John Capon, 'Exiled Bishop of the Martyred Church', *Crusade* (May 1977): 22.

Uganda.[69] Kivengere's own experience in exile energised his preaching of reconciliation. The persecution of Christians seemingly strengthened the church.[70] While institutions such as the legislative and executive arm of government, the judiciary, and the health services collapsed, the church was the only institution that survived Amin's rule.[71]

1.2.5 International Community Watches Uganda

The fifth feature is the fact that Amin's rule gained the attention of the international community as the press and others monitored closely what was happening in Uganda. As later (2002) portrayed by Barbet Schroder's film: *General Idi Amin Dada: A Self Portrait*,[72] Amin appeared as a buffoon. *Time* magazine ran on its front page the picture of Amin with the caption, 'The Wild Man of Africa'.[73] Thomas Melady, a former U.S. Ambassador to Uganda, in 1976 and 1977 published works that exposed Amin's atrocities.[74] Ugandan exiles were also active in creating awareness

---

69. Episcopal Church, 'Bishop Kivengere Describes Persecuted Ugandan Church', Press Release, Episcopal News Service, March 11, 1977, Cited 15 Mar 2012, Online: http://www.episcopalarchives.org/cgi-bin/ENS/ENSpress_release.pl?pr_number=77093.

70. Norman E. Thomas, 'Evangelization and Church Growth: The Case of Africa', *IBMR* 11/4 (1987): 166. Cf.. Kivengere, 'Awesome Growth': 218.

71. For further comments by Kivengere on the Church as the only institution that did not succumb to Amin's reign of terror and also the only institution that gave Ugandans undying hope, see Kivengere, *I Love Idi Amin*, 13. Kivengere explains that the Church in Africa is like the wild African bush fire that burns the grass and before long fresh grass grows up. For breakdown in health services during Amin's rule see, Kivengere, *Address to the National Press Club*; F. J. Bennett, 'A Comparison of Health Community in Uganda with Its Two East African Neighbours in the Periods 1970-1979', in *Crisis in Uganda: The Breakdown in Health Services* (ed. Cole P. Dodge; Oxford, England: Pergamon Pr, 1985), 43–52.

72. Barbet Schroder, *General Idi Amin Dada*, DVD (Criterion Collection; Criterion, 1974).

73. 'Uganda: Amin: The Wild Man of Africa', *Time* (March 7, 1977), Cited 27 Jan 2012, Online: http://www.time.com/time/magazine/article/0,9171,918762,00.html.

74. Schroder, *General Idi Amin Dada*; Melady and Melady, *Uganda*. For a three-way debate between Thomas Melady, Godfrey Binaisa (former Attorney General of Uganda and later President of Uganda) and journalist Carlos Russell on the response that President Carter should make regarding Amin's threat against Americans in Uganda, see Duke Struck, 'Former Uganda Attorney General Godfrey Binaisa, Former United States Ambassador to Uganda Thomas Melady, and Journalist Carlos Russell Debate the Response That President Carter Should Make to Idi Amin's Threats Against Americans in Uganda', Videocassette, *The MacNeil/Lehrer Report* (New York: Educational Broadcasting Corp., 1977).

in the international community about the suffering under Amin.[75] Among them was Kivengere, whose preaching and press engagements[76] contributed significantly to the awareness of the international community and helped to prompt their action. For example, in April 1977, just three months into his exile from Amin (February 1977), he went to the conference room of the U.S. News & World Report to discuss what he saw as Africa's upheaval.[77] Issues he discussed included, 'U.S. military aid to Zaire', where he expressed that 'Any help that America gives an independent African nation resisting outside forces trying to take it over is appreciated', noting that Americans worried too much about being labelled imperialists, colonialists, and exploiters—labels that Russians use to attack America.[78] When America holds back help from African nations resisting foreign powers trying to take over their independence, then Americans 'are playing right into Russia's hands'.[79] This discussion is significant for it highlights his knowledge of the ideologies of America and Russia playing out in Africa and their consequences. Of course, the African country he had particularly in mind was Uganda. After discussing Soviet military aid to African governments, the question of whether Communists are taking over in Africa, lessons on Angola's search for independence in which Russia and Cuba were heavily involved, he carefully exposed the situation in his own country, where the Palestinians, Russians, and Cubans continued to have close dealings with Amin.

Kivengere brought to international attention how the COU, for which he was the spokesman (and 'for the revival'[80]), viewed Amin and his actions: 'We've never regarded our dictator, President Amin, as an enemy of the church. He's never acted that way. His enemies are political—tribal enemies. He rules through arbitrary killing, using the gun instead of the law,

---

75. Nurnburger, 'United States and Amin', 49.
76. E.g., Kivengere, *Address to the National Press Club*; Episcopal Church, 'Persecuted Ugandan Church'.
77. 'How a Ugandan Bishop Views Africa's Upheaval', *U.S. News and World Report* 82 (April 4, 1977): 30.
78. 'How a Ugandan Bishop Views Africa's Upheaval', 30.
79. 'How a Ugandan Bishop Views Africa's Upheaval', 30.
80. Schmidt, *Glorious Companions*, 311.

and there is no constitution except what he happens to think in each day'.[81] Although Amin was not deliberately targeting the church as his enemy, since the majority of Ugandans, particularly the leaders in civil service, happened to be Christians, and since Christians also belonged to tribes and political factions that he happened to think were his enemies, he killed them or ordered their killing—they too fell among the dictator's victims.

Kivengere spoke openly about Amin's paranoia and the anxiety this provoked in the country: 'Tens of thousands of Ugandans have been killed, but all that these killings do is make him feel more and more threatened. Now he is looking for more enemies where they don't even exist. Amin survives by bribing those who work for him, by giving them guns and power. He has Palestinian bodyguards and Russian and Cubans advisors'.[82] 'Everyone watches carefully to spot those who might be anti-Amin. And for anyone accused of being subversive, that is the end'.[83]

Others were beginning to add their voices to the warnings sounded by Kivengere about this situation. In February 1977, the World Council of Churches (WCC) issued an urgent response to the murder of archbishop Janani Luwum:

> [T]he Executive Committee [of the WCC] therefore:
>
> *strongly condemns* those responsible for these killings[84] which took place within hours of President Amin's public promise that the accused would be brought to trial before sentencing,
>
> *urges* an immediate international investigation into the circumstances leading to the deaths of Archbishop Luwum . . . ,

---

81. 'How a Ugandan Bishop Views Africa's Upheaval', 30.
82. 'How a Ugandan Bishop Views Africa's Upheaval', 30.
83. 'How a Ugandan Bishop Views Africa's Upheaval', 30.
84. Luwum was killed together with two government ministers: Arphaxed Oboth-Ofumbi, Interior Minister and Erinayo Wilson Oryema, Minister of Lands, Housing and Physical Planning.

supports the appeal made earlier by the All Africa Conference of Churches [AACC] for such an investigation,

requests the United Nations Commission on Human Rights to undertake a thorough investigation into the systematic and gross violation of human rights in that country, and to take immediate steps to prevent the killing of persons who may now be in imminent danger,

appeals to the nations, especially those of independent Africa, to take actions to prevent further loss of life in Uganda. This situation of brutal oppression does grave injustice not only to the people of Uganda, but to all the people of Africa in this crucial moment in the history of that continent,

appeals to WCC member Churches, through appropriate action in their countries, to affirm their solidarity with the Church of Uganda especially in this year of centennial celebrations [1977] of the coming of Christianity to their land.[85]

Similar condemnations of Amin's inhuman action of murdering Luwum and others came from Amnesty International, the International Commission of Jurists, and the Vatican who said the story of Luwum's murder reported by the government of Uganda was 'unswallowable'. Billy Graham also issued a statement deploring the 'cold blooded murder'.[86]

The awareness campaign of Ugandans in exile, notably Kivengere, helped to mobilize global support for the situation of Ugandans living in exile and those in Uganda. Later in the sermons he is thankful for their support especially the participation of the Christian communities through their prayers, material and spiritual support during Amin's rule. After the overthrow of Amin, he will still appeal for prayers and material support to

---

85. World Council of Churches Executive Committee, 'The Archbishop Has Gone Home to His Lord', *Ecumenical Review* 29/2 (April 1977): 196–197.
86. Matthews, 'Terror and death in Uganda', 50.

help rebuild Uganda, but he is quick to remind them that the only antidote to Uganda's deep wound is the biblical message of reconciliation, which must be at the centre of reconstruction and rehabilitation of Uganda. It is the only hope for Uganda and the world. The international community channelled support through his AEE.

1.2.6 A Christ-centred Leadership

Finally, the most compelling reason for focusing on 1971–1988 is because of the visionary, spiritual, and selfless Christ-centred leadership Kivengere displayed during this turbulent period. Kivengere could confidently stand knowing that his voice was not the only one crying out to the international community. This served to strengthen his leadership. His spiritual leadership in this period was based on his love for his Lord Jesus Christ and upon the reconciliation rooted in Jesus Christ.[87] It was in this period and especially after the fall of Amin (April 1979),[88] that Kivengere mobilized and rallied the nation for reconstruction and rehabilitation, and he did this by means of his powerful preaching of reconciliation. From 23–26 March, 1979, Moshi Unity Conference, consisting of various Ugandan organizations that were in exile from Idi Amin, whose representatives met at Moshi in Tanzania to discuss the future of Uganda and select its new leader for the transition government after the fall of Amin.[89] Kivengere himself was in attendance at the Moshi Unity Conference. At the meeting his leadership ability strongly emerged. 'Bishop Festo himself was approached, with offers of high government office', while others even 'wanted to push him into the presidency but he smilingly refused'.[90] He refused because he 'was committed to his ministry' as a bishop in the church and he also believed that

---

87. Loane, 'Memoirs', 100–05.
88. World Council of Churches Executive Committee, 'The Archbishop', 197; Michael Twaddle, 'The Ousting of Idi Amin: Regime's Swift Collapse Took Tanzania By Surprise', *Round Table: The Commonwealth Journal of International Affairs*/275 (July 1979): 316–221; Al J. Venter, 'Amin's Chamber of Horrors', *South African Journal of African Affairs* 9/2 (1979): 104–10. For an interview about the fall of Kampala and flight of Amin, see Yusuf K. Lule, '"We Stand for Justice": Professor Lule', *New African*/141 (May 1979): 18–20.
89. Legum and Clements, *Africa Contemporary Record*, [Check Legum and Jaquline]; New African, 'Uganda's Historical Moshi Conference', *New African* 141 (May 1979): 14–17.
90. Anne Coomes, *African Harvest: The Captivating Story of Michael Cassidy and African Enterprise* (London: Monarch, 2002), 367.

his job was to bring reconciliation to the government and to build bridges over which the Ugandans can cross.[91] Indeed, in 1979 Kivengere's hour had come: 'For at President Lule's invitation, Festo led the call to all Ugandans for national reconciliation'.[92] His message had become a matter of national political importance.

1.3 The Need For This Study

1.3.1 The Unstudied Kivengere: Preacher of Reconciliation

Kivengere saw himself fundamentally as a preacher of reconciliation. As he told the International Conference of Itinerant Evangelists (1983): 'To all of us who proclaim the good news of God to men and women, God has entrusted the most precious treasure—"The Ministry of Reconciliation"'.[93] His commitment to reconciliation was clearly seen by others. Michael Cassidy, Kivengere's long time friend and colleague—with whom he both co-founded the African Enterprise and preached in tandem[94]—observed that 'reconciliation was the heart of Festo's message';[95] that Kivengere preached 'reconciliation between God and man and between man and man'.[96] Jay Russell observed that in the midst of tribulation in Uganda Kivengere preached 'love and reconciliation'.[97] Quinn wrote: 'Forgiveness, reconciliation and proclamation were the three cornerstones of Kivengere's ministry, which

---

91. Episcopal Church, 'Bishop Kivengere Returns To Uganda'.
92. Coomes, *African Harvest*, 368.
93. Festo Kivengere, 'The Evangelist's Ministry of Reconciliation: We Are Christ's Ambassadors', in *The Work of an Evangelist: International Congress for Itinerant Evangelists* (ed. J. D. Douglas; Minneapolis, Minn.: World Wide Publications, 1984), p. 157, #1.
94. 'Tandem style' is a method of preaching that Michael Cassidy claimed to be 'the East African Revival way' in which two or more speakers, in this case Kivengere, an ordained minister, and a black Ugandan, and Cassidy, a lay minister, and a white South African, preached on the same theme and text. See Michael Cassidy, 'Festo Has Died But He Still Speaks', *AE*/August (1988): 8.
95. Cassidy, 'Festo Has Died But He Still Speaks', 8.
96. Festo Kivengere, *Revolutionary Love* (ed. Dorothy Smoker; Fort Washington, PA.: Christian Literature Crusade, 1983).
97. Russell, 'Ministry of Reconciliation', 304.

continued until his death'.⁹⁸ And Shaw observed that Kivengere preached 'racial reconciliation and reconciliation with God through Christ'.⁹⁹

During the course of his preaching ministry Kivengere generated a vast number of sermons. To date, however, there has been no major study of these sermons. In particular, there has been no study of the centrality of the Christian doctrine of reconciliation in his preaching. The lack of a fuller study of Kivengere's sermons has been to a large degree due to the fact that the only sermons generally accessible to researchers have been those published in book form: *The Spirit is Moving, Jesus our Reality, Love Unlimited, Revolutionary Love, When God Moves in Revival*, and *Hope for Uganda and Beyond*.

The few Kivengere studies that exist¹⁰⁰ have been driven by very different questions from ours. This study seeks to explore, how far is it possible to give a coherent biblical-theological evaluation of the Christian doctrine of reconciliation in Kivengere's preaching from a selection of his sermons between the years 1971–1988? How was he shaped theologically? What is the connection between the content of his message and his style of preaching? As indicated, this study will attempt to make its contribution to these questions on the basis of Kivengere's claim that the Christian doctrine of 'reconciliation is the centre of the Christian gospel'.¹⁰¹

Claims about 'the centre' intersect with similar concerns among Biblical Theologians. The intention in this study is to examine the extent to which Kivengere display a Biblical Theology of reconciliation. Among scholars who have attempted to analyze at least some of his sermons, none have demonstrated any overt concern for analyzing his Biblical Theology. Instead

---

98. Quinn, 'Kivengere, Festo'.
99. Shaw, *Global Awakening*, 107.
100. Cassidy, 'Festo Has Died But He Still Speaks', 8; John M. M. Senyonyi, 'Bishop Festo Kivengere's Philosophy of Evangelism' (M.A. Thesis, Deerfield, Ill.: Trinity Evangelical Divinity School, 1992); Peter B Rwabyoma, 'Bishop Festo Kivengere: An Analysis of His Communication Skills and How He Applied Them in the Mission of the Church in Uganda' (MA Thesis, Cardiff: University of Wales, 2007); Anne Coomes, *Festo Kivengere: A Biography* (Eastbourne: Monarch, 1990); Old, *Reading and Preaching*, 200–03.
101. Kivengere, 'Ambassador For Christ', p. 3, #5.

they focus on elements of his theology such as 'the cross of Jesus', 'the love of Jesus', 'the Holy Spirit', and 'evangelism'.

1.3.2 Sermons at the Periphery

Kivegere's preaching is touched on in passing by those whose interest in him lies elsewhere. Kevin Ward, for example, acknowledged the sermon Kivengere preached on 30 January 1977 at the consecration of Bishop Yoram Bamunoba a few days after the first anniversary of Amin's coup: 'Bishop Festo Kivengere preached a powerful sermon warning government officials of their moral duties before God: "How are you using your authority? . . . To crush men's faces into the dust?"'[102] In 1990, Anne Coomes' *Festo Kivengere: A Biography* appeared—the first (and, to date, the only) major biography of Kivengere.[103] The analysis of the sermons of Kivengere in this study will yield some revisions to Coomes' biography and to those reliant on her. These studies include Senyonyi,[104] Rwabyoma,[105] Stott,[106] MacMaster and Jacobs,[107] Bowen,[108] and two memorial talks about his life and ministry by Senyimba[109] and Ekudu-Adoku.[110] The fact that all these scholars made use of Coomes' for their biographical details, despite each having personal experience of Kivengere, indicates the extent to which Coomes' work has become the benchmark of Kivengere biographies.

---

102. Ward, 'Archbishop Janani Luwum', 214–15.
103. Coomes, *Festo Kivengere*.
104. Senyonyi, 'Philosophy of Evangelism', esp. Chapter I and the section "Literature about Kivengere" under Chapter III, 120–24.
105. Rwabyoma, 'Bishop Festo Kivengere'.
106. Stott, *People My Teachers*, 48–53.
107. Richard K MacMaster and Donald R Jacobs, *A Gentle Wind of God: The Influence of the East Africa Revival* (Scottdale, Pa: Herald Press, 2006), 360–89.
108. Roger Bowen, *A Guide to Preaching* (ed. David Lawrence Edwards and Society for Promoting Christian Knowledge; SPCK International Study Guide; London: SPCK, 2005), 27, 31, 83, 85, 112, 114.
109. Michael Senyimba, 'Festo Kivengere: The Man (Who Never Retreated from Challenges) and His Legacy', Unpublished Paper, delivered at the Bishop Festo Kivengere Memorial Lecture (Kampala, Uganda, May 5, 1991), 1–12.
110. John Ekudu-Adoku, 'The Extent and Implications of His Spiritual and Social Ministry', Unpublished Paper, delivered at the Bishop Festo Kivengere Memorial Lecture (Kampala, Uganda, 1994), 1–22.

From the opening page Kivengere's interest in reconciliation was noted: 'He [Kivengere] travelled widely, preaching reconciliation in Christ'.[111] In 2002 Coomes also published the biography of Michael Cassidy.[112] This book devotes a significant amount of space to Kivengere,[113] and once again, *notes* the importance of reconciliation to Kivengere's life and preaching without *analyzing* it.[114] Further, her focus is the involvement of the African Enterprise in evangelism and reconciliation, in which Kivengere was a central figure—not Kivengere's sermons.

1.3.3 Some Sermons in Focus

1.3.3.1 Inkelaar-de Mos 1988

The first attempt at a sustained reflection on Kivengere's sermons appeared in Charlotte Inkelaar-de Mos' 1988 doctoral thesis.[115] Although her primary interest was the history of the AEE, she made a small but significant attempt to engage with the published sermons of Kivengere, as well as with some additional audio-recorded sermons.[116] After analyzing the sermons in Kivengere's books, *Revolutionary Love* and *Hope for Uganda and Beyond*, Inkelaar-de Mos pulled together seven elements of his theology which she argued constituted Kivengere's message: The Cross, Calvary Love, Reconciliation, Renewal, The Holy Spirit, Fellowship, and Hope.[117] These elements link together in Kivengere's emphasis of the cross, which forms a central place in the teaching of Keswick on sanctification.[118]

---

111. Coomes, *Festo Kivengere*.
112. Coomes, *African Harvest*.
113. For the significant space that Coomes devote to Kivengere in her book, see Coomes, *African Harvest*, 546.
114. Coomes, *African Harvest*, 368.
115. Inkelaar-de Mos, 'Evangelistic Enterprise'.
116. For a list of other sermons of Kivengere that Inkelaar-de Mos accessed for her study, see Appendix 3.
117. Inkelaar-de Mos, 'Evangelistic Enterprise', 62–69.
118. See Chapter Three, 2. 'The Keswick Movement and the East African Revival: The Approach and Context of Preaching'.

Inkelaar-de Mos noted that Kivengere's preaching is characterized by narrative, repetition,[119] and elements of biographical reflection.[120] Concerning the last of these, she points to frequent use of three features of his own biography: (i) the story of his conversion—how he met the Lord at the cross; (ii) the story of his reconciliation with an English missionary he hated; and (iii) an account of how it dawned on him to forgive Idi Amin.[121]

Engaging with Kivengere's sermons 'Love and the Unlovable' and 'Loved into Joy',[122] and asking why and in what way the theological theme of the cross is so central to Kivengere's thinking, Inkelaar-de Mos related its centrality to the story of his conversion.[123] Turning to the sermon 'The Cross and World Evangelization',[124] she summarized it in six related points: the cross is the *message* of evangelism; the cross is the *motivating power* of evangelism; the cross is the *inspiration* of evangelism; the cross is the *prize* of evangelism; the cross is the *uniting power* of evangelism; and the cross is the *drawing power* of evangelism.[125] In dealing with this sermon Inkelaar-de Mos gives her sole mention of reconciliation, observing that according to Kivengere, God was personally present in his Son Jesus Christ on the cross at Calvary and God reconciled himself to the hostile world.

From another sermon, 'Sense Out of Nonsense',[126] Inkelaar–de Mos argues that for Kivengere, the cross freed Paul from his Jewish prejudice against Gentiles. The freedom that Kivengere got from the cross brought him to a personal realization of the love of Jesus for him. Jesus never treated His murderers as 'torturers' or 'them'. With Christ as his model, Kivengere therefore had no option but to forgive Idi Amin. Once again, and as we will see below, Kivengere's sermons link this event also to reconciliation in Christ. Thus Inkelaar–de Mos' helpful study on Kivengere's

---

119. Inkelaar-de Mos does not qualify Kivegere's repetitions, whether thematic, rhetorical, or stylistic.
120. Inkelaar-de Mos, 'Evangelistic Enterprise', 71.
121. Inkelaar-de Mos, 'Evangelistic Enterprise', 71. For the full-blown story see, Kivengere, *I Love Idi Amin*.
122. Inkelaar-de Mos, 'Evangelistic Enterprise', 62.
123. Inkelaar-de Mos, 'Evangelistic Enterprise', 71.
124. Inkelaar-de Mos, 'Evangelistic Enterprise', 63.
125. Inkelaar-de Mos, 'Evangelistic Enterprise', 63–64.
126. Inkelaar-de Mos, 'Evangelistic Enterprise', 64.

contextual message and the style of his preaching certainly touches on key elements which recur constantly in his sermons, but it shows no interest in examining Kivengere's preaching in the light of Biblical theology and does not explore the connection Kivengere makes between these elements and reconciliation.

1.3.3.2 John M. M. Senyonyi 1992

John Senyonyi's 1992 MA dissertation was the first detailed attempt to study Kivengere's sermons. Whereas Inkelaar–de Mos dealt with Kivengere's sermons as a small part of her larger treatment of the history of AEE, Senyonyi's analysis focused directly on the sermons. He observed that the sermons in *Revolutionary Love* are based on Bible stories. Senyonyi only mentions in passing that this book has much to say about reconciliation and he never engages with the sermon 'Love Reconciles'.[127] He acknowledges, however, that Kivengere was inclined to address reconciliation in his post-exile writings,[128] and Senyonyi further suggests that in the post-exile period, Kivengere gave more consideration to the human heart, the cross, and the Holy Spirit.[129]

Sin in the human heart interrupts the flow of the Holy Sprit in our hearts and dampens our hearts, causing them to become less receptive to the purpose of God. But only the Holy Spirit, working through Jesus Christ, can meet man's crying need for forgiveness and cleansing from sin. Although he does not explicitly mention reconciliation in this consideration, Senyonyi draws attention to the idea when he mentioned Jesus Christ who meets man's crying need for forgiveness and cleansing from sin.

Senyonyi identified three 'foundation stones' of Kivengere's approach to evangelism in these sermons: the Cross, the Love of God, and the Holy Spirit.[130] However, for Senyonyi, Kivengere excelled among these in em-

---

127. For Senyoni's in passing comment, see Senyonyi, 'Philosophy of Evangelism', 91. For the sermons 'Love Reconciles', see Kivengere, *Revolutionary Love*, 25–29.
128. Senyonyi, 'Philosophy of Evangelism', 90–91.
129. Senyonyi, 'Philosophy of Evangelism', 93–94.
130. Senyonyi, 'Philosophy of Evangelism', 132–33; Festo Kivengere, 'One Antidote Alone', *Outlook* 16 (June 1979): 1; Festo Kivengere, 'Citizens of the Kingdom', *Outlook* 18 (April 1981): 1.

phasizing the love of God over his peers. Senyonyi observes that this must not be construed to mean that the Revival did not preach the love of God. For already the love of God was preached by the Revival owing to the fact that they preached the message of the cross, which by its nature encompasses the love of God. 'God's love was embodied in the Saviour'.[131] However, Senyonyi argues that unlike other revivalists, the love of God is a subject that occupies much of Kivengere's writings.[132]

From articles by Kivengere in *Decision*[133] and *Outlook*,[134] Senyonyi observes that liberation and reconciliation are common images in Kivengere's writings on the conversion of a sinner to God. Kivengere views humanity as enslaved in sin, thus usurping the centrality of Jesus from our lives. But once a man turns his heart to 'the risen Jesus, living Jesus Christ', liberation from sin occurs. Indeed, to be centred in Jesus Christ is in and of itself liberation. Engaging with this first image, Senyonyi highlights that according to Kivengere, liberation means conversion in Jesus Christ. In effect, we submit that conversion in Jesus Christ cannot be isolated from reconciliation in Jesus Christ.

In the second image, reconciliation, Senyonyi mentions that the 'image of reconciliation is particularly noticeable in his later years'.[135] Senyonyi argues that Kivengere understood reconciliation to be part of conversion: 'to be converted is primarily to be reconciled'.[136] Reconciliation is personal and to be found in Jesus Christ, whose death to save sinners is personal. It is personal because God is personal. God never deals with sin or alienation except personally. Kivengere invites his readers (i.e., of *Decision*, July–August, 1984) to come into that personal reconciliation, now, if they have never done it before.

---

131. Senyonyi, 'Philosophy of Evangelism', 133.
132. Senyonyi, 'Philosophy of Evangelism', 133.
133. Festo Kivengere, 'A Challenge In Love', *Decision* (July 1962): 8–9; Festo Kivengere, 'The Ministry of Reconciliation', *Decision* (August 1984): 4.
134. Festo Kivengere, 'Called to Make Friends', *Outlook* 20 (Fall 1987): 2; Festo Kivengere, 'Are You Starving?', *Outlook* 17 (October 1987): 2; Festo Kivengere, 'Practise Christ's Wholeness', *Outlook* 16 (March 1982): 1.
135. Senyonyi, 'Philosophy of Evangelism', 111.
136. Kivengere, 'Called to Make Friends', 2; Senyonyi, 'Philosophy of Evangelism', 111.

Kivengere, therefore, understands conversion as a life-transforming event. To him an individual who is reconciled becomes a reconciler. Reconciliation came at a heavy cost to God and there never can be easy reconciliation. There has to be deep repentance because the misery of humanity calls for it. Reconciliation comes directly from God, the one who is personally present in Christ, the means by which reconciliation is attained. Senyonyi's study concludes that Kivengere was convinced that all social, political, and economic fragmentation has 'its roots in spiritual fragmentation'; hence, obeying Jesus lays a foundation upon which reconstruction and reconciliation can build.[137]

Senyonyi's helpful study, like Inkelaar-de Mos with whom he never interacted, offers a helpful engagement with Kivengere's contextual message and style of preaching, touching on significant elements in the sermons directly linked to reconciliation: the Cross, the Love of God, the Holy Spirit, the centrality of Jesus, Conversion, and Liberation. However, he does not examine the sermons from the perspective of Biblical theology and he never explores the connection that Kivengere makes between these elements and reconciliation.

1.3.3.3 Peter R. Rwabyoma 2007

Also focusing on *Revolutionary Love*, Peter Rwabyoma does not analyze the sermons from a biblical-theology perspective, but like Inkelaar-de Mos and Senyonyi, he restricts himself to an analysis of Kivengere's *style of preaching*. Rwabyoma also criticises Kivengere's preaching: 'his sermons did not have a logical progression in the form of a three-point sermon'; his preaching 'was like painting in a canvas';[138] 'This method of preaching was so taxing to a hazy memory'.[139] Considering that Rwabyoma had personal knowledge of Kivengere and worked closely with him (he was ordained by Kivengere and served as his chaplain for many years),[140] it seems odd that his evaluation of Kivengere's sermons engaged only with the book, *Revolutionary Love*. With

---

137. Senyonyi, 'Philosophy of Evangelism', 135.
138. Rwabyoma, 'Bishop Festo Kivengere', 45.
139. Rwabyoma, 'Bishop Festo Kivengere', 45.
140. Rwabyoma, 'Bishop Festo Kivengere', 2.

more of Kivengere's sermons at our disposal, this thesis hopes to make a more judicious assessment of Kivengere's style, as well as the *content* of his sermons from a biblical-theological perspective.

It is surprising how the few scholars that have interacted with his sermons have resisted an analysis of the doctrine that so captivated and produced Kivengere's preaching. Failing to engage with the biblical theology of reconciliation in his sermons is to miss the significance of the 'centre of the New Testament' message that shaped his thought, life and preaching. (For a comparison of Kivengere's sermons that Inkelaar-de Mos, Senyonyi and Rwabyoma interacted with, see appendix 3.)

1.4 The Present Study

This study is an inquiry into the role of reconciliation in Kivengere's preaching between 1971–1988 in Uganda and beyond. We will not be concerned in any significant sense with the question of *how* Kivengere delivered his sermons, namely, Kivengere's style and personality in his preaching.[141] Rwabyoma recently analyzed his communication skills and how he applied them in the mission of the church in Uganda. Taking his lead from Coomes and Stott,[142] in addition to his personal knowledge of Kivengere, Rwabyoma noted the positive marks of Kivengere's delivery of his sermons include the following: he was a gifted speaker; he captured his audience with vivid pictures, yet preached his message with delightful touches of African humour; he spoke with incredible natural eloquence; and in his application he was bold and challenging to his audience to respond to God's word.[143]

Concerning his preaching style, Charlotte Inkelaar-de Mos noted that Kivengere's preaching was full of stories, repetition, and elements of biographical reflection. There was frequent use of three features of his own biography: the story of his conversion—how he met the Lord 'at the cross';

---

141. For his style and personality of preaching the gospel in Uganda, see Rwabyoma, 'Bishop Festo Kivengere'.
142. Stott, *People My Teachers*, 49.
143. Rwabyoma, 'Bishop Festo Kivengere', 25–27.

the story of his reconciliation with an English missionary he hated; and an account of how it dawned on him to forgive Idi Amin.[144]

This study does not ignore the above elements of his homiletics, for they are in fact drawn from observations of his sermons.[145] But as important as these may be, this study is not so much interested in Kivengere's *delivery* style. This study is also not primarily concerned with the question of *why* Kivengere picked certain biblical texts to preach reconciliation. *Instead this study focuses on the 'what'—the content. It asks the more fundamental question of whether there is a coherent 'biblical-theological' theme in Kivengere's preaching of reconciliation and, if so, how does it function?* To address this question, this study focuses primarily on the content of Kivengere's preaching and what he does with the New Testament theme of reconciliation in his twenty-six sermons. Thus the concern in this study is to *analyze from a biblical-theological perspective the role of the Christian doctrine of reconciliation in Kivengere's preaching in Uganda and further afield in the period 1971–1988.*

To commence the study five subjects require some explanation.

1.4.1 The Collection

We have noted that the previous studies of Inkelaar-de Mos, Senyonyi, and Rwabyoma utilize only a limited number of Kivengere's sermons, on the whole, those already published. This is understandable, especially given that Kivengere's extant sermons are widely scattered throughout the globe, making collection difficult.[146]

In preparation for the present research, more than 500 transcriptions of Kivengere's unpublished sermons have been collected from different continents and countries: (Africa, United States of America, Europe, Australia, Asia, and New Zealand) and deposited in the Moore Theological College library. Given this wealth of primary material, we are in a much better

---

144. Inkelaar-de Mos, 'Evangelistic Enterprise', 71.
145. See Chapters Five and Six.
146. See Appendix 5 for a catalog of the sermons in my collection. Archives of AEE African Enterprise Offices: Pasadena, Kampala, and Australia were able to give the sermons that are in our collection. Archives of All Souls, Langham Palace, London sent me copies of several sermons and materials.

position than previous scholars to examine Kivengere in general and his preaching in particular. We are now able:
1. to provide a fuller description of Kivengere's sermonic output than ever before;
2. to provide a description of Kivengere's sermonic content;
3. to provide an analysis of Kivengere's sermonic method; and, especially
4. to present a clearer portrait of Kivengere as a preacher, and especially as a preacher of reconciliation.

This large body of sermons in our collection adds to the already existing materials enabling a fuller biography to be constructed and previous errors to be corrected.[147] However, further to this contribution this thesis will in particular,

5. provide an evaluation of Kivengere's sermons from a biblical-theological framework; and,

---

147. Two obvious errors not only serve as examples, but can also set the historical record straight even at this preliminary stage of the thesis. Firstly, in the recent work of Old, twice he designates Bishop Festo Kivengere as the Archbishop of the Church of Uganda: firstly, 'Kivengere served as the Anglican archbishop of Uganda from 1979 until his death in 1988'; and secondly, in the footnote '101. For further information on the life of Archbishop Kivengere' (See Old, *Reading and Preaching*, 198.) However, popular and much loved as Kivengere was, he never became Archbishop of the Church of Uganda; rather Bishop Silvanus Wani the successor of Archbishop Janani Luwum, in Madi and West Nile Diocese was also elected and consecrated to succeed him as Archbishop of Uganda. (See A. D. Tom Tuma and Phares Mutibwa, eds., *A Century of Christianity in Uganda, 1877–1977: A Historical Appraisal of the Development of the Uganda Church Over the Last One Hundred Years* (Nairobi: Uzima Press, 1978), 174.). The second example comes from Kivengere himself, who was not immune from making the occasional error. On one occasion Kivengere tells of the death of two Ugandan Bishops murdered by the fleeing soldiers of Idi Amin at Jinja (in the Kivengere sermon Kivengere, 'In Christ', [#2]. Yet, there is no known historical evidence of the death of *two* Bishops. Those murdered included only one except Bishop, John Wasikye (See David Twinamatsiko, 'The Church of Uganda and the Amin Regime January 25, 1971 Through April 11, 1979' (MA Thesis, Alexandria: Virginia Theological Seminary, 1994). The other was Masete, his school bursar. The larger number of sermons now collected will facilitate a more fully researched biography, not only promising a better biography but also enabling a better understanding of Kivengere's preaching. Again, two examples will illustrate the possibilities, at this preliminary stage. Many scholars are positive about Kivengere's preaching and to such people our collection will further their already good understanding of his preaching. Such voices include, Stott, *People My Teachers*, 48; Rwabyoma, 'Bishop Festo Kivengere'; Coomes, *Festo Kivengere*; Russell, 'Ministry of Reconciliation', 304–07; Inkelaar-de Mos, 'Evangelistic Enterprise'; Senyonyi, 'Philosophy of Evangelism'; and, Old, *Reading and Preaching*.

6. account for the influence and impact of Kivengere's preaching of reconciliation on church and society, both in Uganda and beyond.

1.4.2 Rationale for the Selection

This is the first major study of Kivengere's sermons but it does not aim to be a comprehensive study, for the vast number of sermons collected necessitates a selection to enable a clear focus. With no major study of Kivengere as a preacher, it goes without saying that there has also been no study of particular *themes* in his preaching. This is a biblical-theological evaluation[148] of a New Testament theme in Kivengere's sermons, namely, reconciliation. This theme is not arbitrarily chosen. Reconciliation is clearly a theme of central concern and of great significance to Kivengere's preaching and ministry. Selecting sermons from a particularly significant period of Kivengere's preaching career (1971–1988) provides an even sharper focus, allowing his message of reconciliation to be evaluated against this particularly turbulent period.

The sermons under consideration were orally preached and recorded during the period 1971–1988 and delivered to a variety of audiences in Uganda, Ghana, the United States of America, the Netherlands, Britain, and Australia. Considered together, the sermons disclose issues close to Kivengere's heart—what he believed would effect transformation in his different audiences (individually and collectively). In the sermons, Kivengere names the deep wounds that Ugandans suffered under the rule of Idi Amin in the period 1971–1979, noting how Jesus the reconciler brought healing to Kivengere's own life, and to the situation.

---

148. For an explanation of biblical-theology consistent with the approach adopted in this thesis, so Donald A. Carson, 'Current Issues in Biblical Theology: A New Testament Perspective', *BBR* 5 (1995): 5, 17–41; Donald A. Carson, 'The Role of Exegesis in Systematic Theology', in *Doing Theology in Today's World: Essays in Honor of Kenneth S. Kantzer* (ed. John D Woodbridge, Thomas Edward McComiskey, and Kenneth S Kantzer; Grand Rapids, Mich.: Zondervan, 1991), 39–76. For an excellent biblical theology approach to preaching, see Graeme Goldsworthy, *Preaching the Whole Bible as Christian Scripture: The Application of Biblical Theology to Expository Preaching* (Leicester: Inter-Varsity, 2000). For a working definition of my 'biblical-theological' perspective, see below 4.4.4 'Elements of Biblical Theology'.

As a preliminary step in research, these five hundred sermons were catalogued in orderly sequence, before a selection was made to yield the twenty-six sermons in focus in this thesis. These are grouped into two broad categories: explicit reconciliation sermons, preached from Pauline reconciliation texts (seventeen, studied in chapter 4) and non-explicit reconciliation sermons, preached from passages from the Bible which do not mention reconciliation.

In chapter 5, beside one reflection on reconciliation from Kivengere's pen, we deal with a selection of eight non-explicit sermons in which he preached reconciliation using one key: Jesus Christ—the life, death, and resurrection of Jesus Christ. Each time the text mentions the life, death, and resurrection of Jesus Christ, for Kivengere there is reconciliation.

In this study the non-explicit reconciliation passages act as a control. For the explicit group it could be argued that Kivengere was constrained to preach reconciliation simply because it was mentioned in the text. The non-explicit group, however, shows that he preached reconciliation even when the text did not mention it. Clearly, this is because of the importance that he attaches to reconciliation—it is close to his heart. The catalogue also acted as another point of control in our selection of the non-explicit sermons. From the titles in the catalogue it is fairly easy to identify that Kivengere preached reconciliation over a long period of time wherever he went, even when his passage or address title does not explicitly mention reconciliation.

1.4.3 The Shape of the Study

Preaching arises from, and is, in turn, addressed to a particular human context. In order to evaluate Kivengere's preaching of reconciliation, therefore, this thesis outlines something of his biographical context, paying particular attention to the East African Revival in which his Christian faith was, in turn, born, nurtured and expressed throughout his days (chapter 2). Four key theological influences acknowledged by Kivengere himself are then examined, in order to discover some potential criteria against which the sermons can be evaluated (chapter 3). Kivengere's clear debt to the East African Revival brought him under the influence of the Keswick Movement, albeit with his own African flavour. Decades after his theological education in Pittsburgh, Kivengere acknowledged his debt to Karl Barth, and to Barth's son and Kivengere's New Testament teacher, Markus. Since each of these three influences had a particular concern for 'reconciliation', it is worthwhile to examine this doctrine in their hands, in order to then compare it with the doctrine as expounded in Kivengere's sermons. Because Kivengere's approach to the scriptural text has affinities with Barth's exegetical method, this section will also briefly examine Karl Barth's 'Theological Exegesis' and Markus Barth's input into the Biblical Theology Movement. The fourth and last influence to be examined is the New Testament itself. Kivengere clearly regarded the Bible as his authority, and the New Testament message of *reconciliation* at its centre. It is therefore worthwhile to briefly outline the New Testament's explicit teaching on reconciliation to provide a most significant part of the framework used to analyze Kivengere's preaching on this theme. A reconciliation time-line showing his preaching of reconciliation over the period 1971–1988 is then provided (chapter 4). With these preliminaries dealt with, the sermons themselves will be analyzed. This will be done in two groups: those sermons on New Testament passages explicitly about reconciliation (chapter 5) and those which speak of reconciliation, even though they are purportedly expositions of the New Testament passages which do not explicitly mention reconciliation (chapter 6). The analysis of both groups will also be assisted by an essay Kivengere wrote explicitly addressing the topic of reconciliation. A conclusion (chapter 7) draws together the results and teases out the implications of the entire thesis.

1.4.4 Research Methodology

To analyze the role of the doctrine of reconciliation in Kivengere's preaching in the period 1971–1988 five aspects of each of the twenty-six selected sermons are described. First, a clear sermon title is stated. Second, the sermon is situated in the original context in which it was preached. Third, a statement of the basic shape of the sermon is described. Fourth, a clear description of the sermon flow is described. Fifthly and finally, and most significantly for this thesis, the analysis concludes with a consideration of elements of Kivengere's biblical theology that are linked to, or arise out of, Kivengere's understanding of reconciliation. These five considerations enable the role of the doctrine of reconciliation in Kivengere's preaching, to be exposed, as well as serving as grids through which the influence of that preaching may be, at least to some degree, discussed.

1.4.4.1 Sermon Title

Since no catalogue of Kivengere's sermons was yet in existence one was developed as part of the preparation for this research. It acted as well as a system to provide a unique identification number for each sermon.[149]

1.4.4.2 Situate the Sermon

As the sermons are discussed they are situated according to the original context of their preaching: when, where, who was the audience (congregation). At this point connections are drawn with the historical circumstances of the day or with Kivengere's biography (i.e. chapter 2 or influence as in chapter 3).

1.4.4.3 Sermon Flow

This is followed by a description of the flow of the sermon, giving more focus to the content and how one paragraph in the sermon builds towards the next.

We have indicated paragraphs and pages with the conventions: p. 1, #1 (to be read as page 1, paragraph 1); pp. 1–2 (for pages 1–2); and, 4 mins. (for 4 minutes into the sermon) for those on audio. The transcripts have some obvious weaknesses, including typographical errors, repetition of sentences or phrases, and missing pages. Square brackets are used for the corrections that we make, but these are kept to a minimum to avoid the risk of changing or losing the meaning of Kivengere's point.

1.4.4.4 Elements of Biblical Theology

Each sermon is examined for elements indicating his biblical theology because the *primary* area of interest in the sermons is Kivengere's biblical theology, expressed in his preaching of reconciliation. Since biblical theology is an approach which seeks to explain the Bible on its terms, content is prior to method. God's plan of salvation unfolds step by step through biblical

---

149. See introductory explanation of the catalogue in Appendix 5.

history, centring upon Jesus Christ and his great act of reconciliation. This content then yields a way of approaching the Scriptures in which the details of any one passage are explained against the larger context of the unfolding plan of salvation and this centre. With this perspective in mind, each sermon will be examined for elements of Kivengere's biblical theology related to reconciliation both in terms of his content and the exegetical expository approach that arises from it.

The working definition of biblical theology presumed in this study derives from Graeme Goldsworthy: 'Biblical Theology is a way of understanding the Bible as a whole, so that we can see the plan of salvation as it unfolds step by step. It is concerned with God's message to us in the form that it actually takes in Scripture'.[150] Biblical theology, therefore, strictly speaking, is an approach to understanding the Bible in its entirety. God has revealed himself in human history not on only one occasion but over time, historically (see Heb 1:1–3). But it is also true that the salvific purpose of God centres upon the work of Jesus Christ (see 2 Cor 1:20). But Biblical theology is more than simply history, for God's revelation of himself has implications for human life, for it is 'God's message to us'.

God's grand purposes for the world from creation (Gen 1–2) to new creation (Rev 21–22) are centred on the reconciling work of Jesus Christ; and this great act at the centre of history—Jesus Christ—gave rise to the Christian preaching. Taken hold of by Jesus Christ, Kivengere was himself captured by God's reconciling work centred in Jesus Christ and he found himself a preacher of reconciliation.

1.4.5 The Influence of Kivengere's Reconciliation Preaching

This study does not pretend to be a social history of the impact of Kivengere's preaching. To ascertain how his preaching was received and the impact it made would be a very different inquiry, and, although interesting, well beyond our chosen scope. However, given the nature of preaching, the

---

150. Graeme Goldsworthy, *According to Plan: The Unfolding Revelation of God in the Bible* (Sydney: Lancer Press, 1991), 33. For a definition of 'Biblical Theology' that comes close to Goldsworthy's cf. Geerhardus Vos, *Biblical Theology: Old and New Testaments* (Edinburgh: Banner of Truth Trust, 1975), 5. Vos is explicit on the self-revelation of God deposited in the Bible.

sermons being studied from time to time act as windows into the worlds of both the preacher and his audiences. The sermons therefore provide some insight into what his audiences were experiencing, such as the terrors of Idi Amin's rule, and what they wanted their spiritual leader to understand about their anguish. They also provide insight into what Kivengere himself believed preaching reconciliation can do to heal their deep wounds. For example, Kivengere in the sermon *In Christ: AO: 19790429, #2* (pp. 3–4, #8–#9) said,

> A young lady, lovely highly educated person, lost her brother last year. . . . This man was taken from his home. He . . . was tortured to death. I can't put it in words. I met this man's sister, she said to me . . . , 'I have never felt like I would kill; now, if you gave me a knife, and you put Amin or one of his men in front of me, I will kill'. Now, tell me, how do you change that lady? Tell me, how you change her from this grip of destruction, which has invaded her personality, her children experience that because they feel what their mother is feeling.
>
> I want to tell you we have a stupendous job in Uganda today, not only giving people food to eat . . . there is an area which these services will never meet. For deep down in the human persons there are wounds, which needs one antidote alone. That antidote is found in 2 Cor 5:11–20.

Even if this does not enable conclusions to be drawn about the actual impact made by Kivengere's preaching, it does enable some insight into the impact he was trying to achieve through his preaching. The sermons show, in practice, his vision of reconciliation and what it might achieve.

With the above orientation of this study, we now turn to chapter 2.

CHAPTER TWO
Historical and Biographical Context of Kivengere's Preaching

2.1 A Synopsis

This chapter aims to provide a historical and biographical context for Kivengere's preaching of reconciliation that is as congruent as possible with material in his sermons. In fact, constantly touching upon current events in Uganda and details of his own life, the sermons of Kivengere now collected constitute another body of primary material as relevant for the history of Uganda in this period as for the construction of Kivengere's own biography. The historical context is discussed in two parts (sections 2 and 3): Uganda the nation and Ugandan Christianity, both itemising some of the deep wounds in the country. Section 4 takes up the East African Revival Movement of which Kivengere was a product, a spokesman and a preacher, both in Uganda and further afield. Section 5 presents 'Kivengere's homiletical biography', and section 6 provides a summary of the chapter.

2.2 Historical Context (I): Uganda the Nation

Before dealing with the period immediately relevant to Kivengere's preaching (1962–1988), and although it strictly falls outside the scope of this study, it is necessary firstly to understand the older history of Uganda

(1894–1962) to appreciate the period in which Kivengere was preaching and in order to understand many of his historical reminiscences.

2.2.1 From 1894–1962: The Origin of Divisions and Tensions

Modern Uganda, with its present international boundaries, covers a wide area containing different nationalities, religions and languages, and its distinctiveness has evolved over the years as the boundaries changed.[1] Uganda was created by the British colonial administration in 1894,[2] ushering in a political 'unity', and thus creating a pathway towards the independent nation declared on 9 October 1962. Prior to 1894, the motivation to make Uganda into a nation came from the scramble for territories by the imperial powers, Great Britain, Germany, and France, in the wake of the 1885 Treaty of Berlin.[3] By enforcing the cause to end the slave trade, the treaty legitimised the conquest of African territories.[4]

In the case of Uganda, the main motivating forces for the conquest were the headwaters of the Nile and the wealth of ivory.[5] To their surprise, the new powers discovered that the region had some well-established political constituents, some with 'strong centralised monarchies'.[6] The Buganda Kingdom was 'the largest, most sophisticated, and most prosperous',[7] and according to the explorer, Henry Morton Stanley (1841–1904), Buganda

---

1. See map of Uganda showing the present boundaries on page vi. Along the boundaries are physical features like lakes and rivers—these are features that ironically formerly united the same people groups rather than divide them into separate countries! For an in-depth bibliography on the history of Christianity in Uganda, see Philip Jenkins, *The Next Christendom: The Coming of Global Christianity* (Rev. and expanded ed.; The Future of Christianity Trilogy; Oxford: Oxford University Press, 2007), 764–65. For the different languages and nationalities see, Patrick J. St. G Johnstone and Jason Mandryk, eds., *Operation World* (21st-century ed.; Nunawading: Triune, 2001 [1978]), 641–44.
2. Ian Leggett, *Uganda* (Oxford: Oxfam, 2001), 1.
3. Mark A Noll, *The New Shape of World Christianity: How American Experience Reflects Global Faith* (Downers Grove, Ill.: IVP Academic, 2009), 173.
4. Cedric Pulford, *Eating Uganda: From Christianity to Conquest* (Banbury: Ituri, 1999), 81.
5. Leggett, *Uganda*, 15.
6. Paul Gifford, *African Christianity: Its Public Role* (London: Hurst & Company, 1998), 112.
7. Leggett, *Uganda*, 15.

held much promise for the development of Christianity, commerce and civilization.[8] This promise was realized in at least three ways. First, it became the centre of missionary activities, thus, the Baganda[9] became the first people in Uganda to hear the gospel, to read, write, and to have formal education.

Second, because of its central strategic location in Uganda, Buganda became the practical centre from which the British Colonial administration conducted development in Uganda. Their headquarters were at Entebbe and Kampala became the business district. Third, given that the Baganda had the privilege of being the largest and strongest ethnic group in Uganda, which hosted missionary and political institutions, it is not surprising that they became collaborators with the Protectorate government.[10] Through annexing the bordering kingdoms to Buganda, the Protectorate government provided oversight of local self-government through the use of various treaties with local leaders.[11]

Effectively the British administration indirectly ruled from the centre, using the Baganda as sub-imperialists. This rule had mixed outcomes: a long-standing division between the Protestants, *Bangereza* (English), and the Catholics, *Bafaransa* (French);[12] a perceived north-south divide;[13] imbalance within the Buganda region arising from the central alliance with Buganda;[14] and because the Protestant and not the Catholic influence

---

8. Pulford, *Eating Uganda*, 23.
9. For the different usage of the prefix: *Bu-, Mu-, Ba-, Lu-,* and *Ki-,* (ganda), see J. F. Faupel, *African Holocaust: The Story of the Uganda Martyrs* (2nd ed.; Deacon Books Series; London: Chapman, 1965 [1962]), 8.
10. Samwiri Rubaraza Karugire, *A Political History of Uganda* (Nairobi: Heinemann Educational Books, 1980), 89.
11. Pulford, *Eating Uganda*, 159.
12. Gifford, *African Christianity*, 113.
13. See Leggett, *Uganda*, 19. To the north of the Nile River, were the Nilotic peoples with their set way of life, and to the south of the Nile River were Bantu peoples with a different way of life. Once the colonial administration lumped them together in the new Protectorate, their earlier prejudices and inequalities were also incorporated, thus creating problems that will last in the new Protectorate. For in-depth discussions of the disparities in Uganda see Abdu Basajabaka Kawalya Kasozi, Nakanyike Musisi, and James Mukooza Sejjengo, *The Social Origins of Violence in Uganda, 1964-1985* (Montreal: McGill-Queen's University Press, 1994).
14. Mutibwa, *Uganda Since Independence*.

shaped the country, the nation developed to be part of predominantly Christian East Africa, rather than the predominantly Islamic northern part of Africa. These four outcomes of British rule created a setting, which, by Kivengere's time, led to violence and a deeply wounded country.

2.2.2 From 1962–1988: Deep Wounds Created in the Country

At the time of independence (October 1962), Uganda was already wracked by stark regional imbalances[15] arising from the divisions and tensions carried forward from the colonial era, in which the system of rule was divide-and-conquer politics. Milton Obote (1925–2005) became Prime Minister of the independent Uganda (Obote I) in a shared alliance with the Buganda Kingdom, whose *Kabaka* (King) became the first President. However, this alliance had serious weaknesses and the power sharing soon ended.

The weakness of this alliance erupted in the 1966 crisis, in which Obote suspended the constitution and Amin, then General of the Uganda Army, crushed the Kabaka's palace at Mengo.[16] The Kabaka fled into exile and died in Britain, and the hopes of a newly formed democracy in independent Uganda ceased. This paved the way for Amin to overthrow Obote in the 1971 military coup and rule the nation with terror, murdering Obote's supporters around the country, especially from Lango and Acholi,[17] expel-

---

15. Amii Omara-Otunnu, *Politics and the Military in Uganda, 1890-1985* (London: Macmillan, 1987), 80–82. For a study that examined the emergence of modern Uganda in a region beset with persisting imbalance that led to political contest entrenching violence as an instrument of change, thus heightening the demand for light weapons, see Sabiiti Mutengesa and Dylan Hendrickson, 'Prospects for Addressing Uganda's Small Arms Problem Through Security Reform' (vol. 7; CSDG Papers; Kings College London: Conflict, Security & Development Group, 2007), 9, Online: securityanddevelopment.org.

16. For an in-depth biographical account of the Kabaka Muteesa's strained relations with of Obote, see King of Buganda Mutesa, *Desecration of My Kingdom* (London: Constable, 1967).

17. Discussions on the murders include, Erin Day, 'Uganda', in *World Minorities: A Second Volume* (ed. Georgina Ashworth; Sunbury: Quartermaine House, 1978), 137–41. Day chronicles the slaughter of Acholi and Langi soldiers and civilians whom Amin suspected to be Obote's sympathisers. Day also gives helpful insight into the legal reasons for the massacres based in the decrees that Amin issued in the first two years of his rule. For an anonymous account revealing the massacres of soldiers in Amin's army and other individuals, like the Chief Justice Benedicto Kiwanuka, see Munger and Anon, *Inside Amin's Uganda: More Africans Murdered*, 11–22. Stanley Meisler, 'From Dreams to Brutality', *Nation* 215/15 (November 13, 1972): 463–66. Misler notes the killings

ling the Asian community, and persecuting the church. This lasted until April 1979 when the joint forces of the Tanzania People's Defence Forces (TPDF) and the Uganda National Liberation Front (UNLF),[18] which later formed Uganda National Liberation Army (UNLA), overthrew him.[19]

When the TPDF left the UNLA to manage the nation post-Amin, the old ethnic differences and regional imbalances reasserted their influence. This led to successive short-term governments before the multi-party election of 1980,[20] which saw the return of Obote to presidency for the second time (Obote II).[21] The economy was in ruins, guns were in indiscriminate hands, and, rejecting the elections, Yoweri Kaguta Museveni (1944–) went to the bush and built a guerrilla movement that later captured power in 1986.[22]

Into this troubled context, Kivengere found himself thrust as a preacher of reconciliation.

---

and army excesses, especially the fact that Ugandans treating each other worse than they did the Asians. John S Saul, 'The Unsteady State: Uganda, Obote and General Amin', *Review of African Political Economy* 5 (April 1976): 12–38. Saul discusses Amin's post coup murders. 'Amin's Death Roll', *Transition (Accra)* 49/9/6 (September 1975): 17, 21, 27. W.E.B. Du Bois Institute, in the article lists 571 entries of names of persons executed under Amin's regime with some entries stating brief accounts of the killings.

18. Kivengere explains in a press conference that at Moshi Unity Conference it was decided that since the war was still on-going and other Ugandans were yet to be included in the interim government, it was deemed wise to call it a front. See Kivengere, 'World Vision: with Festo Kivengere', p. 8, #8.

19. Pulford, *Eating Uganda*, 39. Anirudha Gupta, 'Amin's Fall: Would There Be Other Dominoes?', *AQ* 19/1 (June 1979): 4–13. Tony Avirgan, *War in Uganda: The Legacy of Idi Amin* (Westport, Conn: L. Hill, 1982). Twaddle, 'Ousting of Idi Amin', 216–21.

20. Pirouet, *Historical Dictionary of Uganda*, xxiv.

21. Gifford, *African Christianity*, 114. Gifford explains that in December 1980 elections were held, won by UPC, so Obote returned from exile to become President a second time. This election is believed to have been rigged; and, the opposition groups took to the bush to fight Obote's regime. The most important of these groups was Yoweri Museveni's National Resistance Army (NRA)'.

22. Yoweri Museveni, *Sowing the Mustard Seed: The Struggle for Freedom and Democracy in Uganda* (London: Macmillan, 1997). Muhoozi Kainerugaba, *Battles of the Ugandan Resistance: A Tradition of Maneuver* (Oxford: African Books Collective, 2010). Pirouet, *Historical Dictionary of Uganda*, 267–69.

2.3 Historical Context (II): Ugandan Christianity

2.3.1 Missionary Origins

On 30 June 1877, Christianity arrived in Uganda with the first missionaries of the Anglican Church Missionary Society (CMS), who travelled from Zanzibar on the route pioneered by the slave traders. Stanley has proposed the introduction of Christian missionaries, and because he regarded Stanley positively due to his 1875 visit and military assistance, Kabaka Mutesa I (1838–1884) had assented to them coming into his kingdom, Buganda, in the hope that they would give him further military assistance.[23]

A year later one of the key pioneer missionaries of the CMS, a Scottish engineer, Alexander Mackay (1849–1890), arrived.[24] The CMS missionaries brought with them their evangelical tradition.[25] Under the leadership of Henry Venn (1841–1872), CMS kept a clear focus on the primacy of evangelism and operated on the three principles of indigenous churches being self-supporting, self-governing, and self-extending.[26] The principals encompassed a holistic gospel focus. They pioneered and provided Christian education, medicine, and agriculture, and stood against colonial powers over matters of land. These principles shaped the mission work in Buganda and eventually in the rest of Uganda.

---

23. Hansen and Twaddle, *Developing Uganda*, 2.
24. For his brief biography see John C. Lambert, 'Alexander Mackay "The Hero of Uganda"', in *The Romance of Missionary Heroism: True Stories of the Intrepid Bravery and Stirring Adventures of Missionaries with Uncivilised Man, Wild Beasts and the Forces of Nature in all Parts of the World* (London: Seeley & Co., 1907).
25. There is a plethora of materials on the Evangelical Movements in Europe from which the CMS stand in their tradition. A sound understanding of the evangelical movement that emerged in the 17th and 18th centuries as Revival movements within the Protestant circles in Europe see two works: W. Reginald Ward, *The Protestant Evangelical Awakening* (Cambridge: Cambridge University Press, 1992). And, Mark A Noll, *The Rise of Evangelicalism: The Age of Edwards Whitefield and the Wesleys* (A History of Evangelicalism; Nottingham: Inter-Varsity, 2004). For an excellent article on the bounding of evangelical on the basis of the gospel, see, David William Bebbington, 'Towards an Evangelical Identity', in *For Such a Time as This: Perspectives on Evangelicalism, Past, Present and Future* (ed. Steve Brady and Harold Rowdon; London: Evangelical Alliance, 1996), 46. For a good definition of evangelicals see, David William Bebbington, *Evangelicalism in Modern Britain: A History from the 1730s to the 1980s* (London: Unwin Hyman, 1989), 2–17.
26. Pulford, *Eating Uganda*, 39. Kevin Ward, *A History of Global Anglicanism* (Cambridge: Cambridge University Press, 2006), 35.

Kivengere was grateful for the dedication, painful discipleship, and inspiration in gospel work of the foundation laid by CMS. Bishop Alfred Tucker, the second bishop of Eastern Equatorial Province, was the legal advisor on matters of land policy to Ugandans against the British. In his sermon on 'The Love of Christ',[27] and elsewhere,[28] he spoke of the missionaries from Britain walking 800 miles from the coast at Mombasa into Buganda, some dying on the way.[29] He tells of himself being a direct product of missionary evangelism in Uganda and expresses appreciation of the missionaries.[30] If he preached reconciliation in his home country it was from a strong desire to rebuild the nation. When he preached reconciliation abroad, it was from a desire to give back to the churches that sent Uganda missionaries. This is reflected, for example, in his preaching missions codenamed 'From Uganda With Love'[31] or 'From Africa With Love'.[32]

Soon after CMS had come, on 17 February 1879, the first White Fathers arrived in Buganda,[33] Father Simeon Lourdel—popularly known as *Mapera*, a distortion of the French *Mon Père*—and, Brother Amans. Father Lèon Livinhac, the leader of the White Father's party, sent Lourdel and Amans ahead of his group to first meet Kabaka Mutesa. Lourdel was fluent in *Swahili* and it was common knowledge that Mutesa was apprehensive of white men who arrived at his court in large numbers.[34] Livinhac himself

---

27. Festo Kivengere, 'The Love of Christ', Sermon Transcript, July 1977, p. 3, #4–#5, AO: 197707[--].

28. Festo Kivengere, 'Testimony', in *Let the Earth Hear His Voice: Official Reference Volume, Papers and Responses* (ed. J. D Douglas; Minneapolis: World Wide Publications, 1975), 416–17.

29. Kivengere, 'The Love of Christ', p. 3, #4–#5.

30. Festo Kivengere, 'The Unshakable Identity of the Church of Jesus Christ', Sermon Transcript, October 29, 1977, pp. 1–2, #2, AO: 19771029, [#1]. Kivengere, 'Testimony', 416. Festo Kivengere, 'The Release of Forgiveness', in *The Keswick Week 1975: Centenary Year* (London: Marshall, Morgan & Scott, 1975), 27.

31. See Festo Kivengere, 'From Uganda With Love', Sermon Transcript (Preached at Kendall, UK, January 1981), AO:198101[--]*5. This sermon was preached in many Churches in England as a Mission arranged by the Ruanda Mission.

32. Festo Kivengere, *The Spiritual Life of a Pastor*, Videocassette (Sydney: Christian Film Service, 1987).

33. Founded by Charles Lavigerie (then Archbishop of Algiers) in 1867, reached Buganda in 1897. See Adrian Hastings, *The Church in Africa, 1450-1950* (Oxford History of the Christian Church; Oxford: Clarendon Press, 1994), 254–55.

34. J. M. Lukwata, *The First Hundred Years of the Bugandan Church and Her Worship*

stayed behind at Bukumi, on the shore of Lake Victoria, where they began a second mission station.[35] Lourdel met Kabaka Mutesa and gave him gifts—old military uniforms they had bought cheaply from Marché du Temple in Paris[36]—and then sent boats to bring the rest of the party with their goods.[37] Since the Protestant CMS missionaries were already present, the arrival at the court of the White Fathers ushered in religious rivalries: 'The White Fathers at Rubaga, Mutesa's capital, came to the Protestant [church] service, but refuted the message. Mutesa was disturbed. The conflict that swept through central Africa had been launched; it lasted until Vatican II (1962–1965)'.[38]

In the period of Kivengere's ministry, there was some rapprochement between the two Christian traditions. For example, in 1969, the Uganda Joint Christian Council (UJCC) was formed as result of dialogue that addressed the ills that had caused tension between the churches, especially the Anglican and Catholic churches. These two churches worked in solidarity to address the deep wounds Amin had caused.[39] Significantly, Archbishop Janani Luwum (Anglican) and Cardinal Nsubuga (Roman Catholic) jointly went to console Makerere University students when brutally attacked by Amin's soldiers.[40]

Kivengere refers to this incident in which his daughter, Charity, was also involved: 'there are other parts of the world who have seen terrible experiences, like those young people in my country, including my daughter who has had quite nasty experiences as a university student under Amin' (p. 2, #3). Amin's soldiers attacked the university, threw the students through the windows from the third floor, breaking their backs and gashing their heads,

---

(Rome: Ponificium Atheneum S. Anselmi De Urbe, 1991), 24.
35. Peter Falk, *The Growth of the Church in Africa* (Contemporary Evangelical Perspectives; Grand Rapids, Mich.: Zondervan, 1979), 243.
36. Lukwata, *The First Hundred Years of the Bugandan Church and Her Worship*, 24.
37. Glen D Kittler, *The White Fathers* (New York: Image Books, 1961), 149.
38. Falk, *The Growth of the Church in Africa*, 243.
39. Twinamatsiko, 'The Church of Uganda and the Amin Regime January 25, 1971 Through April 11, 1979', 39.
40. M. Mamdani, 'The Makerere Massacre', in *The Debate: University of Dar es Salaam Debate on Class, State & Imperialism* (ed. Yash Tandon; Dar es Salaam: Tanzania Publishing House, 1982), 69–73.

with some losing their eyes. 'My daughter [. . . was] lucky to escape . . .' (p. 2, #3).[41]

Immediately following their joint visit to Makerere, the Catholic bishops and the Anglican bishops (including senior Muslim leaders) met under the chairmanship of Luwum, and issued a letter of protest to Amin expressing their concern over the appalling situation in Uganda, especially the indiscipline in the army. This expression was understood by Amin to amount to a wide denunciation of his military regime.[42] Because Luwum signed them, this provoked Amin's hostility towards him. It was against this background that Amin's government considered church leaders like Luwum who had national and international following, among the opposition to his government to be crushed.[43]

Luwum's background as former bishop of Northern Uganda, Obote's region, coupled with suspicion that he had dealings with Obote who attempted to overthrow Amin in 1972,[44] would seem to warrant Amin and his government's decision to consider him an opposition to be crushed. The

---

41. Kivengere Festo, 'Bishop Festo Kivenger: Press Conference at Trinity Church, USA', p. 5, #12, AO: 10771028. Festo Kivengere, 'Set Free by Christ', Sermon Transcript, April 24, 1980, pp. 2–3, #3–#4. , AO: 19800424*1. On 24th April 1980, he preached at the diocese of Colorado, Denver, during the occasion of 'Youth Night', from John 8:38 on the theme 'Set Free by Christ'. In his preaching, he explains his escape into exile: 'I escaped from Uganda in 1977 with my wife, when we barely could get away, we were sought for elimination after the death of the Archbishop [Janani Luwum]'.

42. Twinamatsiko, 'The Church of Uganda and the Amin Regime January 25, 1971 Through April 11, 1979', 39.

43. For the letters see Appendix 2: Report of a very serious incident at the Archbishops' house in the early hours of Saturday 5 February 1977; A Statement by the House of Bishop of Uganda, Rwanda, Burundi and Boga-Zaire, the Most Reverend Jannai Luwum in Answer to the President's Allegations about Arms found near the Archbishop's house (Voice of Uganda Tuesday 15 February, 1977); A Letter from the House of Bishops to Amin (also reproduced in Michael Cassidy, *Together in One Place: The Story of PACLA December 9–19, 1976, Nairobi* (ed. Gottfried Osei-Mensah; Kisumu, Kenya: Evangel Publishing House, 1978), 290–93.); and, A Response of the House of Bishops of the COU Rwanda Burundi and Boga-Zaire To His Excellency on Wednesday 16 February 1977, at the Conference Centre in Kampala.

44. Enahoro Peter, 'Whither Uganda', *Africa* 16 (December 1972): 13–17. S. Rikahuru, 'Uganda and Amin', *African Red Family*/no. 2 (1973): 41–50. For Obote's alleged take over plans see, Ministry of Information and Broadcasting, 'Obote's War Call to Langis and Acholis against Other Ugandans', Letter (Kampala, Uganda, 1977). Milton Obote, 'Memorandum Outlines Overthrow of Uganda Regime', *Translations on Sub-Saharan Africa* No. 1717 (March 2, 1977): 127–39.

plan to crush his alleged opposition began in the first week of February 1977. Amin meeting with his soldiers from West Nile region, resolved to crush any group of people his government considered to be in opposition to his rule and this set a trail of protests by the COU House of Bishops to Amin. However, Kivengere was also a member of the committee that drafted the letters, and some have found his voice coming through in them. This gives greater poignancy to his latter criticism of Amin's murder of Luwum.[45]

2.3.2 Mwanga's Martyrdoms

With Christianity now planted in Buganda (during Mutesa's reign), and the seeds of conflict between the CMS and White Fathers already planted, it took a new shape when Kabaka Mwanga (1866–1903), the youngest son of Mutesa, ascended to power on Mutesa's death in 1884.

Mwanga inherited an administrative structure under going a radical transformation: prior to his ascendancy to power, his father, Mutesa I, patronised the new cadres of relatively young leaders (many of whom were Christian) and gave them unprecedented influence in the kingdom. This was not to be the case with Mwanga, however, due to his apprehension about the increasing influence of the chiefs.[46] Other factors kept his apprehension high, such as in 1885 when he learned of the German annexation of Tanganyika, when his apprehension was coupled with advice from his Katikiro (Prime Minister), he gave orders to put to death several Christians.

On 30 January 1885, he brutally put to death three Christians, Nuwa Seruwanga, Marko Kakumba and Yusuf Lugalama, mutilating their bodies and burning them to death.[47] The series of events leading to the charge against these three Ugandans began when the CMS missionary, Mackay, rejected the offer of an official legate and a letter for his travel to go south of Lake Victoria, on the premise of personal privacy.[48] It was an unfortunate decision because the legate in the context of traditional Buganda was

---

45. Rwabyoma, 'Bishop Festo Kivengere'. 36.
46. Mark R Lipschutz, *Dictionary of African Historical Biography* (ed. R. Kent Rasmussen; 2nd ed.; Berkeley: University of California Press, 1986), 165.
47. Ward, *A History of Global Anglicanism*, 167. Cassidy, *Together in One Place*, 290–93.
48. Faupel, *African Holocaust*, 88. According to Faupel, 'The Kabaka asked whether he wanted a legate to accompany him; to which Mackay replied that he did not'.

'not an interference with his privacy, but a guarantee that he was travelling legitimately'.⁴⁹ The two Ugandans, who accompanied Mackay, Lugalama and Kakumba, were seen by the administration of Buganda to have accompanied Mackay on his journey without permission. Seruwanga was arrested later because he consorted with Mackay,⁵⁰ and all three were burnt to death at Mpimerebera, just west of Kampala.⁵¹

Late the same year, on 29 October 1885, the 37-year old British Anglican Bishop James Hannington (1847–1885) on his way to Buganda 'to become the first bishop of that young church in central and eastern Africa known at that time as Equatorial Africa',⁵² was murdered in Uganda (at Busoga) before he crossed the River Nile on the order of Mwanga.⁵³ He was killed because of the Buganda belief that anyone who approached the kingdom from the direction of Busoga was considered a threat to the kingdom.⁵⁴ The official route into the kingdom of Buganda was through the route coming from the south of Lake Victoria. In unclear circumstances Hannington unwisely approached the kingdom from the East through Busoga.⁵⁵ Unfortunately, his decision to do so coincided with Mwanga's apprehension of German annexation of Tanganyika, and encouraged by his Katikiro, he ordered the killing of Bishop Hannington, along with his 150 porters from the coast, only six years from the time when Christianity had been planted in Uganda.

His death redefined the course of the history of 'the young church' planted in Buganda.⁵⁶ Just two weeks after the bishop's death, on 15 November, Mwanga ordered the murder of Joseph Mukasa Balikuddembe for daring

---

49. Pirouet, *Historical Dictionary of Uganda*, 106.
50. Faupel, *African Holocaust*, 69.
51. Pirouet, *Historical Dictionary of Uganda*, 106.
52. Kivengere, 'Glorified in Them', p. 2, #2.
53. Kivengere, 'Glorified in Them', p. 2, #2. Pirouet, *Historical Dictionary of Uganda*, 161. For a fuller biography see Dawson, E. C. (Edwin Collas), *James Hannington: First Bishop of Eastern Equatorial Africa: A History of his Life and Work, 1847-1885*, 1849, Cited 21 Feb 2012, Online: http://www.archive.org/details/jameshanningtonf00daws.
54. Kivengere, 'Glorified in Them', p. 2, #2. Pirouet, *Historical Dictionary of Uganda*, 161.
55. Pirouet, *Historical Dictionary of Uganda*, 106.
56. Colin Reed, *Pastors, Partners and Paternalists: African Church Leaders and Western Missionaries in the Anglican Church in Kenya, 1850-1900* (Brill Academic Pub, 1997), 95.

to challenge him about Hannington's murder,[57] and so Balikuddembe became the first Catholic martyr.[58]

On Ascension Day in June 1886, thirty-one Christians—Catholic and Protestant—were massacred. These Ugandan martyrs (there were Banyankole, Banyoro, Batoro and Basoga as well as Baganda) died believing and trusting in Christ as their Saviour.[59] As they died they sang hymns, preached to their persecutors, and expressed strong belief in life after death.[60] Their courage and fortitude rendered a strong witness to those who saw them die.

Despite this Christian memory of these martyrs, secular historians have been highly sceptical of the accounts given by pietistic hagiography, arguing that life at the Kabaka's court was delicate, and that the Kabaka could order execution of his subjects for variety of reasons.[61] The Baganda generally faced death philosophically if the Kabaka so wished! If in this case, the martyrs may be put in this category, then, given the wider context of life in the kingdom of Buganda, the martyrs would fall in the tradition of *Kiwendo* (ritual sacrifice) of a number of victims at the instigation of one of the *balubaale*.[62] Nationalists who support the kingdom of Buganda, like Nuwa Sentongo,[63] have argued that the Christians were rebels against

---

57. Ward, *A History of Global Anglicanism*, 5.
58. For a general bibliography on the topic of Martyrs and an in-depth story of Balikuddembe, see excellent treatments by Faupel, *African Holocaust*. J. P. Thoonen, *Black Martyrs* (London: Sheed and Ward, 1941).
59. Pirouet, *Historical Dictionary of Uganda*, 109; Elizabeth Isichei, *A History of Christianity in Africa: From Antiquity to the Present* (Grand Rapids, Mich.: William B Eerdmans, 1995), 147. For a list of the names of most of the martyrs, see Pirouet, *Historical Dictionary of Uganda*. S. R. Karugire, 'The Arrival of European Missionaries', in *A Century of Christianity in Uganda, 1877-1977: A Historical Appraisal of the Development of the Uganda Church Over the Last One Hundred Years* (ed. A D Tom Tuma and Phares Mutibwa; Nairobi: Uzima Press, 1978), 14–15. Karugire helpfully provides a list of the Uganda martyrs from 31 January 1885 to 27 January 1877, which includes 23 Anglican martyrs and 22 Roman Catholic martyrs, Bishop James Hannington, and a note on the missing names of other martyrs. The list sets out the date, place, and type of execution(s).
60. Isichei, *A History of Christianity in Africa*, 148.
61. For example, the Kabaka ordered the public executions of over 100 Muslim converts to teach others to mend their ways. See D. A. Low, *Buganda in Modern History* (University of California Press, 1971), 22.
62. Christopher Byaruhanga, *Bishop Alfred Robert Tucker and the Establishment of the African Anglican Church* (Nairobi: Word Alive Publishers, 2008), 82.
63. Ward, 'Archbishop Janani Luwum', 20.

the *Kabaka*, 'collaborators', 'stooges of colonialism', and 'traitors to their African heritage'.[64] All these assessments hold a reasonable degree of truth.

Certainly accounting for the death of these Christian people during Kabaka Mwanga's rule is complex. But despite this complexity it is nevertheless true that the Ugandan martyrs displayed deep faith, and a conviction supported by their action of voluntarily death for the cause of the gospel. In this event, whether Catholic or Protestant, Ugandan Christianity finds its identity,[65] and martyrdom acquired great importance for the Ugandan religious communities.[66] 'In the early days, especially during persecution there was no distinction of religion or denomination; we were all Christians'.[67]

The deaths of the Ugandan martyrs is a story which inspires Christians in Uganda who are looking for lessons of sacrifice, models of standing firm for the sake of the gospel, or simply confronting evil. Christians view the martyrdoms from the conviction that the gospel effectively transforms people and that people who are transformed by the gospel remain obedient to their Saviour, even in persecution.[68] However, as time progressed, in 1969, when Pope Paul VI canonised the Catholic martyrs at Namugongo, this attracted opposition from pro-Kabaka Mwanga Nationalists, such as Nuwa Sentongo who objected to the canonising of the martyrs because he regarded them as disloyal servants to the king.

The Nationalists saw these disloyal servants of the Kabaka as worthy of being branded 'collaborators' and 'traitors of African heritage'.[69] The Nationalist view is loaded with a sense of bitterness and disappointment about such people being canonised as martyrs. Despite the Nationalist objections, Christians have continued to exalt the story of the martyrs affirming the local identity and local tradition, especially against pretentions of the state to make new martyrs.[70] As a kind of meta-narrative deep in

---

64. Ward, 'Archbishop Janani Luwum', 201.
65. 'This revolution began a combination of all new and religious groups, but soon developed into civil wars between Muslims and Christians, resulting in a Muslim defeat'. Ward, *A History of Global Anglicanism*, 167.
66. Faupel, *African Holocaust*.
67. Isichei, *A History of Christianity in Africa*, 148.
68. Ward, 'Archbishop Janani Luwum', 201.
69. Ward, 'Archbishop Janani Luwum', 201.
70. Ward, 'Archbishop Janani Luwum', 201.

the fabric of the Christian faith in Uganda, when Amin murdered Janani Luwum, it was viewed as a parallel to the Ugandan martyrs' story.

The parallel did not escape Kivengere. Later he told that prophetically after the death of the Christian martyrs (1885–1887) in the first decade of planting Christianity in Uganda, 'it has come again that at the end of the century, the Archbishop of Uganda, Janani Luwum, has sealed the celebration, or rather has celebrated by sealing the celebrations for 100 years with his blood'.[71] He often encouraged his audience with the witness of the martyrs to the non-Christian king, their executioners and family: '[A]nd before they were thrown into the fire, they burst into song daily, daily singing the praises of the city which God has prepared for us . . . I would have flown and been with Jesus'.[72] Through their witness, that evening 40 adults came to the missionary and asked to be baptized.[73] They rejected to serve the king in the areas of life that were against the will of King Jesus: 'we love to serve you, your majesty, but we can't serve if it offends our king, Jesus'.[74] The murdered pages had refused Mwanga's advance for homosexual practice.[75] Kivengere was impressed that the martyrs displayed a high view of God, even in the midst of the violence inflicted on them. 'They couldn't change their minds because they were captives of God's love'.[76]

2.3.3 Religious Wars in Buganda

Subsequent to Mwanga's rule, Buganda was marked by a complex political instability and a militarisation of the religious groups leading to the

---

71. Kivengere, 'Glorified in Them', p. 3, #2.

72. Festo Kivengere, 'Prayer and Praise', Sermon Transcript, May 10, 1980, p. 14, #27, AO: 19800510*1. Kivengere, 'Glorified in Them', pp. 2–3, #2.

73. Kivengere, 'Prayer and Praise', p. 14, #27.

74. Festo Kivengere, 'The Triumph of God's Glory', Sermon Transcript (Urbana, December 31, 1976), p. 3, #2, AO: 19761231. Kivengere, 'The Triumph of God's Glory', p. 9, #44.

75. Kivengere, 'Prayer and Praise', p. 14, #27. Isichei, *A History of Christianity in Africa*, 147.

76. Kivengere, 'Prayer and Praise', p. 13, #27.

religious wars of the 1880s and 1890s.[77] The Kabaka was overthrown and Mwanga fled to the south of Lake Victoria.[78]

The civil unrest in Buganda continued unabated until the arrival of the Imperial British East Africa Company (IBEAC) in 1888.[79] The Company had been set up in response to the emergence of German interests in East Africa.[80] In 1892 Captain (later Lord) Lugard[81] arrived as the agent of IBEAC, and prevailed with his military might in the religious wars in Buganda,[82] siding with the Anglicans, who were British, whereas the White Fathers were French.[83] Lugard's actions ensured that the Protestant faction, rather than the Catholic or Muslim faction, rose to power in Uganda.[84]

With the Protestants as the leading power, Apolo Kagwa (1869–1926) became Prime Minister. Other Baganda Christian lay leaders, like Ham Mukasa (1871–1956), would later join him in the struggle to be agents of the spread of Christianity.[85] After the revolution settled, other parts of the country, which had kingdom administrations, namely, Bunyoro, Toro and Ankole, replicated this model of spreading Christianity from top to bottom, with reasonable degrees of success. However, in northern Uganda, especially, between the Acholi and the Langi and in Eastern Uganda among the Teso people, this approach was resisted.[86] Nevertheless, this hierarchical pattern prevailed and just before independence (1950s to early 1960s) the religions became aligned with political parties: the Protestants with Uganda People's Congress (UPC) and the Catholic Church with the Democratic Party (DP) adding tensions to the already established religious hatred.

---

77. Ward, *A History of Global Anglicanism*, 167.
78. Falk, *The Growth of the Church in Africa*, 272.
79. Pirouet, *Historical Dictionary of Uganda*, 164–66.
80. Gifford, *African Christianity*, 113.
81. Gifford, *African Christianity*, 113.
82. Falk, *The Growth of the Church in Africa*, 272.
83. Gifford, *African Christianity*, 113.
84. Ward, *A History of Global Anglicanism*, 167; Pirouet, *Historical Dictionary of Uganda*, 224–5.
85. Pirouet, *Historical Dictionary of Uganda*, 261–62.
86. These are different ethnic groups organized differently from the southern predominant Bantu people. See, M. Louise Pirouet, *Black Evangelists: The Spread of Christianity in Uganda, 1891-1914* (London: Rex Collings, 1978).

Kivengere viewed religious tensions in Uganda and more broadly in Africa as due to historical differences, inherited from her missionaries, and as an abiding barrier in the churches. In Kivengere's view, 'the only remedy is Christ's barrier-breaking love'.[87] His sermons in chapter 5 frequently made reference to the reconciling love of Christ that removes the barriers, for it is only in Christ that everything holds together.

2.3.4 Baganda Evangelists Spread the Gospel

The resultant hierarchy of religions placed the Protestant church in the rank of an establishment only comparable to the traditional religion prior to the advent of Christianity.[88] The missionaries created a council of twelve leading Baganda Christians of integrity, drawn from some of the 'heads of households and therefore well suited to lead the small clusters of Christians'.[89] This crucial decision marked the beginning of an indigenous church.[90] From this point on, Buganda increasingly became a centre for evangelization in the Great Lakes Region: 'The Ganda soon began to bring their new faith to others'.[91]

The most celebrated of these Baganda evangelists was Apolo Kivebulaya (1864–1933) who later became a Canon of Namirembe Cathedral.[92] Kivebulaya is remembered as the apostle to the pygmies for taking the Christian gospel into Eastern Congo.[93] Kivebulaya is the shining example of the Baganda evangelists spreading the gospel beyond Buganda. Later Kivengere will encourage theological students at Mukono to emulate Kivebulaya's dedication and passion to preach and spread the gospel.[94]

---

87. Kivengere, 'Bleeding Africa', 29.
88. D. Z. Niringiye, 'The Church in the World: A Historical - Ecclesiological Study of the Church of Uganda with Particular Reference to Post-Independence Uganda, 1962-1992' (Unpublished PhD thesis, Edinburgh: University of Edinburgh, 1992), 40.
89. Niringiye, 'The Church in the World', 41.
90. Niringiye, 'The Church in the World', 41.
91. Isichei, *A History of Christianity in Africa*, 149.
92. For his biography, see Anne Luck, *African Saint: The Story of Apolo Kivebulaya* (London: SCM Press, 1963); Pirouet, *Historical Dictionary of Uganda*, 206–07.
93. William J. W Roome, *Apolo, the Apostle to the Pygmies* (London: Marshall, 1934).
94. Festo Kivengere, 'The Cross Today and Divine Outreach', Sermon Transcript, April 4, 1980, AO: 19800404.

The drive for the Baganda evangelists to spread the gospel had both admirable and less admirable aspects. They spread the gospel with great sacrifice: 'In 1894, eighty evangelists left Mengo [in Buganda], supporting themselves with banana cultivation, and a small stipend from their home church'.[95] Since the genuine impetus of the expansion of the gospel was from the Baganda evangelists, rather than the white missionaries, this is to be seen as *mainly* an African initiative.[96] This became an extraordinary indigenous movement, spreading Christianity within Buganda, to the rest of Uganda and beyond. It exposes as false the notion that 'Christianity was more or less forcibly imposed on unwilling subject populations, for it was Uganda Christians, not expatriate missionaries, who were the pace setters'.[97]

Later Kivengere continued this pace setting by founding the indigenous founded organization, AEE,[98] which provided him a base for his preaching ministry to the rest of the world. Some key foundation members of AEE were Baganda evangelists.[99]

A less admirable aspect of the Baganda evangelists was the fact that they were too closely caught up with British colonial politics. Accordingly, the spread of the gospel was closely tied with political expansion. The British needed local collaborators for their administration and the Baganda were suitable candidates. This choice placed the Baganda into a class of their own within Uganda: they were regarded as civilized and superior to any other Ugandan.

Despite many devoted evangelists, many others fell into the same arrogance that the Buganda political agents displayed, reflecting the domineering tendencies of the British colonial powers. The British esteem of

---

95. Isichei, *A History of Christianity in Africa*, 149.
96. We use the term 'African' aware of the great diversity within Africa; diversity of cultures, language, history, etc. In this case we apply the term in as long as it is helpful to explain the distinction between western efforts of evangelism and 'local' initiatives of evangelism such as the phenomenon in Buganda: voluntarily taking the gospel outside Buganda.
97. Pirouet, *Black Evangelists*, 195.
98. Inkelaar-de Mos, 'Evangelistic Enterprise', 29–40.
99. These include, Zebulon Kabaza, John Wilson. Others include, Misaeri Kauma (bishop of Namirembe diocese, 1885–1994), Michael Senyimba and John M. M. Senyonyi (Current Vice-Chancellor Uganda Christian University, 2011–).

the Buganda was accompanied by a distrust of other tribes. This is well captured in Tosh's attitude to the Lango: 'the Lango are raw savages. The only system that these people can be dealt with is through the intelligence agents as has been done in Bukedi [Eastern Uganda]'.[100] It is not surprising that, by and large, as the Baganda collaborators expanded colonial rule beyond Buganda,[101] their attitude and actions mirrored those of the British colonial administrators.

This decision to make Baganda collaborators or sub-imperialists in Uganda had serious consequences for both the politics and religion in Uganda. Politically,[102] by placing Buganda in its own class above all other tribes in Uganda, British Colonial administration brought Buganda direct resistance from the non-Baganda tribes. At times this developed into hostility and an abiding deep hatred. In acknowledging a fact of deep wounds in the relationship between Baganda non-Baganda, the Ugandan historian Professor Mutibwa comes to the conclusion:

---

100. J. Tosh, 'Small-Scale Resistance in Uganda: The Lango Rising at Adwari in 1919', *Azania* 9 (1974): 51–64. The Baganda agents were aware of their 'class' as collaborators and were proud of it. Consequently, they meted out violence to the people they ruled, thus, evoking anti-colonial resistance, which in Lango turned violent and several Baganda were killed in Ocini area. See, Michael Twaddle, 'Decentralized Violence and Collaboration in Early Colonial Uganda', *JCPS* 16/3 (1988): 71–85; John Tosh, *Clan Leaders and Colonial Chiefs in Lango: The Political History of an East African Stateless Society C. 1800-1939* (Oxford University Press, USA, 1979), 115. In Bunyoro, Kabalega resisted in 'The *Kyanyangire*, 1907' with lasting consequence up to now. See, G. N. Uzoigwe, 'The Kyanyangire, 1907: Passive Revolt Against British Overrule', in *War and Society in Africa* (ed. B. A. Ogot; London: Cass, 1972), 179–212. Bakiga in western Uganda protested the British Colonial rule in 1900–1919. See, Donald Denoon, ed., *A History of Kigezi in South-West Uganda*. (Kampala, Uganda: The National Trust, 1972). Toro resisted their overbearing manners. See, Edward I. Steinhart, *Conflict and Collaboration: The Kingdoms of Western Uganda, 1890-1907* (1st ed.; Princeton: Princeton University Press, 1977), 103. The Lugbara resisted through a 'religious cult—the Yakan'. See, A. King, 'The Yakan Cult and Lugbara Response to Colonial Rule', *Azania* 5 (1970): 1–25.

101. As we explain the collaboration between the Baganda sub-imperialists and the British Colonial administration in Uganda, we are not implying that there was no positive and objective understanding of leadership challenges on the part of the British Colonial administrators. There was. See a case in point in Phares Mutibwa, *The Buganda Factor in Uganda Politics* (Kampala: Fountain Publishers, 2008), 10. '[i]n 1911 the new [British] Governor, sir Frederick Jackson, who did not like the use of Buganda Agents as advisors, condemned the agents and the system; but his opposition to the use of Buganda agents was resisted by some British officials (e.g, the Provincial Commissioner, Eastern Province), and Jackson had to back down'.

102. Mutibwa, *The Buganda Factor in Uganda Politics*, xi.

Whatever may be said today—when we want to [emphasize] reconciliation and brotherhood—it is a fact that not many non-Baganda love Buganda. They harbour a kind of love-hate complex towards the Baganda. On the other hand, the Baganda too harbour a somewhat arrogant attitude towards the non-Baganda, particularly those who come from non-kingdom areas.[103]

Kivengere acknowledges this 'love-hate complex' in his sermons, particularly after the fall of Amin and his solution to it is equally clear. As he returned to Uganda, he told *La Canada Church* that the only antidote to Uganda's deep wounds is reconciliation.[104] Immediately on his return he exhorted his audience at Mukono to take the opportunity of preaching reconciliation as the only hope for the country.[105]

2.4 The East African Revival Movement

Kivengere's preaching of reconciliation must not only be placed against the background of the history of the church in Uganda, it must also be seen as part of the East African Revival.[106] This movement not only helps

---

103. Mutibwa, *The Buganda Factor in Uganda Politics*, xi.
104. Kivengere, 'In Christ', p. 4, #8.
105. Festo Kivengere, 'The Whole Gospel For The Whole World', Sermon Transcript (Preached at Wheaton Bible Church, Illinois, May 1978), AO:197805[--], [#2]. A fuller history of Ugandan Christianity would need to include the Churches, which began to mushroom after Museveni took power in 1986. See further Gifford, *African Christianity*, 307. Gifford, African Christianity and it's Public Role, 307. Since this is very much towards the end of our period of interest, May 1988, they have been ignored in this thesis.
106. For other 'Revival Movements', see the works of Edith Waldvogel Blumhofer and Randall Herbert Balmer, eds., *Modern Christian Revivals* (Urbana: University of Illinois Press, 1993); Richard M. Riss, *A Survey of 20th-Century Revival Movements in North America* (Peabody, Mass.: Hendrickson, 1988). For literature on the East African Revival, see Kevin Ward and Emma Wild-Wood, *The East African Revival: History and Legacies* (Farnham: Ashgate, 2012); Kevin Ward, 'Tukutendereza Yesu', ed. Mark R Lipschutz and R. Kent Rasmussen, *Dictionary of African Christian Biography* (Berkeley: University of California Press, 1986), 113–44; Ward, *A History of Global Anglicanism*, 175–9; Kevin Ward, '"Obedient Rebels": The Relationship between the Early "Balokole" and the Church of Uganda: The Mukono Crisis of 1941', *JRA* 19/3 (October 1, 1989): 194–227;

to account for Kivengere's preaching of reconciliation, but it also helps to trace the evolution of the trajectory of his international preaching ministry, from Kabale (Uganda) to Dodoma (Tanzania); from Dodoma to the United Kingdom; from Dodoma to Australia; from Uganda to America and other parts of the world.

2.4.1 Spread in Uganda

This story of the Revival requires an appreciation of the features that promoted the Revival as it emerged in 1928,[107] with a big breakthrough in the early 1930s, first in Uganda, and then Ruanda, before returning to Uganda with a much more vigorous momentum and moving beyond.[108] It is in this 'second return' from Ruanda to Uganda that Kivengere was swept up in the Revival 'fire',[109] a foretaste of greater things to come in his preaching ministry. Ward focuses on two significant features responsible for the Revival: the sick spiritual state of the Native Anglican Church (NAC), later called 'the Church of Uganda (COU)',[110] and the work of the Ruanda Mission.[111]

2.4.2 The Church of Uganda: The 'Sick' Spiritual State

From the outside, the situation of the church in Uganda—and especially in Buganda—looked successful because of its mission history,[112] but internally

---

Patricia Mary St. John, *Breath of Life: The Story of the Ruanda Mission* (London: Norfolk Press, 1971); Noll, *The New Shape of World Christianity*, 176–87; Colin Reed, *Walking in the Light: Reflections on the East Africa Revival and Its Link to Australia* (Brunswick East, Vic.: Acorn Press Ltd., 2007). Murry Jocelyn, 'A Bibliography of the East African Revival Movement', *JRA* 8/2 (1975): 144–47.

107. Kivengere, 'Awesome Growth', 216.
108. Kivengere, 'Awesome Growth', 216.
109. Kivengere, 'Awesome Growth', 216.
110. See Commission on Canon Law, Doctrine and Liturgy of the Church of the Province of Uganda, *The Provincial Canons of the Church of Uganda* (Uganda: Centenary Publishing House, 1971). 'Canon 1:1 The Name of the Church' states that '1.1.1 The Church shall be called THE COU' and that, '1.1.2 The name of THE COU under this canon shall be understood to mean ANGLICAN CHURCH, in communion with the See of Canterbury (COU 1997:1). Apolo Nsibambi, 'The Importance of the East African Revival (Obulokole)', in *The East African Revival Through Seventy Years (1935-2005): Testimonies and Reflections* (ed. Manuel J. K. Muranga; Kabale, Uganda: Diocese of Kigezi, 2005), 44.
111. Ward and Wild-Wood, *The East African Revival*, 3.
112. A. D. Tom Tuma, 'Church Expansion in Buganda', in *A Century of Christianity in Uganda, 1877-1977: A Historical Appraisal of the Development of the Uganda Church Over*

there was a problem. Founded in 1877, the COU had become complacent. Keen Christian leaders, such as Simyoni Nsibambi,[113] noted that material opportunities opened up by modern society, coupled with traditional culture, had compromised the church, so that its evangelistic fervour and the quality of its Christian discipleship dwindled.[114] Nsibambi's dissatisfaction with the spiritual state of the church began in September 1929, with a meeting with Joe Church at Namirembe, Kampala,[115] when he had 'a hunger and thirst for spiritual reality and for honesty, trust and a new community between Africans, and Africans and Europeans'.[116]

Both Nsibambi and Church were going through their own crisis in life, and they needed a fresh infilling of the Spirit.[117] Both shared their frustration and exhaustion after recent experiences within the church. From the outset, the Revival did not come from the church establishment—bishops, clergy, or missionaries—and the two men sought the experience of 'new birth' from the movement of the Holy Spirit. Joe Church told Nsibambi he was looking for a new infilling of the Holy Spirit and victorious life. From this sharing and reading of the Bible together, they discovered God

---

the Last One Hundred Years (ed. A. D. Tom Tuma and Phares Mutibwa; Nairobi: Uzima Press, 1978), 23. Isichei, *A History of Christianity in Africa*, 149. Isichei, explains the 'outside' success of the Church in Buganda noting how it began to send out missionaries to other rural Churches; Pirouet, *Black Evangelists*. In her book Pirouet discusses the success of the indigenous agents, indicating initial growth, its expansion in Uganda, and claim on page 195: 'Ugandan Christians, not the expatriate missionaries, were the pace setters'.

113. Nsibambi is considered the 'father of the Balokole Movement'. For an accurate explanation on Nsibambi's first name, see Nsibambi, 'The Importance of the East African Revival', 98.

114. Ward and Wild-Wood, *The East African Revival*, 3. For a much earlier concern on the spiritual state of the Church in Uganda, see J. V. Taylor, *Processes of Growth in an African Church* (London: SCM Press, 1958), 62.

115. For a helpful treatment of Joe Church's biography, see chapter 2, 'Joe and Decie Church', in Herbert Henry Osborn, *Pioneers in the East African Revival* (Hampshire: Apologia Publications, 2000), 53–110.

116. Inkelaar-de Mos, 'Evangelistic Enterprise', 9.

117. Brian Stanley, 'The East African Revival', *ERT* 2/2 (1978): 10. In 1926 and 1927, his correspondences requested prayers that God may raise up men 'filled with the Spirit' and that 'this part of Africa may be a great centre for Evangelization and Revival'. Joseph E. Church, *Quest for the Highest: An Autobiographical Account of the East African Revival* (Exeter: Paternoster, 1981), 91. Following his exhaustion he would write, 'We, a sound evangelical mission, came to the end of ourselves' in order that 'God was able to begin work'.

Himself, for, as Joe Church reports, this experience gave him 'the power of Pentecost'.[118] This experience changed everything. Nsibambi, 'the father of the East African Revival Movement',[119] discovered that new birth was not merely doctrine, but was also an experience of holiness based on the foundation of the cross.

In their meeting, the presence of the Holy Spirit exposed Nsibambi and Church to Jesus Christ. They perceived that in him everything was held together—personal issues such as life crises, financial and family problems. Revival even brought the power of the Holy Spirit to bear over the spirits and the supernatural powers that troubled so many in Uganda. Therefore, the solution to the sick state of the church in Uganda lay in new birth rooted in the cross.

2.4.3 The Search for Renewal and Holiness

The Ruanda Mission (now 'the Mid-Africa Mission'[120]) pressed hard for renewal and personal holiness.[121] Ruanda Mission operated as an autonomous mission of CMS in Southwest Uganda: 'to pioneer evangelism in the Belgian territory of Ruanda-Urundi, a League of Nations mandate'.[122] From a conservative evangelical position on the Bible, it promoted 'an urgent quest for renewal and personal holiness as understood by the Keswick movement'.[123]

---

118. Church, *Quest for the Highest*, 66–68.

119. Kevin Ward, 'Journal of Religion in Africa', *JRA* 19/3 (October 1989): 113–144.

120. The new name was introduced to correct the previous impression that Ruanda Mission operated only in Rwanda. It was changes because it is operating in three independent country in Africa, not only in Rwanda, thus, the change. See *Partners Together*/no. 267 (June 1990).

121. For a brief account of the 'Ruanda Mission', see Ward and Wild-Wood, *The East African Revival*, 13–22. Ruand-Urundi, is today two nations—now known as Ruanda and Burundi. At colonial times it first came under the Germans (1890s) and later (after the World War I), came under the Belgian mandate. See Kenneth Ingham, 'Tanganyika: The Mandate and Cameron', in *The History of East Africa* (ed. V. T. Harlow and E. M. Chilver; Oxford: Oxford University Press, 1965), 547–550. In this Chapter, we use 'Ruanda' and 'Rwanda' interchangeably.

122. Ward and Wild-Wood, *The East African Revival*, 3.

123. Ward and Wild-Wood, *The East African Revival*, 3.

Dr. Joseph Church was the pioneer Ruanda missionary at Gahini Hospital in Ruanda.[124] Joe Church and his wife, Decie, joined an earlier missionary party: Leonard Sharp and Algie Stanley Smith,[125] medical doctors serving as pioneer missionaries in Ruanda-Urundi. Before settling in Ruanda-Urundi, Sharp and Stanley worked temporarily as CMS missionaries in Kigezi, Uganda, in anticipation of moving into Ruanda-Urundi.

Their delay at the end of 1919 was due to Belgian suspicion that British missionaries in Ruanda would spy on them, leading to loss of 'the spoils of victory'.[126] Their ministry in Kigezi, however, was highly welcomed by the British colonial administration as a pathway to the destabilisation of the Nyabingi cult, a militant African religion, which resisted the establishment of colonial rule in the region of South Western Uganda.[127] They developed a substantial hospital work in Kissizi (Uganda) and later Gahini (Ruanda), as they maintained their persistent faith in God for a future day of establishing missionary work in Ruanda.[128] By God's grace a pathway opened in 1923, when Eastern Ruanda was let out to Britain to construct a Cape to Cairo railway—an undertaking that was soon neglected.[129]

As they worked in Kigezi, the Ruanda Mission came under the authority of the Anglican Bishop of Uganda, Bishop John Willis (1872–1954),[130] in whom they found a friend and helper. Because of the structure of leadership, the Ruanda Mission endeavoured to remain loyal Anglicans although evangelicals first. Since this was Kivengere's region, it is unsurprising that he later displayed the same commitment to being evangelical first. In Kabale, Kivengere's region, the Ruanda Mission conducted their activities of medi-

---

124. St. John, *Breath of Life*, 59. Church was formerly a founding member of the University Missionary group committed to becoming missionaries or supporting overseas mission.
125. Reed, *Walking in the Light*, 18.
126. Ward and Wild-Wood, *The East African Revival*, 17.
127. Elizabeth Hopkins, 'The Nyabingi Cult of Southwestern Uganda', in *Protest and Power in Black Africa* (ed. Robert I Rotberg and Ali Al'Amin Mazrui; New York: Oxford University Press, 1970), 319ff.
128. For a clear account of the missionary activities of Sharp and Smith, see James W. Katarikawe and John E. Wilson, 'The East African Revival Movement' (Joint MA and MTh Thesis, Pasadena, California: Fuller Theological Seminary, 1975), 30–37.
129. Katarikawe and Wilson, 'The East African Revival', 36.
130. John Willis was the Anglican Bishop of Uganda from 1912–1934.

cal treatment and proclaiming the gospel. The Ruanda Mission being evangelicals first did not stop them from being critical of developments within the Church of Uganda (Anglican), namely, of complacency with African customs that were incompatible with Christianity, and of *bukulu* (clericalism) and its stifling conservatism.

Those of the Ruanda Mission found comrades among the company of the Baganda, notably Semyoni Nsibambi and his brother, Bulasio Kigozi, a deacon of the Anglican Church in Uganda, who had been posted from Uganda to Gahini in Ruanda. Gahini was a Church Missionary Society mission hospital overseen by the Anglican diocese of Uganda. This meant that the Anglican Church in Uganda influenced it both culturally and religiously. There developed a direct link between the hospital staff at Gahini and the church in Uganda. Most of the hospital staff and the leaders of the awakening were Baganda, such as Bulasio Kigozi, or from western Uganda, such as Yosiya Kinuka (1905–1981).[131]

James Katarikawe writes: 'a good team of about 40 volunteer hospital staff, with the head assistant, Yosiya Kinuka, and about twice that number of evangelists from Kigezi, were to follow him later'.[132] Through this relationship, Joe Church, recruited keen Ugandan Christians who became hospital staff at Gahini.[133] This humble missionary never took credit for being the initiator of the Revival, seeing the Revival as purely a movement of the Holy Spirit, using the locals as 'tools'. This said, Joe Church 'understood that his skills as an organizer could be used to further revival'.[134]

2.4.4 Uganda Synod: The Call to Zukuka 'Awake!'

Since the Holy Spirit used locals to bring about revival from the start, it was 'an African Initiative',[135] making an impact on the life and character of

---

131. For a biography of Kinuka, see Osborn, *Pioneers in the East African Revival*.
132. Katarikawe and Wilson, 'The East African Revival'.
133. Ward and Wild-Wood, *The East African Revival*, 4. Kivengere, *Revolutionary Love*, 63.'[S]imeon's brother, Blasio Kigozi, who accompanied Dr. Joe Church back to his hospital at Gahini, Ruanda'.
134. Ward and Wild-Wood, *The East African Revival*, 4.
135. Lipschutz, *Dictionary of African Historical Biography*, 165. Ward, *A History of Global Anglicanism*, 176; Ward, 'Tukutendereza Yesu', 113; Reed, *Walking in the Light*, 85.: 'The East African Revival was at heart an African Movement and its expressions, its emphasis

the church in East Africa and beyond.[136] In September 1935, a major wave of 'Revival fire' occurred in Ruanda. In the following year Bulasio Kigozi brought back from Gahini the message of Revival to the synod of the COU held at Mukono. Although he was still a deacon, the bishop asked Bulasio to address the clergy retreat on the 6 January 1936, prior to the synod.[137] He died before the synod.

James Katarikawe, a student of Kivengere and later a friend of Kivengere in the Revival recalled his emphasis on being reconciled: 'There was no question of fear or compromise on his [Bulasio] part, he urged them to get right with God, let him bring revival in the COU, which it desperately needed'.[138] Kigozi's fervent call: *Zukuka* 'Awake!' appealed considerably to the synod. Katarikawe recalls three questions he wrote down for the synod to ponder: 'What was the cause of the coldness and hardness he discerned in the church? Why were church members allowed to attend Holy Communion when they were known for living immoral lives? What could, and should, be done to correct these matters and to revive the Uganda church?'[139]

His appeal before the synod met seemed prophetic at the time, but this was reinforced by his sudden death just close to three weeks prior on 25 January 1936, perhaps caused by tick fever on his way to the synod from Ruanda.[140] His prophetic message to the synod was recorded in just one word on his gravestone in Luganda: 'Zukuka!—meaning Awake'.[141]

---

and its outworking, shaped by Africa'.
136. Noll, *The New Shape of World Christianity*, 182. For the impact of the Revival in the Mennonite Church in East Africa and beyond, see MacMaster and Jacobs, *A Gentle Wind of God*.
137. Katarikawe and Wilson, 'The East African Revival', 68.
138. Katarikawe and Wilson, 'The East African Revival', 68.
139. Katarikawe and Wilson, 'The East African Revival', 68. Church, *Quest for the Highest*, 122.
140. David B. Barrett, 'Blasio Kigozi', in *Biographical Dictionary of Christian Missions* (ed. Gerald H. Anderson; Grand Rapids, Michigan: Wm. B. Eerdmans Publishing Company, 1998), 262; Osborn, *Pioneers in the East African Revival*, 13.
141. Katarikawe and Wilson, 'The East African Revival', 68. Kigozi's *Zukuka* was later to become the title of Joe Church's book on the biography of Kigozi's life and ministry: '*Awake Uganda! The Story of Blasio Kigozi and his Vision of Revival*'. See Joseph E. Church, *Awake, Uganda!: The Story of Blasio Kigozi and His Vision of Revival* (Uganda: Uganda Bookshop Press, 1957 [1936]).

Following Kigozi's appeal and death, Revival fellowships mushroomed throughout Buganda and well beyond, first within Uganda and soon outside. The Bishop of Uganda, Cyril Stuart (1892-1982),[142] supported the Revival that was going on in Gahini and Kigezi. Kigozi was trained by him and sent to serve as a deacon in Gahini. Stuart supported his concern to bring the fruits of the Revival into the heart of the COU, the Bishop Tucker College, so that the fire of the Revival could then spread to all the parishes in Uganda.

Since preparation for the celebration of the Diamond Jubilee of the Church of Uganda was due in 1937, Stuart's hope was that this occasion would be perfect timing to bring renewal of the church. Preparing for this occasion, Stuart extended the invitation to Joe Church to bring a team from Ruanda to conduct a mission in late 1936 at Bishop Tucker College.[143] Joe Church brought a joint team of whites (Joe Church and Lawrence Barham) and blacks (Semyoni Nsibambi, Yosiya Kinuka, and Erica Sabiiti).[144] On 19–21 June 1936, they all spent the weekend together, sleeping under one roof at the house of Bishop Stuart. It is helpful to note that this joint team not only stayed together under one roof, but that they also preached as a team. Later Kivengere will tell that he preached in tandem with Michael Cassidy,[145] with Bishop Misaeri Kauma and Canon John Wilson.[146]

The mission began on 22 June 1936 in the Bishop Tucker College hall,[147] all tutors dressed in their academic gowns, seated on the platform,

---

142. Cyril Stuart was the Anglican Bishop of Uganda from 1934–1953.
143. Kevin Ward, *Called To Serve: Bishop Tucker Theological College, Mukono: A History 1913-1989* (Kampala, Uganda: Bishop Tucker Theological College, 1989), 11.
144. Erica Sabiti became the first African Archbishop of Uganda, Ruanda, Burundi and Boga Zaire. For his biography see Gerald H Anderson, ed., *Biographical Dictionary of Christian Missions* (Paperback ed.; Grand Rapid, Mich.: Eerdmans, 1999).
145. Festo Kivengere, 'Forgiveness', Sermon Transcript (Preached at Sydney, Australia Bridge '78, 1978), AO: 1978[----]*1. Kivengere, 'From Uganda With Love'.
146. Kivengere, 'The Reconciling Love of Christ', p. 1, #1.
147. For a recent emphasis and broadening of the work of the Gospel using Bishop Tucker College as the launch pad for mission that will penetrate the Ugandan society through the field of Higher Education, see Stephen Noll's argument in favour of renewal for mission work that delightfully parallels Bishop Stuarts's vision for the gospel work in Uganda. Stephen Noll, 'Higher Education As Mission: The Role of the University in the Development of the Church's Ministry and Mission', Unpublished Paper (Uganda Christian University, February 25, 2005), 1–8. Since Bishop Tucker College became a

in a tense atmosphere. However, as the Revival team expounded Scripture in the structure of the Keswick Convention—sin, repentance, the new birth, separation, the victorious life, the Holy Spirit[148]—about forty students accepted the Lord as their personal Saviour. However, this good news of salvation was not good news for all: there were sharp dissenting voices among the faculty! The mission elicited a strong reaction from the faculty at a meeting, which was arranged by the bishop, to think over the follow up of the mission.[149]

As we shall see in chapter 3,[150] Joe Church recalls the Kabale gathering (1935) to have been organized on the same structure of the Keswick Convention. The Revival structure and method of preaching was also the same as Keswick. Although some have argued that the Revival was indigenous to Africa,[151] Kivengere, himself a child and a spokesman of the Revival, does not subscribe to this view: 'maybe our music or other forms of expression have made a certain contribution . . . We have shared Christ and not Africa . . . I don't think there is anything purely African about the Revival'.[152]

According to Katarikawe, the students at Mukono were under instruction not to sing some of the controversial hymns about the blood, for apparently Moody and Sankey hymns were distasteful to some of the faculty.[153] One of the hymns the students kept spontaneously singing was '*What Can Wash Away My Sins? Nothing but the Blood of Jesus*'. Nevertheless, through the mission God had hit the heart of the COU, Bishop Tucker College,

---

University, under the watch of Professor Stephen Noll as its first Vice-Chancellor, the Bishop Tucker Hall has been re-named 'The Principal's Hall'. On the walls of the hall is a spectacular display of the photographs of the former Wardens and Principals of Bishop Tucker College.
148. Katarikawe and Wilson, 'The East African Revival', 71.
149. Katarikawe and Wilson, 'The East African Revival', 72.
150. See Chapter Three, 2.1 'The Early Keswick Convention (1875–1920)'.
151. See Chapter Three, 2.1 'The Early Keswick Convention (1875–1920)'.
152. Kivengere Festo, 'Revival That Was and Is', May 21, 1976, 14.
153. For further discussion on D. L Moody and his innovative song leader Ira Sankey, see Andrew David Naselli, 'Keswick Theology: A Historical and Theological Survey and Analysis of the Doctrine of Sanctification in the Early Keswick Movement, 1975-1920' (PhD thesis, Greenville, S.C.: Bob Jones University, 2006), 107–112.

with the Revival message. It was a foretaste of what was to come in 1941, provoking the Mukono crisis.

2.4.5 The Mukono Crisis

As the Church of Uganda was preparing for the 1937 Diamond Jubilee, strange things were happening around the country as the Revival was spreading.[154] In February 1937, the first of the Jubilee missions opened at Kako (1–10 February), following the Kabale Programme, and then Hoima (19–25 February).[155] Teams of people touched by the conventions spread the message further, even crossing the Nile into Acholi and Lango.[156] Up until 1937 the Revival had touched Rwanda, Burundi and Uganda,[157] but in March and April 1937 it went into Kenya, with a convention at Kabete (30 March–7 April), soon followed by one at Kabare (June), Kenya Keswick Convention, Maseno (September 1938), with ripples extending to Zaire (October 1938) and to the Sudan.

After being invited by Bishop Chambers, a team set off for Tanzania in April 1939, to Katoke, Ngara and Dodoma.[158] When excesses broke out in some quarters at the end of 1939, Bishop Chambers instructed them to cease and so Joe Church disassociated himself from the outcome.[159] Every year since 1937, the tensions between the Revival and the church and the missionaries grew, and at the Namirembe Conference in 1940 (9–16 August) they were almost at bursting point.[160] William Nagenda was by now at Mukono, finding it very difficult to be there.

In May 1941, he and four other ordinands and their young missionary teacher Bill Butler (1939–1962)[161] attended the convention at Kabarole, Toro, and returned determined to fight the ritualistic innovations at

---

154. Katarikawe and Wilson, 'The East African Revival', 73–74.
155. Katarikawe and Wilson, 'The East African Revival', 77–81.
156. Katarikawe and Wilson, 'The East African Revival', 82.
157. Katarikawe and Wilson, 'The East African Revival', 83–91. Inkelaar-de Mos, 'Evangelistic Enterprise', 10.
158. Katarikawe and Wilson, 'The East African Revival', 7.
159. Katarikawe and Wilson, 'The East African Revival', 95–96.
160. Katarikawe and Wilson, 'The East African Revival', 106.
161. He was tutor at Bishop Tucker College 1940–1941 and became General Secretary of the Rwanda Mission of CMS in 1960s/70s. See Ward, *Called to Serve*, 45.

Mukono and the modernist teaching of Warden John Jones.[162] John Jones immediately transferred Bill Butler to Bunyoro and on 22 October he changed the college rules to make it difficult for the revivalists to operate as they had been doing.[163] When they continued unabated, by Monday 27 October 25, Balokole ('the save people')[164] students and the chaplain found themselves ejected from the college, some with only one month until completion, after having acquired the label 'the rebels'.[165] Among those expelled in 1941 were William Nagenda, Eli Ezra Mugamba, Yona Mondo, John Musoke, Erasto Kato, Edward Kakudidi, Mika Mwaru, Mesulamu, and Waiswa.[166]

Called 'the greatest crisis' in the history of Uganda,[167] the 'Mukono Crisis' led to both opposition and furtherance of the Revival. The COU formulated rules against the Balokole, which were enforced in all dioceses except Kigezi, which lay under the Rwanda mission. In that diocese at Kabale on 16 December 1941, the Balokole emergency meeting issued the Kabale Report, which declared the 'Mukono incident' unwisely handled and required the bishop to reconsider the rules hindering the Revival. The bishop did not respond well at the Uganda Missionary Conference, condemning the Kabale meeting as one of the biggest tragedies of the affair.[168]

In January 1942 a request for a Christian Union at Mukono, affiliated with Cambridge University Inter Collegiate Christian Union (CICCU), was rejected as a way of bringing the Revival in the back door,[169] and in the following year, church council meetings and synod passed motions to curb the preaching of the Balokole.[170] On 6 February 1943 the Executive

---

162. Katarikawe and Wilson, 'The East African Revival', 107.
163. Katarikawe and Wilson, 'The East African Revival', 108–109.
164. Ward and Wild-Wood, *The East African Revival*, 5. Reed, *Walking in the Light*, 19.
165. Katarikawe and Wilson, 'The East African Revival', 110. For a more positive title that appreciates 'the rebels', namely, 'Obedient Rebels', followed by an in-depth account of the relationship between the early 'Balokole' and the Church of Uganda, focusing on 'the Mukono Crisis of 1941', see Ward, 'Obedient Rebels', 194–227.
166. Katarikawe and Wilson, 'The East African Revival', 110. Ward, 'Obedient Rebels'.
167. Bishop Stuart in his pastoral letter of 1 December 1941, (p. 110).
168. Katarikawe and Wilson, 'The East African Revival', 111.
169. Katarikawe and Wilson, 'The East African Revival', 112.
170. Katarikawe and Wilson, 'The East African Revival', 112.

Council of Rwanda Mission gave a semi-apology for some of the practices of the Revival, and when the Diocesan Council endorsed the minute, the bishop proclaimed a new way of co-operation (March 1943), but the Balokole including the Kivengere leadership, feeling the apology had been unnecessary, rejected the new way. By May 1944 the synod was seriously considering that the Ruanda Mission should go out on their own.[171]

Despite this opposition, however, the 1941 expulsion of the twenty-six revivalists from Mukono actually caused the Revival to prosper. Whenever they were scattered, they took the Revival message with them. As pastors were caught up in it, so the Revival returned to the COU, especially in the remote areas.[172] After previous unsuccessful attempts, eventually the bishop agreed to have a convention at Namirembe in August 1944 and the Balokole came from all over Uganda and Rwanda-Burundi. It proved a time of great blessing and the most difficult years for the Revival (1941–44) reached a turning point.[173]

In September 1945, a convention in East Africa, the biggest ever held at Kabale, the theme 'Jesus Satisfies', drew delegates from all over Uganda, Rwanda, Burundi, Zaire, Tanzania, Sudan and Kenya. At this convention two young men with their wives and children offered to answer the call to go to Tanzania: Erisa Wakabi who had been expelled from Mukono in 1941 and Festo Kivengere a 22 year old teacher.[174]

2.5 Kivengere the Revival Preacher: A Homiletical Biographical Sketch

Having examined some key features of the history of Uganda and the church in Uganda, in order to set the context of examining Kivengere's sermons, it is also necessary to examine some key aspects of Kivengere's own biography. His homiletical background can be considered in four

---

171. Katarikawe and Wilson, 'The East African Revival', 113.
172. Katarikawe and Wilson, 'The East African Revival', 114–115.
173. Katarikawe and Wilson, 'The East African Revival', 118.
174. Katarikawe and Wilson, 'The East African Revival', 118.

brief sections: 2.5.1 Family Background; 2.5.2 His Conversion; 2.5.3 His Teacher Education; and 2.5.4 Pittsburgh Seminary.

2.5.1 Family Background

2.5.1.1 Aristocratic Upbringing

Kivengere was born in November 1919 to an aristocratic Hima family,[175] spent his early years looking after cattle, and later commenced formal education in church school at Kinyasano.[176] His parents—father, Ntzisira, 'a royal Kyahi clan' and mother, Barungi, a princess, who was 'the favourite daughter of the king',—impressed upon the boy that his grandfather, king Makobore who doubled as 'a military leader' and almost the 'Chief priest' of the *Bahima*, was one of the shrewdest military and 'spiritual' leaders with a great reputation, and a long aristocratic genealogy.[177]

At a time when the British Colonial administration in Uganda was signing treaties with kings, Makobore made Kigezi a very different environment. Administratively, he signed a treaty in 1912 acknowledging the indirect rule of the British.[178] Makobore cautiously welcomed Constance Hornby (1884–1972),[179] a CMS missionary, who left behind a coy catechist, Jacob Byensi. He founded a small mud hut church,[180] spiritually lighting the fire of Christianity that soon consumed, transforming illiterate herdsmen in Kyamakanda, Kivengere's village. When his uncle, Karegesya, succeeded Makobore after he abdicated his throne, Kivengere was allowed to sit and listen to the discussions, in which his uncle sought help from the British government for the Bahima during crisis moments.

The influence of his aristocratic background can be observed in his later preaching ministry in a variety of ways. Although his parents drummed into him the impressive family tree, he later critiqued its harmful effects: 'It

---

175. Senyimba, 'Festo Kivengere: The Man', 3.
176. Rwabyoma, 'Bishop Festo Kivengere', 1.
177. Coomes, *Festo Kivengere*, 26–27.
178. Pirouet, *Historical Dictionary of Uganda*, 8.
179. For a biography of her work in western Uganda, see Elizabeth Traill, *Venturesome Love: The Story of Constance Hornby, 1884-1972* (Handsel Press, Limited, 2011).
180. Coomes, *Festo Kivengere*, 27.

gave them [his parents and Bahima] a feeling of great superiority—which is always very unfortunate and superficial'.[181] His own sense of superiority was 'tamed' by the Christian influence, but it still gave Kivengere 'extraordinary self-confidence and poise' in the midst of western material wealth and 'sophistication'.[182] Kivengere's Christianity also enabled him to critique the temptation to find one's identity in one's class. Preaching at the Lausanne Congress in July 1974, on 'The Cross and World Evangelization', he said: 'Christ destroys our prejudiced way of seeing our fellow men as racial cases, tribal specimens, social outcasts or aristocrats, sinful characters, and religious misfits, by giving us a fresh evaluation of all men as redeemable persons "on whose behalf Christ died"'.[183]

Brought up in a large aristocratic family, where many young children were raised, Kivengere also gained a sense of what it means to care for others. After the collapse of Idi Amin's dictatorship,[184] his memory of his uncle negotiating with the British for the Bahima, inspired him to seek help for Uganda's latest crisis.[185] In his preaching engagements abroad, not only in Britain, but in other parts of the world,[186] with the catch phrase, 'Brethren, pray for us',[187] Kivengere asked for more help for the people of Uganda and Ruanda.

---

181. Coomes, *Festo Kivengere*, 27.
182. Coomes, *Festo Kivengere*, 22–28.
183. Festo Kivengere, 'The Cross and World Evangelization', in *Let the Earth Hear His Voice: International Congress on World Evangelization, Lausanne, Switzerland: Official Reference Volume: Papers and Responses* (ed. James Douglas; Minneapolis: World Wide Publications, 1975), 403–404. Also cited by Schmidt, *Glorious Companions*, 315. From J. D Douglas, ed., *Let the Earth Hear His Voice: Official Reference Volume, Papers and Responses* (Minneapolis: World Wide Publications, 1975), 403–404.
184. Pirouet, *Historical Dictionary of Uganda*, xxxiii–xxxiv. Amin's government fell in April 1979 and by May of this year, the liberation of Uganda was over.
185. Loane, 'Memoirs', 102. In Chicago he addressed Evangelical Relief Agencies on coordination of Relief and Rehabilitation efforts for Uganda and Committee of World Relief of the National Evangelicals. See Kivengere, 'The Church During and After the Regime of Amin', in *Christianity Today*, 54.
186. Kivengere, 'In Christ'. Kivengere, 'From Uganda With Love'. For help with the support of Archbishop Marcus Loan of Australia, see *Church Scene*, 'Appeal for Ugandan Refugees launched', February 9, 1978; 'Ugandan Bishop Visits Brisbane', *Telegraph*, Wednesday, February 8, 1978; 'Help for Uganda Refugees', *The Courier Mail*, February 6, 1978: 'The Appeal is designed to aid at least 50,000 refugees Bishop Kivengere says . . . some of these are students from Makerere University, some are professional people'.
187. For an assessment of the deep level brokenness in the country for which Kivengere

Despite his aristocratic background, Kivengere was born in a cattle kraal and grew up on a staple diet of milk and blood from cattle, sleeping on a hard crucible bed, covering himself with cattle skin. He grew up loving his people and his culture, including the land of the Bahima.[188] This humble background was significant for his self-understanding. Later in his preaching he speaks as one human being to another, always refusing to define himself in terms of gender, ethnicity, and colour. For example, in 1976 he said, 'because of Christ in me, you cannot play with me; no longer any one can sit on top of the other'.[189] Responding to a cynical question by a journalist, David Broadbent, at the National Press Club of Australia in 1979, he said: 'If you meet me by my colour of skin, by my dress, or by my clothes: then you haven't met me . . . I am a human being'.[190] Preaching in the racist apartheid South Africa during AEE missions at Stellenbosch University in 1981, Kivengere will explain his philosophy of colour in the context of reconciliation: 'colour is God's way of dealing with monotony. It is never meant for people to fight over'.[191] His Christian faith had made the aristocrat into just another human being.

2.5.1.2 Religious Upbringing

Growing up in the culture of the Bahima included a religious upbringing.

> I was born in a traditional non-Christian home in Africa. My parents had never heard about Jesus Christ but my father was a very religious man. He worshipped God through the agents of the spirits of our dead ancestors. . . . Being the first born, my father introduced me into this worship very early. He taught me by example. He took me to the worship. We sacrificed together. And yet we never found that god. . . . He remained

---

asks for help from abroad, see J. Paget Stanford, 'Reconciliation in Uganda?', *Third Way* (April 1981): 13–17.
188. Senyonyi, 'Philosophy of Evangelism', 2–6.
189. Kivengere, 'The Triumph of God's Glory'.
190. Kivengere, *Address to the National Press Club*.
191. Kivengere, 'Jesus Came as a Missionary'.

a distant god—someone too far to help you when you need him. That is where I grew.[192]

Although far from biblical Christianity, this religious background, characterized by the notion of 'worship', 'sacrifice', 'ancestors', seeking and never finding, influenced Kivengere towards belief in the Christian God. With this background, belief in the existence of God was a settled matter, but the real problem was: 'how can we know him?'[193]

This question will be crucial to Kivengere's theological thought, interpretation of God, and preaching. Leading up to his conversion in October 1945, Kivengere became aware that God the Creator was not to be reached through his ancestors but through God's Son, Jesus Christ.[194] From then on Kivengere preached the Incarnation (God in his love has come among his people in the person of his Son Jesus Christ of Nazareth),[195] and that the method of reaching God is through meeting Jesus at the cross. As Kivengere succinctly put it on one occasion in 1972: 'not only was God reachable, but [also] he was reaching out to us!'[196]

2.5.1.3 Story-Telling at the Fireplace

An important part of Bahima oral culture was the story-telling lessons at the family fireplace. After supper, Kivengere learned many lessons from the history of his tribe: children's fables, praise songs of past warriors, dramatic recitations of 'one's cows' finer points', and composition.[197] The recitals around the fire at night taught Kivengere skills of how 'to think on his feet, to speak fluently in public on a theme with next to no warning . . . to improvise as he went, to tell stories and to use words to move an audience'.[198]

---

192. Kivengere, 'Testimony', 416.
193. Coomes, *Festo Kivengere*, 38–39.
194. See his sermons in Chapters Four and Five. For example, Kivengere, 'Jesus Came as a Missionary'.
195. Kivengere, 'Christ Has Reconciled the Universe to Himself', p. 5, #7. .
196. Festo Kivengere, 'Christ Puts All Things Together', Sermon Transcript, 1972, p. 5, #9, AO:1972[----]*1.
197. Coomes, *Festo Kivengere*, 35.
198. Coomes, *Festo Kivengere*, 35.

He also learned how to swathe abstract ideas in down-to-earth examples. The Bahima used fictional stories to convey significant truths, such as exciting stories about creation, about their ancestors, and about their tribe.[199] Later Kivengere's preaching is studded with imaginative and pictorial stories used to get his points across to his audience.[200] This firm foundation in oral culture gave him a high regard for linguistic expressions aimed at conveying plain, clear meaning to the listener.[201]

In the company and conversation at the fireplace he learned by experience that people were not a strain but a relaxation: 'It tested your resourcefulness and the way of handling things. It was very good education'.[202] With this earliest informal education in Kyamakanda was well rounded—religious, social-political, and intellectually critical, philosophical—and it all contributed to producing a great orator and communicator, and helped to develop Kivengere's remarkable facility with languages.

As Kivengere travelled more widely, he appreciated different cultures and languages, especially the many languages and dialects of Africa. He was renowned for his ability as a translator. At a Kabale convention he gave notices in seven different African languages.[203] It was in this capacity that he was introduced to Billy Graham, who was so confident in Kivengere's facility with *Swahili* that he told him 'Don't bother to translate literally. You know what I mean. Get that across'.[204]

2.5.2 Kivengere's Conversion: From Agnostic to Preacher[205]

Kivengere never intended to be a preacher, not even a revival preacher. In a most dramatic event, his encounter with the wholly unexpected love of

---

199. Rwabyoma, 'Bishop Festo Kivengere', 25.
200. Rwabyoma, 'Bishop Festo Kivengere', 31.
201. Rwabyoma, 'Bishop Festo Kivengere', 36.
202. Coomes, *Festo Kivengere*, 35.
203. Richard Bewes, 'Man of Africa: Bishop Festo Kivengere of Uganda', *AE* (1979): 7. Rwabyoma does not mention the year of this Kabale Convention. However, his knowledge and competence of fluency in the different languages cannot be doubted. Richard Bewes writes that 'one day Festo preached in Swahili, with the Mennonite Bishop Don Jacobs as interpreter'. See Bewes, 'Man of Africa', 7.
204. Quinn, 'Kivengere, Festo'.
205. This title reflects my appreciation of a snippet of Kivengere's conversion in the sermon, Kivengere, 'Glorified in Them', p. 7, #3.

Christ filled his room and he was convinced that he saw the real and crucified Christ who died for him.[206] The story of his conversion can be pieced together from his first conversion testimony,[207] and from three of his sermons, from 1974,[208] 1982,[209] 1983.[210]

Kivengere recalls being introduced to Christianity 'through a black face',[211] Jacob Byensi, at the age of ten. In 1936, at his boarding primary school in Kabale, while a youngster, he experienced an encounter with the risen and living Lord Jesus Christ.[212] After becoming a teacher he was expected to attend church every Sunday as a requirement of the missionary school at which he taught.[213] He knew about Jesus, read about him, appreciated his ethics, but 'I never met him'.[214] After the 1935 Kabale gathering, the message of the speakers led to the conversion of many who passionately shared the gospel and Kivengere considered them 'fanatics',[215] 'emotional and ignorant'; 'but my attitude never put them off'.[216] However, in 1941 he experienced a second encounter with the Lord Jesus Christ. This particular encounter turned his world upside down and transformed an agnostic into one of Christianity's passionate preachers. His autobiographical accounts enable a portrait of Kivengere to be constructed of his life before and after his second conversion and of the massive reversal this caused. Each of his conversion accounts shows how important reconciliation was to Kivengere, even at this early stage.

His conversion led him to be an evangelist. Once the Holy Spirit baptized the revival converts, they were filled with the love of Jesus Christ, 'and in that we saw the world. Men went out like never before, evangelising their neighbours . . . it became a huge crowd of evangelists. Out of this has

---

206. Kivengere, *Revolutionary Love*, 16–17.
207. Kivengere, 'A Challenge In Love', 8.
208. Kivengere, 'Testimony', 416–417.
209. Kivengere, *Revolutionary Love*, 9–17.
210. 'Reconciliation', Sermon Transcript, AO: 198204[--], [#1].
211. Kivengere, 'Testimony', 416.
212. Kivengere, 'Love and the Unlovable': 12.
213. Kivengere, 'Love and the Unlovable': 12.
214. Ward, *Called to Serve*, 3.
215. Kivengere, 'Love and the Unlovable': 11.
216. Kivengere, 'A Challenge In Love', 8.

grown a fellowship which knows no colour, no race, no denominational barrier'.[217] 'After eighteen years in Christianity I became tired of it; I became tired of missionaries [and their Christian message]; I became tired of church tradition because there was an area which needed to be believed in Jesus and it had not yet been touched'.[218] [. . . But] 'there was an afternoon I shall never forget. . . . I came from the land of the groping . . . it was during that time when I nearly committed suicide because of frustration'.[219]

At this time Kivengere was a young teacher, and 'politically minded'.[220] A teacher and a friend confronted him when Kivengere was on the way home from a drinking party: 'a young African, a friend of mine, with a fresh air of meeting Jesus Christ'.[221] On inquiring why his friend had joy and looked alive his friend explained, concluding with the words: 'I love you'.[222] At this point, 'I exposed my poor life to the love of God in Jesus Christ. I spoke from suffering. I presented my emptiness to the love, which took Jesus to Calvary, and in his amazing grace . . . he entered into the heart of that enemy [agnostic Kivengere] He touched my wounds . . . lifted my burdens . . . forgave my sins . . . liberated me. I got off my knees . . . , got excited!'[223]

Once Jesus 'liberated him', he sent Kivengere to an African whom he hated so that 'we might be reconciled'.[224] He then cycled fifty miles in the hill country of Kigezi to another man, this time the man was an Englishman he hated. At first he protested, but the Lord's voice came to him: 'You hated that man, but I love him, and he is your brother . . . I died for him. I died for you'.[225] Thus his conversion led to reconciliation with his fellow man.

---

217. Festo Kivengere, 'The Work of the Holy Spirit in Evangelization, Individually and Through the Church', in *Let the Earth Hear His Voice: International Congress on World Evangelization, Lausanne, Switzerland: Official Reference Volume: Papers and Responses* (ed. James Douglas; Minneapolis: World Wide Publications, 1975), 277.
218. Kivengere, 'Testimony', 416.
219. Kivengere, 'Testimony', 416.
220. Kivengere, 'Testimony', 416.
221. Kivengere, 'Testimony', 416.
222. Kivengere, 'Testimony', 416.
223. Kivengere, 'Testimony', 417.
224. Kivengere, 'Testimony', 417.
225. Kivengere, 'Testimony', 417.

Kivengere later tells that 'I was the kind of agnostic who is not interested in trying to prove whether there is a God or not'.[226] He simply wanted to be his own manager. He had a problem: 'my sins were dark and threatening against me. Guilt pursued me like a hunting dog after its prey. I was a man ill at ease, young, but fragmented inside, and a victim of perpetual civil war'.[227] He considered the 'saved' people fanatics because they constantly bombarded agnostics like him with 'the message of the cross'.[228] They were 'dangerously personal',[229] because in their preaching they dragged in disturbing subjects even when they started with seemingly safe stories, such as Adam and Eve.

But after crying for help to God in whom he no longer believed: 'God! If you happen to be there . . . I am miserable . . . HELP!',[230] in answer to his cry 'Heaven opened, and in front of me was Jesus. He was there real and crucified for me. His broken body was hanging on the cross, and suddenly I knew that it was my badness that did this to the King of Life. It shook me'.[231] 'In tears, I thought that I was going to hell'.[232]

> [B]ut then I saw his eyes of infinite love which were looking into mine. Could it be he who was clearly saying: "This is how much I love you, Festo!" I shook my head because I knew that couldn't be possible, and said: 'No, I am your enemy. I am rebellious. I have [hated] your people. How can you love me like that?' Even today I do not know the answer to that question. [T]here is no reason in me for his love. . . . The love was wholly unexpected, but it filled my room, and I was convinced. He is the only one who loves the unlovable and embraces the [un]embraceable. In spite of what I was, I knew I was accepted,

---

226. Festo Kivengere, 'Love and the Unlovable', in *Revolutionary Love* (First Edition.; Pasadena, USA: African Enterprise, 1983), 15.
227. Kivengere, 'Love and the Unlovable': 14.
228. Kivengere, 'Love and the Unlovable': 11.
229. Kivengere, 'Love and the Unlovable': 11.
230. Kivengere, 'Love and the Unlovable': 16.
231. Kivengere, 'Love and the Unlovable': 16.
232. Kivengere, 'Love and the Unlovable': 16.

was a son of the Father, and that whatever Jesus did on the cross, it was for me. Ever since that day the cross has been central in my thinking.[233]

In this conversion account, Kivengere recounts the exact circumstances of his encounter with Christ. While we must leave room for later reflection, development and discovery as will be revealed in his sermons, we cannot underestimate the immediate shock waves that reverberated through his mind in the encounter, the effects of which remained with Kivengere for the rest of his preaching life and ministry.

In terms of his belief about *the person* and *work of Jesus Christ* (Christocentricity), Kivengere had to come to grips with the fact that Jesus Christ was real, spoke to him when heaven opened, and he saw him hanging on the cross, an indelible mark of his love for him. The experience would remain imprinted in Kivengere's mind and it meant that Christ crucified was to be identified with God's own love, even for agnostics like the pre-Christian Kivengere. Regarding his belief about the *present* and *future* age, Kivengere formerly believed that God was distant and judgmental, desiring to send him to hell. But now he realized God sent Jesus Christ to die on the cross to bring repentance, forgiveness and reconciliation. Jesus fills empty lives, heals wounds, and liberates from emptiness, which is tiresome and too heavy.

The experience also brought a shift in Kivengere's language from 'a groping, tired, and frustrated young man to acceptance as son of the Father'. He knew that in spite of what he was, Christ's enemy, rebellious, a man who hated people, Christ's acceptance gained him sonship in the family of God. Because he is now a son, Jesus' death on the cross was God's love for him.

Kivengere's conversion caused him to reconfigure his biography, reverse his opposition to the Lord Jesus Christ and pursue the proclamation of the message of the cross. The encounter with the Lord had enormous impact on him, his missionary drive and theological reflection about God's reconciling love, centred in Jesus Christ. His conversion experience crushed the pre-Christian Kivengere—the agnostic, ancestor worshiper—and ushered

---

233. Kivengere, 'Love and the Unlovable': 16–17.

in a brand new Kivengere the Revival preacher, ever excited about Christ's reconciling love.

2.5.3 Kivengere's Teacher Education

After being educated at Kigezi and Mbarara High Schools, Kivengere was trained at the Bishop Tucker Mukono Teacher Training College.[234] On graduating he taught in Kigezi schools from 1940–1945. In 1945, two years after he married Mera Nyinenzangye,[235] they felt called at the Kabale Convention to teach at the Alliance High School, Dodoma, Tanganyika (modern day Tanzania).[236] While gaining good experience as a teacher, during this period Kivengere also travelled all over Tanzania as a preacher of Revival.[237] Towards the end of his service in Tanzania, he went to London University where he graduated with a Diploma in Education.[238] On graduating from London University in 1957, Bishop Alfred Stanway prepared to ordain Kivengere even when Kivengere had not yet considered ordination.[239] A week before the ordination, Kivengere told Bishop Stanway: 'Bishop, I don't feel happy about being ordained, and I wonder whether

---

234. Ward, *Called to Serve*, 3. Ward distinguishes between the Bishop Tucker Memorial Collage (later Bishop Tucker Theological College, now Bishop Tucker School of Divinity and Theology—also designated Faculty of Theology at Uganda Christian University) and Bishop Tucker Teacher Training College: 'from 1920–1955 there was a teacher training course at Mukono, which was government aided. But the purely theological section had to be supported entirely from the Church or CMS funds'.

235. Some of his biographers interchangeably use 'Mera' and 'Merabu' to refer to Kivengere's wife. In this thesis we use 'Mera' which was Kivengere's fond way of referring to his wife.

236. The Church Missionary Society built Alliance High School but run in alliance with the Moravians and the Africa Inland Mission, recruiting staff from within Tanganyika and beyond. See Thomas T. Spear and Isaria N. Kimambo, *East African Expressions of Christianity* (James Currey, 1999), 298.

237. Josiah R. Mlahagwa, 'Contending for the Faith: Spiritual Revival and the Fellowship in Tanzania', in Spear and Kimambo, *East African Expressions of Christianity*, 298.

238. Spear and Kimambo, *East African Expressions of Christianity*, 261. Although in the Book, *East African Expressions* Kivengere is said to have graduated with a BA in Education from the University of London, I find the account of William Rukirande more likely. See Diocese of Kigezi, 'Order of Service For the Church and State Funeral of the Late Rt. Rev. Festo Kivengere' (Government Printer, Entebbe, Uganda, May 29, 1988), 1, Archives of the Diocese of Kigezi.

239. Festo, 'Bishop Festo Kivengere', 1, #1.

this is of the Lord' and bless him, he said, 'I understand, but let us postpone it until [the time when] the Spirit of God says yes'.

Bishop Alfred Stanway of Central Tanganyika diocese arranged for Kivengere to accompany Yohana Omari, the Assistant Bishop of Central Tanganyika, for six months (December 1958 to June 1959) to visit in Australia, to meet 'the CMS staff and supporters in Australia', and to experience Kivengere's 'proven evangelistic skill'.[240] Stanway wanted Kivengere to share the message of the Revival with the Australian Churches, which he did with great success leaving a significant impact.[241] In New South Wales, he spoke at the Katoomba Convention, and CMS summer school at Moss Vale, and the Upwey Convention in Victoria.[242] During this mission, Kivengere was voted 'The Australian of the Week', whose views on racial problems then were 'listened to with much interest by the Governor of New South Wales, Sir Eric Woodward'.[243] In 1959 he also had an important visit to the Northern Territory,[244] where he was well received by the Aboriginal Christians. Some felt his style appealed to the Aboriginal audience. 'In this, the Revival reflected strongly African cultural forms of African teaching, in which tribal lore was couched in myth and legend. This style also related well to an aboriginal audience'.[245] This may, however, reflect the perspective of some missionaries on the Revival preaching,[246] in which Kivengere's 'African style' was contrasted to 'the linear, closely reasoned and often abstract presentations typical of Western Christianity', and ostensibly relied upon 'a "felt", experiential response, rather than to a thought or a logical response'.[247] Following the Australia visit, he made a

---

240. Reed, *Walking in the Light*, 201–205.
241. Reed, *Walking in the Light*, 204–230.
242. 'Bishop Omari Arrives for a Six Months Visit', *The Anglican* (Sydney, December 19, 1958), 1.
243. 'Anglican of the Week', *The Anglican* (Sydney, January 16, 1959), 1.
244. Reed, *Walking in the Light*, 201.
245. Reed, *Walking in the Light*, 223. Max Hart, *A Story of Fire, Continued: Aboriginal Christianity* (2nd ed.; Blackwood, South Australia: New Creation Publications, 1997 [1988]), 73, 77, 88, 205.
246. For a list of missionaries associated with the Revival Movement that were interviewed by Reed for his thesis entitled, *The East African Revival*. The list also appears in his book, *Walking in the Light*, 259–60.
247. Reed, *Walking in the Light*, 223.

preaching visit to the Solomon Islands[248] where the churches were experiencing revival, and he was invited to encourage them with the experience of the East African Revival.[249] Towards the end of 1959, after 13 years in Tanzania, he returned to Uganda where he was appointed Kigezi District Assistant Schools Supervisor.

In 1961, he was appointed Kigezi District School Supervisor.[250] This same year, as a freelance evangelist, he preached at the InterVarsity Missionary Convention, Illinois, where he boldly challenged the missionaries' reticence to be transparent, acting as a damper on the transparency of the brethren: 'How can I open my "box" when the missionaries' "box" is not only closed, but has a lock on it?'[251]

Even before his later theological study, his education and experience as a teacher equipped him with the persuasive skills he later displayed as a preacher.

2.5.4 Pittsburgh Seminary: From 1964–1967

The second major educational influence on Kivengere was his theological education at Pittsburgh Theological Seminary (1964–1967).[252] It was here that his thoughts on reconciliation were brought to maturity through his own reflection under the tuition of his theological teachers.

The forty-three year old Kivengere went to Pittsburgh Theological Seminary after deciding to be ordained. He had already begun to have a ministry beyond Uganda, through his connections with Billy Graham

---

248. John Garrett, *Where Nets Were Cast: Christianity in Oceania Since World War II* (Suva, Fiji: University of the South Pacific, 1997), 362. Garrett, however, goes too far when he states that, 'In 1959 Festo Kivengere, an Evangelical bishop from Uganda . . . Malaitans and Markirans welcomed this Black African Bishop'. Kivengere only became Bishop of Kigezi in 1972, thus, to designate 1959, as the year when Kivengere became Bishop is incorrect.

249. For insight into his messages while in the Solomons Islands, see Festo Kivengere, *The Spirit Is Moving* (Rev. ed.; Pasadena, Ca.: African Enterprise, 1979 [1976]).

250. See 'Biography' in Diocese of Kigezi, 'Order of Service', 3.

251. S. Fife Eric and F. Glasser Aurthur, eds., *Commission, Conflict, Commitment: Messages from the Sixth International Student Missionary Convention* (IVP Series in Creative Christian Living; Chicago: Inter-Varsity Press, 1962), 21–46.

252. For a history of Pittsburgh Seminary, see James Arthur Walther, ed., *Ever a Frontier: The Bicentennial History of the Pittsburgh Theological Seminary* (First Edition.; Eerdmans Pub Co, 1994).

since 1960 when he first interpreted for him during the Moshi and Nairobi public crusades.[253] Billy Graham by the 1960s was probably the most influential American evangelical preacher in America—and the world.[254] Kivengere by mid-1963 decided to have a Western theological education following a short period of deciding how he could best use his gift for life as an itinerant evangelist. Ordination, he decided, was the way to go because his worldwide travels in Christian circles brought home for him the realization that there was a real difference between the lay Christians and the clergy in terms of influence.

The best way for him to attain this influence for his evangelism was to have a Western theological education leading to his ordination. However, the Revival leaders, especially Joe Church, were appalled at this decision because they could not see what Kivengere could achieve by gaining ordination.[255] They feared he would be tainted by American liberal spirituality, and that he would become a White Man.[256] When Kivengere responded by arguing that his call to an international ministry demanded credentials of proper theological education that other clergymen had if he was to interact on par with them in his ministry, the brethren accepted this decision.

Archbishop Leslie Brown of the Church of the Province of Uganda, Ruanda and Boga-zaire, also reacted badly to Kivengere's decision initially. As first he rejected his request to be put forward as an Anglican candidate for ordination on successfully completing his theological education. As the most intellectually able African he had ever met, with a fine Christian character, and remarkable gifts, especially in evangelism,[257] he knew Kivengere had the right qualities. However, he was somewhat taken aback when he learned from Kivengere that he had already made arrangements to go to the Presbyterian Seminary in Pittsburgh. Nevertheless, Brown accepted his de-

---

253. Billy Graham, *Just As I Am: The Autobiography of Billy Graham* (New York: HarperOne, 2007), 410–411.
254. For a study that examined his methodology of preaching and theology, bringing to the fore the powerful influence his message wield in evangelical circles, See Thomas Paul Johnston, *Examining Billy Graham's Theology of Evangelism* (Eugene, Or.: Wipf and Stock, 2003), 403–417.
255. Coomes, *Festo Kivengere*, 228.
256. Coomes, *Festo Kivengere*, 229.
257. Coomes, *Festo Kivengere*, 229.

cision.²⁵⁸ To Kivengere's decision, he was enabled by a three-year scholarship awarded by the United Presbyterian Mission Missionaries' Conference held in 1964 at New Wellington, Pennsylvania.

Just before Kivengere entered Pittsburgh Seminary, Karl Barth toured the United States of America delivering five lectures subsequently published as *Evangelical Theology: An Introduction*.²⁵⁹ The presence of this twentieth century Swiss theological giant caused a massive stir in the States; 'I delivered the first five of these lectures in Chicago and Princeton, and the first one also in Richmond and San Francisco . . . to see myself suddenly engulfed by such an avalanche of "publicity", to which I was quite unaccustomed'.²⁶⁰ The ripples from this visit were still apparent when Kivengere arrived to begin his theological studies in Pittsburgh. Indeed, the impact of a heavyweight New Testament scholar and theologian such as Karl Barth engulfed him, however, even more significantly his public acknowledgement of Karl Barth's influence over him.

> [W]hen I was studying for my theology in America, reading Karl Barth's (pause) great big things . . . (Sustained laughter). We had a professor who was teaching systematic theology and we had come to the atonement and it was a problem with my professor. He found it terribly difficult to teach us about the atonement, and he had twenty theories about atonement (pause)—which we appreciated (laughter).
>
> But I could see that he was embarrassed. He just did not get excited and I was frustrated. I was expecting this course to really hit me hard and fill me and get me deeper and it just flopped. However, when I read Karl Barth I found that actually, Karl Barth was a little brighter than my professor.²⁶¹

---

258. Coomes, *Festo Kivengere*, 229.
259. Charles Dickson, 'Markus Barth and Biblical Theology: A Personal Re-View', *HBT* 17/2 (December 1995): 96.
260. Karl Barth, *Evangelical Theology: An Introduction* (Grand Rapids, Mich.: Eerdmans, 1992 [1963]), v–xii.
261. Kivengere, *The Spiritual Life of a Pastor*. 46.44 mins into the tape. An important incidental evidence for Kivengere's love for Karl Barth's theology and preaching the gospel can also be found well beyond his Seminary period. Michael Cassidy recalls that

With Barth, the father, still firmly in the discussions among seminarians and professors, in September 1964 Kivengere begun his studies at Pittsburgh Theological Seminary, where he soon sat under the lecturing of Barth, the son. In 1964, Markus Barth commenced teaching New Testament at the Seminary,[262] remaining there until 1973, giving Kivengere three years to learn from this mentor before he completed Master of Divinity in 9 May 1967.[263] Pittsburgh Seminary emphasized Scripture,[264] making it a congenial environment for Markus Barth in the 1960s to the early 1970s. In 1959 he had published his great book on reconciliation,[265] which Kivengere absorbed as Markus Barth shared this interest in his lectures. In 1981, eighteen years after seminary, Kivengere in a Special Lecture at Trinity Episcopal School of Ministry (TESM), revealed that Markus Barth taught him New Testament, helped him to clarify his thinking, and claiming further that he had great respect for Markus Barth's scholarship and his colleagues.[266] This

---

like himself in spare moments during mission preaching trips, Kivengere spent much preparation time in solitude: 'He was so steeped in theology, and the Bible, plus the anointing of the Holy Spirit . . . especially anything on the cross . . . Festo was reading—often dense German theology, picking up insights as he went . . . he was thoroughly absorbing'. Amongst these works of 'German' theology were the two Barths. Cassidy further recalls that Kivengere 'really got into the heavies, and this no doubt provided an ever-deepening base for his popular [preaching] ministry'. Coomes, *Festo Kivengere*, 290–291.

262. See relevant sections in Walther, *Ever a Frontier*, 169.: 'Markus Barth came as Professor of New Testament. In 1973 he returned to Switzerland where he occupied a chair in the University of Basel'. Also see under the section, 'Historical Roll of Professors' in Walther, *Ever a Frontier*, 270.

263. See list and of graduating class: 'The Pittsburgh Theological Seminary Class 1966–1967', in Appendix 1. Kivengere's photograph and name is cited in the fourth row, third from the right, between William Kemp and J. Legge; or, tenth column sitting fourth, between S. Becker [above] and A. Nephew [below].

264. Donald E. Gowan, 'In Memory of Markus Barth: A Personal Note', *HBT* 17/2 (December 1995): 95.

265. Markus Barth, *The Broken Wall: A Study of the Epistle to the Ephesians* (London: Collins, 1959). The book's title is drawn from a perspective of Christ's redeeming act (Ephesians 2:14). This book appeared at the time when globally there were evidence of walls built between nations, races, classes, and religious sects; and, its plea is for the oneness in Christ. For threes years, at Pittsburgh Seminary, Kivengere was directly influenced by this excellent resource on reconciliation by Markus Barth.

266. Festo Kivengere, 'A Special Lecture', Sermon Transcript (Trinity Episcopal School For Ministry, USA), 4, #5, AO: 1981[----]*1.

remark is all the more significant for our purposes, because it came out as an incidental remark while Kivengere addressed another topic altogether.

In summer 1965 Kivengere briefly visited Uganda to preach at the Kabale Convention. He later said of the convention: 'St. Paul's word of reconciliation was what we needed, and the Lord's message to the Church of Thyatira poignantly describes the state of danger we were in (Rev 2:18–29)'.[267] Although at Seminary for such a short time, already he was convinced of the message of reconciliation. This experience in Uganda was also helpful for his self-evaluation of his African style of preaching versus the Western influences he was now exposed to at seminary and in American church life.

During his seminary days he was not unreflective on how he was being shaped: he had discovered that he was losing his freshness in communicating with his African brethren. He was after all going to college to prepare himself for ministry in Africa; thus, he wanted to be careful not to lose his understanding of the African way of communicating. He made up his mind that Western influence should help him to clarify his thoughts, but not force him into a set mould. He was going to learn from his brethren in the West and use the relaxed African approach in his preaching.[268]

In 1966 Archbishop Leslie Brown wrote a letter to Bishop William Thomas, suffragan bishop of Pittsburgh, asking him to make Kivengere a deacon, which took place on 11 June 1966 at 11:30 am, St. Stephen's Church, Sewickley, Pennsylvania. Exactly ten years after (1957) when Bishop Stanway said to Kivengere: 'let us postpone it until the Spirit of God says yes'. The right moment for his ordination had come. This had huge implications for his future ministry. He was no longer an itinerant evangelist but well on his way to becoming an international evangelist from the Anglican communion.

In October 1966, at the World Congress on Evangelism, Nzila Simeona (African Inland Mission) and Kivengere (Church of England), represented

---

267. Festo Kivengere, 'Introduction', in *Golden Jubilee Convention: Behold I Make All Things New: The Fifth Kabale Convention* (Kabale, Uganda: Anglican Diocese of Kigizi, 1985), 6.
268. Anglican Diocese of Kigizi, 'Golden Jubilee Convention: Behold I Make All Things New: The Fifth Kabale Convention', Convention Booklet (Kabale, Uganda, August 13, 1985), 6, Archives of Diocese of Kigezi.

Uganda.²⁶⁹ In his address at the congress, Kivengere declared spiritual indifference to God 'symptomatic of a broken relationship with the Lord . . . Christ must be central, and the church totally dependent upon him . . . for a soul-saving ministry'.²⁷⁰ This attack on spiritual indifference he delivered alongside other theologians and church leaders, notably the Australian theologian Leon Morris who addressed the subject, 'Universalism',²⁷¹ based on John 12:32, 'I, when I am lifted up from the earth, will draw all men to myself', a text that ten years later (1976) Kivengere will use to rally the Pan African Leaders Assembly (PACLA).²⁷²

At the close of the conference Billy Graham noted, 'we have seen a change from man's personal responsibility before God, to an entirely new concept of reconciliation which assumes that all men are Christians. Therefore, reconciliation takes a new and non-Biblical meaning'.²⁷³ He concludes the address with an emphatic appeal alluding to 2 Corinthians 5:19: 'We have only one gospel to declare in every generation, and that is, "God was in Christ reconciling the world unto Himself". We have one task—the penetration of the entire world in our generation with the gospel!'²⁷⁴

While it has been fashionable in the 1960s among evangelicals to use the phrase 'the penetration of the entire world in our generation with the gospel!', we might imagine that Billy Graham's appeal meant for Kivengere, a further concretisation of reconciliation in addition to Barth's works he read and Markus Barth's teaching. Recently Hughes Oliphant Old²⁷⁵ discussed five main elements in Graham's preaching: Our Need for Salvation, God has Provided a Way of Salvation, Living the Christian Life, Warning of Final Judgment, and Invitation to Receive the Gospel. Kivengere's preaching of reconciliation reflects these elements of Graham's preaching which in

---

269. See Kivengere, 'World Congress On Evangelism', in *Spiritual Indifference* (presented at the Group III, Kongresshale, Berlin, 1966), 333-34.
270. Kivengere, 'Spiritual Indifference', 1–3.
271. Leon Morris, 'Universalism', in *Hinderances to Evangelism: in the Church* (presented at the World Congress on Evangelsim, Kongresshalle, Berlin, 1966), 1–2.
272. Cassidy, *Together in One Place*.
273. Billy Graham, 'World Congress On Evangelism', in *Why The Berlin Congress?* (presented at the World Congress on Evangelism, Kongresshalle, Berlin, 1966), 13.
274. Graham, 'Why The Berlin Congress?', 13.
275. Old, *Reading and Preaching*, 61–86.

effect reflect the Keswick teaching.[276] The similarities were so great, in fact, Kivengere became known as 'the Billy Graham of Africa'.[277]

The following year, October 1967, Kivengere completed his seminary education, graduating with a Master of Divinity. He returned immediately to Uganda, where Bishop Dick Lyth at St. Peter's Cathedral priested him on Sunday 10 December 1967, in Kabale. A dear friend and clergyman from Northern Uganda, Luwum, then Provincial Secretary, attended his Priesthood. Little did either of them know that exactly ten years from then (1977), Luwum would be murdered by Amin, and Kivengere would be the last bishop and friend to see him alive before fleeing into exile.

2.6 Summary of Chapter Two

In this chapter we have sketched the historical and biographical context of Kivengere's preaching. From 1894–1962, divisions and tensions opened up in Uganda, which left deep wounds in the nation during the period 1962–1988, which includes the years 1971–1988, the period of our investigation. We reconstructed Kivengere's homiletical biography primarily based on material from his sermons, both those under our inquiry and those others of relevance to his preaching biography. We proposed that an understanding of four elements in his life and ministry—his family upbringing of the Bahima, his conversion, his teacher education, and his seminary training at Pittsburgh—shaped his preaching of reconciliation. In this chapter, we have begun to show how the historical and biographical context of Kivengere's preaching, drawn from his sermons, function together in order to illuminate his preaching of reconciliation. The influences upon Kivengere, arising from the historical and biographical context in this chapter, are developed further in the next chapter.

---

276. See Chapter three below under relevant section 2. 'The Keswick Movement and the East African Revival'.

277. The expression 'Billy Graham of Africa' is popularly used to refer to Kivengere but the author of the expression is unknown to me. E.g., Coomes refer to Kivengere with this expression in chapter 14 of her book, Coomes, *Festo Kivengere*, 251.

CHAPTER THREE
Potential Influences on Kivengere's Preaching

3.1 A Trajectory of Influences: Synopsis

This chapter aims to provide a trajectory for analyzing Kivengere's preaching of reconciliation. The first section sets out the approach to preaching that characterized the Keswick Movement, which is the background to the East African Revival Movement. Kivengere not only inherited the Revival approach to preaching of reconciliation, he became its spokesman. The second section discusses Karl Barth's 'Theological Exegesis' and his theology of atonement and reconciliation. As we shall see, Kivengere claimed that Barth consolidated for him what he learned from the Revival. Although he made this comment with particular reference to his teaching on atonement, this thesis will suggest that Kivengere's biblical theology has a great deal of affinity with Barth's 'Theological Exegesis' and they hold in common a focus on reconciliation. The third section outlines Markus Barth's contributions to the discussion of the New Testament doctrine of reconciliation. Since Kivengere is open about his debt to his New Testament teacher, this examination contributes to the next item in our trajectory, for Markus Barth built on his father's 'Theological Exegesis' and specifically dealt with reconciliation, the topic so central to Kivengere's preaching. Although strictly out of sequence, the fourth and last section sketches out the Pauline theology of reconciliation, in order to provide a theological grid for analyzing Kivengere's preaching of reconciliation. Once this trajectory is established, from Keswick to the East African Revival, and to the influence of the two Barths, it becomes clear that each of these influences bequeathed to Kivengere ways of reflecting upon the New Testament doctrine of reconciliation. This trajectory will therefore assist in analyzing his preaching of reconciliation.

3.2 The Keswick Movement and the East African Revival: The Approach and Context of Preaching

3.2.1 Early Keswick Convention (1875–1920)

Kivengere was a product of the East African Revival, which, in turn, had roots in the Keswick Movement. The early Keswick Convention saw itself as 'a spiritual clinic'.[1] The Keswick pattern was to have a five-day convention at which specific New Testament themes linked to the doctrine of sanctification[2] were preached. Andy Naselli[3] summarizes these typical themes as follows: day one, sin; day two, cleansing; day three, surrender; day four, service; and day five, communion (see also table 1 for a slightly more elaborated version).

The British Keswick Movement influenced Joe Church, one of the key pioneer leaders of the East African Revival, with its strong emphasis on personal holiness, infilling of the Holy Spirit, and the 'total surrender' of a believer's life to God. Church, with the other missionaries from the Ruanda Mission and CMS, transported the Keswick pattern to the Kabale Convention of 1935, as Church recalls: 'the Revival brethren gathered for prayers and spiritual renewal where they sang the songs "Spirit of the living God fall afresh on me"; "What can wash a way my sin?"'.[4] These songs were popular in the American and British evangelical circles. Church's debt to

---

1. Steven Barabas, *So Great Salvation: The History and Message of the Keswick Convention* (Eugene, Or.: Wipf and Stock Publishers, 2005).
2. For a synopsis of the major features of sanctification in the historic Protestant view, see Bruce A Demarest, *The Cross and Salvation: The Doctrine of Salvation* (Foundations of Evangelical Theology; Wheaton, Ill.: Crossway Books, 1997), 385–492.
3. See chapters 3 and 4 in Naselli, 'Keswick Theology'.
4. Church, *Quest for the Highest*, 116–17.

Keswick is clear when he recalls: 'The Bible readings were based as always on the Scofield Bible chain reference and a "panorama" presentation of the great themes of Scripture', adding that the subjects were as follows: Tuesday, sin; Wednesday, repentance; Thursday, the New Birth; Friday, 'coming out of Egypt', i.e. separation; Saturday, the Holy Spirit and the victorious life; Sunday, gospel service with eight testimonies; and Monday, a praise meeting.[5] The East African Revival is an extension of the English Keswick teaching. Although there were clear indigenous aspects, the Keswick Movement also just as clearly had elements that were universal.[6] Both in England and in Africa, each day's teaching built on that of the day before, creating a forward momentum for the conference that anticipated a climax in the experience of the participants. Each day's teaching,[7] typical of early Keswick conventions, will now be described in a little more detail.

Table 1: The Early Keswick Convention: 'A Spiritual Clinic and Its Patterns'[8]

Day One: Monday	Day Two: Tuesday	Day Three: Wednesday	Day Four: Thursday	Day Five: Friday
The Diagnosis: Sin	The Cure: God's Provision for Victorious Christian Living	The Crisis of the Cure: Consecration	The Prescription: Spirit-filling	The Mission: Powerful Christian Service

---

5. Church, *Quest for the Highest*, 116–17.
6. Reed, *Walking in the Light*, 83–85.
7. Among the most significant treatments of the progressive nature of Keswick's Convention teaching are Barabas, *So Great Salvation*, 35–36, 148; Charles W Price, *Transforming Keswick* (ed. Ian M Randall; Carlisle, Cumbria: OM Pub., 2000), 194–98; Herbert F. Stevenson, ed., *Keswick's Triumphant Voice: Forty-Eight Outstanding Addresses Delivered at the Keswick Convention, 1882-1962* (London: Marshall, Morgan and Scott, 1963), 14.
8. Naselli, 'Keswick Theology', 136.

3.2.1.1 Day One: The Diagnosis—Sin

On day one the early Keswick convention preached sin—the diagnosis of the human condition. According to Naselli, Evans Hopkins,[9] Keswick's formative theologian, described sin in six ways: 1) 'an act of rebellion against God'; 2) it rules in man, therefore it is not limited to outward violation of God's law; 3) sin includes 'all the inner activities of the soul that are opposed to the mind and the character of God';[10] 4) it is 'moral uncleanness that makes man unfit before God'; 5) sin is 'a spiritual disease with paralyzing effects'; 6) it is a habit that is acquired and 'an indwelling tendency or law that can be counteracted but never eradicated' [see table 2]. This last category constitutes the major distinctive characteristic of Keswick preaching.[11] Therefore, it should be noted that, for Keswick, how long one has been a Christian is not vital because 'the tendency to sin is still there'; one has not yet 'lost the tendency downwards'.[12]

The law of the Spirit in Christ (Rom 8:2) counteracts the law of sin in the believer (Rom 7:23). Early Keswick Convention preachers also taught the possibility of living without 'known sin'.[13] 'But as to known sin . . . There is no mistake in the attitude of our Lord. He says, "Sin no more"; and He would not say that if he did not mean it'.[14] Thus, the early Keswick preached that all Christians have sin (1 John 1:18), but not all do sin (1 John 1:10). When Christians abide in Christ they do not sin because 'the soul lives from moment to moment in the perfect union with the Lord its keeper', therefore 'daily sinning' is not 'an inevitable necessity'. Hence, 'Christ offers to us now and here' the freedom from the power of all known sin. The decisive factor for successful counteraction of sin is the believer's response, which allows the Holy Spirit to counteract their sinful nature.

---

9. Evan H. Hopkins, *The Law of Liberty in the Spiritual Life* (London: Marshall Bros., 1884), 15–38.
10. Hopkins, *The Law of Liberty in the Spiritual Life*, 18–19.
11. Hopkins, *The Law of Liberty in the Spiritual Life*, 34–38.
12. Hopkins, *The Law of Liberty in the Spiritual Life*, 37.
13. Mark Steven Rathe, 'The Keswick Movement: Its Origins and Teachings' (M. A. Thesis, San Francisco, CA.: Simpson College, 1988), 53.
14. Pierson, 'Unsubdued Sin', 104.

Table 2: Hopkins On the Law of Counteraction of Sin[15]

The Law of Sin in the Believer	The Law of the Spirit in Christ	The Law of Counteraction
Dark room.	Light from a candle.	Light counteracts darkness only when the light abides in the dark room.
A rod attached to lead sinks in a tank of water.	The rod floats in a little life belt.	The life belt counteracts sinking only when the rod abides in the life belt.
Evans Hopkins in the sea would eventually sink to the bottom.	Evans in a life belt would float on the surface.	The life belt counteracts sinking only when Evans Hopkins abides in the life belt.
Peter sinks when trying to walk on the water.	Peter walks on water through Christ's power.	Christ's power counteracts sinking only when Peter gazes on Christ.
A hot air balloon without gas rests on the ground.	A hot air balloon soars above the ground when hot gas inflates it.	Hot gas counteracts gravity's effect on the hot air balloon only when the gas abides in the balloon.
Iron by itself is black, cold, and hard.	Iron in the fire is red, hot, and malleable because the fire is in the iron.	Fire counteracts iron's blackness, coldness, and hardness only when the iron abides in the fire.
A young lion is savage and bloodthirsty.	The lion is tame when in the presence of its keeper.	The keeper counteracts the lion's savage nature only when the keeper abides in the lion's presence.

---

15. Hopkins, *The Law of Liberty in the Spiritual Life*, 34.; Evan H. Hopkins, 'Deliverance from the Law of Sin', in *Keswick's Authentic Voice: Sixty-Five Dynamic Addresses Delivered at the Keswick Convention, 1875-1957* (ed. Herbert F. Stevenson; London: Marshall, Morgan & Scott, 1959), 160–61.; Evan H. Hopkins, 'Threefold Deliverance', in *Keswick's Authentic Voice: Sixty-Five Dynamic Addresses Delivered at the Keswick Convention, 1875-1957* (ed. Herbert F. Stevenson; London: Marshall, Morgan & Scott, 1959), 166.; Evan H. Hopkins, 'The Path and the Power', in *Keswick's Authentic Voice: Sixty-Five Dynamic Addresses Delivered at the Keswick Convention, 1875-1957* (ed. Herbert F. Stevenson; London: Marshall, Morgan & Scott, 1959), 302.; A. T. Pierson, 'Unsubdued Sin', in *Keswick's Triumphant Voice: Forty-Eight Outstanding Addresses Delivered at the Keswick Convention, 1882-1962* (ed. Herbert F Stevenson; London: Marshall, Morgan and Scott, 1963), 306.; Andrew Murray, *Abide in Christ: Thoughts on the Blessed Life of Fellowship with the Son of God* (London: Oliphants, 1963 [1895]), 203.

The East African Revival preached about sin with a similar emphasis. They emphasized initial conversion from sin with overwhelming experience of brokenness at the cross, which triggers public confession. In fact, the dominant feature of the East African Revival was the public confession and repentance of sins,[16] accompanied with the practice of restitution.[17] When the early Keswick Movement preaching on sin is placed alongside the East African Revival preaching on sin, a number of expressions in Kivengere's sermons are illuminated. For example, when Kivengere preached on the cross at Lausanne Congress, summarizing the Revival theology of the cross, he spoke of the condition of fallen humanity as one of 'conflicting pulls': 'the outward pull of broken relationships' and 'the downward pull of violent appetites and passions'.[18] However, to Kivengere the sinful nature of man that causes the conflicting pulls can be counteracted in Christ. When he himself preached at the Keswick Convention,[19] he repeatedly spoke about sin: 'there is sin in the believer, that sin which hinders the flow of the Holy Spirit', 'that sin which has made the testimony dry; that sin which has kept a brother at a distance from another brother', and 'that sin which still exists in the new community which Jesus brought about through his death and resurrection'.[20]

In 1975 Kivengere had the honour to preach at the Keswick centenary celebration.[21] He reminded his audience about their Keswick heritage. He

---

16. William Rukirande, 'The East African Revival and the Church in Kigezi: A Personal Experience', in *The East African Revival Through Seventy Years (1935-2005): Testimonies and Reflections* (ed. Manuel J. K. Muranga; Kabale, Uganda: Diocese of Kigezi, 2005), 9.

17. Nsibambi, 'The Importance of the East African Revival', 45.

18. Kivengere, 'The Cross and World Evangelization', 400–01. For an audio version of this talk, see Festo Kivengere, *The Cross and World Evangelization; and Communion Service*, Audio Cassette (International Congress on World Evangelization; Lausanne, 1974).

19. Festo Kivengere, 'Christ the Renewer', in *The Keswick Week 1972* (London: Marshall, Morgan & Scott, 1972), 66–75.; Festo Kivengere, 'Christ the Dynamic of Life', in *The Keswick Week 1972* (London: Marshall, Morgan & Scott, 1972), 183–94.; Kivengere, 'The Release of Forgiveness', 27–34.

20. Kivengere, 'Christ the Renewer', 66–76.

21. The actual year of the Keswick Centenary, the hundredth Convention is 1974. However, the celebration took place in 1975 following interruptions in the sequence of annual gatherings, namely, following the first World War (1914–1918) and during the second World War travel restrictions hindered holding meetings in Keswick. For a historical explanation see, Keswick Ministries, *The Keswick Week 1975: Centenary Year* (London: Marshall, Morgan & Scott, 1975), 8.

spoke of its teaching on sin and provided some of the old diagnosis: 'Now, all through the years at Keswick there has been a concentration on sin in the life of a believer'; '[I]n the Keswick Convention they always start with a reminder of—sin in the heart of the believer'; 'What the Bible calls sin is when you live at cross purposes with the will of the Father'. He also spoke of the Keswick emphasis on the forgiveness of sin: 'There is a tremendous need in 1975, a hundred years since Keswick began, for us to catch a fresh vision of the release which comes when sins are forgiven'.

In short, Keswick preaching on day one establishes living in sin as a major problem for believers that the redemptive work of Christ, discussed on ensuing days, counteracts.

3.2.1.2 Day Two: The Cure—God's Provision for Victorious Christian Living

The main focus of preaching on day two built on day one and was centred on 'God's provision for victorious Christian living'—the cure. There are two categories of Christians: those who have been justified but are yet to have a personal experience of a crisis of sanctification and those who have been justified and have had a personal experience of a crisis of sanctification.[22] If we take Hopkins as emblematic of the Keswick teaching on victorious living,[23] he taught that not all believers are situated positionally 'in Christ', but there is a possibility of living victorious Christian lives.[24] Some believers are experientially situated 'in Christ'.[25] He distinguished between 'the old man' and 'the flesh', noting that the old man refers to the believer's unregenerate life in Adam and 'the flesh' refers to the 'old nature' and remains with the believer until glorification.[26] While believers would distinguish between being 'positioned in Christ' from 'experientially situated in

---

22. Naselli, 'Keswick Theology', 257–60.
23. Hopkins, *The Law of Liberty in the Spiritual Life*, 41–55.
24. Cf. J. Elder Cumming, 'What We Teach', in *Keswick's Triumphant Voice: Forty-Eight Outstanding Addresses Delivered at the Keswick Convention, 1882-1962* (ed. Herbert F Stevenson; London: Marshall, Morgan and Scott, 1963), 23.
25. Hopkins, *The Law of Liberty in the Spiritual Life*, 41–55.
26. Evan H. Hopkins, 'Our Old Man Crucified', in *Keswick's Triumphant Voice: Forty-Eight Outstanding Addresses Delivered at the Keswick Convention, 1882-1962* (London: Marshall, Morgan and Scott, 1963), 172–75; Hopkins, 'Threefold Deliverance', 164–65.

Christ', he contends that believers would not separate the two positions.[27] Only those experiencing fellowship with Christ 'have consciousness of his favour'; they abide in Christ and 'live the Christ-life'. Therefore, believers who do not abide in Christ live 'the self-life'.[28]

Romans 6 was the key Pauline passage used by Keswick preachers in their books, articles, and preaching at the Annual Keswick Conventions.[29] For example, Hopkins reports: 'There was no passage of Scripture that was more frequently to the front'.[30] For the early Keswick preachers, Romans 6 set forth the believer's union with Christ as the ground of sanctification, and because to them some believers are positionally united with Christ, they have the possibility of experientially living the victorious Christian life.[31]

According to Hopkins, sanctification:

> [M]ay be regarded in relation to our own individual condition and conduct—as personal separation from all known sin on the one hand and, dedication to God on the other . . . In this aspect sanctification may be regarded as a personal and definite act of consecration to God. Following the initial act, the habit or attitude of surrender is formed; and a progress is made, so the thoroughness of dedication to God deepens and increases. We may take the word 'yield' as expressive of the main idea involved in such a personal consecration.[32]

---

27. Hopkins, *The Law of Liberty in the Spiritual Life*, 41.
28. Hopkins, *The Law of Liberty in the Spiritual Life*, 41–55.
29. Hopkins, 'Our Old Man Crucified', 172. A vigorous Keswick discussion on the passage (Romans 6) is perhaps Moule's exposition: H. C. G. Moule, *The Epistle of St. Paul to the Romans* (The Expositors Bible; London: Hodder and Stoughton, 1894), 156–80. See also Arthur Tappan Pierson, *Vital Union with Christ* (Grand Rapids, Mich.: Zondervan Publishing House, 1961); Pierson, 'Unsubdued Sin', 100–10; Cf. Barabas, *So Great Salvation*, 89–92.
30. Hopkins, 'Our Old Man Crucified', 172; H. Webb-Peploe, 'Dead unto Sin', in *Keswick's Triumphant Voice: Forty-Eight Outstanding Addresses Delivered at the Keswick Convention, 1882-1962* (ed. Herbert F Stevenson; London: Marshall, Morgan and Scott, 1963), 150.
31. Cumming, 'What We Teach', 23.
32. Hopkins, *The Law of Liberty in the Spiritual Life*, 91–92.

Hopkins described sanctification as a crisis, followed by an experiential process, both aspects being a gift.[33] He argued that experiential sanctification is purely a gift that a believer must willingly accept. Its starting point is a crisis of consecration followed by a process; the crisis to him is 'an act or attitude of consecration'.[34] And the means of sanctification is appropriating the gift by faith alone, not by effort or struggle.[35] The agent through whom God delivers a believer to victorious Christian living is the Holy Spirit. This aspect of Keswick's teaching on sanctification caused great concern. It was the reason why influential preachers like Charles H. Spurgeon and J. C. Ryle never addressed the Keswick Convention.[36] Lloyd-Jones believed that Keswick's teaching had its pedigree in Wesleyanism and its Holiness Movement, which made him suspect its theological accuracy.[37]

Traces of the Keswick call to a victorious life are clear in many of Kivengere's sermons. For example, he emphasizes the believer's need to live 'the Christ-life' as opposed to the 'self' or 'I'.[38] He expressed for his audience from many angles what happens when the believer 'yields' to Christ: Christ becomes 'the centre' of the believer's life; Christ gives the believer 'a new dynamic' to life; Christ becomes 'the foundation' of life for the believ-

---

33. Hopkins, *The Law of Liberty in the Spiritual Life*, 84–104; Cf. Evan H. Hopkins, 'Crisis and Progress', in *Keswick's Authentic Voice: Sixty-Five Dynamic Addresses Delivered at the Keswick Convention, 1875-1957* (ed. Herbert F. Stevenson; London: Marshall, Morgan & Scott, 1959), 332–57.

34. Hopkins, *The Law of Liberty in the Spiritual Life*, 89; Cf. F. B Meyer, *The Christ-Life for the Self-Life [Formerly "A Castaway"]* (Chicago: Moody Press, 1900); J. I Packer, '"Keswick" and the Reformed Doctrine of Sanctification', *Evangelical Quarterly* 27.3 (1955): 157–58.

35. F. B Meyer, *Christian Living* (London: Morgan and Scott, 1902), ch. 1, pp. 1–16.

36. David Martyn Lloyd-Jones, '"Living the Christian Life"—New Development in the 18th and 19th Century Teaching', in *The Puritans: Their Origins and Successors: Addresses Delivered at the Puritan and Westminster Conferences 1959-1978* (Carlisle: Banner of Truth Trust, 1987), 318.

37. Works that support Lloyd-John's claim include C. M. Loucks, 'The Theological Foundation of the Victorious Life' (PhD Thesis, Pasadena, CA.: Fuller Theological Seminary, 1984), 179–38, and esp. 199; B. E. Moyer, 'The Doctrine of Christian Perfection: A Comparative Study of John Wesley and the Modern American Holiness Movement' (PhD Thesis, Milwaukee, Wis.: Marquette University, 1992), 82–84; M. A. R. Maddox, 'Jesus Saves Me Now: Sanctification in the Writings of Hannah Whitall Smith' (PhD Thesis, Louisville, Kent.: Southern Baptist Theological Seminary, 2003), 287–88.

38. For examples of sermons that emphasize 'Christ-life' living, see Kivengere's four thematic addresses in Chapter Six: *Revival Begins at the Cross, Remove the Masks, Peace and Victory for the Christian*, and *the Covenant of Love*.

er; Christ becomes 'the liberator' in the believer's life; and Christ becomes 'the healer' of the believer's life, hence, the believer now lives the victorious Christian life.[39]

Kivengere further illustrates the victorious Christian living with stories and testimonies from the Revival brethren, in that they managed to sustain their Christian testimony in the midst of political turmoil and suffering. Over and again he referred to Janani Luwum's torture and murder by Idi Amin.[40] He also tells in his sermons stories of the brethren suffering in the Mau Mau uprising; yet, still loving their tormentors.[41] He tells similar stories from the Hutu versus Tutsi revolution in Rwanda, and from the 'Simba' rebellion in Eastern Zaire and others from Burundi.[42]

In all the fight against sin and evil, for the Revivalist, victorious living in Christ was not an end in itself. They insisted on absolute moral standards, namely, the Christian life may be lived as a result of salvation in Jesus Christ. For the Revivalist, not even searching for victorious Christian living in Christ may be attained as an end in itself for a believer.

3.2.1.3 Day Three: The Consecration—Crisis of the Cure

A frequent saying at the early Keswick Convention was 'No crisis before Wednesday', because the groundwork for the crisis was laid in the first two days.[43] Because sanctification is a crisis that is followed by a process, the Keswick proponents taught how to experience the crisis so that the process may follow and the sequential structure of the teaching created the conditions at the convention to facilitate this experience occurring. What are the conditions of this victorious life? They taught only two conditions:

---

39. Kivengere, 'In Christ'.
40. In Chapter Five, all the sermons Kivengere preached after the murder of Luwum, for purposes of prayers for the situation in Uganda under Idi Amin, information and awareness of the world about the brutal dictatorship of Idi Amin, and application of God's message of reconciliation into such a world full of brokenness, Kivengere tells of Luwum's following in the footsteps of his Master.
41. For further stories of how the Revival brethren faced the effects of sin manifested in the form of evil descended upon them, see Kivengere's published sermons in Kivengere, *Revolutionary Love* esp. "Love Triumphs in Suffering", 73-82.
42. Kivengere, 'Introduction'.
43. J. Robertson McQuilkin, 'The Keswick Perspective', in *Five Views on Sanctification* (ed. Melvin Easterday Dieter and Stanley N. Gundry; Grand Rapids: Zondervan, 1987), 155.

surrender and faith: 'Let go, and let God'.[44] Here the key is trusting, not trying; resting, not struggling. 'Our efforts' do not play any part in victory, 'they can and do effectually prevent such victory'.[45] In his chapter on 'Victory Without Trying', Trumbull asks: 'What do you consider the most dangerous heresy of today?' and replies: 'The most dangerous is the emphasis that is being given, right in the professing Christian church itself, on *What we do for God*, instead of on *what God does for us*'.[46] As a child of the Revival, it is certain that Kivengere encountered some of this early Keswick teaching emphasizing 'not what we do for God but what God does for us'.[47]

Kivengere's sermons are full of autobiographical illustrations where he struggles with the Lord over some personal crisis in his life but in the end he 'lets go', he surrenders to the Lord; and 'lets God', by faith in God and obedience to his word. Not only in his sermons does he express this surrender to God, but also in his writings and interviews. For example, he writes: '[M]y hardness and bitterness toward those who were persecuting us could only bring spiritual loss. This would take away my ability to communicate the love of God, which is the essence of my ministry'.[48] Kivengere had to ask forgiveness from the Lord and for grace to love President Amin more. This gave his tired soul fresh air. From that moment he knew that he had seen the Lord and he was released: love filled his heart.[49]

Such Keswick piety lasted with him throughout his life. Shortly before his death, he still had the same perspective: 'My vision is not so much what we can do for the Lord, but what the Lord can do for us'.[50] Inherent in these autobiographical statements lies the secret to his preaching ministry. He 'let go' and by faith trusted not what he could do for God, but 'what God can do' by means of his preaching ministry.

---

44. Charles G. Trumbull, *Victory in Christ* (Fort Washington, Penn.: Christian Literature Crusade, 1980), 14, 35, 43.
45. Trumbull, *Victory in Christ*, 126.
46. Trumbull, *Victory in Christ*, 53.
47. Senyonyi argues that Kivengere's preaching was in essence the Revival theology, even though Kivengere added a very valuable building block of the love of God to the already firm foundation of Jesus Christ in revival. See Senyonyi, 'Philosophy of Evangelism', 136.
48. Kivengere, *I Love Idi Amin*, 62.
49. Kivengere, *I Love Idi Amin*, 62.
50. Melhust Kaare, 'Festo's Vision', *AV* August (1988): 3.

3.2.1.4 Day Four: The Prescription—Spirit-filling

The focus of day four was Spirit-filling as the prescription for health, growth and avoiding a relapse. In an address to the 1947 Keswick Convention, Montague Goodman observed that the message of the Spirit-filled life is the central, dominating theme of Keswick Convention, and also constituted the very reason why Keswick existed.[51] At the Keswick conventions, Spirit-filling was a major theme, where the work of the Holy Spirit was presented with the command: 'BE FILLED WITH THE SPIRIT!'[52] Not to be filled with the Holy Spirit was taught as a great sin because the Scripture does not present being filled with the Holy Spirit as an optional matter, but as an obligation for all believers. Spirit-filling began at a believer's crisis of consecration and continued on for as long as a believer maintained a condition of surrender and faith.[53] In effect, the believer may be compared to a vessel filled with water to the brim (see table 3 below).

According to Hopkins, the question in Acts 19:2: 'Did you receive the Holy Spirit when you believed?' shows that 'it is possible to believe, to be born again of the Spirit, and yet not to have the Holy Spirit in the same sense as the apostles received him on the day of Pentecost'.[54]

Table 3: Hopkins Illustrating Spirit-filling[55]

Illustration	Explanation
A cup filled with water	The cup may be full, overflowing, or in periodic need of refilling because of leakage.
A person breathing in air	The same life-giving properties in the air are in that person.
Iron in the fire	Iron by itself is black, cold, and hard, but iron in the fire is red, hot, and malleable because the fire is in the iron.

---

51. Montague Goodman, 'The Wonderous Cross', in *The Keswick Week 1947* (London: Marshall, Morgan & Scott, 1947), 41.
52. J B Figgis, *Keswick from Within* (The Higher Christian Life; New York: Garland, 1985), 57.
53. John. MacNeil, *The Spirit-Filled Life* (London: Marshall Bros., 1894), Cited 22 Nov 2011, Online: http://hdl.handle.net/2027/[u]: nnc1.cr00285420.
54. Hopkins, *The Law of Liberty in the Spiritual Life*, 179.
55. Pierson, 'Unsubdued Sin', 106. Andrew Murray, *The Deeper Christian Life: An Aid*

Kivengere's preaching shows a most significant difference from this Keswick influence. Keswick Spirit-filling becomes Jesus filling the believer. For example, in his address on 'Christ the Liberator', at the Keswick Week of 1972, he said: 'When the Holy Spirit came down on the day of Pentecost . . . He actually came to bring the risen Lord, the one who died, and enthroned him on the heart of a believer and that heart which was in darkness is flooded with light, flooded with liberty: the liberator is inside'.[56]

Kivengere argued that believers want life but they have 'not yet discovered that when you live for your self you become empty'.[57] This fundamental reality of an empty life demands filling. In the sermon 'Love's Quick Way',[58] he could explain: 'I am not always full of love, not always seeing [Jesus] clearly. Self-indulgence has a way of creeping in. Sometimes I am thoroughly empty and have to say so in public. But what I have discovered is that Jesus loves to fill empties! All I need to do is to keep open to him and to admit frankly what's wrong. He does the rest'.[59]

Kivengere quite clearly and explicitly changes 'Spirit-filling' in the life of a believer to Jesus being the *content* that fills the believer's life. However, we hasten to add that he is not countering the Revival tradition in which he was brought up in the aspect of 'Spirit-filling', but he is simply being more precise. Throughout his sermons, Jesus is never separated from the Holy Spirit, but the emphasis and focus of attention must always be Jesus Christ himself.[60]

3.2.1.5 Day Five: The Mission—Powerful Christian Service

The climax of the early Keswick Convention was on day five, focusing on powerful Christian service. The result of a believer, who has experienced

---

to Its Attainment (Fleming H. Revell, 1895), 59. Andrew Murray, *The Full Blessing of Pentecost: The One Thing Needful* (Whitefish, Mont.: Kessinger, 2010 [1908]), 98.

56. Festo Kivengere, 'Christ the Liberator', in *The Keswick Week 1972* (London: Marshall, Morgan & Scott, 1972), 121.

57. Kivengere, 'Christ the Liberator', 120.

58. Kivengere, *Revolutionary Love*, 33.

59. See "Love's Quick Way" in Kivengere, *Revolutionary Love*, 130; Schmidt, *Glorious Companions*, 318.

60. As we shall see, all twenty-six sermons studied here show this focus. See Chapters Five and Six.

crisis of consecration and who has been filled by the Holy Spirit, is the fruit of soul winning and foreign missions. Writing on 'The Sequence of Teaching at Keswick', Barabas concludes: 'In the final analysis, the Christian life reduces itself to this—knowing God's will and doing it. . . . What he expects of us he gives us the power to do, both in sanctification and service. That is the message of Keswick'.[61]

Clearly this final day focus on Mission-Service forms a crucial step between Keswick and Kivengere. Not only because it lies behind the missionaries (like Joe Church, missionary of Ruanda Mission) coming to Uganda in the first place, but it also helps to access other later influences on Kivengere. For example, Keswick conventions spread all over the world as a result of this Mission-Service emphasis. In Australia the offshoots of the Keswick Conventions include the Katoomba Convention, started in 1903. Forty-three years later (1946), a distinct pattern of Keswick progressive teaching could still be seen in Loane's drafted outline for the Katoomba Convention: 'Monday, The fact of Sin in the Regenerate Life; Tuesday, the Way of Victory and Separation; Wednesday, the Fullness of the Holy Spirit; Thursday, the Call to Surrender; Friday, the Challenge for Service; Saturday, Missionary Day'.[62] The Belgrave Heights Convention in Melbourne started in 1918, the Katherine Christian Convention in Darwin started in 1969, etc. These conventions, in turn, played a role in recruiting for CMS Australia, leading to Kivengere's friends in Tanganyika and, through this link, to his further ministry in Australia (and beyond).

This focus on Mission-Service also extended its influence directly on Kivengere's call. His own missionary call to Tanganyika came at the 1945 Kabale Convention.[63] On day five, the appeal for believers to go out into mission service was made. He responded to it. This focus on reaching out in mission shaped Kivengere's life. It also shaped his preaching of reconciliation. For example, in the sermons Kivengere exhorts his audience to reach out into the world with good news. Even without the Convention Week he took the Keswick message of reaching out in Mission-Service and made it

---

61. Barabas, *So Great Salvation*, 155.
62. Stuart Braga, *A Century Preaching Christ* (Sydney: Katoomba Christian Convention, Limited, 2003), 82.
63. See Chapter Two, 4.5 'The Mukono Crisis'.

transportable to many different places. What was done across a week in the convention was now done within one sermon.

Kivengere took the Keswick emphasis of bathing every work of evangelism in prayer,[64] practical Bible living,[65] and a great ministry of literature. Later he published a few of his sermons[66] as a ministry of literature that he hoped could bring encouragement to the discouraged and transformation to believers. He tells in his 'Preface' to *I Love Idi Amin*, 'It is a book of praise to encourage those who feel discouraged because of the circumstances in which they find themselves'[67] and in the 'Preface' to *Revolutionary Love*: 'I pray that the shared messages of this book—by the power of the Holy Spirit—you will open up to this revolutionary love of Christ and experience a radical transformation of the foundations of your entire systems of life'.[68]

3.2.2 Modern Keswick Convention (1950s–)

As we will see in the analysis to follow, the influences of this pattern of teaching can clearly be detected—but not without some modifications—in Kivengere's preaching. Keswick began to change, however, with the arrival of John Stott and Billy Graham, who brought a new emphasis in their

---

64. For a few examples of his relying on prayers see, Kivengere, 'Ambassador For Christ', p. 4, #7–#8, p. 6, #10–#11. Kivengere, 'In Christ', p. 1, #3, p. 7, #12. Kivengere, 'The Reconciling Love of Christ', pp. 9–10, #12. 'Jesus Came As A Missionary of Reconciliation', Sermon Transcript, p. 1, #4, AO: 19820521.

65. His sermons in Chapters Five and Six show his devotion to practical living of the Christian faith as illustrated by his numerous testimonies of how he related with his enemies, his wife, and his colleagues.

66. For example, Festo Kivengere, *Hope for Uganda and the World: The Secret of Rehabilitation* (Rev. ed.; Pasadena: African Enterprise, 1981). Kivengere, *The Spirit Is Moving*. Festo Kivengere, *When God Moves* (Rev. ed.; Pasadena: African Enterprise, 1976). Kivengere, *Revolutionary Love*. and Festo Kivengere, *Love Unlimited* (ed. Dorothy Smoker; Glendale, Ca.: G/L Regal, 1975). Besides these he was a regular contributor to *Outlook Magazine*.

67. See 'Preface' in Kivengere, *I Love Idi Amin*. Kivengere, 'Ambassador For Christ', p. 4, #7–#8, p. 6, #10–#11.

68. See 'Preface' in Kivengere, *Revolutionary Love*, 8.

preaching at Keswick.[69] This will not only have an impact on Kivengere but he himself will play a role in the modern Keswick.[70]

It was only in the late 1950s and into the 1960s that the Keswick Convention message began to be transformed so that its message increasingly differed from the early emphasis on sanctification. John R. W. Stott addressed the convention for the first time in 1962, and then in 1964 he gave an address that was published as *The Baptism and Fullness of the Holy Spirit* (republished in 1975 as part of the Keswick centenary celebration[71]). However, it was his preaching on Romans 5–8 in 1965 that provoked 'some controversy', because it specifically countered the earlier Keswick preaching, by correcting the notion of 'progressing in Christian experience from the struggle of Romans 7 to the victory of chapter 8'.[72]

Besides correcting aspects of the early Keswick theology, Stott's style of exposing biblical passages was marked by clear, analytical, and deep biblical understanding; and an unwavering emphasis on the centrality of Jesus Christ.[73] Being involved in the modern Keswick movement contributed to Kivengere's growth.[74] He confessed a special debt to John Stott's preaching: 'He [John Stott] put me to shame! I would listen to him in the morning, all neat and clear. . . . He has taught me lessons of grace and discipline for

---

69. We do not need to be specific about the Keswick Convention (1921–1950) even though this was the period when Kivengere was growing up in the Keswick teaching. Our main contention for this is simple: the patterns of Keswick teaching remained the same as demonstrated by Joe Church at the Kabale gathering.

70. See his addressees at the *Keswick Week* of 1972 and 1975: Kivengere, 'Christ the Renewer', 66–76. Kivengere, 'Christ the Liberator', 116–22. Kivengere, 'Christ the Dynamic of Life', 183–94. Kivengere, 'The Release of Forgiveness', 27–34.

71. John R. W Stott, *John Stott at Keswick: A Lifetime of Preaching* (ed. Keswick Ministries; Milton Keynes, UK: Authentic Media, 2008), 284–367.

72. Stott's 1965 series was published as John R. W Stott, *Men Made New: An Exposition of Romans 5-8* (American ed.; Grand Rapids: Baker Book House, 1984). Cf. John R. W Stott, *The Message of Romans: God's Good News for the World* (The Bible Speaks Today. New Testament Series; Leicester, England: Inter-Varsity Press, 1994), 189–260.

73. Most of his Keswick addresses are published in Stott, *John Stott at Keswick*. A distinctive mark of the exposition is the centrality of Jesus Christ.

74. As he attended and gave addresses at the Keswick Convention, he continued to grow in the light of their teaching. His addresses at the Convention include Kivengere, 'Christ the Liberator', 116–22 (AO:19720711); Kivengere, 'Christ the Dynamic of Life', 183–94; Kivengere, 'The Release of Forgiveness', 27–34.

which I am deeply grateful'.[75] Clear Bible exposition with its emphasis on the centrality of Jesus Christ no doubt reinforced the strong emphasis on the centrality of Christ in Kivengere's preaching of reconciliation.

Billy Graham was the main speaker at the convention's centennial in 1975.[76] In reviewing the Keswick history, he spoke of its move away from the emphasis upon individual sanctification up to the 1920s, towards the ecumenical spirit expressed in the slogan 'All One in Christ': 'I associate the concept of *Biblical unity* with Keswick. I love your motto, "All one in Christ Jesus". . . . The denominational barriers that existed then are hard for us to understand today. Christians felt deeply about their particular and peculiar distinctions, and thought their own way was right, and others were wrong'. He illustrated the new ecumenical spirit by speaking of the variety of people at the convention: Anglicans, Quakers, Presbyterians, Baptists, Congregationalists, Methodists, Brethren 'and even Americans!'[77] The 1975 convention was different from the previous conventions because it embraced 'people from all nations and kindred and tongues, who stand before the Lamb in heart and in spirit'.[78]

The ecumenical spirit of the modern Keswick, so applauded by Billy Graham, was not new for Kivengere. Even by the 1930s the Revival in East Africa displayed the same spirit, embracing the Mennonites, the Lutherans, the Anglicans, and Africa Inland Mission, among others. However, Kivengere's involvement with modern Keswick and his friend Billy Graham would further reinforce these commitments.

In sum: analyzing Kivengere's preaching requires a consideration of influences of Keswick and the Revival over him. Within the discussions of Keswick and the Revival approach and context of preaching, a basis for analyzing the sermons has been provided. In particular, Kivengere's sermons should be analyzed in terms of Keswick teaching, which is the background of the Revival. In particular, the sermons should be analyzed in such a way as presumes a continuity between Keswick and Revival emphasis on sin,

---

75. Bewes, 'Man of Africa', 3–7.
76. Billy Graham, 'A Hundred Years of Blessing and Glory', in *The Keswick Week 1975: Centenary Year* (London: Marshall, Morgan & Scott, 1975), 101–07.
77. Graham, 'A Hundred Years of Blessing and Glory', 103–04.
78. Graham, 'A Hundred Years of Blessing and Glory', 103–04.

victorious Christian living, Spirit-filled life, Biblical unity, prayer, practical holiness living, ministry of literature, missionary outreach, active social concern, and prayer. Attention must be given where he publicly acknowledges their influence and where he had moved on from Keswick and Revival teaching. The position of Kivengere as a spokesman of the Revival and a speaker on more than one occasion at Keswick must be borne in mind. This establishes his close link and acquaintance with the Keswick and Revival teaching and approach to preaching.

3.3 Karl Barth's Influence: 'Theological Exegesis' and Reconciliation

To discern the influence on Kivengere of Karl Barth's 'Theological Exegesis' and his work on 'The Doctrine of Reconciliation',[79] we undertake an inquiry into Barth's method of 'Theological Exegesis' and the doctrine of atonement or reconciliation. Kivengere gave explicit testimony to his debt to Karl Barth.[80]

3.3.1 Kivengere's Reference to the Influence of Karl Barth

In 1984, as Kivengere addressed the topic of tensions in ministry, he mentioned ministers having an attitude of 'professionalism', which made them look down on the laity. Laity, however, when excited about their faith are a beautiful thing and they can minister to you greatly. They may make theological mistakes, but they are fresh, and often they are right. In this context he gave an illustration about the laity of his country, and as he does so, he makes reference to the influence of Karl Barth in his own theological training. This remark is all the more significant for our purposes, because it came out as an incidental remark while Kivengere addressed another topic altogether.

---

79. Karl Barth, *Church Dogmatics* (ed. G. W. Bromiley and T. F. Torrance; trans. G. W. Bromiley; Edinburgh: T&T Clark, 1936), IV/1.
80. See Chapter Two, 5.4 'Pittsburgh Seminary: From 1964–1967'.

[W]hen I was studying for my theology in America, reading Karl Barth's (pause) great big things . . . (Sustained laughter) we had a professor who was teaching systematic theology and we had come to the atonement and it was a problem with my professor. He found it terribly difficult to teach us about the atonement, and he had twenty theories about atonement (pause)—which we appreciated (laughter).

But I could see that he was embarrassed. He just did not get excited and I was frustrated. I was expecting this course to really hit me hard and fill me and get me deeper and it just flopped. However, when I read Karl Barth I found that actually, Karl Barth was a little brighter than my professor. (Laughter) However, what surprised me, was when I was reading what this great theologian wrote, I found he wrote things which I had heard my people express who had never been to school. Almost word for word. And really that – that really shook me.

Here is a little fellow, a herdsman, never been to school, converted at the age of forty-five from paganism, illiterate, comes into the experience of the Lord Jesus, preaches Christ and him crucified, teaches himself how to read the Bible, and comes out with some of the most beautiful theological statements; about the blood, redeeming love, the liberty, . . . I couldn't believe it. And I even put in my notes the name of that man I am referring to. He still is active and he has brought many, hundreds and thousands of people to Jesus Christ.[81]

The reality of this connection between Kivengere and Karl Barth is the basis for conducting our second step in the trajectory for analyzing Kivengere's sermons.

---

81. Kivengere, *The Spiritual Life of a Pastor*, 46.44 mins into the tape.

3.3.2 Karl Barth's 'Theological Exegesis'

Markus Barth is acknowledged as his father's 'representative in America' and in particular his father's biblical theology.[82] Since Kivengere confessed his debt to Markus, his New Testament teacher, presumably through him he also imbibed Karl Barth's Biblical Theology and his 'Theological Exegesis'.

Throughout his career Barth attached great importance to biblical exegesis.[83] According to his friend Eduard Thurneysen,[84] Barth's biblical exegesis 'has grown out of the work of preaching, and it serves the proclamation of the church'; Barth 'does not project theological speculations out of his mind; he is not concerned about a system'; but 'he is and he remains a student and teacher of Holy Scriptures'. This being so, 'Whoever tries to understand him as other than this will not understand him at all'.[85]

Barth's exegesis has been described as 'Theological Exegesis', because it always keeps an eye on the *Sache*—the subject-matter, which is God. Whereas previous studies of Barth on Scripture have emphasized either his hermeneutical principles or his treatment of the historical-critical method,[86] we are here primarily concerned with the theological *content* of Barth's interpretation and his *approach* to theological exegesis.

---

82. Dickson, 'Markus Barth and Biblical Theology: A Personal Re-View', 96. Donald E. Gowan, describing the role of Markus Barth in America, notes that Markus taught New Testament at Dubuque Theological Seminary (1953–55), the Divinity School of the University of Chicago (1956–63), and Pittsburgh Theological Seminary (1963–72). See Gowan, 'In Memory of Markus Barth: A Personal Note', 93.

83. Bruce L. McCormack, 'The Significance of Karl Barth's Theological Exegesis of Philippians', in *The Epistle to the Philippians* (40th ed.; Louisville, KY: Westminster John Knox Press, 2002), v-xxv.

84. Karl Barth and Eduard Thurneysen, *Revolutionary Theology in the Making: Barth-Thurneysen Correspondence 1914-1925* (Louis: John Knox Press, 1964).

85. Barth and Thurneysen, *Revolutionary Theology in the Making*, 13.

86. Recent hermeneutical studies include Richard E Burnett, *Karl Barth's Theological Exegesis: The Hermeneutical Principals of the Römerbrief Period* (Wissenschaftliche Untersuchungen Zum Neuen Testament. 2. Reihe; Tübingen: Mohr Siebeck, 2001). For studies on Barth's use of the historical-critical method see, Christina A. Baxter, 'The Movement from Exegesis to Dogmatics in the Theology of Karl Barth, with Special Reference to Romans, Philippians and Church Dogmatics' (PhD Thesis, University of Durham, 1981); McCormack, 'The Significance of Karl Barth's Theological Exegesis of Philippians'. On Barth's interpretation, see Mary Kathleen Cunningham, *What Is Theological Exegesis?: Interpretation and Use of Scripture in Barth's Doctrine of Election* (Valley Forge, Penn.: Trinity Press International, 1995). For recent critique of different aspects of Barth's method and theology, see David Gibson and Daniel Strange, eds., *Engaging with Barth: Contemporary Evangelical Critiques* (Nottingham: Apollos, 2008).

Richard E. Burnett has examined three related aspects of Barth's commitment to theological exegesis: the popularity of his exegetical courses, his use of exegesis to correct an emphasis on methodology at the expense of content, and the claim that he originated 'pneumatic' exegesis.

Firstly, it was chiefly because of the interest in his biblical exegesis in his Romans commentary that he was appointed to his first teaching post.[87] After the announcement at Göttingen, Barth's exegesis courses were 'more often, if not always, more popular than his courses in dogmatic or historical theology'.[88] In Barth's first semester at Göttingen, his course on *The Epistle to the Ephesians* had between fifty and sixty students, as opposed to that on the Heidelberg catechism, which had only about fifteen.[89]

Barth taught his exegetical courses at his own initiative because, at the time, it was what he knew best and was most qualified to teach, bringing insights from his earlier pastoral ministry in Safenwil.[90] This combination of scholarship and pastoral insights earned him the reputation of approaching his exegetical courses with due seriousness.[91]

Secondly, Barth's use of exegesis to correct an over-emphasis on methodology is exemplified in his second exegetical work, *Die Auferstehung der Toten* (1924). Barth 'saw it as his task to "uphold and continue the attempt of a theological exegesis" not at the expense of—much less in opposition to —historical questions and concerns, but as a necessary corrective'.[92] With regard to 'the decisive historical orientation of the appointed New Testament scholars of today', he recognized it was no doubt considered a 'scandal and outrage' that their problems seemed of 'little or no interest to me at all'.[93] Barth's concern for content over method drove him to explain 1 Corinthians by reference to the resurrection of the dead, the decisive act of God's self-revelation.

---

87. Burnett, *Karl Barth's Theological Exegesis*, 23.
88. Burnett, *Karl Barth's Theological Exegesis*, 25.
89. Burnett, *Karl Barth's Theological Exegesis*, 25.
90. Burnett, *Karl Barth's Theological Exegesis*, 25.
91. Burnett, *Karl Barth's Theological Exegesis*, 25.
92. Burnett, *Karl Barth's Theological Exegesis*, 26.
93. Burnett, *Karl Barth's Theological Exegesis*, 23.

Thirdly, Barth's theological exegesis was forged in the context of a decade-long discussion of 'pneumatic exegesis', which some claimed emerged with him.[94] Although he did not quickly dismiss the discussion, he was not entirely happy with the label. In the preface of his next exegetical work, the commentary on *Philippians* (1927), Barth succinctly stated, 'I do not propose to enter here into dispute concerning pneumatic exegesis . . . Although, if I am not mistaken, I am one of those who occasioned it, yet this unpleasant catch-word at all events is not my coining'.[95] 'I ask readers not to say to me too quickly (as a few in Germany have said to me all too quickly), that I am not an exegete or rather: that I am a "pneumatic" exegete. The reproach which is said in the word "pneumatic" may well fall back heavily on those who so easily raise it'.[96] To Barth, his critics were much taken up with debate on method, in which he is not interested.

Whatever the position of his critics regarding his theological exegesis,[97] Barth remained committed to it. This is clearly and forcefully illustrated by his farewell speech to a group of his students in Bonn on 10 February 1935, shortly before officially being dismissed from teaching in Germany due to his refusal to take 'an unqualified oath of allegiance to Adolf Hitler',[98] which every teacher in schools and universities was required to take. In the speech he told the students: 'Take now my last piece of advice: exegesis, exegesis, and once more exegesis!'.[99]

Despite Barth's suspension from his official teaching role, he continued for eight consecutive weekends, delivering a series of sixteen lectures on the

---

94. For a catalogue of wide-ranging discussions on 'pneumatic exegesis', see Burnett, *Karl Barth's Theological Exegesis*, 27–28, n. 68.
95. Karl Barth, *Theology and Church Shorter Writings 1920-1928* (The Preachers Library; London: SCM Press, 1962), 286.
96. Karl Barth, *The Epistle to the Romans* (trans. Edwyn Clement Hoskyns; Translated from the 6th ed.; Oxford: Oxford University Press, 1933), ix.
97. For a list of contemporary evangelical critics of Barth's theology, see Gibson and Strange, *Engaging with Barth*. Others include, H Jackson Forstman, *Word and Spirit: Calvin's Doctrine of Biblical Authority* (Stanford: Stanford University Press, 1962), 146–7; Helmut Thielicke, *Modern Faith and Thought* (Grand Rapids, Mich.: Eerdmans, 1990), 17.
98. Burnett, *Karl Barth's Theological Exegesis*, 30.
99. Burnett, *Karl Barth's Theological Exegesis*, 30.

creed, which were published that same year (1935).[100] On officially concluding his lecture series, during the question and answer session two questions that he was asked directly linked with his exegetical method. In his effort to put forward theological exegesis, Barth discovered that he still had to clarify his relationship to 'pneumatic exegesis' and how he understood the link between theological exegesis and the science of history.[101] Barth left Germany at the end of May 1935 for a teaching post at Basel, where he remained the rest of his life, and where he became a prolific writer, producing his famous *Church Dogmatics*. Barth's exegesis continued to attract criticism,[102] but his commitment to theological exegesis never diminished.[103]

3.3.3 Barth's Hermeneutics

Barth was indifferent to his critics' preoccupation with hermeneutics as a subject,[104] because he disagreed with its claimed significance. From the very beginning of his *Römerbrief* period, Barth recognized that 'no theological or exegetical method could lead to God'.[105] In the first volume of his *Church Dogmatics*, he stated the reason for his rejection for his critics' hermeneutics. There is 'no method of Scriptural exegesis which is truly pneumatic, i.e., which articulates the witness to revelation in the Bible and to that degree really introduces the *Pneuma*'.[106]

---

100. Karl Barth and J. Strathearn McNab, *Credo: A Presentation of the Chief Problems of Dogmatics with Reference to the Apostles' Creed; Sixteen Lectures Delivered at the University of Utrecht in February and March, 1935* (London: Hodder & Stoughton, 1936).
101. Barth and McNab, *Credo*, appendix, Question II, 177–79, 186–91.
102. E.g., those who continued to refer to him as *Pneumatiker* include, Forstman, *Word and Spirit*, 146–7; Thielicke, *Modern Faith and Thought*, 17.
103. Baxter, 'The Movement from Exegesis', 445–65. Burnett's examines Christiana Baxter's article, Christina A. Baxter, 'Barth - a Truly Biblical Theologian', *Tyndale Bulletin* 38 (1987): 3–27. In particular, her unpublished PhD thesis which puts forward statistics to support his view that Barth's interest in theological exegesis was never extinct; rather the later volumes of *Church Dogmatics* that Barth produced contains twice more theological exegesis than his earlier writings, which explain the distinction between *pneumatic exegesis*, and the relationship between theological exegesis and the science of history.
104. E.g., Rudolf Karl Bultmann, 'The Problem of Hermeneutics', in *New Testament and Mythology: And other Basic Writings* (trans. M. Ogden Schubert; Philadelphia: Fortress, 1984), 69–94.
105. Barth, *The Epistle to the Romans*, 57, 110, 137.
106. Barth, *CD*, 1/1, 183.

The fact that Barth did not acknowledge the significance of his critics' hermeneutical questions—such as those asked by Ernest Fuchs, 'How do I come to understand?'[107]—created discomfort within the guild.[108] In 1953, Barth rejected Ebeling's invitation to attend a conference on theological method,[109] seeing it as useless, since he had already made known his position: to use methodology to understand God was too narrow. In Barth's opinion, 'The question of the right hermeneutics cannot be decided in a discussion of exegetical *method*, but only in exegesis itself'.[110]

For Barth, the antidote for the malaise was theological exegesis. Exegesis should be understood not from the human standpoint, which was the preoccupation of modern theology, but from the viewpoint of God. Because the discussion is not merely anthropological but theological, Barth regarded it as improper to insist that human thoughts about God form the backbone of the contents of the Bible. Rather it is the thoughts of God about men: 'The Bible tells us not how we should talk with God but what he says to us; not how we find the way to him, but how he has sought and found the way to us'.[111] Barth's entire theological revolution was based on this discovery. 'The reality of God precedes the possibility of God, that the being of God precedes all human questioning'.[112]

Consequently, 'God is not self-evidently *the object* of human investigation nor is he *the answer* to the human question, the human dilemma, the human crisis'.[113] God is free. Barth saw the prevailing anthropological perspective contradicting itself in that in theory it acknowledged that the being of God precedes human questioning but in practice it consequently betrayed the implications of this claim. At times it did so in the name

---

107. James McConkey Robinson, *The New Hermeneutic* (New York: Harper & Row, 1964), 136.

108. Robinson, *The New Hermeneutic*, 31f. Gerhard Ebeling, 'Word of God and Hermeneutics', in *Word and Faith* (Philadelphia: Fortress, 1963), 317.

109. Burnett, *Karl Barth's Theological Exegesis*, 34.

110. From a letter from Karl Barth to Gerhard Ebeling, 7 December 1952, cited in Eberhard Busch, *Karl Barth: His Life from Letters and Autobiographical Texts* (Grand Rapids, Michigan: W B Eerdmans, 1993), 390.

111. Burnett, *Karl Barth's Theological Exegesis*, 35.

112. Burnett, *Karl Barth's Theological Exegesis*, 35.

113. Burnett, *Karl Barth's Theological Exegesis*, 36.

of providing 'a firmer, more "objective" and more "scientific" foundation for theology', or at times 'for apologetic reasons'.[114] Gradually, with ever increasing forcefulness, the human questions, situation, and condition became 'a matter of principle the starting point of theology, the basis and presupposition for discussing the being of God'.[115]

Barth 'Theological Exegesis' can be briefly described as follows:
1. The Bible—the word of God—the Old and New Testament, is emphasized as a place where God discovers us, not where we discover God. The Bible is the arena in which the living God comes in his reconciling love to humanity who is alienated from him by sin, and God, in Jesus Christ, reconciled humanity;
2. The word of God in the Bible is to be heard as God speaking to the listeners from and in the text. Thus, God stands in and behind the text;
3. What is important is to be discovered by God and not so much to discover God in the text;
4. The important message is that 'God found the way to us', God came into our situation;
5. God is a living subject in the Bible in whose presence we are confronted by his word. Barth's main concern was to proclaim this word of God to the broken world and not to discuss human thoughts about God. He is keen to affirm the reality of God as present in history and now; and,
6. The *Sache*—subject-matter, is God.

3.3.4 Barth: the Sache—The Subject-matter, God

The work of Keith Condie (focusing on Barth's *Resurrection of the Dead* [1924])[116] and Bruce McCormack (focusing on Barth's *Commentary on*

---

114. Burnett, *Karl Barth's Theological Exegesis*, 36.
115. Burnett, *Karl Barth's Theological Exegesis*, 36; Barth, *CD*, 1/2: 4: "It [Protestant Theology] has actually become a fundamental presupposition."
116. Keith Condie, "'Of God': Karl Barth and the Coherence of 1 Corinthians', in *The Wisdom of the Cross: Exploring 1 Corinthians* (ed. Brian S Rosner and Moore Theological College. School of Theology; Nottingham: Apollos, 2011), 32–56.

Philippians [1928])[117] will assist in understanding the inner logic and approach of Barth's exegesis. Whereas some accuse Barth of either straining or bending the text, or presenting illegitimate exegesis, each of these two commentators, while aware of some of its weaknesses, nevertheless illuminate Barth's theological exegesis clearly.

Barth's reading of 1 Corinthians on the *Resurrection of the Dead* (1924), demonstrate how he went about doing theological exegesis. Barth considered the text of 1 Corinthians as Scripture. Standing behind and issuing from the biblical text is the 'divine voice of God'.[118]

With such an understanding, it is not difficult to see why the key to understanding 1 Corinthians does not lie in the fact that it is a written text from the apostle Paul to the Corinthians in the first century. Rather than focusing upon what Paul is doing, a more crucial question is: 'what kind of text is this?' The interpreter must sit under this text, because the text itself gives witness to the active presence of God,[119] thus, it 'displays an internal logic—as Christian Scripture, it is from God and about God, and that presupposes unity'.[120] Paul, therefore, is not philosophising. He is preaching. He is showing how we ought to think from the standpoint of Christ.[121]

We are now in a position to understand how Barth reads 1 Corinthians chapters 1–14 with all its problems.[122]

In chapters 1–4, the Corinthians are puffed up with the human disease of egoism and are totally blind to see that all they have is coming 'from God'. Barth's focus here is on the foolishness of the cross and he does not mention the resurrection, which Paul will major on in chapter 15. In chapters 5–6, Paul is critiquing the disease that has affected the church. The Corinthian Christians should realize that the death of Christ at Calvary on the cross is God's price for their lives. They are not free to do what they like outside Christ. In chapter 7, Paul offers a warning against hubris in the area

---

117. McCormack, 'The Significance of Karl Barth's Theological Exegesis of Philippians', v–xxv.
118. Condie, '"Of God": Karl Barth and the Coherence of 1 Corinthians', 37.
119. Condie, '"Of God": Karl Barth and the Coherence of 1 Corinthians', 37.
120. Condie, '"Of God": Karl Barth and the Coherence of 1 Corinthians', 37.
121. Condie, '"Of God": Karl Barth and the Coherence of 1 Corinthians', 37.
122. Condie, '"Of God": Karl Barth and the Coherence of 1 Corinthians', 38–43.

of sexuality. Chapters 8–10 give instruction on how to live for the glory of God, noting that human freedom and knowledge must never be a source of pride. Freedom is only to be used of God. In chapter 11, Paul critiques human self-assertion, which does not recognize the magnitude of the distinction between the human and the divine God, and is therefore unable to recognize the Lordship of Christ. In chapters 12–14, in the mix of the gift of the Spirit of God and the squabbling in the Corinthian church, the Corinthian Christians appear unredeemed and they are called to unity and order. In chapters 1–14, Paul is critiquing a form of flourishing Christianity that had become an end in itself. This kind of Christianity is a kind of 'rearing up against God'.[123] However, all that the Corinthians have is summed up in the phrase: 'of God' or 'from God'.[124]

1 Corinthians 15 contains the solution to all the problems in the first 14 chapters. God's revelation of the *Resurrection of the Dead* must inform all Christian practice, and give a sharp critique of the Corinthian church.[125] The Corinthians had a twisted understanding of their eschatology because they did not have a correct understanding of the theology of the resurrection of the dead.[126] The twisted view of the Corinthians was to deceive themselves that what happened to Christ in the world was the total picture for Christian experience. They were wrong. The fundamental point they missed is this: they must first die, and more significantly, they were to reckon with the reality of the resurrection of the dead, which they had failed to do. Barth is clear: God has revealed the reality of resurrection of the dead, and this is something that must inform Christian practice, because the church was founded on this singular revealed truth.

The Corinthian Christians must turn away from their egoism, embrace the resurrection, which is the gospel and the foundation of the church, and look forward to the future fulfilment of God's purposes.[127] But the

---

123. Condie, "'Of God': Karl Barth and the Coherence of 1 Corinthians', 43.
124. Condie, "'Of God': Karl Barth and the Coherence of 1 Corinthians', 42.
125. Condie, "'Of God': Karl Barth and the Coherence of 1 Corinthians', 43.
126. David R Hall, *The Unity of the Corinthian Correspondence* (vol. 251; Journal for the Study of the New Testament Supplement Series; London: T&T Clark International, 2003), 32–41.
127. Condie, "'Of God': Karl Barth and the Coherence of 1 Corinthians', 44.

Corinthians are not doing this because of their lack of the knowledge *of God*. Barth is not so taken up with God that in his analysis of the Corinthian situation human action is ignored. He recognizes that the future has been reconstructed by the act of Christ's resurrection. Love is the life for the future (chapter 13), since it will last forever, and by God's grace this future starts now as human beings begin to love.[128] This recreation is very powerful; it changes people, history, and everything,[129] and it is therefore the hope for humanity.

Barth's Theological Exegesis of 1 Corinthians reveals a set of important issues for our study. Barth's Theological Exegesis enables him to concern himself with the *Sache*—the subject-matter, God. This leads him to be astonished at the word of God. He is concerned with the big theme: resurrection. It is the subject that Paul is using to confront the Corinthians and bring them to the realization that all that matters in their lives flows *from God*. He is not so much concerned with their experience; he is concerned with the source of their experience, God. He does not deal with the text verse-by-verse. His method is focused on understanding what the text *means* and not what the text *meant*.

Kivengere's sermons show a great affinity with Barth's approach: he is concerned with the subject matter, God, and his Son Jesus Christ. Using theological exegesis, he does not expose biblical text for every verse: he uses large units of text with his 'big idea' being reconciliation centred in God's Son, Jesus Christ. His starting point for explaining the reconciliation between God and man, and man and man, is the cross. From the cross he works outwards.

Finding meaning and purpose in life in this world, involves the encounter between God, the context, and Paul, the author. The relating of God and humanity involves tensions: 'inner tension' and 'inner dialectic' of the Bible.[130] What does it mean for a fallen humanity to face God? In Barth's

---

128. Cf. J. B Webster, *Barth's Earlier Theology: Four Studies* (London: T. & T. Clark, 2005), 84–88.

129. R. Dale Dawson, *The Resurrection in Karl Barth* (Barth Studies; Aldershot: Ashgate, 2006), 4f, 46f, 60.

130. McCormack, 'The Significance of Karl Barth's Theological Exegesis of Philippians', xvii.

theological exegesis the interpreter must understand the author well enough 'to allow the author to speak in my name and I can speak in his name'. To understand an author well, there is no need to require an experience, out of which the author was then driven to write, but it requires understanding 'the author as a *witness*, not as subject of interest in his own right'.[131] The *Sache*—the subject-matter of the Bible, God, is more than the history. It concerns the gospel—the message of what God did in history through his Son Jesus Christ and what he continues to do through Jesus Christ in his kingdom. This indeed is the driving force behind Barth's concern with the *Sache*—the subject-matter, God, as Barth interprets the Bible. The 'real history', the time that God has revealed himself to humanity in the Bible, is beyond the reach of a historian, and so the method of interpreting the biblical text rests in recognizing that the *Sache* is not an object of clear and obvious ideas for historical critics; they are not in control of God.

Barth's approach to the biblical text in which the Bible is not merely an object that is floating freely at the disposal of preachers, but instead they are enmeshed in the *Sache*, will shine in all Kivengere's sermons. The sermons show that God came in his Son Jesus Christ, the reconciler. His sermons reveal Kivengere dealing with Jesus Christ, face-to-face, often in a conversation, right from his time of conversion. He wrestles with God, the subject matter. He does not merely preach the reconciling love of God, but he reconciles his audience as the word of God demands and as his personal encounter with God confirms.

3.3.4.1 Barth: The Significance of Reconciliation

The doctrine of reconciliation is a major part of Barth's magnum opus, the *Church Dogmatics*.[132] Barth placed reconciliation in a central and strategic category that expresses the core of the gospel. Barth's comprehensive treatment of the doctrine of reconciliation has been described by David Muller as a theological treatment that is indeed 'unsurpassed in the history of Protestant theology and perhaps in the entire history of the

---

131. McCormack, 'The Significance of Karl Barth's Theological Exegesis of Philippians', xviii.
132. Of the fifteen volumes in Barth's *Church Dogmatics*, five are devoted to the doctrine of reconciliation.

church universal'.[133] Barth's work has the distinction of bringing together Christology, Soteriology, Hamartiology, Pneumatology, and Ecclesiology under an all-encompassing analysis of 'The Doctrine of Reconciliation', as such locating 'reconciliation' at the very centre of his *Church Dogmatics*. In fact the outline of the broad sweep of the *Church Dogmatics* expresses his biblical theology moving from creation, through reconciliation and towards redemption in the resurrection of the body. The precise reason for this is because 'reconciliation' represents the 'centre of Christian knowledge'.[134] In June 1953 Barth himself claimed that 'to fail here is to fail everywhere, while to be on the right track here makes it impossible to be completely mistaken in the whole'.[135]

This is important to our concerns, because, Barth's understanding of reconciliation would pass on to Kivengere directly through reading his works and indirectly through his son, Professor Markus Barth. Kivengere later echoed Barth's view of the centrality of reconciliation in the New Testament, indeed the Christian gospel, and it constituted the theoretical framework of his preaching.[136]

3.3.4.2 The Doctrine of Reconciliation

Fred H. Klooster summarizes Barth's extensive treatment of reconciliation in *Church Dogmatics*.[137] The background to Barth's doctrine of reconciliation is his view of covenant and sin. The covenant of grace is the presupposition of reconciliation,[138] although this does not mean that the covenant historically precedes reconciliation.[139] As much as it may be referred to as the presupposition of reconciliation, this covenant can be known for what it is; this may be done in the light of Jesus Christ who is the reconciliation.[140]

---

133. David L. Müller, *Foundations of Karl Barth's Doctrine of Reconciliation: Jesus Christ Crucified and Risen* (Mampeter: Edwin Mellen Press, 1990), 251.
134. Barth, *CD*, IV/1, ix.
135. Barth, *CD*, IV/1, ix. Cf. Webster, *Barth's Earlier Theology*, 14.
136. Chapter Five, Kivengere, 'Ambassador For Christ', p. 3, #4.
137. Fred H Klooster, 'Karl Barth's Doctrine of Reconciliation: A Review Article', *WTJ* 20/2 (My 1958): 170–84.
138. Klooster, 'Karl Barth's Doctrine of Reconciliation', 171.
139. Klooster, 'Karl Barth's Doctrine of Reconciliation', 171.
140. Klooster, 'Karl Barth's Doctrine of Reconciliation', 171.

The covenant of grace originally existed between God and man, and it was disturbed and jeopardised. However, its purpose is now fulfilled in Jesus Christ, who is himself reconciliation.[141]

Because the 'covenant is a broken covenant', Barth considers it 'necessary to speak of sin as a presupposition of reconciliation'.[142] Just as the covenant of grace can only be understood 'in the light of Jesus Christ the reconciler', this is also true for sin.[143] While Barth insists that sin, like covenant, 'may only be known in the light of Jesus Christ the reconciler', he recognizes the need to first examine some aspects of the doctrine of sin to set him up for a proper discussion of the doctrine of reconciliation.

3.3.4.3 Reconciliation—Covenant and Sin

Barth defines the covenant as 'Immanuel'—'God with us'.[144] This definition has a universal dimension: 'it is for all men to all places'.[145] Barth has only one covenant—the covenant of grace, and its focus is the eternal will of God. 'God elected man to a covenant with himself, and created Heaven and earth and man himself for the sake of this covenant'.[146] There is another reality to the covenant: its fulfilment took the form of atonement because of man's sin. Barth's view of sin is simple—it is breaking the covenant. Here Barth is not referring to the covenant of works Reformed theologians have traditionally derived from Genesis 2 but to a covenant of grace, even if only vaguely outlined and in Barth's terms.[147]

Although Barth sought to maintain the historicity of the biblical story, his interpretation read Genesis 1 to 3 as *saga* or legend.[148] Orthodox Reformed theology regards it as historical, but despite Barth's persistent, quiet and yet intense debate with Rudolf Bultman seeking to retain a greater historicity for the biblical narrative, Klooster is dissatisfied that Barth

---

141. Klooster, 'Karl Barth's Doctrine of Reconciliation', 172.
142. Klooster, 'Karl Barth's Doctrine of Reconciliation', 171.
143. Klooster, 'Karl Barth's Doctrine of Reconciliation', 171.
144. Barth, *CD*, IV/1, 3–21.
145. Klooster, 'Karl Barth's Doctrine of Reconciliation', 172.
146. Barth, *CD*, IV/1, 68.
147. Klooster, 'Karl Barth's Doctrine of Reconciliation', 172.
148. Klooster, 'Karl Barth's Doctrine of Reconciliation', 172.

'still continues to regard Genesis 1 to 3 as *Saga* or legend'.[149] In this biblical saga, Adam (which refers to man) 'owes his existence directly to the creative will and Word and act of God without any human intervention'.[150] The saga tells of Adam's fall, describing the character of sin for the rest of world history. Sin can 'only say No where God says Yes . . . It can only break down . . . But the divine Yes which sin negates and by which it is negated is the Yes of God's covenant with man which is the mystery of creation—the covenant of grace concluded in Jesus Christ from all eternity and fulfilment and revealed in time'.[151] At the same time, Adam's fall points ahead to the great moment of reconciliation.

For Barth, therefore, reconciliation will have primarily a man-ward direction.[152] Repeatedly Barth speaks of reconciliation to mean the conversion of man to God:

> Neither here nor in Romans 5 does he (Paul) speak of an enmity of God against man which is removed from the atonement . . . The hurt which has to be made good is on our side . . . God does not need reconciliation with men, but men need reconciliation with Him, and this verse [2 Cor 5:19] tells us that God has made this reconciliation, and how he made it . . . And the goal is undoubtedly this complete conversion of the world to Him.[153]

3.3.4.4 *The Components of Barth's Doctrine of Reconciliation*

Klooster's description of Barth's doctrine of reconciliation is summarized in table 4.

---

149. Klooster, 'Karl Barth's Doctrine of Reconciliation', 172.
150. Barth, *CD*, IV/1, 507f.
151. Barth, *CD*, 139f.
152. Klooster, 'Karl Barth's Doctrine of Reconciliation', 174.
153. Barth, *CD*, IV/1, 174.

Table 4: The Subdivisions of the Doctrine of Reconciliation[154]

Church Dogmatics	IV/1°	IV/2°	IV/3°
A Christology	very God	very man	God-man
B Doctrine of Sin	as pride	as sloth	as falsehood
C Soteriology (objective)	justification	sanctification	sanctification
D Ecclesiology (community)	awakening	quickening	sending
E Soteriology (individual)	faith	love	hope

While showing the broad scope of Barth's doctrine of reconciliation, this table also illustrates Barth's Christocentric approach to reconciliation. The *content* of the doctrine of reconciliation is the knowledge of Jesus Christ, who himself is 'very God, and very man, and in the unity of the two the guarantor and witness of our atonement'.[155] Because the three Christological aspects of Barth's doctrine of reconciliation will prove significant in analyzing Kivengere's preaching of reconciliation, they merit further brief discussion.

3.3.4.4.1 Jesus Christ—'very God'

Barth affirms that Jesus Christ, the 'very God', is the God who humbles himself. God is 'the reconciling God', who in his freedom crosses the frontier, which is 'a yawning abyss', thereby humbling himself by becoming

---

154. Klooster, 'Karl Barth's Doctrine of Reconciliation', 174.
155. Barth, *CD*, IV/1, 79.

man.[156] In his humiliation, 'God emerges from the impenetrable mystery of Godhead, which has become so dreadful to the sin of man, and gives himself to man and to be known by man'.[157] In giving his Son to the world, God 'sets at stake his own existence as God'.[158] This act of God's 'self-offering' and 'self-hazarding' is the reason to claim that Jesus Christ is 'very God'. In Jesus Christ, God himself humiliated himself. Barth reasoned that, 'The false gods are not capable of self-humiliation', but in this act of God, self-humiliation, we find the meaning of Christmas and Good Friday. According to Klooster, it is in the act of 'humiliation of very God' that 'Barth recognizes the priestly office of Jesus Christ'.[159]

It is against this Christological aspect—very God—that Barth develops his understanding of sin, soteriology, and ecclesiology (see B–E table 5). Sin viewed in the light of atonement, for Barth, is 'the opposite of what God does for us in Jesus Christ in condescending to us, in humbling himself, in becoming a servant to take to himself and a way from us our guilt and sickness'.[160] His soteriological deduction is that salvation involves 'the divine verdict in Jesus Christ by which man is justified'.[161] God alone decided to justify man from his guilt. This decision of God is universal: it concerns all men of all times and places. So, by this verdict, all men are justified.[162]

Additionally, Barth makes deductions from the first Christological aspect regarding man's subjective hearing, seeing and accepting objective reconciliation. As Barth, explaining the work of the Holy Spirit, notes that although justification occurs for all men, 'subjective appropriation of salvation' occurs only in the Christian.[163] Through the Holy Spirit, individuals are awakened to faith. 'That God did not owe his Son, and in that Son himself, to the world, is revealed by the fact that he gives his Spirit to whom

---

156. Barth, *CD*, IV/1, 82.
157. Barth, *CD*, IV/1, 82.
158. Barth, *CD*, IV/1, 75.
159. Barth, *CD*, IV/1, 134.
160. Barth, *CD*, IV/1, 172.
161. Barth, *CD*, IV/1, 145.
162. Barth, *CD*, IV/1, 148.
163. Barth, *CD*, IV/1, 148.

he will'.[164] Because of the self-humiliation of God and in the light of justification, the Holy Spirit awakens the church. So, when that verdict of God is heard by men, in their inner fellowship, 'there arises in their outward assembly a new humanity'.[165]

Kivengere makes frequent references to this humiliation. The brokenness of humanity concerned God, so he 'crossed frontiers' and came to man, lighting up our darkness and yet not diminishing his deity. Kivengere's sermons frequently emphasize the cross as the means God used to cross the yawning abyss between man and God, and the priestly role of Jesus.[166] It is interesting to notice that, despite Barth's huge emphasis on justification, Kivengere does not teach justification in his sermons, even in his Romans 5 sermons. If he absorbed Barth's teaching on justification, he may have assumed it under the umbrella term of 'reconciliation'. A comparison with Barth therefore raises interesting questions for this study: in his endeavour to preach reconciliation in Jesus Christ as the only antidote to bleeding Africa,[167] why was he so silent on justification?

3.3.4.4.2 Jesus Christ—'very man'

In discussing Jesus as 'very man', Barth deals with his state of exaltation, the kingly office, sin, sanctification, church and the individual.

He links Jesus Christ, 'very man', to 'man exalted and therefore reconciled by God'.[168] 'The reconciliation of the world with God takes place in the person of a man in whom, because he is also true God, the conversion of all men to God is an actual event'.[169] Jesus is a true man, like all other men in every respect. Because 'He is altogether man just as he is altogether God', that is 'how he is the reconciler between God and man'.[170] 'To say that God was truly and altogether in Christ means this man was born like

---

164. Barth, *CD*, IV/1, 148.
165. Barth, *CD*, IV/1, 151.
166. His sermons in Chapters Five and Six mention the cross as the starting point of explaining reconciliation and its outworking in the life of believers.
167. See his sermons on Romans 5:1–11 in Chapter Five.
168. Barth, *CD*, IV/1, 79.
169. Barth, *CD*, IV/1, 130.
170. Barth, *CD*, IV/1, 183.

all of us in time, who lived and thought and spoke, who could be tempted and suffer and die and was in fact tempted, and suffered and died'. 'To say man is to say creature and sin and this means limitation and suffering' . . . 'both of these have to be said of Jesus Christ'.[171]

Barth explains the importance of this unity of God with his creature in five carefully weighed statements. Firstly, 'in Jesus as the one true man is the conversion of all to God', thus, the realization of true humanity. Secondly, 'since in him God was bound, so too in him man has become like God'. Thirdly, 'as in him man was bound, so too in him man is made free'. Fourthly, 'as in him the Lord became a servant, as too in him the servant became a Lord'. And, fifthly, he concludes, 'That is the atonement made in Jesus Christ in the second aspect'.[172] Clearly for Barth, the conversion of man to God took place in him, and this is the point of reconciliation of all men, and also it is the fulfilment of the covenant.[173] Following the above explanation, Barth turns to make deductions in regard to sin, soteriology and the work of the Holy Spirit (see table 5, B2–E2). Sin now shows the aspect of sloth, 'the opposite of what God did in Jesus Christ, the servant who became Lord, to exalt man—not to deity but to His own right hand in fellowship of life with himself'.[174] Because of the covenant fulfilled, 'God himself has already exalted him. Therefore man must not wilfully fall'.[175] However, the fact that man does fall shows his sin as sloth. Barth deduces the soteriological dimension: in Jesus Christ the direction is given in which the sanctification of man is accomplished.

Sanctification is objective, hence it may be said that all men are sanctified. Not only God's verdict, justification, but more so his direction, sanctification, has been pronounced over all.[176] As for the church, the Holy Spirit is involved in life-giving, quickening and inner up-building of the church

---

171. Barth, *CD*, IV/1, 131.
172. Barth, *CD*, IV/1, 131.
173. Klooster, 'Karl Barth's Doctrine of Reconciliation', 177.
174. Klooster, 'Karl Barth's Doctrine of Reconciliation', 178.
175. Barth, *CD*, IV/1, 143.
176. Barth, *CD*, IV/1, 147.

or community. In regard to the individual, the Holy Spirit quickens him in love so that he follows the sanctifying direction.[177]

It is certainly true that all twenty-seven sermons are clear about reconciliation between God and man, and man with each other. Kivengere understands reconciliation to have happened at a cosmic level because Jesus died for all. His opening prayers in the sermons focus the Holy Spirit as the one who illuminates Jesus Christ and in the sermons in chapter 5, especially the four thematic addresses, the role of the Holy Spirit in quickening the church or community and individuals is brought to the fore.

3.3.4.4.3 Jesus Christ—'God-man'

Barth's third and final Christological aspect of the doctrine of reconciliation is the union of Jesus Christ as 'God-man'. 'As the God who humbles himself and therefore reconciles man with himself, and as the man exalted by God and therefore reconciled with him, as the One who is very God and very man in this concrete sense, Jesus Christ is one'.[178] Barth understood the 'God-man' to mean, 'the Son of God who is this man'; and, 'this man is the Son of God'. He now brings together in this third aspect the two previously described dialectical elements: Jesus Christ.

The name 'Christ' identifies the first; and the name 'Jesus' identifies the second, noting that the name Jesus Christ brings them together without fusion.[179] The new thing in this third aspect is the prophetic office of Jesus Christ. The third office concerns the revelation of the previous two aspects. Jesus is the reconciliation because he is 'very God' and 'very man' and Jesus Christ is the revelation since he is both of these two in unity, the God-man. Jesus Christ is the guarantor, because 'He who is himself the material content of the atonement, the mediator of it, stands securely with man as well as with God that it is our atonement—he himself being the form of it as well as the content'.[180] In line with his previously articulated view of revelation,[181] he states that this prophetic office, 'does not involve the con-

---

177. Klooster, 'Karl Barth's Doctrine of Reconciliation', 178.
178. Barth, *CD*, IV/1, 135.
179. Barth, *CD*, IV/1, 136.
180. Barth, *CD*, IV/1, 137.
181. Barth, *CD*, 1/1 and 1/2.

tent of truth', but 'the character of truth', which truth Christ 'himself has guaranteed and pledged'.[182]

Again, from this third aspect, Barth makes deductions for the doctrines of sin, soteriology and ecclesiology. Against the background of Jesus Christ as God-man, sin is falsehood: 'We have to see that that which is told us is true: that Jesus Christ is Lord who became a servant for us, and the servant who became Lord for us'.[183] However, man in disobedience chooses to live in falsehood. Regarding soteriology, Barth explains it in reference to calling noting that man's calling, 'like justification and sanctification, is pronounced over all'.[184] He then turns to the Holy Spirit and his work in the church. Barth deduces that, 'When men hear the promise, inwardly and outwardly, these men are together ordained to be the community sent out as a witness in the world and to the world'.[185] The Holy Spirit constitutes the church, a 'missionary community', which 'in its particular existence', the church 'stands vicariously for the world'.[186] When the individual hears the promise, which causes the individual to have hope, then the individual's calling is defined. When the individual accepts the divine promise to eternal life, and in temporal life, the lesser fulfilment of enjoyment of fellowship in the covenant, by way of reconciliation, the covenant in them is attained.

Our goal in the above section has been to state Barth's Theological Exegesis and his doctrine of reconciliation as another benchmarks, which we shall use to analyze Kivengere's sermons.

3.4 Markus Barth's Link to Kivengere

In 1981, in a special lecture he gave at Trinity Episcopal School for Ministry, USA, Kivengere revealed: 'Marcus Barth was my professor of New Testament . . . I respected [his] scholarship'.[187] Kivengere also openly

---

182. Barth, *CD*, IV/1, 138.
183. Barth, *CD*, IV/1, 143.
184. Klooster, 'Karl Barth's Doctrine of Reconciliation', 179.
185. Barth, *CD*, IV/1, 152.
186. Barth, *CD*, IV/1, 152f.
187. See Kivengere, 'A Special Lecture'. Kivengere, 'A Special Lecture'. His link with

acknowledged the help of Markus to clarify his theological thinking when he joined the seminary at Pittsburgh: 'I expected him to give me a few clarifying points and Markus Barth did that'. This succinct autobiographical statement reveals his self-acknowledged debt to Markus's influence, all the more significant because it is an incidental remark eighteen years after the seminary at Pittsburgh, showing that Markus Barth was an abiding influence on his life and thought.

Markus Barth was known for his commitment to the Word of God as Scripture, his dedication to thoroughness, and his obvious joy in discovering new things in Scripture.[188] 'Believing that if one finds in Scripture only confirmation for what one has always believed, one has probably not listened closely enough',[189] Markus helped Biblical Theology to be taken seriously at Pittsburgh Seminary, and at Chicago University. In fact, Markus Barth contributed more widely to the American Biblical Theology Movement.[190] Each of these features of Markus's renown can be traced in Kivengere, who also set before his hearers diligence, thoroughness, and a commitment to the Word of God, and a joy of discovering new things in Scripture. But for our purposes, it seems clear that Markus Barth also influenced Kivengere in his Biblical Theology. Markus was also, of course, another instrument through which Kivengere came, albeit indirectly, under the influence of Karl Barth.

Trinity Episcopal School for Ministry came through the founding Australian Principal, his Tanzanian 'Godfather' mentor, Bishop Alfred Stanway with whom he had special links since his days at Alliance High School, Dodoma. 'To their great surprise, Alf [Alfred Stanway] was invited on the recommendation of John Stott to be the founding President of Trinity Episcopal School for Ministry in Pittsburgh, Pennsylvania. The school as yet did not exist, but it was as though all Alf's experiences were a preparation to date. So he responded positively and in 1975 they moved to America. Over the next few years the College was established and continues to flourish'—From a brief biography of Bishop Alfred Stanway, John Wilson, 'Bishop Alfred Stanway - Heroes of the Faith', *The Melbourne Anglican* (March 2011), Cited 2 Feb 2012, Online: http://melbourne.anglican.com.au/NewsAndViews/TMA/Heroes%20of%20the%20Faith/Bishop%20Alfred%20Stanway%20-%20Heroes%20of%20the%20Faith%20-%20March%202011.pdf.
188. Gowan, 'In Memory of Markus Barth: A Personal Note', 93.
189. Kivengere, 'In Christ', p. 3, #1.
190. Dickson, 'Markus Barth and Biblical Theology: A Personal Re-View', 96.

Growing out of a 1961 lecture, Markus Barth in 1964 published his *Conversation with the Bible*,[191] dealing with the contents of the Bible, the authority of the Bible, and the interpretation of the Bible. On the contents, Markus argues that the Bible tells how the free God has called man to be his free partner in covenant with himself.[192] As for the authority of the Bible, he argues the Bible presents Jesus Christ as the spiritual criterion of the author's spirited interpretation and no method but only the Holy Spirit can guarantee a proper understanding of the text.[193]

As with his father, Markus Barth saw the theological task as an engagement with the real issues of the world and his theology of the redemptive work of Christ boldly addressed itself to the real life situation in the world—where men are constantly building walls between races, between nations, between classes, and even between Christian denominations.[194]

Writing in the middle of the darkest days of the Cold War, his belief that the gospel should engage with the world is strong: 'to propose in the name of Christianity, neutrality or unconcern on questions of international, racial or economic peace—this amounts to using Christ's name in vain'.[195] This commitment to engaging the world clearly finds an echo in Kivengere, as does its explicit connection with reconciliation:

> [T]o say 'Christ' means to say 'reconciliation' or to say 'peace'. (2:14, 17) . . . Christ is that reconciliation which is greater and stronger than the hostility . . . If he 'is peace', then he is by nature a social, even a political event, which marks the overcoming and ending of barriers, however deeply founded and highly constructed these appear to be . . . When this peace is deprived of its social, national, or economic dimensions, when it is distorted or emasculated so much that only 'peace of

---

191. Gowan, 'In Memory of Markus Barth: A Personal Note', 94.
192. Markus Barth, *Conversation with the Bible* (New York: Holt, 1964), 69.
193. Barth, *Conversation with the Bible*, 104.
194. See comment on the inside cover of Barth, *Broken Wall*.
195. Barth, *Broken Wall*, 38–39.

mind' enjoyed by saintly individuals is left—then Jesus Christ is being flatly denied.[196]

Markus Barth employed the language of Ephesians (2:14–22) to explain brokenness: 'wall of division', 'broken down', 'enmity between man and God', 'barriers', 'alienation', 'those far off and near'; and that 'Christ has reconciled men with God!'[197] He is explicit that only Jesus brings peace and reconciliation, implying that he effected peace 'in his blood' (Eph 2:13), 'in his flesh' (Eph 2:15), 'in his body . . . through the cross' (Eph 2:16). He argues that Paul's words—'blood', 'flesh', 'one body', and 'one spirit'—points to nothing else except 'Christ himself'.[198] By 'Christ himself', Paul did not primarily mean Christ's words, his example, his suffering or his miracles. Rather, Paul means his whole humanity—his self-sacrificial death on the cross ('The sacrificial words "blood" and "flesh" set the tone of the argument').[199] The cross (Eph 2:16) is mentioned as the means of reconciliation (cf. Col 1:22, Heb 2:14; and John 1:14). Markus argues that, to us, the death of Christ is painful, shameful, and humanly without a doubt it is a defeat and a deplorable end under human enmity and God's wrath, instead of reconciliation and peace. However, in Ephesians, the self-sacrificial death of Christ on the cross results not in misery and defeat, but in 'at-one-ment' or reconciliation.

The influence of Markus Barth no doubt shines through in Kivengere's constant use of this same vocabulary as he preaches reconciliation.[200]

It has been necessary to state Markus Barth's extension of his father, Karl Barth's Biblical Theology and doctrine of reconciliation, alongside each other as Kivengere publicly acknowledged his debt to both. This will help in determining their influence over his approach to preaching reconciliation. With these potential influences on Kivengere clearly stated,

---

196. Barth, *Broken Wall*, 38–39.
197. Barth, *Broken Wall*, 33–37.
198. Barth, *Broken Wall*, 40.
199. Barth, *Broken Wall*, 40.
200. Kivengere expounds Ephesians in the same way as his New Testament teacher. (See the start of this section.) This debt to Markus Barth may have been further reinforced by their common association with Presbyterianism.

the way is opened for another trajectory—a theological understanding of reconciliation in the New Testament, which is a pre-requisite for recognizing the influence of Pauline doctrine of reconciliation on Kivengere and for assessing his biblical theology of reconciliation.

3.5 Reconciliation in the New Testament

In the synopsis of this chapter, we introduced the trajectories in this chapter and noted that even though out of sequence with the rest (Keswick, the Revival, Karl Barth and Markus Barth) a theological understanding of reconciliation is necessary. Understood purely from the perspective of frequency, reconciliation within the New Testament may be considered a minor theme. Reconciliation is found largely within Pauline letters,[201] and only in four chapters: Rom 5:9–11, 2 Cor 5:18–20, Col 1:20, and Eph 2:16. Nevertheless, reconciliation has received a significant amount of attention from Pauline scholars, because, despite the infrequent occurrence of the specific vocabulary, it is a key New Testament concept. Among major New Testament themes that scholars have studied, reconciliation has generated several monographs,[202] a

---

201. This study works with the traditional view that the letters that bear the name 'Paul' were penned by the apostle. This is consistent with Kivengere's own view. It is of course, a subject of debate in Pauline scholarship.

202. See examples of monographs published on reconciliation after the work of Ralph Martin (Ralph P. Martin, *Reconciliation: A Study of Paul's Theology* (Revised ed.; Grand Rapids: Zondervan, 1989 [1981])[originally published in 1981].) Peter Stuhlmacher, 'The Gospel of Reconciliation in Christ: Basic Features and Issues of a Biblical Theology of the New Testament', *HBT* 1 (1980): 161–90; Hans Jürgen Findeis, *Versöhnung - Apostolat - Kirche* (Forschungen zur Bibel; Wurzburg: Echter, 1983) especially its treatment of Romans 5:10–11 and Colossians 1:20–22; Cilliers Breytenbach, 'Versöhnung: Eine Studie zur Paulinischen Soteriologie', *WNANT* 60 (1989): 59–79; I. Howard Marshall, 'The Meaning of Reconciliation', in *Unity and Diversity in New Testament Theology: Essays in Honor of George E. Ladd* (ed. George Eldon Ladd and Robert A Guelich; Grand Rapids, Mich.: Eerdmans, 1978), 117–32; Stanley E. Porter, *Katallassō in Ancient Greek Literature, with Reference to the Pauline Writings* (Estudios de filología Neotestamentaria; Cordoba, Spain: Almendro, 1994); Stanley E. Porter, 'Reconciliation and 2 Cor 5,18-21', in *Corinthian Correspondence* (ed. Reimund Bieringer; Bibliotheca Ephemeridum Theologicarum Lovaniensium; Leuven: Leuven University Press, 1996), 693–705; Stanley E. Porter, 'Peace, Reconciliation', in *Dictionary of Paul and his Letters* (ed. G. F. Hawthorn, Ralph P. Martin, and D. G. Reid; Downers Grove, Ill.: InterVarsity, 1993), 695–99; Seyoon Kim, '2 Cor 5:11–21 and the Origin of Paul's Concept of "Reconciliation"', *NovT* 34 (1997): 306–84; Joseph A. Fitzmyer, 'Reconciliation in Pauline Theology',

plethora of scholarly and specialist articles,[203] and discussions in the various commentaries.

---

in *No famine in the Land* (Missoula, Mont: Scholars, 1975), 155–77; Michael Wolter, *Rechtfertigung und Zukünftiges Heil: Untersuchungen zu Röm 5, 1-11* (Walter de Gruyter, 1978); among others.
203. E.g. see, Mark R. Amstutz, 'Is Reconciliation Possible After Genocide? The Case of Rwanda', *JCS* 48/3 (2006): 541–65; Elazar Barkan, 'Historical Reconciliation: Redress, Rights and Politics', *JIA* 60/1 (2006): 1–15; Georges Casalis, 'Reconciliation Through Christ as Basis for Living with Others and Living for Others', *Communio Viatorum* 2 (1961): 103–16; Anthony J. Chvála-Smith, 'The Politics of Reconciliation in 2 Corinthians 5', in *Proceedings, Eastern Great Lakes and Midwest Biblical Societies, vol 11, 1991* (Cincinnati: Eastern Great Lakes & Midwest Biblical Societies, 1991), 210–21; Arville Earl and Sheila Earl, 'Committed to the Ministry of Reconciliation: Moving Beyond Conflict in the Balkans', *Rev. Exp.* 104/3 (Summer 2007): 603–21; Joseph A. Favazza, 'Reconciliation: On the Border between Theological and Political Praxis', *Journal for the Study of Religion and Ideologies* 3 (2002): 52–64; Bruce W. Fong, 'Addressing the Issue of Racial Reconciliation According to the Principles of Eph 2:11-22', *JETS* 38/4 (1995): 565–80; F. Forster, '"Reconcile": 2 Corinthians 5:18-20', *CTM* 21/4 (1950): 296–98; N. S. L. Fryer, 'Reconciliation in Paul's Epistle to the Romans', *Neotestamentica* 15 (1981): 34–68; Hulitt Gloer, 'Ambassadors of Reconciliation: Paul's Genius in Applying the Gospel in a Multi-Cultural World: 2 Corinthians 5:14-21', *Rev. Exp.* 104/3 (Sum 2007): 589–604; D. Leslie Hollon, 'Reconciliation: Pastoral Reflections and Resources', *Rev. Exp.* 104 (2007): 442–62; Clark Hyde, 'The Ministry of Reconciliation', *Saint Luke's Journal of Theology* 31/2 (Mr 1988): 111–25; Ross Langmead, 'Transformed Relationships: Reconciliation as the Central Model for Mission', *MS* 25 (2008): 5–20; John D'Arcy May, 'Reconciliation in Religion and Society: A Conference in Honor of Irish Ecumenist Michael Hurley SJ', *Mid-Stream* 33/3 (1994): 346–49; Jens Meierhenrich, 'Varieties of Reconciliation', *Law and Social Inquiry* 33/1 (Winter 2008): 195–231; James R. A. Merrick, 'Justice, Forgiveness, and Reconciliation: The Reconciliatory Cross as Forgiving Justice: A Response to Don McLennan', *ERT* 30/3 (2006): 292–308; Itumeleng J. Mosala, 'The Meaning of Reconciliation: A Black Perspective', *JTSA* 59 (1987): 19–25; Rafi Nets-Zehngut, 'Analyzing the Reconciliation Process', *International Journal on World Peace* 24/3 (2007): 53–81; Peter T. O'Brien, 'Col 1:20 and the Reconciliation of All Things', *RTR* 33/1 (1974): 45–53; David W. Shenk, 'The Gospel of Reconciliation Within the Wrath of Nations', *International Bulletin of Missionary Research* 32/1 (2008): 2–9; Victor Sinclair, 'The Sovereignty of God in Reconciliation, with Karl Barth as a Guide', *Irish Biblical Studies* 18 (1996): 156–69; D J. Smit, 'The Truth and Reconciliation Commission -Tentative Religious and Theological Perspectives', *JTSA*/90 (1995): 3–16; Malcolm Tolbert, 'Theology and Ministry: 2 Corinthians 5:11-21', *Faith and Mission* 1/1 (Fall 1983): 63-70; Miklós Tomka, 'Religious Identity and the Gospel of Reconciliation', *Religion in Eastern Europe* 29/1 (2009): 20–28; Thomas M Tripp, Robert J Bies, and Karl Aquino, 'A Vigilante Model of Justice: Revenge, Reconciliation, Forgiveness, and Avoidance', *Social Justice Research* 20/1 (2007): 3–34; Ann Belford Ulanov, 'Practicing Reconciliation: Love and Work', *ATR* 89/2 (2007): 227–46; Miroslav Volf, 'The Social Meaning of Reconciliation', *Transformation* 16/Jan-Mar (1999): 7–12; Miroslav Volf, 'Forgiveness, Reconciliation, and Justice: A Theological Contribution to a More Peaceful Social Environment', *Millennium* 29/3 (December 1, 2000): 861–77, Cited 22 Nov 2011; Miroslav Volf, 'The Final Reconciliation: Reflections on a Social Dimension of the Eschatological Transition', *Modern Theology* 16/1 (2000): 91–113.

It is beyond the purpose of this study to comprehensively survey the literature on 'reconciliation'. Instead we propose simply to outline the New Testament's theological understanding of reconciliation. This will give us yet another perspective from which to analyze Kivengere's sermons. As we will see, Kivengere claims that reconciliation is 'the centre of the Christian gospel'.[204] Some awareness of the treatment of this theme by others will therefore assist the evaluation of Kivengere's use of this doctrine in his sermons,[205] providing a sounding board as we ask: how did Kivengere interpret and preach reconciliation to his various audiences?

This discussion will also help to situate Kivengere's preaching in the wider context of New Testament scholarship. The question of reconciliation as 'the centre' of Paul's theology, which has been a matter of debate for many years, was current at Kivengere's time.[206] The discussion also touches on larger questions in Biblical Theology,[207] such as the question of how

---

204. E.g., Kivengere, 'In Christ', p. 3, #1. Kivengere, 'Ambassador For Christ', p. 8, #1. Cf., Kivengere, 'The Ministry of Reconciliation', 1, where Kivengere claims, "reconciliation is the lifeblood of the evangelist's message."

205. See Chapters Five and Six.

206. Joseph Plevnik, 'The Center of Pauline Theology', *CBQ* 51/3 (1989): 461–78; E. P Sanders, *Paul and Palestinian Judaism: A Comparison of Patterns of Religion* (London: SCM, 1977), 461–78; Ernst Käsemann, *New Testament Questions of Today* (The New Testament Library; Philadelphia: Fortress, 1969), 1969; C J A. Hickling, 'Centre and Periphery in the Thought of Paul', in *Studia biblica 1978, 3* (Sheffield: JSOT Pr, 1980), 199–214.

207. Here we do not have in mind the Biblical Theology Movement. We are reluctant to deal with the Biblical Theology Movement in this study because it is littered with fundamental conceptual difficulties, which only are made obvious by Barr's work (James Barr, *The Semantics of Biblical Language* (Oxford: Oxford University Press, 1961); James Barr, *Biblical Words for Time* (2nd ed.; London: SCM, 1969); James Barr, *The Bible in the Modern World: The Croall Lectures Given in New College, Edinburgh in November 1970* (London: S.C.M. Press, 1973)). C.f. Brevard S. Childs, *Biblical Theology in Crisis* (Philadelphia: Westminster, 1970). Attempts to revive and defend or revive the Biblical Theology Movement include, James D. Smart, *Past, Present and Future of Biblical Theology* (Westminster, U.S.: John Knox Press, 1980); John Reumann, ed., *The Promise and Practice of Biblical Theology* (Minneapolis: Fortress Press, 1991); Francis B. Watson, *Text, Church and World: Biblical Interpretation in Theological Perspective* (Grand Rapids, Mich.: William B. Eerdmans, 1994); Francis B. Watson, *Text and Truth: Redefining Biblical Theology* (Edinburgh: T&T Clark, 1997); Steven J. Kraftchick, 'Facing Janus: Reviewing the Biblical Theology Movement', in *Biblical Theology: Problems and Perspectives: in Honor of J Christiaan Beker* (ed. S. J. Kraftchick, Charles D Myers, and Ben C. Ollenburger; Nashville: Abingdon Pr, 1995), 54–77; Scott J Hafemann, ed., *Biblical Theology: Retrospect and Prospect* (Downers Grove, Ill.: InterVarsity Press, 2002).

to hold the unity of Scripture together with the 'different faces'[208] of the biblical witness, links between Scripture and history, vocabulary, themes, typology, promise-fulfilment, salvation history and unity of viewpoints.[209] The language of 'centre' found in Kivengere's preaching of reconciliation[210] is one aspect of the on-going debates. What is 'the centre'? Is it better to talk of 'the foundation'? Or, is it better to talk of 'in Christ'?

The following inquiry does not pretend to hunt for, or to deny, that there was a 'centre' of Paul's theology. This language of 'centre' is certainly part of Kivengere's vocabulary, but, in this section, the notion is raised not to arbitrate on the question itself but to provide a conceptual context for his preaching.

In the following inquiry we will be asking, 'How does New Testament scholarship help us to understand reconciliation?' in order to assist us to evaluate Kivengere's preaching of this theme. For this concept, the New Testament uses two Greek verbs καταλλάσσω and ἀποκαταλλάσσω 'to reconcile' and one noun καταλλαγή 'reconciliation'. Paul explains humanity being reconciled to God καταλλάσσω: (Rom 5:10–11; 2 Cor 5:18–20; Eph 2:14–17; and Col 1:20–22). The verb, καταλλάσσω, simply means 'The exchange of hostility for a friendly relationship'.[211] Outside the epistles, in Matthew 5:24 the verb form διαλλάγηθι, rendered 'become reconciled', is used within the context of righting a relationship with a brother before approaching the altar to make one's offerings and in Acts 7:26, συνήλλασσεν, is rendered 'reconcile', within the context of resolving a dispute between two brothers.

---

208. The use of 'different faces' is deliberate. On close examination, the Bible has different parts, we refer to here as 'faces': Old Testament—the Law, the Wisdom, and the Prophets; and the New Testament—the Gospels and Epistles. Put together, in a biblical theology framework, the themes within both the Old Testament and the New Testament, mirrors the need for some kind of unity, while maintaining the distinct nature of each 'face'.
209. See Gerhard F Hasel, *New Testament Theology: Basic Issues in the Current Debate* (Grand Rapids: Eerdmans, 1978), 184–203. For other unity points—Jesus Christ, the Gospel, the Kingdom of God, Love, Kerygma, Proclamation of the word, God's plan of Salvation, Eschatology, and faith—see John Reumann, *Variety and Unity in New Testament Thought* (Oxford Bible Series; Oxford: Ox. Univ. Press, 1991).
210. See Kivengere, 'Ambassador For Christ', p. 3, #5. Kivengere, 'In Christ', p. 3, #7–#8.
211. W. Arndt W. F., Danker and F. W and Gingrich W. F Bauer, 'A Greek-English Lexicon of the New Testament and Other Early Christian Literature' (Chicago: University of Chicago Press, 2000), 521.

Paul was the first author to speak of the offended party, God, as being the initiator of reconciliation.²¹² Reconciliation begins with God who reaches out in his grace. It is not surprising that scholars like Ralph Martin have vigorously defended the argument that reconciliation is the centre of Paul's theology of salvation.²¹³ The sermons studied in this thesis show that Kivengere also championed this view.

In view of the Pauline presentation itself and the use made of it by Kivengere, it is important to deal with (1) Paul's own experience of reconciliation, which runs implicitly behind his letters and (2) Paul's teaching on reconciliation (2 Cor 5:14–20, Rom 5:1–11, Eph 2:14–18, and Col 1:19–22). Clearly, this will help in our analysis of how well Kivengere preached reconciliation in Paul's understanding. Did he get Paul correctly? Did he broaden the concept of reconciliation in his preaching? Did he leave out some important themes in the passage that are linked to Paul's understanding of reconciliation?

3.5.1 Paul's Experience of Reconciliation

In 1981 Seyoon Kim argued that the whole of Paul's gospel had its genesis in the complex experience on the Damascus road.²¹⁴ He refers to it directly and indirectly in his ministry (Gal 1:15–16; Phil 3:4–11; Col 1:23, 25; Eph 3:2–11).²¹⁵ The experience radically changed Paul's worldview and touched the whole of his life and theology.

The pre-Christian Paul was a pious Jew of Tarsus by birth, a Pharisee by training, a Roman citizen by upbringing, and a religious zealot by faith. He lived as a perfect Jew according to the Law and the Prophets. Paul

---

212. Porter, *Katallassō in Ancient Greek Literature, with Reference to the Pauline Writings*.
213. Martin, *Reconciliation*; Ralph P. Martin, 'New Testament Theology: A Proposal; The Theme of Reconciliation', *ET* 91/12 (1980): 364–368; Ralph P. Martin, 'Reconciliation and Forgiveness in the Letter to the Colossians', in *Reconciliation and Hope: New Testament Essays on Atonement and Eschatology, Presented to L.L. Morris on His 60th Birthday* (ed. Robert Banks; 1st ed.; Exeter: Paternoster, 1974), 104–24; Ralph P. Martin, 'New Testament Theology: Impasse and Exit; The Issues', *ET* 91/9 (1980): 264–269. For a similar argument see Marshall, 'The Meaning of Reconciliation'.
214. Seyoon Kim, *The Origin of Paul's Gospel* (Wissenschaftliche Untersuchungen Zum Neuen Testament. 2. Reihe; Tubingen: Mohr, 1981).
215. Kim acknowledges that there were many others before him who have pointed to Paul's allusion to his Damascus road experience. See Kim, *Origin*, 13–20.

meticulously kept the Ten Commandments. He followed the Pharisaic model of living that life directed by the tradition of the elders. In the eyes of the Jewish law he was considered blameless (Phil 3:6). He persecuted the church, since to him belief in a crucified Messiah was scandalous (1 Cor 1:18–23; Rom 9:23–33).

Jesus of Nazareth crucified in Jerusalem, confronted Paul as a living person in terms that Paul could not deny: Jesus was the Son of God raised and now the Saviour of the world. Paul the persecutor of the church, an 'enemy' of God, surrendered to Christ when he was confronted with this radical new reality. His own experience of the reconciling grace of God was overwhelming.[216]

Paul's experience of reconciliation on the Damascus road significantly shaped his subsequent articulation of his theology of reconciliation. This is relevant because most of Kivengere's sermons make reference to Paul's Damascus road experience in close parallel to his own reconciliation with God.

3.5.2 2 Corinthian 5:11–20

In 2 Corinthians 5:11–20, Paul defends his apostleship following suspicions aroused by his detractors.[217] Paul has the true credentials of apostleship. Without a recommendation letter from the apostles that had been with Jesus when he was still on earth, what would deter his Corinthian detractors from believing that Paul was a self-made apostle? In his own defence Paul concentrated on reconciliation.[218]

In verse 13 (εἴτε γὰρ ἐξέστημεν, θεῷ εἴτε σωφρονοῦμεν, ὑμῖν, 'For if we are out of our minds, it is for God: if we are of sound mind, it is for you'), Paul seeks not to present himself as a 'hero'. Rather, no matter the

---

216. For excellent essays on the significance of Paul's conversion on his life and thought, see Richard N Longenecker, ed., *The Road from Damascus: The Impact of Paul's Conversion on His Life, Thought, and Ministry* (Grand Rapids, Mich.: W.B. Eerdmans Pub., 1997); Alan F Segal, *Paul the Convert: The Apostolate and Apostasy of Saul the Pharisee* (New Haven: Yale U.P., 1990).
217. Ralph P. Martin, *2 Corinthians* (vol. 40; Word Biblical Commentary; Waco, Tex.: Word Books, 1986), 118–119.
218. For an extensive discussion on Paul's allusion to the Damascus road experience as a defense of his conversion and linked it with reconciliation, see Kim, '2 Cor 5:11–21 and Origin', esp. 268–71.

state of his mind, all he does is for God and not for himself. 'ἐξέστημεν', 'to be out of one's mind',[219] could refer to insanity. But working from the dative 'θεῷ', 'to God', this would not be of any value to God. Instead the verb emphasizes either the stress of intense spiritual emotion or elation. It is likely that the intense moment Paul is alluding to is his Damascus road experience. The experience so gripped Paul that his ecstatic behaviour towards God was then rational and controlled (σωφρονοῦμεν)[220] towards the Corinthians (ὑμῖν).

In verse 14 Paul explains the reason (γαρ) for this change, as being a judgment (κρίναντας), concerning the importance of why Jesus died on the cross for all, as he grasped the scope of God's love for him and the universe. This love of God συνέχει, 'compelled' him to live his life for Jesus Christ and to serve Christ (v 15). The death of Christ compelled Paul to a have a selfless attitude towards the Corinthians because in the death of Christ he found Christ's love for him (v 15).[221] In his death Christ represented the sinner (ἄρα οἱ πάντες ἀπέθανον) and died as a substitute for the sinner (καὶ ὑπὲρ πάντων ἀπέθανεν, 'And he died for all'), and this constitutes the binding force by which the sinner is then constrained (14a), leading to 'moral renewal'.[222] With this explanation of the love of Christ, and the renewal it brought, Paul's response to his detractors is complete. The work of Christ motivates and excites Paul to live and proclaim the love of Christ.

Out of his new conviction about the importance of the death of Christ (vv 14, 15) arises, in consequence (ὥστε) a turning point in his life (v 16)—'from now on', 'ἀπὸ τοῦ νῦν' after which he can view nobody simply 'according to the flesh', but only in the light of Christ's love for them. This moment is not 'from the present moment, the time of writing',[223] but 'from the time he saw that one had died for all'.[224] Most New Testament scholars

---

219. Martin, *2 Corinthians*, 126.
220. Martin, *2 Corinthians*, 126.
221. Martin, *2 Corinthians*, 132.
222. Martin, *2 Corinthians*, 132.
223. Alfred Plummer, *2 Corinthians* (Edinburgh: T&T Clark, 2000), 176.
224. Charles Kingsley Barrett, *A Commentary on the Second Epistle to the Corinthians* (London: Adam & Charles Black, 1976), 170.

agree that Paul here refers to his Damascus road experience, the moment when he became aware that Jesus Christ died for all.²²⁵

Verse 17 explains the new way Paul sees people, also drawing upon his Damascus road experience: ὥστε εἴ τις ἐν Χριστῷ, καινὴ κτίσις· τὰ ἀρχαῖα παρῆλθεν, ἰδοὺ γέγονεν καινά, 'So if anyone is in Christ, there is a new creation, everything old has passed away; see, everything has become new!' 'New creation'—'καινὴ κτίσις'—is a general and global claim of the reality of the new hope brought about by the death and resurrection of Jesus Christ, which he himself has already experienced when he was made new in Christ.²²⁶ This is sealed with a statement about 'the former things' and 'the new things' (cf. verses 15–16)—an allusion to Isaiah 43:18–19 (τὰ ἀρχαῖα μὴ συλλογίζεσθε, 'Do not remember the former things, or consider the things of old'. I am about to do a new thing (ἰδοὺ ποιῶ καινά); do you not perceive it?).

Paul then anchors this new creation, so much part of his own experience as well as his message, in the reconciling work of God (v 18). The clause τοῦ καταλλάξαντος, 'the one who reconciled us', is indicative of God's past action rooted in the 'mediation of Christ', διὰ Χριστοῦ. God initiates reconciliation, and then he commits the message of reconciliation to his servants, especially Paul (δόντος ἡμῖν τὴν διακονίαν τῆς καταλλαγῆς). Some take the two aorist participles, καταλλάξαντος ἡμᾶς, 'having reconciled us' and δόντος ἡμῖν, 'having given to us', as pointing to Paul's own conversion experience on the Damascus road and as an experience of reconciliation.²²⁷ God has given us a ministry of reconciliation, ἡμῖν διακονίαν; 'ministry' thus designated Paul's office as a preacher of reconciliation through the cross of Christ.

---

225. For example, see Jan Lambrecht, 'The Favorable Time', in *Studies on 2 Corinthians* (ed. R. Bieringer and Jan Lambrecht; Bibliotheca Ephemeridum Theologicarum Lovaniensium; Louvain: Leuven University Press, 1994), 96; Christian Wolff, 'True Apostolic Knowledge of Christ: Exegetical Reflections on 2 Corinthians 5:14ff', in *Paul and Jesus: Collected Essays* (ed. A. J. M. Wedderburn; JSOT Supp. 37; Sheffield: JSOT Press, 1989), 145–60; Philip Edgcumbe Hughes, *Paul's Second Epistle to the Corinthians: The English Text with Introduction, Exposition and Notes* (Grand Rapids, Mich.: Eerdmans, 1962), 197–201.

226. Barrett, *Second Corinthians*, 174.

227. L Joseph Kreitzer, *Second Corinthians* (New Testament Guides; Sheffield: Sheffield Academic Pr, 1996), 109.

In verse 19 Paul gives three actions of God: (1) in Christ, God was *reconciling the world;* (2) God was reconciling to world *to himself;* and, (3) God was present *in Christ* reconciling *the world*.²²⁸ The work of God in Christ means Paul's ministry 'is a setting forth of the word of proclamation',²²⁹ that is, the preaching of reconciliation. This had a hortatory side, in which Paul tells the Corinthians that 'God has made peace with the world'.²³⁰

Here we read: ὡς ὅτι θεὸς ἦν ἐν Χριστῷ κόσμον καταλλάσσων ἑαυτῷ, μὴ λογιζόμενος αὐτοῖς τὰ παραπτώματα αὐτῶν, 'in Christ God was reconciling the world to himself, not counting their trespasses against them'. Paul explicitly speaks of his personal experience of Christ (θέμενος ἐν ἡμῖν τὸν λόγον τῆς καταλλαγῆς, 'He has committed to us the word of reconciliation').

Although Paul as a Pharisee may have felt estranged from God before his Damascus road encounter with Christ, this encounter showed him that as a persecutor of the church he had been opposed to God and his purpose. But the encounter showed Paul in a very clear way one significant fact of God's character. God is not holding his sin against him. Instead, God forgave him and reconciled him, despite him being an enemy of God's church, and in reality an enemy of God! The act of God's reconciling him and giving him the message of reconciliation to proclaim overwhelmed him, totally grasping his entire being.²³¹

Verse 20 holds the key to Paul's argument in verses 18–21. Paul appeals to the Corinthians to embrace the fruits of divine reconciliation, even though they have run away from his gospel; and, to accept his offer of friendship.²³² Paul's statement that 'God making his plea through us' shows his recognition of his task of calling people to become friends of God. And, as he offers friendship with God, this also brings estranged human beings together.

To summarize, Paul's experience on the Damascus road was a real encounter with God in which he grasped the love of God displayed in Jesus'

---

228. Martin, *2 Corinthians*, 132.
229. Martin, *2 Corinthians*, 154.
230. Martin, *2 Corinthians*, 155.
231. Wolff, 'True Apostolic Knowledge of Christ: Exegetical Reflections on 2 Corinthians 5:14ff', 93–94.
232. Martin, *2 Corinthians*, 155.

death and was thereby reconciled to God. This love of God compelled him into a ministry of proclaiming God's reconciling work in Christ, and inviting people to become friends with God which will also entail that human enemies will become friends. Reconciliation with God through the love of God in Christ makes a person a new creation, whose new identity is found in Christ, and who now only views others from the perspective of Christ' death for them. This is the enormous impact of reconciliation on the Apostle Paul, and it now shaped his ministry of reconciliation.

3.5.3 Romans 5:1–11

Because the letters of Paul arise from his ministry of reconciliation, it is no surprise that they contain explicit teaching on this topic, commonly acknowledged by scholars. Romans 5:1–11 opens with a linking phrase: 'Therefore, having been justified by faith', relating it to the section before. The inferential conjunction, οὖν 'therefore' shows δικαιωθέντες 'having been justified' or 'since we have been justified', and the participle δικαιωθέντες resumes its content. Paul is concluding what was in the section before.[233] The term 'justification' is a legal expression referring to a situation in which God pronounces a believer righteous, drawing the believer into a right relationship with himself ἐκ πίστεως 'by faith'. This brings the following benefit: εἰρήνην ἔχομεν πρὸς τὸν θεον 'we have peace with God'. Peace is used here not in the narrow sense of the absence of hostilities, but in the broader sense of the well being or salvation of a God-fearing believer.[234] This peace is only realized through Jesus Christ, the one in whom the sins of the world are removed.

The second benefit of justification is access to the grace of God (v 2), once again 'through Christ' and 'by faith'. Paul makes reference to the 'grace in which we stand', a state into which God's saving work transfers a believer.[235] In this new state of grace, the believer is no longer under the law, but under grace—a state which includes justification and *all* that God

---

233. Richard A Young, *Intermediate New Testament Greek: A Linguistic and Exegetical Approach* (Nashville, Tenn.: Broadman & Holman, 1994), 191.
234. Douglas J. Moo, *The Epistle to the Romans* (The New International Commentary on the New Testament; Grand Rapids, Mich.: W.B. Eerdmans Pub. Co., 1996), 229.
235. Moo, *The Epistle to the Romans*, 300–01.

gives the believer in Jesus Christ.²³⁶ Having been justified by God, gained peace through Christ by faith, καυχώμεθα ἐπ' ἐλπίδι τῆς δόξης τοῦ θεοῦ, 'we boast in [the] hope of glory of God', καυχώμεθα. This boasting is the believer's joyful confidence in the state of 'the glory of God'—a state that was lost because of sin but will be restored to the believer at the end of time.²³⁷ Being justified even enables this joyful confidence in tribulation (καυχώμεθα ἐν ταῖς θλίψεσιν).

This arises (vv 3–5) from knowing εἰδότες, the outcome of tribulation in God's good plans; that ὑπομονὴ 'perseverance' will come because of tribulation, and this ὑπομονη will bring about δοκιμή, 'character'.²³⁸ δοκιμή in turn will bring about ἐλπις, 'hope', of the glory of God. Paul emphasizes in verse 5a that this 'hope [does] not disappoint' ὅτι 'because' God has poured out his love in our hearts. The perfect verb ἐκκέχυται, 'has been poured out' emphasizes 'the completed action of a past action or process from which the present state emerges'.²³⁹ The 'love of God' is given in full experience, poured into our hearts in the past and now within us,²⁴⁰ through (διὰ) the Holy Spirit.²⁴¹

In verses 6–8 Paul uses ὑπερ 'in place of' four times in reference to the substitutionary atonement of Christ.²⁴² Ἔτι γὰρ Χριστὸς . . . ὑπὲρ ἀσεβῶν ἀπέθανεν 'For yet Christ . . . died in place of irreverent [people]'. ἀσεβῶν 'irreverent', 'impious' or 'ungodly', refers to 'violating norms for a proper relationship to deity'.²⁴³ In verse 6, the expression 'while we were helpless' may refer to a range of situations—illness, sickness, incapacity, or

---

236. Moo, *The Epistle to the Romans*, 301.
237. Moo, *The Epistle to the Romans*, 301–02.
238. William F Arndt, *A Greek-English Lexicon of the New Testament and Other Early Christian Literature* (ed. Frederick W Danker and Walter Bauer; 3rd ed.; Chicago: University of Chicago Press, 2000), 256.
239. Daniel B Wallace, *Greek Grammar Beyond the Basics: An Exegetical Syntax of the New Testament* (Grand Rapids, Mich.: Zondervan, 1996), 577.
240. Moo, *The Epistle to the Romans*, 305.
241. Young, *Intermediate New Testament Greek*, 92.
242. Young, *Intermediate New Testament Greek*, 101–02; Stanley E. Porter, *Idioms of the Greek New Testament* (2nd ed.; Biblical Languages. Greek; Sheffield: JSOT Press, 1994 [1992]), 176–77.
243. Young, *Intermediate New Testament Greek*, 82.

limitation.[244] Considering that Paul refers to the situation of man as 'helpless', he is emphasizing that the people for whom Christ died are unable to do anything to help themselves out of their situation except by the help of Christ. Paul's statement 'at the [right] time', most likely refers to the time when Christ died—when men were helpless.[245] When Paul uses ὑπὲρ in the three verses 6–8, the unexpected sacrifice of Christ comes to the fore. He died 'in place of' sinners, as a substitute for those who deserve death because of their sins.

Paul's statement in verse 8, συνίστησιν δὲ τὴν ἑαυτοῦ ἀγάπην εἰς ἡμᾶς ὁ θεός 'but God demonstrates his own love for us' seen in the light of the contrastive δε, clearly indicates that Paul is speaking about the love of God for believers and not the believer's love for God. This is particularly so because of the reflexive pronoun ἑαυτοῦ.[246] God took the initiative when he συνίστησιν 'demonstrated' his love for humanity. The verb συνίστησιν is used in the present tense for a past act 'to provide evidence of a personal characteristic or claim through action'.[247] The demonstration of God's love is shown by the clause ὅτι . . . Χριστὸς ὑπὲρ ἡμῶν ἀπέθανεν '[in] that Christ . . . died in place of us'.[248] As with 2 Corinthians 5, the death of Christ is the demonstration of the love of God.

As in verse 1 Paul begins verses 9–11 with δικαιωθέντες 'having been justified' and οὖν 'then', concluding his argument by πολλῷ 'how much more',[249] Paul assures his readers that because God has already justified them, they can be sure that God will treat them well in the future. Believers gain God's justification ἐν τῷ αἵματι αὐτοῦ 'by the blood of Christ'. Clearly, 'blood' signifies the death of Christ as a sacrifice for sins.[250] If this was the enormous cost expended for God's enemies, how much more will he do for

---

244. Moo, *The Epistle to the Romans*, 306.
245. Moo, *The Epistle to the Romans*, 307; Young, *Intermediate New Testament Greek*, 98; Wallace, *Greek Grammar Beyond the Basics*, 376–77.
246. Moo, *The Epistle to the Romans*, 307–08.
247. Arndt, *A Greek-English Lexicon of the New Testament and Other Early Christian Literature*, 973.
248. Arndt, *A Greek-English Lexicon of the New Testament and Other Early Christian Literature*, 723.
249. Wallace, *Greek Grammar Beyond the Basics*, 166–67.
250. Moo, *The Epistle to the Romans*, 310.

his friends? The result of being justified is σωθησόμεθα . . . ἀπὸ τῆς ὀργῆς 'we will be saved . . . from the wrath [of God]', that is, the eschatological wrath.[251]

Paul then explains (γαρ). This confident assertion about the future (v 10): εἰ γὰρ . . . κατηλλάγημεν τῷ θεῷ 'For since . . . we became reconciled with God', this 'became reconciled' is parallel to 'having been justified' (v 9). Justification is a legal term applied to God declaring a believer righteous, but reconciliation is a relational expression referring to bringing together or making peace between enemies.[252] Paul's expression ἐχθροι 'enemies' (of God or Christ) makes the contrast clear. Because humanity is hostile towards God, and their sins have justly incurred the wrath of God, it is fair to view this enmity in both directions. But God's reconciliation removed this enmity 'through the death of his Son', Jesus Christ. This action of God leads to the assurance that believers will be saved. The clause πολλῷ μᾶλλον 'by how much more' makes it clear that the salvation ἀπὸ τῆς ὀργῆς 'from the wrath [of God]' will certainly take place, since the death of Jesus has already done the hard thing. And, the means of salvation is ἐν τῇ ζωῇ αὐτοῦ 'by his life' or δι' αὐτοῦ 'through him'.[253]

Paul's use of the temporal present participle καταλλαγέντες 'after being reconciled' demonstrates that reconciliation, like justification, is an act that happened in the past, but the effects continue in the present and will continue in the future. Paul also views the result of believers' reconciliation as something for which they can boast in God. Boasting in God is set in the context of the assurance of salvation from God's eschatological wrath, and the means by which they can boast is Christ. The clause δι' οὗ νῦν τὴν καταλλαγὴν ἐλάβομεν 'through whom we have now received [the] reconciliation' declares Christ as the means of the believer's reconciliation with God.

---

251. Arndt, *A Greek-English Lexicon of the New Testament and Other Early Christian Literature*, 720–21.
252. Moo, *The Epistle to the Romans*, 312.
253. Moo, *The Epistle to the Romans*, 312.

3.5.4 Ephesians 2:14–18

Although not without challenge,[254] scholars identify Ephesians 2:14–18 as a complete passage,[255] and this view is adopted here. Paul's opening words, for 'he himself is our peace' (v 14) introduces the vital theme of 'peace'.[256] Christ is the mediator of peace from God (Rom 5:1; Col 1:20) and he gives peace to believers (2 Thess 3:16); indeed, Christ is himself that peace. This is made clear by three participles. He is the one (ὁ) who ποιήσας 'made', λύσας 'destroyed', and καταργήσας 'abolished', in the clause ὁ ποιήσας τὰ ἀμφότερα ἓν καὶ τὸ μεσότοιχον τοῦ φραγμοῦ λύσας, . . . τὸν νόμον τῶν ἐντολῶν ἐν δόγμασιν καταργήσας. Christ removed the barrier that existed between Jews and Gentiles, to form out a new entity, of believing Gentiles and believing Jews, namely, the church.[257]

Formerly there was τὴν ἔχθραν 'the hostility', now in Christ, is ἡ εἰρήνη ἡμῶν 'our peace'. Paul here refers to two parties, Jews and Gentiles, made into one by Christ when he expressed that τὰ ἀμφότερα ἓν 'the both one'. Formerly there was disunity between the Jews and Gentiles but now in Christ there is unity.

Paul explains the wonder of Christ's reconciling work that brought peace to us four times in the passage (vv 14, 15, 17 [twice]).[258] Paul continues with the explanation: καὶ τὸ μεσότοιχον τοῦ φραγμοῦ λύσας, τὴν ἔχθραν ἐν τῇ σαρκὶ αὐτοῦ 'and has broken down in his flesh the dividing wall of hostility'. The word φραγμός denotes a sense of 'fencing in' or 'fortification'. The law required the Jews to be separate and holy.[259] The law became the source of hostility between Jews and Gentiles. The hostility, in the body of Christ, was nullified (καταταργήσας) 'put to death'.

---

254. Thorsten Moritz, *A Profound Mystery: The Use of the Old Testament in Ephesians* (vol. 85; Supplements to Novum Testamentum; Leiden: E.J. Brill, 1996), 25–29; Ian H Thomson, *Chiasmus in the Pauline Letters* (vol. 11; Journal for the Study of the New Testament. Supplement Series; Sheffield: Sheffield Academic Press, 1995), 84–86.
255. Peter T. O'Brien, *The Letter to the Ephesians* (The Pillar New Testament Commentary; Grand Rapids, Mich.: Eerdmans, 1999), 192.
256. O'Brien, *The Letter to the Ephesians*, 192.
257. O'Brien, *The Letter to the Ephesians*, 199.
258. O'Brien, *The Letter to the Ephesians*, 193.
259. James D. G. Dunn, *The Partings of the Ways Between Christianity and Judaism and Their Significance for the Character of Christianity* (vol. 2; London: SCM Press, 2006), 82.

The clause ἐν τῇ σαρκὶ αὐτοῦ 'in his flesh' refers to the crucified Christ. This statement has parallels in verse 13, 'by the blood of Christ' and verse 16 'through the cross'.[260] This is governed by the participle, καταργήσας 'having rendered inoperative'.

Verse 15: Paul states the first reason for rendering the law inoperative is the purpose clause: ἵνα τοὺς δύο κτίσῃ ἐν αὐτῷ εἰς ἕνα καινὸν ἄνθρωπον 'that he might create in himself one new man in place of the two'. He had earlier discussed the division between the two groups—Jews and Gentiles. Now the result of the two (τοὺς δύο) being created into one new person is rendered by the clause ποιῶν εἰρήνην 'making peace'. The context of the 'making peace' explains that 'he is our peace' (v 14). Christ made Jews and Gentiles one, destroyed the middle wall of partition, rendered inoperative the law, and that in turn was for the purpose of making one new person and the ultimate result of this was peace.

At this juncture, a careful look at the text indicates that Christ' death did not simply bring about a universal redemption so that Jews and Gentiles are reconciled. Indeed, most Jews would not concede to this view either. Markus Barth argues that since the context of Paul's statement here does not mention faith, Christ unites the Jews and Gentiles and the unity is not limited to Jewish and Gentile born-again Christians.[261] All Jews are included: the faithful and the rebellious.[262] There is no point in preaching a message of salvation to the Jews.[263]

Contrary to Markus Barth's interpretation of this passage,[264] the text does not clearly suggest that Gentiles have been accepted into the people of God—Israel. Rather, the context assumes that the believing Jews and Gentiles make up this new humanity. Paul is speaking to a community of believing Gentiles: he had thanked God for their 'faith' in Jesus (Eph

---

260. Romano Penna, *Paul the Apostle: A Theological and Exegetical Study* (Collegeville, MN: Liturgical Press, 1996), 37–40.

261. Markus Barth, *Israel and the Church: Contribution to a Dialogue Vital for Peace* (Research in Theology; Richmond: John Knox Press, 1969), 95.

262. Barth, *Broken Wall*, 122, 128.

263. Barth, *Israel and the Church*, 108–15.

264. For a critique of Markus Barth's interpretation of this text, see O'Brien, *The Letter to the Ephesians*, 203.

1:15),[265] and preceding this passage he had said that Gentiles are saved by grace through 'faith' and they are his workmanship in Christ (Eph 1:8–10). Gentiles who were far off but now in Christ were brought near by the blood of Christ—that is, through redemption and forgiveness (Eph 1:7), and that Jews and Gentiles were reconciled through the cross and the message of reconciliation was preached to the Gentiles and to Jews (Eph 2:13–17).[266]

In short, Paul in this context is speaking about a believing community of Jews and Gentiles, not all humanity. It is against this background that Paul expects that the good news of Christ's redemption and reconciliation is to be preached by the church to both Jews and Gentiles with the expectant result that those who will believe will belong to this new community, the one body created by Christ out of his blood and flesh.

At the opening of verse 15b with the conjunction ἵνα Paul is stating that Christ 'might create in himself' and that Christ 'might reconcile'. The verb ἀποκαταλλάσσω 'to reconcile' is only found here and in Colossians 1:20, 22. The use of the double prefix 'ἀπο-' and 'κατα-' is the intensified form of ἀλλάσσω.[267] The significance of Paul's use of the ἀλλάσσω 'exchange', links with exchange of hostility to a friendly relationship.

The clause τῷ θεῷ διὰ τοῦ σταυροῦ 'to God through the cross', makes reference to God whom the believing Jews and Gentiles are reconciled. This is indicated by the indirect object τῷ θεῷ. The reconciliation was done διὰ τοῦ σταυροῦ 'by means of the cross'. Reconciliation enacted a costly price: the death of Christ, the Son of God.[268]

After explaining how peace was accomplished between believing Jews and Gentiles and between them and God, Paul now draws the content and result of that peace (vv 17–18). Christ is not merely 'our peace' but he also came to preach peace (cf. v 14). O'Brien suggests 'the expression *and preached peace* echoed Isaiah 52:7' and that 'the rest of the verse

---

265. O'Brien, *The Letter to the Ephesians*, 204.
266. Andrew T. Lincoln, 'The Church and Israel in Ephesians 2', *CBQ* 49/4 (1987): 605–24; Fong, 'Addressing the Issue of Racial Reconciliation', 565–80.
267. For a detailed discussion of the emphatic prefixed from of ἀποκαταλλάσσω see Porter, 'Peace, Reconciliation', 697–99.
268. For a study of the means of reconciliation by the Son of God, see Barth, *Broken Wall*, 33–45.

approximately follows Isaiah 52:19'.[269] The peace was preached to those who were 'far off', namely, unredeemed Gentiles who were without Christ. They were alienated from Israel and his covenant. Then there were those who were 'near', namely, unredeemed Jews (vv 12–13).

Verse 18: Christ preached peace to Jews and Gentiles with the result ὅτι δι' αὐτοῦ ἔχομεν τὴν προσαγωγὴν οἱ ἀμφότεροι, 'so that through him we both have the access'. We access him ἐν ἑνὶ πνεύματι πρὸς τὸν πατέρα, 'in one Spirit to the Father'. The numeral ἑνὶ 'one' suggest the idea of unity πρὸς τὸν πατέρα 'to, or with the Father'.

To summarize, Paul explains the unity of Jews and Gentiles. The two formerly separate groups, Jews and Gentiles separated by the law, have now been made one in Christ (v 14). Christ has created in himself the two separate groups into one new entity (v 15). Christ reconciled them into one body (v 16) and we both have access in one Spirit to the Father (v 18). This new union that Christ brought replaced the old enmity. Before conversion the two groups were distinctly Jews and Gentiles, but after conversion they are one new person in Christ. It is through the death of Christ that both groups are brought together in one body (v 16) and one Spirit (v 18).

3.5.5 Colossians 1:19–22

In Colossians 1:19–20, Paul explains that God reconciles sinners to himself, by means of the blood of his Son. The consequence of this reconciliation is broad, for it is all-inclusive, affecting not merely humanity, but also the whole universe: 'and through him to reconcile all things to himself, having made peace through the blood of his cross; through him, I say, whether things on earth or things in heaven' (Col 1:20). The clause δι' αὐτοῦ 'through him' makes obvious that God's Son, Jesus Christ, is the mediator through whom God brought about 'complete reconciliation' (cf. ἀποκαταλλάξαι).[270] Paul's statement that God has brought complete reconciliation for humanity and the universe, through Christ's death, implies that Christ has gained salvation for all.

---

269. O'Brien, *The Letter to the Ephesians*, 206. (Emphasis in the original).

270. The preposition ἀπό suggests the sense of intensity or completeness. S Lewis Johnson, 'Studies in the epistle to the Colossians. IV, From enmity to amity', *Bib. Sac.* 119/474 (July 1962): 143.

It is therefore logical to believe that, for Paul, 'complete reconciliation' of all things means that God's proper rule over all creation will be restored. Elsewhere Paul writes: ἀνακεφαλαιώσασθαι τὰ πάντα ἐν τῷ Χριστῷ, through Jesus, God will reign over all things because 'all things will be summed up in Christ' (Eph 1:10).

For Paul, the target of God's reconciliation is sinful humanity. As Christ removed the barrier that stood between God and mankind, Christ took care of the wrath that comes on the sons of disobedience (Col 3:6). Since that barrier has been removed, it does not mean that reconciliation has been appropriated. The act of reconciliation in the death of Christ does not in itself apply reconciliation to the individual. Rather, 'it is provisional and makes possible the reconciliation of the individual'.[271] Even if some people do not appropriate the reconciliation, this does not detract from the reconciling work of the Father. Because of his love, it is already in place, because Christ became 'sin on our behalf' (2 Cor 5:21).

In verse 21 Paul's message then narrows to focus on the unbeliever's estrangement from God: 'you were formerly alienated and hostile in mind, engaged in evil deeds'. He contrasted the Colossians' former and present conditions by the words ποτε 'formerly' (v 21) and νυνὶ δε 'yet now' (v 22). This points up the dramatic change in the believer's quality of life that was accomplished by God (cf. Eph 2:11–13; Col 3:7–8; Phlm 11).[272] 'Formerly' they were ἀπηλλοτριωμένους 'alienated' from God (cf. Eph 2:12; 4:18). This alienation was born out of ignorance.

This ignorance was a spiritual, not an intellectual, lack of knowledge (Eph 4:18). The same passage in Ephesians speaks of the unbeliever ἐσκοτωμένοι τῇ διανοίᾳ 'being darkened in mind'. As enemies (ἐχθρούς) of God (Col 1:21), the unregenerate are definitely 'hostile' toward God, and this relationship is in some way reciprocated by God.[273] In light of God's dealings with sin in the Old Testament and his dealings with his enemies in

---

271. John F. Walvoord, 'The Person and Work of Christ, Part XIII: Reconciliation', *Bib. Sac.* 120 (1963): 8.
272. Peter T. O'Brien, *Colossians, Philemon* (Word Biblical Commentary; Milton Keynes: Word, 1987), 66.
273. Edwin Hamilton Gifford, *The Epistle of St. Paul to the Romans* (London: J. Murray, 1886), 114.

the New Testament (e.g. he will put 'all his enemies under his feet', 1 Cor 15:25), the wrath of God is an active element against his enemies, not just a passive attitude (Rom 1:18).

According to Romans 8:7, φρόνημα 'the mindset' of the flesh is enmity against God, and this hostility manifests itself in deeds of wickedness.[274] Just as faith will manifest itself in a tangible way in the believer's overt actions toward others, so also will powerful and sinful states of mind be revealed ἐν τοῖς ἔργοις τοῖς πονηροῖς 'in evil deeds' (Col 1:21).

After establishing the extent of the believer's former condition (1:21), Paul then disclosed the purpose of the reconciliation, παραστῆσαι 'to present',[275] along with a description of the means 'in his fleshly body through death'. In stressing the fact of Jesus' 'body of flesh', Paul blatantly renounced any of the dualistic philosophies that might have seeped into the Colossian church and fully upheld the integrity of Christ's Person, by linking the incarnation and the atonement.[276]

The prepositions Paul used support this interpretation: ἐν speaks to the issue of the sphere of the uniting operation before death, and διά points to the instrumental cause.[277] By identification, believers are positionally ἁγίους 'holy', ἀμώμους 'blameless', and ἀνεγκλήτους 'beyond reproach'. And they are to manifest these qualities in their Christian walk.[278]

---

274. William Hendriksen, *Exposition of Colossians and Philemon* (Grand Rapids, Mich.: Baker Book House, 1964), 83.

275. E. K. Simpson and F. F. Bruce, *Commentary on the Epistles to the Ephesians and the Colossians* (London: Marshall, 1957), 78.

276. O'Brien, *Colossians*, 68.

277. διά may refer to two meanings: (1) offering a sacrifice, and (2) present a legal placement of a case before a court. See Fritz Rienecker, *A Linguistic Key to the Greek New Testament* (ed. Cleon L. Rogers; trans. Cleon L. Rogers; vol. 2; Grand Rapids, Mich.: Zondervan, 1980), 569.

278. Eduard Lohse, *Colossians and Philemon: a Commentary on the Epistles to the Colossians and to Philemon* (ed. Helmut Koester; trans. William R. Poehlmann and Robert J. Karris; Philadelphia: Fortress Press, 1971), 65.

3.6 Summary of Chapter Three

This chapter has selected relevant material against which to analyze Kivengere's sermons in the next two chapters. Influences from the Keswick Movement, the East African Revival Movement, evangelical leaders, especially Billy Graham and John Stott, Karl Barth and Markus Barth all contributed to shaping Kivengere and his preaching of reconciliation. Additionally, we provided an overview of the Pauline experience of and teaching on reconciliation. This will form an additional background against which Kivengere's thought on and preaching of reconciliation can be evaluated.

CHAPTER FOUR
Kivengere's Preaching Reconciliation: A Reconciliation Time-Line

4.1 A Synopsis

Since Kivengere not only preached reconciliation from explicit reconciliation passages (chapter 5), but also from non-explicit reconciliation passages (chapter 6), investigation into the role of the doctrine of reconciliation in his preaching requires that this study give a sketch of the chronology of his preaching, revealing that it was not something that came about abruptly, but something that he thought about carefully and preached over an extended period.[1] Such a chronology will also help to monitor any development as he preached reconciliation in the context of Uganda's deep wounds.

The survey of the chronology of his sermons on reconciliation provides an outline of the process by which the doctrine of reconciliation became central to his preaching during the period 1971–1988. It falls into three periods: before, during, and after his exile from Uganda by Idi Amin.

---

1. For the genesis of his engaging and preaching reconciliation see his conversion story, chapter Two, 5.2 'Kivengere's Conversion: From Agnostic to Preacher'.

4.2 Before Exile (September 1971–February 1977)

In September 1971, Kivengere preached at Santa Barbara, USA, on the reconciling love of God that brings a surprise of joy and peace to believers.[2]

In November 1971, after returning to Uganda, he found himself as a member of the Kigezi diocesan council embroiled in a provincial church row. Because of ethnic divisions, Namirembe and West Buganda dioceses threatened secession from the province of the COU. Consequently, when President Amin learned of this intention, he called a meeting at Kampala and forced the provincial delegates to come up with a lasting solution to the problem, declaring that he did not want a divided church. By this move, and to everyone's amazement, Amin, a Muslim, 'saved the church'.

On Sunday 28 November 1971, a resolution of the plenary session sent to President Amin, affords clear evidence of a corporate commitment to end the division: '1. *On Secession*: We are all agreed that we are against secession of any Diocese from the Province of the COU, Rwanda and Burundi'.[3] The Archbishop and the Bishops of the COU later (15 August 1973) sent a pastoral letter to the Churches of the Province of Uganda, Rwanda, Burundi and Boga-Zaire: 'We are grieved to know that there have been divisions among us brethren which have resulted in bitterness, hatred and judging each other . . . We urge all of you attend to worship, attend Bible study for prayer and fellowship together in all places of worship as one group in Jesus Christ'.[4]

This incident illustrates the bitter divisions, differences, and disagreements that existed in the life of both church and nation by 1971. It also shows the important role that Kivengere's preaching was already taking. For, into this tense conflict, Archbishop Erica Sabiti asked Kivengere to preach and, in order to bring his audience to acknowledge the problem, repent, forgive each other, and enjoy healing and unity. He chose Philippians

---

2. Kivengere, 'Surprised by Joy'.
3. Festo Kivengere, 'His Excellency the President', Sermon Transcript, November 28, 1971, AO:19711128. The resolution of 28 November 1971 was signed by Archbishop Erica Sabiti (Archbishop of Uganda, Rwanda and Burundi) and sent to President Amin.
4. Festo Kivengere, 'Divisions in the Church', Sermon Transcript, August 15, 1973, AO:19730815.

2:1–7 and preached reconciliation.[5] The following year, while preaching on the same theme and text (Phil 2:6–7) to an American audience, he reflected on the November conference, explaining that he not only preached reconciliation, but gave an altar call in which the delegates were to be reconciled to each other before they received communion.[6]

Kivengere had his own opportunity for practical reconciliation that same year (1972) in Glion, Switzerland, when preaching on reconciliation to an Africa Enterprise meeting arranged for fellowship between the South Africa and East Africa branches. In his opening session, Kivengere started with a testimony, that while praying and expressing his love to Christ for a couple of hours before the session, he had heard an unmistakable inner voice saying to him: 'I know you love me, but do you love Michael?' He admitted that 'he had to confess a lack of love' for Cassidy, but then told how the Lord then poured love into him.[7]

Reconciliation was then preached by his actions, as Donald Jacobs, chairman of the meeting, recalled: 'Having given us his witness, Festo crossed the room and embraced Michael before us. This was a moment, which had about it the aura of eternity. The fellowship between the South Africa and East Africa teams was built upon that little walk of ten steps that Festo took towards Michael'.[8]

In July 1972, Kivengere also spoke at the Keswick Convention in England on reconciliation focused in Christ under different titles: 'Christ the Renewer' and 'Christ the Liberator'.[9] However, in the first topic, his message focused on reconciliation using the language of 2 Corinthians 5:17 when he said: 'Christ is at the centre of renewing the man . . . This is why St. Paul uses lovely expressions like, "When, therefore, any man—any woman—is in Christ, he becomes a new creation"—a fresh person all together . . . Then the world will become aware that here are men once fragmented, but now whole again'.[10] In Africa they are seeing reconciliation.

---

5. Kivengere, 'Surprised by Joy'.
6. Kivengere, 'Christ Puts All Things Together'.
7. 1972: Switzerland, African Enterprise team meeting. Coomes, *Festo Kivengere*, 292.
8. Coomes, *Festo Kivengere*, 292.
9. Kivengere, 'Christ the Renewer', 66–75. Kivengere, 'Christ the Liberator', 116–122.
10. Kivengere, 'Christ the Renewer', 67–68.

Using the language of Colossians 3:10–11 to strengthen this point he said: 'You have put on the new man, the new nature, which is being renewed in the knowledge after the image of its Creator—renewed—and here then there cannot be Greek and Jew, circumcised and uncircumcised, barbarian or Scythian, slave or free man; but Christ is all, and is in all'.[11]

In the second topic, 'Christ the Liberator', he preached on reconciliation from 2 Corinthians 5:19: '[v 19] is wonderful—The fact is that God was acting in Christ to turn the world's enmity to himself into friendship, that he was not holding men's sins against them, and that he placed upon us the privilege of taking to men who are hostile to him this offer of his friendship'.[12] God's action in Christ was to enable men and women to live for him. 'The resurrection was a seal that he accomplished a mighty work for you. Your liberation was sealed with his own blood'.[13] With this action, 'a mission of reconciliation is given to the one who was a miserable self' concluding with an exhortation: 'Maybe tonight you are going to begin to experience in a deeper way the ministry written in blood of reconciliation. A wounded world can never be healed except by a wounded hand. When love fears to bleed, it ceases to bless'.[14]

On 10 October 1973, Kivengere preached at Fuller Seminary Chapel, USA, on the theme: Delivered—Set Free (Heb 13:11–12).[15] As a lay evangelist, 1962, he was at Fuller speaking in their chapel services, now, he is glad to be back. On giving thanks for the training of two Ugandan ministers, John Wilson and James Katarikawe, he made a historical claim: 'we need them to be able to share the good news with their people at this very great need in the continent of Africa' (p. 1, #1).[16] Turning to his passage, Hebrews 13:11–12, he explained reconciliation using the sacrificial language: sin . . . was always connected with separation vertically and

---

11. Kivengere, 'Christ the Renewer', 74.
12. Kivengere, 'Christ the Liberator', 118.
13. Kivengere, 'Christ the Renewer', 120–21.
14. Kivengere, 'Christ the Renewer', 121–22. Kivengere, 'Christ the Renewer': 121–22.
15. Festo Kivengere, 'Delivered—Set Free', Sermon Transcript (Preached at Fuller Seminary, Pasadena, California, October 10, 1973), AO:19731010.
16. Indeed, John Wilson and James Katarikawe, on completion of their MA studies at Fuller, returned to Africa and worked very hard with AEE, under the leadership of Kivengere.

horizontally between God and man, and between man and man' [. . . but] 'Jesus Christ who replaced these sacrifices for sin, had to suffer . . . in order that he may bring those who were separated right in' (p. 2, #3–#5). Again he makes a fundamental New Testament claim: 'This of course [is] the central message of the New Testament' (p. 3, #6). In Jesus Christ, we have a way out from all barriers: at the cross, barriers were crossed out and Jesus introduced men to God and men to men. There is reconciliation without explicit mention of the word reconciliation (p. 8, #18).

In October 1973, Kivengere preached at Channel City, Santa Barbara, USA, on the theme: 'The Problems of the New Nations of Africa' (Genesis 4).[17] After naming the problems of the new nations in Africa: racism, tribalism, barriers scattered all over in Africa—the spectrum of education, cultural, social and historical barriers, ideological differences in politics, language differences (pp. 1–4, #1–#9). Turning to his text, he explains that Cain killed Abel because of his insecurity (p. 5, #11). Reconciliation was in view. He concludes: 'what we need and I believe is what I preach: the love of Jesus Christ can break those miserable fences and introduce men to men and brothers together' (p. 9, #21).

On 24 October 1973, at Calvary Baptist Church, Washington, Kivengere preached on the theme: 'Abundant Complete Life: Revival' (John 10:10).[18] He preached reconciliation using Pauline language: For Paul, holiness, 'is coming into right relationship with God' (p. 3, #6). He alludes to Philippians 2: 'When eternity took flesh and bone and became what you Christians call incarnation' (p. 3, #7). Jesus' coming among us is revival. Reconciliation is never far away. He tells of his conversion story in which he was reconciled to the Lord and lists the places where he has been telling this story, including Australian Aborigines (p. 9, #23). Kivengere tells the impact of his preaching on one young man who said to him: 'You know when you were talking in the service this morning, you referred about writing a letter about someone you do not like. I am going home to write a letter.

---

17. Festo Kivengere, 'The Problems Of The New Nations Of Africa', Sermon Transcript (Preached at Channel City Club, Santa Barbara, California, October 1973), AO:197310[--].
18. Festo Kivengere, 'Abundant, Complete Life', Sermon Transcript (Preached at Calvary Baptist Church, October 24, 1973), AO:19731024*1.

... the New Testament message means that you are going to do something about it'. In this statement is reconciliation in action.

14–18 November 1973, Kivengere at Pittsburgh, Untied States of America, speaking at Pittsburgh Mission, on the theme: 'Abundant Life' using the story of the prodigal Son (Luke 15).[19] The correct title of this parable should be 'the parable of the Father', because Jesus told this story about the father's love. It is a story that tells how much the father loved the son (p. 3, #5), 'who lived so much that when he died, he lived again'. He is with the father's open arms ready to embrace the unembracable and to forgive from the cross (p. 14, #18). Without mentioning reconciliation, he used language of reconciliation: 'the cross', 'fathers arms' 'embrace the unembracable'.

In 1974, Kivengere's preaching schedule was in his view 'one of the busiest I have ever heard in spreading the Good News of our Lord'.[20] From 16–25 July 1974, at the Lausanne Congress on World Evangelization,[21] where his sermon on the cross, which he gave on the last day, during the plenary, turned out to be of great significance to evangelicals all over the world.[22] The sermon was intended by Kivengere to bring together all the

---

19. Festo Kivengere, 'Prodigal Son', Sermon Transcript (Preached at Pittsburgh, Pennsylvania, November 1973), AO: 19731114-18.

20. Festo Kivengere, 'The Bishop's Charge to the Synod', Sermon Transcript, 1975, AO: 1975[03--?]. He reports further: 'January I was in Australia and Papua New Guinea, and Hong Kong. In May I was in Japan ... and on to Germany, Switzerland and England. In July I was in Switzerland for an International Congress. In October and November I was in England and N. Ireland. In September I was in the USA before I joined others in England. So I went round the world one and a half times!'.

21. For details of the proceedings of the July 1974 'Lausanne 1' Congress on World Evangelization, see John R. W. Stott and Lausanne Committee for World Evangelization, eds., *Making Christ Known: Historic Mission Documents from the Lausanne Movement 1974-1989* (Carlisle: Paternoster Press, 1996). Kivengere was not only a preacher at the congress but he was one of the executive members instrumental in organizing the congress. Its main focus was the Great Commission, 'enabling the whole Church to take the whole gospel to the whole world'. See David Claydon, ed., *A New Vision, a New Heart, a Renewed Call: Lausanne Occasional Papers from the 2004 Forum for World Evangelization* (Lausanne Occasional Papers; Pasadena, Calif.: William Carey Library, 2005), ix.

22. See Festo Kivengere, 'The Cross And World Evangelization', Sermon Transcript (Given at International Congress on World Evangelization, Lausanne., July 25, 1974), AO: 19740725, discussed below. As the last sermon, it brought the previous messages on the cross of Christ together and rallied everyone to evangelize the message of reconciliation.

previous thoughts expressed during the Congress and to 'commission' the delegates to go out into the world and evangelize.

Kivengere preached this significant sermon into this context. It shows his carefully considered thought, choice of words, and illustrations as he preached reconciliation with emphasis on the work of Jesus Christ on the cross. Indeed, the fact that he was a speaker not merely at such an important evangelical Congress but also the speaker on the last plenary session with the task to draw together all the thoughts discussed at the conference during the week,[23] show in part his influence and impact upon the life of the evangelical world at the time. His rallying and 'commissioning' the evangelicals to preach reconciliation centred in the cross of Jesus Christ, show the recognition of his preaching gift by other evangelical leaders.

He emphasized Christ's redemptive, reconciling love for all mankind.[24] Kivengere's preaching of reconciliation displayed his theology of the cross. The cross was where God entered into our struggle, resolved all the conflicting pulls ending our despair of ever reaching God through futile man-made means (Gal 4:4). The cross gives a 'new right centre', bringing wholeness as a result of removing the 'conflicting elements' standing between individuals and groups. Kivengere declared this theology of the cross to be the 'hope for my beloved . . . Africa with all its conflicting problems'.[25]

Thus, in 1974, as Kivengere sought to mobilize an international audience to world evangelization, not only did he preach reconciliation, but he was already proclaiming this message as the hope for solving Africa's

---

23. Seven burning questions of the day were discussed at this Congress: The relationship of evangelism and social concern as a matter raised by the rapid growth in awareness of poverty and injustice in the world and the effects of natural and human-made disasters; unity, diversity and cooperation among Christians as raised by the post-World War II development of the ecumenical movement in the World Council of Churches; the uniqueness of Jesus Christ as raised by the question of promoting tolerance to other religions; the validity of missions as raised by the question of the call for a moratorium of missions that had been issued by some Two-Thirds World church leaders; the work of the Holy Spirit in evangelism as a matter prompted by the rapid growth of Pentecostal and Charismatic churches; Religious liberty and human rights as a question raised by heightening awareness through modern media of the infringement of these rights in many parts of the world; and, the relationship of the gospel to culture as a matter raised by its spread into many cultures and the self-consciousness of these cultures in the post-imperial independence movements.

24. Kivengere, 'The Cross And World Evangelization'.

25. Kivengere, 'The Cross and World Evangelization'.

conflicts. Still in July 1974, presumably within the diocese, he conducted 'The Mission of Reconciliation', which he praised God for the mission. Seven months later (March 1975), he reports on this mission in his charge to the diocese.[26]

In February 1975, when preaching for the Ghana Mission,[27] he urged revival based on the cross: Revival Begins at the Cross; Remove the Masks; Peace and Victory for the Christian; The Covenant of Love.[28] He exhorted his audience to see how God is moving in West Africa, just as he did in East Africa. In these addresses, his main focus is cross of Christ—the place where Jesus' death and resurrection gained reconciliation for all. However, he does not explicitly mention reconciliation, but uses the word renewal to refer to reconciliation.

In July 1975, the bishop flew to England where he again preached at the Keswick Convention.[29] He emphasized forgiveness: 'There is tremendous need in 1975, a hundred years since Keswick began, for us to catch a fresh vision of the release which comes when sins are forgiven'.[30] 'Forgiveness brings release' . . . What do we mean when we say "forgiveness"? We simply mean the barriers, which stood between me and my God, have been removed . . . no matter what effort I put out; no matter what techniques I

---

26. In his diocesan charge of 15 – 18 March 1975, Kivengere reports that the Convention took place in July: 'The Mission of Reconciliation. How we praise God for the mission of last July'. See Kivengere, 'The Bishop's Charge to the Synod'.

27. The addresses were published in Festo Kivengere, *When God Moves in Revival* (Wheaton, Ill.: Tyndale House Publishers, 1977 [1973]). [Is the last word of the title "Revival" or "Renewal"?] 'I have written this little book about revival based on four talks I gave in Ghana', Kivengere, *When God Moves in Revival*, 10.

28. For the sermons, see Chapter Five.

29. Kivengere, 'The Release of Forgiveness', 27–34. He joined his friends Billy Graham and John Stott as speakers. See, Graham, 'A Hundred Years of Blessing and Glory', 101–107. John R. W Stott, 'God's New Society (1) New Life (Ephesians 1:1-2:10)', in *The Keswick Week 1975: Centenary Year* (London: Marshall, Morgan & Scott, 1975), 43–52. John R. W Stott, 'God's New Society (2) New Life (Ephesians 2:11-3:21)', in *The Keswick Week 1975: Centenary Year* (London: Marshall, Morgan & Scott, 1975), 65–74. John R. W Stott, 'God's New Society (3) New Life (Ephesians 4:1-5:21)', in *The Keswick Week 1975: Centenary Year* (London: Marshall, Morgan & Scott, 1975), 101. John R. W Stott, 'God's New Society (4) New Life (Ephesians 5:22-6:24)', in *The Keswick Week 1975: Centenary Year* (London: Marshall, Morgan & Scott, 1975), 123–133. Also see these addresses published as Stott's address, 'God's New Society: Ephesians', in Stott, *John Stott at Keswick*, 293–367.

30. Kivengere, 'The Release of Forgiveness', 28.

used, they were useless'.³¹ He further preached reconciliation without mentioning it, using the language of Colossians 1: 'he invited the brethren to look at him, and he sees that he is greater than the world: "In whom all things cohere, apart from whom everything breaks apart'.³²

'Forgiveness came in the Person of Jesus Christ' . . . 'He loved me so much, he hated my sin so much, that he bled for it, and the blood speaks of the power of the self-sacrificing God in Jesus Christ. He took me with my sins to Calvary; and there—the miracle of his love—took the mess that I was, and the burdens which were crushing me, upon his mighty shoulders; and he took the papers one after another and wiped me clean'.³³ The bishop adds that forgiveness is not an experience merely to be enjoyed: 'you have to go out . . . forgive. And as you forgive, you are continually being forgiven . . . that is how release comes . . . when you stand before the cross'.³⁴

This address shows him preaching reconciliation to Keswick evangelicals in a form that expressed strongly the gospel's objection to personal efforts to overcome the barriers between a believer and God. Clearly reconciliation not only has the *theological* meaning (vertical relationship) of the death of Christ reconciling people to God, but also the *social* meaning (horizontal relationship) of Christ's death reconciling people to each other.

Kivengere flew home from England via Westmont, Illinois, USA, where he preached reconciliation, emphasizing the right balance between relationships: between God and man (vertical relationship) and between human beings (horizontal relationship). He argued that his audience must know the flooding love of God if they were to have a personal experience of Jesus Christ.³⁵

At the Kabale Convention July 1975, he chose the theme 'Christ's Love Reconciles Us'.³⁶ The first convention was held in September 1935

---

31. Kivengere, 'The Release of Forgiveness', 28.
32. Kivengere, 'The Release of Forgiveness', 29.
33. Kivengere, 'The Release of Forgiveness', 31–32.
34. Kivengere, 'The Release of Forgiveness', 33.
35. Kivengere, 'His Flooding Love'.
36. Coomes, *Festo Kivengere*, 335. Anglican Diocese of Kigizi, 'Golden Jubilee Convention', 7. Cf. Rukirande, 'The East African Revival', 7. Rukirande reports the theme simply as 'RECONCILIATION'.

at Rugarama, Kabale, lasting for a week with the topics that Katarikawe (chapter 2) and Joe Church (chapter 3) referred to: Sin, Repentance, New Birth, Coming out of Egypt, and the Holy Spirit.[37] Since 1935, every 10 years the brethren gather at Kabale for a weeklong meeting. The meeting has became designated the 'Kabale Convention'.

When Kivengere later (August 1985) reflected upon this convention, he wrote: '[E]xternal pressures from dictators, such as Idi Amin . . . was [a] blessing in disguise, as it acted like a heavy pressure upon us and kept the cracked body from breaking in pieces!' His solution to the 'cracks' in Uganda and East Africa was clear: 'So St. Paul's word of *reconciliation* was what we needed'.[38]

With the theme of the convention 'Christ's Love Reconciles Us', even before convention week Kivengere was preaching this message very practically. In July 1975 he went to the governor of the Southern Province, Bashir Juma, to reconcile with him following the anti-Christian policies that the governor was instituting against Kivengere, as the bishop of Kigezi, for opposing the brutality of Amin's soldiers on the civilians in that region.[39] After Governor Bashir's senior officers beat a Christian girl just for fun, Kivengere had advised her to write a protest to the governor. Bashir suspected the letter was from the bishop, and he was furious.[40]

At the convention, as the bishop highlighted 'Christ's love reconciled us', many people repented together, 'some openly, others quietly'. This convention happened during Idi Amin's rule 'when many people were being killed in Uganda because of their faith'.[41] Despite these troubles, many people from all over the world attended, largely because of their friendship with Kivengere. The presence of international guests at the convention raised its profile and exposed these international visitors to Kivengere's preaching of reconciliation and to its effects.

---

37. Rukirande, 'The East African Revival', 2.
38. Anglican Diocese of Kigizi, 'Golden Jubilee Convention', 6, emphasis in the original.
39. James Dixon Douglas, *The Work of An Evangelist* (World Wide Publications, 1984), p. 160, #34.
40. For the account, see Kivengere, *The Spiritual Life of a Pastor*, approximately 26 mins into the tape.
41. Rukirande, 'The East African Revival', 7.

In 1975, Kivengere preached in Seattle, USA, on the theme: 'The Renewing Presence of Christ in Evangelism' (Luke 24:30–36).[42] On bringing greetings from churches in East Africa, in particular Uganda, he explains evangelism using the language of reconciliation: 'the good news that when the fullness of time came, God sent his Son, born of a woman, born under the law of the Jewish community as well as under the laws of human race as a whole'. Jesus was born purposely 'to gather the children of the tree of curse from the cold of estrangement from God into the warmth of God's unchanging love as is demonstrated in Jesus Christ himself' (p. 1, #1). It is good news because the broken pieces of the human heart are put together. Out of this he produces a new man. 'No other hands can pick up the fragments and out of it create a whole man, except the hands of love: the wounded hands of the Son of God (p. 2, #5). There is reconciliation without explicitly mentioning it.

In May 1976, while a delegate at the World Council of Churches meeting being held in Nairobi, Kenya, he preached at the Nyayo National Stadium on the theme 'Jesus Frees and Unites'.[43] Centred on Galatians 5:13 and Genesis 3, his message called his audience to reconciliation. They were living in a broken world at a time when the world was desperate for freedom and unity that can only be found in Christ the reconciler.

In December 1976, he returned to Nairobi for a follow up meeting to the 1973 congress on mission and evangelism held in South Africa. The 1973 congress had proposed the idea of a Pan-African Christian Leadership Assembly (PACLA), to rally the rising generation of African Christian leaders, so that the church in Africa might face the emerging challenges, such as rapid growth of the churches in Africa, as well as turbulent cultural and political change.[44]

---

42. Festo Kivengere, 'The Renewing Presence of Christ in Evangelism', Sermon Transcript, 1975, AO:1975[----]*6. The sermon does not mention month and day.
43. Festo Kivengere, 'Jesus Frees and Unites', Sermon Transcript, May 24, 1976, AO: 19760524.
44. For a full account of the challenges that AEE met in organizing the meeting, see Cassidy, *Together in One Place*, 25–38. For a further explanation of the upcoming PACLA by Kivengere the year before, see Festo Kivengere, 'Our Bodies: Temples of the Holy Spirit', Sermon Transcript, 1975, AO: 1975[----]*5.

PACLA took place in December 1976, but only after AEE had overcome obstacles caused by theological and political differences between two major groups. Ever the preacher of reconciliation, Kivengere wrote to the two opposing groups:

> I am a firm believer in John 12:32, 'When I am lifted up from the earth I shall draw all men unto myself'. As long as the drawing is to Jesus Christ I am not ashamed to invite all men, from every persuasion, to meet under the same gospel. The essence of evangelical truth is not in the neat expressions used in the Creeds, but the essence is the Lord Jesus Christ and him crucified. I believe that this is open enough for all men of all persuasions to come and have their persuasions re-examined, renewed and revalued . . . an assembly with one simple aim: to bring God's people together to face the challenge of living for Christ on the continent of Africa together.[45]

The *primary* aim was to draw together Christian leaders from all over Africa with all their theological differences and 'preach' 'reconciliation' to them with the hope of encouraging them to further preach the gospel of 'reconciliation' which was desperately needed in Africa through their different churches.[46]

Later Kivengere described the occasion when a white South African, Professor David Bosch,[47] giving a paper before 800 African Christian leaders, touched by the Spirit of God, broke down and wept as he presented his Christian paper on healing relationships (p. 8, #2).[48] 'The love of Christ had penetrated this man's heart'. Bosch's pain, however, was not just for the participants at the PACLA, such as Kivengere himself ('I was among them',

---

45. Cassidy, *Together in One Place*, 27.
46. For an excellent report of the meeting see, Cassidy, *Together in One Place*.
47. See Cassidy, *Together in One Place*, 130. It is clear that Kivengere is referring to Professor David Bosch of South Africa's address at PACLA in Nairobi. Bosch's paper was entitled, 'The In-Between People'.
48. Festo Kivengere, 'Broken Relationships Restored', Sermon Transcript (USA, March 1977), p. 8, #2, AO: 1977[0314?].

p. 8, #2) who went and embraced the weeping Bosch but for the many Africans who are not in the conference.

To understand something of what Kivengere was going through in the midst of Bosch sharing, one would need to remember that way back in 1969 Kivengere was already 'Preaching the Good News that in Jesus the barriers come down—between God and man, and between man and man. [I]n him is reconciliation'.[49] This reconciliation was not just for the top church leaders and theologians at the conference,[50] but its influence will filter down from Nairobi to Soweto and other parts of South Africa. From this meeting, the fire for a follow up meeting for South Africa region was formed for a South African Leaders Assembly whose main agenda is perusing and preaching reconciliation.

4.3 The Exile (February 1977– May 1979)

Prior to February 1977, Kivengere was based in Uganda, although preaching elsewhere in Africa and internationally. As we have seen, the message of reconciliation had already been on his lips for some time before the worsening situation in Uganda forced him to flee the country to escape from Amin.[51] For the next two years he was a refugee in exile, and from his base in Pasadena, USA, he continued to preach reconciliation.

In 1977 the centenary celebrations of the COU (1877–1977)[52] were marred by Uganda's complicated politics that now directly affected the church. Early in February,[53] Archbishop Luwum and his seventeen bishops

---

49. Cassidy, *Together in One Place*, 17.
50. The theologians at the conference include, Prof. David Bosch, Michael Cassidy, Archbishop Luwum, etc. See Cassidy, *Together in One Place*, 297–99, Appendix 6.
51. Wood, 'The Bishop and Idi Amin', 26–28.
52. Jan Jelmert Jørgensen, *Uganda: A Modern History* (London: Taylor & Francis, 1981), 307. See, Kivengere, 'Jesus Came as a Missionary', p. 1, #4; Kivengere, 'The Love of Christ', p. 3, #4–5; Festo Kivengere, 'Broken Relationships Restored', Sermon Transcript, October 26, 1977, p. 1, #1, AO: 19771026*1; Kivengere, 'The Unshakable Identity', pp. 2–3, #3.
53. For the letter, see Cassidy, *Together in One Place*, 290–293.Cassidy and Osei-Mesah, *Together in One Place*, 290–293, 'Appendix 2: Letter from the Late Archbishop Janani Luwum and Bishops of Uganda to President Amin'. The letter protested against the brutal

signed a forceful letter to President Amin, complaining about the killings and disappearances occurring in the country. This resulted in the murder of three of the organizers of the centenary celebrations: Charles Oboth-Ofumbi (Internal Minister) and Lieutenant Colonel Erinayo Oryema (Minister of Lands),[54] and, on 17 February, Archbishop Janani Luwum. Amin's murder of Janani Luwum deeply affected Kivengere and the entire COU.

Fearing he might be next, on 20 February Kivengere fled Uganda.[55] The account of his escape then became a regular part of his preaching during his exile. In March, he preached in the chapel service of World Vision, in Monrovia, USA, giving a succinct account of the murder of Archbishop Luwum, which had made the news all around the world. He placed the story in the context of the greater story of Jesus steadfastly and determinedly setting his face to go to Jerusalem (Luke 9:51).[56]

But his language of reconciliation was not far away. Drawing upon the language of 2 Corinthians 5:14: 'The love of God constrains me', he stressed that this is the reason why 'we [the house of bishops] made presentations [to Amin]'; 'this is why His Grace [Archbishop Luwum] spoke with the president on the 14 February for a long session—a clear, truthful, Christian presentation' (p. 8, #22); and this is why 'we stood on the 16 [at the mass meeting of government officials, army, church leaders, ambassadors called by Amin]' (p. 8, #22).

On 16 October 1977 the misery of the Ugandans becomes the platform from which Kivengere called upon his audience at Fremont, California, to be agents of reconciliation, 'Ambassadors For Christ in a Miserable World' (2 Cor 5:18).[57] He links Amin's murder of Luwum and the ongoing

---

search of the homes of Archbishop Luwum and Bishop Yona Okoth (Bukedi diocese, and later Archbishop of Uganda) by Amin's State Research Bureau; the intimidation of civilians by the security agents; the war against the educated; and the threat to life and property by the security agents.

54. J. Bowyer Bell, *Assassin: Theory and Practice of Political Violence* (New Brunswick: Transaction Publishers, 2005), 132.

55. Festo Kivengere, 'Let Your Life And Power Go Out', Sermon Transcript, June 1977, p. 1, #1, AO: 197706[--].

56. Festo Kivengere, 'Festo Relates His Escape Story', Sermon Transcript, March 1977, AO: 197703[--]. This sermon was later aired in 1982 on an AE Pasadena radio broadcast.

57. Kivengere, 'Ambassador For Christ'.

persecution in Uganda to 'the fallen nature of humanity'. As an ambassador of Christ, each member of his audience can pray for and help Ugandans. Kivengere appeals to the body of Christ at Fremont Presbyterian Church to work within the framework of the universal church under the Lordship of Christ.

Kivengere is preaching ten months after he fled into exile from Idi Amin (17 February 1977), so the misery in the world, in particular Uganda's suffering under Amin, is very much on his heart. Kivengere has since known the frustration of being misunderstood by some U.S. senators through his friend Don Jacobs,[58] and his wife has cautioned him no longer to be speaking in public about Idi Amin because their children in Uganda have been victims of assassination attempts,[59] even though he had forgiven Idi Amin four months ago. Even though he is in exile, Kivengere is still busy traversing the globe, preaching the gospel. He is also concerned with informing the wider world about the situation in Uganda,[60] especially the churches and asking for their prayers for Uganda and support of Ugandan refugees. A much clearer picture of prayer and support that he is seeking

---

58. For his connection with his friends in the Mennonite Church like Don Jacobs, who linked him with the U.S. Senators, see chapter One, 2.3 'Campaign for Ugandan Refugees and Coffee Farmers'. After his addresses to the U.S. Senators about what was going on in Uganda Don was approached by staff persons asking him whether the addresses were Kivengere's campaign to replace Idi Amin: "Is Festo planning to become Uganda's Bishop Markarios"? . . . I finally confided to Festo what was being said in the corridors . . . He picked his Bible, tucked it under his arm, walked a step or two and said, "This is my politics, the word of God, and I have no ambition greater than to preach the mighty word of God", reports Coomes. See Coomes, *Festo Kivengere*, 372–73.

59. See 'News Makers: Exiled Bishop here to beat freedom drum', *The Australian*, February 6, 1978. 'One of Bishop Kivengere's four daughters, Charity (the others are Peace, Joy and Hope) was beaten by Amin's soldiers and still bears the scars, he says'. Coomes reports that 'Every time Festo gave an interview to the BBC or an American radio reporter about Amin and Uganda, she [Mera] would round on him furiously: "Peace [one of their four daughters] is killed it will be your fault!'. See Coomes, *Festo Kivengere*, 273.

60. See, Episcopal Press and News, March 8, 1979: 'The Friday night banquet will feature exiled Ugandan Bishop Festo Kivengere, whose banquet speech will tell the story of his escape from Uganda after threats to his life following the assassination of Archbishop Luwum in 1977'. See, 'Anglican Fellowship of Prayer to Meet', *Episcopal News Service*, March 8, 1979, Cited 30 Dec 2010, Online: http://www.episcopalarchives.org/cgi-bin/ ENS/ENSpress_release.pl?pr_number=79076. Accessed 30th December 2010. Kivengere, *Address to the National Press Club*.

for Ugandans, especially refugees throughout the period in exile is illuminated by the documentation of his Australian agenda just four months after this sermon.

He wrote an appeal to Australian Christians saying 'Please hear the cry of my country's refugees. My burden is to give release to these people—to share with them the love of Christ and the eventual reconstruction of Uganda. These people need life's essentials while they try to find shelter, pick up their education or find a job'.[61] One of Kivengere's main concerns is that 'the country is undergoing a tremendous drain of brainpower. I feel deeply for them because I too escaped narrowly'.[62] Kivengere not only invited his audience to enter the scene of his message with the spiritual and social needs of Ugandans. Kivengere also has had political concerns. Because of what he is going through and especially his concern for the people of Uganda, he makes strong political statements.

The statements focus clearly his political hope: 'Countries fortunate to have democratic Governments should speak more forcibly against President Idi Amin's rule of Uganda'. 'By speaking up more in international assemblies such as the United Nation, free countries could do a great deal to bring pressure on president Amin to stop "dehumanization" of [his] subjects'.[63] At this stage as he comes to preach this sermon, Kivengere believed that Amin's downfall was inevitable. He asks: 'Show me a dictator right through history who did not eventually fall'.[64] He is careful to undergird his political statements with Scripture, as Scripture directly addresses the subject he is dealing with. So he said, 'God never allows anyone to take the authority upon themselves to remove lives at will, violently, and this is what Amin is doing. The regime is writing its own death warrant'.[65]

One of his main sources about Uganda is from his staff at the African Enterprise Office in Nairobi, Kenya, where many Ugandan refugees

---

61. See Church Scene, 'Appeal for Ugandan Refugees Launched', *Church Scene*, February 9, 1978. 'Ugandan Bishop Visits Brisbane', *Telegraph*, February 8, 1978. 'Help for Uganda Refugees'. 'The Appeal is designed to aid at least 50,000 refugees Bishop Kivengere says . . . some of these are students from Makerere University, some are professional people'.
62. See 'Help for Uganda Refugees'.
63. See 'Appeal by Bishop: Speak on Uganda', *Sydney Morning Herald*, February 6, 1978.
64. See 'Appeal by Bishop'.
65. See 'Appeal by Bishop'.

fleeing from Amin would first report for help. In the face of the misery of Ugandans, Kivengere expects his audience to be ambassadors of reconciliation for Christ to a miserable world (2 Cor 5:18); hence the appeal to his audience to be 'Ambassadors for Christ in this miserable world'.

Kivengere's appeal arises from two fronts. Firstly, the ongoing persecution in Uganda and what he calls 'the fallen nature of humanity'. Amin killed Luwum and is still killing Ugandans as a result of the fall of humanity. And, secondly, each member of his audience is called to be 'Ambassador for Christ' (2 Cor 5:20). For this reason, they have a role to pray and help Ugandans. Kivengere's appeal has the effect of stirring the body of Christ at Fremont Presbyterian Church to work within the framework of the universal church under the Lordship of Christ, to be 'Ambassadors for Christ' in a suffering and miserable world telling people to become friends of God.

In October 1977, at Saratoga Evensong, USA, in a 'Bishop Festo Mission', Kivengere preached reconciliation with the theme 'Broken Relationships Restored'.[66] His message focused on God breaking down the barriers that men and women built between him and us. 'When Christ came, the only purpose of his mission was to restore broken relationships between these human beginnings and this God from whom they came; and, having restored their vertical relationship with the father, God, then the horizontal relationship between man and man was restored'.[67]

In October 1977, Kivengere was awarded the International Freedom Prize in Oslo, Norway. The recognition distinguished him internationally as one who performed outstanding feats in defence of freedom.[68] In his defence of freedom and human rights, reconciliation was the message he used to address issues of oppression and injustices in Africa.[69]

In May 1978, he was preaching reconciliation at Wheaton Bible College at a mission conference.[70] Noting that the church is a new community

---

66. Kivengere, 'Broken Relationships Restored'.
67. Kivengere, 'Broken Relationships Restored', p. 6, #12.
68. Olson Warwick, 'Festo Kivengere—The King's Grandson Who Became a Greater King's Servant', *AE* (May 1988): 6.
69. See Chapters Five and Six. The introductory part of his sermons in which he first explain the injustices and oppressions of the suffering people in Uganda, South Africa and other parts of the world, before applying the gospel message of reconciliation.
70. Kivengere, 'The Whole Gospel For The Whole World'.

created out of the suffering of Christ, he deplored the divisions within the church in Africa. By 1978, the church in Africa is afflicted with foreign ideologies that have become isolating forces. The only message that can heal the wounds and brokenness of Africa is Calvary-love.

On 29 April 1979, one week before his return to Uganda from exile, Kivengere preached at *LaCanada* Presbyterian Church, Pasadena, California.[71] The focus of his message was reconciliation between God and man, and between man and his neighbour. Reconciliation is the only antidote to Uganda's deep wounds. Food, clothing, medicine and shelter are important, but they cannot go deep enough into wounded hearts in order to bring transformation. Kivengere saw the needs of Uganda post-Amin, and summed it in three words: Return [Relief], Reconstruction, and Reconciliation (p. 3, #7–#8). All are important, but to Kivengere, reconciliation is to be put 'in the centre' 'at the bottom' as 'the foundation' (p. 3, #7–#8). There are deep wounds opened in Uganda, such as the desire for revenge over family members who have been murdered (p. 3, #7–#8). No matter how much relief is given, it won't deal with such deep wounds, which only have one antidote: reconciliation (p. 4, #8).

4.4 After the Exile (May 1979 to May 1988)

On 10 May 1979, Kivengere addressed a press conference arranged by World Vision, in Nairobi, Kenya, soon after the Nairobi City Mission.[72] In his address, he explains his primary role as a minister of reconciliation in Uganda post-Amin, spelling in detail what they agreed at Moshi Unity Conference for the transitional government since Amin's rule had fallen.

In January 1980, he preached reconciliation through the risen Lord (from Heb 10:9) to the First United Methodist Church, Texas.[73] On 22 April 1980, Kivengere flew to Pasadena, where he preached reconciliation

---

71. Kivengere, 'In Christ'.
72. Kivengere, 'World Vision: with Festo Kivengere'.
73. Kivengere, 'Costly Breakthrough'.

at All Saints Episcopal Church.[74] He reported the exciting job of reconstruction and rehabilitation in Uganda, noting that it was 'a very tough job'. He acknowledged that they are preaching to thousands of widows who come with little babies in their hands. Their fathers have been eliminated during the terrible reign of Amin (p. 6, #19): 'you stand there and tell of the hope, love, which can put them together. This is not easy preaching, brethren' (p. 7, #20).

As Kivengere preached reconciliation to Ugandans, it brought him into direct confrontation with the politicians: 'as soon as you preach the message of God's love, the possibility of his redeeming grace, then you open new spheres to embarrass yourself'. Because the people become uniquely important, you cannot therefore 'forget their political freedom, social needs, stand in society, feeding their body'. In this way he finds himself speaking with politicians on behalf of those who are being unjustly treated. 'The gospel has opened our eyes to the value of God's harvest' (p. 8, #26).

On 10 May 1980, at Long Island, New York, during a diocesan conference, he preached reconciliation from Luke 24:30–35 on the theme: 'The Resurrection or Burning Hearts'.[75] After explaining about the situation in Uganda which resulted in their escape into exile where they lived for two years before returning back, he brought greetings from millions of Christians in Uganda who went through the fire of persecution and harassment under Amin (p. 1, #1). Eight years under Amin created broken hearts. Even though Amin is gone the problems are still there (p. 2, #5). He thanked them for their prayers that enabled them to return to Uganda.

Using the language of reconciliation, he explains from the text the misery of the disciples on the 'Dark Friday' Jesus died and the difference that death made. Jesus' death and resurrection made a new day to the community. 'It was a new day because the wounds which human beings have incurred through sin now [are] healed. The breakdowns of human experience can now be picked up' (p. 6, #12). Out of the breakdown, Jesus created a new community.

---

74. Festo Kivengere, 'Divine Sensitivity', Sermon Transcript (Preached at Santa Barbara, California, April 21, 1980), AO:19800421.
75. Kivengere, 'The Resurrection or Burning Hearts'.

Jesus explains to his disciples the meaning of his wounds. 'And the cross became a shining experience of hope, the centre of healing of a broken community' (p. 6, #12). This is the message of the cross. If Christians saw it, 'broken relationships would have been healed by the wounded hands. Racial tensions would never have existed' (p. 7, #13). In the presence of Jesus who died and rose again, 'walls are smashed, and alienations are removed. God and man are brought together'. In the presence of the bleeding God, man discovers his brother; and, a new authentic identity (p. 7. #13)—there is the language of reconciliation.

The message of reconciliation springs from the cross. He told the story of how on 10 February 1973, Amin ordered his soldiers to shoot three Christian men of his church in public at Kabale stadium, before a crowd of 3,000 people.

> The first [public] executions in the history of Uganda. Twelve Ugandans are going to be shot in their respective towns by firing squad. Why? They are subversives. I had a big problem as a newly consecrated bishop. I had to go to Amin and make a protest . . . I sat with him for one hour. I poured my heart out . . . I challenged Amin . . . I did not expect to return. I was in pain because Ugandans were going to be shot . . . Ugandans created in the image of God . . . Ugandans for whom Christ died . . . I went round Uganda preaching and telling everybody the victory of the risen Christ (pp. 9–10, #21).

The following Sunday Kivengere preached in the area of one of the three men who was shot dead. There were about 3,000 people there. All in sadness, but when he told them the message of their son, 3,000 people burst into a song of praise (p. 11, #23). In this story, Kivengere concludes with a challenge that every man and women whose eyes have been opened by the message of the cross, the gospel message, has a responsibility to tell others how much God loves them (p. 11, #23). Again, there is a language of reconciliation.

On 5 October 1980, at St. Andrew's Presbyterian Church, Newport Beach, California, on the occasion of World Communion Sunday, he preached reconciliation from Luke 22:14–20, from the theme: 'The Master Came Down'. On bringing greetings from brothers and sisters in Uganda and East Africa as a whole, he reports that their prayer support in many ways, sympathy and in participation under God, has supported 'the ministry of his reconciling love to be proclaimed'. The ministry now has grown into many aspects—'not only to proclaim the very needed word of reconciliation, and if there has ever been a time, in the history of Africa when the message of reconciliation is needed, that time is today' (p. 1, #2).

This historical claim, echoes a similar historical claim he made seven months ago at Mukono Chapel. However, here he adds the scope to include Africa. It is not surprising, since by 1971 when he founded his AEE, his vision has been to preach reconciliation throughout African cities and universities.[76]

A year ago Amin was defeated, but Uganda has remained with 'very deep wounds, which need God alone to heal' (p. 2, #3). Besides the deep wound, from his knowledge as the first National Chairman of Relief and Rehabilitation of Uganda, he lists more: there are more than a half a million orphans and widows, pain of shattered lives, embittered lives, men and women almost given to an attitude of revenge, guns in indiscriminate hands, famine caused by drought and insecurity (p. 2, #3). To this gruesome picture of his preaching context, he adds the South African wounds: 'I was preaching in Cape Town, Durban, Soweto, Johannesburg and Pietermaritzburg . . . preaching in a situation . . . people are starving out of a famine of inhuman relationships' (p. 4, #7). Reconciliation is not far away from his explanation of the suffering in Africa.

Paraphrasing Jesus' words from the text, 'this is the New Covenant God has made with shattered humanity', he explains that the blood symbolises 'the suffering love for humanity', 'healing love for broken humanity', 'reconciling love for alienated humanity' (p. 7, #12)—there is reconciliation in his explanation. In Soweto as well as in Kampala where guns and dead bodies are everywhere, 'politicians making their noises as usual . . . and they have promised us another utopia', the medicine to this problem is in the covenant that Jesus based on the self-sacrificing love (p. 8, #13).

---

76. See Chapter Two, 2. 'Reconciliation and Kivengere's Sermons'.

If Soweto, Kampala, Northern Ireland, and the United States are going to heal, there is going to be a movement downwards (Phil 2:5–11) like that downward movement which Jesus took in order to meet men and women in the arena of their brokenness (p. 8, #14). Jesus came to restore us to our humanness (p. 9, #15). This is the Christian hope. In Pretoria he challenged a government minister for crowding the people in Soweto and he visited his friend Desmond Tutu whose passport had been removed by the government because of his outspokenness.[77] In the seeming hopelessness of suffering in South Africa, there was still hope—hope in the New Covenant which God has established at the cost of the life of his Son Jesus Christ (p. 11, #18).

Desmond Tutu in the hopelessness still saw himself and his country in the light of this hope: 'Because I believe in Jesus who died and rose again, I am a member of the community of hope' (p. 10, #18). In Desmond Tutu's hope, reconciliation is in view for Kivengere, when as he said: 'But he [Desmond Tutu] is a member of that body which was broken for us and it was broken that human beings with broken relationships may be made whole again' (p. 10, #18),—there for Kivengere is reconciliation.

On the 7 October 1980, Kivengere preached at the University Club, Pasadena, on the theme 'Compassion Harvest', drawing upon Matthew 9:35–36.[78] He described what he saw when he looked upon the crowds of Uganda:

> [W]hen you look at the people, you know that they have got wounds; you know among them there are widows, orphans, created by Amin; you go to Karamoja and you find that schools have been closed because of starvation; you first give porridge and then preach the gospel. That is the holistic nature of the gospel in the world of 1980 (p. 3, #4).

---

77. Jake C. Miller, *Prophets of a Just Society* (New York: Nova, 2002), 129. For the retuning of his passport, see, John Allen, *Rabble-Rouser for Peace: The Authorized Biography of Desmond Tutu* (New York: Simon and Schuster, 2006), 189.
78. Kivengere, 'Compassion Harvest'.

He spoke of a 'gun culture' in Uganda, caused by so many guns left in indiscriminate hands by the fleeing Amin soldiers. After the Karamojong 'helped themselves' to the guns from the deserted Moroto Army barracks after the Uganda National Liberation Army (UNLA) overthrew Amin, they used them to raid cattle, killing many innocent people.

He also reported on his opportunities to preach through AEE organized missions in Southern Africa. In Zimbabwe, the 'Fox Fire' sent out young people who love the Lord Jesus into camps of the guerrilla fighters (p. 15. #14). From Pretoria he went to Soweto, a city where he and Michael Cassidy preached in a situation that Kivengere described as 'politically confused and rather bloody' (p. 6, #15). He observed that 'we need to be liberated by the love of God [through] the ministry of reconciliation' (p. 6, #17).

On 26 October 1980, at Christ Church Overland Park, Kansa City, USA, Kivengere preached reconciliation on the theme: 'How a Person can be Sure of his Right Relationship with God' (2 Cor 8:9). As he stated five months ago, again, he tells that Amin is gone from Uganda, but he has left his trail with over half a million widows and orphans. The need care and love. The church is the agent of reconciliation, reconstruction, and rehabilitation (p. 2, #7).

Kivengere explains reconciliation from the perspective of the cross using the language of grace: 'Let us go to the cross. There you will see when love becomes grace' (p. 5, #19). When love loves to the point of saying 'My father, please forgive these men, they don't understand what they are doing'—at that point of loving the unlovely, of welcoming the enemy, of forgiving the sinner, of embracing the unembracable, and of welcoming the unwelcome—the New Testament, then says now love is grace (p. 6, #20). Earlier he said that 'Jesus came full of grace' (John 1) (p. 5, #16). 'Grace is radical love' (p. 6, #20). There is reconciliation, but being explained from the New Testament perspective of the cross using the language of grace. He explains with the story of Janani Luwum whom Amin murdered, a wonderful man of God, a great preacher, that once you know this amazing love, amazing grace, you become exposed (p. 10, #29).

In December 1980, in a Christmas message he dictated over telephone from London to Nairobi, the theme was 'Jesus Came as Light and Life for Men' (John 1:6–11). Early in the year Kivengere addressed himself strongly on the message of reconciliation and now he closed the year and looks into the feature for Uganda and beyond with the same conviction that reconciliation is the only message and hope. After recalling his recent mission trips to Switzerland and Holland, he reports his recognition and award: 'yesterday at the World Council of Churches headquarters I received the Edward Browning award for the ministry of evangelism in which I have been engaged. Of course, it was quite an experience as my friend Emilio Castro introduced me with beautiful words in the chapel of WCC. . . . I was given an opportunity to share the message and I spoke from Romans 1:14–16. . . . They kept me very busy speaking to various committees'.

In the light of Jesus' words in John 1:6–11, 'And in Him (Christ) was life and the life was the light of men. And the life kept shining in darkness and the darkness has never succeeded in putting it out', he sees these words absolutely fitting life in a world rushing headlong into chaos as in Africa—mentioning Uganda, Zimbabwe, South Africa and other parts of the world (p. 1, #4–#5). He lists the chaos as seen in 'politics, economics, social relationships, homes, and intellectual understanding' (p. 1, #4–#5). Looking at the world without the light, which comes from Our Lord and Saviour Jesus Christ, it is not a hopeful world. Reconciliation is not far away.

Apart from the light, Jesus Christ in whom there is life and light for men, 'men are engulfed in destructive darkness' and there is no understanding because darkness takes away the ability to see. Christmas draws us near and the light shines in darkness and God steps into the chaos of men and women he created in his image (p. 2, #6).[79] God's practical stepping in his Son into our chaos is his love for us. He insisted that: this is the only hope for Uganda and South Africa; this is the only hope in this chaos; the only message which can restore sense into this human nonsense; the only message which can really take hold of broken pieces, put them together and create a new community made up of men and women with a new relationship based on his unbreakable love; this is the only message which can heal (p. 2, #6).

---

79. Festo Kivengere, 'Jesus Came as Light and Life for Men', Sermon Transcript, December 25, 1980, AO: 19801225.

He sees so much brokenness in life—wounds incurred by men against each other and against themselves. The Christmas message is a message of reconciliation, because God became man and in him is life. This life is the very light of everyman. Even in darkness and chaos, the light has proved stronger than the darkness because it is based on God's love, which is stronger than death (p. 2, #7).

The things he shared are so blatant and clear in Uganda, however, 'this message has proved the only message and hope for the hopeless, the only message with a centre for the centre-lessness, which we feel and hear. This is the only message with direction where life seems to be going in circles of utter meaninglessness'. He is praising God that when all seemed dark, God stepped forward and his coming has brought not only hope but also real life. 'Jesus has come. And love has increasingly overcome death, hatred, resentment'. The reconciliation language of Romans 5 is employed here: while we were still sinners, helpless, Christ died for us.

He concludes that the central message of Christmas is 'restoration, reconciliation and healing for all people everywhere, particularly my people in Uganda and for Africa in general: A continent of hope'. Kivengere sees Africa suffering from 'destructive ideologies, greed of men, wars', and he prays for God to 'save us from this chaos and restore us to himself' (p. 3, #8–#9),—there Kivengere ends the year with the message of reconciliation that is close on his heart.

In October 1981, accompanied by Bishop Misaeri Kauma (Namirembe diocese) and Rev'd John Wilson (AEE), Kivengere travelled to England for a mission arranged by the CMS Ruanda Mission, code-named 'From Uganda with Love' (Luke 10:25).[80] This mission had been planned for May 1979, which Kivengere had postponed in order to return to Uganda soon after the fall of President Idi Amin. At that time, although hundreds of thousands of pounds were lost in bookings for venues and accommodation, the organizers had agreed that Kivengere should return to Uganda (p. 1, #1). They preached in several churches, which were always packed beyond the seating capacity of the churches. The Archbishop of Canterbury, Robert

---

80. Kivengere, 'From Uganda With Love'.

Runcie, awarded each of them with the St. Augustine's cross, for outstanding work of spreading the gospel with the Anglican Communion.

In the sermon, Kivengere reported about the situation in Uganda since 1977 to 1981, both negative and positive. The purpose of this message was to fulfil an earlier aborted mission because Kivengere had to return to Uganda as soon as Kampala fell to the joint TPDF/UNLF and to update the UK churches and friends of Uganda on the ministry of reconciliation in Uganda post-Amin.

He tells them they are back to share with Britain what Christ means to Ugandans in the difficult times they experienced (p. 1, #1). Linking his message to the text (Luke 10:25), he explained the segregative attitude of the Jews displayed by the religious teacher who asked Jesus to tell him 'who is my neighbour?' This is the problem in Uganda, including Britain, Northern Ireland, Zimbabwe and Soweto (p. 3, #4). He links back to Jesus' parable of the Good Samaritan. There are many people lying by the roadside, perhaps not beaten up by bandits. He gives a long list of situations of suffering not uncommon to Britain and Uganda: unemployment, inflation, dictatorship, racial segregation, broken experiences, etc. (pp. 5–6, #6–#8).

He concludes that reconciliation is within view. 'The world needs a rediscovery of who is my neighbour' (p. 9, #11–12). To discover him is a disturbing experience; Christians in Uganda are discovering that you cannot discover your neighbour and sit back. They [Bishops of COU] had to go to Amin to plead for justice knowing the dangers involved. 'But there is no way you can preach the good news and sit back' (p. 9, #11–12). When a Christian tell a person that 'God loves you and died for you', it makes the person become very important, thus, the person's justice, rights, and welfare becomes 'a very important business for you the preacher' (p. 9, #12).

Kivengere then proceeds to explain how three years after the fall of Amin's rule, together with his AEE organization and colleagues, addressed the broken state of the human heart and body of the Karamojong during the natural calamity, namely, the famine that hit hard the Karamoja region.[81] Despite the famine, elsewhere he tells of the problem of a gun cul-

---

81. Coomes, *Festo Kivengere*, 404. Large parts of Northern and Eastern Uganda were affected by the famine, especially Karamoja region. Kivengere visited Karamoja himself and described the situation: 'The little children who came and put their frail hands in

ture that complicated life in Karamoja. In 1979, when Idi Amin's soldiers fled from the approaching liberators, the joint TPDF and UNLA, they left behind them sub-machine guns and hand grenades in the Moroto army barracks, where the Karamojong warriors 'helped themselves to them'.

Traditionally among the Karamojong there existed a culture of raiding cattle but using primitive weapons: spears, bows and arrows. Now they upgraded their military strength and intensified raids among themselves, ambushing travellers, especially trucks they suspected were carrying foodstuff or money, leading to the loss of many lives ('10,000 people died'). Fear of being attacked as one travelled in the Karamoja region was real and travelling was a very risky thing to do. But because the love of Christ compels Kivengere and his AEE teammates to reach out to the suffering with the love of Christ, they left their comfort zone and took the risk to travel in the dangerous roads of Karamoja, taking the gospel of reconciliation to the suffering Karamojong.

Kivengere as National Chairman for relief in the country and as a preacher of reconciliation travelled in person to Karamoja to inspect the distribution of foodstuff, medicine, seeds and hoes for cultivation. Kivengere was not a bystander or never offered mere lip service to the suffering Karamojong: he was practical. How? He tells them that 'we preached the gospel and then we gave soup and beans' (pp. 2–3, #3). Their style of preaching practically brought the Lord Jesus into people's lives by meeting 'their *physical* and *spiritual* needs'.

Kivengere's approach seeks to follow the Lord Jesus' model, 'He [Jesus] feeds the hungry, heals the sick, touches the untouchables, forgives the guilty' and this is "beyond comparison"' (pp. 2–3, #3). He adds that in universities and schools in Uganda, the human condition is full of 'suffering, pain, loneliness, and shattering experience' (pp. 2–3, #3).[82] Regarding these situations he posed the questions: any antidote? Words?

---

mine . . . I felt the heart beat of suffering humanity . . . bellies and extended arms legs like matchsticks . . . I was moved to tears'.

82. For an example of a shattering experience in one University, Makerere, see Pirouet, *Historical Dictionary of Uganda*, 240–42. '[O]ne woman student suffered multiple rape. Throughout the day batches of students including some women were taken in lorries to Makindye Barracks were they were roughed up . . . There were further violence on the campus in the afternoon when some soldiers returned, apparently against orders'.

The bishop clearly aims in the introduction to name the suffering in Uganda, especially Karamoja. He also named the theological framework that drives his preaching of reconciliation in the face of suffering such as famine in Karamoja. Now he tells his audience that in the difficult situations in Uganda, there have been moments 'beyond human ability to cope with, but Jesus gives the ability to cope with the situation' (p. 3, #5).

After the murder of Archbishop Luwum, President Amin's soldiers took his body buried away from his cathedral in the city to his home church in [Kitgum].[83] For four days 5,000 Christians who had come to bury his body at his cathedral held a service without his body since the government had transported it to Kitgum so that they may not see the torture inflicted on the body. At the service, they were praising and singing their hallelujahs at his cathedral, St. Paul's Cathedral.[84]

On 2 November 1981, at Pasadena office, USA, Kivengere preached reconciliation at the AE staff, from the theme: 'I am the Light of the World' (John 8:1–12).[85] Jesus said he is the light of the world; those who follow him don't walk in darkness. He lists darkness to include mistaking each person and simply categorising them according to work or gifts. He exhorts the staff 'when you are in that light here in Pasadena, each one of you is very precious, to each other, when your commitment is not only to the Lord vertically, but it is to the other person horizontally'. Kivengere is telling them to live reconciled lives with God and with each other.

In February 1982, two years since he returned from exile, Kivengere preached at Presbyterian Church Missionary Commitment, Detroit. He urged his listeners to take the love of Christ out into the world, the message of reconciliation. Christ is the dynamic by which they can reach out into the world, because he came as a missionary of reconciliation.[86]

---

83. Pirouet, *Historical Dictionary of Uganda*, 230.
84. St. Paul's Cathedral Namirembe, located in Kampala city, serves a double function: first as the official seat of the Bishop of Namirembe diocese; secondly as the Provincial Cathedral of the COU. It is in this latter respect that Kivengere refers to as his Cathedral. The official seat of Archbishop Luwum (as Bishop of Kampala diocese) is All Saints Cathedral, Kampala.
85. Festo Kivengere, 'I Am The Light Of The World', Sermon Transcript (Preached at Pasadena, California, November 2, 1981), AO: 19811102.
86. Kivengere, 'Jesus Came as a Missionary'.

On 16 February 1982, at Pasadena, California, USA, on the occasion of the 20th anniversary of AE, Kivengere preached reconciliation (2 Kgs 4).[87] After explaining the history of AE, its connection with Pasadena and Kivengere, he looks back at the history of Africa and tells of open doors for missions in African, in particular Uganda (pp. 1–3, #1–#4).

Kivengere now tells of reconciliation as an indispensible need in Uganda. 'The president and his cabinet members told of their lack of what it takes to rehabilitate the twisted Ugandans, their morals shattered, the economy in shambles and they are exploiting each other' (p. 6, #9). The Christian evangelists and minister have got what it takes to rehabilitate Uganda—reconciliation message. He ends with a story of reconciliation between a man who planed to kill another man but on hearing the message of reconciliation was transformed: 'he went to the man he intended to murder, and put it right, asked for reconciliation, the other man was a Christian' (p. 9, #14). This is the work AEE is involved in: the ministry of reconciliation.

In April 1982, in Israel, Kivengere preached reconciliation on the occasion of 'Celebration of Evangelism'. This sermon was a result of the successful mission in Egypt in 1978 that involved Jews, Arabs, and missionaries in Haifa, Jerusalem and Tel Aviv.[88] In the sermon he gave a clear and succinct testimony of his conversion to illustrate how conversion is synonymous with reconciliation.

On 10 October 1982, Kivengere preached to packed services in England, with a message emphasizing a new way of looking at Jesus—a way that gives you a new understanding of the world.[89] In Israel, he saw reconciliation together with 250 people who just gazed in amazement, because the unthinkable had happened. An Arab and a Jew in each other's arms, reconciled when planes were flying over their heads, preparing for bombing; yet here was an Arab and a Jew 'weeping together, getting reconciled' (p. 9, #14). Using medical language, he tells that 'it was as if the Arab was given new optics, and he saw in the Jew, no longer just a Jew representing an enemy camp, but a brother created in the image of God the Father of Jesus

---

87. Festo Kivengere, '20th Anniversary of African Enterprise', Sermon Transcript (Preached at Pasadena, California, February 16, 1982), AO: 19820216.
88. Coomes, *Festo Kivengere*, 419.
89. Kivengere, 'A New Way of Seeing Jesus'.

Christ and redeemed at the price of a redeeming blood' (pp. 9–10, #14). This reconciliation represented 'a new way of seeing' (cf. 2 Cor 5:16). He makes a flashback to the theme in Ephesians 2:14: 'the two, as they stood there embracing, they represented Ephesians chapter 2, two become one' (p. 10, #14). He is explicitly preaching reconciliation.

On 15 July 1983, Kivengere had the opportunity to address the Amsterdam assembly of International Itinerant Evangelists.[90] The focus of his message was the ministry of reconciliation that has been handed to us as a precious treasure. The church must recover the preaching of reconciliation wherever it is not being taught or being taught inappropriately. Reconciliation must be taught in the context of Jesus Christ.

In 1984, Kivengere contributed an article entitled, 'Bleeding Africa', to *Proclaiming Christ in his World,* dedicated to his friend Sigurd Aske on his seventieth birthday.[91] In the article, he states his carefully considered philosophy of social and political reconstruction that reconciliation through the cross of Christ is needed to overcome socio-political problems. The title of his article carries the negative overtones of haemorrhage and violence: 'I am, however, convinced that bleeding experiences have all along marked the continent of Africa with their indelible marks'.[92]

Historically Africa bled profusely through bloody tribal and clan hostilities and wars that left behind 'a trail of deep, bleeding wounds, of widows, orphans, slaves and cripples. Africa paid and still pays dearly through those destructive and violently executed wars'.[93] Socially, there are still barriers in African societies accented and largely protected by several features. He lists the features: 'language, "status quo", tribal and clannish taboos, physical appearance, superiority in power between the "rule" and the "ruled"'. Although these social barriers were not responsible for bloodbaths as in the case of tribal wars, 'they were responsible for the formation of impenetrable barriers of alienation, with the resulting bitterness and hatred. These

---

90. Kivengere, 'The Evangelist's Ministry of Reconciliation'.
91. Kivengere, 'Bleeding Africa', 25–29.
92. Kivengere, 'Bleeding Africa', 25.
93. Kivengere, 'Bleeding Africa', 25.

embittered attitudes in turn produced wounded hearts and lives and twisted them in the direction of revenge and violent relations'.[94]

The origins of modern bloody revolutions in Rwanda and Burundi between the Hutu and Tutsi tribes fighting against each other in the early sixties, and the displacement of innocent people in Mbarara-Bushenyi Districts in Western Uganda have their origins in the long-standing hatred between Hima and Iru tribes. 'The destruction of the accumulated properties of the well-to-do by the have-nots in Uganda in the seventies, the bloody overthrow of the Emperor in Ethiopia, all focus on the social conflicts based on the exploitation of the powerless by the powerful'.[95]

Economically, 'Africa has bled almost to death'. Its own kings and chiefs have exploited it. The upsurge of the industrial revolution in Western Europe and colonial expansion over new territories saw the desperate demand for raw materials and manpower to feed the mushrooming industries. Moreover, slave trade, with its philosophy of getting rich quickly, bled Africa almost to death. 'The slave trade cost 'bleeding Africa' millions of lives, and left behind a trail of deserted villages and heritage of deep gaping wounds of hatred, fear and vulnerability among the people of Africa. The economic exploitations which still suck the blood of the common citizen is still in our era of post-political independence'.[96]

Politically, 'Bleeding Africa' continues to have its political fragmentations that are based on tribes, kings, and empires. Conflicts from the ambitions of the emperors over boundaries and territorial expansions have remained part of African history, which by its very nature is full of violence.[97] Western European colonialists made this situation more complicated with their 'scramble for Africa'. Tribes were divided down the middle by the new colonial boundaries without regard for the people. The present nations of bleeding Africa are shining examples of the colonial fragmentation of Africa. 'The struggle for political independence has cost Africa dearly both in human blood and ideological hostilities which has sent millions into

---

94. Kivengere, 'Bleeding Africa', 25–26.
95. Kivengere, 'Bleeding Africa', 26.
96. Kivengere, 'Bleeding Africa', 26.
97. Kivengere, 'Bleeding Africa', 27.

mass graves'. He sees many millions of Africans living in refugee camps: 'In fact, at the present, Africa is a huge refugee camp'.[98] Bleeding Africa is full of forgotten people on the roadside of life—men, women, and children starve to death in the camps without food, water, medical care and security.[99] More blood has been shed in the post-independence era than before in most African nations. For example, Nigeria in the so-called 'Biafran War' lost a million people and 'In my country, precious lives have been violently eliminated because of party differences'.[100]

Racial hostilities have caused more bitterness, resentments, and discriminatory policies that breed injustices. Those who are discriminated against perennially and persistently experience the 'internal bleeding' that result in damning walls of repression and endurance that wash the nation with waves of blood such as the case of South Africa's discriminations and repressions.[101]

Spiritually, bleeding Africa in her search for the real living God has suffered greatly. 'African people are religious to the core. God is not reasoned into being, but is almost taken for granted'. However, when gropers after him turned to their own natural fears out of which taboos were developed, it enforced the practice of witch doctors and priests, which in some tribes encouraged the killing of twin babies and whole communities being massacred. 'The dawn of hope, of coming out of this haunted world of vicious spirits, came when God sent missionaries of the Good News to Africa'.[102]

Missionaries were God's messengers by whom he touched their hearts; he had opened their eyes to see Jesus, the light of the world. The missionaries shared the good news in action, teaching people to read God's message, established schools to enlighten the minds, and hospitals to heal the bodies.[103] The healing message of God's love in Christ was proclaimed. 'Like the woman of Mark 5:25–29, Africa "had been subject to bleeding" for many years. "She had suffered a great deal at the hands of many doc-

---

98. Kivengere, 'Bleeding Africa', 27.
99. Kivengere, 'Bleeding Africa', 27.
100. Kivengere, 'Bleeding Africa', 27.
101. Kivengere, 'Bleeding Africa', 27.
102. Kivengere, 'Bleeding Africa', 28.
103. Kivengere, 'Bleeding Africa', 28.

tors, and had spent all she had, yet instead of getting better, she grew worse. This was the turning point in the woman's history of suffering—"She heard about Jesus". Then "she came up behind him', she touched his cloak and her bleeding stopped"'.[104]

In all these, 'the answer to the perennially bleeding Africa is to hear about Jesus, come up following him and touch him'. In St. Peter's words: '"By His wounds" Africa's bleeding will be healed (1 Pet 2:24). It is in the bleeding love of Jesus that the historical scars of Africa will be turned into landmarks of praise to the God of love intervening in human affairs. It is the love of Christ alone which will break down the alienating and hostile walls of social structures and introduce men to a new society of God's children (Eph 2:12–18)'.[105] He emphasized that 'it is only in the sin-forgetting love of Jesus that our greedy exploitation of the world and each other will be exposed, judged and removed, and a fresh approach to the use of material things will take place'. Jesus teaches us that 'sharing with each other will bring more joy than selfish accumulation of wealth at the expense of the less fortunate'.[106]

Kivengere concludes that the love of Jesus alone can expose political opportunism and manipulation of people for power. Jesus alone can open the eyes of those who are called into politics to see the people they are meant to serve with new eyes, so that they might change policies to favour the welfare of the people.

The cross of Christ and the experience of his self-giving love is the antidote for Africa's poisonous racial discrimination and estrangement. Christ's barrier-breaking love is the only solution to the religious tensions that 'Africa inherited from her missionaries, and which are still acting as barriers in the churches'. Whatever the problem, 'only wounds heal wounds', and 'only the bleeding Christ can heal the bleeding Africa today'.[107]

In August 1985, Kivengere had an opportunity to put his gospel-shaped political philosophy into practice. On 27 July the military took control of

---

104. Kivengere, 'Bleeding Africa', 28.
105. Kivengere, 'Bleeding Africa', 28.
106. Kivengere, 'Bleeding Africa', 28.
107. Kivengere, 'Bleeding Africa', 28–29.

the country through a coup d'état, and Kivengere in a letter of 23 August, drafted a proposal for discussion at the House of Bishops on the need to encourage reconciliation between the leaders of the military government and rebels.[108] He proposed three things. First, that a government of national reconciliation should be formed. Second, if this government is formed, it must not be on political party lines. Thirdly, the army and the fighting rebels must lay down their arms and enter into a discussion for peace. Kivengere hoped that out of such a discussion would come a specific role of a Military Commission, which would reconstruct the existing Uganda Armed Forces into a National army. This reconstruction of the army would entail 'the de-tribalization of the Armed Forces'.

The present situation, therefore, demands that the COU must put forward a clear statement as to what should be done. This clear statement should be given to the press and shared with brethren in other churches in different parts of the world so that they could pray and help in bringing constructive ideas for Uganda. Such a statement, he cautions, does not mean the authorities will bow to the church, but that they will know the mind of the church about peace, justice and stability.

Kivengere's suggestions end with a personal confession that these were his personal thoughts, resulting from prayer and deep thought about the country. They did not arise simply because of the recent coup, but he has been thinking in this direction for quite some time. He gave his suggestions in the context of reconciliation and peace for the nation. A ripple of his message for peace and reconciliation was reiterated in the neighbouring Kenya in a call for reconciliation between the church and politicians.[109]

In March-April 1986, reconciliation was still a clear issue on his mind. Following the ascendency of President Yoweri Kaguta Museveni to power on 26 January 1986, from the military government of Tito Okello, Kivengere was optimistic that Museveni will restore peace. With this hope, he wrote:

---

108. Festo Kivengere, 'Proposal For Discussion at the House of Bishops Regarding Peace Talks for Uganda Government After the Coup D'état', Unpublished Proposal, August 1985, Archives of the Church of Uganda, Uganda Christian University. AO: 19850823.
109. 'Bishop Muge Faces a Barrage of Attacks', *The Weekly Review* (September 19, 1986): 6.

'Now comes a challenge to the Christian community in Uganda. Our ministry of reconciliation has never been needed as much as it is today'.[110]

In August 1986, Kivengere preached reconciliation at the fifth Kabale Convention, 'which could not take place in 1985 because of the war in Uganda'.[111] This was the Jubilee year (50 years) of the East African Revival. Kivengere explains the milestones in the revival's journey of forty-nine years, emphasizing that 'The centrality and supremacy of the Lord Jesus Christ permeated the whole movement from the start and continues to be the only valid reason for its continuation'.[112] He explains that the theme for 1975 Kabale Convention was 'Christ's Love Reconciles Us'; and, at the August 1985 Kabale Convention he explains that it was 'the first year of the unsearchable rich blessings of the Redeemer!' The Jubilee Year was set aside for four reasons: the proclamation of liberty throughout the land (the world) to all its inhabitants; the release of every slave (oppressed person); the reunion of every family (the separated ones); and the reconciliation and restitution of all wrongs.[113]

In the summer of 1987, Kivengere recalls that God gave them 'extra strength to share the message of his reconciling love'.[114] Their message was based on 'preaching Jesus Christ—crucified, risen, alive, and moving among his people'.[115] The Kenyan team was started in 1976 at the Pan African Leadership Assembly, a conference that was spearheaded by AEE. This conference is the turning point for AE because it became known to church leaders all over Africa: 'our ministry of reconciliation through Jesus himself became the message to run with'.[116] This message, Kivengere and his team used to address racial feelings that were hindering fellowship among them. He argued that if they were going to work with each other, then they must

---

110. Kivengere Festo, 'Good News For Uganda', *Outlook* 19/No. 2 (April 1986): 1.
111. 'Interview with Bishop Kivengere on the Nature of the Revival in East Africa', *AV* (February 1987): 3–5.
112. Festo Kivengere, 'Golden Jubilee Convention', in *Behold I Am Making All Things New* (Kabale, Uganda, 1975), 4.
113. Kivengere, 'Golden Jubilee Convention', 7–8.
114. Festo Kivengere, 'Reflections on a Dynamic Ministry', *Outlook* 20/3 (1987): 7.
115. Kivengere, 'Reflections on a Dynamic Ministry', 7.
116. Kivengere, 'Reflections on a Dynamic Ministry', 7.

be willing to come into the light to the Holy Spirit and experience healing. Only then can they go out and preach the gospel.[117]

In spring 1988, Kivengere published what would be his last public reflection, 'Unshakable Love',[118] before his death in May from malignant leukaemia.[119] Reconciliation, never far away from his thought, he wrote: 'Love sent Jesus, and it was love that made him walk for 33 years in the world. Every step was love, whether it was feeding the hungry, giving eyes to the blind . . . he could sit with a broken hearted woman at the well of Sychar . . . It was all love . . . The love of Jesus Christ on the cross and his blood on the cross can cleanse any sin . . . Any one is redeemable, for he loves us to the very end'. The language of 'the cross', 'broken heart', 'His blood', and 'redeemable' all are linked to reconciliation.

4.5 Summary of Reconciliation Time-line

The progress of Kivengere's preaching of reconciliation from 1971–1988 has been sketched. As we have seen, some years he preached reconciliation more than others. The chronology presented here is based primarily on the twenty-six sermons under our study. However, we have included other sermons that we deem to be of relevance to this study.[120] Given the sketch above, it is clear that he had been preaching reconciliation throughout his career.

We now turn to look at a few sermons he preached on the message of reconciliation.

---

117. Kivengere, 'Reflections on a Dynamic Ministry', 7.
118. Festo Kivengere, 'Unshakable Love', *Outlook* 21/1 (1988): 2.
119. 'Bishop Kivengere Seriously Ill in Nairobi', *Outlook* 21/1 (1988): 1.
120. For example, Kivengere, 'Divisions in the Church'; Kivengere, 'The Cross And World Evangelization'; Kivengere, 'Jesus Frees and Unites'; Kivengere, 'Festo Relates His Escape Story'; Kivengere, 'World Vision: with Festo Kivengere'; Festo Kivengere, 'God's Short-Cut To Humanity', Sermon Transcript (Preached at Christ Church Greenwich, CT, May 11, 1980), AO: 19800511*1; Kivengere, 'Compassion Harvest'; Kivengere, 'Costly Breakthrough'; Kivengere, 'Right Relationship With God'.

CHAPTER FIVE
Explicit Reconciliation Passages

5.1 A Synopsis

We begin our investigation into the role of the doctrine of reconciliation in the preaching of Kivengere by examining eighteen (18) sermons he preached from the Pauline passages that explicitly mention reconciliation.[1] As mentioned in chapter 1, the sermons are examined from a biblical-theological perspective. We argue in the investigation that Kivengere's sermons show two main points: reconciliation is 'the centre' of the New Testament and it is the Christian gospel, and the sermons exhorted his different audiences to 'be reconciled with God' (2 Cor 5:20) and then be reconciled with their fellow human beings as part of God's remedy for a broken world. One without the other is of no use: both are equally important and cannot be separated from each other.

---

1. The six sermons are from **2 Corinthians 5:18–20**: Kivengere, 'Ambassador For Christ'. Kivengere, 'In Christ'. Kivengere, 'The Cross Today'. Kivengere, 'The Reconciling Love of Christ'. Kivengere, 'Jesus Came as a Missionary'. Kivengere, 'Reconciliation'. This is followed by four (4) sermons he preached from **Romans 5:1–11**: (1) 'Surprised by Joy'. (2) Festo Kivengere, 'God's Intervening Love', Sermon Transcript (Preached at Presbyterian Church, Aurora, Illinois, July 29, 1975), AO: 19750729, [#1]. (3) Kivengere, 'The Love of Christ'. And, (4) Festo Kivengere, 'Life in Jesus', Sermon Transcript (Sydney, Australia, 1978), AO: 1978[----], [#1].'Life in Jesus': AO: 197802[--], [#1]). Followed by three (3) sermons he preached from **Ephesians 2:14–18**: (1) His Flooding Love: AO: 19750729, [#2], (2) 'Broken Relationships Restored': AO: 1977[----], (3) The Whole Gospel for the Whole Church: AO: 197805[--], [#2]. And, three (3) sermons he preached from **Colossians 1:19–22**: (1) Christ put all things together: AO: 1972[----], (2) The Unshakable Identity of the Church of Jesus Christ: AO: 19772910, [#1], and (3) 'Christ has reconciled the Universe to Himself': AO: 1979[05?--], [#2]).

In the process, this study considers several questions: (a) What is reconciliation according to Kivengere? (b) How does Kivengere's understanding of reconciliation compare with Pauline doctrine of reconciliation that we set up in chapter 3? (c) Does Kivengere exposit all, or overlook some? (d) What does Kivengere believe about preaching reconciliation? (e) Why does he preach and how does he preach reconciliation? (f) What aims does Kivengere have in preaching reconciliation? And, (g) what evidence do his sermons show for potential and actual impact of his kind of preaching reconciliation?

Answering these questions, we seek to analyze the role of the doctrine of reconciliation in Kivengere's preaching during the period 1971–1988 in Uganda and further afield. We are not aware of any study that has analyzed the role of the doctrine of reconciliation in Kivegere's preaching or even attempted to critique the connections between reconciliation and its related themes in his preaching.

5.2 Kivengere's Framework for Explaining Reconciliation

In the first sermon under our inquiry,[2] evidence for Kivengere making use of a New Testament framework around which he hangs his coherent thought and explanation of the Christian doctrine of reconciliation in his preaching is found in his call to prayer (p. 3, #5). He makes a major claim: 'reconciliation is the central message of the New Testament' (p. 3, #5). This assumed New Testament framework of explaining the Christian doctrine of reconciliation will feature throughout his sermons.

Kivengere's claim makes an assumption that is extended throughout his sermons; namely, reconciliation is securely based upon expectations generated by the Old Testament of the coming of Christ and the fulfilment of the Old Testament promises of God.[3] Kivengere appreciates the fact of rec-

---

2. Kivengere, 'Ambassador For Christ'.
3. E.g., see Festo Kivengere, 'Jesus is the Fulfilment of the Old Testament', Sermon Transcript, n.d., p. 4, #10, AO: [--------]*2.

onciliation as a central unifying theme in the New Testament. His sermons will show that, for him, reconciliation is not only found within Pauline letters but it is also found more broadly within the New Testament.

5.3 Reconciliation According to Kivengere

At the outset we need to be clear about what reconciliation is according to Kivengere in relation to (a) his understanding of how God relates to and rules over his created world, (b) how Kivengere views God's rule over history, in particular the history of Uganda and the suffering nations of Africa and beyond, and (c) how Kivengere explains the way the reality of (a) and (b) is affected by God's initiative of coming in his Son Jesus Christ into the brokenness in his world to redeem it.[4]

The way Kivengere explains reconciliation in the sermons will show that he was well acquainted with the context of his different audiences: cultural, religious, political and social life of the nations (Uganda and further afield) and its peoples with whom his preaching painstakingly engaged. More significantly his biblical theology started with the cross to explain reconciliation and how it works in the heart of believers, and applies to the context of his various audiences.

Kivengere considers that reconciliation has two dimensions: divine and human. His understanding of the divine-human (theological-social) dimensions of reconciliation comes clearly to the fore in the first set of six explicit reconciliation sermons.[5] First, we will see that right from the outset, his opening prayers clearly focus on reconciliation in Jesus Christ. For example, He reveals in these prayers that Jesus should shine so that when they catch the shining face of Jesus, 'they will see the reconciling love of Christ and become friends of God'.[6] On another occasion he prayed for the coming of Jesus 'into the arena of human confusion' [. . . and] 'put broken

---

4. Kivengere, 'Ambassador For Christ'.
5. The six sermons are from 2 Corinthians 5:18–20: Kivengere, 'Ambassador For Christ'. Kivengere, 'In Christ'. Kivengere, 'The Cross Today'. Kivengere, 'The Reconciling Love of Christ'. Kivengere, 'Jesus Came as a Missionary'. Kivengere, 'Reconciliation'.
6. Kivengere, 'Ambassador For Christ', p. 3, #6.

pieces [of humanity] together'.[7] At Mukono, he tells in his opening prayer that 'Jesus came to us on Good Friday'.[8] By mentioning Jesus' coming, he already focuses on reconciliation. Reconciliation begins with God who comes to man. These three examples already show the theological and social dimensions of reconciliation.

Second, as Kivengere explains reconciliation in his opening prayers to his explanation of reconciliation in the body of the sermons, he moves from the thought of 'old ways of keeping accounts' including sin, to 'a new creation' that has come about because of reconciliation in Christ Jesus.[9] Before his audience has 'caught the vision of Christ' from the cross for God's fresh doing, he credited his audiences with 'deep wounds', which have created hatred and a shattered society; 'tribes have slaughtered tribes' and 'racial tensions have made people enemies'.[10]

Into this terrible human situation, God has made Christ to be sin for all, with the result that their sins need no longer be held against them, and friendship between them and with God, and with each other is now possible. There is no more enmity. Now they are friends of God. Their new centre is located in Jesus Christ, who in his self-sacrificial love died on the cross and by his death for all, set man free from the paralyzing effects of sin.

Because this good news has been entrusted to them, they are now reconcilers,[11] and 'ambassadors for Christ in a miserable and broken world'.[12] Those who have embraced this reconciliation in Jesus Christ have a new identity in Christ, and they have become broader and can now proclaim on behalf of God this friendship that God has extended to his enemies. The analysis of the sermons will show that across the course of these sermons, Kivengere refines his understanding of reconciliation.

---

7. Kivengere, 'In Christ', p. 1, #1–#2.
8. Kivengere, 'The Cross Today', pp. 1–2, #2–#4.
9. Kivengere, 'Ambassador For Christ', pp. 4–5, #10–#11.
10. Kivengere, 'Ambassador For Christ', p. 5, #11.
11. Cf. Chapter One, 3.2.2 'John M. M. Senyonyi 1992'. Senyonyi has pointed out that for Kivengere, conversion is synonymous with being a reconciler.
12. Kivengere, 'Ambassador For Christ', p. 16, #29–#30 .

5.4 Explicit Reconciliation Sermons (I): 2 Corinthians 5:18–20 in Context

5.4.1 'Ambassadors For Christ': AO: 19771016[13]

5.4.1.1 Situating the Sermon

Kivengere preached this sermon at Fremont Presbyterian Church, Sacramento, USA, on 16 October 1977, at a Sunday morning Worship Service (9:30 am).

5.4.1.2 Preliminaries

After expressing gratitude for the opportunity to be with them and for being well looked after (p. 1, #1–#2), Kivengere encouraged them to continue to put their love in practice. 'True love makes ordinary things into extraordinary things'. He compared true love to the love of Christ, which he pictured like the developing fluid in photography, which brings out the image from the dark photo. That is why the love of Christ is called redeeming love, because it [brings] into being the qualities which you never thought were there' (p. 2, #3–#4)—which is what he wants to share on this occasion. He urges the congregation 'please don't hold back God's developer in you', for this would lead to their 'gifts being overshadowed'.

Kivengere then calls his audience to pray through the Holy Spirit to work in the hearts of his audience so that they 'may catch a fresh vision of "renewal and reconciliation"' (p. 3, #5). The bishop makes a claim about reconciliation that will feature throughout his sermons: 'This is, of course, the central message of the New Testament, and may I say it is the message more desperately needed in our world today, where we are increasingly becoming strangers in the world of God',—'the world in which God sent his [S]on'. 'Because God did that, that is why we still feel called upon to tell the world that it is still a redeemable world'.

---

13. The title 'Ambassadors For Christ' is taken from the climax of the sermon's message (see p. 16, #29–#30), although the sermon transcript does not mention it specifically. Kivengere's appeal to his audience at Fremont, to take home the new title of 'Ambassador', marks his desire and the heart of his message in the sermon. In this way we give the sermon a clear and focused theme that captures the sweep of Kivengere's message.

5.4.1.3 Prayer

The prayer that follows asks Jesus to shine upon his word so that the audience might see his face and 'catch a vision of who we are, and where we are and why we are here' (p. 3, #6).[14]

5.4.1.4 Introduction

After passing on greetings from Uganda, from whence he came earlier this year (Feb 1977) (p. 3, #6), Kivengere recounts the rapid changes from the conference that he attended at the Mount Hermon Church[15] in January that same year along with some members of the congregation and the minister. When he returned to Uganda he was 'caught in the crossfire' (p. 4, #7–#8) surrounding the murder of Luwum.[16] The conference was God preparing him for the latter.

He unfolds the story of the murder of Luwum and his own traumatising experience of the situation to help them enter into that pain. 'Human courage fails but the only courage that remains absolutely free and powerfully liberating is the love of Christ' (p. 4, #7–#8). His use of the language of 'the love of Christ' in the statement is referring to reconciliation.

He thanked them for their prayers for the difficult days of 16–20 February that year,[17] in which 'a man had stood his ground' demonstrating

---

14. In later sermons he uses the language of 'catching fresh vision of Christ'; he asks: 'where does Christ find us?' He is quick to answer that 'Christ finds man out there in the world, lonely and estranged'; and that when Christ returns 'all the hang-ups will be hung up'. See Kivengere, 'The Triumph of God's Glory'.
15. At the Mount Hermon Conference centre during the Pastor's Conference, he preached reconciliation based on the life, death, and resurrection of Jesus. See Festo Kivengere, 'The Pastor's Joy', Sermon Transcript (Preached at Mount Hermon, California, January 20, 1977), AO: 19770120.
16. See Twinamatsiko, 'The Church of Uganda and the Amin Regime January 25, 1971 Through April 11, 1979' especially chapter II, "The First Attack on Amin's Regime" and chapter III, "The Death of the Archbishop.". Cf. Kivengere, *I Love Idi Amin*. Pirouet, *Historical Dictionary of Uganda*, 228–31. Ward, 'Archbishop Janani Luwum', 200–24.
17. There is a plethora of literature by Kivengere on the precise facts of what happened on this occasion, including a press address by Festo Kivengere, 'Bishop Festo: On Events in Uganda', February 1977, pp. 3–5, #13–#21, AO: 197702[--]. After returning from exile, his first pastoral to Muyebe Archdeaconry recaps this occasion, see Festo Kivengere, 'The Task of Rebuilding', Sermon Transcript (Muyebe Archdeaconry, July 9, 1979), pp. 3–5, #6–#10, AO: 19790709. For an in-depth interview that reveals what took place on this occasion, see Capon, 'Exiled Bishop of the Martyred Church'.

the 'glory of him [Jesus Christ] who redeemed him'.[18] Kivengere details the Kampala thanksgiving service for Luwum. The grave prepared for the Archbishop's body was next to Bishop Hannington, martyred in 1885,[19] so both men could 'be together a witness of the love of Christ' (p. 5, #9).[20] Because the body of Luwum was not released to them,[21] however, they left the grave open, while hundreds of thousands stood around it to hear the words from the first Easter morning, 'Christ is [not] here. He has risen'.[22] The words evoked an immediate outburst of praise (p. 5, #9).[23] This death was not treated as an experience of hopelessness, but as a triumphant resurrection (p. 6, #10–#11).[24]

The prayers of this congregation are appreciated. Presumably as signs of God answering them, Kivengere notes that churches are packed out in Uganda and that many young people are responding. It makes him 'want to run back home'!

---

18. On the death of Luwum, see further John Sentamu, 'Tribalism, Religion and Despotism in Uganda: Archbishop Janani Luwum', in *The Terrible Alternative: Christian Martyrdom in the Twentieth Century* (ed. Andrew Chandler; London: Cassell, 1998), 147–49. Ward, 'Archbishop Janani Luwum', 200–24.
19. See Chapter Two, 3.2 'Mwanga's Martyrdoms'.
20. Also see Kivengere, *I Love Idi Amin*, 56. cf. Coomes, *Festo Kivengere*, 56–07.
21. Capon, 'Exiled Bishop of the Martyred Church', 20. He explains what Kivengere was told on asking for Luwum's body: 'Don't you ask any more about it'. Cf. Coomes, *Festo Kivengere*, 364.
22. For an eyewitness account of the service, see Ward, 'Archbishop Janani Luwum', 217–19. Ward expressed what he saw and heard at the service in a succinct way. For example, that Bishop John Wasikye preached the sermon and Archbishop Sabiti declared the words: '"He [Christ] is not here, he is risen". Luwum also has gone to be with the risen Lord. We too should be willing to die for our faith'. However, he disputes Sentamu's account of Luwum's missing body and that Luwum never received a Christian burial saying, 'This is incorrect'. For Sentamu's account that is rejected by Ward, see Sentamu, 'Tribalism, Religion and Despotism in Uganda: Archbishop Janani Luwum', 144–58. Regarding the historical dispute between Ward and Sentamu over Luwum's body and service, this sermon is bent towards Ward's account: there was a Christian service which Ward himself attended, not Sentamu; and, at Mucwini in Kitgum diocese, the home Church of Luwum, there is Luwum's grave dug by Idi Amin's soldiers and Luwum's remains are buried there.
23. Kivengere, *I Love Idi Amin*, 56. The outburst of praise is the song 'Precious Saviour', in *Golden Jubilee Convention: Behold I Make All Things New: The Fifth Kabale Convention* (Kabale, Uganda: Anglican Diocese of Kigizi, 1985), 25.
24. Christians in Uganda like Kivengere saw the death of Luwum as a triumph over the power of evil. Coomes, *Festo Kivengere*, 375–76.

5.4.1.5 Exposition

Kivengere focuses upon Paul's language of appearing 'beside ourselves', which he labels 'eccentric' (pp. 7–8, #12–#16). He sets Paul's statement against the background of his pre-Christian days as a fanatical persecutor of Christians who was changed by the love of God and so became more balanced. 'The cross of Christ, the love of Christ [v 14] is a balancer'. 'It balances our extremes'. The love of Christ changed Paul's entire outlook. Kivengere alludes to Philippians 3 to fill out the story. Paul was a 'bigot of a man'—a narrow conservative; and, yet he was 'changed by the cross of Christ . . . the love of Christ'. The love of Christ was demonstrated at the cross. 'God made him sin or treated him as sin for us although he had no sin'. He explains that God's purpose for this is 'that we who are sinners by nature might become the righteousness of God, through and in him'.

This is the 'exciting message' and this excitement is what makes Paul appear like an eccentric. 'The love of Christ has completely replaced the former criterion', and become his new 'base upon which life has completely received a new meaning'. It gripped him and, rather than imprisoning him, it broadened him from being 'a narrow human being'.

Kivengere notes that in the second part of the passage, Paul speaks of the love of Christ: Christ died for all and so all died; and the great revolution, which changed Paul, was that 'he discovered that all men were loved equally by the Lord Jesus Christ'. For a Jew, this was revolutionary: 'The cross is an embracer' of all people. This gave Paul a completely new vision. All human beings were 'all as good as dead morally'.

Bridging the gap between preacher and his audience, he said, 'So we are all in the same boat' (p. 10, #19–#20). Paul, the Pharisee, realized that despite his blameless former life (Phil 3) he is the same as everyone—all have sinned (Rom 3:23). 'Christ died for all for one reason alone', so all may live for Christ (v 15). 'The centre has changed'. It is now Christ, and 'that centre has completely reoriented my direction'. 'I have discovered my true [centre] in the love of Christ. Christ does not destroy. He does not destroy your self, but he gives your self a completely new value, new meaning and ability'.[25]

---

25. The transcript renders 'sense' and we have replaced it with 'centre' for purpose of

He gives you freedom and a new identity (p. 11, #21–#23). Until Christ becomes the centre, a person remains a prisoner. Our preacher illustrates with a man with 'an unforgiving spirit' after rebels had murdered his father. As he heard the 'voice from the cross', it opened his heart and he began 'to breathe the fresh air of God's forgiving love'. The bishop then brings it back to the text—'Christ died so that all of us who are now alive may not live for themselves but for him who died and rose again for them' (v 14); and he then pointedly asks his audience: 'so has that taken place in you?'.

When you come to Christ, your values are changed, and you no longer evaluate men by colour or race (p. 12, #24–#26).[26] 'Christ died for all therefore all can no longer be understood from a merely human standpoint', for when a person experiences this love they become completely new, with a new centre. He lists the changed centre: you no longer value men according to whether they are black or brown, Americans or British or Germans, Chinese or Russians, Africans—Ugandans or Nigerians. There is a new vision. Kivengere then again makes his appeal: has that happened in your case?

He illustrates from his own life, using the story he later wrote up in *I Love Idi Amin*.[27] Six weeks after his flight into exile, he was in church at All Soul's Langham Place, London, on Good Friday 1977 (8 April) and heard the prayer of Jesus from the cross 'Father forgive them'.[28] The bishop realized that if Idi Amin had been among the soldiers that day Jesus would have prayed for *his* forgiveness. Kivengere was led to repentance for his sin of bitterness towards Idi Amin, and asked to be given grace to forgive Idi Amin. He is one of those for whom Christ died.[29]

Our preacher explains 'that reconciliation comes from God' with 'joy and hope' (p. 15, #27–#28). God's work of forgiveness brings a new start. This could not happen without the death of Christ: 'to do that he had

---

clarity of the sentence.
26. At the end of #26, we jump to #28: (p. 14) either the page is missing or the transcript is incorrectly numbered. In any case, we do not detect any missing content.
27. Kivengere, *I Love Idi Amin*.
28. Kivengere, *I Love Idi Amin*, 62.
29. For the same story see Kivengere, *I Love Idi Amin*, 62.

to die'. He breaks abruptly to ask his audience whether they count other people's sins? When you do, it makes you miserable.

Kivengere illustrates from counting his wife's sins, which makes him become a cold judge, feeling miserable (p. 16, #29–#30). Then comes the contrast: 'God does not do it that way. He offers his free friendship, he who refuses that friendship exposes himself to the hottest judgment naturally'. But Jesus came to save not to judge (John 3:17) but 'once you reject that love, then eternity cannot change, then you are in the grip of eternal judgment'.

Without explaining Paul's use of the word '*us*' by stating its reference to the original setting,[30] Kivengere jumped to state that God has committed to *us* the word of reconciliation. Each one of you is a reconciler: 'Ambassadors for Christ in this miserable world'. He asks: 'Will they take home the new title of ambassador?'

Kivengere's language of 'us' suggests that at this point in the sermon he is not using the language of 'apostles'[31] any more. Rather, he is using the language of 'us'—all whom God has reconciled to himself and given the 'ministry of reconciliation'. Is Kivengere right in his use of 'us'?

Biblical scholars have debated the correct meaning of the use of 'us'.[32] Paul Barnett reports three categories:

> 1. The first category are scholars like Furnish[33] and Bultman[34] who take it that in the two references above, 'us' refers to the community of believers;

---

30. Martin, *Reconciliation*, 104. 2 Corinthians 5:18 suggests that 'Paul used the language both personally ('reconcile us') and universally ('the world').

31. Paul Barnett, *The Second Epistle to the Corinthians* (The New International Commentary on the New Testament; Grand Rapids, Mich.: W.B. Eerdmans Pub., 1997), 300–01. Barnett, asserts: 'the apostle is God's partner and fellow worker, empowered by God, through whom God speaks and who, as such, shares the dignity of the OT prophet who declared, "Thus says the Yahweh"'.

32. Barnett, *2 Corinthians*, 304.

33. Victor Paul Furnish, *II Corinthians* (Bible. English. Anchor Bible. 1964; N.Y.: Doubleday, 1984, 1984), 317.

34. Rudolf Karl Bultmann, *The Second Letter to the Corinthians* (Minneapolis: Augsburg Publishing House, 1985), 161.

2. The second category of scholars like Thrall,[35] are persuaded that the first reference to 'us' is referring to Paul and that the second reference is to believers; and,

3. The third category of scholars, who do not link the two references hold that the first is pointing to both the community of believers and pointing to the apostles.[36]

According to Barnett, the two occasions when reference is made to 'us' clearly apply in the first place to Paul, reference to all believers notwithstanding (3:18; 4:14; 16–5:10). As the wider aspects of the passage unfold (5:11–6:13), within which our text falls, it becomes clear that 'us' refers (1) in a narrow sense to the apostle Paul, and (2) Paul the writer who explicitly speaks about his ministry in an autobiographical way (2:14–7:4). Barnett further argued that 'Paul to whom God has given this ministry and word will immediately address the Corinthians, calling directly on them to be reconciled to God and to his apostle (5:20–6:2, 11–13)'.[37]

Given Barnett's clear historical interpretation of Paul's use of 'us' in the context of the passage, we may tentatively say that Kivengere is not interested in a historical investigation of the text but bent towards a theological interpretation of the text. Here we spot an element of his 'Biblical theology' of apostles.

Although the first person plural ('us'/'we') in the passage refers to Paul and the apostles,[38] Kivengere broadens the reference to all believers, which hints at a different view of the role of the apostles in salvation-history, while at the same time showing how significant he feels reconciliation is for every Christian. Lying behind his belief is the influence from both Keswick and

---

35. Margaret E. Thrall, *The First and Second Letters of Paul to the Corinthians: Commentary* (The Cambridge Bible Commentary. New English Bible; Cambridge: Cambridge University Press, 1965), 1.430.
36. E.g., Barrett, *Second Corinthians*, 176. Murray J. Harris, '2 Corinthians', in *The Expositor's Bible Commentary: With the New International Version of the Holy Bible* (ed. Frank E. Gaebelein, J.D. Douglas, and Dick Polcyn; Grand Rapids: Zondervan, 1992), 354. Alfred Plummer, *A Critical and Exegetical Commentary on the Second Epistle of St. Paul to the Corinthians* (vol. 34; The International Critical Commentary; Edinburgh: T. & T. Clark, 2000 [1915]), 182.
37. Barnett, *2 Corinthians*, 304–05.
38. Porter, 'Peace, Reconciliation', 696.

Revival thrust of mission as a calling for every believer to participate in the mission of God,[39] which in this case is the ministry of reconciliation.

5.4.1.6 Summary from 'Ambassadors For Christ': AO: 19771016

The purpose of this sermon was primarily for his audience to 'catch a fresh vision of renewal and reconciliation' because God is actively involved with the increasingly strange world. The world is still redeemable because God sent his son Jesus Christ who invites enemies of God to be his friends through the voice of believers who are called to be his ambassadors to the miserable world.

The introduction of the sermon shows great brokenness in Uganda where many people are living like strangers in God's world. His description of the brokenness and suffering in Uganda under Idi Amin, which climaxed in the murder of Luwum and his own flight into exile, seems to demonstrate to his audience what living 'the love of Christ' means in a world of brokenness. Thus, his explanation of the clash between the harsh powers that be in Uganda, symbolized in Amin, and living as witness for the love of Christ, symbolized in Luwum and Kivengere himself, hints at his understanding of the social and theological implication of reconciliation.

Kivengere's handling of the passage (2 Cor 5:11–20) shows that he is not an expositor in the sense of exegeting the passage verse-by-verse. This will come through in all his sermons. Without openly acknowledging influence by Karl Barth, the sermon shows great affinity with Barth's Theological Exegesis. He is more concerned with God who came in his Son Jesus Christ to redeem this strange world. His starting point of explaining reconciliation is God who sent his Son into this strange world, so that he may reconcile 'us' back to God and with one another.[40] Also the intense focus on the individual Christian's present experience found in both Keswick and the Revival that has probably contributed to his deficient view of the role of apostles in salvation-history is detectable. Nevertheless, the rest of

---

39. See Chapter Three, 2.1.5 'Day Five: The Mission—Powerful Christian Service'.
40. See chapter three, 3.3 'Barth's Hermeneutics' and 3.4 'Barth: the *Sach*e—The Subject matter, God'.

his explanation of reconciliation shows that he had great affinity with the Pauline understanding of the doctrine of reconciliation.

His treatment of reconciliation moves from the view of a new creation brought about by the love of Christ to that of reconciliation. Before the conversion of the Corinthians, God credited them with sin and now Christ died for their sins. A new creation has now made new life possible. God's messengers ('us') can now openly proclaim the possibility of the new life and people can be reconciled to God. The concept of sin for which Christ died on the cross is emphasized. There is also a close link between sin and the language of justification (pp. 7–8, #12–#16). And, he discussed the need to proclaim reconciliation as ambassadors for Christ (pp. 7–8, #12–#16).[41]

The way he views reconciliation dictated his way of preaching it. Deliberately, he bridged the gap between the preacher and the audience. He used illustrations from real life experiences in his African context: one from a bitter unforgiving young man, his bitterness to Idi Amin, and keeping records of the wrongs of his wife. From the cross, Jesus Christ the reconciler brought forgiveness and repentance into the heart of the situation.

5.4.2 In Christ: AO: 19790429, [#2]

5.4.2.1 Situating the Sermon

Kivengere preached this sermon at *La Canada* Presbyterian Church, California, on 29 April 1979, at a Sunday Worship, one week before Kivengere returned to Uganda from two years in exile.

Poised on his return, this particular sermon provides a brilliant insight into his thought about preaching reconciliation at this point in the history of Uganda. This sermon may actually express his fundamental manifesto of hope for the suffering world, and especially for post-Amin Uganda.

With the fall of Kampala on 11 April 1979 to the joint military forces of the TPDF and UNLF,[42] President Amin fled the county, but the liberation of the rest of the country, especially the eastern and northern parts, was still

---

41. See Chapter 5.2 'Kivengere's Conversion: From Agnostic to Preacher'. He links conversion in Christ to being a reconciler.
42. Gupta, 'Amin's Fall', 4–13. S. I Mmbando, *The Tanzania-Uganda War in Pictures* (Dar es Salaam: Longman Tanzania, 1980). Twaddle, 'Ousting of Idi Amin', 216–21.

going on. The remnants of fleeing Amin soldiers continued to kill people indiscriminately as they surrendered to the liberation forces or fled for their life. At the famous Moshi Unity Conference in Tanzania (23–26 March 1979),[43] an interim government was formed with President Yusuf Kironde Lule as the interim President. Our preacher was in attendance and played an important role, reconciling the different Ugandan groups opposed to Idi Amin who were fighting among themselves.[44]

Kivengere is feeling both excited at the news of the fall of Kampala and the prospect of returning home, and yet daunted by the huge and difficult task of rehabilitating the country. As a particular challenge, he wonders what message to take to Ugandans? Knowing that they had deep wounds in their personalities, that there is bitter hatred, and that the economy is in a shambles, he asks for continued prayers from the *La Canada* audience for him and his wife and for Uganda. It was to *La Canada* church he came when he first fled into exile in the USA in February 1977,[45] where he narrated the ordeal of the horrors going on in Uganda. In effect it is his home church and he has a very close relationship with his audience.

The impact of the message would have been enormous considering this intimacy. He spoke with excitement and high degree of openness, with a sense of urgency for them to support him spiritually and materially.

5.4.2.2 Prayer

Kivengere's prayer already sets the scene for this sermon majoring on reconciliation by mentioning Jesus coming 'into the arena of human confusion, [to] put the broken pieces together' (p. 1, #2). He prays for a greater impact of the Holy Spirit and the 'power of your undying love' for the people and for the Lord's help for himself as he shares with them 'in the excitement of what you are doing in the world'.

---

43. Pirouet, *Historical Dictionary of Uganda*, 255–57.
44. See Chapter One, 2.6 'A Christ-centred Leadership'.
45. See Kivengere, 'Bishop Festo Kivengere: On Events in Uganda', p. 5, #20.

5.4.2.3 Introduction

Excited that he is preaching on the last Sunday before he returns home to his diocese after an absence of two years,[46] where he hopes to be preaching the following Sunday (p. 1, #3),[47] Kivengere links this excitement to the fact that the congregation's prayers have been answered in the recent events in Uganda.[48] Unexpectedly, a provisional government is beginning to restore proper structures in Uganda after 'the last eight years of destruction', which has 'just now come to an end'.[49] Kivengere quickly adds that all is not yet completely well, for two Anglican bishops were killed and other killings have taken place as Amin's troops fled (p. 2, #5),[50] and some parts of Uganda are not yet liberated. Despite this, however, 'liberation has come' and 'jubilation is there'.[51]

Kivengere sees the miraculous hand of God behind President [Julius Kambarage] Nyerere's intervention (p. 2, #5),[52] and he once again links this with the prayers of his congregation: 'you are a participant in the liberation of Uganda'. God sees human tears and he answers prayers. After repeating his observations about God's delight in answering prayers and how the congregation 'have had a part' in these things, Kivengere reflects on his imminent return. He recalls his first visit to *La Canada* just after his escape,

---

46. For the account of his return into the country, see Coomes, *African Harvest*, 369–89. Coomes, *Festo Kivengere*, 355–67.
47. For a description of how Kivengere dropped everything including a mission in the UK where he was to be the guest evangelist and focused on immediate return home, see Coomes, *African Harvest*, 368.
48. For the major recent events in Uganda regarding the overthrow of President Amin, See, Gupta, 'Amin's Fall', 413. Twaddle, 'Ousting of Idi Amin', 216–21. Lule, 'We Stand for Justice', 18–20.
49. See Pirouet, *Historical Dictionary of Uganda*, 226–27. Lule was the interim President of Uganda at this time for 68 days.
50. Twinamatsiko, 'The Church of Uganda and the Amin Regime January 25, 1971 Through April 11, 1979', 84–87.
51. For an example of jubilation by Makerere University students, see James Tumusiime, *Uganda 30 years, 1962-1992* (Kampala: Fountain Publishers, 1992), 197.
52. For President Nyerere's justification of Tanzania's action (declared war) on President Amin, see, Okoth, 'OAU and the Uganda-Tanzania War', 152–62. Avirgan, *War in Uganda*. Caroline Thomas, *New States, Sovereignty and Intervention* (New York: St Martin's Press, 1985). Noreen Burrows, 'Tanzania's Intervention in Uganda: Some Legal Aspects', *The World Today* 35/7 (1979): 306–10. Gupta, 'Amin's Fall', 4–13. Komba Marcelion, 'Amin's Pillage in the Kagera', *Africa* 89 (January 1979): 12–17.

and the horrors that he told about on that occasion, and their solidarity with him (p. 2, #6).

Now that their prayers have been answered, he and his wife are about to return and he requests continued prayer, for things will be difficult (p. 3, #7–#8). Uganda's needs are summed up in three words: Return [Relief], Reconstruction, Reconciliation.[53] Each is important, but Kivengere clearly states that reconciliation is 'in the centre' 'at the bottom'. 'As a foundation, that is what is needed in Uganda today'.[54] Deep wounds have been opened in Uganda, and no matter how much relief is given, it won't deal with such deep wounds, which only have one antidote and that antidote is found in 2 Corinthians 5:18 (p. 4, #8).

Kivengere's introduction sets his future preaching ministry of reconciliation in post-Amin Uganda against the backdrop of the horrors of Uganda during Amin's rule (1971–9). Amin's government with all its brutality is no more. It has left behind huge and complex problems which are not easy to deal with such as deep wounds arising from the desire for revenge for murdered family members,[55] ethnic hatred, half a million widows and orphans, a shattered economy. Joint military forces of the Tanzanian Peoples Defence Forces (TPDF) and Ugandan National Liberation Front (UNLF) have brought physical liberation from Amin's regime and Western NGOs are prepared to give essential relief items such as medicine, blankets, etc., devoting enormous amounts of resources in responding to the needs of Ugandans. But Kivengere is clear that this support cannot penetrate to the wounded heart of Ugandans and transform them. Much as the issues that have caused deep wounds on the hearts of Ugandans are physical, in a very real sense they are fundamentally spiritual. The liberation war that got rid

---

53. See Coomes, *Festo Kivengere*, 386. Dudley Seers, *The Rehabilitation of the Economy of Uganda: A Report* (London: Commonwealth Fund for Technical Co-operation, Commonwealth Secretariat, 1979). For a study of the problems facing rehabilitation of Uganda, see D. Rothchild and J.W. Harbeson, *The Political Economy of Rehabilitation in Uganda* (African Studies association, 1980), 15–18. However, the Uganda National Liberation Front (UNLF) that ousted Amin, requested for Commonwealth team to visit Uganda and assess the task of reviving the economy. The approach of the later works does not have reconciliation as Kivengere offers to be at 'the centre' of reconstructing Uganda.
54. See Kivengere, *Hope for Uganda and the World*, 19.
55. See Omongole R Anguria, ed., *Apollo Milton Obote: What Others Say* (Kampala: Fountain Publishers, 2006), 92.

of Amin's rule, and the material support from the Western world would go a long way to help Ugandans in their suffering, but neither could heal and transform these deep wounds.

The new situation, for Kivengere, raises the question of what message the church in Uganda should be preaching. As a side issue, but still linked with a broader mission of the church universal, what should churches such as *La Canada* that are friends of Uganda be doing in a world faced with increasingly deep wounds? Kivengere boldly proclaimed the doctrine of reconciliation as the only antidote to deep wounds in post-Amin Uganda.

5.4.2.4 Exposition

As in the previous sermon, Kivengere stresses 'anyone', including in his explanation 'African or American, black or white'—thus bringing preacher and audience together (p. 4, #10), the 'old things that have passed away', stressing that 'it is not simply sin, narrowly conceived by evangelicals as breaking the moral code', but 'all the ways of . . . "*keeping accounts*"', and Paul's excitement about the 'new', explaining that this is God turning enemies into friends, as so we come to the heart of the sermon: reconciliation .

'We are men and women [who] have incurred deep wounds to each other, where hatred has shattered every society, where tribes have slaughtered tribes. Racial tensions have made people enemies',[56] for which deliverance is needed. He then resolves this message into one word: 'friend'.

---

56. See Ronald C. Potter, 'Race, Theological Discourse and the Continuing American Dilemma', in *The Gospel in Black and White: Theological Resources for Racial Reconciliation* (ed. Dennis L Okholm; Downers Grove, Ill: InterVarsity Press, 1997), 27–36. For an engaging discussion on the complex nature of racism in the American context, ranging from history to tradition, from culture to religion and from economics to politics, see Donald A. Carson, *Love in Hard Places* (Wheaton, Ill.: Crossway Books, 2002), 87–108. Douglas R Sharp, *No Partiality: The Idolatry of Race & the New Humanity* (Downers Grove, Ill.: InterVarsity Press, 2002). For how one feels about another person in a different race, see, Michael O Emerson and Christian Smith, eds., *Divided by Faith: Evangelical Religion and the Problem of Race in America* (Oxford: Oxford University Press, 2000), 88–91. Bruce L Fields, *Introducing Black Theology: 3 Crucial Questions for the Evangelical Church* (3 Crucial Questions; Grand Rapids, MI: Baker Academic, 2001), 67–69. We must note that even though these scholars are writing at the beginning of the twenty first century (Carson: 2002, Sharp, 2002, Emerson and Smith: 2000) with the exception of (Potter: 1997), within the American context, they put their finger on a crucial problem that expands well beyond the twentieth century, thus, making Kivengere's message relevant to the American audience.

He strengthens the point by recalling Jesus' words in John 15: 'I have made you friends' (p. 5, #11). With no further explanation Kivengere uses these words to return to the present situation: 'So, my friends in America. . . .' As he returns this is the *only message* for those in Uganda so deeply wounded (p. 5, #11). It is not surprising that Ugandans are not only in great spiritual need, but also in social need, e.g. the community is shattered, a half a million orphans, etc., for the human body houses the spiritual and physical needs. The bishop wants to tell them 'Christ has invited you to become friends again', but he asks if they will hear it? (p. 6, #11)

Our preacher's scepticism of whether Ugandans in their great bewilderment may listen to Christ's invitation for them to become his friends arises from 'the last eight years of destruction' (p. 1, #3), and 'open deep wounds' (p. 3, #7–#8). They could easily reject a human message that may not touch their needs, their wounds.

But Kivengere is an ambassador for Christ (p. 7, #14), and his hope is understandable, for he goes only by 'Eternal love and the power of the Spirit' (pp. 6–7, #12). He identifies with the pain of Ugandans, and he recognizes the great message of reconciliation that Christ extends to make Ugandans his friends, but despite being excited, he struggles to find the words to express the message of this love. So, once again, he requests the *La Canada* congregation to pray for him (p. 7, #12).

To conclude Kivengere uses an illustration of a father and son reconciled by their wife and mother on her deathbed (p. 7, #12). 'Upon the dying heart of the mother, the father and the son, enemies, were brought back, and from the moment the enmity ended [when] the mother died, the friendship of the father and the son began again' (pp. 6–7, #14). 'This illustrates what happened on Calvary's cross'. The bishop's illustration gives the message of reconciliation between God and man, ending enmity and gaining friendship on the cross at Calvary.

In paraphrasing 2 Corinthians 5:18–19, our preacher said, firstly, that Paul told the Jews, Greeks, and Gentiles that 'we are ambassadors of God's eternal love'. Secondly, that we 'stand in the name of Jesus, calling upon you in his name as if God is making his appeal to you through us' (p. 7, #12). And, he brings the message home with, 'Uganda needs that, so does America, and so does the world' (p. 7, #12).

Again he asks for the congregation's continued prayers, especially at this time. 'Don't stop because this is the greatest moment in church history in Uganda. This is where the gospel, the Good News, makes sense. This is where preachers should recover'. He hopes those in America will ask the Holy Spirit to cause every Christian to 'stand in [the] bleeding human arena and . . . shout it out': 'In Christ Jesus, God has offered humanity, every human being, a chance to become friends again first with him and then with each other' (p. 7, #12).

Our preacher's imminent return to Uganda will mean becoming involved in the job of preaching reconciliation. The church in Uganda stands poised at this historical moment to give Ugandans the only antidote (p. 4, #8), thus, he directly asks again for prayer from the congregation: 'will you pray for that'. To pray for the church [to preach reconciliation] and then the government can build upon this reconstruction (p. 7, #13).

5.4.2.5 Summary of In Christ: AO: 19790429, [#2]

Kivengere's sermon was preached in the context of his close relationship with *La Canada*, his home church since fleeing into exile. It was there he first revealed the horrors of Amin's persecution of Ugandans and now he addresses this church as he comes to the end of his exile. Although in the previous sermon he had links with the church and received great love from them, at *La Canada* his existing relationship is deeper.[57] The strength of his deeper relationship is evident in him three times asking for prayers for his wife, himself and their ministry in Uganda and the situation in Uganda to which they return.

In this call to prayer, he shows himself as a child of the revival and the important place that fervent prayer of believers had for the work of spreading the gospel both in the Keswick and Revival gatherings.[58]

It is difficult to quantify how much material support he got from *La Canada*, although he had been able to make a home in exile among them. When Kivengere turned to introduce his excitement and hope of returning

---

57. Kivengere, 'Introduction', 13.
58. See Chapter Three, 2.1 'Early Keswick Convention (1875–1920)' and 2.2 'Modern Keswick Convention (1950s–)'.

to Uganda in a week's time, his message had two clear elements. He reports on the situation of brokenness and the ongoing Liberation War in Uganda, which has seen Kampala fall to the liberators. Secondly, he explained the clear Scriptural message that he is taking to Uganda: the message of reconciliation. It is the only message that can penetrate the wounded hearts of Ugandans and bring healing and transformation. However, it is a difficult task and so he is sceptical if Ugandans will listen to the message given their deep wounds.

As in the previous sermon, his exposition has affinity with Barth's theological exegesis. The miraculous hand of God was behind President Nyerere and God cares for the suffering of his people and he answers prayers. He follows Paul's explanation of reconciliation in the passage. However, an important element that he did not mention in the first sermon is God turning 'enemies into friends'. The concept of enmity as the context out of which deliverance is needed is not actually found in the passage. The notion is of sin and trespasses. Kivengere is open to this notion.

The connection between the social and theological implication of reconciliation is clear when Kivengere charged his audience to 'pray' for the church in Uganda at this greatest moment in church history in Uganda to recover from the persecution of Amin and now to preach the message of reconciliation, the foundation upon which the government can build reconstruction and rehabilitation of Uganda. This repeats with slight variation Kivengere's earlier belief that God cares for his suffering people. However, it also includes the whole world, as his message of reconciliation is for Uganda, America, and the world (p. 7, #12).

His illustration of a father and son upon the dying heart of a wife and mother parallels that reconciling act of God in Jesus Christ at Calvary. This shows an element that was significant to his preaching: practical living out of reconciliation in broken lives/families. He also used Scripture to interpret Scripture when he recalled Jesus' words on friendship to illuminate his point on the need for reconciliation.

5.4.3 The Cross Today and Divine Outreach: AO: 19800404

5.4.3.1 Situating the Sermon

Our preacher delivered this sermon in March 1980, in Uganda, at the chapel of Bishop Tucker Theological College, Mukono. It was on Good Friday (4 April).

In the previous sermon, Kivengere was set to return to Uganda with a message of reconciliation. Eleven months after his return to Uganda he is now at the 'powerhouse' or 'the hub of the church of Uganda',[59] speaking to ministers of reconciliation at 'a historical moment for the church in Uganda'.[60] It is a moment in which the church leaders must take the opportunity to preach reconciliation. The church must recover the opportunity for preaching the gospel to a community living with deep wounds.

After his return from exile in May, during 1979 to 1980, Kivengere travelled around his diocese, just to be present and to be re-united with his folk. This was a very emotional time.[61] 'I feel my role is reconciliation, and [I] am not ashamed of saying that word of reconciliation in any platform and particularly in political platform which becomes increasingly [a]lienating'.[62] He also travelled around the country preaching reconciliation and also in his capacity as the first National Chairman of relief in post-Amin Uganda.[63] This travel left him deeply moved by the state of the country. Now in a delightful move he comes to preach reconciliation at the premier theologi-

---

59. The term 'powerhouse' or 'the hub of the Church of Uganda' to refer to the role and place of Bishop Tucker School of Divinity and Theology, formerly Bishop Tucker College, has recently been brought to the fore in discussions at the faculty and within the Church of Uganda following a passionate presentation by Edison Kalengyo. See Edison M. Kalengyo, 'The Place and Role of Bishop Tucker School of Divinity and Theology in Uganda Christian University and the Church of Uganda', Unpublished Paper, delivered at Archbishop Janani Luwum Memorial Lectures (The Ankrah Foundation, Mukono, Uganda, February 13, 2006), 1, 4.
60. Kivengere, 'In Christ', p. 4, #8.
61. Festo Kivengere, 'Nyaruhanga', Sermon Transcript, July 1979, AO: 197907[--]*3. Kivengere, 'Bishop Festo Kivengere: On Events in Uganda'. Kivengere, 'The Task of Rebuilding'. Festo Kivengere, 'Festo Kivengere's Return', Sermon Transcript, n.d., AO: [--------]*1.
62. Kivengere, 'World Vision: with Festo Kivengere', p. 6, #6.
63. Kivengere, 'Divine Sensitivity', p. 3, #4.

cal college of the province of the COU, the college that in 1945 had the 'Uganda Crisis',[64] and he preaches on Good Friday.

5.4.3.2 Prayer

Kivengere's prayer sets the scene for his sermon focusing on reconciliation by mentioning Jesus' coming 'down to us, on Good Friday' (p. 1, #2). He prays for this 'Good News' to penetrate the hearts of his BTTC audience, transform them, and send them into the world, with zeal to proclaim the wonder of the Lord. Although Kivengere does not make any open acknowledgement in the sermon of Keswick or the Revival, their emphasis and passion on reaching out into the world with the good news of salvation, stands behind Kivengere's prayer with a focus on the reconciling Lord Jesus Christ, the source of reaching out.

5.4.3.3 Introduction

In a long introduction majoring on the death of Jesus on the cross on Good Friday, including 'calculated' repetitions meant to emphasize his points on self-centredness and Jesus' selfless love, Kivengere clarifies the first part of his theme 'The Cross Today'.

Kivengere opens with greeting of 'Peace!' (p. 1, #3), which in the sermon fulfils one aim, namely, his identification with 'the kind of peace which Jesus gives unto you'. BTTC 'Holy Week Mission' of March 1980 is a 'lovely mission'. He links the lovely mission to the fact of Christ's death on the cross (p. 2 #3) and asked them not to downplay the significance of Good Friday. He appeals to their memory ('May I remind you', p. 2, #3). Good Friday shows the importance of the historicity of Jesus.

He names the dangers of simply inheriting 'tremendous interpretations', as a theological community, namely, 'spiritual enlightenments', 'the Bible itself', 'the letters of Paul' and 'all concentrations on the cross'. His main message, what brought about Good Friday, concerns Jesus' death on the cross and its relevance for today (1980). He begins with the shattering experience of the cross and how it 'mends or recreates broken things' (p. 2, #3). He refers to all false hopes such as the experiences of Peter and Mary

---

64. See Chapter Two, 4.5 'The Mukono Crisis'.

Magdalene after the death of Jesus, which must first be shattered, bringing about 'a new undying hope'. The Holy Spirit, who came at Pentecost, threw light on the action of God in sending Jesus Christ to die on the cross for our sins, making what is now Good Friday 'the greatest day of Good News' (p. 2, #4). The Holy Spirit came to lead us into 'all truth'. For this reason 'men who used to be offended by the cross became disciples, proclaimer of nothing but the cross' (pp. 2–3, #4). These men became caught up in 'the grip of [his] liberating power today', which brings Kivengere to the heart of his message: The Cross Today and Divine Outreach.

Kivengere's call to preach at Mukono was on the last day of the mission. This contrasts with the last day on the Keswick sequence,[65] and so its influence is felt here too. As the mission comes to 'the conclusion', Kivengere expresses his interest in the topic: 'today I want to share with you the outreach', that 'which thrusts people into the world' (p. 2, #3). The basis of Kivengere's claim is this: 'God in the cross shows us his outreaching hand' (p. 3, #4). God has put such outreaching hand into effect, Paul insists, 'in the cross'. He stresses that the outreaching hand of God 'shatters all the traditions', including for the benefit of his 'Anglican audience',[66] the 'Anglican tradition'.

There are many lives lost 'even in the church' because of the desires that invade people's bodies (p. 3, #4). He advised the young people to 'look at the cross'. That is the place where divine outreach begins.

The bishop then proceeds to draw their attention to reconciliation as God reached out through Jesus Christ, when He 'entered the open arena of human hostility', through the cross, leading to his divine outreach, where our lives are exposed to the cross.

5.4.3.4 Exposition
Turning to his text, 2 Corinthians 5:14, he tells BTTC 'how the divine outreach sets men and women free to go out' (p. 4, #4). 'Christianity

---

65. See Chapter Three, 2.1.5 'Day Five: The Mission—Powerful Christian Service'.
66. Up until this time BTTC only trained Anglican ministers for the Anglican Church in the East Africa region. Since former BTTC became a faculty of UCU in 1997, it began to take theological students of other Christian denominations such as Lutheran, Pentecostal Churches, Methodists, on a smaller percentage.

comes from the cross, and the cross never hugs itself, it releases' (p. 4, #4). Kivengere's language of the cross 'releasing' sinners was also used frequently at Keswick.[67] The same language will have an impact on his audience who in turn will take it into the different churches around the country and beyond. Kivengere links them back to the central point in the text, reconciliation: 'in this chapter (2 Cor 5: 13ff.) we read about reconciliation', and about 'the message [on] what Jesus did [on the cross]' (p. 4, #5).

Just like Paul who was 'answering criticisms' from those Corinthians who are saying that Paul is 'mad'; 'too excited about the death of Christ'; 'too emotional'; and 'you are not using your reason' (p. 4, #5); so too Kivengere brings his point home, 'if we appear to you as if we are mad, it is for God's sake'. He calls his audience to literally hear this message from the text saying, 'Listen to that' (p. 4, #5).

He asks: 'are we eccentric?' A madman he argues 'does things [in a way] different from other people' and to his Corinthian audience, Paul 'seems to work from a completely different centre'. Paul has a real reason to be eccentric, for verse 14 expresses that 'we are under the control of the love of Christ' (p. 5, #5). For clarity of meaning, Kivengere paraphrases it for his audience, 'let me use another modern way, we have discovered a completely new centre, for action'. Kivengere defines of 'the centre' as located in Jesus Christ, and now, Jesus controls us (p. 5, #5).[68]

The bishop wants to tell them it is not only the dynamic but also 'the power which changes our courses' (p. 5, #5). The power makes us sit 'under the rule of the love of Christ'. In using the language of 'the centre' Kivengere has reconciliation at the centre of his thought. His primary point in verse 14 is that Jesus has been shown to be 'the centre' by which 'we are ruled' by his love.

As in the previous two sermons he explains similar points from the passage: the love of Christ rules us, and in his love for us, he died on the cross for us, and this was the most revolutionary experience any man could have from a Jewish perspective (p. 5, #5). The Balokole in Uganda, many of

---

67. Kivengere, 'The Release of Forgiveness', 27–34.
68. Cf. Kivengere, 'Ambassador For Christ', p. 10, #19–#20. Kivengere, 'In Christ', p. 3, #7–#8.

whom would have been part of his audience, understand the emphasis on the death of Christ, the Son of God, and the revolution he has brought to believers in whom is now a new 'tribe' in Christ. Among the Balokole there is no emphasis on gender (male or female), tribe, roles, and race,[69] but these were real issues in Uganda. The influence of the Revival on him can be discerned here.

Kivengere's emphasizes that, once his audience are 'caught in this [compelling] love of Christ' (p. 7, #6) and he becomes 'the controlling force' in them, then Christ's compelling love will 'push them [to reach] out' into the world as it did with the early missionaries who travelled from Europe via Mombasa into Uganda.[70] His thought on the missionaries is just like the Corinthian's criticism of Paul (p. 4, #5). Some of the missionaries walked on foot for several miles from Mombasa into Uganda as if they were 'absolutely mad' (p. 7, #6). The missionaries had never seen any faces in Uganda. They faced hostile tribes. Some died on the way from disease and wild animals. 'Don't you think they are a bit insane?'

The reason behind such madness was the compelling love of Christ, which Kivengere later called 'divine dynamite' (p. 8, #7). The accent is upon the object of that love—their fellow Ugandans and all men. Thus the exhortation to abound in the love of Christ will push the audience at Mukono out and cause them to abandon their comfort, as the missionaries did. The bishop noted that 'at times it will involve facing death from diseases'.[71] They should continue to preach the gospel of Christ's love, taking a leaf from the missionaries: that is the reason 'why you are here. That is the reason I am preaching today' (p. 7, #6).

He links back to the passage noting that, 'The cross penetrated the man [Paul], applied by the Holy Spirit, into the heart [of Paul] which was completely tight, melted Paul's tight heart, and opened [his] eyes that saw [the cross]' (p. 7, #6). If there is any moment in the sermon when Kivengere's great desire to see his audience reach out into the world with the message of cross, then it is here. Kivengere passionately and intimately caught the

---

69. MacMaster and Jacobs, *A Gentle Wind of God*.
70. Reed, *Walking in the Light*, 40–51.
71. Cf. Bulasio in Chapter Two, 4.4 'Uganda Synod: The Call to *Zukuka* 'Awake!'"

attention of his audience by using the biography of Paul, a preacher of reconciliation. 'I tell you my brethren, the writer of this chapter, ran like a madman from Jerusalem to Cyprus to Rome, even to Spain, to Galatia, to Ephesus, you name it . . . you simply had no way of stopping that little man' (p. 7, #6). He was 'a little man, but a man absolutely aflame' (p. 7, #6).

Although perhaps stronger, Paul's experience is similar to Kivengere's own experience of preaching reconciliation in Uganda and beyond. He gave earlier examples of local evangelists like Kivebulaya, and we may add Bulasio Kigozi, and William Nagenda, whom he knew would have been in their memory even if he did not explicitly mention these men. He also mentioned some early missionaries to Uganda from overseas like George Pilkington and Alexander Mackay. Besides all these would have been the Revival Movement teams who strongly encouraged outreach by laity all over East Africa and beyond—including the young Kivengere.[72] His audience would have understood these examples.

This would endorse his expression of Paul, 'a little man, but a man absolutely aflame', suggesting that he had a broad knowledge of Paul and is expecting to see a church or preachers similarly aflame in post-Amin Uganda. Now, he tells the brethren (young men and women of Uganda) to become aflame for Jesus. The bishop boldly affirmed this need: 'yes indeed, we are tired of flabby religion' in which, 'you have no muscle to run and all you do is become very churchy'.[73]

It would not be correct to assume that every church of Uganda was flabby. Nevertheless, there was enough evidence to Kivengere that prompted him to speak 'prophetically' into the specific social moment of Uganda. He understands the country very well as he travels around the country in his national role and preaching ministry. Kivengere's bold critique of the state of COU was a definitive illustration of his vision for her in post-Amin Uganda. This is an important period for the church to help the country recover by preaching reconciliation to the suffering community of Uganda,

---

72. See Chapter Two, 4. 'The East Africa Revival Movement'.

73. C. S Lewis, *Mere Christianity* (A revised and amplified edition, with a new introduction, of the three books "Broadcast Talks", "Christian Behaviour" and "Beyond Personality."; London: Fontana, 1955).

but it needs the fire of Jesus, the one who died for all so that they may live for him. 'I am saying this to challenge you at Mukono. Today there is a tremendous amount of religion which is comfortable, self-centred, we need to be released, we need a new centre, a new dynamic' (p. 7, #6). A later account by Ward suggests that the church may have heeded Kivengere's 'prophecy': 'Individuals and communities discovered the importance of a strong Christian faith to make sense of existence in a hostile world'.[74]

Our preacher returns to the Bible passage by alluding to a gospel text: 'for unless a grain of wheat . . . falls into the ground and dies, it remains alone, but when it dies, you can't stop it from multiplying, it enters the liberty of multiplication'. With this text (John 12:24), he brings back his audience to where he started: the story of Good Friday. His audience would know of the text and its link to the self-sacrificial death of Jesus.

Good Friday means when divine power in the love of Christ was released for humanity, 'the first man whom love reached was right by the side of the Saviour'. He was 'a desperate case of a criminal and a terrorist', who had committed 'murder for political purposes in the city like Barabbas who also was a gang leader' (John 18:40). The man was hanging on the cross with the Master. The outreach of love gets to him and he made a confession to Jesus. 'You, Jesus, are king and remember me in your kingdom'.

5.4.3.5 Summary of The Cross Today and Divine Outreach: AO: 19800404

In the first set of sermons, Kivengere used the vocabulary of 'Peace' (p. 1, #3) only once and even within the sermon he used it in the context of greeting as a kind of peace that Jesus gives. He does not explain further. However, he will elaborate more the connection between peace and reconciliation in the set of sermons on Romans 5:1–11 and Colossians 1:19–20, where the act of reconciliation is identified with the making of peace through the blood of Jesus Christ who died on the cross for all.

While Kivengere's exposition of the cross of Christ is linked with his starting point of explaining reconciliation and its link to sin, repentance and forgiveness (p. 4, #5), and also the language of the centre is again

---

74. Ward, *Called to Serve*, 24.

raised as in the previous sermons and answered in terms of Jesus Christ, his method of exposition of the passage still parallels Barth's 'Theological Exegesis'. Barth was concerned that we should hear what the Bible is telling us, how God has sought and found the way to us.[75] Kivengere urged his audience to listen to what God is saying to his audience from the Scripture, telling them to 'Listen to that' (p. 4, #5).

Kivengere's vision for Uganda post-Amin can be discerned at two levels. Firstly, a year ago at *La Canada*, he said that Uganda was at a historically significant moment. Secondly, now a year later, he is at the hub of the COU and enforces the same claim, noting that the church must recover and preach reconciliation. These two instances assume his visionary role of a preacher of and out of revival, fully operating at the centre of the nation, mobilizing the nation for transformation, reconstruction, and rehabilitation using the biblical message of reconciliation between man and God and man and man. He did this by preaching the reconciling love of Jesus Christ. These occasions also reveal the type of benefit that Uganda would have from the fruits of being blessed with Revival preachers: Luwum, and now Kivengere his contemporary. God's outreach to the world through Jesus' reconciling love, demonstrated in his Good Friday death on the cross, moved early missionaries to and within Uganda, with the message of reconciliation that penetrated men and women, breaking down barriers of race, tribe, gender and class. It is a message that compels believers to reach out into the broken world, and his audience like Paul will reach out with the message.

5.4.4 'The Reconciling Love of Christ': AO: 198110[--], [#1][76]

5.4.4.1 *Situating the Sermon*

This sermon was preached in Sheffield, United Kingdom, in October 1981. Kivengere, Bishop Misaeri Kauma (Namirembe diocese), and Reverend

---

75. See Chapter Three, '3.3 'Barth's Hermeneutics'.
76. We took this theme from Kivengere's main focus in the sermon: 'we are talking about the reconciling love [of Christ] (pp. 1–2, #2).

John Wilson (AEE), went to England on a mission code-named 'From Uganda with Love'.[77] The CMS Ruanda Mission, England, made the arrangement. This was a mission that fulfilled the mission of May 1979, which was postponed when Kivengere returned to Uganda soon after the fall of President Idi Amin.[78]

5.4.4.2 Preliminaries

Kivengere opens with an expression of joy and thanks for the welcome accorded his teammates. 'Glory be to the Lord Jesus Christ' (p. 1, #1). One of the distinguishing marks of the East African Revival has been to preach in tandem.[79] Giving personal testimonies of the love of God expressed giving glory and praise to God for what he is doing in his world, especially the life of brethren, is recognized in the sermon. Jesus Christ comes through as having the central and upper place in their testimonies.[80] Under this influence, a testimony comes through this sermon.

5.4.4.3 Introduction

Kivengere's introductory remarks already set the stage, focusing on reconciliation by observing that when his audience sang the song 'how beautiful [God] is' (pp. 1-2, #2), he and his teammates saw in their faces 'a demonstration of His reconciling love'. 'It is only that love which can wash ugly faces clean'. Clearly he is using the language of 2 Corinthians 5:14.

Our preacher expressed that this was done in 'blood and sweat' on the cross of Calvary. 'It was in absolute nakedness, loneliness, utter helplessness, outside a city, in a violent mob, nothing was really beautiful that day'. The link in this statement with the previous sermon[81] is that it expresses that the Good Friday experience was not 'good', as we might define it today. He

---

77. For similar sermons also preached during the same mission, see Festo Kivengere, 'Jesus Is Good News', Sermon Transcript, October 1981, AO: 198110[--]*2. This sermon was also preached on another occasion under the title, Festo Kivengere, 'Jesus: The Treasurer', Sermon Transcript, August 27, 1982, AO: 19820827.
78. Coomes, *Festo Kivengere*, 411–13.
79. Noll, *The New Shape of World Christianity*, 169–70. Cassidy, 'Festo Has Died But He Still Speaks', 1–8.
80. Ward and Wild-Wood, *The East African Revival*, 45–110.
81. Kivengere, 'The Cross Today', p. 2, #3.

immediately adds that the story of the sinful human heart is disastrous. It has left wounds in Uganda: 'a few hundred widows and orphans found in the church' and a dreadful state of suffering that has affected the personalities of people, especially those whose dear ones have been 'eliminated' by the dictator Idi Amin.[82]

However, despite the negative picture of the horrors of Uganda, pictures that he explained in his introductory remarks in the previous two sermons, there is hope for Uganda. Because of 'the extraordinary love of Christ' (pp. 1–2, #2), his people are not finished. The extraordinary love of Christ is preserving Ugandans in the face of their great suffering, something his audience would be keen to understand because of their long involvement in the unfolding story of the gospel in Uganda.

5.4.4.4 Exposition

Kivengere launches into the gist of what he is talking about: 'that reconciling love, first, must be a liberating love' (pp. 3–4, #3). 'It must set men and women from these hang-ups'. By 'these hang-ups' Kivengere is referring to a situation of suffering which is terrible and which is paralyzing humanity.

A year ago he visited [Archbishop] Desmond Tutu at his home in Soweto. The context of the visit was the preaching of reconciliation in South Africa together with his African Enterprise Team leader, Michael Cassidy, with whom he had been preaching reconciliation all over Africa since 1971.[83] The bishop's story reveals not only his preaching of reconciliation in the situation of the blacks suffering under the apartheid regime,[84] but also his close link with Desmond Tutu well before formation of the notion of 'Reconciliation and Forgiveness',[85] which later became the dominant theses of the South African Truth and Reconciliation Commission (1995–1998). Kivengere's deliberate visit to Desmond Tutu at his home in

---

82. Coomes, *Festo Kivengere*, 398–403.
83. See Chapter One, 2. 'Reconciliation and Kivengere's Sermons'.
84. Kivengere, 'Bleeding Africa', 29.
85. Tutu's assumes a distinction between the 'reconciliation' and 'Forgiveness' as two notions constructed and accepted by South African in the Truth and Reconciliation Commission.

Soweto, when he is reaching out with the gospel of reconciliation,[86] implies that he was dealing with a leader at the forefront of seeking liberation from the oppressive and segregative regime in South Africa. This needs to be asserted against the current scholarship on reconciliation in Africa, especially South Africa, where there has been a tendency to explain away reconciliation and forgiveness by reference to political liberation.[87]

He comes to Tutu as one who has seen the power of God in the horrors of Uganda and in his own person. He forgave Amin, and now he 'embodied in himself' reconciliation as an ambassador of Christ for reconciliation. He found Tutu believing in the hope of this risen Christ. He then met with the South African leaders in government and confronted them with the message of reconciliation as he did with the minister of internal affairs on this occasion. Tutu is aware of *who* and *what* Kivengere is on this visit. In the foreword to Kivengere's authorized biography, Tutu writes in appreciation of Kivengere's preaching: 'He proclaimed the love of Jesus Christ so passionately and eloquently and was truly an ambassador of Christ in carrying out a wonderful ministry of reconciliation in his strife-torn Uganda'.[88]

Kivengere's story tells of a very difficult situation that he found in South Africa, 'Men and women seething with frustration, disappointment, anger and bitterness' (pp. 3–4, #3). They could not hear the gospel. Yet Kivengere is there to preach the gospel of reconciliation. He then tells of a miracle that he saw. 'And we [Michael Cassidy and Kivengere] not only wanted to preach reconciliation, we stood there and embraced in the stadium before the blacks and the whites and the browns. . . . we began to tell the amazing miracle which the Spirit of God does when he opens the heart wide, smashes the barriers open, fills the empty heart with God's love and then life begins to tick again' (pp. 3–4, #3).

Life in South Africa was full of racial hatred. As Michael Cassidy shared his testimony of how Jesus liberated him from racial prejudice, all the

---

86. Kivengere, 'Bleeding Africa'.
87. Gunnar Theissen, 'Common Past, Divided Truth: The Truth and Reconciliation Commission in South-African Public Opinion', Unpublished Paper presented at the International Institute for the Sociology of Law (Onati, Spain, September 22, 1999), Cited 15 Mar 2012, Online: http://userpage.zedat.fu-berlin.de/~theissen/pdf/IISL-Paper.PDF.
88. Coomes, *Festo Kivengere*, 9.

stadium clapped, as they could see Kivengere, a black Ugandan, proclaiming with Cassidy, a white South African, the love of Jesus with all that they had (pp. 4–5, #4).[89] Kivengere moves on to explain from Paul's biography, noting his education under Gamaliel and his obedience to the Old Testament Scripture (p. 6, #6), and his Damascus road encounter that led him to be reconciled with God through Christ. He was dramatically changed by eternal love. He links this with what God is calling him and other Ugandans to do—in addition to meeting the physical needs with food, medicine and clothes to proclaim divine-man reconciliation.

Kivengere recalls the strength of Luwum's ministry of reconciliation (p. 6, #7). 'My archbishop died in Kampala. A tremendous reconciler . . . Straight he went until he died as an ambassador of reconciliation'. He wants to tell his English congregation that they may not suffer as Ugandans do but there are situations that keep them apart, and they need 'the redeeming love of Christ'. This love will liberate them and set them free from being 'self-centred'.

Kivengere proceeded to assert that 'we in Uganda feel that the church is irrelevant if it fails to carry on the message of being ambassadors of reconciliation' (p. 6, #8). No matter how busy his audience may be, 'primarily we are all called, . . . if you believe in Jesus . . . then you immediately become an ambassador [of reconciliation]'. After explaining what it means to be an ambassador for Christ, he then declared that there is a deeper disease at the heart of Ugandans. Not only was Idi Amin 'diseased', but also the Ugandans were themselves. Kivengere does not elaborate on what he means by saying that Idi Amin and Ugandans themselves are 'diseased'. Later he will refer to a greater power bigger than one man, Amin, in Uganda: the power of evil. We can confidently, state that the power of evil working in Amin and Ugandans themselves, is in view.

Kivengere concluded by affirming that 'you are ambassadors of Christ' (p. 6, #8), so they should go out and stand in the name of Christ and tell the people that 'God is offering you friendship with Himself, please

---

89. See, *African Enterprise*, Pasadena, 'Highlights of our 1985–86 ministry': 9–11: besides his message of inter-personal reconciliation, Kivengere influenced Cassidy to bring together 100 key South African Church leaders of all races and denominations to a meeting that gave birth to the National Initiative for Reconciliation (N.I.R) in 1985.

take His offer tonight'. He illustrates with the story of how they have been preaching for one week in the UK from this theme and have seen literally thousands of people committing their lives to Jesus Christ, and he asks: 'what is happening here in Sheffield?'

Kivengere finished by saying that even though there is still suffering in Uganda, there is hope because 'they have been given wings to fly' (pp. 9–10, #12). If there are people in the congregation who are feeling weighed down by difficult circumstances, they should open up to Jesus who will give them the ability to go through it (pp. 9–10, #12). His prayer for them is that 'God may help you tonight to open up and see that the world is waiting for me, an ambassador' (pp. 9–10, #12). He used an illustration borrowed from his friend, Bishop Yohana Omari,[90] who in 1955 at his consecration and enthronement as bishop in Tanzania compared the ambassador of Christ with a little donkey whose role was to carry Christ down the street in Jerusalem (pp. 9–10, #12). Will you say, 'Lord, I too would like to be your donkey [?]'.[91]

5.4.4.5 Summary of 'The Reconciling Love of Christ': AO: 198110[--], [#1]

This sermon makes a contribution to this study, namely, Kivengere's starting point of explaining reconciliation is the cross of Calvary where in absolute nakedness, loneliness, and utter helplessness, Christ demonstrated his reconciling love that washes ugly faces clean (pp. 1–2, #2). This approach leads him to explain the consequences of the sinful human heart that left wounds in Uganda. Not only does his approach show him as a Christ-centred preacher, but also it reveals his biblical theology of the cross.

Kivengere's preaching of reconciliation in Uganda prepared him for his South African ministry of preaching reconciliation, during which ministry he visited Tutu. Without his openly stating it in the sermon, it is a well known fact that when Amin murdered Luwum, Kivengere fled into exile and became very bitter with Amin. However, when on a Good Friday at All

---

90. From December 1958 to June 1959, Kivengere visited Australia with his friend Bishop Yohana Omari for six months for speaking engagements to different Churches.
91. Stott, *People My Teachers*, 50. Coomes, *Festo Kivengere*, 305. Kivengere, *I Love Idi Amin*, 23.

Souls Church, London, he wrestled with the words of the Lord from the cross, 'Father forgive them', he forgave Amin. He then wrote the story in his 1978 book, *I Love Idi Amin*. Forgiveness and reconciliation became the cornerstone of his message and life as a result of the situation in Uganda. By 1978, Tutu was aware of this story of Kivengere and the situation in Uganda. Now Kivengere comes to South Africa, and makes a contribution to the terrible situation in Apartheid South Africa, preaching the gospel of reconciliation. His visit to Tutu had an influence and impact on Tutu, who later applauded the life and gospel of reconciliation Kivengere preached, observing that Kivengere was a true ambassador of Christ.

His influence on Tutu makes him one of the forerunners of the South African TRC. This point will become more evident in later sermons where he expressed clearly his role in preaching reconciliation in South Africa and at the Pan African Leaders Assembly. Kivengere's open embracing of Michael Cassidy in the stadium before blacks and the whites in South Africa arose because the message of reconciliation that he is preaching smashed barriers down.

He is preaching the Pauline message of reconciliation in which Paul was not only 'shaken' by his Damascus road experience, but by the understanding that the reconciling love of Christ on the cross embraced him. Within the context of this embrace, Paul, a former enemy of God, came to the realization that Christ accepted him despite his past enmity against God. He realized that this acceptance was not only for him, but the acceptance is also extended to others, whom now Paul does not judge because of his new identity in Christ. Kivengere understood this message and applied it to his love of Christ and the people of Christ, including Michael Cassidy, whom elsewhere he refers to as 'my miracle brother' who has 'come to Christ too and I am stuck with him'.[92]

In terms of the preaching of reconciliation in the harsh context of Uganda under Idi Amin, he located Luwum as a tremendous ambassador of reconciliation (p. 6, #7). When the church is not carrying out the ministry of reconciliation, an irresistible verdict is passed on it: it has become

---

92. Cassidy Michael, 'Foreword to Second Edition', in *Revolutionary Love* (2nd ed.; Monrovia, Ca.: African Enterprise, 2001 [1983]), 5.

irrelevant. Behind this statement is Kivengere's understanding of Christ at the centre of the church. He discussed this more clearly in the set of sermons on Colossians 1:19–20, where he will explain that in Christ, everything holds together, and so the church can hold together only if Christ is at the centre, and only then can the church be relevant in its ministry. Central to the ministry of the church is reconciliation in Jesus Christ. So he can assert that the church in Uganda believes that if the church has stopped preaching reconciliation as its role, then it has become irrelevant.

The impact of this sermon is further revealed when he explained that their weeklong mission in England saw literally thousands of people commit their lives to Jesus Christ (p. 6, #7). He prayed that *God*, the subject of his message, would help his audience to reach out into the world that is waiting. His emphasis on God, who in Jesus sets men and women free from their hang-ups, is the subject of his mission. Behind this understanding is his way of viewing the world through the lens of God, which approach, once again, has an affinity with Karl Barth's 'Theological Exegesis'.[93]

His illustration of the donkey taking Jesus down the street in Jerusalem reveals the Revival influence on him through his friend Bishop Yohana Omari.[94] Later he tells this same story at his consecration and enthronement as Bishop of Kigezi diocese. Additionally, his Revival influence stands behind his appeal to his audience to open up tonight. At Keswick, each day had its own moment of climax that led to 'total surrender' to the Lord Jesus Christ, and the messages are clearly focused at the heart and transformation of believers.[95] However, the climax of the Keswick and Revival teaching and preaching was on day five. In this sermon Kivengere reduces the week long pattern and daily messages to one sermon with a climax: 'tonight open up and see the world is waiting for me, an ambassador'; 'God is offering you friendship with himself, please take his offer tonight' (pp. 9–10, #13). He is citing gospel narrative to illuminate his point of reaching out into the world with the message of the reconciling love of Jesus.

---

93. See Chapter Three, 3.3 'Barth's Hermeneutics'.
94. See Chapter Two, 5.3 'Kivengere's Teacher Education'.
95. See Chapter Three, 2.1 'Early Keswick Convention (1875–1920)'.

5.4.5 'Jesus Came as a Missionary of Reconciliation': AO: 19820221[96]

5.4.5.1 Situating the Sermon

This sermon was preached on the 21 February 1982 in Detroit, USA, on the occasion of 'Missionary Commitment'. Kivengere had been in Uganda for two years since returning from exile, preaching the doctrine of reconciliation. Now he has been invited to preach at the Presbyterian Church.

5.4.5.2 Introduction

As in his previous sermons in this chapter, Kivengere opens with greetings from East Africa, especially Uganda, recalling with thanks their prayers for the difficult situation they were going through; and, in praying for them they participated in the liberation from Idi Amin's murderous rule, in which 'some of us narrowly escaped death' (p. 1, #4).[97]

As in the previous sermons, he preaches the reconciling love of Christ, he names the brokenness of the people of Uganda, his own encounter in the situation, and Jesus' own encounter of brokenness that gained God's love for humanity. Since he escaped death from Amin, he has been involved in 'a great challenging missionary movement' (p. 1, #4), and it is no coincidence that this is happening following the fact that his background is of a missionary church—the COU that has recently celebrated its centenary. He links his missionary involvement to his early childhood when a black evangelist [Byensi] introduced him to Jesus Christ at about 10 years old (p. 1, #4). He was taught to read and the first book he read was the gospel according to St. Luke in his mother tongue [*Rukiga*].

From that point on he began his missionary evangelism by reading to the boys and girls in the village 'the story as Luke records it in his Good News'. He looks back over the years at the missionary zeal and activity of the black evangelist who had little education 'but the best that he had, he

---

96. We took the title of this theme from the words of Kivengere in this sermon as it best captures the heart of the sermon.
97. Michael, 'Forward', 5.

shared with [the] boys and girls and therefore started Christianity in the village and here I am, excited about it all'.[98]

5.4.5.3 Exposition

As in the previous sermons, Kivengere refers to Paul's former life as a persecutor of the church (pp. 5–6, #7). Only after Paul's experience on the road to Damascus, Paul could say: 'The love of Christ, now is the controlling dynamic of my life'. 'It becomes *the dynamic by which I can change the world*'.

Kivengere stressed that when a church comes under the love of Christ, 'It becomes an infectious community'. He illustrates the 'infectious' nature of such a church with the example from the Anglican Church in Uganda. In a critical way he said that the Anglican Church in Uganda, unlike the Presbyterian, is '"loaded" with a heavy tradition of liturgy, which can weigh heavy on the feet of believers, like the Jewish tradition'.

But the Presbyterian Church[99] was the context in which he was critiquing the liturgy of the Anglican Church in Uganda, before it caught the vision of Jesus Christ. His audience, whose traditions did not weigh heavily on its members, would have felt the impact of the critique as he brings a new perspective of the church from a different theological emphasis.

On a positive note, he drove the message home for his audience by illustrating how the Anglican Church in Uganda got out of the situation: 'The spirit of God breathed in and the Christians caught the vision of Jesus Christ'. Before, 'they were sitting in [the] church like spectators'. Now, the situation became different. The 'fire of his love began to burn', 'And the dumb began to sing', 'The deaf began to hear the voice' and 'The blind began to see God's world and men became very precious'. Here is a direct link to his opening prayer.

Our preacher merged this with his text, as if it were spoken by Paul on the Damascus road experience when he said, 'Now the love of Christ is [the] dynamic that controls our life'. Kivengere believed 'that is how we can change the world'. This is the heart of Kivengere's sermon. He emphasizes

---

98. Kivengere, *I Love Idi Amin*.

99. There are different 'traditions' among the Presbyterians but here we assume that Kivengere is referring to all Presbyterian traditions.

that, 'Not by any other means, except by the love of Christ' (pp. 6–7, #8). It is what 'God recognizes as a key which opens hearts of men and women even enemies'. Although Kivengere does not mention explicitly the language of reconciliation, by emphasizing 'the love of Christ as a key that opens the heart of men and women', he is alluding to it at this stage in the sermon. But towards the end of the sermon, he will be explicit about the need to embrace the 'ministry of reconciliation' (see p. 12, #24). Kivengere once again applies this message to the two contexts: America and Uganda. 'The dynamic is love, with that you can change America, with that I change Uganda' (p. 7, #9).

As the mission comes to a conclusion, he hopes that his audience will see that 'Christ died for all, therefore all were dead, there was no one better' (p. 7, #9). He repeats the same Pauline explanation of the passage that he gave in the previous sermons, again raising the question of 'centre' and answering in clear terms: 'Jesus who came and love became a new centre'. Kivengere sees no more living for self as 'the centre'. Kivengere adds another important element in his sermon that Paul would see the death of Christ on the cross differently: 'I saw a completely new world' (pp. 7–8, #9).

Kivengere said that 'in Uganda many people thought that Amin was the big problem'. But for him, 'Amin was only an instrument in the hands of the demons'. 'The greater power of evil was bigger than Amin and it is we Ugandans'. This point he made earlier in the previous sermon. From his opening prayer in which he mentions the blind, it is likely that the 'blind hearts' of Ugandans exacerbated the evil in Uganda. It is not unreasonable that the same was true of Amin as it led him to cause a lot of deaths in Uganda. Not surprising, therefore, when the bishop reported that 'The hearts are blind until the love of Christ sets the men and women free, we don't see each other' (p. 9, #10).

Again he repeats his illustration that he used in a previous sermon of how this love of Christ practically works in the lives of believers, recalling a practical demonstration of it during their public preaching of reconciliation in Soweto stadium South Africa. He challenged the young people in his audience: 'to make a decision to tell others about the love of God', which they have in their heart because 'the love of Christ is now the centre'.

As in the previous sermons he explains again his points on the language of 'the centre', stressed the death of Christ for 'everyone', and the possibility of 'new life' when the love of Christ, 'penetrates and make people completely new and fresh' (p. 12, #13). 'This is God's truth'. 'That's what my country Africa desperately needs'.[100] His audience that night should 'embrace the ministry that God has given them' (p. 12, #14): 'The ministry of reconciliation', adding that *'Jesus came as a missionary for reconciliation'*. For this reason, Kivengere sees that there is hope to redeem the miserable world: 'it is [still a] redeemable world' (pp. 12–14, #15).

Unlike before when he made personal appeals to the heart of his audiences to embrace the love of Christ and become reconcilers and ambassadors for Christ to a miserable and broken world, on this occasion he made 'altar calls' for those who are prepared to join others in the 'dynamic of the Holy Spirit to change the world for my Saviour'. Even without Kivengere's direct acknowledgement of his sources of influence over this method of preaching, from our discussion in chapter 3 he clearly stands in the same tradition as Keswick, the Revival, and Billy Graham, with preaching that is focused at the heart of the audience, making 'altar calls' in response to the truth of the word of God being proclaimed.[101] Kivengere extended the invitation of the President of Uganda, Dr [Apollo Milton] Obote, who said to him 'if you [Kivengere] can find 200 Christian teachers with degrees in science and mathematics, bring them into Ugandan schools, we want our schools to have . . . the Christian standard'.

5.4.5.4 Summary of 'Jesus Came as a Missionary of Reconciliation': AO: 19820221

This sermon contributes to this study in many ways. First, Kivengere's utterance that 'Jesus came as a missionary of reconciliation' (pp. 12–14, #15) constitutes explicitly part of the title of this thesis: 'missionary of reconciliation'. He came and took the centre stage in the life of a believer, following

---

100. Kivengere, *Hope for Uganda and the World*, 19.
101. For a description of Billy Graham's altar calls, see Bennett David, *The Altar Call: Its Origins and Present Usage* (Lanham, Maryland: University Press of America, 2000), xiii. He helpfully notes the interchangeable uses of 'public appeal' and 'public invitation' to refer to altar call (p. xv).

his death on the cross, which expressed his love for all. Only through his death on the cross is humanity able to see God and to see one another. This truth of God, Kivengere not only believed but also saw as the desperate need of his country and Africa. Jesus is the content and message of reconciliation. He is the means and message by which Uganda, America, and the world may be changed.

Secondly, for the most part in the sermon Kivengere makes reference to God, who is the subject of his message. Because God is the truth that his audience need to know, he appealed to them to embrace God's ministry of reconciliation entrusted to us.

Thirdly, he mentioned without discussion the powers of demons and evil in Uganda. Amin is only an instrument in the hands of demons. This recognition of Ugandans struggling with evil and demonic powers is a hint at Kivengere's being knowledgeable in Scripture such that behind this comment is his recognition of Scripture's exhortation that 'our struggle is not against flesh and blood' but a struggle against certain destructive forces and their ideologies. Struggle against 'powers of this dark world' and against 'rulers' and 'spiritual forces of evil in heavenly realms' (Ephesians 6:10–18). Kivengere's search for reconciliation in Uganda so full of evil acts[102] recognizes the struggle in the world against the powers of evil, which for Ugandans is real. Preaching reconciliation in such a context calls for prayer and discernment 'in the spirit' (Ephesians 6:18), to be at the core of his ministry of reconciliation in a country bathed in innocent blood. It also hints at his belief that preaching reconciliation is truly a matter of understanding and knowing God's power and the victory over evil won on the cross of Calvary. Evil spiritual forces (Eph 6:12), must be seen as part of brokenness in the world and the antidote to this brokenness is the message of reconciliation.

Lastly, and finally, in his extension of the invitation from President Obote for 200 Christian teachers to come and teach in Ugandan Christian schools and raise the standards, lies a hint of President Obote's recognition of Kivengere's impact and influence in the life of Uganda even though he

---

102. For example, one evil in Amin is reported that he admits to eating humans! See 'Amin Admits Eating Humans, Vow to Return', *Sub-Saharan Africa Report* 2192 (December 21, 1979): 122–23.

hails from the Revival fellowship. His contribution to Uganda was well beyond church circles.

5.4.6 'Reconciliation': AO: 198204[--], [#1][103]

5.4.6.1 Situating the Sermon

This sermon was preached in the Israel, in April 1982. The occasion was the 'Celebration of Evangelism'. It was a follow up of a successful evangelistic mission that took place at Assuit, Egypt, 6 March 1978, where Kivengere preached reconciliation from the theme: God's Love (1 John 3:16).[104] It comes at the time when our preacher had been working behind the scenes to mediate peace in the Middle East.

5.4.6.2 Introduction

Kivengere started by giving a testimony of his conversion,[105] acknowledging the preaching of the Revival, which he hated: 'They made me uncomfortable . . . they sang when they should be quiet . . . when they talked about Jesus, they related him to their daily personal life' which he did not like (pp. 3–4, #9–#11). He then reveals his message to them: 'Let me tell you something about reconciliation because this is what I want to share with you'.

Using a practical illustration of how the brethren showed practical reconciliation to him, a former agnostic, and knowing that they had been praying for him to trust Jesus with his life, desiring that he should change from being argumentative, they rejoiced with him and one of them literally lifted him up, putting him on his shoulder on the occasion of his conversion. Kivengere wondered whether the man who lifted him knew that he

---

103. In the sermon Kivengere said, 'Let me tell you something about reconciliation because this is what I want to share with you' (pp. 3–4, #9–#11).
104. Festo Kivengere, 'God's Love', Sermon Transcript, January 6, 1978, AO: 19780106. For two sermons he preach while on the same mission but the day before, see Festo Kivengere, 'For Me To Live Is Christ', Sermon Transcript (Evangelical Presbyterian Church, Cairo, Egypt, March 5, 1978), AO: 19780305*1. Festo Kivengere, 'Compelling Calvary Love', Sermon Transcript (Preached at Salvation of Souls Church, Cairo, Egypt, May 5, 1978), AO: 19780505.
105. See Chapter Two, 5.2 'Kivengere's Conversion: From Agnostic to Preacher'.

was enacting the story of the lost sheep in Luke 15. When the lost sheep was found, the shepherd took it and put it on his shoulder and carried [it] rejoicing (p. 5, #13). Reconciliation between man and man follows reconciliation with the father who first loved the sinner.

5.4.6.3 *Exposition*

Kivengere stated that 'reconciliation is not just a question of putting your thoughts right' (pp. 5–6, #14). 'It comes out of a heart liberated by the love of God. He rejected the idea that reconciliation can be part of the formal administrative side of church life: 'You cannot pass a minute about reconciliation in a [church] committee'. The brethren loving him the way they did, they set him free. 'And the next day I was on the road, village-to-village being reconciled', without knowing what to expect, trembling at moments; yet, he went because 'it is not a question of expertise. It is just love, love compelling'. He 'argued' with the Holy Spirit against going to put right the hatred he had with a relative, however, he had to go. To his surprise, his relative, who was not a Christian, forgave him and embraced him because 'Jesus created this unique way of removing barriers between us' (p. 6, #15).

He tells one more example of his conflict with Governor Bashir, a Muslim, over the beating of one of his Christians by a soldier under the authority of the governor (pp. 7–8, #16–#19). This encounter resulted in a conflict but was resolved with reconciliation. Hatred developed between them and went on for some time. However, under the prompting of the Holy Spirit, Kivengere drove 92 miles to the Governor's office at Mbarara, and sought reconciliation after first putting right what caused the hatred between them. 'And when I finished the governor was taken aback because I read [to] him Romans 13, with his permission'.

On reconciling, Bashir asked Kivengere what he could do to further develop the restored relationship. Kivengere asked him to open the 1975 Christian Convention in his diocese, which he happily did (pp. 7–8, #16–#19). This was an act of reconciliation. Present at the opening and preaching on the occasion was Archbishop Luwum, whom Kivengere acknowledged as 'a man absolutely on fire for the Lord'.

Before closing, Kivengere then gave a few words, which he thought to be very important: 'Verse 14 of 2 Corinthians chapter 5, this is what I call the basis of reconciliation' (pp. 8–9, #20). He paraphrased the verse: 'The love of Christ leaves me no choice, controls me, says Paul'. As in the previous sermons he refers to Paul's pre-Christian life, and comes to the conclusion that Paul is no longer making conclusions for himself: 'the love of Christ has taken over'. 'That is where reconciliation begins'. It starts with the love of Christ taking over. 'Without that, reconciliation is just a technique'. The love of Christ is so powerful such that Paul came to the conclusion that 'Christ died for *all* who are living here in Israel and in Uganda'.

By emphasizing *all* he brought the audience to be at one with him (pp. 8–9, #20), for it is language that bridges the gap between himself and his audience, as is, 'my dear friends' (p. 9, #22). 'Reconciliation is not my work, nor is it your work' (pp. 9–10, #22). 'Through Christ God has reconciled us unto himself, or changed us from being enemies into his friends'. He repeats the point he made in the previous sermons that God is the author of reconciliation. 'God broke through the greatest barrier—between a Holy God and sinful man'. On breaking the barriers, he 'brought back men and women to himself at the price of dying for them. It is all done by God, not man' (p. 10, #24–#25).

'God is now speaking through us. We are speaking on behalf of Christ, telling the world of Israel, Uganda, South Africa, [and] America' (p. 11, #27). He wonders how else you can heal or bring back people who have suffered so much from the murder of their loved ones, listing: 'brothers, sister, mothers, fathers as it is the case in Uganda' (p. 11, #29). They are 'harbouring deep-seated bitterness such that at times tears cannot roll from their eyes; they just dry up'. He illustrates the horrors of Uganda with a story of how in 1973, in Kabale stadium, three men were killed by a firing squad at the order of President Amin. But before they were shot in public, 'as a Christian brother and a minister', he went and preached reconciliation to them.

Kivengere then tells his audience to preach reconciliation in Israel, Uganda, and South Africa: 'this is the message of God' (p. 14, #39). 'It is the message that God has given his children, 'you are on the team of God's ambassadors of God's reconciliation'. His audience needs to join the spirit of God and move forward like a beautiful fragrant perfume in Israel. He asks: 'when you see an Arab and an Israeli embracing, isn't that a perfume?'

5.4.6.4 Summary of 'Reconciliation': AO: 198204[--], [#1]

One of the striking features of Kivengere's belief about what reconciliation is not, which in all his sermons is only found here, is his conviction that reconciliation is more that a question of putting your thoughts right. 'Reconciliation comes out of a heart liberated by the love of God'. For Kivengere, the implications of this understanding of reconciliation is crucial. Firstly, it is significant for what it is, namely, it is a gift from God. Secondly, he objects to the notion that 'reconciliation can be part of a formal administrative side of church life'.

His argument is based on two considerations, namely, if the church committee passes a minute about reconciliation (presumably he is referring to social reconciliation), it becomes a question of what he called 'a technique' (pp. 8–9, #20). For Kivengere, reconciliation must spring out of the love of Christ that compels a believer to love with 'the love of Christ'. This love, he argues, leaves believers with no choice but to love because Christ has taken over.

This point needs to be seen in the broader picture of Kivengere's understanding of reconciliation. Kivengere placed the foundation of reconciliation in the context of the covenant of grace.[106] In this way reconciliation is given a more secure and firm biblical theology. Outside the covenant context, reconciliation degenerates to a mere attempt at peaceful co-existence.

Evident in this sermon is repetition of the link between enmity as the state from which deliverance is needed, which is not found in the Pauline text of 2 Corinthians 5:11–20. However, he correctly follows Pauline thought of sin and trespasses. He links the brokenness in Uganda, South Africa and America to one solution: God's sacrificial death of Christ.

His expression that 'God is now speaking through us' hints at his theological exegesis, similar to that of Karl Barth.[107] He gave the illustration of preaching in 1973 at Kabale stadium, packed with 3,000 people who had witnessed the public execution of three fellow Christians by firing squad,[108]

---

106. See Chapter Six, 3.4 'The Covenant of Love'.
107. See Chapter Three, 3.3 'Barth's Hermeneutics'.
108. Of the three men killed by firing squad, only once in his sermons he mentions one Bitwari of Nyaruhanga, whom he describes as 'our dear brother'. See Kivengere, 'The Task of Rebuilding', p. 14, #26.

which reveals the potential impact of his message of reconciliation in a Uganda full of brokenness. A week later he preached at the home of these three men and the families became born again, together with many others in the village. The sermon shows his broad commitment to mission and discipleship in the context of injustice upon Ugandans inflicted by Amin's rule.

5.4.7 Conclusions on the First Set of Six Sermons

Listening to the sermons has shown that they consist of two main parts: the socio-historical context of Uganda (and beyond) and the theological exposition of reconciliation. In the first category, the socio-historical context, there was much brokenness in Uganda, especially arising from the horrors of Amin. The atrocities of Amin are linked to complex issues: ethnic, political, religious and demonic/evil. What has emerged is that in a deeply broken world, especially Uganda, during and after the rule of Amin, faithful Christian proclamation of reconciliation—God's initiative to restore himself to man and man to man (2 Cor 5:18–20), according to Kivengere, can be envisioned in direct relationship with God's unfinished vision of His mission.

His mission simply is: reconciliation. He came in his son Jesus Christ as a missionary of reconciliation, he then entrusted to believers to ask enemies of God to become friends of God. This is seen in the way Kivengere engaged with the historical and social basis of brokenness and deep wounds that Christians in Uganda and beyond had. He found himself witnessing for Christ in this context—including facing and coming to grips with his own brokenness, which was similar to what other Christians in Uganda faced during the period 1971–88.

With a theological exposition of 2 Corinthians 5:11–20, Kivengere preached the biblical message of reconciliation, emphasizing the love of Christ, displayed on the cross. This love of Christ made Paul seem eccentric. Kivengere brought out for his audiences two metaphors of reconciliation: the cross as a 'balancer' and the cross as 'embracer'. Reconciliation is necessary and it is precisely the reason the love of Christ was displayed on the cross for humanity that had become enemies of God.

Kivengere used the concept of enmity, for the state for which deliverance is required, but about which Paul is silent in this text (2 Cor 5:11–20). This is a deficiency in Kivengere's theological exposition. However, for the most part he had read Paul correctly. The love of Christ originates with God, the author of reconciliation. In Christ, God's love for sinners (his enemies) is demonstrated through the coming of Christ into the arena of the human situation, bringing a new 'identity'.

The foundation on which reconciliation, the good news to a broken world, is based, is the death of Jesus Christ as the historical event of God's self-sacrificial love for sinners (enemies of God). This love is the hope for humanity. The hope is realized when the Holy Spirit illuminates Christ's redemption for the world. This redeeming love for Christ is a broad concept, broader than perhaps the notions of 'sacrificial death'[109] or 'penal substitution',[110] in the understanding emerging in Kivengere's preaching of reconciliation.

Regarding biblical exposition, he is not an expositor in the sense of verse-by-verse like his evangelical friend John Stott.[111] He is instead focused on the big theme of reconciliation centred in Jesus Christ. This approach and theology has affinity with Karl Barth's 'Theological Exegesis' that concentrates on the *Sache*—the subject-matter, God, the heart of the Bible. Also elements of Barth's doctrine of reconciliation, such as the link between covenant, sin and reconciliation, find an echo in Kivengere's understanding of reconciliation. But more striking is the way Kivengere explains reconciliation, making his starting point to be God in his Son Jesus Christ on the cross, who died for all and brought forgiveness and repentance of sins, thus making us reconcilers and ambassadors for Christ. Also, in the sermon, influences from Keswick and the Revival are detectable in the sermons.

---

109. For a way of explaining the sacrificial death of Christ, see John R. W Stott, *The Cross of Christ* (20th ed.; Nottingham: Inter-Varsity Press, 2006 [1986]). For a rather controversial explanation see, Mark D Baker and Joel B Green, *Recovering the Scandal of the Cross: Atonement in New Testament and Contemporary Contexts* (2nd ed.; Downers Grove, Ill.: IVP Academic, 2011 [2000]).

110. Brian Vickers, *Jesus' Blood and Righteousness: Paul's Theology of Imputation* (Wheaton, Ill.: Crossway Books, 2006).

111. See Chapter Three, 2.2 'Modern Keswick Convention (1950s–)'.

Explicit Reconciliation Passages   231

In his vision of preaching reconciliation in Uganda and at *La Canada*, he made a significant historical claim that in the history of Uganda, the church stood poised to recover the preaching of reconciliation. For Kivengere, with preaching the message of reconciliation, there was hope for Uganda and beyond. He mobilized the nation for reconstruction and rehabilitation using the message of reconciliation.

5.5 Explicit Reconciliation Sermons (II): Romans 5:1–11 in Context

5.5.1 Surprised by Joy: AO: 197109[--]

5.5.1.1 Situating the Sermon

Kivengere preached this sermon at All Saints Santa Barbara, California, USA, in September 1971, during a mission gathering.[112]

The sermon does not get to verses 10–11.

On 25 January 1971, Amin ascended to power in a military coup in Uganda, and since then the situation in the country is very fresh on Kivengere's heart.[113] By Easter time (April) he was in Ghana to lead a Scripture Union house party, by which time Coomes reports that 'as always for Festo, everything began and ended with the cross, and it was from here he seems to have tried to make sense of Amin'.[114]

5.5.1.2 Preliminaries

The apostle Peter led the early Christian fellowship. He led people 'drawn together, not ("necessarily") organizationally, but rather drawn by "agape", the undefeatable love of God as expressed in Jesus Christ on the cross' (p. 1, #1). As always, mentioning the love of God, the cross of Christ, people

---

112. From the recollections of the memory of an eyewitness account, Keith Jesson in an e-mail of 6 September 2010 to the author states that, 'The message Surprised by Joy: AO: 197109[--] was one given during a Mission to All Saints, Santa Barbara, CA in Sept. 1971. The meetings each evening were in a home with 50 or more [people in attendance]'. I am indebted to Keith Jesson for sharing this information with me.
113. Kivengere, 'Awesome Growth', 218.
114. See Coomes, *Festo Kivengere*, 286.

gathering around Jesus, reconciliation is in view. The undefeatable love of God is 'the magnet that the Holy Spirit used to draw all sorts of characters together' in the fellowship.

5.5.1.3 Introduction

Kivengere proceeds to note that 'no other power on earth could have drawn such a group of people [together]', forming such a 'united group of people' (p. 1, #2).[115] 'Only the power of the cross could do it'. Reconciliation is not far away. The cross became the centre of the Christian church. As early as 1971, Kivengere was already using the language of 'the centre', in regard to 'the Christian church'.[116] In later years he emphasized the 'centre' to be located in Jesus Christ.[117]

Kivengere announces his current interest in Paul. Paul is 'a man whom I now very much like to read' (p. 3, #5). He clarifies for his audience the distinction between reading 'St. Paul'—that is, 'his letters' and reading 'St. Paul', 'a person in whose heart the love of God has done a miracle'. 'Paul is a man we love to hear from'—thus, bridging the gap between the audience and the preacher ('we') and directly acknowledging Pauline influence as early as 1971. Paul 'was a man surprised by the love of God'. For Paul, 'the good news of God simply meant [that] men and women [are] put right with God and with each other, that is all'.[118]

Kivengere then lists some facts about Paul's biography.[119] Kivengere wishes his audience to understand that even for a theologian like Paul ('an

---

115. The most helpful comment for illuminating Kivengere's description of the temperaments of the early Church ('led by Peter', p. 1, #1) is in his Book *The Spirit Is Moving*, 20. 'their [the early disciples] hearts and minds had a lot of hangover and doubts, like Thomas; they were bad tempered, like John and James, the sons of thunder'.

116. Kivengere, 'Surprised by Joy', p. 10, #19–#20.

117. Later years include, Kivengere, 'The Cross Today', p. 5, #5. Kivengere, 'In Christ', p. 3, #7–#8. Kivengere, 'Jesus Came as a Missionary', p. 7, #9.

118. This is true, in general, of Pauline reconciliation. So, Michael Bird: 'Reconciliation emerges as a counterpart to justification. It marks the end of alienation and hostilities between humanity and God, it mends the rapture in the creator-creature relationship, it occurs through or in Christ (specifically his death), God no longer reckons sin to sinners and its result is peace—not peace as a subjective experience, but the objective state of peace between warring parties' in *A Bird's-Eye View of Paul: The Man, His Mission and His Message* (Nottingham, England: Inter-Varsity Press, 2008), 106.

119. See Chapter Three, 5.1 'Paul's Experience of Reconciliation'.

expert in the Old Testament' p. 3, #5), the good news is simple. With reconciliation in view, he notes: 'when Jesus came in his amazing grace and simplicity, Jesus ushered into the arena [of the human situation] his amazing good news', which good news he observed that it was 'so simple that the simple folks in Judea understood him'.[120]

Without explaining the biblical concept of the coming of 'Jesus in his amazing grace and simplicity', and who 'the simple folks of Judea' were, Kivengere proceeds to give two examples of how the good news worked in 'the life of the simple folks in Judea', alluding to two gospel stories to illuminate his point: 'the women who followed him [Jesus] were set free; one after another' (p. 4, #5), and 'the sick [people who] experienced the new touch of healing; deeper than the physical healing'. When Jesus heals, he touches the entire personality—the physical, the mental, and the psychological and 'the person becomes a completely new creature'. Kivengere is again using the language of 2 Corinthians 5:17, though with the modification from 'new creation' to 'new creature'.

5.5.1.4 Exposition

He explains that 'it is through faith that we have been put into a right relationship with God' (p. 4, #7). We, therefore, are at peace with him [God], because of what our Lord Jesus Christ has done for us. 'Through him [Christ], we possess the entrance into the grace in which we stand'. This statement of Paul had an impact on Kivengere, as he explicitly acknowledges: 'I love that word', namely, 'Through him (Christ)'. He loves what Paul is saying because Paul is plain and he is saying that 'there is no more any distance at all'; 'it has been taken care of'.

For Paul, the means by which God's grace is accessed is 'through Christ'.[121] This explains Kivengere's excitement about the New Testament.

---

120. For an excellent discussion on the life of the simple folk in Judea especially in the gospel according to John, see Timothy J. M Ling, *The Judean Poor and the Fourth Gospel* (vol. 13; Monograph Series Society for New Testament Studies; Cambridge: Cambridge University Press, 2006).

121. See, David Fisher, *The 21st Century Pastor: A Vision Based on the Ministry of Paul* (Grand Rapids, Mich.: Zondervan, 1996), 86. He comments that Paul understood 'grace' as 'God acting in accordance with his own character and being'; and, 'grace' is more than a divine attribute but is 'God himself'.

This leads him to the heart of the theme of this sermon: Surprised by Joy.[122] He asserts that 'we have possessed the entrance into this grace in which we stand and our pride is in the glorious hope which God has given to us' (p. 5, #8). The bishop links Jesus Christ to an eschatological fact: Christ is 'the glorious hope' that we have from God on which our life should be built for now and in the future.

Speaking from his 'personal experience' of being brought up in a Christ-less society, he recalls: 'my father was a practicing religious man in his society. Call it paganism, animism, . . . he was a sincere seeker' after God (p. 5, #8),[123] but he never found Christ, leading to frustration.[124] However, in Christianity, we have 'a faith not for seekers but a faith for finders', and this 'is the exciting news of the New Testament' (p. 6, #8). He lists examples of finders in Christianity, including Andrew who in excitement went and told his brother, James, that they have found the Lord, and Mary Magdalene who went and told the sceptical disciples that she found the Lord (p. 7, #9).

Kivengere wants his audience to have deep Christian character, which comes out of suffering, such as Peter and John had; they were publicly humiliated before the Jerusalem council but left the council 'so excited and went out singing' (p. 7, #9). Their suffering and humiliating experience took the councillors aback.

The kind of character displayed by Peter and John produces hope that 'never lets us down'. 'God's love has been poured into our hearts through the Holy Spirit' (pp. 7–8, #9). The Holy Spirit is working in our hearts because he 'has been given to us'. According to Paul, 'the Christian hope never becomes glorious until the Holy Spirit has poured God's love into our hearts like a flood' (p. 8, #9).

---

122. See, C. S Lewis, *Surprised by Joy: The Shape of My Early Life* (London: Geoffrey Bles, 1955). Kivengere mentions C. S. Lewis' allusion to give the title of the sermon. Lewis, in this book, tells of his quest for joy: a spiritual journey that led him from Christianity in his early days as a youth through atheism and then back into Christianity.

123. cf. John S Mbiti, *Introduction to African Religion* (London: Heinemann Educational, 1975), 19.

124. See, Kivengere, 'Testimony', 416–17. '[M]y father was a very religious man. He worshipped God through the agents of spirit of our dead ancestors. He was seeking after God like most Africans do'.

He linked the picture of 'flooding our hearts' with the recent (1969) floods in Santa Barbara, which had disastrous consequences.[125] 'The love of God comes like a huge flood and sweeps through the heart which was full of doubts' (p. 8, #9). 'For this love, which has come by the Holy Spirit, whom God has given to us as a gift'. Again by mentioning the love of God, reconciliation is in view.

His earlier equation of God's love with the gift of the Holy Spirit, given through the death of Christ on the cross of Calvary, would have prepared the way for his further message. In the larger purpose of God, the historical fact is that 'The Lord Jesus died in order that men and women may receive the Holy Spirit, because apart from him you can never cry, "Abba. Father"' (p. 8, #9).[126]

Kivengere wishes his audience to hear this message. He asks: 'May I repeat that'? (p. 8, #10) Elsewhere, Kivengere explained that after Jesus' death and glorification, the Holy Spirit came.[127] Kivengere here makes for his audience a fundamental affirmation in the context of the love of God. Without the Holy Spirit 'you will never cry, "Abba, Father" (p. 8, #10), explaining that 'Abba' in Aramaic means 'Daddy', and 'that is exactly what Christ called God' (p. 8, #9).

It is helpful to note that in the years prior to 1971 when Kivengere preached this sermon, the theological debate on Jesus' use of language of 'Abba', looked to the figure of Joachim Jeremias' 1967 book, *Prayers of Jesus*,[128] followed later by his 1971 book, *New Testament Theology*.[129] However, in the 1980s and 90s many scholars have questioned Jeremias' view that Jesus used this term to mean an individual address to God in

---

125. K. Fauchald, 'A Survey of the Benthos of Santa Barbara Following the January 1969 Oil Spill', *California Marine Research Commission* 16 (1972): 125–29.
126. For his thoughts advanced on the working of the Holy Spirit see, Festo Kivengere, 'The Work of the Holy Spirit in Evangelization, Individually and Through the Church', in *Let the Earth Hear His Voice: International Congress on World Evangelization, Lausanne, Switzerland: Official Reference Volume: Papers and Responses* (ed. James Douglas; Minneapolis: World Wide Publications, 1975), 277–78; Kivengere, *The Spirit Is Moving*, chap. 2.
127. See Kivengere, *The Spirit Is Moving*, 16.
128. See Joachim Jeremias, *The Prayers of Jesus* (Philadelphia: Fortress, 1978 [1976]).
129. See Joachim Jeremias, *New Testament Theology* (The New Testament Library; London: SCM Press, 1971), 1:61–68.

the context of prayer in Palestinian Judaism.[130] Kivengere's explanation promises to make its impact upon his audience through engaging them by rendering 'Abba' for his twentieth century audience as 'Daddy'.

He adds his testimony saying that 'that is exactly the relationship which Jesus introduces me into' (p. 8, #10). 'Jesus removed the old covenant' [the law]. In the old covenant, Kivengere 'treated God as a distant, threatening figure'. But now, the situation is different. 'God becomes my Father so that I can say to him, 'Daddy, my Father'. Kivengere is indirectly speaking about reconciliation in stating that 'God becomes my Father' on the basis that 'Jesus removed the old covenant' and now there is no more distance between God and himself. Kivengere tells his audience that the new relationship he has with God is 'a tremendous experience, I have no words to express it, and words don't express it'.

He defines his new relationship in one word: 'faith'. Faith 'is confidence in that love which will never let you down'. Faith is simply 'a response to God's love' (p. 9, #10). When people respond to this action of God, as recorded in the New Testament, 'We discover [that] God is now my Father'. Again, reconciliation is in view.

The Holy Spirit, 'the agent who introduces strangers into citizenship [of God's Kingdom]' (p. 9, #10), took him as he was, alienated from God by his sins, before the cross of Calvary as one of those debtors who 'have no penny to pay' for his sins, and opened his eyes to see that on the cross of Calvary, Christ paid all the debt for his sins,[131] and immediately he was surprised by joy.

---

130. These scholars include, Barr, James, 'Abba Isn't "Daddy"', *JTS* n.s. 39 (1988): 28–47; James H Charlesworth, Mark Kiley, and Mark Harding, eds., 'A Caveat on Textual Transmission and the Meaning of Abba: A Study of the Lord's Prayer', in *The Lord's Prayer and Other Prayer Texts from the Greco-Roman Era* (Valley Forge, Penn.: Trinity Press International, 1994), 1–14; Bruce Chilton, 'God as "Father" in the Targumim, in Non-Canonical Literatures of Early Judaism and Primitive Christianity, and in Matthew', in *Judaic Approaches to the Gospels* (University of South Florida International Studies in Formative Christianity and Judaism; Atlanta, Ga.: Scholars Press, 1994), 39–73; Géza Vermès, *Jesus the Jew: A Historian's Reading of the Gospels* (London: Collins, 1973), 211–13.

131. Kivengere seems to be having 'justification' by faith alone in God in mind by mentioning that 'Christ paid it all for him' at this point, however, his stress in a moment is shifted to reconciliation.

His relationship has changed, so he can cry 'Abba, Father'.[132] His heart was flooded with 'wave after wave of this amazing love of God' (p. 9, #10). Kivengere does not directly label this amazing love of God, experienced in the changed relationship from estrangement to a 'Father-Son relationship', as reconciliation. Nevertheless, this description depicts nothing less than reconciliation.

The presence of Jesus is what excited Paul. 'This is how God demonstrates his love to all men' (p. 10, #14). He links the point of God's love for his audience emphasizing 'all men'. Our preacher lists examples to include 'all men' in Africa, America, Europe, China, and India. God demonstrates his love for all men in 'That while we were still strangers, and sinners and rebels, Christ at that time died for those who don't love him'. Kivengere adds his glosses to Romans 5:8: 'still strangers', 'and sinners', 'and rebels', 'Christ at that time, for those who don't love him' (p. 10, #14). Even though he does not explicitly talk about 'justification' of all men by faith alone, it is in view.

'When he [Jesus] walked through the streets of that city nearly two thousand years ago, a lonely figure who could hardly carry a piece of wood on which he was going to hang, he demonstrated' . . . 'The greatest demonstration God had ever displayed before human eyes'. Paul told the Galatians: 'Christ was portrayed or placarded', before you: 'crucified'. His crucifixion was a pubic display, God demonstrating 'this is how much I love you'.

Kivengere has been swept by the wave of the love of God and 'He introduced me into a new relationship' (p. 8, #10). Others were also touched for 'the wounded hands picked up all human beings including myself, in fact that's why anytime I speak about him I get excited' (p. 12, #12). He wants them 'to catch the vision of the drama of God's love', which is compatible with the story of the death of Christ on the cross at Calvary. So he articulates for them the intrinsic relationship between the cross, the suffering of Christ, and the love of God for them.

---

132. Cf. Paul's thought that God sent his son to redeem those under the law so that 'we might receive adoption as sons' (Rom 8:15) and since believers are considered sons of God, through the Holy Spirit of God, they are able to cry out, 'Abba, Father!' (Gal 4:4–5; Rom 8:23).

The bishop tells his audience to 'look at the cross' (p. 11, #11), 'picture themselves standing before the cross', and 'seeing' the way that 'Jesus got to the cross, falling, bleeding, with thorns around his Head' for their sake. They should 'not [have] pity [on] Jesus; the cross never demands pity'. They should look at the cross until 'the cross pierces through the walls of his [the sinner's] resistance'.

Using the language of the old hymn 'When I Survey the Wondrous Cross', Kivengere concludes this point with two related remarks. First, 'this is what God is doing for all men', and this action of God caught up with Paul unprepared, driving him 'almost mad'.[133] Second, Paul was 'a man frozen with hatred and pride', yet God's action through the light of the Holy Spirit enabled him to see 'the demonstration'.

He illustrated from stories of people he met during his mission trips to Indonesia ('Dec 1971', p. 12, #14) and the Solomon Islands ('Feb 1971' p. 15, #14), how sinners 'are rescued' (p. 12, #24) from their sins and set free when they catch the vision of the love of Christ. He used the language of 2 Corinthians 5:17, but he modified it from 'a new creation' to 'a completely new man'. He adds that he too caught that vision: 'He loved even me' (p. 12, #14). He made reference to Paul, who caught this vision on the Damascus road experience (p. 12, #14).[134]

5.5.1.5 Summary of Surprised by Joy: AO: 197109[--]

In the sermon, reconciliation is simply stated as 'the good news of God'. This good news is about having a right relationship between God and man and a right relationship between man and man. This good news must be proclaimed in simple terms. Paul, a theologian and expert in Jewish Law, presented the good news in a simple way to his Roman audience. Jesus also presented the good news in a simple way to the simple folk in Judea.

---

133. Kivengere alludes to Acts 9:3: 'A bright light from Heaven suddenly flashed around him'. For a broader discussion on the impact of this light on Paul for his theology and ministry, see Kim, *Origin*. Kim argued that the Damascus revelation of the exalted Christ taken as the image of God provided the origins of Paul's Christology, and Paul's transformation soteriology. Consequently, for Kim, Paul's visionary experience resulted in the gospel that Paul preached, especially Paul's doctrines, namely, justification and reconciliation.

134. See chapter Three, 5.1 'Paul's Experience of Reconciliation'.

Simplicity in presenting the gospel was also an important feature of the Revival and clearly here significant for Kivengere.

In all the sermons that we have so far listened to, Kivengere's clearest and most open acknowledgement of Pauline influence on him is found in this sermon. As early as 1971, an important year in Kivengere's preaching as well as important for this study,[135] he reveals his passion for Paul, 'a man in whose heart the love of God has performed a miracle'. In keeping with his own preaching ministry, Kivengere is fascinated by Paul's reconciliation experience that arose out of his preaching ministry. This acknowledgement and fascination with Paul and his letters is helpful to understand Kivengere's close reading of Paul and his letters elsewhere.

A further insight into Kivengere's fascination with Paul arises from his statement: 'a man we love to listen to'. As a revival preacher and a Mulokole, listening to testimonies of how God is transforming his enemies into believers and giving them the ministry of reconciliation excites him. The excitement rests on the fact that for a Mulokole, the permanent nature, attitude, and doing of God to sinners is reveal in a radical way. He loves Paul's letters and life experience because everything he says about reconciliation, at a personal, social and political level, can be properly understood in the light of God's doing.

Whereas in the first set of sermons we have listened to Kivengere use the concept of enmity, which Paul is silent about, it is striking that in this particular sermon, when Paul talks about enmity, Kivengere is silent. He makes no comment reflecting Paul's argument that those who were once enemies of God, but have now been reconciled by the death of Jesus Christ on the cross, may now be sure that they will gain salvation by the life of Jesus Christ.[136]

Paul envisaged a previous situation in which the enmity is to be taken as mutual. Nevertheless despite his enmity, God in his love demonstrated in the death of Jesus Christ on the cross for all, has already acted and provided the means of dealing with sin and its consequences that paralyzed the

---

135. See Chapter One, 2. 'Reconciliation and Kivengere's Sermons'.
136. See Chapter Three, 5.3 'Romans 5:1–11'.

relationship between God and man previously. The life of Jesus Christ in his self-sacrificial death for sinners was the price paid.

Kivengere does not explain justification of sinners by faith alone. Paul states this to be a current experience of believers, noting that if God has justified sinners by the blood of Christ, then they may be certain they will be delivered at the last judgment. Kivengere also ignores the wrath of God on the last day of judgment, which plays a prominent part in this.

Given that Kivengere articulates the intrinsic relationship between the cross, the suffering of Christ, and the love of God for them, he is more focused on the fact that Christ on the cross has brought reconciliation and gained final salvation for them. They are no longer enemies of God. Since this transcript is missing verses 10–11, it is difficult to speculate if in the sermon he went on to explain reconciliation from the missing verses.

Although it is difficult to speculate that he would have done so, because Kivengere's primary interest is explaining reconciliation, demonstrated in the death of Jesus on the cross, and since Paul explicitly mentions reconciliation in verses 10 and 11 as the climax of the passage, it would have most certainly been in his view. If so, this may well explain why he was silent about justification in verse 1, either because his focus was elsewhere, or because he simply assumed it.

While Kivengere explained reconciliation in the passage using Pauline terms such as 'through him', 'peace', 'hope', 'suffering', and 'love', he introduced from the gospel the term 'Abba, Father', to illuminate his point on the work of Jesus Christ on the cross. The term 'Abba, Father', is also in Romans 8. For Barth, this cry is 'the sum total of the Christian life'.[137] He described this work of Jesus on the cross with the expression 'demonstration', linking it to an activity in the recent memory of his audience: demonstrations in America.

---

137. Karl Barth, *Church Dogmatics IV.4: The Christian Life. Lecture Fragments* (trans. G. W. Bromiley; London: T. & T. Clark, 2004), 52.

5.5.2 God's Intervening Love: AO: 19750729, [#1]

5.5.2.1 Situating the Sermon

Kivengere preached this sermon at Aurora, USA, on 29 July 1975 at a four-day mission conference in 'a church or community setting'.[138]

Kivengere is preaching this sermon within the last six months of the year. He has been through major events in his preaching locally and internationally. Locally, in February, he had been preaching in 'the Ghana mission' and back in his diocese he had participated in a joint ecumenical walk with the Roman Catholics.[139] In April he preached at the consecration of his assistant bishop, William Rukirande, addressing himself directly to President Amin who was in attendance, telling him that Uganda 'needs citizens whose hearts are united by the love of God'.[140] Reconciliation was in view.

Internationally, in July he preached at the centenary of the Keswick Convention in London in the company of his friends, Billy Graham and John Stott.[141] Coomes reported this message emphasized the racial, tribal, political, and denominational bitterness that has dominated the African continent and church.[142] However, Kivengere's message at the convention simply focused on the release of sins that forgiveness brings.[143] This 'burden' of the release of forgiveness stood behind his sermon at Aurora.

5.5.2.2 Prayer

Kivengere is thankful to God because 'when the fullness of time came you [sent] your beloved Son Jesus Christ' (p. 1, #2)[144]—thus, bringing recon-

---

138. Reconstructing the occasion from the sermon, Kivengere's two statements are helpful, namely, 'these next four days may see the reality of God's intervening love in the circumstances of each and everyone' and, 2. '[W]hen God brings a mission or special meetings in a Church or a community it is to specifically meet needs' (p. 2, #4).
139. Coomes, *Festo Kivengere*, 331.
140. See Coomes, *Festo Kivengere*, 332.
141. Kivengere, 'The Release of Forgiveness', 27–34.
142. See Coomes, *Festo Kivengere*, 333.
143. Kivengere, 'The Release of Forgiveness', 27–34.
144. In the Old Testament, Jesus the Messiah was promised to come through the line of King David; and, in the New Testament, God fulfilled this promise through sending the Messiah, a greater David to be born of the virgin Mary. For Kivengere this is no vague or

ciliation into the opening prayer. Jesus was sent 'to bring God's intervening love for us' (p. 1, #2). He prayed for God to set 'each and everyone free' to experience 'the fullness of life in Christ Jesus'.

5.5.2.3 Introduction
After the prayers that already focused on reconciliation, Kivengere expressed his appreciation for their invitation, remembering with gratitude the lovely evening he had together with them earlier in May that year (1975). He brought 'the love and greetings' of the Christians in East Africa who are praying for their four-day conference (pp. 1–2, #3). Kivengere then launched straight into his topic—'God's intervening love' (p. 2, #4).

5.5.2.4 Exposition
This is a relevant topic for his audience because 'God never steps from where he is to where his people are without knowing [that] there are specific felt needs in the lives of his people' (p. 2, #4). 'God's intervening love' simply means 'God's stepping forward when you need and I need him desperately' (p. 2, #5) Kivengere's language bridges the gap between the preacher and his audience ('you' and 'I').

He speaks of 'God's love moving towards the separated one' (p. 2, #5). As they have been reading in Romans chapter five, 'there are the righteous' as Paul states. God has acted in history for 'us'. 'God has *justified* us' [Rom 5:1], 'at the appropriate time', 'while we were still helpless' [Rom 5:6], and 'God has poured his love into our hearts through the Holy Spirit whom he has given to us' [Rom 5:5], making 'us righteous' (p. 2, #6).

Kivengere then jumps to explain the purpose and place of man within creation. 'God created you and created me, not because we were absolutely essential', but 'because God is love. He stepped forward in love and created man he loved' (pp. 2–4, #6–#7). The purpose for which God created man is 'for fellowship'. Using relational language (horizontal) he emphasized that God created man 'for community', 'for communion', and 'for relationship'. But 'man broke away from God' (vertical relationship) and

---

casual reference to whatever time it might be. It is the historical fact that at the right time Jesus came.

has remained in his state of a 'protesting conscience', which has led to 'a crisis situation'—that is, 'the broken state of man and society'. Kivengere pointed to evidence of this 'crisis situation of man' all around the world. He lists examples, including Chicago, Paris, London, Uganda, Vietnam, and not least Aurora, where he listened to the radio reporting of murders the morning of 29 July 1975.

'Externally there could be different mitigating circumstances but essentially the problem is the same. Deep down we live with separation from God'—that is, we live with sin. The clear personal pronoun that Kivengere uses for his Aurora audience cannot be missed: 'we'. This is indeed a 'striking personal dimension' that he tells them given the personal actors that he stated—'God' and 'we'. He desires that his audience should know that there is 'action' undertaken here: 'we live with separation from God'—that is, we live in sin'.

The 'Scriptures say that the breaking away from God made us utterly helpless to help ourselves'. The story of the fall of man (Gen 3) that Paul tells his audience (Rom 5:12ff.) is now the story of his Aurora audience. So, 'the more efforts we put out the more helpless we become to remedy the situation'. . . . 'and that is the situation we read in Romans chapter seven verse twelve onwards to twenty-five'.

Kivengere now explains the implication of this text for his personal life ('the crisis situation of man', pp. 2–4, #7), saying: 'I simply don't understand myself because every time I try to do right I do the wrong, the desire to do right I have, the ability to do it I do not have, so I don't understand my own actions' (pp. 2–4, #7). He then asks: 'am I two men in one [?] Am I divided' [?]. So the 'I' situation that has left man in crisis led Kivengere to ask another question in wonder: 'what a confused human being I must be [?]' as described in verse 24. The answer to the questions Kivengere posed to his audience now begins to emerge.

According to Kivengere, 'Paul says, thanks be to God. God's intervening love came exactly when we need it' (pp. 4–5, #8). He linked the timing of the coming of the 'intervening love of God' to the story of Genesis 3, saying: 'It was [like] when it happened in the Garden of Eden'. Kivengere links back to his text, on the subject of helpless humanity that he had earlier hinted (See, p. 2, #6) saying: 'For we read here, [that] when we were still utterly helpless and miserably rebellious, and running away from God, and breaking all the time, God took it upon himself to do something and this action was initiated by love alone' (p. 5, #9). To Kivengere, 'God justified us', and the basis for our justification from sin, so that we may be 'righteous' with God, is 'his love for us' that moved his Son 'Jesus Christ to go and die on the cross to reconcile us to God', giving us peace with God and with one another.

So God's action 'in Jesus Christ' on the cross sorted out the 'helpless situation' of man (p. 5, #9). The means through which the helpless situation of man from sin was 'redeemed', 'was realized through Jesus' speaking out on the cross, 'Father forgive them for they don't understand what they are doing' [reconciliation]. Kivengere pointed out that 'we' (thus, bridging the gap between his Aurora audience and the preacher) needed 'a word from the cross and there on Calvary's cross God spoke to our situation'.

'God's word is action'. So 'when God spoke in love he acted in love' and 'he became naked on the cross of Calvary but it was love in action entering our nakedness' (p. 5, #9). 'God entering our nakedness' has theological and social implications of living as Christians in Aurora in 1975. 'God's dynamic action takes[s] helpless people and introduce[s] them into new life' (p. 6, #11). This is 'reconciliation' even if he does not use the word 'reconciliation'. Reconciliation starts with God, he restores relationship with helpless man and sets him at peace with God/self, and with 'others'.

God's action of 'reconciling love' that took 'helpless people' and introduced them into 'a new life' turns 'his enemies into friends' (p. 6, #11). He paraphrases the text adopting God's voice and adding his own glosses: 'I want to make you into a friend but I paid a tremendous price', that is, 'not counted in dollars' but 'counted in drops of blood and sweat'. 'It cost God everything in Jesus to make you a friend again' and 'not only did God speak in reconciliation on the cross of Calvary, but God spoke effectively' (pp. 6–7, #12). 'God's word on the cross affects men, it is a word [. . . that] changes men'.

Becoming 'a friend of God' through the death of Christ on the cross raises for his audience two important points. Firstly, the fact that Christ's death on the cross at Calvary was a story depicting 'the reconciling love of God for helpless man', means that they are now drawn in to be part of that story since 'the reconciling love of God' moved Christ 'to die on the cross for them', and their 'new life' is to continue daily 'in Christ'.

Secondly, this 'new life' continues daily because of their 'new identity' in Christ. 'If God acted in so costly a way on the cross to make you his friend' then 'whenever you hear the message you are invited to act in response' (pp. 6–7, #12). To illustrate 'the social' as well as 'the theological' implications of this 'reconciling love of God' and its 'new life' now working in believers in Uganda, Kivengere tells of a politician[145] who came forward at the Kabale Jubilee celebration of 1975,[146] before fifteen thousand people and gave his testimony of the liberation Jesus gave him.

Relationships between 'Christians and God and Christians and Christians are broken relationships caused by sin' (pp. 7–8, #15). The politician illustrated that, 'The love of Christ has broken the barrier' between him and others in the community, including his pastor. 'The pastor was as much to blame as the politician', however, they 'both came as men, not as a politician or as a pastor, they came as human beings'. Here is reconciliation, and for Kivengere, 'this is how practical reconciliation is in Christ' (pp. 7–8, #15). 'That is the New Testament. It is real' (pp. 7–8, #15). The message of reconciliation has both theological and social implications for daily living.

Kivengere hopes that his audience will expose themselves 'to this message of reconciling love' because 'there is a word for every one of us' to embrace (pp. 8–9, #16). On a personal note, he admits to the difficulty he has 'with a wrong attitude' to others and every time 'after preaching' he makes effort to 'reconcile' with the brothers and sisters in the congregation.

Kivengere believes that God is going to remove the barriers among his audience since the essence of the Christian faith is 'God's intervening love'. 'This love is not satisfied until they respond with a "yes"' (p. 9, #18). Kivengere ends with prayer for Jesus to touch with his wounded hand,[147]

---

145. Throughout Kivengere's sermons under our inquiry, he has the 'wisdom' of not telling the names of people that he uses in his illustrations. Beyond the sermons under our inquiry, he explicitly tells on very few occasions. Nevertheless we raise this comment to show that Kivengere is not in the 'habit' of using names of people outside the Bible in his illustrations.

146. See, Chapter Two, *Jubilee Celebration*.

147. In mentioning the 'Jesus' touch of his wounded hand' reconciliation is in view.

the individual lives of his audience and thanking Jesus for coming to us and speaking the 'wonderful word to those of us who were absolutely helpless'. In this closing prayer, just as in the opening prayers, he focused clearly on reconciliation (p. 9, #20).

5.5.2.5 Summary of God's Intervening Love: AO: 19750729, [#1]

Kivengere's opening prayers have a direct link with reconciliation, the main subject that he is expounding with a view to bringing about the transformation of his audience.

This single big theme of reconciliation shows Kivengere the preacher: he is focused. It is not surprising that the year before, at Lausanne Congress, the theme of reconciliation was focused in the life and work of Jesus Christ on the cross,[148] and, this year the same focus on the life and work of Jesus is explained with an emphasis on the love of God.

Since entering seminary at Pittsburgh in 1964,[149] Kivengere continued to focus on this theme of reconciliation—Billy Graham's call of October 1966 that we have only one gospel to declare in every generation: 'God was in Christ reconciling the world unto Himself' (2 Cor 5:19).[150]

Kivengere in this sermon is clear more than elsewhere in his sermons on the importance of Scripture for his preaching reconciliation. In the previous sermons, he first reads the texts aloud to let the word of God speak before the preacher does. Here he underpins the significance of letting Scripture speak before the preacher with the expressions: 'Scripture says', 'For we read here', 'As we have been reading in Romans chapter 5', and 'God's word is action'.

See his article, Every time Kivengere speaks of the language of 'healing', 'deep wounds' 'wounded hand', 'bleeding Africa', 'Africa's bleeding', 'bleeding woman' (Mark 5:25–29), 'bleeding Christ', 'scars', reconciliation is in view.

148. Festo Kivengere, 'The Cross and World Evangelization', in *Let the Earth Hear His Voice: International Congress on World Evangelization, Lausanne, Switzerland: Official Reference Volume: Papers and Responses* (ed. James Douglas; Minneapolis: World Wide Publications, 1975), 400-04. For audio version, Festo Kivengere, *The Cross and World Evangelization; and Communion Service*, Audio Cassette (International Congress on World Evangelization; Lausanne, 1974).

149. See Chapter Two, 5.4 'Pittsburgh Seminary: From 1964–1967'.

150. See Chapter Two, 5.4 'Pittsburgh Seminary: From 1964–1967'.

As God speaks to us through his words, those words at the same time search the preacher as well as his audience. In relation to this sermon, Kivengere is aware that God has spoken the message of his love through Scripture not only to his audience but also to him as preacher. Through Scripture, God spoke in his love for humanity: 'Father forgive them for they do not know what they are doing'. Kivengere believes these words of God are not mere words of God but are also actions of God. He acted in love by sending his Son Jesus to die on the cross for the sins of all humanity, thereby granting forgiveness to all in the words of Jesus on the cross: 'Father forgive them'. Kivengere believed God was speaking to us and found him with bitter hatred of Amin. He asked God to forgive him and so he forgave Amin.

The impact of this message from Scripture is seen in the Ugandan community. Lives are being changed as words of Scripture are heeded on being set free by Jesus Christ. On being set free by Jesus Christ, Christians are reconciling with each other. The result of heeding the words of Scripture is practical reconciliation in Jesus Christ. Scripture speaks the word of reconciliation to individuals and to the community and that is why in Uganda a politician is saved and immediately reconciled with his enemies and the community.

In the sermon, twice he refers to peace as linked with the reconciliation, something he never mentioned in the previous sermon in this second set of reconciliation sermons. Mention is made of enmity as the state for which deliverance is required, but on embracing Christ, believers gain peace. Kivengere strongly expressed that when God speaks reconciliation from the cross, he speaks effectively and his words changes men. Here alone among all his sermons Kivengere speaks about the 'yes' of God being pronounced in the sinners favour.

While he does not openly acknowledge any influence from Karl Barth's 'yes' of God,[151] in relation to the covenant of grace fulfilled in Jesus Christ, his language echoes a favourite Barthian expression. Barth also links his covenant of grace to the story of Genesis 1 to 3, and in this sermon, Kivengere links the barriers which God's love will pull down, and for which

---

151. See Chapter Three, 3.5.2 'Reconciliation—Covenant and Sin'.

his audience need to respond with 'yes', to have its origin in Genesis 1 to 3. Again, with clear affinity with Barth's theological exegesis, especially the *Sache*—the subject-matter, God,[152] Kivengere's explanation has a clear focus on God: 'God has justified us', 'God created man', 'man broke away from God', 'deep down we live with separation from God', 'thanks be to God', 'reconcile us to God', etc. God is the subject matter and he explains the reconciling love for his audience starting with God.

5.5.3 'The Love of Christ' AO: [197707--][153]

5.5.3.1 *Situating the Sermon*
Kivengere preached this sermon in New York City at a missionary gathering (p. 1, #1).

5.5.3.2 *Introduction*
The transcript of this sermon begins with a continuation from an earlier part of the sermon in which he tells them: '[T]he New Testament calls that kind of love, grace' (p. 1, #1). We will assume in what follows that the missing opening pages do not undermine the integrity of this sermon.

5.5.3.3 *Exposition*
He explains that 'grace is love underserved, unearned' (p. 1, #1). When that love comes within the reach of a life, or when it is brought by grace into the radius of that saving hand of Jesus Christ, that life can never be the same'. Grace has a way of filling empty gaps in life. This 'grace comes in the person of that unspeakable Jesus, and the gaps are filled'. That grace 'saved a wretch like me' (p. 1, #1).

The narrative features in this definition of grace cannot be missed. As Campbell rightly remarked: 'Among the features that suggest narrative is

---

152. See Chapter Three, 3.3 'Barth's Hermeneutics' and 3.4 'Barth: The *Sache*—The Subject-matter, God'.

153. This sermon transcript is missing the usual preliminary information—thus, we have given an overarching title, 'The Love of Christ', which is broad enough to capture Kivengere's message in the sermon. However, a sub-theme found in the sermon would be 'The value of Life in Christ' (p. 4, #6–#7).

a striking personal dimension largely conveyed by the activity of personal actors, who usually undertake actions, often in relation to one another, and to whom events occur' adding that such 'stories are especially useful types of texts for giving an account of the behaviour, actions, history, and or accomplishments of people (or most personally of personal actors).[154] He desires that his audience would understand that there is indeed 'an amazing personal dimension' in the story that the New Testament calls grace. He describes the personal dimension in two ways: 'that unspeakable Jesus', and 'a wretch, me'. There is 'action' undertaken here by Jesus with reference to a 'wretch'. By Kivengere pointing to Jesus as the 'object' of faith, the saving work of Jesus is placed in the larger New Testament story of God's love for the world.

Kivengere jumps to thank the missionaries that brought the gospel to Africa: 'May God bless you, particularly whenever I participate in missionary endeavours, it reminds me of something I can never express, because I am a direct product of the message which was brought to Africa through the missionaries' (p. 1, #1)[155]—thus bridging the gap between him and his audience. 'Missionaries did not bring God to Africa. Africa had God before any missionary came'. The missionaries brought 'the message' of which he is a direct beneficiary of the love of God. The missionaries came and preached 'him [Jesus] who left his divinity and entered into the mess of humanity, and took the case of human misery so seriously that he became man for men' (pp. 2–3, #3). Again, reconciliation is not far away.

In his father's traditional religion, they were seekers after God but never found him (pp. 1–2, #2). Some 'people who don't know Africa think that was foolish paganism', but 'Not at all. It was the most meaningful way of seeking a meaningful relationship with God'. In mentioning their search for a meaningful relationship with God, reconciliation is in view.

---

154. Douglas A. Campbell, 'The Story of Jesus in Romans and Galatians', in *Narrative Dynamics in Paul: A Critical Assessment* (ed. Bruce W. Longenecker; Louisville, Kent.: Westminster John Knox, 2002), 99.
155. Over the years he has openly been indebted to missionary endeavors of evangelism in Uganda. For example, his address at the 1972 Keswick, Kivengere, 'Christ the Renewer', 66–67. In 1974: Kivengere, 'Testimony', 416. In 1975: Kivengere, 'The Release of Forgiveness', 27.Kivengere, 'Christ the Renewer', 66–67.

Kivengere was very alert to the moods of scholarship about African Traditional Religion in the 1960s to the 1970s and well beyond that time. Many scholars were interested in the encounter between Christianity and African Traditional Religion.[156] Secondly, there were 'voices' such as Emil Ludwig, a German biographer and writer, who asked, 'how can the untutored Africans conceive God? . . . How can this be'?, adding that 'Deity is a philosophical concept which savages are incapable of framing'.[157] To clarify for his audience the difference between Christianity and African Traditional Religion in regard to accessing a meaningful relationship with God, he objected to the notion that his father's religion was foolish paganism.

With his father's religion, they were 'seeking for a meaningful relationship with the creator' (pp. 1–2, #2), even if problematic at several points. The key problem was that 'we had never found that meaningful relationship with that creator, which, when experienced, the seeker can sit back

---

156. The list could begin with: Kwesi A Dickson and Paul Ellingworth, eds., *Biblical Revelation and African Beliefs* (London: Lutterworth P., 1969); John S Mbiti, *African Religions & Philosophy* (2nd ed.; Oxford; Portsmouth, N.H: Heinemann, 1990 [1969]); John S Mbiti, *The Crisis of Mission in Africa* (Mukono: Uganda Church Press, 1971); John S Mbiti, *New Testament Eschatology in an African Background: A Study of the Encounter Between New Testament Theology and African Traditional Concepts* (London: Oxford University Press, 1971); Barrett, David B., ed., *African Initiatives in Religion; 21 Studies from Eastern and Central Africa* (Nairobi: East African Publishing House, 1971); and continue with: Aylward Shorter and Eugene Kataza, eds., *Missionaries to Yourselves; African Catechists Today* (Maryknoll, N.Y: Orbis Books, 1972); Peter Sarpong, *Ghana in Retrospect: Some Aspects of Ghanaian Culture* (Tema: Ghana Pub. Corp, 1975); Edward H Berman, ed., *African Reactions to Missionary Education* (Publications of the Center for Education in Africa; New York: Teachers College Press, Teachers College, Columbia University, 1975); E. Bolaji Idowu, *African Traditional Religion: A Definition* (Maryknoll, N.Y: Orbis Books, 1973); Byang H Kato, *Theological Pitfalls in Africa* (Kisumu, Kenya: Evangel Pub. House, 1975); Erasto Muga, *African Response to Western Christian Religion: A Sociological Analysis of African Separatist Religious and Political Movements in East Africa* (Kampala: East African Literature Bureau, 1975); Benjamin C Ray, *African Religions: Symbol, Ritual, and Community* (2nd ed.; Upper Saddle River, N.J: Prentice Hall, 2000 [1976]); Robert Cameron Mitchell, *African Primal Religions* (Major world religions series; Niles, Ill: Argus Communications, 1977); Charles R Taber, ed., *The Church in Africa, 1977: Papers Presented at a Symposium at Milligan College, March 31-April 3, 1977* (South Pasadena, Calif: William Carey Library, 1978); Kofi Asare Opoku, *West African Traditional Religion* (Accra, [Ghana]: FEP International Private Limited, 1978); Tokunboh Adeyemo, *Salvation in African Tradition* (2nd ed [1979] ed.; Nairobi, Kenya: Evangel Pub. House, 1997 [1979]).

157. Cf. James Henry Owino Kombo, *The Doctrine of God in African Christian Thought: The Holy Trinity, Theological Hermeneutics, and the African Intellectual Culture* (Studies in Reformed theology; Leiden; Boston: Brill, 2007), 204.

in security and sing, "Amazing Grace, I am now safe. All is well"'. 'That is what was lacking'.

At this point, he turns back to his point of gratitude to the missionaries for not bringing their culture to Africa: 'the missionaries be blessed for not coming to preach their culture' (pp. 1–2, #2). He lists the missionary cultures: American, German, and British. 'American culture could never save African culture, because American culture cannot save itself' and that they 'were messed up cultures like any other one'—again, bridging the gap between preacher and audience by referring to 'any other one'.

The missionaries came and preached Jesus who came into the mess of humanity and reconciled humanity to God (pp. 2–3, #3). 'The word became flesh for flesh' [cf. John 1]'. He said: 'that is the centre of the good news. You catch the vision of that one, you can't stay where you are'. Kivengere has placed Jesus at the 'centre' of the gospel and intimately linked 'reconciliation' with this gospel: 'He [Jesus] left his divinity and entered into the mess of humanity'.

'For God moved from where he was to where we are so that we might be lifted from where we are to where he is' (pp. 2–3, #3).[158] 'That is the New Testament'. For Kivengere, in telling his audience 'that is the New Testament', the gospel of reconciliation is in view. 'He came down, symbolically down, in despair' to the 'fragmented'.

He emphatically tells them of the nature of the work of Jesus Christ to humanity: 'and no other good hands could pick up humanity and put together'. 'Human efforts were put forward by people of good wishes like philosophers[159] and intellectuals, however, 'there were no hands with ability to pick up broken pieces of a human life and put them together and create a whole new man again, except the wounded hand [Jesus' hand]'. In a

---

158. Cf. Kivengere, 'His Flooding Love', p. 2, #4–#5.AO: 19750729 [#1], (p. 2, #4–#5). He talks of God moving from where he is into the human mess; Kivengere, *When God Moves*; Kivengere, *The Spirit Is Moving*.

159. cf. his 'favorite' philosopher that he likes to critique, German philosopher Nietzsche. 'Many modern philosophers, like the famous German atheist, Nietzsche, have become prophets of despair. They struggle with the problem of how to make life meaningful, and in the end they say all you can do is to know you are utterly meaningless: accept it, and face it, feed on it, commit suicide! For some people suicide is the literal result of alienation from God' (Kivengere, *When God Moves*, 12).

meticulous contrast with 'human efforts . . .', by which man successfully failed to 'create a new whole man', 'not broken into pieces', Kivengere tells them, 'except the wounded hand' of Jesus.

Even though unmentioned, two passages are in view here: 'By His wounds' (1 Pet 2: 24) and 'a new society of God's children' (Eph 2:14–18).[160] Kivengere's audience would not have missed his clear emphasis on both the *nature* of the work of Christ, namely, the work of reconciliation ('pick up humanity and put together') and the *fact* of reconciliation. And the fact that reconciliation is God's initiative: God [is] on the move after the beloved, like a shepherd seeking the lost sheep until He finds it. ([cf. Luke 15:6] "Rejoice with me I have found my lost sheep"), Jesus. My, that was good news' (p. 3, #4–#5).

Kivengere returned to the missionaries and the reason why the Africans accepted the good news the missionaries preached. 'The message spoke to our needs, for we were seeking for meaningful relationship with the creator' and 'in Jesus Christ the meaningful relationship was established' and 'That is why I am a Christian today'. This is a clear reference to 'reconciliation' even without the language, for he refers to establishing a meaningful relationship 'in Jesus Christ'.

To let his audience appreciate the significance of the message of 'the love of God', which moved the missionaries from their home countries to evangelize Uganda, he recalled the history of the missionary preaching in Uganda. They preached 'the good news' on coming to Uganda. The centenary of the gospel work in Uganda will be held in December 1977. From Mombasa [situated on the coast of the Indian Ocean in Kenya] to Uganda, the first bunch of missionaries from Britain walked '800 miles without roads, and the first group of missionaries died on the way'.[161]

The first Bishop [James] Hannington 'was murdered, speared to death'.[162] He said to the chief, 'You have killed me, but my blood has opened the way to enter your country'.[163] Kivengere notes: 'And so the missionaries came'.

---

160. See Kivengere, 'Bleeding Africa', 28.
161. See Chapter Two, '3.1 Missionary Origins'.
162. Faupel, *African Holocaust*, 125.
163. Pulford, *Eating Uganda*, 63.

He asks: 'Do you know why?' In answer to his question, he tells them that 'this was not a business of culture. This was men and women compelled by the love of Christ, because it was God who loved those Africans, not mere men'. Kivengere uses the message of reconciliation using the language of 2 Corinthian 5:14, when he referred to missionaries being 'compelled by the love of Christ'. Still using the language of 'love of Christ' he says: 'Other than the love of Calvary, no one could have stepped where we were: it was too tough'.

From the subject of 'the love of Christ' that compelled the missionaries from Britain to go to Uganda, he shifted to 'the love of Christ' that moved Paul in excitement to Jerusalem 'bound in the Holy Spirit'. 'This is St. Paul speaking, . . . Listen to the words': 'And now behold I am going to Jerusalem bound in the Spirit, not knowing what shall befall me there, except that the Holy Spirit testifies to me in every city that imprisonment and affliction await me' (p. 3, #4–#5). 'That is exactly the context in which I want you to see what is the value of life' (p. 4, #6–#7). By pointing to 'affliction and imprisonment that awaits Paul', as a testimony from the Holy Spirit, Kivengere is drawing the attention of his audience to the ministry of Paul and the larger story of life under the overarching theme of 'the love of God'.

Kivengere then goes on to propound three things that are a 'must' for life on the basis of the testimony he read from Acts 20:22. First, 'life must have a direction' (p. 4, #6–#7), second, 'life must have a motivation' (pp. 5–6, #8), and his audience must testify to the grace of God because the world is waiting for this message (p. 9, #13).

He now links back to his main text, Roman 5:4–5: 'And God has flooded our hearts with the love of himself whom he has given us'. 'The Spirit of Christ takes possession of a young man, or a young woman, a girl or a boy, and gives you that tremendous dynamic which motivates your life' (p. 6, #9). As in the first set of explicit reconciliation sermons, the language of Christ as the dynamic that motivates the life of a believer is used here. 'Paul had that dynamic'—that is, Paul had Christ at the centre of his life.

He asks: 'have you ever known it? Do you have the Spirit in you to motivate you, so that you can move in New York, in Uganda, in a confused world where men are breaking apart? Where men are slaughtering each other for nothing? Amidst tribal wars, wars of ideology, racial tensions?' ... 'We need a motivating dynamic in order to move in the direction of his redeeming love', 'the world is waiting for you' (p. 6, #9). Kivengere is aware of the cultural, political and social context of what is happening in Uganda and New York and the world, and he believes that reconciliation in Christ is the message that his audience needs.

Kivengere adopts a confessional tone using the image of 'flood' from life in relation to the 'love of him [Christ] whom God has given us'. When the Spirit of Christ takes possession of men and women and gives them the tremendous dynamic that motivates a life centred in Christ, there is 'reconciliation'.

'Jesus Christ died for New York, whatever happens, whether your banks fall flat, Jesus still loved your city, because He loved the people and died for them' (pp. 6–7, #10). Kivengere speaks of 'reconciliation' using the language of which he has been using in the sermon up to this point, namely, 'the death of Christ [5:5, 8] and 'the love of Christ'.

The formula 'Jesus died for us' was a significant confession in Pauline epistles.[164] Relevant for our purpose in regard to Kivengere's message about 'the death of Jesus Christ' for his audience in New York, is the conclusion drawn from Gibson's study that, in the formula of 'Jesus died for us', against the context of Paul's Roman audience, some have read it of a 'hero' dying for the welfare of the city and their indigenous land. 'The death of others, especially the 'noble death' is always undertaken in attempt to rescue or defend one's own'.[165] Perhaps against a similar 'hero culture' in the USA, 'the death of Jesus Christ for New York' would have had its own contemporary nobility.

But, when compared with how Paul applies 'the death of Jesus Christ' a clear contrast emerges: Jesus Christ was not a simply a 'hero'. He was the Son of God, 'in the very form of God' (Phil 2:6) who died for others:

---

164. Jeffry B. Gibson, 'Paul's Dying Formula: Prolegomena to an Understanding of Its Import and Significance', in *Celebrating Romans, Template for Pauline Theology: Essays in Honor of Robert Jewett* (ed. Sheila E McGinn; Grand Rapids, Mich.: Eerdmans, 2004), 21–22.
165. Gibson, 'Paul's Dying Formula: Prolegomena to an Understanding of Its Import and Significance', 25.

sinners, enemies of God. A significant point here for Paul is that 'the death of Jesus Christ' is a pathway for believers to humility and servanthood. Kivengere found in Paul's story with his Roman believers a story for his New York audience. When he tells: whatever contemporary hero overtones in the phrase 'Jesus Christ died for New York', especially when explained by 'whatever happens'—bringing in their current 'suffering', etc., their banks have fallen flat—It is the sacrifice of the Son of God for sin that profoundly changes reality. 'Jesus still loves their city because he died for them'.

Kivengere's proclamation to his audience to themselves, in true Keswick style, then turns to a call to mission. Both preacher and audience have the same call. 'There are people who are waiting to hear that God so loved them that he died for them' (p. 9, #13). 'This is the ministry which every Christian has received from the Lord Jesus Christ to testify to the grace of God in Jesus Christ. . . . Jesus came to the world as Redeemer, Saviour, full of grace and truth, and now out of his fullness all of us have received grace upon grace' (p. 9, #13). 'This is the ministry which God has given you my dear friends'. They have 'received the ministry to testify to the grace of God as if it is in Jesus Christ' (p. 9, #13). The world is 'waiting to hear' (p. 9, #13).[166]

5.5.3.4 Summary of 'The Love of Christ' AO: [197707--]

As we have hinted in chapter 2 and developed in chapter 3, the English Keswick movement, deeply influenced by the American holiness tradition, taught that the Christian believers should have a 'second conversion', beyond the first.[167] Kivengere was a child and spokesman of the Revival, and by 1977 he was also a spiritual leader and spokesman of the COU house of bishops. This sermon shows a distinctive element of the Revival, which was different from the Keswick teaching on a 'second conversion'.

Like other Balokole, Kivengere focused on initial conversion with the overwhelming experience of brokenness at the cross, which triggers a public

---

166. The transcript ends at this point without his usual way of concluding in prayer.
167. See Chapter Two 4. 'The East African Revival Movement' and Chapter Three, 2 'The Keswick Movement and The East African Revival: The Approach and Context of Preaching'.

confession of sins with restitution.[168] Unlike the emphasis of the early Keswick movement on Spirit-filling of believers, Kivengere's explanation emphasizes the cross-centred filling of gaps because his understanding of the cross is synonymous with Jesus Christ. God's grace comes in the person of Jesus Christ, who fills gaps in the life of believers. Kivengere's own testimony reinforces the message, which he boldly proclaimed because Jesus saved him and filled the gaps in his life.

This Jesus-centred message moves on from the Keswick emphasis on Spirit-filling. In fact, if Kivengere were alive in Uganda today, where a growing Pentecostal revivalism focuses largely on Spirit-filling,[169] he would almost certainly object. The focus and emphasis for him is the person of Jesus Christ. His absolute focus on the love of Christ is immediately practical. The cross displays the love of Christ and this is manifested to him at his conversion,[170] after which he runs to reconcile with his enemies. Christ reconciled him to God (theological dimension of reconciliation) and sent him to reconcile with his enemies (social dimension of reconciliation).

Using the language of grace, the undeserved love of God, makes Kivengere see the person of Jesus when any life encounters the saving work of Christ as grace of God. It will not remain the same. It affected the missionaries, who had to bring this love of Christ to Uganda and not bring their culture; it affected him, bringing him out from the ancestral worship of his father. The message, brought by the missionaries, is bearing fruit in Uganda and soon after this sermon was preached the celebration of its growth and spread was celebrated in December 1977.

This sermon clearly stated that the missionaries came and preached reconciliation by their proclamation of Jesus as the Son of God who left his divinity and entered into the mess of humanity, and took the case of human misery so seriously that He became man for men.

---

168. See Chapter Three, Chapter Three, 2.1.1 'Day One: The Diagnosis—Sin'.

169. For discussion on Pentecostalism as new form of Revivalism in Uganda and its emphasis on spirit-filling, see Kasibante Amos, 'The Challenge of the New Pentecostal Churches to the East African Revival: The Confluence of Two Movements in my Life', in *The East African Revival: History and Legacies* (Kampala, Uganda: Fountain Publishers, 2010), 90–110.

170. See Chapter Two, 5.2 'Kivengere's Conversion: From Agonistic to Preacher'.

5.5.4 'Life in Jesus': AO: 1978 [02--?], [#1]

5.5.4.1 Situating the Sermon

Kivengere preached this sermon in Sydney, Australia, 1978, on the occasion of 'Bridge 1978'.[171] This 'Bridge 1978' was a mission, which 'aimed at preparing the ground for the following year's Billy Graham crusade' and it was also 'a success in raising interest and cash for AEE's work among the Ugandan refugees'.[172]

5.5.4.2 Preliminaries

Kivengere opens with greetings from 'Christians on the continent of Africa', expressing joy for both Michael [Cassidy] and himself, representing, AEE at the mission (p. 1, #1). Kivengere preached this sermon in tandem with Cassidy.[173] Playing on the mission slogan, he announced he would 'purposely share the miracles of His grace in situations which are absolutely the very opposite of what you may call "bridge"'. However, in his usual style, Kivengere himself bridges the gap between himself and his audience. His sharing is 'not just words nicely put together by ministers and preachers for church-going people', because 'We are not actually living in a coordinated world'. The world is 'increasingly becoming a world of bewilderments, a world of puzzlements'. In Africa, they are discovering that 'only in Jesus the crucified, Jesus Christ, that a hope for a dis-coordinated continent and a dis-coordinated experience in human society can find its answer' (p. 1, #2).

5.5.4.3 Exposition

After reading aloud from Paul's epistle to Ephesians 2:12, Kivengere's exposition began (pp. 1–2, #3–#4). Paul was writing at the time in history when there was 'so much disintegration, and yet there was so much enlightenment'. 'This was the Roman [E]mpire. This was the height of Greek philosophy. This was when Judaism was at its height'. Paul is writing when he had 'tried every possible way to make life a success, in his way'.

---

171. Coomes, *Festo Kivengere*, 386.
172. See, Coomes, *Festo Kivengere*, 386.
173. According to Braga, preaching in tandem was a regular part of the Katoomba Convention in the early days. See Braga, *A Century Preaching*, 76.

He refers to his audience as 'brethren', thus again, bridging the gap between the preacher and his audience. He appealed to their memory in order to come to the heart of his message: 'remember that time'. He makes the same point in several ways, focusing 'that time', never to be forgotten (p. 2, #5). 'Scripture divides life very simply in this way'. 'At that time. . . . You were separated from Christ'. 'Life is divided by the simple fact of Jesus Christ. Life before he came, [and] Life after he had come'. He asks: 'what was life before he came'? 'Paul tells us what it was': 'you were separate from Christ'. 'Paul says, "Life separate from Christ is one divided life"', . . . 'Separate from Christ, life is like a big forest in which you wonder alone'.

He tells nevertheless of a young American millionaire whose life was miserable, until he discovered 'the secret, that apart from Christ, life is divided' (pp. 4–5, #5). Using his own autobiography, he tells: 'I was a stranger to my self. . . . Without Christ everything is strange' (p. 4, #6). He links back to the Genesis 3 story. 'No wonder Adam went and hid in the garden of God. Everything around that man Adam became a strange experience. Even his wife sounded a strange woman. Even God who gave him life became a strange God, from whom to run'.

Using Adam as an 'everyman', he expands his experience to others: 'there are many people who run away from God'. However, when Jesus Christ comes and deals with them things that were strange begin to have a new meaning (p. 4, #6). 'Jesus makes all the difference in life, I can tell you' (p. 4, #7). Kivengere then links back to his text: 'St. Paul says, apart from Christ, life was absolutely a strange experience all along', but 'with Christ comes something completely new'. Jesus 'has removed enmity and estrangements and dividedness' and he has 'introduced the element which Paul calls, "Peace", "Holiness', "integration"'. 'Finding your true identity in his love' leads you not to walk as a stranger but to 'walking as a child at home'.

Kivengere hopes that his audience will 'discover the true and fresh meaning of life when Jesus has been welcomed into the affairs of your life tonight' (p. 5, #7). He asked God to bless them as he concluded his message.

5.5.4.4 Summary of 'Life in Jesus': AO: 1978 [02--?], [#1]

Preaching in tandem, the Revival influence on his style of preaching is certainly evident. However, tandem was not a new way of preaching to Australia, in particular with the Sydney diocese. This was a common feature of Keswick, and it therefore came to the Keswick influenced by the Katoomba Convention in its early days, and, after lapsing for a time, 43 years after the start of Katoomba Convention, Loane revived it.[174] However, the significant thing about Kivengere preaching in tandem with Cassidy, is that it enabled him to practically demonstrate his own reconciliation to his 'miracle brother'[175] from apartheid South Africa. This displayed 'life in Jesus'.

He has been preaching in tandem with Cassidy since way back in 1970,[176] when he travelled with Cassidy to America, preaching the message of reconciliation from 2 Corinthians 5.[177] Now, in 1978, alongside Cassidy still, he appeals to his audience to accept Jesus today. This is a mark of Revival influence, directly linked with the message of reconciliation for after a week of preaching the climatic last day is the day to appeal to them to accept Christ.

While in the previous sermons he consistently brought greetings from Uganda or East Africa, especially from the brethren who were always praying for his preaching missions around the world, in this sermon he brings greetings from the entire 'continent of Africa'. In the previous year he had been awarded the Freedom Prize for speaking out on human rights in Africa.[178] His gospel message of reconciliation now addressed not just human rights, but all of life on the African continent.[179] In his Australian 'Bridge 1978' address, he refers to Africa, linking it to Jesus Christ as the solution to bewilderment in life.

---

174. For Loan's revival of tandem preaching at Katoomba Convention, see Braga, *A Century Preaching*, 76.
175. Michael, 'Forward', 5.
176. A list of Audio sermons preached in tandem by Kivengere and Cassidy include, Tapes: 116–123 (back inside cover) of Kivengere, *Love Unlimited*.
177. See Chapter One, 2. 'Reconciliation and Kivengere's Sermons'.
178. See Chapter Four, 3. 'The Exile (February 1977 – May 1979).
179. This mission was also to prepares Australia for the 1979 evangelistic crusade of Billy Graham.

The greetings from Africa are linked with reconciliation in Jesus Christ. The brethren on the African continent are described in the sermon as 'finding Jesus', the reconciler. Greetings from them, therefore, is a way of expressing the love of Christ presently at work among believers. This is the God whose message Kivengere comes to share.

In the sermon, his biblical theology of creation is evident. God created the world and yet the world is experiencing brokenness. 'Life separate from Christ is one divided life', and 'Separate from Christ, life is like a big forest in which you wander alone'. However, there is hope because Jesus came into the situation. More significant, his biblical theology of time is brought to the fore. He explains life before and outside Christ and life in and after Christ. He is using Paul's understanding of time in Romans 5:6, 'at that time' God sent his son.

He does not make any links to Paul's similar view of time in Galatians 4:4 '*In the fullness of time* God sent forth His Son . . . that he might redeem those who were under the law'.[180] Nevertheless, he recognized that human history is redemptive history and time serves the outworking of God's purpose. After Christ comes, time is for living a life of reconciliation.

In terms of reconciliation, Kivengere explains that 'apart from Christ life was absolutely a strange experience all along', but when Christ came, he removed enmity, estrangements, and dividedness and introduced peace, holiness, and integration. With the influence of Keswick preaching, emphasizing on the last day of the convention commitment to Jesus Christ and service to him, Kivengere appeals to his audience to welcome Jesus in the affairs of their life tonight, and they will discover the true and fresh meaning of living a reconciled life in Jesus Christ.

5.5.5 Conclusion

This section has examined individually the second set of Pauline reconciliation sermons, those from Romans 5:1–11. We now draw together common threads. Influences from Keswick, the Revival, Karl Barth and Paul can be discerned, informing Kivengere's preaching of reconciliation.

---

180. Emphasis added.

Kivengere teaching of reconciliation basically followed Paul's understanding in the passage. However, as in the previous sermon where he displayed one major deficiency (in his biblical theology of Pauline apostleship), in this second set of sermons he displayed two major deficiencies. First, Kivengere does not mention and explain justification, whereas Paul uses the concept of reconciliation to back up what he says about justification. In Paul's thought, reconciliation is already present in verse 1 of Romans 5. For him, the result of justification is peace with God and all the benefits it brings, especially access into a relationship based on grace of the undeserved love of God. Although Kivengere affirms God's grace, he does not mention justification at all.

Secondly, Paul states that God has justified sinners by the blood of Christ, and this means believers will be delivered from the wrath of God at the last judgment, because they were once enemies of God, but now they have been reconciled with God by Jesus' death. In contrast, Kivengere is silent about the wrath of God. Because he is strong in the sermon on the place of Scripture speaking before the preacher and because in explaining reconciliation in Christ Jesus, he takes the cross of Christ as the first and last point, leaving out these significant points made by the apostle seems to be an anomaly.

5.6 Explicit Reconciliation Sermons (III): Ephesians 2:14–18 in Context

5.6.1 His Flooding Love: AO: 19750729, [#2]

5.6.1.1 Situating the Sermon
Kivengere preached this sermon at Westmont Presbyterian Church, USA, on 29 May 1975.

5.6.1.2 Introduction
Kivengere's introduction already focuses on reconciliation, for he tells that he is grateful to be back at Westmount to 'share something of the love of Christ' (p. 1, #2).

5.6.1.3 Exposition

Kivengere recaps the central idea of the message he gave the previous day: 'Christ rescued us from the power of the dominion of darkness' (p. 1, #2). As he paraphrased: 'Christ rescued us from the dominion of confusion',[181] he set the scene for his message on reconciliation.

'The centre of the essence of [Christian] religion is putting wrong relationships right'. Kivengere's understanding of the Christian 'religion' as that which has the 'potential' for positive change in theological and social relationships, is in view.[182] Putting wrong relationships right is 'Initially between man and God, and then as a result between man and man' (p. 1, #2). Clearly, Kivengere is speaking about reconciliation even though he does not use the word. For Kivengere, if the relationship between man and God, and man and man, is right in any person's life, then, 'That life is complete'.

'But what is Christian perfection?' (p. 2, #3) . . . 'It simply means right relationship with God, right relationship with man as a result, and usually we confuse the two'. This confusion comes from stressing one side of reconciliation at the expense of the other, leading to a reaction from others.

It is possible to care *only* about the vertical relationship with God. When you stress seeking a perfect relationship with God, you forget the world, and ignore what happens with others. This mentality is bound to meet a reaction against it. However, it is also possible to emphasize the horizontal relationship, to 'Forget about the vertical relationship, what matters is the horizontal [relationship]'.[183]

---

181. See Kivengere, 'God's Intervening Love'.

182. There are numerous recent studies that lend support to the positive role of reconciliation, especially social, political and economic well-being. For example, see Mark R. Amstutz, 'Human Rights and the Promise of Political Forgiveness', *Review and Expositor* 105 (2007): 553–77; Barkan, 'Historical Reconciliation', 1–15; Will Kymlicka and Bashir Bashir, eds., *The Politics of Reconciliation in Multicultural Societies* (Oxford; New York: Oxford University Press, 2008); Amy Benson Brown and Karen Poremski, eds., *Roads to Reconciliation: Conflict and Dialogue in the Twenty-First Century* (Armonk, N.Y: M.E. Sharpe, 2005); A. Gasparini, 'Globalisation, Reconciliation and the Conditions for Conserving Peace', *Global Society* 22/1 (2008): 27–55; Langmead, 'Transformed Relationships', 5–20; Shenk, 'The Gospel of Reconciliation Within the Wrath of Nations', 2–9; Tripp, Bies, and Aquino, 'A Vigilante Model of Justice', 3–34.

183. A growing number of scholars continue to deal with either vertical or horizontal or both aspects of emphasis include, F. F. Bruce, 'Christ as Conqueror and Reconciler', *BS* 141/564 (1984): 291–302; Walvoord, 'Reconciliation', 3–12; Thomas B. Talbott, 'The New Testament and Universal Reconciliation', *Christian Scholar's Review* 21/4 (1992):

Kivengere calls his audience 'to the balance of the New Testament' (p. 2, #3). The two sides, 'right relationship with God' (theological) and 'right relationship with man' (social), are caught up in one decisive deed. God put right his relationship with man, and so man can now put right his broken relationship with his fellow man. This now defines the life and existence of all human beings wherever they are.

The New Testament is clear about the right balance. 'The balance of the New Testament is that "God so loved that he became man" [John 3:16]. Isn't that tremendous?' (p. 2, #4). Even if he had not become man, 'He would still love men, but it would be absolutely unpractical kind of loving'. The emphasis here, for Kivengere, is plain: 'it is never a dichotomy of only the vertical, or only the horizontal. Never at all' (pp. 2–3, #4). He is commending a view of reconciliation in this present world that promotes human dignity, justice, love, forgiveness, peace and reconciliation.

Kivengere presents two reasons for the right balance: Firstly, 'If you stress the vertical alone, it becomes impractical, it becomes speculative [Christian] religion'; and, secondly, 'If you stress the horizontal alone, you consume each other' (p. 3, #4). Throughout history, humanity has consumed each other with disastrous consequences: racial and political exploitation, war, etc. Kivengere's exposition labours to correct any lack of a right balance and his solution is clear. 'So, we need a balance and the balance is in the coming of Jesus Christ' (p. 3, #5). 'He [Christ] came to make life a balance' (p. 3, #5), noting that, 'I came that they may have life, and that they may live it to the full or "abundantly"' [John 10:10 NKJV]. Humanity tends to stress horizontal relationships, making 'I' [self] the centre of life, with the disastrous consequence of consuming each other,[184] because without Jesus, the target of humanity is self. Jesus said, 'He who loves his life' [John 12:25 NKJV] to which Kivengere modifies using his glosses: 'He

---

376–94; O'Brien, 'Col 1:20 and Reconciliation', 45–53; C. J. Burdon, 'Paul and the Crucified Church', *ET* 95 (1984): 137–41; Margaret E. Thrall, 'Salvation Proclaimed, Pt 5: 2 Corinthians 5:18-21: Reconciliation with God', *ET* 93/8 (My 1982): 227–32; John Murray, 'The Reconciliation', *WTJ* 29 (1966): 1–23; Leon Morris, 'Reconciliation', *CT* 13/8 (1969): 331–32.

184. Cf. Kivengere, *When God Moves*, 11. 'Self-centredness is the greatest enemy of spiritual life'.

who loves himself', 'He who makes himself at the centre', 'He who makes his life all there is about it', consumes it.[185]

However, 'He [Christ] came vertically, to introduce you to God, and in doing that he healed your horizontal confusion' (p. 4, #5). The starting point of putting right the horizontal relationship begins with a balanced relationship with God. Kivengere speaks first of Jesus coming 'to introduce you to God'. Only then does he speak of the direct consequence of this 'introduction', in terms of human relationships.

'He [Jesus] transferred us into a completely new kingdom of relationships where men and women, properly related to God, find that their human relationship are balanced, and healed, and given a new essence' (p. 4, #5), . . . 'the kingdom of the Son of his love'. 'God so loved the world' [John 3:16] that in the new kingdom, 'the relationship is no longer based on self-achievement, but on love', warning that the word 'love' 'can be thoroughly empty in the 20 century'.

Noting that 'anyone' 'who loves, walks in the light, anyone who hates walks in darkness' [1 John 2:10] (pp. 4–5, #6), Kivengere asks: 'Isn't this remarkable?' (p. 5, #6). If 'God the source of life is love, not to love is to be cut from the source of life, at least spiritually' (p. 5, #7). 'Man out of relationship with God is a walking civil war' (pp. 5–6, #8).[186] 'In other words, men with conflicts unresolved' (p. 6, #8), 'Men and women with battles inside'. 'Once you keep the integrator out of your life, you just continue breaking'.

Even in dreadful situations, the love of Jesus in a believer can never be corroded. He describes the hatred among tribes in Burundi leading to the death of 15,000 people: 'there are thousands of widows in the churches and we lost nearly twenty pastors in that terrible massacring' (p. 7, #10).[187]

---

185. Cf. Kivengere, *When God Moves*, 12–13. 'Many modern philosophers, like the famous German atheist, Nietzsche, have become the prophets of despair. They struggle with the problem of how to make life meaningful, and in the end they say all you can do is to know you are meaningless: accept it, face it, feed on it, commit suicide! For some people suicide is the literal result of alienation from God'.

186. William Barclay, *Many Witnesses One Lord* (London: S.C.M., 1966), Chapter Four. 'The Law has made him [man] a split personality and a walking civil war (Romans 7:13–25).

187. René Lemarchand, 'Le Genocide De 1972 Au Burundi: Les Silences De L'histoire', *Cahiers d'études Africaines* 167/42.3 (2002): 551–67; René Lemarchand, *Burundi:*

When God's love flooded the heart, a headmaster of a school could still sing of the love of Jesus to his tormentors. He is an example of a life flooded by the love of God.

He asks his audience: 'Is your heart absolutely set on fire by the love of Christ?' (p. 11, #18). His use of the language of 'set on fire', draws upon that of the Keswick and the Revival, and his use of 'the love of Christ', refers to reconciliation,—as seen in the previous sermons. The young people at Westmont should make God an integral part of their lives, flooding their lives with His love, like the young schoolteacher who triumphed in his dreadful situation. God gave him the ability to love his enemies: 'a re-enactment of Calvary' (p. 11, #18). He appeals to his audience: 'If you are not right with him who is the King of love' you 'should get right, please' (p. 12, #18).

Once again, in true Keswick and Revival style, he appeals for personal reconciliation, then moves on to a call for 'dedication to ministry'. 'I don't mean that you are all going to become clergymen, or pastors, or priests, I mean that in the true sense you are priests of the new King' (p. 13, #18). 'Under the compelling love of Christ', his audience has an obligation to Christ: 'you cannot consume your life upon yourself, it is going to be used [by Christ]' . . . 'commit your life to Jesus Christ and His love on the cross'. This will lead to them being practically involved in the ministry of sharing 'Christ's love for the world'. In all this exhortation, reconciliation is clearly central.

5.6.1.4 Summary of His Flooding Love: AO: 19750729, [#2]

In this third set of sermons, this first sermon is by far the clearest presentation of Kivengere's view of reconciliation. Reconciliation is putting the right relationship with God (theological) and putting right the relationships between man and the man (social), and the New Testament calls for a right balance between the two. 'God so loved that he became'. Because

---

Ethnocide as Discourse and Practice (Woodrow Wilson Center series; Washington: New York, N.Y: Woodrow Wilson Center Press; Cambridge University Press, 1994); René Lemarchand, *Burundi: Ethnic Conflict and Genocide* (1st ed.; Woodrow Wilson Center series; [Washington, D.C.]: Cambridge; New York, NY: Woodrow Wilson Center Press; Cambridge University Press, 1996); among others on the killings and tribal conflicts in Burundi.

reconciliation is based in the love of God, and Jesus Christ came into the human situation, there is no dichotomy between the theological and social dimensions of reconciliation. One without the other is of no use. The love of God transforms both the theological and social dimensions of life.

According to Paul, God saved those who were sinners, raising them from the dead, as it were. Earlier in the epistle (v 7) he noted that they had received redemption from Christ, and this redemption comprised the forgiveness of sins by the blood of Christ. Kivengere does not address himself to this. Paul further speaks of the relationship between Jews and Gentiles who were formerly alienated from the people of God—Israel and his covenants, who have now been brought near by the blood of Christ, through an action which makes the two: Jews and Gentiles in one people of God (vv 14–18). Again, Kivengere is silent on these clear points of Paul's teaching.

Paul's stress that Jews and Gentiles have both become part of the people of God is clearly tied with their reconciliation to God himself. For Paul, to be reconciled with God is synonymous with becoming part of his people. Christ destroyed the hostility between Jews and Gentiles. Both need to be reconciled with God and as a core part of their reconciliation with God, with each other. Kivengere does not in any way address this aspect of Pauline teaching. It is highly likely that his theological exegesis may account in part for this. His theological exegesis focused on God, the main subject whom his audience should look: 'right relationship with *God*' (p. 2, #3) '*God* so loved that he became' (p. 2, #4), 'man out of relationship with God is a walking civil war' (pp. 5–6, #8).

Although he does not mention the Jew and Gentile question, he clearly stressed interpersonal reconciliation. Reconciliation between God and man comes about as Christ takes centre stage in the life of a believer. But as he introduces believers into a relationship of reconciliation with God, he also brings about reconciliation between man and man. Kivengere's theological exegesis enables him to explain reconciliation for his audience starting with God, the source of love, and therefore love becomes another emphasis in the sermon. He views the kingdom of God as the kingdom of love because it is ruled by the love of Christ.

From the first sermon in the first set of sermons until this present sermon, Kivengere consistently exhorts his audience to commit their lives to

Jesus who reconciles them to God and also to one another. Just as the Keswick and the Revival conventions came to a climax in their call to mission and ministry, Kivengere was also clear that the next step for them is to reach out into the world, preaching reconciliation, which in this sermon he calls 'Christ's love to the world' (p. 13, #9).

5.6.2 'Broken Relationships Restored': AO: 1977[0314?][188]

5.6.2.1 Situating the Sermon

The bishop preached this sermon in 1977 somewhere in the United States of America, during the occasion of a 'Mission Night' to 'Episcopalians' and 'other Christian brothers coming from different traditions'.[189] The exact date and church is unknown, but there is a high probability that he preached the sermon between 14 March 1977 and end of March 1977.[190]

5.6.2.2 Preliminaries

Kivengere introduces this sermon with greetings from the Christian brothers and sisters in Uganda to his audience—'Episcopalians and other Christian . . . traditions', gathered on the mission night (p. 1, #1).[191]

---

188. We have taken the theme of this sermon from Kivengere's catchphrase that summarized his message, namely, 'Restoring broken relationships vertically first, horizontal as an outcome' (p. 5, #1).

189. On more than one occasion in the sermon, Kivengere refers to his audience as 'Episcopalians', or 'the Episcopal Church', and 'other Christian brothers coming from different traditions'. See pages: 4, 11–12, and 13 of this sermon.

190. Coomes' report provides some helpful insight to locate the possible date. First, she reports that on 14 March 1977, at *La Canada* Presbyterian Church, Kivengere addressed an overflowing congregation of 1,200, where the *Los Angeles Times* of 14 March 1977, reported Kivengere telling his audience that 'Christians should shout louder against the forces of destruction' and Coomes also report that 'he [Kivengere] urged that it was the job of the Americans to protest to the United Nations'. Secondly, Coomes report that the Washington post of 25 March 1977, in Washington DC, ran his story of Luwum's death in many columns quoting Kivengere saying that 'the good name of our country [Uganda] can only come back when the law replaces the gun' adding that he called for America's help in 'exerting international pressure'. Moreover she provides a more compelling lead which is linked with Kivengere's 'defence' in the sermon.

191. The section running from pages 1–8 in this sermon is transcribed and presented as one long paragraph. However, the following pages (8–15) are presented into 'normal' paragraphs. For clarity and flow of Kivengere's thoughts in the sermon, I have created paragraphs for every new idea in the sermon that appears in the first eight pages.

That year (1977), the COU was celebrating its centenary, 1877–1977,[192] to 'remember [the year] when the message, of the light of the Good News cross[ed] over from Europe, Britain in particular, into Uganda, by means of missionaries' (p. 1, #1).

The missionaries were 'men and women quite ordinary, but in whose hearts the love of Christ had opened new ways of understanding the needs of men and women'. The love of Christ enlarged their horizon so that 'they saw beyond the comfort of their country'; and it 'ushered them into the human arena of need, exactly in the same way as when God broke through the barriers that we sinful men and women had built between us and him'. Already reconciliation is in view, for Kivengere is using the language of 2 Corinthians 5:16: 'the love of Christ' and God breaking through the sinful barriers that men and women had built between God and them, is clearly Kivengere's way of speaking about reconciliation.

Over the years, Christianity in Uganda has grown and spread considerably (p. 1, #1). Its centenary celebration is exciting news. The gospel 'has humanized the dehumanized society' of Uganda. Africa, once known as the '[D]ark [C]ontinent', has seen the success of the light of the good news though some 'areas . . . in human experience' are yet to see this light. He attributes his being a bishop in exile to the presence of dark areas of human experience, alluding to his broken relationship with President Amin.

'Why should I be here as an exile?' . . . 'I have never been involved in politics in any form'. 'I am quite content to go on preaching the gospel, I don't aspire to the presidency' (p. 2, #1).[193] And so, once more, 'why should I be here as an exile?' . . . 'It is because of the dehumanizing elements of evil, which the Bible calls sin'. Kivengere explained that the biblical language of 'sin'[194] simply means 'when humanity lost or missed its target'.

Kivengere then begins to lay further foundations for what will come later in the sermon: broken relationships restored. 'Man [is] created in God's image', in order for God to have 'fellowship with him' (p. 3, #1).

---

192. Tuma and Mutibwa, *A Century of Christianity in Uganda, 1877–1977*.
193. At the time of appointing ministers in President Yusuf Lule's government, there was proposal of Kivengere's name to be Vice-President.
194. In the transcript, it is rendered 'sins', however, we use 'sin' because it reads correctly without the plural.

Man should therefore not miss this target by living for other categories in life: 'colour, money, cars, politics, ideologies, youth, old age'. Kivengere's discussion of the 'image of God' (Gen 1) sets him up for discussing the fall, broken relationships, and then the reconciling work of Christ. The biblical-theological flow is clear.

Kivengere then bridges the gap between himself, the preacher, then a refugee in exile, and his audience, telling them that their country, the United States, 'is not exempted', for many of them came as refugees. 'The blacks' didn't come as refugees, but as slaves, as a result of the greed of both the Whites and the African chiefs who sold their people. In this way, Kivengere evokes the contemporary racial tension in the USA between African American and White American. He then simply declares 'we need a recovery'.

As he concludes his introduction, Kivengere returns to his living in exile because he is regarded as a threat to Idi Amin. To understand this comment, it is important to realize how his 1977 exile was so deeply ingrained on his heart.[195] A broken relationship between him and President Amin led him into exile. But now he tells his audience that rather than being a threat, 'I love him [Amin], I am bound to love him'. 'Having been loved by the son of God, for whom I didn't have anything to do, but because of his outgoing love, he considered me one of those who needed redemption and came my way' (p. 3, #1). As in Paul's statement in 2 Corinthians 5:14, Kivengere considered himself a recipient of reconciliation from God. This led him to the conclusion that 'I owe a debt to every person in the world'—even Amin his tormentor!

That God's love is creative and not destructive is a powerful thing that left Kivengere with no option but to love (p. 3, #1). Kivengere is ready to expound the text, but first he makes a summary of his long introduction: 'tonight we have a mission, Ugandans [are out] there, they love Christ, the gospel came, it [re-] humanized or brought back people into a completely new relationship' (p. 4, #1).

---

195. Kivengere, *I Love Idi Amin*.

5.6.2.3 Exposition

Turning to the biblical passage, he calls their attention to what they have heard tonight in Ephesians 2:14–18 (p. 4, #1). Kivengere's exposition opens with illustrative biographical information about Paul, gleaned from Philippians 3. Paul was one 'who knew what I [Kivengere] am talking about'. Kivengere asks: 'How many Episcopalians can say that?' and bridging the gap between the preacher and his American audience he asks, 'How many of us can say that?'

Continuing to follow Philippians chapter 3, Kivengere explains that by 'righteousness' Paul always meant 'right relationship between him and God', and 'ultimately between him and the neighbour because that was Jewish too'. According to this kind of standard of living, which could be reached by meticulously keeping the [T]en [C]ommandments, Paul said 'I was blameless'.[196]

Turning to Philippians 3 enables Kivengere to allude to Paul's conversion before getting to Ephesians chapter 2. He links the circumstances of Paul's conversion to the overall context of his letter to the Ephesians with a simple conjunction 'And' to emphasize what is following the point. '"And" then in Ephesians, he [Paul] talks in picture language, [presenting a] realistic portrayal of what is going on in society'. He does not explain specifically which society—although he adds that Paul, 'spoke at the time of his own age'.

After mentioning in passing the context of the passage, Kivengere is set to determine what the text means for his audience: 'But if you bring that [S]cripture closer you can see our own age in 1977'. To do so, he jumps back to Paul's audience, listing them: 'there were categories of men, the Romans, the Governors, the Jews, the Religious, the Pharisees, the conservatives, [the] Perfect ones, Separatists, the Greeks, philosophically minded ones, the rational ones, the publicans, the outcasts of society, the women, the despised group, sexually . . . the categories were all there' (p. 5, #1). They had different categories including 'a special one called the Barbarians, people who cannot speak good Greek'. Kivengere then concludes: 'so you

---

196. See Chapter Three, 5.1 'Paul's Experience of Reconciliation'.

see you had all those [factions], and classes of people and fences went up, and relationships were up to zero'.

Christianity 'is faith in Jesus Christ'. So when Christ came, 'the only purpose of his mission was to restore broken relationships between these human beings and this God from whom they came' [vertical relationship]'.[197] And, 'the horizontal relationship[s] between man and man were healed'. That is Christianity; it points to the cross (p. 5, #1). You look at the cross, 'what do you do?' (p. 5, #1). At the cross, you see 'the vertical God came to restore broken relationship with man; God so loved the world [John 3:16]'. 'The horizontal God in eternal and undefeatable love, opening his eternal embrace to the unembraceable, to receive the outcasts, to forgive the sinner, that is the cross' (p. 5, #1).[198]

The bishop prepares his audience to further receive the New Testament message by quoting an Old Testament passage. 'I am going to use a little passage from the Old Testament in order to bring the New Testament into the Old Testament' (p. 5, #1). . . . 'sometimes the Old Testament being [H]ebraic speaks in picture language and helps us to get there'. Like the Hebrews, Kivengere saw truths in pictures.[199]

---

197. For discussion by scholars who are sympathetic the purpose of 'the ministry of reconciliation' and the relationship between 'reconciliation' and 'atonement', see J.I.H. McDonald, 'Paul and the Preaching Ministry. A Reconsideration of 2 Cor 2:14–17 in its Context', *JSNT* 17 (1983): 81–93; David L. Turner, 'Paul and the Ministry of Reconciliation in 2 Cor 5:11-6:2', *Criswell Theological Review* 4 (Fall 1989): 77–95; John W. De Gruchy and Steve De Gruchy, *The Church Struggle in South Africa: 25th Anniversary Edition* (London: SCM, 2005), 43–52; Reimund Bieringer, 'Paul's Understanding of Diakonia in 2 Corinthians 5,18', in *Studies in 2 Corinthians* (ed. R. Bieringer and J. Lambrecht; Leuven: University Press, 1994), 413–28; Victor Paul Furnish, 'Ministry of Reconciliation', *Currents in Theology and Mission* 4/4 (1977): 204–18; Jan Lambrecht, 'Reconcile Yourselves . . . : A Reading of 2 Corinthians 5:11–21', in *Studies on 2 Corinthians* (ed. R. Bieringer and Jan Lambrecht; Bibliotheca Ephemeridum Theologicarum Lovaniensium; Louvain: Leuven University Press, 1994), 363–412; Adolf Koeberle, 'Reconciliation and Justification', *CTM* 21 (1950): 641–58; Vincent Brummer, 'Atonement and Reconciliation', *Religious Studies* 28 (1992): 435–52; Martin H. Franzmann, 'Reconciliation and Justification', *CTM* 21/2 (1950): 81–93.
198. See Miroslav Volf, *Exclusion and Embrace: A Theological Exploration of Identity, Otherness, and Reconciliation* (Nashville, TN: Abingdon Press, 1996).
199. Coomes, *Festo Kivengere*, 291. 'Hebrews saw things in pictures. . . . Festo had the amazing capacity to see the Word of God at both the immediate level and also the subterranean, picture level. He always saw the picture beyond'.

For Kivengere, this method of textual interpretation is helpful because 'It brings historical events into the spiritual experience so that you can see the spiritual in the historic'. Here, as elsewhere, Kivengere sees that the past has its history distinct from the events of the present and yet he desires there to be continuity between the past history and the present events. He brings past and present together not only in his general interpretation of the Bible, but especially in the reconciliation passages. Here he names the historical mess and suffering in the church and nation of Uganda and beyond, and then makes the connection between this real life historical facts of brokenness in the world and the biblical message.

In a sentence, he summarized his message: 'Restoring broken relationships: vertical first, horizontal as an outcome'. His Old Testament illustration is taken from 'Joseph, the young man, the son of Jacob' and his broken relationship with his brothers.

After a straightforward retelling of the story in a lively way, he said, Joseph's brothers determined among themselves: 'Let us put an end . . . to him not to make us feel uncomfortable' (p. 6, #1). He asks: 'Jealousy, is that a strange thing? Can you say that jealousy was only a peculiar weakness among the Hebrews? And that it doesn't take place in America?'

He proceeds to give meaning to the text: 'Don't you know there are people who have murdered other people's characters? Murder, is not just taking a gun—the tongue is the best murderer', even in the church, there are hearts bleeding because the tongue cut deep. 'Oh unhealed wounds' (p. 6, #1).

Joseph suffered when they sold him as a slave but God changed it round. 'Joseph is a wonderful type of Christ, through the tomb'; he ended up becoming a prime minister of Egypt. He asks: 'How do you restore broken relationships?' Although Joseph was as good as dead, he was always alive in the hearts of his fellows and betrayers; and, they needed to be cured from 'the smashing guilt, which haunted them' (p. 7, #1). They had to come to terms with the truth: 'painful the truth was, as long as they evaded the truth, they evaded peace'.

He jumps to the last part of the story. Joseph declares himself when his brothers were unsuspecting with tears streaming down their cheeks (p. 7, #1). He used figurative language to describe Joseph's emotion: 'the heart weeping loud', 'love bleeding, therefore love redeeming', 'weeping love, therefore able to restore the relationship (p. 8, #1). 'How can you restore broken relationships: between husbands and wives? Between blacks and whites in Africa? (p. 8, #2). Here he emphasized the social implications of reconciliation, using strong African values—families, and peoples of Africa.

Christ is restoring broken relationships among Christians. He tells a graphic picture of reconciliation that took place at the Pan African Leader's Assembly (PACLA).[200] PACLA took place in December 1976 in Nairobi, the first meeting of its kind organized under the chairmanship of Kivengere and his colleagues Michael Cassidy and Osei-Mensah. The primary aim was to draw together Christian leaders from all over Africa with all their theological differences and 'preach' 'reconciliation' to them with the hope of encouraging them to further preach the gospel of 'reconciliation' which was desperately needed in Africa through their different churches.[201]

Back to the sermon, Kivengere described the occasion when a White South African, Professor David Bosch,[202] giving a paper before 800 African Christian leaders, touched by the Spirit of God, broke down and wept as he presented his Christian paper on healing relationships (p. 8, #2). 'The love of Christ had penetrated this man's heart' (p. 8, #2). It is important for us to note here that Kivengere's careful choice of Bosch's 'case' of brokenness for the sermon is significant for his audience to grasp the depth and scope of the reconciling work of Christ and to realize that it had an important part in Kivengere's engaging of the minds of his audience with the practical outworking of reconciliation.

Bosch's pain, however, was not just for the participants at the PACLA, such as Kivengere himself ('I was among them', p. 8, #2) who went and embraced the weeping Bosch (p. 8, #2) but for the many Africans who are not in the conference. To understand something of what Kivengere

---

200. See Chapter Four, 2. 'Before Exile (September 1971– February 1977). See further Cassidy, *Together in One Place*, 129–33.
201. For an excellent report of the meeting see, Cassidy, *Together in One Place*.
202. From Cassidy and Osei-Mensah's account *Together in One Place*, 130, it is clear that Kivengere is referring to Professor David Bosch of South Africa's address at PACLA in Nairobi. Bosch's paper was entitled, 'The In-Between People'. Cassidy and Osei-Mensah report that Bosch claimed that 'Reconciliation takes place when two opposing forces clash and somebody gets crushed in between'.

was going through in the midst of Bosch sharing, one would need to remember that way back in 1969 Kivengere was already 'Preaching the Good News that in Jesus the barriers come down—between God and man, and between man and man. [I]n Him is reconciliation'.[203] This reconciliation was not just for the top church leaders and theologians at the conference,[204] but its influence will filter down from Nairobi to Soweto and other parts of South Africa. From this meeting, the fire for a follow up meeting for the South Africa region was formed for a South African Leaders Assembly whose main agenda is perusing and preaching reconciliation.

After Kivengere's description of Bosch's testimony, he concludes the purpose of the story with two points. First, Bosch embraced hundreds of the participants, weeping together, not because he gave them something, but because the 'love [of Christ] has broken barriers down' (p. 9, #2). Secondly, 'Reconciliation, restoration of broken relationships began because of Christ' (p. 9, #2). Relating this back to the biblical story, he tells: 'Joseph wept, *revealed himself to them* [his brothers], and that is a criterion for healing relationships. Only that tonight, a greater than Joseph is here [Jesus Christ]' (p. 9, #2).[205] [. . . and] 'you and I have a brother, Jesus Christ, the one who was rejected, the one who was crucified, whose cross we remember' (p. 9, #2). On that cross a voice comes out. 'I am your brother. *I am Jesus*'.

Joseph's brothers were at a distance, and at a distance you never know the heartbeat of another man. Our preacher bridges the gap between himself and the audience saying, 'As long as there is that distance, I remain a strange black man, you remain a strange white man'. As he returns to the text he stresses that 'Joseph said, "Please come close, feel the heartbeat", don't you hear the New Testament words, the Lord Jesus saying to his disciples on the day of resurrection, in Jerusalem, "come, touch me, feel my wounds, that I am he. And don't be afraid". Same thing only this is a small picture' (p. 9, #3).

---

203. Cassidy, *Together in One Place*, 17.
204. The theologians at the conference include, Prof. David Bosch, Michael Cassidy, Archbishop Luwum, etc. See Cassidy, *Together in One Place*, 297–99, Appendix 6.
205. Emphasis added.

Kivengere then painted the picture of 'undefeatable love', when he tells that 'I am your brother, Joseph, whom you sold into Egypt', 'I am still your brother Joseph' (p. 10, #3). He drives home the message for his audience using the New Testament picture of the Calvary experience saying: 'The same love which made the Son of God on the cross of Calvary cry when they were driving the nails in his hands, "Father forgive them, they are my brothers, they don't understand what they are doing" is still there. That love is 'The criteria for restoring broken relationship' and it 'lies in the wounded heart of Jesus Christ'. Reconciliation is not far away. His use of the language of Calvary is linked to the Keswick and Revival influence. To them, Calvary expressed the emotionalism of the death of Christ on the cross.

When love is undefeatable like this, the New Testament calls it grace. Grace is 'love unearned, undeserved, unexpected'. The gospel is exciting 'because you are absolutely shocked into love. That God should have loved such people like us; that Joseph should have reacted the way he reacted, that is the greatest shock'. The New Testament calls that radical love. 'Love which refuses to give up; refuses to be defeated'.

Kivengere now turns to tell the story of the cross. The Son of God steps into that confusion, destructive as it is, full of all the meanness of sin (p. 11, #4). He takes the whole load to Calvary, declares on the cross: 'It is finished'. 'God crossed to us. So we may cross over to him, and then to each other'. He asks: 'Have you crossed?' Reconciliation is once again, in view.

Then comes the characteristic appeal: 'Tonight God is expecting you to act radically' (p. 11, #5). 'Radical' is positive. It 'does not mean destruction, it can mean constructive, activity, at the price'. He illustrated by referring to the murder of Luwum, shot dead in Kampala on 16 February 1977, after being taken from in front of Kivengere. 'Archbishop Luwum loved his Lord radically'. He knew what it would cost him to speak out 'against the evil forces, which were dehumanizing lives in Uganda', but he still spoke. That 'is radical love'.

Reflecting upon those terrible days, later scholars debate whether Luwum over-estimated the potential positive effect of his speaking against evil in Uganda.[206] Kivengere had no doubts about it. Luwum's radical love

---

206. For example, Mary Craig, *Candles in the Dark: Six Modern Martyrs* (London: Hodder

for Ugandans, particularly the persecuted and oppressed, moved him to unreservedly confront Amin's evil. When people act in the love of Christ like Luwum, then they 'are liberated'. 'They are no longer captives of self-centredness. They are more human, they are wide open, [and] America needs that' (p. 11, #6). 'You my dear Episcopalians and Christian brothers coming from different traditions, what sort of Christianity do you profess? Where does it lead you? Do you still sustain broken relationships?'

Using his testimony of how he came to forgive and love Amin,[207] Kivengere illustrated how that night his audience might gain reconciliation. 'It is not a question of choosing to love him; I am stuck with him. Because my Lord acted that way, and I am a follower of Jesus, that is my option, I don't have two' (p. 11, #6). 'I have only one option, one commandment I give you, love one another' and before that, 'love your enemies, pray for those who persecute you form the bottom of your heart'. 'That is the New Testament, it is his words'.

'As we start the mission, the mission has one message for you, that tonight you bow your heads and you say, "Lord Jesus, I have someone I have refused to forgive, I am suffering from a kind of estrangement, spiritually I can hardly breathe Lord Jesus, so feel this poor heart of mine, forgive my fumes of hatred and resentment (p. 12, #6). He links back to the Genesis 45 passage: 'after Joseph had said that he kissed them, fellowship . . . and they began to speak to him. Restored relationships start tonight'. Only then 'mission will be meaningful in this part of your United States. Then the Episcopal Church is going to experience new life as members cross the road [to ask each other for forgiveness] (p. 12, #6). In his entire explanation, reconciliation is clearly in view.

He further illustrated with a testimony about what the Lord has been teaching him and his wife in their 34 years of marriage: 'home has become a school and I speak of revival in the kitchen, bedroom, where you sit together and sort out the messes which came yesterday, those nasty relationships which become tight' (p. 13, #7). 'Most of the things which soil

---

and Stoughton, 1984), 164. 'But Janani had been mistaken in one thing, at least in the short term. He assured his wife that even if Amin killed him, "my blood will save the nation". So far it has not done so'.

207. For a full-length of the story, see Kivengere, *I Love Idi Amin*, 62.

relationships, which poison homes, are not necessarily big'. Behind these words lies the influence of the Revival, always concerned about every moment's walk with the Lord.[208] He names the painful 'road' to reconciliation via forgiveness, then exhorts his audience to 'Go and start tonight if you have got an occasion to do that'.

He concludes the sermon with an altar call. 'There is a special place over there, so that anyone tonight who felt that the spirit of God quietly, gently, firmly, clearly has whispered something in your heart . . . we give you a chance, and those who may want to ask questions avail yourself of the opportunity. This is your mission' (p. 14–15, #7). He prayed for 'the loving physician, the wonderful Saviour, to come by your Holy Spirit and enter the arena of each heart, pick up our broken pieces and recreate a new man, new woman' (p. 15, #7). Kivengere's climax here is clearly reconciliation, without him even mentioning the word.

5.6.2.4 Summary of 'Broken Relationships Restored': AO: 1977[0314?]

When Kivengere's understanding of reconciliation in this sermon is placed side by side with Paul's understanding of reconciliation in the text,[209] Kivengere, again, does not follow Paul strictly. His starting point of explaining reconciliation is the cross of Jesus Christ.

At the cross, you see the 'vertical' God who came in his Son to restore broken relationship with God and man, and with each other. God in his undefeatable love opened his eternal embrace to the unembraceable, for their sins to be forgiven. This forgiveness was gained through the cross. This is an act of God's love for sinners and the world. This love of God, expressed in the cross, is the only criterion for restoring broken relationships. This love of God lies in the wounded heart of Christ.

Although his explanation has affinity with Paul's understanding of how God saved sinners, bringing about forgiveness of sins by the death of Jesus on the cross, Kivengere is still silent about the relationship between Jews

---

208. See Chapter Three, 2. 'The Keswick Movement and the East African Revival: The Approach and Context of Preaching'. Cassidy, 'Forward', 3, in Kivengere, *Revolutionary Love*.
209. See Chapter Three, 5.4 'Ephesians 2:14–18'.

and Gentiles. The closest he comes is acknowledging that Paul 'spoke at the time of his own age' (p. 4, #1). His main focus was explaining reconciliation using the cross as his starting point and contrasting it with the Old Testament narrative of the broken relationships between Joseph and his brothers to illuminate the practical outworking of the reconciling work of Jesus in relationships. He asks his audience: don't you hear the New Testament words of Jesus: 'come, touch me', 'feel my wounds', 'father forgive them, they are my brothers', 'it is finished'. He states that God, in Jesus Christ, crossed to us.

He believes that because God crossed over to us, and reconciled us to God and to one another, then entrusted this ministry to us, we must therefore proclaim reconciliation centred in Christ Jesus. Kivengere preached reconciliation using practical illustrations from everyday life—his marriage. In the sermon, he called on his audience: 'tonight be reconciled with God'. Consequently, he designated an open space at the mission gathering, and invited his audience that night to make a decision to be reconciled with God and with one another. The sermon shows Kivengere telling the Episcopal Church that they will experience new life when they cross over to Jesus Christ. Behind this 'altar call', as in the previous sermons, again lies the influence on the Keswick, the Revival and the Billy Graham crusades.[210]

All this is motivated by Kivengere's conviction that reconciliation is the central message of the New Testament and it is the message by which God will bring healing and transformation to the world. Such a message had a huge potential impact upon the life of his audience, and he wished them to take hold of it.

---

210. For an excellent assessment of the use of or absence of alter calls in preaching, see David, *The Altar Call*.

5.6.3 The Whole Gospel for the Whole Church: AO: 197805[--], [#2]

5.6.3.1 Situating the sermon

Kivengere preached this sermon in May 1978, at Wheaton Bible Church, Chicago, USA, on the occasion of a Mission Conference held in the morning (p. 1, #4).

5.6.3.2 Preliminaries

Kivengere is grateful for the invitation to 'this great church well known for its biblical [teaching] and missionary vision' (p. 1, #3). He brings greetings from 'the young churches of that great continent of Africa'. In the last hundred years, 1878–1978, 'Africa has known tremendous activity of missionaries and the planting of churches'.

5.6.3.3 Prayer

Kivengere calls his audience to pray so that the Holy Spirit may widen their horizons, help them understand, and so they might 'catch a fresh vision of the redeeming love of God for the Africa of 1978' (p. 1, #3). As noted in the first set of sermons, whenever he uses the language of catching a fresh vision, reconciliation is not far away.

5.6.3.4 Exposition

Kivengere now turns to the exposition of the passage (Eph 2:14–22). After reading the passage aloud, he asks: 'Did you hear in the passage before us that there are those two aspects?' (p. 2, #5). The first is 'the church, a strange miraculous community. Created as it were from chaos', . . . 'borne of the sufferings of the Lord'.

Dwelling on the world of Paul's time, he identifies the issues that Paul repeatedly spoke about in Ephesians 2:14–22: 'killing the enmity' [v 14], 'breaking down walls of separation' [vv 15–16], 'killing the estrangement and alienations' [v 19]. Out of his suffering, broken body, Christ brought a new community into an existence that was completely strange [v 19] (p. 2, #7).

'It simply couldn't make sense in Ephesus', and at 'Corinth, even in Jerusalem'. The only way this community came about is found in [v 16]: 'in his body', 'through the cross', 'by his blood', 'through suffering'—out of that came a new community: the church (p. 3, #7).[211]

Kivengere brings this first point into connection with the church in Africa: 'how on earth can I say there is an African church?' (p. 3, #8). Kivengere is quick to answer his question in a well-defended argument (apologetic): 'If the church came into being the way we read here (in Eph 2:14–22)', and 'If the church is a community born out of the suffering, the wounds of the Master, Jesus Christ, the Son of God producing it, creating it, bringing it into being', then, 'This community is born at a cost—"out of pain, suffering, the blood and eternal sacrifice"—of the Son of God'.

Kivengere believes that it is reasonable to say that the church 'can't be identified with Africa or America or Europe or Asia'. 'The essence of the church has nothing to do with those categories'. Closing the gap between his audience and himself, Kivengere asks: 'don't you feel as I do feel that Christianity is suffering from ideal words?' 'We [say there are] no alienations, and yet we accept even in the evangelical churches—alienations exists. Isn't that strange?' He points out the following facts: 'we speak about no estrangement', yet we have estranged people among those who say 'I am born again'. And, 'we speak about "no Jew, no Gentile" and yet there are lovely people who love the Bible so much that they isolate one another for its sake'.

Kivengere declares that 'The cross is practical' (p. 3, 10). Jesus practically died and rose again (p. 4, #10). 'He practically broke the barriers'. The reason the barriers exist is because we are sinners. The church, according to Kivengere, 'cannot be identified with a particular culture, continent, group of people, class or language' (p. 4, #10).

'It is an African church because it is in Africa *per se*'. . . . 'But that church is not of Africa. It is a church of Jesus Christ in Africa'. The expressions of this church must be African, otherwise, the old complaint that missionaries

---

211. For an excellent treatment of this subject see the contribution of his Professor Markus Barth, on the subject in his—a title linked with Christ's redemptive work.

brought their cultures and imposed them on poor innocent blacks will continue.[212]

Contrary to what his audience might have expected, he bridged the gap between them and himself saying that as a black man, 'no missionary ever imposed their culture on me'. Just like the West copied 'from the Greeks and the Romans'—and 'some of us (Blacks, like himself) copied a lot from the Western world'. 'We hope that the West and the Western world would copy a few things [from us] into its culture'. . . . 'No culture can live in isolation'.

There is a church in the continent of Africa—the church of Jesus Christ. But 'what sort of continent?—And, 'what is the African world?' (p. 4, #12). The African world is that world he read about in Ephesians [chap 2] and with much hope he says that Africa today [1978] is 'a wonderful continent of wonderful possibilities more than ever before', full of 'millions of people waiting to listen to the gospel presented in its true simplicity'.

He lists several reasons for conflicts in Africa: conflicting ideologies, conflicting cultures, tribal misunderstandings, isolation and divisions— 'even today [1978] in Africa, the Christian church is being [accused by politicians] of being a catalyst for isolationism and division' (p. 4, #12).[213] Kivengere is aware these claims are exaggerated—although he admits that there is a point to them.

Along with 'the wonderful gospel message of Jesus Christ' the missionaries also brought their traditions. That he [Kivengere] is wearing the robes of an Anglican bishop demonstrates that 'Anglicans brought Anglicanism',

---

212. For a fair discussion on this criticism, see Ferdinando Keith, 'Christian Identity in African Context: Reflections on Kwame Bediako's Theology and Identity', *JETS* 50/1 (March 2007): 121–43, esp. 142–43.

213. For excellent in-depth discussions on different ideologies, political, and socio-religious affairs in Africa before and during the period of Kivengere's preaching, see Ali Al'Amin Mazrui, *The African Condition: A Political Diagnosis* (London; New York: Cambridge University Press, 1980); Ali Al'Amin Mazrui, *The Africans: A Triple Heritage* (1st ed.; Boston: Little, Brown, 1986); Ali Al'Amin Mazrui, ed., *The Warrior Tradition in Modern Africa* (vol. 23; International Studies in Sociology and Social Anthropology; Leiden: Brill, 1977); Ali Al'Amin Mazrui and Hasu H Patel, eds., *Africa in World Affairs: The Next Thirty Years* (New York: Third Press, 1973); Robert I Rotberg and Ali Al'Amin Mazrui, eds., *Protest and Power in Black Africa* (New York: Oxford University Press, 1970); Ali Al'Amin Mazrui, *Towards a Pax Africana: A Study of Ideology and Ambition* (The Nature of human society series; London: Weidenfeld & Nicolson, 1967).

adding 'Not that [wearing the robes] is necessary at all. Except of course for fishing purposes in certain waters'. Missionaries came from different traditional churches, and so the churches they established followed their respective traditions (p. 4, #13). This was fine in itself, except that the traditions were turned from being 'bridges [to cross]', to 'means by which communities [churches] became isolated from one another' (p. 5, #13).

'Other isolating forces entering Africa include 'political ideologies such as Marxism, capitalism, and socialism' (p. 5, #14). Each one of them is affected by 'the sin of man', and they become 'isolating forces'. Africa 'has become an arena for the battles of ideologies'.[214] But into Africa, despite this hotbed of isolating forces, 'come[s] a church'.

In this setting, the church is essential because it has 'the only message which can heal the wounds and the brokenness of a continent like Africa'. Kivengere believes that they can heal only after they themselves have been liberated. 'We cannot heal our suffering continent unless we stretch out our hands and put them in the hands of another brother, and another sister—and see each believer as a wonderful product of Calvary'.[215] 'Then we can move into the shattered arena. Then we can bring the broken-hearted people of our continent'. 'Then we can meet the refugees and look them in the eyes and say to them, Jesus, only Jesus, is the hope that you can receive' (p. 5, #15). Once again Kivengere has reconciliation clearly in view.

With the African church, you cannot take a chance by letting the church become 'a victim of culture' (p. 6, #15). 'There are as many African cultures as there are tribes'.[216] If this happens the church would loose its vision and, 'as a prisoner to its culture it will no longer heal'. Will they pray for the church? (p. 6, #16). 'Africa is a continent full of millions of people waiting to listen to the gospel presented in its true simplicity' (p. 7, #19).

---

214. Kivengere, Interview
215. Cf. Kivengere, 'Bleeding Africa', above.
216. For an in-depth bibliography of the African tribes and cultures, see 'Select Bibliography' in Mbiti, *African Religions & Philosophy*, 278–82.

5.6.3.5 Summary of The Whole Gospel for the Whole Church: AO: 197805[--], [#2]

In this sermon, Kivengere's doctrine of reconciliation shows a great affinity with Paul's. Paul's language of the cross is evident: 'killing the enmity', 'breaking down walls of separation', 'killing estrangement and alienations', estrangement of Jews and Gentiles, the new community brought out of the body of Christ. Interestingly, these were the same expressions that Markus Barth used, drawing from his interpretation of Paul's text under our inquiry.[217]

Writing in the context of great suffering due to the cold war, Barth was convinced that the gospel must be relevant to the world and the church must preach the gospel of reconciliation centred in the redeeming work of Christ. Picking up Paul's vocabulary of 'peace', and drawing upon his teaching that Jew and Gentiles have been reconciled to become the new people of God (Israel), Markus boldly rebuked neutrality or unconcern with the practical, that is with social aspects of reconciliation, international, racial, and economic peace. To say 'Christ' or 'peace' is synonymous with reconciliation.

Preaching at a mission conference in exile only slightly over a year since he fled from the horrors of Uganda, Kivengere clearly reflects his professor's concern for the social implications of preaching reconciliation in a broken world. He emphasizes that the church of Jesus Christ in Africa is 'a strange miraculous community created [by Jesus] from chaos—borne out of the suffering of the Lord' (p. 3, #5). Once again, however, he does not explain the Jew-Gentile question of a new people created through the body of Christ, reconciled to God, and made part of the people of God. Important as this point may be for Paul and Markus Barth, Kivengere passes over it to explain the divisions within the church in Africa, which has led to isolation, alienations, and barriers between tribes within churches based on race, nationality and class (p. 3, #8). Embarrassingly, politicians have accused churches of acting as catalysts of isolation and division. A living example of this accusation, well known to Kivengere, was the division within the COU

---

217. See Chapter Three, 4. 'Markus Barth's Link to Kivengere'.

that was a security threat, which prompted Amin to force a solution.[218] At the core of these and other negative divisive forces (Marxism, capitalism, and socialism) causing hatred and bitterness lies 'the sin of man'.

The solution to these problems in Africa is the same solution that Paul mentions in the hatred and divisions of Jews and Gentiles, namely, the preaching of reconciliation in Jesus Christ. The opportunity to preach this gospel in Africa is wide open and Africans are waiting for this gospel to be preached in all its true simplicity.

Learning from Paul and Markus Barth, Kivengere saw reconciliation as an obligation of discipleship even if it may be difficult to assess the impact of this message, preached at the gathering of a mission event. It clearly shows Kivengere's vision for healing the divisions and isolations of Africa through preaching reconciliation.

5.6.4 'No More Distance in the Love of Christ': AO: 19801014, [#1][219]

5.6.4.1 *Situating the Sermon*
Kivengere preached this sermon on 14 October 1980, in Western Missouri, Kansas City, USA, at a diocesan youth rally.

5.6.4.2 *Preliminaries*
Kivengere opens by asking his audience to spend a little time being quiet in the 'presence of him' whom they will remember in the Eucharist, and 'in whose love we are going to participate' (p. 1, #1). By mentioning Jesus as 'him' and his love, reconciliation is already in view.

---

218. See Chapter Four, 2. 'Before Exile September (February 1971–1977)'. See Amin's address to the religious leaders in Uganda, Idi Amin, 'Speech by His Excellency the President, General Idi Amin Dada on the Occasion of Meeting Moslem Leaders', Unpublished Speech, November 22, 1971, Archives of the Church of Uganda.

219. We borrowed this theme from Kivengere's concluding paragraph of his exposition in the sermon where he said, 'Thank you for listening and I hope that this little message[,] "No more distance but in the love of Christ we are together. And that is what makes life worth living', (p. 10, #34).

5.6.4.3 Prayer

Kivengere focused his prayer on reconciliation, mentioning Jesus' 'miracle which brings us together—the miracle of your love' (p. 1, #1). He prayed that they may see how much Jesus loved them and 'become men and women for whom you died and rose again'.

5.6.4.4 Introduction

Kivengere brings greetings from the 'Christian brothers and sisters in Uganda' and 'other parts of Eastern Africa' (p. 1, #2). There are literally thousands of young people in Uganda who gather together like the youth in the present rally. They gather together from their desire to seek and find Jesus—and indeed, they are finding Jesus. Kivengere came on this occasion to share with them 'the Lord Jesus Christ'. Again, reconciliation is not far away.

Kivengere begins with his conversion testimony.[220] As in the sermon discussed previously,[221] where he critiqued his father's ancestral worship, this time he has a different focus: the role of the mediator between God and man. 'The only problem is when you worship God through the medium of human hearts you are very likely never to go to him, because human spirits act like humans' (p. 1, #3). As well as exposing the distance between God and humanity in his father's religion and revealing his anthropological insights, his critique shows the rigour of his theological thought on the relationship between God, Jesus Christ, and man. Reconciliation is in view.

He hopes that Christians understand that they are people who have 'found the way' (p. 2, #4) because 'In the Acts of the Apostles . . . the believers in Jesus were not called Christians first . . . They were always known as the people of the way' [Acts 11:26, 'At Antioch', p. 2, #4). 'You remember Jesus said, "I am the way"', therefore the Christians are the people who have found the way of bringing a relationship between God and humanity.

---

220. See Chapter Two, 5.2 'Kivengere's Conversion: From Agonistic to Preacher'.
221. Kivengere, 'The Love of Christ', pp. 1–2, #1–#2.

5.6.4.5 *Exposition*

As he read the text (Eph 2:13), Kivengere stressed: 'You were far away', including in his explanation being 'at a distance'. Our preacher then asks his audience: 'And you know when that gap began?' (p. 3, #8). 'It was when Adam and Eve as we read in the Old Testament—created in the image of God', (p. 3, #9), 'so that they may have fellowship with God', 'so that he could be a human being', 'He turned away from God because he wanted something for himself'. As soon as they 'turned away from God, they lost the way'.

'They were in darkness hiding in God's garden', God the creator, their friend and not enemy, came to them but on hearing 'God coming' to them they ran away. 'I don't see the reason why they should have run', . . . 'They should have come with joy to meet their Father'. But, instead, they hid when God asks: 'Adam where are you?' They hid away from God because 'They have lost the Way'.

'When you lose the way to God you lose the way to your fellow men. You can't lose your way to God and still know your people' (p. 4, #14). 'Amin murdered half a million Ugandans in eight years'. When the way is lost we remain in darkness and do not see another human being properly so they become to us dangerous people, and the only way to deal with them is 'to eliminate' them.

At Stellenbosch University, South Africa, he spoke of naming the distance and brokenness of the people: 'lovely young people who would be together'—blacks, browns, and whites—'not at all, they are kept apart' (p. 4, #13). It is a miserable situation to see in that country a group of 'strangers [are] are living together'. It is hard 'to make sense out of that' because the people are living at a distance. 'But don't think that it's only in South Africa. No. [It is] even here in America'.

In Uganda, 'men treat each other as strangers even in home[s]'. Children can be strangers to their parents. Husbands can be strangers to their wives and wives can be strangers to husbands (p. 4, #14). 'It is that distance which Paul says, once you were at a distance from God and therefore you became strangers to God and strangers to one another' (p. 5, #16). He stresses that Jesus' 'love becomes the power which draws all sorts of people, young and old, black and white and brown together' (p. 5, #20). Paul's explanation of 'the new creation' that draws together the Jews and Gentiles who were separated enemies as now, reconciled in Christ as one 'new creation'.

He stressed that all 'humanity today' (by then 1980) are suffering because of standing at a distance [from God, and from one another] (p. 7, #25). He lists the countries suffering: South Africa, Uganda, Ethiopia, and in the USA, Buffalo, Kansas City. When we stand at a distance, we do not see one another. We see only categories: blacks, whites, brown, the poor, the rich, and also the religious.

He tells his audience about preaching reconciliation in South Africa during apartheid (racial segregation) 'I told the students [that] you young people in South Africa can change your country without destroying it . . . it's always young people who are not victims of their prejudices . . . who can see where the old people do not see. And particularly if you receive Jesus' eyes'.

Referring to the text he says 'So, in these few words "you were once at a distance but now you have been brought near, through the blood ('of Christ', p. 8, #27), which means through the [sacrificial] love [of] Christ'. 'And Jesus' love [made him] sacrifice himself', so that we from Uganda, you from the States, the blacks, the whites . . . [we can] come together' (p. 8, #26–#27). Kivengere tells them his philosophy of racism, pointing out why we are created as different and why we should come together. Again reconciliation is in view.

He highlights how racism in South Africa has created distance between blacks and whites: 'You have been fighting over colour'. 'The whites hate blacks and the blacks hate whites' (p. 8, #26). Moreover, both fear each other. He asks: 'who told you that colours were made to be fought over?' 'I haven't seen you fight over your cardigans and your black and brown suits and white shirts'. 'You accept those but you can't accept a human being'. After asserting this distance, he offers a solution, with reconciliation in view.

'God does not like monotony, so he doesn't like only white faces'. 'So he puts in blacks so that when you are tired of looking at the white, you've got a holiday'. 'When you are tired of looking at blacks you look at whites and you have a break'. 'So they laughed and we laughed together'—thus bridging the gap between the preacher and his audience. The bishop then made his point: 'The good things, which God gives us, becomes the means by which we fight each other. We hate one another [a]s if it was a mistake'.

Kivengere concludes his point on reconciliation with an illustration he used before,[222]—how Jesus removed the distance between him and a white English missionary whom he hated in Uganda (pp. 8–10, #28–#32). For his audience to deal with the problem of distances in life, they need the message of reconciliation. The force of the impact of this message is in his concluding words: 'Then you can heal America. Then you can heal Uganda, then you can heal one another' (p. 10, #33). Kivengere hopes that his audience will take the message: 'No more distance but in the love of Christ we are together' (p. 10, #34) and 'that is what makes [life] worth living' (p. 10, #34).

5.6.4.6 Summary of 'No More Distance in the Love of Christ': AO: 19801014, [#1]

This sermon concludes the set of sermons on Ephesians 2:14–18. Kivengere focused on the death of Jesus Christ as a miracle of God's love that removed the distance between God and man. Before his conversion, he worshipped a distant God who would be accessed through ancestral spirits. Ancestral spirits are beset with difficulties making it important for the spirits to mediate between God and man. As we have seen, Kivengere commonly explains reconciliation by starting with Jesus Christ, coming into our situation, to die on the cross to bring reconciliation. However, on this occasion, he starts with Jesus, 'the way'. Once Jesus is found, he leads the lost back to God. He is 'the way' to God and to fellow men (p. 4, #14).

Kivengere uses the Pauline language of reconciliation drawn from 2 Corinthians 5, 'the new creation', to illuminate the relationship between Jews and Gentiles, which Paul states in the text Ephesians 2. Kivengere illustrates from the great brokenness he found at Stellenbosch University, South Africa. Drawing his illustration from the political situation in South Africa to his own marriage shows the scope of reconciliation ranges from one person in a family to national conflicts.

---

222. Kivengere, '*Love Reconciles,*' 28.

Kivengere's philosophy of racism, found only in this sermon of the twenty-seven sermons analyzed in this study, has revealed his biblical theology of creation, in which he appreciates God's creation and diversity of colour and people. With this biblical perspective of creation, he reconciles blacks and whites in his audience, by encouraging them to appreciate the creation of God and diversity.

Again, justifies as the Keswick and the Revival convention reached a climax in their call for commitment to Jesus and dedication to his service, Kivengere calls his audience to a life of reconciliation in Jesus Christ. Only then can their service for Jesus bring healing can be brought to America, Uganda, or to one another.

5.7 Explicit Reconciliation Sermons (IV): Colossians 1:19–22 in Context

5.7.1 Christ Puts All Things Together: AO: 1972[----]

5.7.1.1 Situating the Sermon
Kivengere preached this sermon in 1972, somewhere in the United States of America.

5.7.1.2 Preliminaries
Kivengere is not ashamed to testify that 'another one intervened in the affairs of my life', picked him from the road of life, and 'put the pieces together' (p. 1, #1). In referring to 'life as a road' it is possible that he is alluding to Paul's Damascus Road conversion experience, and his own experience, which he links with reconciliation in Jesus Christ.[223]

5.7.1.3 Prayer
Kivengere's prayer already introduced reconciliation when he focused 'the love of Christ in the fellowship' (p. 5, #8). Jesus is 'the king of glory, who left heaven for our sake'. He prayed that 'there are wounds to be healed',

---

223. See Chapter Two, 5.2 'Kivengere's Conversion: From Agnostic To Preacher'.

and that 'there are burdens to be lifted', and 'loneliness to be filled'. Clearly, without explicitly mentioning the word, the prayer is very focused on reconciliation.

5.7.1.4 Exposition

Kivengere again lets the Scripture speak before his exposition, by reading aloud the letter, before explaining why it is written (pp. 5–6, #9). Colossians was written 'to answer the question posed by the Jews, in order to have a right relationship with God, you need to keep the commandments and ceremonies'.

You don't need to keep the Ten Commandments to be put right with God. You need Christ who is the fullness of God. When you find Christ, 'you are put right with God'. That 'answers the questions posed by the Greek philosophers of their time', who believed that 'to reach God you need to go through a hierarchy of sparks representing God, like a ladder'. To the Greek philosophers, 'if you can be clever enough to explain them and to go through them without getting ashamed, ultimately you may get to God'. His audience does not need that 'because Christ is the Head'.[224]

There is no doubt in Kivengere's mind that 'it is all about the centrality of the Headship of Jesus Christ' (p. 6, #10). For Paul, 'it was Christ who rescued us from the grip of the power of darkness', 'He transferred us into the kingdom of his dear Son'. Two things happened. A transfer took place and the transfer happened 'In the grip of darkness'. He asks: 'what is darkness?' 'Darkness means confusion'.

Kivengere emphatically explains that 'Jesus came', and his coming 'took a rescuing, it was not an easy job at all'. He rescued us at a price that 'cost him blood and sweat, and darkness, and loneliness, on the cross of Calvary', so that he may 'rescue us from that terrible confusion into which we had landed ourselves'.

---

224. Kivengere's line of reasoning here is clearly advancing an emphasis on Christ, something that New Testament scholars noted as a characteristic of Christianity in the first century. Among these scholars, see Richard Bauckham, *God Crucified: Monotheism and Christology in the New Testament* (Didsbury Lectures; Carlisle: Paternoster, 1998), 25–42; Larry W Hurtado, *Lord Jesus Christ: Devotion to Jesus in Earliest Christianity* (Grand Rapids, Mich.: Eerdmans, 2003), 29–53; N. T Wright, *The Climax of the Covenant: Christ and the Law in Pauline Theology* (Edinburgh: T&T Clark, 1991), 56–136.

Kivengere is not surprised that sometimes people in their excitement jump, cry, sit, laugh, and fall on hearing this message (pp. 6–7, #11). People are surprised, because 'they did not expect it'. 'You were just absolutely outside there, and he, Christ, rescued us from the power of this darkness, transferred us into the kingdom of his Son'.

Kivengere points out two things. First, Christ is the subject of their faith, and he is responsible for making reconciliation. Of course, behind the work of Christ, God the father is in view, as the one who sent Jesus Christ to reconcile everything in himself from sins, confusions, and darkness. Second, the cross is the central place where Christ's action of rescuing humanity occurred.

In verse 15, 'It is Christ who is the perfect likeness of the invisible God. He is the supremacy of all creation' (pp. 7–8, #12). Kivengere notes the answer 'to the agnostics of the Greeks who thought that there were other powers other than Christ'. 'For Christ is the agent by whom all things were created in heaven and upon the earth'. 'Visible and invisible, spiritual powers all beings created in him', whether they be thrones, or lordships or authorities, or powers, they were all under Him. 'He is the agent and the goal of all creation'. Christ is the focus of all creation.

'Not only is he [Christ] the goal of creation, he exists before everything else'. 'He is therefore before you, he is therefore before me, and he is therefore before everybody, he is the foundation. In Christ, 'you are standing on something eternal—unshakable'.[225] He concludes: 'He [Christ] is there, underneath are the everlasting arms, and unless they hold you and hold me, we are just like that'.

To understand Kivengere's allusion to the hymn 'underneath are the everlasting arms', one needs to appreciate that by 1972 Idi Amin had already killed about 90,000 people in Uganda. Kivengere sees that Ugandan believers can only trust in the 'strong and everlasting arms of Jesus' to live.[226] The

---

225. Cf. The Unshakable Identity of Jesus Christ: AO: 19772910.
226. The Elisha Hoffman' hymn (1887), used by the Revival, lie behind this image of protection:
What a fellowship, what a joy divine,
Leaning on the everlasting arms;
What a blessedness, what a peace is mine,
Leaning on the everlasting arms.

words of Moses lie behind the hymn: 'The eternal God is your refuge, and underneath are the everlasting arms' (Deut 33:27). Moses' experience of ups and downs in his wilderness years led him to know that no matter how low he may sink, underneath are the everlasting arms of God to lift him up. Uganda under Idi Amin, the situation of the COU with its ethnic divisions that he will mention in this sermon, the killings and horrors of Uganda, can make you sink, but underneath are the everlasting arms of God. 'Christ is there, underneath are the everlasting arms and unless his arms hold you and me, you are just like that'.

'Everything else holds in him, coheres, in him'. This means 'apart from him [Christ] everything else falls apart'. The focus is 'in Christ'. He lists things that will not hold outside Christ: government, life as it is, business, marriage, and Christian experience. Kivengere emphasizes the 'in him [Christ]', which is connected to reconciliation language in the text: 'In him all things cohere'.

Illustrating God's reconciling work 'in Christ', he explains a deep rift that had been going on in the COU on a provincial scale. It was a reflection of the division in the country according to tribal, political, and economic 'interests', but Christ in whom all things hold together saved the rift from degenerating further. Passionately and painfully Kivengere names the past wounds of his church to illustrate how 'in Christ', situations of deep wounds, divisions are healed and held together 'in Christ' alone.[227]

On 28 November 1971, for 'those of you who use the calendar of the church, it was called Advent Sunday' (pp. 13–14, #19). He saw a situation that he described as 'unique'. A 'unique' meeting of the COU was called at the Kampala International Conference Centre. The uniqueness of the meeting lies in the nature of the invitation, the nature of the problem, and the message that was preached at the meeting.

In attendance of the meeting were the archbishop of the COU, Erica Sabiti, and the House of Bishops (nine bishops), representatives of Senior Clergy (Archdeacons) and clergy, the laity. There were 350 delegates for

---

Leaning, leaning, Safe and secure from all alarms;
Leaning, leaning, Leaning on the everlasting arms.
227. See Chapter Four, 2. 'Before Exile (September 1971– February 1977)'.

the entire Province of the COU (pp. 13–14, #19). They were 'thoroughly embarrassed' because of the whole Province of COU had almost broken to pieces (pp. 12–13, #18). 'The extent of the confusion' in the church was seen in the shattered disagreements between the different groups in the church: disagreements between 'Bishops and Bishops', disagreements between 'dioceses and dioceses', and disagreements between 'synods and synods' (pp. 12–13, #18). 'Oh, the confusion that came' (pp. 13–14, #19).

In the larger context of the confusion, because this confusion had the potential to degenerate into a national security problem, President Amin, a Muslim, invited the delegates of the COU to come to a meeting at Kampala International Conference Centre. He put it to the delegates: 'Come and sort out your differences and find a solution, because . . . We are scared when God's people are disunited' (pp. 13–14, #19). Kivengere emotionally exclaimed: 'A Muslim inviting Christians who preach reconciliation and love, who have even experienced revival. Imagine!' (pp. 13–14, #19). Kivengere at this point is explicit about reconciliation, whereas before he did not use the word.

Several historical works have echoed and overshadowed the event because of different concerns that they deal with. Nevertheless, they still give evidence or hints on how Amin, a Muslim, forced the COU to reconcile among themselves.[228] It is not surprising that out of this awkward situation it was later frustrating for a spiritual leader like Luwum to try and save the face of the church before a Muslim President who was well aware of the weakness of the church, namely, ethnic division.

'We came, oh, we were half dead. Three hundred and fifty of us, we sat' (p. 14, #20). 'You have never seen a more embarrassed church than that' (p. 14, #20). . . . 'Our [Archbishop], a lovely man, full of God's Holy Spirit, there he was. Some didn't like him, [because of] tribalism' (p. 14, #20). 'Church politics, everything was just falling apart. Oh, synods of course,

---

228. For example, Mark A. Noll and Carolyn Nystrom, *Clouds of Witnesses: Christian Voices from Africa and Asia* (Downers Grove, Ill.: IVP Books, 2011), 112. They only mention in passing the deep tribal divisions which Archbishop Erica Sabiti faced in providing spiritual leadership in Uganda under Amin, and his focus on the brutal murder of Luwum by Amin. He is still dealing with the ethnic problem in political circles but surely it was also the same political and ethnic problems reflected in the division within the COU.

met, passed resolutions, things fell apart. Diocesan councils sat and sought means, passed resolutions again, things kept on falling apart, because you see committees can never bring reconciliation' (p. 14, #20). Again, whereas before when he did not explicitly mention reconciliation, now he clearly stated it.

Although reconciliation between the bishops and delegates occurred in this meeting, it must be stressed for the benefit of appreciating fully the embarrassing situation that Kivengere is naming here, that tribal and ethnic division within the COU was a manifestation of a complex and much broader national political division than merely religious division within dioceses.[229] Kivengere noted that 'reconciliation came from Jesus Christ when he died on the cross' and 'not from church committee meetings'—thus, 'a resolution [of church committee meetings] is not a means by which you can be reconciled'. While church committee meetings may come up with a 'resolution about reconciliation', they are 'not the source of reconciliation'. The source and means of attaining true 'reconciliation' is Jesus Christ who died on the cross. For Kivengere, a resolution of a church committee meeting, 'may lead to reconciliation but usually it doesn't'.

Kivengere's Revival background emphasized personal ownership of sin and personal confession of sins accompanied by restitution among the brethren.[230] They were never interested in a group or church committee resolutions about reconciliation. They insisted that the Christian life could only be lived as result of salvation in Jesus Christ.[231] For them, of whom Kivengere is a good example, Christian life begins and ends at the cross of Jesus Christ. For this reason, church committee resolutions about reconciliation are not reconciliation that comes from Jesus Christ.

Ten years later, Kivengere will visit young Desmond Tutu in his home in South Africa while on a mission to preach the message of reconciliation

---

229. See Mujaju, 'Political Crisis', 67–85. Akiiki discusses Amin's view of Church strife as a threat to government. See also M. Louise Pirouet, 'Religion in Uganda under Amin', *JRA* 11/1 (1980): 13–29. COU File, 'Amin's meeting with religious leaders in Kabale'.

230. See Chapter Three, 2.1.1 'Day One: The Diagnosis—Sin'.

231. See Chapter Three, 2.1.2 'Day Two: The Cure—God's Provision for Victorious Christian Living'.

at the height of Apartheid.[232] He will be encouraged to know that Tutu has great hope in Jesus Christ even in the midst of racism against the blacks. Because Kivengere's theology of the cross is Christocentric,[233] and his Revival focus on Jesus' working in transforming the life of a believers,[234] he was hopeful that the future of South Africa lies in Jesus Christ changing lives and not the gun and violence. He encourages reconciliation that comes from having a personal relationship with Christ and translates itself into a social relationship with each other.

Tutu fought for reconciliation, first as a liberation struggle against the white domination of the blacks during apartheid, and later when President Nelson Mandela[235] asked him to chair the South African Truth and Reconciliation Commission (TRC).[236] The TRC was a way of encouraging truth telling about injustices inflicted and reconciliation of the offender and offended parties.

Kivengere narrates in detail the message he preached from Philippians 2, which led the COU delegates to repentance and reconciliation.[237] 'Christ is the only one that can put things together'. 'In Him all things'—and for him 'all things, mean all things cohere' (pp. 17–18, #27). Reconciliation, for Kivengere, is not far away. Kivengere believes that AEE has a message for Africa, Asia, and everywhere, 'by which men and women can again be put together' (p. 22, #32). This is why he is preaching reconciliation in the States. 'There is hope for our world [and] there is hope for every life'.

---

232. 'The Reconciling Love of Christ': AO: 198110[--], [#1].
233. See further Festo Kivengere, 'The Cross of Christ', Sermon Transcript (Preached at Eugene, Oregon, April 19, 1979), AO: 19790419*2. Kivengere, 'The Cross Today'. Festo Kivengere, 'The Cross at the Centre', Sermon Transcript, AO: [--------]*71. , among others.
234. Festo Kivengere, 'Revival Begins at the Cross', in *When God Moves in Revival* (Wheaton, Ill.: Tyndale House Publishers, 1977 [1973]), 11–21.
235. Anthony Sampson, *Mandela: The Authorised Biography* (New Ed.; New York: HarperCollins, 2000).
236. Desmond Tutu, *No Future Without Forgiveness* (London: Rider, 2000). Hugo Van der Merwe and Audrey R. Chapman, *Truth and Reconciliation in South Africa: Did the TRC Deliver?* (University of Pennsylvania Press, 2008). Johan Mostert and Mervin van der Spuy, 'Truth and Reconciliation', in *Forgiveness, Reconciliation, and Restoration: Multidisciplinary Studies from a Pentecostal Perspective* (ed. Geoffrey W. Sutton and Martin William Mittelstadt; Eugene, Ore.: Pickwick Publications, 2010).
237. See Chapter Four, 2. 'Before September (September 1971– February 1977)'.

5.7.1.5 Summary of *Christ Puts All Things Together:* AO: 1972[----]

Kivengere followed the Pauline approach in this chapter, emphasizing the person and the work of Jesus Christ on the cross. He used the language of Ephesians 6:12, referring to the powers of darkness. Jesus liberates us from the powers of darkness and he forgives our sins.

He shows affinity with Barth's way of taking God as the subject matter. God in Jesus Christ reconciled everything to himself and the cross is where reconciliation happened. Christ came to our situation. He is the invisible image of God and the focus of creation.

The Revival influence is detectable. The message of reconciliation is the message that AEE is taking everywhere in the world. This is in line with the Keswick and Revival focus of serving the Lord in reaching out with his message to the world. AEE is reaching out with a message that puts men and women together. This is the reason for his preaching in the United States of America. There is hope for the world and everyday life.

5.7.2 The Unshakable Identity of the Church of Jesus Christ: AO: 19771029, [#1]

5.7.2.1 Situating the Sermon

Kivengere preached this sermon on 29 October 1977, at Grace Cathedral, California, USA, on the occasion of their convention.

5.7.2.2 Preliminaries

Kivengere is introduced to the convention by James Paulding who announces his topic: 'The Unshakable Identity of the Church of Jesus Christ' (p. 1, #1), and that he is bishop of Kigezi, a gifted preacher, and currently a refugee in exile. Because of 'his faithfulness to Christ', his church (COU) 'for six years had increasing hardships, suffering and persecution'. Kivengere comes to preach as 'a brother in Christ', 'a representative of the church in Uganda', and in the midst of the 'persecution and martyrdom' in Uganda, the COU is still 'one of the most vibrant and alive churches in the world today' [1977].

5.7.2.3 Introduction

Kivengere opens with an expression of thanks for the tremendously warm welcome and expressed on behalf of the COU his thanks for their concern, love, and prayers during 'our time of need' (pp. 1–2, #2).

Immediately he draws upon the Keswick slogan; telling the Episcopal Church that Scripture states: 'You are all one in Christ Jesus'. They have cared enough to support the COU, and as the distance of miles across oceans no longer created a barrier. Two years before, when Billy Graham addressed the centenary of the Keswick Movement, he also spoke on their Scriptural slogan, 'All One in Christ', emphasizing the need for churches to care and work with each other.[238] Just two years after that centenary Kivengere used the Keswick catch-cry to the COU and the Episcopal Church.

The missionaries that the Episcopal Church sent to Uganda, such as James Paulding,[239] have done tremendous work 'producing fruit', and the COU is 'a product of missionary activities'.[240] As a young church, it will be celebrating its centenary that year (1977).[241] Kivengere is thankful to God that, within the first century of the Christian church, we have seen the hand of God doing miracles in that country. When the missionaries came to Uganda, they were pioneers of education, medicine, and agriculture, and they stood against colonial powers over matters of land.[242] The missionaries 'preached the love of Jesus Christ' and 'they never isolated the whole needs of man'. Reconciliation is not far away with his reference to 'the love of Jesus Christ'.

God has blessed the work of the missionaries. He cites the example of Bishop Alfred Tucker, who also was the legal advisor on matters of land policy to Ugandans against the British, his own people and Bishop

---

238. Graham, 'A Hundred Years of Blessing and Glory', 101–04.
239. James Paulding and his wife first came out as missionaries of the Episcopal Church to work in Uganda at the Bishop Tucker College in 1969–73, after parish work returned on the faculty of Bishop Tucker in 1987, died at the College in 1988. See Ward, *Called to Serve*, 36.
240. For a list of some 693 CMS missionaries who served in Uganda between 1877–1977, mentioning the years of service, see Tuma and Mutibwa, *A Century of Christianity in Uganda, 1877–1977*, 175–87.
241. As part of the activities to mark the centenary celebration of the COU, see a series of excellent articles in Tuma and Mutibwa, *A Century of Christianity in Uganda, 1877–1977*.
242. See Chapter Two, 3.1 'Missionary Origins'.

Hannington, murdered in Uganda (pp. 2–3, #3). He is also thankful for the witness of hundreds of Ugandans, who became martyrs in the first ten years of the church. Of their witness, he alluded to Tertullian's famous statement: 'so the blood of the martyrs remains the seed of the church'. But the bloodshed did not stop there. 'We ended the centenary as we began'. The first decade produced 'the Uganda Christian martyrs' and at the close of the century, Luwum was martyred, and his blood sealed the centenary.[243] 'The church blesses only when the church bleeds' (pp. 3–4, #4).[244]

Kivengere links it to Jesus' dealing with 'the wounds of a bleeding world'. Jesus, the founder and head of the church, 'so loved this world with its bloody wounds and in the end died in the very exercise of healing the world'. 'Therefore, the church must stand where its [H]ead has always stood'.

5.7.2.4 Exposition

Kivengere enters the exposition with a careful explanation of what it means for the church to be 'the salt and light of the earth'. He names the evil that Idi Amin committed against Ugandans, and what Luwum experienced in facing the evil of Amin with the gospel. 'Because of the kind of experience I have been in, but even long before that, I have come to the conclusion that the church must rediscover its 'unshakable identity' in Jesus Christ (Matt 5) if it is not going to lose its ministry this century' (p. 4, #5).

He links his warning to a biblical text: 'the salt of the earth', noting that 'salt never arrests the decay in the thing it is trying to save without being dissolved in the thing itself'. In the same way, 'the church must be prepared to suffer in the world' (p. 4, #5). The church should 'not always expect that it [can] stop the corruption of the world and get away with it'. Luwum stood against the destructive corruption of President Idi Amin's regime, 'as firmly and clearly as the grace of God worked in his heart'.[245] He stood, 'as

---

243. See Chapter One, 3.2 'Mwanga's Martyrdoms'.
244. Kivengere, *I Love Idi Amin*, 13.
245. For an account of his stand against the rule of Amin, Ford, *Janani*; Ward, 'Archbishop Janani Luwum', 199–224. See Noll and Nystrom, *Clouds of Witnesses*, 121. 'Luwum was standing next to a fellow bishop, Festo Kivengere, and whispered, "They are going to kill me. I am not afraid".'

a minister of the gospel with the concerns of those who suffer written upon his heart' (pp. 4–6, #6), knowing 'what the price was going to be'. Luwum 'made several representations to President Amin'.

'If the church shies away from getting too involved then the church either disintegrates or simply bows to the squeezing of the world in which it lives but of which it is not' (pp. 5–7, #7). Jesus said 'You are in the world, but you are not of the world', the church does not have the option to stay away. In Colossians 2:6, 'As you therefore have received Christ Jesus, the Lord, so walk or live in him accordingly'. 'He is the invisible image of the invisible God', so the church, 'is a community which has restored the image of God', thus, 'the church is a witness in the world', and 'That is primary'.

Jesus is 'the unchanging rock for he was there before everything else was created and therefore, the church is not just beating about the bush'. 'The church has an unchangeable, absolute foundation'. Everything in the world does change, but there remains one unshakable and unchanging foundation for the church, 'Jesus Christ' ('Col 1).

'The church is not a confused community'. If we suffer from confusion it is because we [have] shifted from the centre. He sees Christ as the one who is 'the centre' of the church, the one who 'gives the church its image', and the one who is the church's 'true identity'. Kivengere believes that 'the world needs to be redeemed from its self-destruction' (pp. 7–8, #8), thus becoming 'a community of those who have been redeemed, restored, brought back to its normality'. 'It is a pity that the church has lost its normality'.

In talking about 'redemption' of the world, Kivengere is talking about redemption as the message that the church can tell to a confused world. In Christ, 'all things are held together'. The cohesion of the church does not depend on its understanding theologically. He is not against theology, but this category is 'not strong enough to give us the kind of unity in diversity that we need'. It is in him that all things of the church hold together. Again, reconciliation is not far away.

'I would like you to ask the Spirit of God as members of this great church in America today that he may actually print it upon your hearts, that you are a community which knows cohesion'. 'All things hold together in the Head'. A shift from the Head or the centre then you are going to experience breaking. According to the same message of 'holding together in Christ', 'church history is a witness that the church of Jesus Christ can no longer cohere apart from the Lordship of Jesus Christ'. In other words, he is talking about vertical relationship with Christ. Reconciliation is brought by Christ.

Still speaking of a shift from Christ, Kivengere adds that Paul concludes: 'When that becomes the case, all other categories fall down'. Christ is 'all in all'. To Kivengere, 'immediately that becomes the vision of the church, it becomes undefeatable'. This is because the 'presence of the Risen Christ in the middle of the church gives the church its unconquerable nature' (pp. 8–9, #). 'I am a lover of referring to Scriptures because the church has no other textbook except this one' (p. 9, #9). 'And in the textbook given to the saints for our instruction, for our rebuke, and for our enlightenment, you have these words', in which many things are mentioned by Paul, who himself 'was caught up in the confusions of the church'. 'All the problems you are discussing here in the diocese were with Paul' singling out a critical issue for the Episcopal Church at that time, 'including the ordination of women. If you read carefully, they are not brought in the language of the twentieth century but they are there' (p. 9, #9).

On this basis, he sees that 'there has never been an ideal church', in fact he believes that 'the only ideal in the church is Jesus Christ'. 'Romans 12, Paul says, "do not allow the world [around you] to squeeze you into its mould. 'Paul says, "Let us be transformed in our minds by the power of the Holy Spirit so that we may live according to the will' of God. The will of God is the will of love, which love 'is in Jesus Christ'. It is that 'love alone which can redeem our broken world'. Reconciliation is in view.

Kivengere prescribed three more issues that the church should not allow: 'legalism to enslave our spirituality (Gal 5:1)' (p. 10, #10), 'tradition to strangle life out of the church'; and 'religiosity . . . to supplement the truth and the living reality in Jesus Christ'. St. Paul calls these three things 'shadows'. Kivengere then jumps to state the 'terrible [and] nasty situations in oppressive regimes of the world', listing: Uganda, South Africa, Rhodesia, Ethiopia, and Guinea Bissau. He then asks: 'where is the ray of hope?'

Kivengere answered his question by saying that 'you have the ray of hope' because you have got 'the Son of righteousness who has healing in his wings' (p. 9, #9). By the 'Son of righteousness' he means 'Jesus Christ'. Jesus is 'the centre of the church', and also 'the centre is a community full of excitement'.

Kivengere uses an illustration of 'what makes his diocese tick?' (pp. 12–14, #12). Although his diocese still was many problems such as financial short-comings and is filled with a number of dry roots which need life, nevertheless it is 'an exciting diocese because of the Lordship of Jesus Christ' that is right 'at the heart of that diocese' and this makes 'all the difference in the world'. 'Jesus Christ the Lord' takes 'the centre in the ministry', 'in reconciliation when people don't agree'.

Kivengere reflects on how he saw a church warden at the Holy Communion ask for 'forgiveness from the living Lord'. They proceeded to have Communion reminding them of 'the bleeding reconciling hands of the master' (pp. 12–14, #12). Kivengere recalls that they 'all sat down and the Spirit of God penetrated the congregation and there was much reconciliation that day and the people were born into the kingdom, and homes were reconciled'. People who were at loggerheads 'were reconciled'. Kivengere then asks: 'Don't you think you need this [in] the church today?' This is what makes the church of Jesus Christ tick with life.

He concludes with a challenge: 'Let the Spirit of the Lord penetrate our church, liberating the lay men and women, setting the priests on fire because America desperately needs the testimony of the a reconciled, reconciling church of Christ' (pp. 12–14, #12).

5.7.2.5 Summary of The Unshakable Identity of the Church of Jesus Christ: AO: 19771029, [#1]

The exposition opens with an explanation on being salt and light in the world. The world is a rough place where many Christians in Uganda have been murdered, like Janani Luwum, a minister of reconciliation with concerns of people who suffer written on his heart. In his diocese, reconciliation takes the centre stage of ministry because Jesus Christ is also the centre of the church and community with his reconciling love. He describes Jesus as the bleeding reconciling master.

The impact of this sermon to the Episcopal Church is direct: it is to let the Spirit penetrate the church, liberate laymen and women, 'setting their priests on fire' for Jesus. This is prophetic message that he spoke into the specific social moment of the American community, and it focused on reconciliation: America desperately needs the testimony of a reconciled and reconciling church.

5.7.3 'Christ has Reconciled the Universe to Himself': AO: [estimated after May 1979], [#2]²⁴⁶

5.7.3.1 Situating the Sermon
This sermon was preached in Dr. Schuller's Church at Garden Grove, California, USA.

5.7.3.2 Introduction
Kivengere notes 'our Lord and Saviour takes one across barriers', whether territorial, tribal, racial, or denominational (p. 1, #1). Reconciliation is in view.

5.7.3.3 Exposition
After reading the text, Colossians 1, Kivengere then followed the word of God with his exposition. He notes that outside in God's world, all is not well. 'Men's hearts are breaking' (pp. 1–2, #2). In Uganda, 'we know situations where a church like this would be three quarters widows. The husbands are not to be found because they have lost their lives in the confusion of the world'.²⁴⁷

He moves from the world to his text, 'Christ exists before everything else. And everything else holds together in him' (pp. 3–4, #3). The church of which you are members is his body and he is the Head.

'There is no part of the universe in which the topmost place is not his'. 'God in all his completeness made his home in him, in Christ'. It was God's

---

246. Kivengere preached the first sermon in the morning from 1 Peter 2. See in this sermon, #2, pp. 1–2, he said, 'I want to read a passage which I think is suitable for our evening today. . . . The first letter of our apostle Peter, chapter two. And it is a beautiful passage, pardon[;] it's Colossians rather than Peter. I preached on Peter this morning, that is why I referred to him'. We have not yet been able to locate the first sermon.
247. Kivengere, 'In Christ'. Kivengere, 'The Reconciling Love of Christ', pp. 1–2, #2.

decision to effect through him an act of universal reconciliation to himself, of everything in heaven and on the earth. And it was through his decision, that by the cross God brought the whole universe into a right relationship with himself.

The bishop then explains that the uniqueness of his message that evening derives from what they heard: 'the centrality of Jesus Christ as the one who is at the bottom', 'the foundation of the universe'. 'Christ is the only one in whom the universe and all who inhabit it cohere or are held together', 'apart from Christ everything remains fluid', 'He is the foundation'. However, Kivengere then asserted, 'the foundation alone is not enough'.

'There is cohesion' in which 'things hold together', or, without it, 'fall apart'. 'Adam, the first representative of the human race, lost his bearings, lost his boundaries of destiny within which he could be completely free'. Freedom is meaningless if it does not have 'boundaries of destiny'. From that time on we have all experienced that life is breaking apart all the time' (pp. 3–4, #5). After bridging the gap between the world of the text and the world of his audience, Kivengere proceeds to explain the ground for reconciliation, without explicitly stating the word.

'The fall of humanity in Adam' led to 'the disintegration of life repeatedly', noting that 'homes break, life itself keeps on breaking'. In Africa, despite receiving political independence, 'we became the means by which we broke that which we wanted to build'. 'The very freedom one claims, one smashes that freedom, because freedom can only be freedom within the context of God'.

In Uganda, you hear stories of bloodshed and tribal conflicts. Humanity has continually experienced fighting, such as Arabs and Israelites fighting, yet they are all from 'the same ethnic group', the same historical background. They are not the only ones breaking in conflict.

The fundamental problem with 'the falling apart' is because 'I remain unpredictable until you see me in Jesus Christ' (p. 5, #7). To him, 'you simply cannot discover who I am until you find me in him who picked me up, put my broken life together', and out of 'the broken pieces brought out a man'.

Kivengere sees two important dimensions of the broken life of man restored in Jesus Christ. First he says, 'We are miracles of grace'. The 'broken life of man' can only be put together by 'the grace of God'. Secondly, he sees that the 'wounded humanity' can only be 'put together' by 'the wounded hands of Jesus'. He emphasized that *only* the wounded hands, 'could bring wounded humanity together' and that *only* 'the bleeding heart of the Son of God' could produce 'cohesion where there was disintegration'. 'This is the miracle of the New Testament message'. Clearly he is talking about reconciliation brought about by the work of Christ on the cross. Jesus Christ is the means for the reconciliation for humanity.

In Luke 4:18, Jesus is 'the good news' because he announced that 'The Spirit of the Lord is upon me, for I have been anointed to preach the good news to the poor, to give sight to the blind, to take captives and to release them to live, to the oppressed to experience liberty, and to proclaim the acceptable year of the Lord'. 'He is good news for the broken humanity'.

Kivengere then comes to the heart of the sermon and, this time he is explicit: reconciliation. First he explains his testimony leading to his explanation of how God reconciles man to himself. The work of Christ, drawing all men to himself is an on-going work: 'this continually happens when Christians experience the redeeming act' (pp. 6–7, #9). 'I am standing here as a witness of that redeeming act' (pp. 6–7, #9). Once alone and broken up, 'I was becoming a victim of life and yet he created me that life may become a joy to me'.

Referring to his audience as 'my dear friends'—thus, bridging the gap between the audience and the preacher—he moved on to explain the basis of reconciliation. If you have never known what happened on Calvary, there 'God [was] putting broken men and women together', and this act of God, 'cost him blood, and sweat, and nakedness'. Jesus 'put his blessed hands into the mess of humanity, and out of the mess he created a new community called the church'.

He is using the language of Ephesians 2. The church is a new community. 'It was God's decision to effect through him an act of universal reconciliation to himself'. 'God' is the subject and 'him' [Jesus] is the agent of reconciliation. This great 'act of universal reconciliation', brings a hostile universe back into friendship with himself. Jesus' death on the cross for all gives reconciliation a universal scope. It is God's 'act of universal reconciliation'. God has reconciled humanity 'back into sonship, back as children'.

Kivengere is using the language of the 'prodigal son' in the Gospel of Luke 15, adding a twist: 'These prodigals of humanity'. Again, he echoes the Keswick week using the language of 2 Corinthian 5:19–20, God reconciling with man and sending man out to ask people to be God's friends: 'And then cleansing them, restoring them, filling them, healing them, and sending them'. 'The cross was not lovely'. In fact, 'the cross was a realistic approach of God to humanity' (p. 7, #10): outside the city, a man—Jesus Christ—hung in blood and sweat, in utter loneliness and weakness. The outstretched arms of Christ embraced such a world—slowly, gently, steadily—until the world found itself upon the chest of the Son of God.

When reconciliation happens in Christ, out of that broken humanity you see miracles emerging. 'Through Jesus' death on the cross', 'God brought the whole universe to himself', reconciled the world through 'the death of Christ on the cross'. Again with a story previously recounted, that of the schoolmaster who witnessed to his murderers about the love of Christ before they shot him (pp. 7–9, #11–#13).[248]

5.7.3.4 Summary of 'Christ has Reconciled the Universe to Himself': AO: [estimated after May 1979], [#2]

Kivengere gives Scripture the priority to speak before the preacher by his reading it first. This feature of his preaching is common in his previous sermons. He reads aloud the text to be heard before he expounds it, thus letting the word of God from Scripture speak to his audience. His attitude of reading out the word aloud is in itself a biblical theology attitude that the word ought to be the preached word. It is by this uttered word and hearing it that his audience comes to respond to the message of reconciliation.

In line with Pauline interpretation of Colossians, he emphasized the unity of everything in Christ, the foundation upon which all things hold. Christ is also the one who gives coherence of all things. Because of the fall of man Christ had to bring reconciliation as a solution to the consequences of the fall.

A contribution of this sermon to this study is its recognition that Kivengere preached this message to his audience, assuring them that the

---

248. See Kivengere, 'His Flooding Love', p. 7, #10.

brokenness and wounds in life are put together and healed by the wounded hands of Jesus, the one who produces cohesion. Reconciliation is brought by the work of Christ and the death of Christ for all gives reconciliation a universal scope.

And, evidence of echoes from the Keswick calling to a life surrender to Christ and dedication to Christ in his service is present.

5.8 Conclusion of Chapter Five

Serving the wider question of the role of the doctrine of reconciliation in Kivengere's preaching, 1971–1988,[249] this chapter has analyzed a sample of 17 explicit reconciliation sermons, asking such questions as: 1. What is reconciliation according to Kivengere? 2. How does Kivengere's understanding of reconciliation compare to the Pauline doctrine of reconciliation 3. Does Kivengere exposit all, or overlook some? 4. What does Kivengere believe about preaching reconciliation? 5. Why does he preach and how does he preach reconciliation? 6. What aims does Kivengere have in preaching reconciliation? and, 7. What evidence do his sermons provide for potential and actual impact of his kind of preaching reconciliation?

Tentative findings have emerged. Reconciliation according to Kivengere starts with God. God so loved the world that in the person of the son, he came into the darkness and confusion of humanity, reconciled man back to himself and reconciled man with each other. Even more significantly, God in Jesus Christ reconciled all things (Col 1:19). Kivengere views this reconciliation to be firmly and securely rooted in God who in his Son Jesus Christ restored the world to God's purposes. The reason God reconciled humanity to himself was to recover the original fellowship between God and humanity at creation.

Reconciliation is a long and costly journey, costing the life of Jesus Christ. In Uganda at the opening of the century from the missionaries to the 100-year celebration of the gospel in Uganda, it cost the life of the Ugandan martyrs. Towards the closing of the century, Luwum sealed the celebrations

---

249. See Chapter One, 1. 'Thesis'.

of a century of gospel work in Uganda with his blood. Reconciliation is synonymous with conversion to Christ. Kivengere's own experiences of forgiving Amin and not hating him, of reconciling with an English missionary he hated, of reconciling with William Nagenda, Michael Cassidy, and Mera his wife, is a two-way journey. It firstly requires humility to accept the forgiveness that Christ has brought, and only then, you can repent to Christ of wrongs done against God and against other human beings, then extend forgiveness to those who have wronged you and whom you have wronged.

Reconciliation so mattered to Kivengere that he sought every opportunity to reconcile. This is even evident in the way he preached: he constantly bridged the gap between himself and his audience. After putting right his relationship with God he then moved to put right any wrong relationships with others. The scope of reconciliation ranged from one person to many groups, for God is interested in one person and many people as well. Reconciliation demands that he put right things in life that affected himself and other individuals. He no longer kept records of wrongs. He put right relationships that affected the fellowship. He asked the church to forgive him for wasting their time and the time of God over a dry sermon he preached. He also preached reconciliation to whole nations, to long- divided peoples like blacks and whites in Apartheid South Africa, or to similar racial tensions in America. Reconciliation not only brought restoration of fellowship with God, through forgiveness of sins, but Kivengere found God at work extending his kingdom even now.

This ministry of reconciling, one person, or within a whole nation, shaped his way of being a peacemaker. Reconciliation was central to his Christian ministry, because he believed it to be the centre of the Christian gospel. He pursued reconciliation at the Moshi Unity Conference in Tanzania where Ugandans of all shades of life were present. Thus, he pursued reconciliation well beyond the Christian community. Because he believed that the Lordship of Christ meant that everything held together in Christ, this shaped his pastoral practice of extending reconciliation to 'excluded' communities even outside the church.

The sermons have shown that Kivengere engaged publicly with Ugandan political authorities to hold them to account, or, in his words: 'to help the Uganda government lead better' her citizens, under God. Several times he confronted Amin and Obote about conditions of brokenness in the nation. Soon after the fall of Amin, there was enormous need for relief, reconstruction and rehabilitation of Uganda. Children were dying from measles for lack of drugs and health personnel to treat them. So in his preaching engagements in the USA, he shouted abroad for help and prayers to address these urgent and degenerating health conditions. Against the background of the bad governance of Ugandan leaders that had resulted in the state of brokenness, he reminded the church of its primary calling to preach reconciliation in the nation, and the church should never lose this calling or compromise it.

Reconciliation is a costly road. Janani died, being misunderstood as opposing Amin. Kivengere himself fled in exile. Shortly before the Moshi Unity Conference (23–26 March 1979), Kivengere was disappointed when he met Obote and found in him a politician planning to regain power and yet when he met Nyerere he found in him a nationalist planning to support Ugandans to get out of their situation of suffering in exile. When he got to the conference, though frustrated with the political divisions among Ugandan politicians in exile, he nevertheless painfully led both sides of the opposition across the bridge.

The sermons have shown Kivengere leading the way for Christians not to be observers, but to become reconcilers, even in the midst of deep divisions and conflicts. As reconcilers they will keep watch over the forces of spiritual and physical evil, that combine to bring brokenness in the world, as it was in Uganda under Amin. The gospel message of reconciliation prevails, even in such circumstances

All seventeen sermons treat reconciliation explicitly, basically following Paul's treatment. However, one sermon made no explicit mention of reconciliation, even when the text explicitly mentions reconciliation.[250] Mostly reconciliation was never far away, as he laid the ground for explicit mention of reconciliation. The cross was the starting point for his explicit treatment of reconciliation, and different themes linked with the cross helped Kivengere to explain reconciliation between God and humanity, between

---

250. Festo Kivengere, 'Life in Jesus', Sermon Transcript (Sydney, Australia, 1978), AO: 1978 [02--?].

each other. These themes include, 'the love of God', 'grace', 'hope', fellowship, the Holy Spirit, prayer, peace.

Taken together, the explicit Pauline reconciliation passages reveal a coherent treatment of reconciliation to which, for the most part Kivengere adhered. The sermons, as in the Pauline passages, show 'us'—human beings as enemies of God because of 'our' sins, which alienate 'us' from a right relationship with God. Again, as in the Pauline passages, Kivengere presents God as the source of reconciliation. He has demonstrated 'in Christ' or 'through Christ' his reconciling love by the action of Christ who came into our messy situation, lived and died on the cross to forgive our sins. Through his costly self-sacrifice death on the cross, we are reconciled to God and fellow man. However, in some instances he was silent about some concepts Paul linked with reconciliation, especially the Jew–Gentile relationship. Once he showed a defective biblical theological theology of Pauline Apostleship.

Kivengere's refusal to speak of justification or the wrath of God when expounding Romans 5:1–11 raises serious questions about the adequacy of his doctrine of reconciliation. How does it sit with the eschatology of the New Testament, which so clearly expects a 'Day of Christ' that will involve a salvation, that is always salvation from the wrath of God? Does Kivegere's reconciliation only relate to the problems of this world, not those of the next?

These observations therefore generate some major questions for further inquiry at a later date. What do the sermons show about Kivengere's view of God's wrath and justification?

In the sermons we have found out that for Kivengere, God has entrusted the ministry of reconciliation to us. Brokenness in the human heart can only be addressed by the gospel of reconciliation. Due to sin, man alienated himself from God and lived a life of enmity and hostility to God. Through Christ, God was pleased to reconcile to himself all things.

All the influences discussed in chapter three can be determined in these sermons. The Keswick and Revival topics and sequence of preaching was evident, with the change that a weeklong sequence of preaching is brought into one sermon. His exposition shows great affinity with Karl Barth's theological Exegesis. He is concerned with the *Sache*—the subject-matter,

God, who came in his son Jesus Christ and reconciled us back to God and with each other. The big theme with which he concerned himself in the sermons was reconciliation, centred in the person and work of Jesus Christ. Because of his Keswick and Revival background, his concern with individual Christian experience led him into a deficient biblical theology of the role of apostles in salvation-history, despite his great affinity with the Pauline doctrine of reconciliation.

These sermons were preached in a variety of places (Uganda, United States of America, England, Israel, and Australia), to a range of different audiences (mission gatherings, church worship, theological students and faculty). Although the actual impact of the sermons on their hearers is difficult to ascertain, they show clearly enough what Kivengere himself was aiming to achieve and his vision of what he thought reconciliation would achieve. In Uganda, he aimed at healing the deep wounds that had been created by Amin's rule, ethnic conflicts, and bad governance. Using his words, 'the only antidote' to Uganda's wounds is reconciliation. His vision was to touch hearts that were full of the attitude of desire to revenge using the message of reconciliation. This message started with God who sent his son Jesus Christ into our darkness and in his self-love demonstrated in his death on the cross, change him, led him to reconcile with his enemies. This message was still fresh and it is the hope of Uganda. He does not say if this message will be complete with the final return of Jesus Christ (Rom 8:18–39; Rev 21–22:5).

In seeking to accomplish his vision of preaching the message of reconciliation in Uganda, Kivengere openly acknowledged in his illustrations and testimonies in the sermons the reality of destructive conflicts in Uganda's history. At the centre of this history is the church in Uganda, especially the COU which has been caught up in the historical conflicts of ethnic divisions and association with political parties with the consequence that the church has been caught up in church and State conflicts. However, the church in its discipleship and mission of preaching reconciliation has continued even in the midst of State violence, which in Amin's case led to the murder of Luwum and Kivengere fleeing to exile.

In Kivengere's vision of preaching reconciliation in Uganda, he noted clearly that there are other sources of brokenness outside Amin and

Ugandans, namely, evil spirits. These sources are dealt with by the death and blood of Jesus Christ. His vision for dealing with the post conflict situation is plain: first embrace Jesus Christ, and he will give you the ability to face any situation: unresolved past, haunted memories.

In foreign places, he preached the same message of reconciliation in Jesus Christ as the hope for the world. His audiences must be reconciled with God and with each other, maintaining the right balance between the two dimensions of reconciliation. One without the other is of no use. This message of reconciliation is what he used to mobilize the world for peace that comes from God as a result of reconciliation and it is the message he used to encouraged his audience to reach out in service of making people friends of God. Because he considered this message from God so important, he preached reconciliation throughout his life and ministry, even from passages in Scripture that do not explicitly mention reconciliation. With this in mind, we turn to chapter 6, and to sermons where he preached reconciliation from non-explicit reconciliation passages.

CHAPTER SIX

Non-Explicit Reconciliation Passages

6.1 A Synopsis

Since Kivengere not only preached reconciliation from explicit reconciliation passages (chapter 5), but also preached reconciliation from non-explicit passages, in this chapter we analyze a representative sample of sermons focusing on reconciliation, even though this is not as explicit in them. Alongside our planned catalogue of sermons,[1] these sermons will act as a further 'control' to show that reconciliation was close to his heart, that it shaped his attitude to life—to others, to his enemies, and to himself.

As the chronology in chapter 4 shows, Kivengere preached reconciliation throughout 1971–1988, which gave him sufficient time to reflect on the topic and upon its importance for the continuing mission of God in the world. In this chapter, our sample of eight sermons on non-explicit reconciliation passages and one reflection on reconciliation from Kivengere's own pen, will show that, on each occasion, he preached reconciliation as the climax of the cross. The message of reconciliation aimed at bringing hope and recovery for sinners, and to heal their wounds, and bring about their transformation.

---

1. See Appendix 5.

6.2 Four Sermons on Non-Explicit Passages

6.2.1 The Cross: AO: 19740725[2]

6.2.1.1 Situating the Sermon

Kivengere preached this sermon at Lausanne, Switzerland, on 25 July 1974, on the last day of the International Congress on World Evangelization.[3] The influence of the Keswick sequence of preaching is discernable, for Kivengere is true to the Keswick tradition of using the last day to send believers out into the world to proclaim the gospel.

6.2.1.2 Preliminaries

Kivengere opens with an expression of humility as he is preaching 'about the eternal secret of God coming to man' (p. 1, #1). Speaking of 'God coming to man' already lays the ground for reconciliation. Because of the miracle, which took place at Calvary's cross, Kivengere would say, 'I am the man and Christian I am today',[4] Kivengere's indirect way of saying that he is now reconciled to God.

He sees his audience standing on 'the most holy ground' and asks for their prayers to the Holy Spirit so that he may speak. He asks that they should hold back their clapping and bow their hearts 'at the feet of eternity', so that their conscience will be melted at the cross, and their eyes opened to see the 'bleeding world', in the bleeding wounds of him who died for the world. On day one Keswick focused on holy living,[5] but here Kivengere brings that teaching at the opening of his message. Keswick and the Revival also similarly emphasized the death of Jesus on the cross, and the preciousness of his cleansing blood shed to save sinners. This perspective no doubt informs Kivengere's grace tones as he calls his audience to bow their hearts 'at the feet of eternity', and to see the 'bleeding world', in the bleeding wounds of Jesus.

---

2. For an edited version of the sermon Transcript see, Kivengere, 'The Cross and World Evangelization'.
3. See Reconciliation Time-line (under 1974) in Chapter Four.
4. See Chapter Two, 5.2 'Kivengere's Conversion: From Agnostic to Preacher'.
5. See Chapter Three, 2.1.1 'Day One: The Diagnosis—Sin'.

6.2.1.3 Exposition

His exposition is from Romans 1:16. He immediately seeks to highlight the context of the passage. Paul focuses on that tremendous vision of presenting the gospel to the Roman Christians. 'I owe a debt to all men, to the Jews (the religious), to the Greeks (the sophisticated), and to the ordinary man on the street or in the village' (p. 1, #2). He asks: 'How did that happen?' 'In the vision of him who died and rose again from the dead, whom St. Paul calls Jesus Christ and him crucified' (p. 2, #2). This, for Kivengere, 'is the very heart of evangelism'.

Kivengere explains the meaning of the cross as God's self-sacrificing love for humanity (p. 2, #3). The cross means 'something deeper, wider, eternally outreaching, and embracing broken humanity in a mighty embrace'. Without using the word 'reconciliation' he accurately provides its description.

Appealing to his audience as 'dear brethren' he calls them to the cross for 'cleansing in the precious blood of Jesus' (p. 2, #4). He appeals to them to recall all that God has been teaching them in the ten days at the Congress: 'with hushed hearts, with ready minds, will you gather all [that] God has been teaching you and exercise your intellect, your spiritual gifts, your understanding of the word and bring all of it to the cross?' He is not asking his audience to respond to his appeal to draw near to the cross as a consequence of mere oratory.[6] They should draw near to the cross because the theology of the cross is in the centre and the heart of his theological thought (p. 2, #4). He uses the language of 'the centre' and 'the heart' to state that 'without the cross theology is like the dry bones in Ezekiel's vision in the valley'. In contrast to lifeless or dead theology, a living theology 'takes its blood from Calvary, and when Calvary is not there all that remains is . . . confusing words'.[7] The cross addresses itself primarily to man. This is illustrated by his answer to the question 'where does the cross find man?'

The cross finds man standing in the world; it finds man actually crossed out, standing alone, torn apart with conflicting pulls (p. 3, #5). Kivengere's

---

6. See Chapter Two, 5.3.1 'Story-telling at the Fireplace'.
7. Here Kivengere like Barth desires that theology should shine like a living voice in the communion of the saints. See Webster, *Barth's Earlier Theology*, 9.

answer clearly depicts the reason God reconciled men to himself, without using the word reconciliation. He describes a 'conflicting pull' between the upward and downward which leaves man 'crossed out, standing alone, torn apart, with no solution in his own power: for there is no ladder, no way of ever getting there, he stands in suspense'. His audience is aware of the downward pull of base desire, to deterioration into meanness. He would not be surprised if some of his audience leave the congress 'thoroughly angry, pulled outward to fight and to resent'.

This tension between the 'upward pull and the downward pull' arises when the centre becomes 'I'. He recalled his conversion story, as a young teacher, personally broken, fragmented, resenting his brokenness because of the sin in him, hating the world, hating man (p. 3, #6).[8] He lost his centre and therefore became eccentric and thus took the direction of darkness instead of the direction of light (p. 4, #6). Everywhere in the world there is a tremendous amount of eccentricity and 'where do you go when you have no other centre except yourself?' Kivengere's use of the language of 2 Corinthians 5:13, which is linked to the concept of reconciliation when his text does not call for it, strengthens our argument that reconciliation to Kivengere was close to his heart. As the reconciliation time-line in chapter 4 has shown, it was a subject he had long thought over and he had become convinced that it was the important message to preach. That he preaches reconciliation when the text does not demand this is a clear indicator of its importance to him.

When 'self' becomes the centre of your life, it makes a mess of lives, of relationships, and this is illustrated by a broken world, and broken homes even in evangelical circles (p. 4, #6). Man standing in the darkness of his relationships is 'where God finds man'. God 'took that position very seriously, and stepped from where he was . . . and he came right into that terrible chaotic existence'. 'For God so loved this world that he gave his beloved son' (Jon 3:16). When the beloved Son came, he did not keep from responding to the deep-seated need of man, but 'he came 100% to where

---

8. See Chapter Two, 5.2 'Kivengere's Conversion: From Agnostic to Preacher'.

man was'. Here Kivengere echoes Karl Barth's emphasis that 'God found his way to us'.[9]

In coming to man's chaotic situation 'He put his hands into the situation', as illustrated in his baptism in the River Jordan. 'He refused to be counted apart from the broken men and women, in Africa, in America, all over the world'. This locates him at the centre of God's reconciliation with man, and men with each other. When Christ came rushing to the rescue of humanity, he took his place among them, put his hand into their lonely trembling hand, and hope entered humanity (p. 5, #7). Every time Kivengere talks of 'God coming to us' or 'Jesus coming into our situation', 'putting his hands into our lonely trembling hands', Kivengere is echoing Barth's way of talking about reconciliation 'In Christ . . . God himself has stepped among us'. That was merely a beginning, 'the climax is coming'. He points his audience to the future, expecting God to do more 'for God, did not stop there. He addressed himself to the deepest human need' (p. 5, #8).

He wants his audience to know precisely what is the deepest human need. 'Primarily my greatest need, and your greatest need, and the needs of men among whom we preach, is their deepest-seated human guilt' (p. 5, #9). He is emphatic about this need: 'this is the shattering experience of all men everywhere, no matter whether you cover it with psychological words or theological expressions, or sociological understanding, it is still there!' The Keswick diagnosis of sin,[10] no doubt influences him to emphasize the problem of guilt, using himself as an illustration: 'you feed me, you dress me up, you make me physically fat, I am still a suffering man unless you deal with my guilt'. Here is an insight into the secret of Kivengere's belief that *context* is immaterial, what matters most is *content* addressed to the heart of man where guilt, the consequence of sin, resides.

'The cross comes with its divine origin purposely to meet my need in my relationship to God. A bridge is created' (p. 5, #9). He recalls a 'Negro' spiritual song 'that wonderful ladder of Jacob, the cross' (p. 5, #9). He links back to explain the expression 'divine origin': the cross originates from the love of God—love stooping down and answering my question

---

9. See Chapter Three, 3.3 'Barth's Hermeneutics'.
10. See Chapter Three, 2.1.1 'Day One: The Diagnosis—Sin'.

and removing the barrier between me and God, as if Jesus says, 'the original state is now possible, I am the way up there' (p. 6, #9). Once again echoing Barth, he is clearly preaching[11] that God comes to humanity in his reconciling love.

The cross goes down deep into man's deterioration. The cross is deep—its depth is so great that there is no need that the cross cannot meet (p. 6, #10). If there is deep hatred, underneath it lies that deep redeeming love of the Son of God, and in the depth of its outreach it meets man's deterioration—the tendency to go down to base desire and become its victim. Because the cross is like it is 'in its outreach it goes right up there and finds men fighting other men', such as 'black and white resentments and hostilities'.[12] He asks: 'what does the cross do?' The cross deals 'with my hostilities, and restores relationships between man and man because it has already restored my relationship with God'. Here he clearly speaks of the horizontal (social relationship) and the vertical (theological relationship) in reconciliation.

How does Christ restore 'my inward fragmentation?' 'The cross of Jesus Christ is love going right into my psychological confusion and answering the questions which no psychiatrist can deal with, and puts a broken man together'. Kivengere explains how God in Jesus Christ, reconciled man back to himself and men to each other. 'No wonder the cross is, therefore, the message for humanity. It is the message for evangelism my dear brethren'. In this statement, he accomplished two things. Firstly, by using the phrase 'my dear brethren', the preacher and the audience come together. So he is using language that closes the gap between them. Secondly, in telling his audience that the cross is the message of evangelism, he is informing their understanding of a theology of evangelism.[13]

---

11. See chapter three, 3.3 'Barth's Hermeneutics'.

12. On becoming a Christian, Kivengere no longer look at the identity of men to be found in groups like blacks or which. See Chapter Two, 5.1.1 'Ancestral Upbringing'.

13. In the period leading up to 1974, few books had been written on a theology of evangelism to help with this problem unlike other areas of theology, namely, systematic theology and missions. The reasons for not writing it are beyond the scope of our inquiry. Here we simply acknowledge a problem that Kivengere is providing a corrective to. For the few helpful works on a theology of evangelism, in a chronological order since 1949, see among others, Judson Eber Conant, *No Salvation Without Substitution* (Grand Rapids, Mich.: Eerdmans, 1941); Samuel Marinus Zwemer, *Evangelism Today: Message*

'Evangelism is never going to come simply because we have had long papers presented at Berlin or at Lausanne' (p. 7, #11). . . . 'Those may enlighten us, but they can never be the substance of evangelism', for this will always be 'Jesus Christ, him crucified'. To illustrate he referred to men in Uganda who could only read Saint Mark and Saint Luke's gospels. These men were never educated in any school; yet, they stood in the marketplace and preached the gospel with some success.[14] This kind of evangelism allows Kivengere to reinforce his argument by drawing upon the East African Revival. 'In fact, I was converted under men who, when they talked about hell, they wept. When they talked about heaven they laughed. When they talked about the need of a sinner, you saw it portrayed in their eyes'.[15] There is his open acknowledgement of influence from the Revival as early as the days of his conversion.[16]

The key to their message was the cross, not merely their persuasive words. It is not surprising that he concludes: 'the cross is the heart of evangelism, it is the heartbeat, and it is the message'. Without the cross, 'The power to heal broken hearts, broken homes, broken relationships is lost'. His use of such phrases: 'heal broken hearts', 'broken lives', and 'heal broken relationships' are indicative that reconciliation is not far away from his mind.

The cross speaks to the guilt of man; it speaks to his condemnation by a holy God, speaking of eternal forgiveness (p. 8, #12). This message is wonderful for it brings 'the blood which speaks sweet messages when the heart is guilty and the conscience is burdened'. His language is always linked to reconciliation: the cross, the guilt of man, condemnation by God, forgiveness, the guilty heart of a burdened conscience. All these phrases help him to explain reconciliation in the person and work of Jesus on the

---

Not Method (New York: Flemington H. Revell Company, 1944); Henry Cook, *The Theology of Evangelism: The Gospel in the World of To-Day* (London: Carey Kingsgate Press, 1951); Taito Almar Kantonen, *The Theology of Evangelism* (Philadelphia: Muhlennerg Press, 1954); Julian N. Hartt, *Towards a Theology of Evangelism* (New York: Abingdon Press, 1955); C. E. Autrey, *The Theology of Evangelism* (Nashville: Broadman, 1966); A. Skevington Wood, *Evangelism: Its Theology and Practice* (Grand Rapids, Mich.: Zondervan, 1966); Ernest D. Pickering, *The Theology of Evangelism* (Clarks Summit, PA: Baptist Bible College Press, 1974).

14. Kivengere, 'Awesome Growth', 217.
15. For the experience he described, see Kivengere, *Revolutionary Love*, 17–23.
16. See Chapter Two, 5.2 'Kivengere's Conversion: From Agnostic to Preacher'.

cross. Behind the use of these expressions stands the same Pauline theology of reconciliation that Kivengere expounded in the explicit reconciliation passages.[17] Kivengere's reference to man's guilt, which God alone can deal with, shows affinity with an aspect of Karl Barth's Christology, Jesus Christ, 'very God'.[18]

The cross is 'the motivating power of evangelism' (p. 8, #13). Like Paul a new vision of the cross brings to our attention 'the wonder of his incredible redeeming love and our own wretchedness' (p. 8, #13). In the final analysis we 'discover that there is no one too far gone at all', every case is forgivable. Using the language of 2 Corinthians 5:14, like Paul 'he felt compelled by the love of Christ' . . . and said] 'we have come to the conclusion that if Christ died for all men including myself then men are all redeemable'. Kivengere is preaching the message of reconciliation when his text does not call for it. When hearts catch the vision of the redeeming love on the cross of Calvary, humanity takes on a new colour (p. 9, #14). Once again, reconciliation is in view.

He also used the language of Ephesians 2:14–18: 'barriers are broken down', adding his own glosses: 'race can speak to race'. The concept of reconciliation is clear as he moves on. 'Paul, a sophisticated Pharisee [with] segregating power, and a bigot of a man who loses his bigotry, his segregating fences and begins to speak to men everywhere'. Again he returns to the language of 2 Corinthians 5:13. When he asks: 'what has happened to Paul?' Kivengere answered: 'the cross has pierced the heart of Paul and broken down the barriers'. Clearly, therefore, for Kivengere the cross achieves reconciliation.

Forgiveness to all, the cross was the inspiration of evangelism and there was no other: 'God breathes through the cross upon evangelism and only then men become evangelists everywhere' (p. 9, #14). This was his own experience, for the cross had lit a fire that burned within him and others who suffered for Christ in Uganda to the point of shedding their blood. Here the story of the Uganda martyrs is in view.[19]

---

17. See Chapter Three, 5. 'Reconciliation in the New Testament'.
18. See Chapter Three, 3.5.3 'The Components of Barth's Doctrine of Reconciliation', the relevant section 3.4.4.1 Jesus Christ —'very God'.
19. See Chapter Two, 3.2 'Mwanga's Martyrdoms'.

'God in his incredible love for us treated Christ as a sinner who knew no sin, for us sinners, that we may be brought into right relationship with him' (p. 11, #17). This is from 2 Corinthians 5:21 that he is paraphrasing and he is excited at what God has done for us according to that text: 'isn't that tremendous?' . . . 'If this is what God went through that he may bring us into right relationship with himself, what about you? what about me?',—thus, bridging the gap between preacher and audience. Again, behind the discovery of what God has done, is Markus Barth's influence of getting excited at the insight of discovering something new in the text.[20]

His two questions underscore the need to recognize and act by bringing 'men into right relationship with God and with each other'. Clearly he refers to reconciliation. 'Do we take these things seriously?—God took it very seriously' (p. 11, #17). Christ being made sin for us shows this, for God 'treated Christ who knew no sin as sin' and he adds his own glosses 'for me, for you'. He asks: 'what did you do to deserve that?' '[Nothing] at all . . . you were an enemy, I was still an enemy when Christ came my way'. Kivengere is here using the language of Romans 5:6, which is about reconciliation. Already halfway into the sermon, on a non-explicit passage, Kivengere is clearly preaching reconciliation by drawing in the language of passages explicitly about the doctrine. This demonstrates that he attaches great significance to reconciliation.

'Therefore, mark this, my dear brethren, an evangelical is a man who is going to love as a necessity from Calvary, not one who throws stones in the name of truth at other people'. 'This is where evangelicals are called, including myself, to stand in front of Calvary and see what is happening there',— thus, bridging the gap between the preacher and audience. Without mentioning the texts, he recalls examples of how Christ loved people: 'and we see love pouring down to the criminal and to the soldiers and to everyone from Jesus'. Bringing home his message, he asks 'are we catching the vision?' . . . 'Before you criticize, love more. Before you throw your truth at a man, put it in the envelope of love and give it to him' (p. 12, #17).

This manner of communicating truth and love is challenging because: 'the price of evangelism is the cross. The cross is the price God paid for my

---

20. See Chapter Three, 4. 'Markus Barth's Link with Kivengere'.

sin and yours'. By including himself alongside his audience, he bridges the gap between himself ('my') and the audience ('yours'). Using the language of the cross as 'the centre' of the good news, reconciliation centred in the cross is in view.

There are divisions among evangelicals. Using an illustration from Africa of growing millet too close to explain crowding together, he observed that evangelicals crowd all sorts of gifts together, leading to divisions and schisms (p. 13, #18). He directs them to look at the situation in the light of the cross, specifically, the issue of money and paternalism. If they want to lose paternalism in missionary activity, they should come to the cross. Will they? Kivengere had observed paternalism in missionary activity in Uganda.[21] Missionaries from Britain were paternalistic, perhaps more than anyone else, because the British were then ruling Uganda.[22] Without stating when and where, he simply told of a time when all came to the vision of Calvary: 'Africans and missionaries, repented of their meanness and they became a body of men and women witnessing together irrespective of their colour and background'. Clearly this illustration speaks of reconciliation, even though he doesn't use the word.

He prefers to use of the word 'the cross' which he said did a quick work in removing paternalism. At the cross is where you lose it all (pp. 13–14, #19). His people saw the vision, 'took their bags and walked miles and miles' (p. 14, #20). Christ had the terrible experience of knowingly facing the cross in the Garden of Gethsemane. He was pressed hard but he accomplished it. He explained that Jesus was under pressure to come where we are. 'He jumped into it without sparing anything'. This was the reason why these evangelists were at Lausanne. He is excited about what Christ did at Calvary. Isaac Watts was excited about the same when he wrote his famous line: 'Were the whole realm of nature mine that were in offering far too small. Love so amazing, love so divine, demands my life and my all'. This is the testimony of a man caught in the vision of the cross who states:

---

21. The reason for this paternalism that Kivengere observed in Uganda, according to Colin Reed, was an attitude to do with the western racism that caught up with CMS missionaries in Africa. See Reed, *Pastors, Partners and Paternalists*, 10.
22. See Chapter Two, 2.1 'From 1894–1962: The Origin of Divisions and Tensions'.

'my whole life is no longer meaningful except I put it all at his feet, that it may be redeemed'.

Kivengere appealed to them not to leave the congress without experiencing the 'melting' from the cross. He wants to see their lives changed. He tells them to re-examine their relationships and see how they are doing in the light of the cross. The cross is where God embraces humanity and where humanity can shake hands and cultures can become a means of communication instead of being barriers of separation. Kivengere calls for reconciliation without explicitly using of the word.

Pressing his point on the need for self-examination he rejects the notion of colour as a basis for not having fellowship with another brother (p. 15, #20).[23] Repeating the testimony of his conversion, he said he was one of the worst of bigots, prejudiced and cold, but now, because the cross had set him free, he was happy to have fellowship with everybody, those who are white, black, yellow or brown.[24] Set free by the cross 'one day I was compelled to go and embrace a missionary, and in person say "I am sorry I hated you, but now you are my brother, the cross has set me free. I want to be your brother"'. Although he does not use the word, here Kivengere illustrates how reconciliation has changed his attitude towards self, others, and life.

When he stresses the work of the cross as the drawing power in evangelism, it is because the cross requires them to take their responsibility seriously—not merely speaking empty words deprived of action. 'Aren't there people here you would like to shake hands with? People you have resented, feared, or suspected?' Kivengere is not merely preaching the message of reconciliation, he is reconciling them with God and with each other. He gave an example of the World Council of Churches who needed to feel the warmth of love obtained from Calvary by evangelicals. 'You don't get in fellowship by theological resolutions' (p. 16, #20). He quotes John 12:32 '[A]nd I, when I am lifted high up from the earth, will draw all people to myself'. It is fellowship in Christ that draws believers together.[25]

---

23. See Chapter Two, 5.1.1 'Aristocratic Upbringing'.
24. See Chapter Two, 5.2 'Kivengere's Conversion: From Agnostic to Preacher'.
25. See Chapter One, 3.3.1 'Inkelaar-de Mos 1988'.

He appeals to them to let the power of Jesus draw all men to himself emphasizing that it is not a method, a technique or a programme (p. 16, #21). To draw men in fellowship with God only by passing theological resolutions is to leave them in suspense and confusion. The cross of Christ draws men like a magnet.[26] Their meeting at Lausanne was a result of the drawing power of evangelism: Christ (p. 16, #22).

Kivengere then comes to his last point that the cross is the uniting power in evangelism (p. 17, #22). We lack unity, because we think that in order to be united we need to experience the same thing. But unity never comes that way. Rather the cross draws men from their sins, from their isolation, and draws them to the centre, changing their eccentricity and making them Christ-centred and therefore normal. By once again using the language of 2 Corinthians 5, Kivengere has reconciliation in view.

With Christ at the centre, differences are forgotten and gifts are used. He links the times of revival with the Spirit of God pouring out gifts. In the East African Revival people dreamt dreams, saw visions, and spoke in ecstatic utterances. The spirit gives the gifts because it has all been purchased on the cross (p. 17, #22). Kivengere desires that they bring their different spiritual gifts to the cross of cleansing, especially the divisive attitudes of those who claim to speak in ecstatic utterances.

He illustrates the misuse of these gifts when one brother says to another 'I can't have fellowship with you unless you do the same' (pp. 17–18, #22). He desires that they take their pride to the cross for cleansing so that the gifts will flow to build the body of Christ. In conclusion he pleads with his audience for humility of heart and asks that they look in the face of Christ and open their heart to him, and let Christ's love break the barriers (p. 18, #22). Without explicitly mentioning it Kivengere is preaching reconciliation.

At this point, he introduces an explicit reconciliation passage (Matt 5:24) urging them to be reconciled with each other before they bring their gifts to the altar.[27] This is particularly significant for, even though he is preaching

---

26. See Kivengere, 'Surprised by Joy', p. 1, #1. Kivengere, 'The Evangelist's Ministry of Reconciliation', p. 159, #22.
27. See chapter three, 5. 'Reconciliation in the New Testament'.

from a non-explicit text, he has so preached reconciliation that he needs to draw upon an explicit text to make his conclusion. This strengthens the argument of this thesis that reconciliation was close to his heart.

Kivengere recalls the reconciling message in Matthew where Christ refers to the obligation and responsibility to others with whom there may be barriers. If there is a barrier between 'you and your brother, [or] between you and an unconverted man, please be open to the Holy Spirit that he may apply the almighty love of Christ. Then you may have to leave your gift on the altar and go and be reconciled to that man or that woman and then come and preach a lovely evangelical sermon' (p. 18, #22). In his own life, there were times he desired to go and preach before putting right the strained relationship with another. But only after putting things right can one go in the power of the cross to preach the message that liberates humanity, heals the sick, helps the weak, and recovers the sinner (p. 19, #22).

He asks God's blessing upon them that they each receive, embrace and bless each other as they go away from Lausanne. He tells them to be excited, fired up to preach the gospel because churches are waiting, the world is waiting, and for them to tell 'our age' the good news.[28] 'Let the whole world hear his voice till he comes to rule forever and ever [Amen]'.[29] In true Keswick tradition,[30] Kivengere has used the last day of the convention to send the crowd out into the world in mission service.

6.2.1.4 Summary of The Cross: AO: 19740725

In this sermon, without the text calling for reconciliation, he preached that reconciliation comprised obligation and responsibility in the context of relationships to others with whom there are barriers: between 'you and your brother (man and woman)', and between 'you and unconverted man'. Only when this is put right, can a believer preach the love of

---

28. See Chapter Two, 5.4 'Pittsburgh Seminary: From 1964–1967'. He echoes the evangelical phrase that was used in the 1960s of penetrating the entire world in our generation.
29. This was the theme of the 1974 Lausanne Congress. See the title of the Congress in Douglas, *Let the Earth Hear His Voice*.
30. See Chapter Three, 2.1.5 'Day Five: The Mission Powerful Service'.

Christ—reconciliation (p. 18, #22). This reconciliation liberates humanity, heals the sick and recovers sinners (p. 19, #22).

Reconciliation is grounded in the cross where relationships are restored. In the cross, Christ has restored broken people back to God and to each other, removing the barriers between people and God and making the original state of fellowship now possible (p. 6, #9). The hostilities of men, and their struggles with sin and its consequence, guilt, are dealt with in the cross. Thus, reconciliation can be realized when people acknowledge wrongs done against each other motivated by the compelling love of Christ from the cross, which extends forgiveness, and brings restoration of fellowship in the love of God. Without the cross the power to heal broken hearts is lost, for the cross is the heart of evangelism.

Later at the World Congress of Itinerant Evangelists held in 1983 in Amsterdam, he further refined his explanation of reconciliation. It is the lifeblood of the evangelist's message. After close to a decade he has moved from emphasizing the cross as the heart of evangelism and explicitly focused his language on reconciliation as the lifeblood of evangelism. This can also be taken to show that his heart had wanted to speak about reconciliation for over ten years. What was implicit in 1974, became explicit in 1983.

In 1983 Kivengere notes that there is more that the Lord is to do, beyond dying on the cross (p. 5, #8). The cross is the most important thing about the person and the work of Jesus Christ to be preached, but the climax of the cross is reconciliation, which justifies his claim that it is the lifeblood of the evangelist.

This is what Kivengere preached in the 1974 sermon without explicitly mentioning it. Although his text was from Roman 1:16, which clearly does not mention reconciliation, Kivengere's exposition still has clear connection with Paul's understanding of reconciliation. Kivengere's grounding of reconciliation in the cross, which to him is synonymous with the person and work of Jesus Christ, drew in the language of 2 Corinthians 5:14, Ephesians 2:14, and the language Romans 5:6. This suggests clearly the Pauline doctrine of reconciliation has made a profound effect on him, even shaping his message when the text in front of him does not demand it.

The influence of the Revival is also both in this and other sermons, detectable (p. 7, #11). The Revival also influenced his perspective of understanding unity, spiritual gifts, and their use to build the body of Christ (p. 17, #22). He talked about being converted under Revival men who talked about hell, heaven, and the need of a sinner. However, it is very interesting to notice that while Kivengere certainly spoke about the need of the sinner, he himself does not talk about hell and heaven. The eschatology of the Revival seems to have disappeared, even if its views on the plight of man are retained, for this helped him to always focus his message to the heart of believers.

Previously, Kivengere was in attendance at the October 1966 Berlin Congress on World Evangelization, when his life-long friend, Billy Graham 'commissioned' the participants, using a common evangelical phrase dating back to the end of the nineteenth century 'the penetration of the world in our generation with the gospel!'.[31] The singular task was to declare in their generation that 'God was in Christ reconciling the world unto himself'.[32] It is not surprising that Kivengere, now at Lausanne Congress, proclaims reconciliation as a singular task that is close to his heart and his vision is for the evangelical world to proclaim this gospel.

The fact that Kivengere used a gospel reconciliation text Matthew 5:24, which is not his theme text, shows the significance of the subject to his heart. He also made reference to John 12:32: 'I, when I am lifted up from the earth, will draw all men to myself', and linked it with reconciliation, which comes to believers by means of the death of Jesus Christ on the cross. It is significant to note that the Johannine text was used at the October 1966 Berlin Congress on World Evangelization by the Australian Scholar Leon Morris. Morris later published *The Atonement: Its Meaning and Significance*,[33] which emphasizes sin is the barrier, sin must be dealt with, there is a real hostility between God and sinners, reconciliation is God's work, reconciliation proceeds from the love of God, and the reconciliation must be received—with clear echoes of Keswick. At the Berlin Congress, he

---

31. See Chapter Two, 5.4 'Pittsburgh Seminary: From 1964–1967'.
32. See Chapter Two, 5.4 'Pittsburgh Seminary: From 1964–1967'.
33. Leon Morris, *The Atonement: Its Meaning and Significance* (Leicester: Inter-Varsity Press, 1983).

made the point that Jesus was telling us the means by which he was to die (v 33), and 'not how many people will be saved'.[34]

Because Morris's presentation came immediately before Kivengere's presentation on Spiritual Indifference,[35] and because of his interest in the subject of atonement and reconciliation, it is possible that Morris influenced Kivengere's understanding of reconciliation from this text. Even so, Kivengere moves one step further. For Kivengere, reconciliation is rooted in the cross-work of Christ and the target of reconciliation is restored fellowship between God and sinners. But not only is estrangement, alienation, and enmity ended in Christ, but the good news is that a loving relationship with God is gained. He does not only get pardon by God—he gets *God himself*. Morris' presentation help him to arrive at this point.

6.2.2 The Triumph of God's Glory: AO: 19761231

6.2.2.1 Situating the Sermon

Kivengere preached this sermon on 31 December 1976, USA, at Urbana on the Keswick pattern as part of a five-day mission. He preached on the last day of the mission gathering. Among notable evangelical leaders present on the platform were his long-time friends Billy Graham and John Stott.[36] Seventeen thousand students attended the conference held at the

---

34. Morris, 'Universalism', 310.
35. Kivengere, 'Spiritual Indifference', 333–34.
36. The speakers include, *John W. Alexander*, president of Inter-Varsity Christian Fellowship-USA, Madison, Wisconsin; *Edgar S. Beach* staff member of Wycliffe Bible Translators, assigned to Guatemala and president of the Inter-Varsity Christian Fellowship chapter at the University of Illinois at Urbana during his senior year; *Chua Wee Hian*, General Secretary of the International Fellowship of Evangelical Students; *Edmund P. Clowney*, President of Westminster Theological Seminary, Philadelphia, and Professor of Practical Theology; *Eric Frykenberg*, a retired, though not inactive, missionary; *Samuel T. Kamaleson*, Vice-President-at-large for World Vision International; *Elisabeth Elliot Leitch* served in Ecuador among Colorado, Quichua and Auca Indians from 1952 to 1963; *A. Donald MacLeod*, General Director of Inter-Varsity Christian Fellowship-Canada since 1975; *Isabelo Magalit*, Associate General Secretary of the International Fellowship of Evangelical Students in East Asia; *John M. Perkins*, founder and President of Voice of Calvary Ministries in Mendenhall and Jackson, Mississippi; *Helen Roseveare*, staff of the Missionary Training College of the Worldwide Evangelization Crusade; and, *Lemuel S. Tucker*, a student at Westminster Theological Seminary, Philadelphia, Pennsylvania, former president of the Inter-Varsity Christian Fellowship chapter and the Fellowship of Christian Athletes.

University of Illinois. Again, as in the previous sermon, the influence of the Keswick sequence of preaching, culminating into a climax and challenging believers to go out into the world and be involved in the mission of God is clearly evident.

6.2.2.2 Preliminaries

Kivengere's introductory prayer already focused on reconciliation without explicitly using the word by mentioning Jesus coming into the world— 'when all was dark, you entered the gloom, brought the sons of dust into the amazing glory'.[37]

6.2.2.3 Introduction

Kivengere opens by expressing his inadequacy to address such an important topic: 'The Triumph of God's Glory', which he described as the 'very heart of your salvation and mine' (p. 1, #1), thus bridging the gap between his audience ('your') and preacher ('mine'). The triumph of God's glory climaxes in the second coming of the Lord Jesus and that alone should excite his audience. But they have to begin where the triumph begins: where they are (p. 1, #2). It is the triumph of God's glory in their daily experiences in America, Africa, and all over the world, which leads to the tremendous excitement of the second coming of Jesus. Using an illustration from his 1959 visit to the Solomon Islands,[38] he tells a story of how a young man was shaken, affected by this glory of Jesus Christ. Already, by focusing on Jesus Christ, reconciliation is in view.

6.2.2.4 Exposition

His message focuses on John 17:22: 'I have given them the glory that you gave me, that they may be one as we are one'. He started with an appreciation of a biblical theology of glory from the Old Testament leading him to glory in the New Testament, centred in Jesus Christ. The love of God, which he also referred to as the glory of God in the Old Testament, struck

---

37. The sermon transcript does not pick this opening prayer but the original audio sermon (attached to this thesis) clearly present the opening prayer.
38. Garrett, *Where Nets Were Cast*, 362. Kivengere, *The Spirit Is Moving*, 10–11.

the people with a sense of awe and fear. Jesus has given his glory to sinful man and not angels. 'Abraham lost the weaknesses of age, began to praise God and to count the stars' (p. 4, #17). He became a man with a tremendous, exciting vision because 'the glory liberated him'. And without being systematic about the order of events, after Abraham, he jumped to Isaiah before Moses: 'Isaiah spoke the evangel, the good gospel, and in Isaiah 53 he discovered the Messiah'. 'Moses was the same because at eighty years old, he led his people from slavery into freedom'.

He then invited them to move on to see the fullness of the glory of God in the New Testament. Jesus Christ, the one whom God particularly sent as the visible image of the invisible God, has come, and now 'people no longer need be frightened by the glory' (p. 4, #18), because 'the distance has been removed'. 'The glory of God in Jesus Christ triumphed over distance'. Even if he never uses the word, Kivengere is clearly referring to reconciliation.

He asks: 'Where does Jesus begin?' (p. 4, #19) 'Pre-existent time'. He wants them to see the glory which God gave him because God loved him before the foundation of the world. The link with reconciliation here is that 'God overcomes the distance between eternity and time'. The eternal one 'has moved to where men in their finite experience are'. Kivengere echoes Barth's Christological explanation of God, who in Jesus Christ humbled himself and crossed the barrier of sin to us. This happened when Jesus set at stake his own existence as God by moving first to us.[39] Reconciliation begins with God coming to us, even though Kivengere is not using the word reconciliation.

Kivengere marvelled at this coming of Jesus to us, overcoming the distance between eternity and time: 'What a coming!' With his confessed influence of Markus Barth over his joy in discovering new things in Scripture and that if one finds in Scripture only a confirmation of what one has always believed, then one has not listened closely enough to Scripture;[40] it is not too much to claim that Kivengere's confession on the coming of Jesus hints at his insight on the nature of God in the coming of Jesus that Kivengere saw. Fascinated by it he reduced it to three words: 'what a

---

39. See Chapter Three, 3.5.3 'The Components of Barth's Doctrine of Reconciliation'.
40. See Chapter Three, 4. 'Markus Barth's link to Kivengere'.

coming!' This is even further strengthened by the influence over him by Markus's commitment to the Word of God, believing that there should be joy on discovering new things in Scripture.[41]

'Can you imagine God becoming a baby so that he may pick us in our weakness? Can you imagine God who is almighty putting such limitations around himself? Condescending to be like you and me, in utter weakness?' (p. 4, #20) 'In so doing he removed the barriers between the perfect God and broken humanity'. He picked up the pieces, 'put them together', and out of those broken pieces of men and women in Africa, America, Asia, 'he created a new man'. Using the language of Ephesians 2:14–18, and talking about 'putting together', 'out of broken pieces', 'created a new man', Kivengere is explicitly explaining reconciliation.

This concept of Jesus' reconciliation is powerful: 'Because he became a human being, no longer can we accept any external differences' (p. 5, #21).[42] Kivengere highlighted for his audience both the theological and social implications of the concept of reconciliation in Jesus Christ. He tells that Jesus 'gives my African-ness a completely new value. For that reason, "you simply cannot play with me any longer"'.[43]

The implications of the coming of Jesus are clear: 'Apart from Jesus, human beings are broken up, fragmented, bits and pieces, hating one another because they hate themselves' (p. 5, #21). He is not surprised at what is happening in the world among people who do not believe in Jesus Christ: 'they are men and women with a civil war inside, and therefore battles and wars go on all the time —broken homes, tribal wars, racial tensions, conflicts everywhere, until he comes'.

Jesus 'became one of us in order to make us what we should have been'. God's glory or God's love has triumphed over our disintegration and that is a remarkable experience (p. 5, #22). 'What a beautiful, wonderful Saviour! What an almighty God!'[44] Not only is the concept of reconciliation lying behind Kivengere's explanation of Jesus' birth, it is there behind his expla-

---

41. See Chapter Three, 4. 'Markus Barth's link to Kivengere'.
42. See Chapter Three, 5.1.1 'Aristocratic Upbringing'.
43. See Chapter Three, 5.1.1 'Aristocratic Upbringing'.
44. See Chapter Three, 4. 'Markus Barth's Link to Kivengere'.

nation of Jesus' growth. 'Not only was he born, not only did he become one with us, but he became with us. Emmanuel: God present with us' (p. 5, #23). There is Barth's understanding of covenant as Immanuel, God with us. A covenant focussed on the eternal God, and which has been fulfilled in the form of atonement.[45] 'Jesus comes—Emmanuel, God with us—and accepts our infirmity'. 'This is salvation triumphing over loneliness, isolation, and meaninglessness. No wonder people who have no Jesus are disciples of nihilism. What can they do? Life is empty. It is lonely. It is a forest of strange experiences'.

Behind his simple 'Jesus comes', Kivengere has the concept of reconciliation in view. Life is empty and lonely without Jesus coming into it to give meaning. He narrates the circumstances leading to the Calvary cross and he juxtaposes this with marvelling at the love of Jesus. 'The glory of God picked up all the things, which broke humanity; all the nasty experiences of our sinful nature, all the accumulated guilt, and he put them on the shoulders of the God-man, steadily, firmly, like a rock' (p 6, #25). His mention of the 'God-man' echoes Barth's understanding of God-man.[46] Reconciliation is not far away.

Again he marvels at Jesus' action of love for us: 'Oh what a life!' Painfully 'Jesus moved into Gethsemane. He moved to the hill of Calvary. He lifted that wood on which he was going to hang and he died'. He asks: 'Is there any glory in death?' (p. 6, #26) 'That is the essence of the glory of the New Testament'. 'There is no Christianity if you remove the essence of the death of Christ' . . . 'the death of Christ is the climax of love'. God is love, for he asserts: 'His radiant character is his love, and love shines more when it is willing to die for the beloved. This love so loved broken humanity that it took all the judgment and [the entire] burden and went on the cross and hung there like a criminal'.[47]

However, Jesus was not a criminal. Instead, Jesus accepted human criminality (p. 6, #27). Jesus lifted our sins on 'his mighty shoulders, upon his

---

45. See Chapter Three, 3.5.2 'Reconciliation—Covenant and Sin'.
46. Chapter Three, 3. 3.5.3 'The Components of Barth's Doctrine of Reconciliation', the relevant section 3.4.4.3 Jesus Christ—'God-man'.
47. For the purpose of clarity we have replaced the phrase 'the entire' with 'all the' which appears in the original transcript.

heart; he triumphed over it for you and me'. What happened on the cross? Two criminals were hanging—between them, in the centre, the glorious Jesus. 'His face was marred beyond recognition. One man on one side became angry and bitter and rejected Jesus in utter despair' (p. 6, #28). The other fellow, 'His eyes were opened, his heart was melted when he heard, "Father, forgive them for they don't know what they're doing" (p. 6, #29). Immediately the man who was dying as a criminal was ushered into the presence of glory, liberated from despair, removed from darkness. What a discovery!' Again, Kivengere's statement 'What a discovery', is consistent with a possible influence from Markus' exhortation to his students to be excited at what they have discovered in the text.[48]

You mean this man who is hanging on the cross is a king? The cross is his throne? The thorns the crown? A shattered body, a kingly body? A naked body covered with robes of a king? What a discovery! (p. 6, #29) Again he gets excited about over discovering something new in the text. He discovered that the glory of God overcame the despair of this criminal, the triumphing glory of God. Love overcame the barrier, and the man was ushered into the presence of God's glory (p. 6, #30). Here again he is telling of reconciliation without explicitly using the word.

When Jesus tells the man: 'Don't you wait for long. Today you and I are going to share paradise' . . . 'That was victory, the greatest victory, the climax of the glory. And it is because of this we talk about his return with glory' (p. 6, #30). If this were removed, 'his return would be a terrible threat'. 'Humanity would be consumed like dry grass in a fire'.[49] However, 'because of what happened on the cross of Calvary, you can lift your eyes and your head and you look in the face of the eternal king and say, "King, when you come back, remember". And he does remember, for you have been engraved in his palms, says the prophet Isaiah'. For Kivengere, to look in the face of the eternal King is to catch the vision of reconciliation from

---

48. See Chapter Three, 4. 'Markus Barth's Link to Kivengere'.
49. For a similar expression of destruction using the imagery of grass commonly found in the African grasslands, see Kivengere, *I Love Idi Amin*, 13.

the cross,[50] and to look at the cross is the starting point of divine outreach.[51] Thus, reconciliation is in view.

'Jesus was buried and he was resurrected'. 'Jesus' death overcame the sin and the guilt and the separation' (p. 7, #32). 'Jesus' resurrection conquered death, the last enemy of mankind'. The last enemy of mankind makes men tremble and it makes clever men weep (p. 7, #32). Death is a point of despair, 'a point of departure, the dead end of the road'. However, there is good news. 'Jesus entered the realm of death, three days in battle, down there in grip with the terrible enemy of mankind, he killed death . . . and changed the whole nature of death'. To a Christian, 'death is not a departure but an arrival. It is no longer a dead end but the beginning; no longer darkness but the dawn of a new life'.

His audience was so gripped by his explanation of 'Jesus' defeat of death',[52] that they interrupted the flow of the sermon with applause, causing Kivengere to pause before he could continue his explanation.[53] Listening to the audio version of the sermon, the impact of the oratory of the sermon upon his audience is evident.[54] Reconciliation is not far away from Kivengere's explanation of 'Jesus' defeat of death'. It is in the body of his flesh, through his death and resurrection, that we are reconciled to God; that we have a new life. In this sense, the language of Ephesians 2 is what he is using to explain reconciliation without mentioning it.

The death and resurrection of Jesus is crucial for his audience to understand the mercy and the grace of God. 'Not only men and women, who are born again, but the whole of humanity and the whole of the universe

---

50. See Chapter Five, Kivengere, 'Surprised by Joy', p, 11, #11.
51. Kivengere, 'The Cross Today', p. 3, #4. Kivengere, 'Broken Relationships Restored', p. 5, #1.
52. I am indebted to Peter G Bolt for this phrase 'Jesus' defeat of death', the title of his book. See Peter G. Bolt, *Jesus' Defeat of Death: Persuading Mark's Early Readers* (First edition.; Cambridge: Cambridge University Press, 2003). Bolt shows Jesus casting back the shadow of death in Mark's Gospel, and he argues that this pushing back the shadow of death was a primary strategy for Jesus' final defeat of death in resurrection, which Kivengere's explanation of Jesus' defeat of death in the resurrection alludes to as 'the dawn of a new life'.
53. To hear the applause and deep passionate and emotional explanation of this theological truth on death, not a departure but an arrival for a Christian, listen to the audio sermon, 26 minutes into the sermon.
54. See Chapter Two, 5.1.3 'Story-telling at the Fireplace'.

will be under his feet and you will come with him' (p. 8, #40). His resurrection has an impact upon believers in the time before their resurrection. The future in which we shall discover the depth of mercy and grace has actually reached back into our present.[55] Consequently, 'to be human' he desires that his audience should understand that the future has been reconstituted by the fact of Christ's resurrection. Kivengere's understanding of the resurrection shows affinity with Barth's.[56] For Barth, the resurrection has reconstructed the future and it changes history—everything is changed. For Kivengere, this understanding of resurrection, he asserts, must inform all Christian practice. With this understanding it must not come as a surprise that Christ will put all humanity under his feet.

Kivengere asked if his audience knows what resurrection has done to history? To him, because of resurrection, 'history for a Christian is no longer a monotonous cycle, like a Buddhist's prayer, which makes you feel tired and get bored; rather, for a Christian "there is no boredom"' (p. 8, #41). '[Christian] history has a direction, and the direction is towards [the risen] Jesus Christ'.

He desires that his audience should know that Jesus Christ 'is the goal of history because in him all things are completed'. 'It is he who fills all things with himself' (p. 9, #41). Kivengere's language of 'in him all things are completed' is the language of Colossians 1:16, 17 which links reconciliation with the person and work of Jesus Christ. In addition, Jesus 'filling things' recalls Kivengere's re-focusing of the Keswick emphasis on being filled with the Spirit.[57]

Keswick taught that all believers must be filled with the Holy Spirit. Kivengere also recognized the place of Spirit-filling in the life of a believer. Elsewhere he explains that 'the Holy Spirit comes and introduces us into the presence of the cross of our Lord and Saviour',[58] and 'He never shows you your sin without showing you your Saviour'.[59] He has, however, moved on from Keswick, by emphasizing Jesus 'who fills all things with

---

55. See Chapter Three, 3.4 'Barth: the Sache—The Subject-matter, God'.
56. See Chapter Three, 3.4 'Barth: the Sache—The Subject-matter, God'.
57. See Chapter Three, 2.1.4 'Day Four: The Prescription—Spirit-filling'.
58. Kivengere, *The Spirit Is Moving*, 14.
59. Kivengere, *The Spirit Is Moving*, 16.

himself'. He is consistent in his teaching on this point: in 1972 at the Keswick Convention in England,[60] in 1983 in the sermons 'Love's Quick Way',[61] and now 1976, he asserts that there is the tendency to isolate the Holy Spirit, Jesus Christ, and God the Father from working together: 'this is confusion'.[62] Behind his focus on Jesus as the one to fill the life of believers, reconciliation is not far away.

With Jesus filling their hearts, his audience 'can stand up from Urbana and can face this redeemable world' because the world 'is still redeemable' (p. 9, #43). 'And as the world looks at you, thousands of you—my heart beats fast—can the world despair when disciples, 17,000 of them, are in tune with the king of glory?' He does not only share from his heart his vision of evangelists reaching out into the world with the gospel of Christ, but in a more passionate and personal appeal, he directly challenged each of them: 'Tune up, will you? Get your attention focused on Jesus Christ and his coming back to take his kingdom'. He again asks a more personal question: 'what is your part in that kingdom?' In tune with his Keswick and Revival influence, Kivengere addresses the gospel message to the hearts of believers and challenges them to reach out in mission into the world.

He is aware that some members of his audience are trembling but he encouraged them to know that 'This triumphant glory makes weak men strong, makes cowards into warriors'. Using the experience from part of the rich Christian heritage that shaped and has remained a clear feature of the gospel in Uganda, the story of the Uganda martyrs,[63] he encouraged them to stand up for the gospel. He prayed for God to bless his audience as they give their hearts, not to defeat, not to stumbling, not to endless discussion, but to the eternal completion of grace, which is glory (p. 10, #46).

As he is drawing the sermon to a close he exhorts them about a number of points. As they leave Urbana, he tells them to go while singing because Christ in them is the hope of glory. As they put to use all the tools that God has given them during the conference, the Spirit will remind them

---

60. See Kivengere, 'Christ the Liberator', 121–22. Kivengere, *Revolutionary Love*, 33.
61. Festo Kivengere, 'Love's Quick Way', in *Revolutionary Love* (First Edition.; Port Washington, Pennsylvania: Christian Literature Crusade, 1983), 33.
62. Kivengere, *The Spirit Is Moving*, 14.
63. See chapter two,2 3.2 'Mwanga's Martyrdom'.

of one important thing: 'He, the king of glory, is triumphant'. He lists the areas over which the triumph of Christ reigns: America, communist Russia, China, and Africa (p 10, #48). For Africa he adds, 'with its conflicting elements'.[64] In the case of Uganda, the increasing number of atrocities that Amin was committing is in view. He lists the areas over which the reign of Jesus prevails, the church 'with its wickedness' inclusive (p. 10, #49). Without qualifying what he means by the 'wickedness' of the church, he plugs straight to challenges: 'I am in the procession. Are you there?' (p. 10, #49).

Again, as with Keswick, Kivengere ended the convention with a direct appeal to the heart of the believers. He reduced the sequence of the Keswick week-long gathering into one long address, ending with a heart full of songs: Hallelujahs, but to the King, not to the speaker. He appealed for repentance: if they have a sin to repent, it can still be forgiven. He gave them a sure hope of the gospel: 'Jesus is coming back' (p. 11, #51). 'Signs are here'. He invited them to come to Africa and encouraged them to go to India and to China, as ambassadors of the glorious King (p. 11, #53). Standing behind his sending them out into the world is the love or the glory of the triumphant King Jesus who has given them the message of reconciliation.

6.2.2.5 Summary of The Cross: AO: 19740725

Kivengere preached reconciliation from his theme text (John 17:22), which does not explicitly mention reconciliation. On the one hand it is clear that the passage mentions the glory of God, which is given to Jesus Christ. On the other hand, there are indications that once Kivengere defined the glory of God as the love of God, centred in Jesus Christ, then it became clear to him that reconciliation was in view. Once he stated that 'the glory of God in Jesus triumphed over distance', and then asks: 'where does Jesus begin?' (p. 4, #19), he is already moving towards reconciliation, because for him, Jesus came into the human situation, and by using the language of Ephesians 2:14–18, reconciliation was never far away.

---

64. For Africa's 'conflicting elements', Kivengere has in mind some of the upheavals that he discussed in the US News and World Report, See chapter one, 2.5 'International Community Watches Uganda'. Also see Kivengere, 'Bleeding Africa', 25–29.

With his theological exegesis, which has affinity with Barth's understanding of the *Sache*—the subject-matter, God, Kivengere explained the coming of God in Jesus Christ and his death and resurrection. His explanation of the resurrection echoes Barth's understanding of that event.[65] This sermon shows Kivengere's clear and strong conviction about the centrality of the death and resurrection of Jesus and its implication for Christian living. Evidence of affinity with Barth's explanation of the life, death and resurrection of Jesus Christ is detectable. Similarly his treatment of the content of the eternal God fulfilled in the form of atonement is also seen. And, Kivengere also shows affinity with Barth, in his explanation of Jesus as 'God-man' who decisively dealt with our sin. His Theological Exegesis and the doctrine of reconciliation shaped his preaching, and his belief that the primary role of the church is to preach the message of reconciliation.

The sermon also shows some influence on him by Markus Barth's New Testament teaching, which has helped him to discover in the coming of Jesus the awesome nature of God's glory. Markus Barth's encouragement of his students to always be excited about new insights they have discovered in Scripture parallels Kivengere marvelling at the passage of John 17:22. 'God has given his glory to sinners and not angels?'

The influence of Keswick and the Revival is clear, but Kivengere has moved from emphasizing Spirit-filling to Jesus himself filling the life of believers. This development is consistent across the period 1972 to 1976, when he continued to emphasize Jesus as the one who 'fills empties'. Also he is clear about the important role that the Holy Spirit plays in the life of believers besides Jesus and God the Father, all working together. He addressed the mission bringing together elements of the week-long Keswick teaching into one long address: he expounds the gospel with a focus on Jesus Christ, the reconciler, ask the audience to repent of their sins and receive forgiveness from Jesus and he encourages them to reach out into the world with the gospel, using illustrations from the story of the young Uganda martyrs.

His choice of this story was relevant to the young missionaries at Urbana, because it empowered them to recognize the 'powers that be' that

---

65. See Chapter Three, 3.4 'Barth: The *Sache*—The subject-matter, God'.

Non-Explicit Reconciliation Passages 339

are against the gospel in the world. Such powers as shown by Mwanga murdering the Uganda martyrs, need the reconciling message of Jesus to deal with them. The death and resurrection of Jesus is a sign of the presence of God at work in his world, triumphing in a procession led by Jesus Christ, thus transforming lives. Because of the importance of this message to him, it is not surprising that Kivengere preached reconciliation even from non-explicit reconciliation texts.

A clear picture of the potential impact of the message has emerged. First, the recognition and invitation of Kivengere to come and address the mission of 17,000 young missionaries at Urbana is a clear sign of his recognition by other evangelicals of all persuasions. With his preaching reconciliation even from a non-explicit passage, he impacted the life of his audience as they openly applauded and interrupted the heartbeat of his message. In turn those who have attended his message would carry the message of reconciliation around the world.

6.2.3 'A New Way of Seeing Jesus': AO: 19821012, [#1][66]

6.2.3.1 Situating the sermon
Kivengere preached this sermon at Holy Trinity Church, Cambridge, England, on 10 October 1982.

In a long introduction, Kivengere spoke of the horrors going on in Uganda and some of Uganda's positive response to the message of reconciliation.

6.2.3.2 Preliminaries
Kivengere thanked the congregation at Holy Trinity for welcoming him (p. 1, #1). He was not new to this audience but had taken a while before he returned to Cambridge and so it was his joy to see them turn up in large numbers. The previous night he had been preaching to the congregation at Holy Trinity, Cheltenham, which comprised Christians from different churches.[67] They turned up to hear him share 'the joy of serving our Lord

---

66. We have taken this from Kivengere's confession in the sermon: 'a new way of seeing', 'turn your eyes and see me' Revelation 3:20, (p. 18, #26).
67. Festo Kivengere, 'Sermon on 1 John 3:11', Sermon Transcript (Preached at Cheltenham, Gloucestershire, November 10, 1982), AO: 19821110.

Jesus in human chaos'. Already, at the outset, Kivengere focused on the Lord Jesus Christ, and by now we might suspect that every time he mentions Christ, reconciliation is near.

He brought greetings from Uganda his homeland, where tens of thousands of Christians still rejoice to see others come to know Jesus. They 'are praying for the mission, to know the truth of John's words about Jesus: "And light keeps on shining in darkness, and darkness has never succeeded in putting it out" (John 1:5)'. As the sermon will later reveal, when he speaks of light shining in the darkness of the world, he is already preparing to speak of reconciliation.

6.2.3.3 Introduction

Kivengere takes his audience on a historical and spiritual journey of the situation in Uganda during and after Amin. He alerts them to the presence in Uganda of a bigger force than Idi Amin and Ugandans: the presence of evil powers (pp. 1–2, #2), alluding to Ephesians 6:12. This point we noted earlier under the explicit reconciliation sermons.[68] His audience could easily fail to recognize that behind the men and women in authority, there are spiritual forces of evil. By 1982 Ugandans are engulfed in 'darkness and despair,' but Kivengere announces 'Jesus Christ, the only hope' (p. 2, #2) in such a dark situation.[69] At the end of August 1981, at Bweranyangi, West Ankole diocese in Uganda,[70] they had a Christian meeting in which 'we finished on Sunday August 29 with 22,000 Christians, singing and praising, and we saw hundreds come to Jesus Christ the only ray of hope' (p. 2, #2).

Kivengere evokes a contest between the forces of evil operating in Uganda and the victorious power of Jesus working in the life of believers. This gathering of Christians directly continues both the Keswick and

---

68. We noted his mention of evil powers in Uganda in the sermon, Kivengere, 'Jesus Came as a Missionary', p. 6, #8. However, his in this sermon he is much clearer about the powers of evil working in Amin and Ugandans.
69. See further his explanation for the hope of reconstructing and rehabilitating Uganda and hopeless situations in the world, Kivengere, *Hope for Uganda and the World*.
70. This was the place he preached the powerful and controversial sermon from Acts 20:22–28 at the consecration of Bishop Bamunoba to the political leaders of Amin's government. See chapter two above.

Revival meetings.[71] The climax of the meeting drew a response from the believers to reach out into the world and do God's will. At Bweranyangi, this saw a response of many believers coming to Jesus, the only hope for Uganda. Given that in 1979, he said that the only antidote to Uganda's deep wounds is reconciliation,[72] this may be read into his statement two years later when he claims: 'Jesus is the only ray of hope'.

Since 1980, in Kigezi diocese, which did not suffer from the wars and famine that hit northern Uganda, and especially Karamoja, children were dying from measles 'at the rate of 10,000 little children per year' (p. 4, #6). The depth of this alarming situation led to his recent 'cries and shouts' for help while preaching in America. Some medical pharmaceutical organizations 'got together and they donated 60,000 vaccines' (pp. 4–5, #6). 22,000 children in Kigezi diocese were immunised against the killer disease, with American doctors working solidly for three weeks (p. 5, #6). He shared the needs of the people within the framework of the love of God (p. 4, #6). Again, when Kivengere mentions the love of God and alleviation of social needs, reconciliation may not be far away.

In one of Kivengere's open air lunch hour preaching ministry to 1,000 to 2,000 people in the city of Kampala (p. 6, #6), a Ugandan man who had planned to murder another man, on hearing his preaching and singing, stopped and listened to the simplest words: 'Come to me', says Jesus Christ, 'all of you who are exhausted and burdened, and I will refresh you' [Matt 11:28] (p. 6, #8). After a few explanations, 'The Holy Spirit opened his heart, the man accepted the light'. Here is the connection between darkness and light he mentioned in the introduction of his message. Reconciliation with God and man to man is reported. Ugandans accepted the light, 'Jesus became a living Saviour, and in this practical way Africans accept Jesus, not philosophically, but practically'.[73]

This positive story constitutes a sharp contrast with the negative picture of indiscriminate killings going on in the country. Now he tells of a brutal murder of one of his staff at a coffee shop in Kabale on 23 March 1980,

---

71. See Chapter Three, 2.1.5 'Day Five: The Mission—Presence of Christian Service'.
72. Festo Kivengere, 'In Christ', Sermon Transcript, AO: 19790429, [#2].
73. Cf. Kivengere, 'God's Intervening Love', pp. 7–8, #15.

400 yards from where he was having a committee [meeting] (p. 7, #10). 'I came rushing to find one of my staff with a bullet in his heart—dead. I was so angry that I thought they would shoot me too'.

Faced with a situation close to anarchy, how did Kivengere bring healing or preach reconciliation in Uganda? How did he witness the love of God in such a hostile world? In 1979 on his return from exile,[74] he had predicted that the church in Uganda would be faced with a hard job and now living in Uganda is clearly terrifying. Under the leadership of Obote II, there is freedom of expression (p. 8, #12), however, there is a feeling of helplessness about the 'destructive and utterly miserable political situation'.

Kivengere and others have talked about the insecurity with Obote. 'We have seen the president' (p. 8, #11) . . . 'Not once, not twice, several times'. Obote 'expresses a certain amount of helplessness about the situation', however, he lacks 'the ability to change that situation'. Kivengere has come to the conclusion that the political situation in Uganda is 'very complicated, very destructive, [and] utterly miserable'. He asks his audience to pray that 'God who calls men and gives them positions may give them wisdom and authority to arrest the situation before it takes away a million people' (p. 8, #11). Kampala, the seat of political action, is in a terrible mess. He does not want his audience to blame the mess on tribalism[75] but bad governance and to consider the fact of the spiritual vision of Ephesians 6 as a possible source of brokenness in Uganda.

To reconstruct Uganda, not only the urgent needs of returning Ugandans whose homes were destroyed must be met, but even more importantly a spiritual reconstruction must take place. Ugandans need to be taught that love and forgiveness are the best weapons for reconstruction.

---

74. Kivengere, 'In Christ', p. 6, #11.
75. See Chapter One, 2. 'Deep Wounds in Uganda'. For an in-depth discussion on how corruption of power and wealth caused the violent disorganization of Uganda society, ruining Amin's rule, for which now Kivengere is trying to make sense of the messy situation, see Aidan Southhall, 'Social Disorganization in Uganda: Before, During and After Amin', *JMAS* 18/no. 4 (1980): 627–56.

6.2.3.4 Exposition

Using the context of Uganda our preacher calls his audience to live *in* and *under* the biblical story Revelation 3:1–21. How do we happen to go on as Christians in Uganda? Christianity was born 'Not in a lovely church' like Holy Trinity Cambridge. 'It was born in the wind, in utter violence outside the city of Jerusalem' (pp. 8–9, 12).

Revelation is a book about 'seeing the Lord', in 'a completely new way' (p. 9, 14). His language is reminiscent of reconciliation language of 2 Corinthians 5:16 even if he has not yet mentioned reconciliation. As in the previous sermons in this chapter, this use of reconciliation language when the text does not call for it shows it was close to his heart. This concern immediately issues in stories illustrating human reconciliation, such as in Haifa,[76] where he saw 'an Arab Chief Magistrate, before 250 Christians leaders of all denominations, Arabs and Jews, giving his testimony' (p. 9, #14). This testimony resulted in reconciliation, which represented 'a new way of seeing' (cf. 2 Cor 5:16). He makes a flashback to the theme of reconciliation in Ephesians 2:14. 'The two [the Arab Chief Magistrate and the Jew he embraced] as they stood there embracing, they represented Ephesians chapter 2, two [Jews and Gentiles] become one' (p. 10, #14). Again although preaching from the non-explicit passage Revelation 3, he draws in his over-riding concern by alluding to an explicit Pauline reconciliation passage.

Kivengere now explained that John—the seer, the Apostle—was in exile ('suffering persecution', p. 10, #15) on the island of Patmos as a result of his faith, giving an indication that John's community of believers were exposed to 'the powers that be' (p. 10, #15), an allusion he is making from Romans 13:1. John's community was filled with 'fear and trembling'—it was a difficult time to see. Yet, 'this is the time [that] the risen Lord, the glorified Christ decided to give the apostle new optics again' (p. 10, #15).

He emphasized the words of the seer: 'I saw', 'Look', 'See' (p. 10, #15), 'And I turned to see . . . then I saw one who looked like the Son of man', 'When I saw him I fell down, because I saw in a new way'. I saw in him the kind of glory which made me fall down. It was a new seeing. Again,

---

76. Cf. Reconciliation': AO: 198204[--], [#1], p. 14, #39.

this is the language of 2 Corinthians 5:16, and he imports connotations of reconciliation as taught in that passage (pp. 10–11, #15).

The church, 'for example, in chapter three had lost its spiritual ability to see' (p. 11, #16). All was not well with the church in Laodicea. Although they thought they were 'Rich, but you are poor. You are blind'. . . . "You are blind and you are poor, I counsel you buy from me gold refined in the fire, so that you can become rich, and white clothes to wear, so that you can cover your shameful nakedness, and a salve to put on your eyes, so that you can see' " (Rev 3:18), and again he asks: But see what? 'The next verses say, "Those whom I love, I rebuke". To Kivengere therefore, 'Love is the way God makes people see. It is God's way of exposing those who are utterly blinded'.

'I stress the word "see" because when you hear that Ugandans are slaughtering other Ugandans, please mark that it is because they don't see them' (p. 11, #16). 'They don't see the person', instead they 'see a category'. They are just a member of a tribe, a member of a political party, an opposition, a dangerous person. Their ability to see is lost.

On the other hand, 'Christians are a seeing community' and 'in times of revival the spirit of God opens the eyes of the church and the church becomes a seeing community' (p. 11, #17). For example, 'the evangelical Revival here in England, after seeing the Lord, your sons and daughters went like fire all over the place'. This alludes to the fact that missionaries from England scattered around the world. He confessed himself to be a direct product of missionaries who came from England: 'that is why am standing here . . . I was evangelized by members of Ruanda Mission'.[77] Joe Church, a pioneer missionary of the Ruanda Mission, in his student days was influenced by Frank Buchman's Oxford Group movement, and he came as a missionary from England to Ruanda but had much dealing in Uganda, in particular the Revival in Kivengere's area.[78] He introduced some of the features of the Oxford Group movement such as public confession of sins, which became a key feature of the Revival meetings. The medical

---

77. The transcript does not state the names of the missionaries nor the mission agency. However, in chapter Two, we noted that both Rwanda Mission and CMS collectively evangelized western Uganda, in particular the Kigezi region.

78. See Chapter Two, 4.3 'The Search for Renewal and Holiness'.

doctors Leonard Sharp and Algernon Stanley Smith and their wives Esther Sharp and Zoe Stanley Smith joined Joe Church. Stanley Smith had been active in the CICCU at a time when in its history, it had disassociated itself from the Student Christian Movement over the question of the trustworthiness and the authority of the Bible.[79] Both groups had a close connection with the CICCU and the Oxford movement.[80] Clearly he acknowledges the influences of the Keswick convention and the Revival over his life and ministry with delight.

He returns to the point about being unstoppable once the 'love of Christ penetrates the people of God wherever they may be and under whatever circumstances' (p. 12, #19).[81] 'There is an urge, a dynamic in them which is nothing but what Paul [said], "And the love of Christ compels me". Urges me on. I am a captive of the love and therefore I am free' (pp. 12–13, #19). Although a 'captive' of the love of Christ, Kivengere sees that Christ has 'broken my chains of selfishness, opened my traditional eyes which were blind' so now 'I can move in freedom' (p. 13, #19). He is preaching reconciliation using the language of 2 Corinthians 5 every now and again, as he does throughout the sermon. His language of reconciliation in this sermon leans more towards the love of Christ than the cross.

From this point on in the sermon, Kivengere returns to the situation in Uganda, telling stories that illustrate the suffering of individuals and asking his audience to see what they can do about the different situations that he has shared.[82] He tells them that 'you can feed people and clothe them', yet 'they will still fight and kill each other and commit suicide' (p. 18, #26); 'they need a deeper healing' (p. 18, #26). He prays for God's blessing on them as 'you respond to the world of your brothers and sisters' (18, #26). The Keswick focus for the last day of the convention about mission outreach is once again apparent.

---

79. Tatlow Tissington, *The Story of the Student Christian Movement of Great Britain and Ireland* (London: SCM, 1933), 380–88. Douglas Johnson, *Contending for the Christian Faith* (Leicester: Inter-Varsity Press, 1979), 69–78.
80. See Ward and Wild-Wood, *The East African Revival*, 6, 14.
81. Cf. Kivengere, 'The Cross Today', p. 7, #6.
82. See 'Introduction' of this sermon (pp. 1–2, #2–p. 8, #11).

It is also there as he prayed that God will 'touch the young people's hearts, and let them move forward' into the world; that God will 'send them like fire to touch the hearts of mothers and fathers, businessmen and women', so that 'in the end they may become practicing members of your healing community' (p. 18, #26). For the purpose of this thesis it is noteworthy that Kivengere's concluding prayers are introduced by an explicit reference to reconciliation picking up all the implicit hints already in the sermon he asks them to 'pray that the church will never fail in its ministry of reconciliation, for that is absolutely central' (p. 18, #26).[83]

6.2.3.4 Summary of 'A New Way of Seeing Jesus': AO: 19821012, [#1]

Once again, Kivengere preached reconciliation from a text (Rev 3:1–21), which does not explicitly call for reconciliation. As before he used the language of reconciliation found in 2 Corinthians 5 and Ephesians 2 to highlight his point of reconciliation. Twice towards the end of the sermon, he explicitly mentioned reconciliation. Since reconciliation is the message that the church must never fail to preach, and the only ray of hope for Ugandans, it is clearly the central message on his heart. He has thought over reconciliation for a long time (since his conversion) and now in 1982, it is still the message to be preached to bring healing to Uganda—and to his Cambridge audience.

His method of preaching reconciliation, theological exegesis, helps him to focus on what he sees as the central concern of the gospel, which means he does not get into the details of the world behind the text, but rather focuses on the world of the text.[84] From the text, he sees the love of God, which he brings to address the issues going on in Uganda.

Politically, he desires that there should be no more bloodshed, lest a million others will die. Ugandans slaughter each other because they do not have a new way of seeing. They see tribalism, political parties, opposition and dangerous persons. Ugandans need to recognize the power of an evil,

---

83. Cf. Kivengere, 'In Christ', p. 7, #13.
84. Cf. Chapter Three, 'Barth: the *Sache*—the Subject-matter, God'. Kivengere like Barth is concerned with listening to what the text is saying and therefore listening to the text from the stand point of Christ.

which only the power of Christ can defeat, and to gain a new way of seeing other in the context of the love of God. Christians therefore need to preach the message of reconciliation, love and forgiveness to recover their lost ability to see the love of God (p. 11, #16).

The potential impact of this message on the churches in the United Kingdom can be discerned at several points. Preaching at Holy Trinity Church, Cambridge, with its long history of gospel and mission focus, suggests that the message of reconciliation, so desperately needed in Uganda, would also encourage them to pray for Uganda. They would also renew their relationship with God and with each other. Kivengere is absolutely certain that Jesus Christ is the only ray of hope for transformation in Uganda. From this same burden for peace, three years later, he will draft a carefully considered position paper to be debated by the House of Bishops proposing a way forward for peace, so development can follow after.[85] His proposal is for the two protagonists, the Uganda National Liberation Army and the National Resistance Army to stop fighting and the church should help them to form 'a government of national reconciliation' and this reconciliation must not be based on a false understanding, namely, 'reconciliation means peace at any price'.[86] 'Peace must have a solid foundation if it is not going to turn into chaos'.[87]

6.2.4 The Pastor's Joy: AO: 19770120

6.2.4.1 Situating the Sermon

Our bishop preached this sermon in California, USA, at Mount Hermon Christian Conference Centre, during a Pastor's Conference the following month. He preached this sermon on 20 January 1977, only to return to Uganda to be caught up in the cross-fire of the murder of Luwum (16 February 1977).[88]

---

85. Kivengere, 'Proposal For Discussion at the House of Bishops'.
86. Kivengere, 'Proposal For Discussion at the House of Bishops'.
87. Kivengere, 'Proposal For Discussion at the House of Bishops'.
88. See 1977: Time-line above.

6.2.4.2 Introduction

Kivengere calls his audience to remember Jesus' words to his disciples when they were going through moments of apprehension: 'I tell you these things that your joy may be complete' (p. 1, #1)—thus, launching straight to his subject: The Pastor's Joy.

6.2.4.3 Exposition

He read Paul's words: 'Peace to you all brethren, and grace' (p. 1, #2). Kivengere then explains that 'peace comes through grace'. Grace simply means 'that kind of love that you never deserve'. He links that love to Calvary's cross. It is made available for those 'unlovely characters such as we are'—thus, bridging the gap between preacher and audience. 'Grace' he said has multiple meanings: one of them is 'charming, attractive, that which is beautifully drawing'. 'That is exactly Jesus'. He asks: 'wasn't he full of grace and truth so that he could speak the hardest truth and yet attract those who hated him?'

Peace means 'wholeness of life' as opposed to a life of a believer living in defeat of sin, which tears apart the soul of a believer (p. 2, #3). 'Sin is civil war within the soul'. His explanation of sin mirrors Keswick teaching on sin.[89] Setting the stage for his explanation of the joy of a minister, he tells of a couple, African pastors, whose life and marriage had 'lost its beauty, its charm, and its attraction' (pp. 2–3, #5–#7). The ravages of sin 'don't even spare a minister, they come and they make us feel terribly embarrassed' (p. 3, #7).

Our preacher now turns to his subject of a minister's joy. He lists those areas where joy is never to be sought: the success of a minister, being nice, fellowship of the brethren, and commitment to a spiritual discipline (p. 4, #9). Kivengere recalls John's account of the resurrection (John 20: 19, 20), of which he says: 'I think this is a classic, it really is a classic' (p. 5, #5). It offers encouragement to those who are 'tired, shattered, disappointed, frustrated, in gloom'. This is 'the greatest victory in the human history', 'the greatest victory had been won' and the world has never been the same

---

89. See Chapter Three, 2.1.1 'Day One: The Diagnosis—Sin'.

(pp. 5–6, #11–#14),⁹⁰ but the disciples were still afraid of the Jews who had crucified Jesus.

He links the situation of disciples' misery to his audience. There are miserable circumstances in the life of a minister—failures in the congregation such as disagreement among elders, blunders of Christians, ministry scandals (pp. 6–7, #15–#16). In such circumstances, there is no love of one another. He bridged the gap between his audience and himself when he said, 'whatever your Jews [things to be afraid of] are. I have got mine, plenty of those in Uganda' (p. 8, #18).

Our preacher turns to his text: John 20:19–20. He reports that 'Jesus came' and joined them. Jesus is the subject matter of the sermon and focusing on his coming, reconciliation is in view. His coming was good news (p. 8, #18). 'Jesus came and stood in the centre'—the place that was occupied by fear and frustration. The language of the centre is here used in reference to Christ. 'He is good news for bad people'. To illustrate the solution to the disciple's problem, he recalls the words of John, 'Jesus Came', stood amidst them and said: 'Peace be with you'. 'Shalom' —'an ordinary Hebrew word of greeting' (p. 8, #19). He then alludes to John 14 where Jesus had promised them peace: 'My peace I give to you. My peace I leave with you' (p. 9, #20).

Kivengere tells his audience that as they sit at the conference, they may be going through a similar experience to the disciples. He provides a way out in Jesus' words: 'Peace be with you'. On saying these words, Jesus showed his disciples his hands and his side, repeatedly. The purpose was to show to them the cost of purchasing their peace (p. 10, #21). Again by focussing on peace and the wounds of Jesus, reconciliation is in view. The disciples no longer need to 'suffer from a broken heart'. Peter no longer needs to live with guilt and Thomas no longer needs to live with doubt. Jesus' death on the cross demonstrated how much he loved them—'I loved you to the very end' (p. 10, #22).

---

90. For Karl Barth, the resurrection was foundational because 'the world in which we live is the place where Jesus Christ rose from the dead'. See Barth's *A Letter to Great Britain From Switzerland* cited in Peter G. Bolt, 'Introduction', in *Christ's Victory Over Evil: Biblical Theology and Pastoral Ministry* (England, Nottingham: Apollos, 2009), 9. See also Keith Condi's emphasis of importance of this point for Barth in Chapter Three, 3.4 'Barth: The *Sache*—The Subject-matter, God'.

The bishop tells his audience that the disciples found the meaning of the cross, a complete new dimension of peace (p. 11, #23). 'They stood in the sea of the resurrection' (p. 11, #24). Resurrection 'penetrated their lives', 'liberating every part', 'answering their questions', 'brightening up the horizon'. It answered the past, and made the present absolutely exciting. The disciples then rejoiced when they saw the Lord. Kivengere links that to the minister's joy, emphasizing that the conflict that deprives the minister of joy is answered by persistently and continuously seeing the Lord. Here he is alluding to the language of reconciliation in 2 Corinthian 5:14–17. Jesus asked the disciples to 'come and touch' him, because he wanted them 'to experience resurrection'—'the power of his resurrection so that they may become the resurrected community'. This, he said, is the secret to the minister's joy (p. 11, #24).

Using images of bumps from the rough African roads, he likens the rough circumstances in the life and ministry of a pastor to the spiritual road that a minister travels. The minister can only travel successfully with the help of the Holy Spirit who gives the minister the ability to get over the bumps. He calls them to remember that they can only face situations in the power of the risen Christ (p. 13, #27). When he said 'Peace be to you', it was because 'he paid the price' and says you can afford 'to come and admit that things were not right and I will put them right for you' (p. 13, #28). 'Every failure is redeemable because it is within the radius of the resurrection power' (p. 13, #28). Here Kivengere is speaking about reconciliation even though he does not explicitly use the word.

For this juncture, Kivengere explicitly tells his audience about reconciliation. 'So come to the mercy seat', says the Hebraic writer, "Come with boldness, your brother is the President of heaven, he has got the authority there, Satan cannot stand in front of you"' (p. 13, #29). He then alludes to Zachariah 3 when Joshua stood in dirty garments as a priest, terribly embarrassed because priests were supposed to wear clean white linen.

Our bishop then tells his testimony of conflict with a brother,[91] during a preaching mission when he became jealous of his success (pp. 14–16, #30–#33). When he asked his brother to forgive him, 'The dear brother

---

91. Chapter Two, William Nagenda on preaching in US at InterVarsity mission.

got up and embraced me and we were both in tears of reconciliation' (p. 16, #33). When this reconciliation happened, they were in joy; they both saw the Lord together.

After this story, he appealed to his audience to bring to the Lord any person with whom they are not in good relationship (p. 16, #34), to bring them 'the one who died purposely' to 'liberate', 'release', and so to lose their 'broken-heartedness' (p. 16, #35). Kivengere is explicit about reconciliation without any mention of reconciliation in his text. This can be explained because every time he mentions the death of Christ on the cross he automatically links reconciliation, since this is the subject matter (*Sache*) that is important to him. The central message of the Bible is that, in Christ's death and resurrection, reconciliation and peace is attained for all.

'You and I in our ministry need to always repent' . . . 'ministers have forgotten to repent'—'to change your attitude about your brother and about our Lord, and also about yourself' (p. 17, #36),—thus, bridging the gap between the preacher and audience. Jesus rose from the dead to give man the capacity to recover from the terrible negative attitude to life into the positive and exciting attitude to life. 'This is a redeemable world because Christ died and rose again'. Again, because he has already mentioned it explicitly, it is clear that reconciliation is in view in this statement.

Kivengere wants to tell them never to despair even if the situation in their congregation is like that of the valley of dry bones in Ezekiel. 'The resurrection speaks against despair of every kind'. 'That Jesus rose from the bones of the dead tells you there is no situation in your church which is unredeemable' (p. 17, #37). Again Kivengere bridges the gap between preacher and audience: 'You and I are witnesses', (p. 18, #38) who were dead in trespasses and sin but are now rejoicing because of Christ Jesus. He emphasized again that they should not depend on their success but on the Lord daily (p. 18, #38).

Kivengere is excited to preach the gospel in Uganda because the Lord is here. When a person responds to the gospel saying 'I have accepted Jesus Christ', the entire congregation sings as if the whole country has been saved. They use the expression 'Singing the converts into grace', welcoming them with songs of Zion, loving and rejoicing with them (pp. 18–19, #39). He asks them to sing a little more when one struggler comes home because

Jesus said himself, "There is joy in heaven over one sinner who repents"' (p. 19, #40).

When Christ is enthroned upon the hearts of his people, that is Pentecost. Rather than begin at speaking about speaking in tongues, dreaming dreams, and prophecy, the vision of Pentecost was 'And I saw heaven open and this Jesus whom you crucified, God has raised him from the dead, giving him that exact authority and power of the right hand' (p. 19, #40). He exhorts them saying 'catch that please'.

Kivengere urges them to go home saying 'Oh my heart is swimming with unspeakable joy, full of glory because I have seen the Lord afresh'. Kivengere appeals to his audience to bring before the risen Christ their burdens: fears, hang-ups about people, hang-ups from ministry, failures of the church and theological hang-ups. They have a fresh opportunity in the power of the Holy Spirit to come into the presence of the risen Christ (p. 20, #41).

6.2.4.4 Summary of The Pastor's Joy: AO: 19770120

Although peace is closely linked with reconciliation (Rom 5:1–11, Col 1:20), the passage from John does not explicitly mention reconciliation. Although he speaks from a gospel, he preaches assuming connection between reconciliation and peace.

The contribution of this sermon to this study is its role in his call to pastors: to be reconciled with Christ in whom every weakness is redeemable in the power of resurrection. When the pastors keep the habit of repentance, they will change their attitude to the Lord, their brothers, and to self. The reconciliation which he commends to the pastors has three dimensions: God reconciled with man, man reconciled with fellow man, and each reconciliation with self. Five years later (1977) he will still be commending the three-fold aspects of reconciliation: with God, others, and self. He appeals to them to bring their burdens to Christ.

Non-Explicit Reconciliation Passages 353

6.3 Four Thematic Addresses

Kivengere gave the following four thematic addresses in West Africa, Ghana, in (1973),[92] with pastors as his primary audience, although later published (*When God Moves in Revival*)[93] for a wider readership. Kivengere tells stories of what God is able to do when his people are ready to follow him. Taking his example from East Africa, he exhorts his audience in Ghana to start at the cross of Christ, removing their masks, learn the way of 'shalom', and renew love's covenant.

A short introduction to the four addresses focuses on conversion to Christ. 'When God began to bless the church in East Africa we were dead: evangelical, biblical, orthodox, but dead' (p. 9, #2). He tells that in the areas, where he was a schoolteacher in a mission school, God began to move among young people who knew that he was an agnostic (pp. 9–10, #3). His own brother of 'Nine years old, he came forward with his New Testament in his hand' (p. 10, #4) and preached God's message that led to the conversion of about twenty boys. Unconverted teachers, him included, were sitting down: 'I should have gotten up and gone forward, but I was too proud' (p. 10, #4).

6.3.1 Revival Begins at the Cross

6.3.1.1 Exposition
Kivengere opens with an explanation of the word 'revival'. If you write the word carefully with 'I' in the centre, then you put a line through the 'I', it becomes a cross (p. 11, #1). Revival begins by crossing out the 'I', which is at the centre, turning it into a cross (p. 11, #2). From the outset Kivengere is using the language of the centre focussed on Christ. Reconciliation in Christ is in view.

---

92. In a second series of his address to Pastors in Ghana in July 1977 (Congress on Evangelization), Kivengere reveals in his opening address his indebtedness to Pastors in Ghana: 'I owe you because my first book that was ever published under my name started here . . . From the talks [I] share[d] with pastors at Trinity College some years ago'. See Pastor's Conference: AO: 19770612. The published version gives the year 1973.
93. Coomes, *African Harvest*, 369.

Self-centeredness, he reasoned, is the greatest enemy of the spiritual life, because by putting yourself in the centre, you drive God out (p. 12, #5). 'Once you and I are alienated from him to whom we owe our existence, we can never be truly alive, no matter what this world gives us' (p. 12, #6). Kivengere lists the things his audience may fill their lives with and be successful and empty at the same time: 'you may get the best education', 'you may become a millionaire' (p. 12, #16). Referring to 'Many modern philosophers, like the famous German atheist, Nietzsche, [who] have become prophets of despair' (p. 12, #16), he notes they struggle with the problem of how to make life meaningful. In the end, all they can say is that 'you are utterly meaningless . . . commit suicide!' 'For some people suicide is the literal result of alienation from God' (pp. 12–13, #6).

He recalls how in 1938 at boarding school he went to swim—but did not know how to swim. He sunk in the river without help from the boys (p. 13, #8). He was helpless. Kivengere links his helpless situation in the river to the helplessness of many people in the world who are struggling to be better but are becoming worse all the time and then giving up in despair (p. 13, #9). 'This situation is what Paul meant when he said that we were all dead—not that we were all dead physically, but that we were all helpless as a corpse' (p. 14, #11).

'That is why Jesus died in helplessness on the cross. The helplessness was not his but mine' (p. 14, #13). Kivengere lists the works of Jesus on the cross for us: 'He carried our sins and our sicknesses. He was wounded for our transgressions, bruised for our iniquities, and the punishment, which should have fallen upon us, fell on him instead. He took the responsibility for what we did. He accepted the consequences of our rebellion. Because of our selfishness, Jesus went to the cross' (p. 14, #15), alluding to Isaiah 53.

'This is why I said that revival begins by turning the I into a cross' (p. 14, #16). 'He who is eternal comes to take his place right in the centre—not on one side, not just near, but right in the centre'. Kivengere uses this statement to explain to his audience what the cross did. 'The cross cancels out the self, and replaces that self by Jesus Christ'. He lists the result of Jesus replacing self at the centre: 'your dry experience becomes fullness', 'what was empty is no longer empty' and 'what was helpless experiences power'. The love of Christ releases you from self to 'a sense of freedom' (p. 15, #18).

Once again, here he uses language that we have already seen him using in connection with reconciliation, and he has so far in this address moved from the cross to the love of Christ.

The bishop tells them his testimony: 'The reviving grace of God did not meet me in a cathedral or a church; it met me on the road to life'.[94] God does not meet us as a mass, but he meets us individually along the road of life (p. 15, #20). He turns the message on his audience: 'What happens when Jesus meets you? The cross of Jesus forces evil into the open so that he can deal with it like a physician. Like a surgeon he operates on the evil that enslaves you, the evil that breaks lives and homes. Love forces evil into the open at Calvary' (p. 16, #22). He counteracts the negative image of the cross that some people give 'that the cross is death'. On the contrary, 'the cross speaks of life in conflict with death, life defeating death' (p. 16, #23).[95] Kivengere links his statement to Jesus' words: 'Jesus said I came that they may have life' (p. 16, #23). Jesus does not come as your Judge but as your counsel for defence.[96] That you cannot accept yourself but you are accepted 'is good news of the New Testament'. Without explicitly mentioning it, here is reconciliation for Kivengere.

'The cross is not a theory, it is not a doctrine, it is not sentimental feeling. The cross is practical. It is God moving in love to meet violent men and women, facing violence and suffering for us' (p. 16, #25).[97] The Christian can stand anything because 'your faith was born in violence', it was born in 'blood and sweat in the loneliness of Calvary' (p. 16, #25–#26). The God of the cross is the God of the wounded hands, and therefore he can touch the wounds of humanity without fear' (pp. 16–17, #26). Kivengere reflects Barth's Christological aspect of reconciliation. Jesus Christ is very God, the reconciling God, who in his freedom practically crosses the frontier of the separation between God and man, and for man he faced man's life that is in conflict with death.[98] Thus God defeats death on the cross,[99] and in Christ

---

94. See his conversion, Chapter Two, 'Kivengere's Conversion: From Agnostic to Preacher'.
95. Kivengere, 'The Triumph of God's Glory', p. 6, #27.
96. See chapter Three, 3.5.3 'The Components of Barth's Doctrine of Reconciliation'.
97. See chapter Five, Kivengere, 'The Whole Gospel For The Whole World', p. 4, #10.
98. See chapter Three, 3.5.3 'The Components of Barth's Doctrine of Reconciliation'.
99. For an excellent discussion of how God in his Son Jesus defeats death in Mark's

restores the relationship between God and man. Reconciled in Christ, the Christian can therefore 'stand anything'.

Kivengere encouraged those who are afraid of their failings: 'I want to encourage you, revival does not come to respectable Christians' . . . 'The basis of revival is men and women shattered by their failures—aware that all is not well, helpless to do anything about it' (p. 17, #27). Again, this encouragement echoes the Keswick sequence of teaching of sin on Day One.[100]

Referring to what he calls an 'extreme word', Kivengere recalls Jesus' words: 'Blessed are those who are hungry, and are thirsty, for they shall be satisfied' (p. 17, #28). He tells his audience not to imagine that they will work hard with their own fingers and get what they want. Better hands have already done it for them. Their part is to respond to him who did it (p. 17, #28). To illustrate their part of responding to Christ, our preacher then narrated his testimony of conversion when Christ met him on the road going back from drinking to his house (pp. 17–21, #29–#43).[101]

Kivengere concludes his address with the observation that revival is not a spectacular event that happens in the clouds (p. 21, #44). 'It's in your own life. Revival does not require big meetings with famous speakers. Revival begins with you. It is the eruption of God's grace shaking you utterly, through and through' (p. 21, #44). When this happens, his audience should know that they are in the presence of a wonderful person called Jesus Christ. 'Revival begins in his presence. Let him begin in you' (p. 21, #44). In the sermon, he uses the language linked with the cross that he will later bring into close connection with reconciliation: 'He carried our sins and our sicknesses', 'He was wounded for our transgressions', 'bruised for our iniquities', 'He took the responsibility for what we did', 'He accepted the consequences of our rebellion', and 'Jesus went to the cross'.

6.3.1.2 Summary of Revival Begins at the Cross

Kivengere's address focussed on reconciliation centred in Jesus Christ when he explained the work of Jesus Christ and the person of Jesus Christ on the

---

Gospel, see Bolt, *Jesus' Defeat of Death*. Bolt argues that Jesus' final defeat of death in resurrection is yet to happen.

100. See Chapter Three, 2.1.1 'Day One: The Diagnosis—Sin'.

101. See Chapter Two, 5.2 'Kivengere's Conversion: From Agnostic to Preacher'.

cross: he carried our sins and sickness, he was wounded for our transgressions, bruised for our iniquities and punishment and accepted the consequence of our rebellion. However, he also explained reconciliation using the language of Romans 5:6 (p. 14, #11). As before, Jesus is presented, as the one who fills empty lives, and the God of the cross is the God of the wounded. All this focus on reconciliation shows that it is close to his heart and it is his primary message to be preached to bring transformation. Besides the influence from Paul, the influence from Barth has also been detected. Since the sermon speaks of God's movement in revival, the Revival influence is also clear.

The message had potential impact to bring encouragement to the wounded in Africa, those who are not satisfied, and those who are thirsty. They do not need to work at gaining these things because the hand of Jesus has done it for them. Kivengere preached because he believed that the wounded hand of Jesus would bring transformation and healing.

6.3.2 Remove the Masks

6.3.2.1 Exposition
God called Moses up into Mount Sinai for fellowship with him and Moses returned with such a glow that no Israelite dared look him in the face (Exod 34: 29–34) (p. 24, #1). However, this glory tended to fade after a while, thus Moses made a mask so that the people might not see the fading glory (p. 24, #2). He asks: 'what does Paul say about it?'

'Moses wore a mask but we have been brought under a covenant where you don't need a mask' (p. 24, #3)—thus, bridging the gap between preacher and audience. Without explaining the covenant at this stage, he goes straight to what happened when Moses came into the presence of God: wanting to gaze right into the face of the glory, Moses took off the mask, gazed at the glory and caught it (p. 24, #4).

Kivengere links the glory that Moses saw with the statement of Jesus in his prayer to the Father: 'The glory which thou has given me I have given to them (John 17:22)' (p. 25, #4). Three years later (December 1976) this statement was to be the theme of his Urbana address.[102] 'Under the new covenant of the grace of Jesus Christ, every kind of character is taken care of . . . Just take off your mask and look in the face of glory'. Moses saw God's glory in the burning bush. He caught the vision of the eternal God. Here, he is using the language, which he used in the explicit reconciliation sermons: 'catch the vision of God'.

The bishop tells of another incident, the prophet Balaam, who refused to listen to God (Num 22) (p. 26, #9). He asks: how did God deal with him? God did not send a senior prophet to help him. God did not choose a more eloquent prophet to deliver his message. But 'God chose a donkey to speak to Balaam' (p. 26, #9). 'The Bible says the donkey spoke, and when it spoke the Lord opened Balaam's eyes to the truth' and he drew together the two stories saying, 'The bush is aglow. The donkey speaks. God is at work' (p. 26, #9–#10).

Kivengere tells his audience that some of them are just like donkeys: so depressed that they can't speak for God or jealous of the gifts that God has given to others (p. 26, #11). For a second time he used the expression 'new covenant' without explaining it: 'Your case has been taken care of in the new covenant of Jesus Christ . . . use your one gift, even if you are only a donkey. Remember, it was a donkey that carried the Lord into Jerusalem' (p. 26, #11). By referring to 'the new covenant of Jesus Christ', Kivengere echoes Barth on the covenant of grace, which for Barth, the fulfilment of this covenant took the form of atonement because of man's sin.[103]

He learned what it means to be 'a donkey' for Christ from the Revival. A dear brother in Tanzania[104] explained to a Revival fellowship on the eve of his consecration as bishop in the Anglican Church, that when Jesus rode in Jerusalem in triumph, he sat on a donkey. Underneath the bishop's robes

---

102. See Kivengere, 'The Triumph of God's Glory'.
103. See Chapter Three, 3.5.2 'Reconciliation—Covenant and Sin'.
104. His friend Yohana Omari, who became the Assistant Bishop of Central Tanganyika diocese, told the story. Alfred Stanway arrange for Kivengere and Omari to visit Australia arranged for six months (December 1958-June 1959). See Chapter Two, Reed, *Walking in the Light*, 201–05.

that will be put on him will be a donkey, himself, to carry his Lord downtown (p. 27, #13).[105]

Kivengere appealed to his audience to remove their masks, for two reasons. First, a mask prevents them from 'gazing into the face of Jesus and catching the glory' (p. 28, 16). Masks can hide them from God, even though God already knows them better than they know themselves. Second, a mask prevents people from knowing them as they are (p. 28, #16–#17). He illustrates with an example from his marriage when he would put on a mask but this did not help their marriage relationship: 'There was a wrong attitude. I was critical. I was hard, and too proud to admit it' (pp. 29–20, #18–#23).

But as soon as the medicine—'the work of Jesus Christ who made me see my mask, and who took my mask on himself'—tears the mask away, they were then in each other's arms. 'We call those moments "re-weddings"', by which he means beginning again. 'Now grace has brought us together. There has been confession of sin and we have turned and looked at the glory of the Lord with "unveiled face"' (p. 31, #24). Without explicitly using the word, Kivengere's illustration shows reconciliation with God and with each other.

'Immediately love is released, fellowship is warm, and no longer strangers to one another' (p. 31, #25). Kivengere then guesses at Peter and John's relationship with each other on the day of Pentecost: 'On the day of Pentecost, Peter felt safe with John and John felt safe with Peter and the rest of them' (p. 31, #28). The masks had been removed. He further illustrates with the story of how the spirit of God entered into his heart and released him from the bondage of jealousy over the preaching gift of his brother (p. 31, #29–#32).[106] He asked his audience if they find it easy to go to their friends, husbands and wives and say "I am sorry' (p. 32, #33). 'When Jesus died on the cross was it easy?' (pp. 32–33, #33–#34). The death and resurrection of Jesus on the cross was to release people who are captive to

---

105. He used this same story of Bishop Yohana Omari at his consecration and enthronement as Bishop of Kigezi in 1972.
106. William Nagenda, his Revival friend and mentor, is here referred to as 'my brother'. The occasion of this incident was the international Student's conference in Chicago, USA, 1961.

sin because sin makes people its slave. It must be brought into the open, confessed and laid upon Jesus (p. 33, #34). Again, reconciliation is not far away with his explanation of the work of Jesus upon the cross.

With his revival background Kivengere says: 'The examples I have given you are simple and practical, to show how we lose our freedom. It's not just in the big spiritual experiences, but also in the smaller, moment-by-moment incidents of daily life'.[107] If the believer allows the Spirit of God to apply the work of Jesus to these little things, the believer will walk in freedom of the Spirit daily: 'for the rest of your life' (p. 33, #35).

Linking the freedom in Christ to his experience for the past thirty years he says 'the Spirit of God is so fresh that I feel today as if I am just only beginning. Revival is a life of new beginning' (p. 33, #36). 'The final verse of 2 Corinthians 3 reminds us that revival is not the end—it is just a life of new beginnings' (p. 34, #37). Without mentioning reconciliation, he tells: 'if you have become aware that there is a mask somewhere in your relationship with God or with another person, or in your own inward life, then I ask you to let the Holy Spirit tear it off' (p. 35, #41). He illustrates how the reconciliation comes about when the Holy Spirit in the presence of Jesus tears off masks. He used a story of a man who killed many people during the Mau Mau uprising in Kenya. The man spoke about the love of God shown to him when he asked be forgiven from killing sixty people. He was forgiven by a woman whose husband he had killed (pp. 35–36, #42–#48). Kivengere concluded, 'Don't hinder the transformation that the Spirit of God wants to carry out in your life' . . . 'ask the Holy Spirit to give you joy of forgiveness in the place of the burden and guilt of sin' (p. 36, #48). There is reconciliation.

6.3.2.2 Summary of Remove the Masks
Throughout the sermon, the influence of the Revival is detectable from his illustrations and testimony. Kivengere's address used different passages, which did not explicitly call for reconciliation (Exod 34:29–34, John 17:22, Num 22, and 2 Cor 3). His explanation nevertheless focused on

---

107. See Chapter Three, 2.1.2 'Day One: The Diagnosis—Sin'. For a testimony of how Kivengere lived and practiced the Revival life style of paying careful attention to details in life every moment, see Michael, 'Forward', 3.

reconciliation every time he explains Revival using the image of masks. The use of the language of the 'new covenant of grace in Jesus Christ' to explain reconciliation stands out. In the previous sermons, he did not frequently use reconciliation, however, here he is explicit on the expression. Although this expression 'New Covenant' may also suggest an affinity with Barth's understanding of the covenant of grace, which he considered to be the presupposition of reconciliation.[108]

He believes that when his audience begins at the cross, removes the masks from their faces, and gazes at Jesus, they will catch the vision of the glory of God. Kivengere frequently used the language of catching the vision in the explicit reconciliation sermons.[109] Once they remove the masks, they will see the need to reconcile with God and with each other. Reconciliation is preached from texts, which do not mention it.

6.3.3 Peace and Victory for the Christian

6.3.3.1 Exposition

Kivengere opens with Jesus' Easter morning greeting to his disciples: '*Shalom* or Peace!' (p. 37, #1) Before his death and resurrection, Jesus had seldom used this greeting to his disciples. 'The disciples all lacked peace'. The world in which we live itself lacks peace: 'a world of conflict and wars' (p. 38, #2). He lists examples of this lack of peace: 'There are people in the world who have forgotten to laugh'. 'There are families where laughter is rare'. 'When wounds are not healed, and when the shame which one has incurred because of sin is not taken away, how on earth can you have real peace?' (p. 38, #3)

Linking peace to reconciliation, Kivengere used a story of repentance among the elders of an Anglican church in Africa during and after the Communion service. As the words of Holy Communion were read from the Prayer Book, 'you in particular who earnestly and sincerely have repented of your sins, and are in love and charity with all your neighbours,

---

108. See chapter three, 3.5.1 'The Doctrine of Reconciliation'.
109. E.g., Kivengere, 'Surprised by Joy', p. 12, #12. Kivengere, 'Ambassador For Christ', p. 3, #6. Kivengere, 'Jesus Came as a Missionary', pp. 5–6, #7. Kivengere, 'The Love of Christ', pp. 2–3, #3. Kivengere, 'The Whole Gospel For The Whole World', p. 1, #3.

and intend to lead a new life from now, come forward' (p. 38, #4), the elders at those words went to the back of the church as the Holy Spirit caught them red-handed, convicted them of their unrepented sins, lack of love and charity to neighbours right inside the same church (p. 39, #4–#7). One of the elders said, 'under God, we sat together for the first time'. 'We agreed that we should allow God to break our hostilities and enmities, and we came back' (p. 39, #7). In this story Kivengere is telling his audience about reconciliation with God and between men with each other. For him, peace is attained following the reconciliation in Jesus Christ.

On the first Easter day, Jesus rose from the grave. He tells the story of the broken-hearted disciples in two gospels: John 20:1–18 (pp. 39–41, #7–#17), the story of the frightened disciples in John 20:19–23, (pp. 42–44, #18–#25), and the story of the confused disciples in Luke 24:13–25 (pp. 44–45, #26–#32). Summing up these gospel accounts he said: 'This is what the resurrection did for them. . . .] He brought them peace, the thing they could not get anywhere else' (p. 45, #33).

Finally he wants his audience to listen to Paul: 'I want you to listen to Paul speaking. He was a wonderful missionary, a dear brother, born again in a wonderful way, used mightily by God. Many of us have become Christians through his testimony' (p. 45, #33). He commended Paul's message in 2 Corinthians 5:12–14, the message of the love of Christ, which is a reconciliation message. The link between this message and peace is summed up in his words: 'Thanks be to God. He rose from the dead. He's going through the world, but first of all triumphing in every corner of your life. And he wants every part of you to shout, "Victory! Triumph! Peace!' (p. 52, #3)

6.3.3.2 *Summary of Peace and Victory for the Christian*

Kivengere's message reflects the Pauline understanding of reconciliation and the influence of Paul's life on his life and testimony on his life (p. 45, #33). Earlier language referring to reconciliation is used, 'wounds healed', and 'peace'. He explicitly mentions reconciliation in his illustration of elders reconciling at the words from the prayer book.

The influence of the Revival is detected in his love of and fascination with testimony about conversion and what God is doing in the life of believers

(p. 45, #33) and the Keswick influence of victorious living in Christ triumphing over every corner of a believer's life (p. 52, #3). Behind his gospel explanation of the resurrection lays reconciliation. None of the passages explicitly speak about reconciliation, but he preached reconciliation using the Pauline understanding in 2 Corinthians 5:11–14. Reconciliation brings transformation. It did for Paul, and it did for him. Christ is still doing and he wants everyone to be a reconciler: Christ wants every part of you to shout peace (p. 52, #3).

6.3.4 The Covenant of Love

6.3.4.1 Exposition

Kivengere tells his audience that 1 Samuel 18 describes the 'covenant of love'. The covenant was portrayed in the Old Testament and fulfilled in the New Testament, when the Lord Jesus poured out his blood on the cross for the forgiveness of sins' (p. 52, #2). A Biblical covenant is between the greater (God) and the lesser ('you and I', p. 52, #3). 'It is never a covenant between equals. All the initiative is from the greater to the lesser', hence the name 'covenant of love' (p. 52, #3). Kivengere invites his audience to 'to come and respond to God's covenant of love' (p. 52, #5). Here he shows an affinity with Barth's explanation of covenant, linked with reconciliation.[110]

He described the love that brought David in the King's house from verses 1–5: 'The background is simple. It's about David, a shepherd boy from Bethlehem, the son of Jesse; King Saul, the first King of Israel; and Jonathan, the royal prince, the heir to the throne' (p. 52, #5). When Jonathan finished speaking to Saul, 'the soul of Jonathan (his entire personality) was knit to the soul of David'. 'And Saul took David that day, and would not let him return to his father's house' (p. 52, #5). Despite David's poor background, Jonathan loved him with his own soul.

Kivengere then links this love with Ephesians 1:6: 'accepted in the beloved' (p. 54, #10). He tells his audience that they need a spiritual covenant to stay in the kingdom of God (p. 54, #13). He turns back to verse 4 where

---

110. See chapter three, 3.5.3 'The Doctrine of Reconciliation' and 3.5.2 'Reconciliation —Covenant and Sin'.

Jonathan stripped his robe and gave it to David, took off his armour for protection and gave it to David, took his fighting sword that was on him and gave it to David, took his bow and gave it to David and took his girdle of strength and gave it to David. He wants to tell his audience to get the picture of a covenant of love: 'I want you to get the picture: Here was a Shepherd boy; there was a prince . . . why? . . . the two have changed places. That is the meaning of the covenant of love' (p. 55, #15).

The bishop then compared this with Philippians 2:5–11. Jesus, although by nature God, stripped himself of all the glory and emptied himself and became man—the poor man, became a servant, a slave; he became a criminal; and he died on the cross in nakedness and shame (pp. 55–56, #19). 'That is not Jonathan, but a "greater than Jonathan": one who stands by even as you read these words, Jesus Christ the Prince of glory' (p. 56, #18). He links this 'Prince of glory' to the hymn about the wondrous cross on which the Prince of glory died. Kivengere drives the message home for his audience when he explained the love of God for them: 'I have loved you with everlasting love . . . he strips himself and takes off his righteousness, the garment of a Prince. He covers you with it' (p. 56, #20). He lists the actions of Jesus' love to believers: 'he himself puts on your rags and tatters. He takes his armour of protection and salvation, and he gives it to you. . . . He takes his girdles of strength and gives it to you' (p. 56, #20).

Our bishop tells us that that is what Paul means when he says, 'He who knew no sin, God made him sin, or treated him as sin, so that we who are sinners might be made the righteousness of God through him' (p. 56, #21). This is Pauline language of reconciliation (2 Cor 5:21). Now the covenant is complete. He asks: 'you need forgiveness?' He is quick to answer that all they need: peace, strength, victory, 'he has given it' (p. 56, #23). They are more than conquers through him who died and rose again. He appealed to them not to despise themselves, but to go wherever God is sending them in Ghana, Africa and the rest of the world (p. 58, #30). He also appealed to them to make a covenant of love with the Lord: 'it is an unchanging covenant and it's based on love. When it takes you into custody, you are eternally secure' (p. 60, #38). Again, reconciliation is not far away.

6.3.4.2 Summary of the Covenant of Love

Kivengere preached reconciliation from 1 Samuel 18:1–5 which does not mention reconciliation. It is in this address that Kivengere used the clearest expression of the covenant of love or the covenant of grace, linking it to reconciliation. His explanation shows an affinity with Barth's doctrine of reconciliation rooted in the covenant of grace. He linked the Pauline passage which links the concept of reconciliation (2 Cor 5:21) with the Old Testament passage of 1 Samuel 18:1–5, and the Pauline passage of Philippians 2:5–11. These links brought out the concept of reconciliation that was close on his heart as he used them to highlight his points. They need a spiritual covenant to stay in the kingdom and Christ, the head of the kingdom, died in nakedness and shame, stripping himself of his glory and became man. The result of this death was to bring reconciliation between God and man, and man with each other. The impact of this was to be felt in Africa and the rest of the world through the witness to this love by his audience.

6.4 Kivengere's Theological Reflection

6.4.1 The Evangelist's Ministry of Reconciliation: We Are Christ's Ambassadors: AO: 19830715

6.4.1.1 Situating Kivengere's Theological Reflection

On 15 July 1983, at Amsterdam, the Netherlands, Kivengere addressed 4,000 evangelists from 133 nations of the world. His 'theological reflection' on reconciliation was intended to prepare them to do 'The Work of An Evangelist', in a world that is desperately searching for hope that will only come through Jesus Christ.

'To all of us who proclaim the good news of God to men and women, God has entrusted the most precious treasure —"The Ministry of Reconciliation"' (p. 157, #1). 'The cry for peace (wholeness of life) and reconciliation (harmony in relationships, friendships instead of hostility) is as old as humanity' (p. 157, #1). 'The fact that we are ever struggling to be at peace with ourselves and with our environment and with others is a confession that our relations have radically been deranged' (p. 157, #2). There is an on-going struggle: 'we are ever struggling'—thus, bridging the gap between the preacher and the audience. The struggle to be at peace is on three fronts: with self, with environment, and with others.

'This cry for peace and reconciliation in the human heart is the object of God's reconciling act in and through Christ, and "him crucified". Thus, we have peace with God (the end of the war of an alienated conscience) and wholeness of life restored through our Lord Jesus Christ (Rom 5:1)' (p. 157, #3–#4). Kivengere focusses the attention of his audience on the heart of the gospel that they have believed and the gospel, which they proclaim: Jesus Christ, and 'him crucified'.

Using Paul's statement, 'Through whom we have gained access by faith into this grace in which we now stand' (Rom 5:2), he encouraged them to 'become the essence of our gospel' (p. 157, #4). He asks: 'But how did the hostilities, the hostile attitudes and reactions against God, come to an end?' (p. 157, #5) It came to an end in Jesus Christ: 'we were reconciled to him [God] through the death of his Son'. In the beginning when God created the world from nothing, like an artist, he planned to create one creature for fellowship with himself' (p. 157, #6). God created man out of dust of the earth, and lovingly stooped low and breathed the breath of life into him. Man became a living person: 'the image of God!' (p. 157, #6) Here he draws his audience to God, the subject matter. God desires that they should know his purpose in creating the human being: to live in peace with God.

The human person was meant to be, 'a living person', whole, at peace with God from whom he came. This was life in its fullness. 'Man at peace with God was at peace with himself, at peace with his fellowman, and at peace with the world, his home' (p. 157, #6). Only reconciliation can restore 'our relations that have radically been deranged' (p. 157, #2).

6.4.1.2 The Need for Reconciliation[111]

Kivengere's reflection then provides a clear account of the need for reconciliation. When man disrupted his fellowship with God by moving away

---

111. In 1985, Kivengere published an article with the title, 'Need For Reconciliation': 1–2, in the *Hope Bulletin*, a magazine of African Enterprise, Kampala, Uganda devoted to a teaching Ministry and to provide information and items for prayer and praise. The

from God, the centre of man's life, to become self-centred, man inevitably became 'eccentric', 'deranged' (p. 157, #7). Man lost the fellowship with God and he lost the axis of his life, and so his life became wild and out of control, as would a spaceship out of orbit. 'The inner wholeness was shattered, alienated, and uncoordinated; man was invaded by a host of evil influences' (p. 157, #8).

Kivengere's explanation of the mess that man has caused by falling away from God, the source of peace, underlines the centrality of the need for the evangelist' work: 'the ministry of reconciliation'. At a distance from God, man dreaded God's presence, and in his fright man became hostile to God. Kivengere reinforced the hopelessness and helplessness of man: 'This continued discomfort and dread of God made man an enemy of the very one to whom he owed his life' (p. 157, #8).

Kivengere is already looking beyond the helpless situation of man to reconciliation: 'As God is the source and creator of all that is, estrangement from him means estrangement from everything that he created—so man became a fugitive in God's world, and a stranger to his fellowman. His own life was full of discords and breakdowns!' [. . . and] 'This condition squeezed a persistent cry of, O wretched man that I am! Who will rescue me from this life—which is a living death? from every man's inner person' (p. 157, #10). God will send his Son Jesus Christ to bring reconciliation and peace which man had lost. The evangelists will speak this good news as ambassadors of Christ.

6.4.1.3 The Source of Christian Reconciliation which Restores Peace in Life

By now the evangelists know from Kivengere's earlier explanation that it is 'Through Christ', that 'God was pleased . . . to reconcile to himself all things (Col 1:19, 20)' (p. 158, #11). As he explains the source of Christian reconciliation, from which peace in life is attained, a sense of the work of

---

article was a short version of his 1983 Amsterdam reflection on 'The Evangelist's Ministry of reconciliation: We are Christ's Ambassadors (2 Corinthians 5:18–20)'. I am grateful to the editor then, Fred Bazarabusa, for information and access to this article. Fred Bazarabusa currently is adjunct lecturer in the Department of Mass Communication, Uganda Christian University, Bishop Barham University campus, Kabale.

the evangelist dawns deeper in them, as Kivengere gradually exposes the brokenness of the relationship that man caused between God and humanity: 'for when man broke away from fellowship with God, he broke God's heart of love. Man's defiance of God provoked an impenetrable barrier—God's holy barrier of judgment against sin in man' (p. 158, #12). Behind this statement is the language of judgment from Romans 5. Unlike in the previous sermons in chapter 5 on Romans 5, he had been silent on the judgment of God, but here he is clear about the judgment as a result of man's defiance of God. However, even when he has broken his silence on the judgment of God, he does not see the judgment as 'wrath to come' but leans towards 'chaos in the present' when he notes that 'God's holy judgment is against sin in man'.

The evangelists, too, in some sense would have felt in their sin 'utterly helpless', 'as helpless to do anything for themselves as a dead body in a coffin is helpless to raise itself' (p. 158, #12). But there is the good news: 'God, in his incredible self-giving, outgoing love, stooped low again to redeem and restore his rebel back into friendship with himself'—there is reconciliation. This becomes a reality as the evangelists are to speak as Christ's ambassadors through whom God, as it were, will call others to become friends of God (p. 158, 12). They are to speak as Christ's ambassadors because they have been handed a precious treasure—'the ministry of reconciliation'.

6.4.1.4 The Nature of Christian Reconciliation
Since God 'was personally present in Christ, reconciling—bringing a hostile world back into friendship with—the world to Himself (2 Cor 5:19)', then this statement shows some things about Christian reconciliation (p. 158, #13). To him there are three things that constitute the nature of Christian reconciliation: it is personal, it is communal, and it is universal.

6.4.1.4.1 Reconciliation is Personal
The nature of Christian reconciliation is personal. Kivengere draws his audience to God and to themselves. 'The personal God of the Bible can deal with human sin and rebellion only at a personal level, in an individual or in a community'. This engages the evangelist with an idea of the scope of their work as ambassadors for Christ.

6.4.1.4.2 It is Communal

'As man's alienation is never limited to himself but affects his relations with his fellow human persons, so he must be reconciled to the members of the human community' (p. 158, #15). His reflection provides a moment of practical ministry: 'This is the practical effect of reconciliation upon our daily living'. He supports this explanation with the language of reconciliation drawn from outside the Pauline reconciliation language (Matt 5:24): 'First go and be reconciled to your brother; then come and offer your gift', so said the Reconciler, the Lord Jesus Christ. 'He still says so tonight at Amsterdam to all of you—"ministers of reconciliation"—in this hostile, alienated, embittered, deeply fractured world!' (p. 158, #15). The work of the evangelist is clearly a treasure entrusted to them by God. The influence of Keswick and the Revival is detected in his calling upon believers to make a decision for God and to reach out into the world to serve him.[112]

6.4.1.4.3 It is Universal

Christ's reconciling death on the cross is the power by which God intends 'to reconcile all things': things on earth, things in heaven—in the presence of God—to himself, thus making peace—ending hostilities in men's hearts, against him and against one another (Col 1:19, 20). His audience would therefore have had their perspective on Christ and his death focused with a universal edge.

Kivengere desires that the evangelists do the ministry of reconciliation for they know that 'Things here on earth affected by man's rebellion are no longer whole as in heaven' (p. 158, #17). The evangelists know from their work that 'Hostile forces of evil still vie for power (pre-eminence), but Christ's victorious death broke down the walls of hostilities and alienation and made the universe redeemable'. But his audiences are also aware that Christ gave himself up for all. Consequently, all are within the radius of his self-sacrificing love. Moreover, none are too far out of his love. In this paragraph, Kivengere echoes Paul's language of reconciliation from Ephesians 2 and 6, where he sets salvation in the context of hostility of the powers of evil.

---

112. See Chapter Three, 2.1.5 'Day Five: The Mission—Powerful Christian Service'.

6.4.1.5 *The Method of Christian Reconciliation*

Once Kivengere has observed that the break in relations between man and God was so wide and the wound so deep, he then impressed it upon his audience that 'God chose the most radical method to redeem this desperate situation' (p. 158, #18). Jesus came into the human situation, Jesus chose to live in the hopeless situation of man, and he died on the cross for our sin.

6.4.1.6 *He Entered the Arena of the Broken Relations at the Lowest Point*

Jesus chose to be born a baby like the rest of us. He fully became the Son of God broken human person. And, he shared fully in our breaks, without himself breaking down. He chose to live where life had its sting—of poverty, injustice, misunderstandings, unpopularity, hunger, and thirst.

Kivengere reflected on 'things', noting that 'things which make life sour, and relations strained to a breaking point' were Jesus' daily experience in life. But Jesus' life on earth was reconciliation in demonstration (p. 158, #20).[113] Evangelists need not look further than the gospel records of Jesus' daily life to see that 'Christ is indeed our peace'. Wherever Jesus was, men and women with all their strains and stresses of living flocked to him (p. 158, #20). 'And he healed them all' (p. 158, #20).

Clearly, Jesus is the subject of living among humanity where life had its sting, and as Jesus' ambassadors, the evangelists have the responsibility to bring Christ where life has its sting. We see the "Way" going, and we see the "Truth" revealing, and the "Life" living!' (p. 159, #22) In Jesus, men saw the grace that welcomed them all and men also saw the authority that demanded their immediate response of commitment and obedience (p. 159, #22). With his mention of 'the grace that welcomed all', 'the love of God'; reconciliation is in view because in the love of God, Jesus welcomed all.

Kivengere notes that the presence of Jesus 'was as much an invitation as his words' (p. 159, #22). As Kivengere was explaining the work of Jesus, the evangelists would have been drawn to the work of Christ in their ministries. 'Whenever he walked, prayed, taught, healed, or fed the hungry, it was as

---

113. See earlier discussions including, Kivengere, 'The Reconciling Love of Christ', pp. 1–2, #2. Kivengere, 'Jesus Came as a Missionary', p. 9, #10. Kivengere, 'Surprised by Joy', p. 10, #14.

if he was always saying, "Come to me, all of you who are exhausted and are carrying heavy loads. And I will refresh you"' (p. 159, #22). Our preacher appealed to his audience: 'Brethren, this Christ is our reconciliation'. Here he clearly echoes his teacher, Markus Barth, who explains that 'Christ' is 'reconciliation'.[114]

Jesus was never in places for himself. Wherever he was, he was, and still is, 'for us' (p. 159, #22), bringing together the preacher and audience, as well as bridging the gap between the preacher and audience.

6.4.1.7 Christ Went all the Way to the Cross For Us

Kivengere stresses that the climax of God's method to achieve reconciliation is 'clearly demonstrated for us to see in his death on the cross' (p. 159, #23). When Jesus describes his death in terms of a 'creative power', 'a drawing magnet', and 'I, when I am lifted up from the earth will draw all men to myself' (John 12:32), Kivengere links it with James Denney's argument on reconciliation: 'We do not preach that Jesus died' rather, 'that he died for us, and in particular that he died for our sins' (p. 159, #22). In 2 Corinthians 5:21, Paul poignantly describes the way God did it. Thus, in a graphic expression bringing in reconciliation, 'God made Christ] who had no sin to be sin for us, so that in him we might become the righteousness of God' (p. 159, #22). The death of Christ gained reconciliation for all.

6.4.1.8 The Effects of Christian Reconciliation and Peace

If the death of Christ for all gained reconciliation for all, this was reinforced by the self-sacrificing love of God in Christ that removed the barrier of God's offended holiness by lifting the heavy burden of its broken demands on sinful man (p. 159, #23). The love of God, 'lifted man from his moral impotence and paralysis', sensitised his heart, thus calling repentance into being. The result of this love of Christ, when it restores the enemy of God into God's friend, is a liberating experience: reconciliation of humanity at four levels, 'reconciliation with himself', 'reconciliation with his neighbour', 'reconciliation with his community', and 'reconciliation with his Father's world'.

---

114. See Chapter Three, 4. 'Markus Barth's link to Kivengere'.

At this point in his reflection, Kivengere makes a crucial point: 'reconciliation and the resulting peace is not just one of the Christian doctrines in the New Testament, it is the lifeblood of all Christian doctrines' (p. 159, #24). Here Kivengere explicitly acknowledges what is being argued in this thesis: reconciliation was central in his preaching. This claim forms a central thread that runs throughout his preaching in the period under our inquiry: 1971–1988. Now at Amsterdam (1983) five years away from the end of his preaching ministry, this central theme is well developed and clearly articulated by Kivengere as he passed it on to the world (all the 133 nations assembled at Amsterdam). As he heads towards the end of his preaching ministry, the impact of his preaching reconciliation is potentially expanded throughout 133 nations of the world.

Kivengere emphasized for the evangelists the centrality of reconciliation. Where preaching reconciliation is shied away from, 'the church (Christ's body) suffers from a kind of spiritual malnutrition or anaemia'. He stressed that 'where it is altogether shunned, the body starves to death, and preaching becomes dry rhetoric'. However, he warns that 'where reconciliation is overemphasized in isolation, out of context from the living Lord Jesus, confusion and heresy are inevitable' (p. 159, #26).

As ambassadors of Christ, evangelists have a duty to balance the preaching of reconciliation. He is aware that in some sections, the church has isolated itself from the ministry of reconciliation, and in other parts, the church has been preaching reconciliation out of context from the living Lord Jesus, the reconciler. Here Volf comes close to his position on reconciliation when he recently (1999) discovered a 'deeply disturbing absence of sustained attempts to relate the core beliefs about reconciliation to the shape of the shurches' social responsibility'.[115] Volf noted that the doctrine of reconciliation has been reduced to the reconciliation of the soul with God—thus, it 'has a theological and personal meaning, but no wider social meaning'. Moreover, he discovered that there are those who criticise this kind of teaching and take up the concept of 'liberation', rigorously

---

115. See Volf, 'The Social Meaning of Reconciliation', 8.

pursuing freedom, and justice, as the only proper way of responding to social problems.[116]

For Kivengere, the right balance is not simply a theological explanation in abstract. He is correcting an anomaly in the church that has lost sight of the centrality of 'the ministry of reconciliation'—a treasure handed to us by God, in which Jesus is the subject matter of reconciliation. When Jesus is sidelined in the preaching of reconciliation, then the world's need for reconciliation will remain untouched. 'The heartbreaking, senseless, and destructive conflicts in different countries of the world, based on race, tribe, colour, political ideology, ethnocentrism, tribocentrism, are loud cries of our race saying to you and to me, "What a miserable life this is! Who will rescue us from this living death?"' (p. 159, #28) It is only preaching Christ-centred reconciliation that brings transformation in the life of individuals and community.

6.4.1.9 Reconciliation and the Evangelist

Kivengere tells the evangelists that they need reconciliation before attempting to be involved in the ministry of reconciliation. 'The cries of our race saying to you and to me', 'What a miserable life this is! Who will rescue us from this living death?"', (p. 159, #28), demands that they first be reconciled with God. 'Hearing such a cry, you and I are ready to shout back in Paul's words, "But thanks be to God through our Lord Jesus Christ"'. Here he bridges the gap between preacher and audience, but he also gives the way out of this vicious circle of negative action and reaction (p. 159, #29). In the face of the world's crisis, Kivengere and his audience can be thankful to God for his son Jesus Christ: 'Christ is our reconciliation'. 'Through him' reconciliation is gained.

Sometimes words refuse to come because the proclaimer (the preacher), 'has refused to obey or has explained away the Lord's command, "First go to your brother and be reconciled to him, and then come and [preach, teach, counsel, sing] offer your gift!"' (p. 159, #30) But, 'An unreconciled evangelist cannot effectively minister reconciliation. Only reconciled hearts

---

116. See Volf, 'The Social Meaning of Reconciliation', 9.

are God's instruments for healing deep hurts and bridging wide gaps in relationships' (p. 159, #30).

The key task of the evangelists is plain: 'God has given us the ministry of reconciliation. And so tonight, if Amsterdam is going to mean healing and revival, I am going to call you not only to commit yourself to this ministry, but first to put right your relations with God, and then with your brother' (p. 159, #31). Because they must first put right their relationships with God, self, and environment, he asks: 'What are your hang-ups? Where and on whom are they hanging?' (p. 159, #31) It is through them that God's task will be carried out and as such the time has come to let the Holy Spirit hang any of their hang-ups on the cross.[117] In this paragraph Kivengere is not only preaching reconciliation, but he is reconciling the evangelists to God and to one another. In doing so he is formally following the Keswick and Revival patterns.[118]

All his audiences' questions and fears related to broken relationships will find counter-parts in Kivengere's six questions:

1. What are the spiritual barricades which are blocking the spirit of reconciliation from flowing out and across to your brother?
2. Are you asking me the old question, 'And who is my brother?' The one for whom Christ died and to whom he is sending you, saying, 'First go and be reconciled to your brother, and then come back and offer your gift'.
3. Do I have to give in to the wrongdoer?
4. Am I supposed to be a party to his sin?
5. Am I not commanded to have no fellowship, no dealings with such?
6. If I step forward to be reconciled to the one in the wrong, am I not compromising justice? (pp. 159–60, #31)

---

117. cf. *The Triumph of God's Glory: AO: 1976*. At the 1976 Urbana conference (International Students' Conference) on world Evangelization, he to 17,000 students who are going out to be involved in evangelism, he told them that 'your hang-ups will be hanged on the cross'. To him the cross is the solution to all their problems.
118. See Chapter Three, 2. 'The Keswick Movement and the East African Revival: The Approach and Context of Preaching'.

To all the above six questions, he encouraged his audience, 'Let us remember that reconciliation stems from self-sacrificing love'—thus, bridging the gap between him and his audience (p. 160, #32). The liberating power of the self-sacrificing love, 'lies in forgiveness, which is always a miracle' (p. 160, #32). Kivengere is not merely telling them about the self-sacrificing love of Jesus, but it is something that is real as he experienced it in his personal life and ministry: 'No one ever forgives without suffering. It costs to forgive! And costs dearly. That God forgives is a divine miracle' (p. 160, #32).

The centrality of reconciliation to his preaching is once again, abundantly plain. 'The power of his justice and his mercy working in harmony, restoring the alienated wrongdoer, is the heart of "the good news of God"'. The evangelists should know that 'justice' and 'mercy' couldn't be realized independently of each other. It is not the task of the evangelists to bring about justice in their power, but as the evangelists present the good news of God's reconciling love in Jesus Christ, then in the power of Christ, his justice and his mercy, working in harmony, will restore the alienated wrongdoer.

'Mercy is not the opposite of justice', but instead injustice is the opposite of mercy. 'God has nothing to do with injustice in his central work of liberating the guilty through his reconciling love'. 'The price of reconciliation is full identification with the guilty in order to arouse hope for liberation and restoration (2 Cor 5:21)' (p. 160, #32). Such an understanding of the centrality of reconciliation has been at the heart of Kivengere's preaching for his whole Christian ministry in 1983. He now desires the same for the evangelists.

6.4.1.10 Practical Points for Peace and Reconciliation
At this point he warns the evangelists: 'The chains that tie you down and hinder you from moving may lie where you least suspect them!'; 'In the sensitive but seeming trifles of your relationships with your dear wife, your children, your fellow team members! First, go and be reconciled . . . then come and offer your gift (Matt 5:23, 24)' (p. 160, #33). Kivengere used a practical illustration from his own preaching ministry in Uganda to demonstrate how he first had to 'go and be reconciled' with a Muslim, Governor Bashir of western Uganda.

He recalls that a few years ago under the regime of terror in his country, Uganda, he entered into a situation of strained relations with the Governor of western Uganda, his region. The cause was of little significance; but Kivengere's reaction to Governor Bashir's unjust action is crucial. 'I reacted with a certain amount of righteous anger, which in itself was not wrong. He reacted to my reaction publicly with a vehement resentment! I learned of his violent reaction and became justifiably more angry' (p. 160, #34). Kivengere recalled that he did not realize that he was getting into a tangle. But soon the Holy Spirit began his work of disentangling him. The Holy Spirit reminded him that 'If you are offering your gift at the altar and there remember that your brother has something against you, leave your gift there in front of the altar. First go and be reconciled . . . then come and offer your gift' (Matt 5:23, 24)' (p. 160, #34).

'I responded like the theologian in Luke 10:29 by asking, "And who is my brother?" Certainly, Lord, you can't mean that Muslim Governor? The Spirit reaffirmed to my conscience by saying, "Yes, I mean Governor Bashir—the Muslim!"' (p. 160, #34) Kivengere was left with only one option—to go. He went to Governor Bashir, his governor, with a certain amount of trepidation inside but he found him open to talk. He shared his part in their tangled relations, repented of his over-reaction to the governor's action, without justifying the reason for his reaction. 'The rest I left to the Lord; and as usual he did a good job of it, for the governor and I ended as friends'. Consequently, Governor Bashir offered to come 90 miles and open the spiritual renewal convention (Kabale Convention). Kivengere concludes the story: 'Death ended in resurrection through reconciliation and peace between us'. Here, he lifts their eyes from the ruin in which the conflict between himself and Governor Bashir was set to end. This would have been a situation of death; especially because of the fact of the indiscriminate military powers that Amin had given his soldiers like Bashir to deal with any situation the way they saw fit!

As he drew his reflection to a conclusion, he exhorted his hearers to remember that 'God treated Christ who had no sin, like sin for us—sinners—that we might become the righteousness of God through him' [2 Cor 5:21]. A costly identification, which achieved our reconciliation on the cross; now Paul is declaring to us, "We are therefore Christ's ambassadors"—of reconciliation! Holding out to all men God's offer of his friendship to them!' (p. 160, #35) . . . 'But if there is still a hostile reaction tucked away in one corner of your heart, you are guilty of frustrating Christ's reconciling love tonight, and of making sad the Holy Spirit' (p. 160, #36). Kivengere in his final appeal to them is expecting that they will do the work of an evangelist: 'the ministry of reconciliation'. This is reinforced by his passionate appeal: 'Let the chains, which are binding you, be broken by the power of his love. Let the Holy Spirit flood your heart with the love of God. Then, on the mission of reconciliation and peace, you can sing with Charles Wesley:

My Chains fell off,
My heart was free,
I rose, went forth,
And followed Thee' (p. 160–61, #36).

Here at the conclusion, Kivengere's greatest 'wake up call' to the evangelists is both passionate and intense. As they seek to go back and to the work of an evangelist, as they too would have expected, Kivengere called upon them in his strongest possible terms: 'Rise up! Come out! And follow him tonight!'.

6.4.1.11 Summary of The Evangelist's Ministry of Reconciliation: We Are Christ's Ambassadors: AO: 19830715

Kivengere's reflection lays out his carefully considered doctrine of reconciliation and its role in the ministry of an evangelist. His doctrine has a broad structure that enabled him to contain the themes he has dealt with on previous occasions, as discussed in chapter 5 and in this chapter. His structure reveals the need for reconciliation; the source of Christian reconciliation which restores peace in life; the nature of the Christian reconciliation which he divides into personal, communal, and universal; the method of Christian reconciliation, he entered into the arena of the broken relations at the lowest point and he went all the way to the cross for us; the effects of

Christian reconciliation and peace; reconciliation and the evangelist; and practical points for peace and reconciliation.

The reflection shows that, according to Kivengere, reconciliation and the resulting peace is not just one of the Christian doctrines in the New Testament, it is the lifeblood of all Christian doctrines. It is the message to be preached by evangelists if the church of Jesus Christ is not to suffer a kind of spiritual malnutrition or starvation. The doctrine of reconciliation is to be preached, rooted in Jesus Christ, lest confusion or heresy arise. But the evangelist must first be reconciled to God and to fellow man, before preaching the gospel of reconciliation as an ambassador of Christ. Kivengere viewed the ministry of reconciliation as a precious treasure from God entrusted to us, and his audiences are exhorted to have this same perspective on reconciliation.

While Kivengere preached reconciliation mainly using the language of reconciliation from Pauline texts, he also drew upon other gospel reconciliation passages.

Clear evidence of his influences can be determined in this theological reflection. His theological exegesis has affinity with Barth's approach and elements of Barth's Christological doctrine of reconciliation are discernable. The Revival influence of sequential preaching building to a climax and 'commissioning' believers into the world to preach, is clear as he follows the same patterns.

This reflection had the potential impact of influencing the understanding of reconciliation by the evangelists for 133 nations, putting the doctrine of reconciliation afresh to the churches of the world through their messages as they returned home. Perhaps it helped to correct a wrong doctrine of reconciliation or to restore the right balance of the doctrine, or to improve the practical preaching of reconciliation.

6.5 Conclusion on Non-Explicit Reconciliation Passages

This chapter has examined eight sermons that touched on the theme of reconciliation comprising of four sermons from non-explicit reconciliation passages,[119] and four thematic addresses.[120] The findings from these sermons were supplemented by examining a late theological reflection on the doctrine of reconciliation by Kivengere.[121] This material acts as a control to the sermons on explicit reconciliation passages. They show that he preached reconciliation even when the text does not mention reconciliation, thus revealing reconciliation as of central concern to Kivengere.

The sermons have shown that Kivengere attached great importance to the doctrine of reconciliation. This doctrine was so close to his heart that he believed that it is a precious message entrusted to believers by God to be preached to redeem the world. It is the heartbeat or the lifeblood of the evangelist's ministry. It is not simply another doctrine of the New Testament but it is the central message of the Christian gospel.

The primary role of the church of Jesus Christ, therefore, according to Kivengere is to embody and preach the message of reconciliation to a broken world. If this doctrine is properly preached, Kivengere believes that it will bring healing, satisfaction and transformation to Africa, America or anywhere in the world. He is convinced that there is still more that the Lord will do before he return. In the meantime, the message of reconciliation is to be preached and this is the primary message that the church must preach.

For his part, Kivengere's preaching shows influences from Keswick, the Revival, Karl Barth, and Markus Barth, alongside the influence of Paul himself and his doctrine of reconciliation. The method of his preaching reconciliation in the non-explicit passages shows great affinity with Barth's Theological Exegesis. The Old Testament and the New Testament texts that he expounded were the place of discovering God, and his nature and work in Jesus Christ, which gave rise to expressions of wonder, like 'what a discovery', 'what a coming'. He discovered the fascinating nature and love of God, demonstrated in Jesus Christ. He discovered the love of God who

---

119. Festo Kivengere, 'The Cross And World Evangelization', Sermon Transcript, 1974, AO: 19740725.Kivengere, 'The Triumph of God's Glory'. Kivengere, 'A New Way of Seeing Jesus'.Kivengere, 'The Pastor's Joy'.

120. See *Revival Begins at the Cross, Remove the Masks, Peace and Victory for the Christian, The Covenant of Love*.

121. Kivengere, 'The Evangelist's Ministry of Reconciliation'.

reconciles alienated humanity back to God. And, God, in Jesus Christ, came and redeemed humanity from alienation, making man his friend. This is good news. This good news God entrusted to believers who are reconcilers with this message into the world as God's ambassadors. This message brings peace, healing, and transformation into the situation of brokenness in the world.

The addresses in this chapter show the significance of preaching reconciliation rooted in Jesus Christ and preaching a Christ-centred doctrine of reconciliation. Whether he was in Africa or abroad, the content of his message was reconciliation, centred in Jesus Christ. That is what mattered more than the context of his preaching, important as the various contexts were. His theological exegesis helped him to stick to the subject matter, God, in Jesus Christ, who reconciled us and gave us the ministry of reconciling people back to God. There lies his methodological genius.

The distinctive contribution of these sermons is that they show the breadth of his understanding of the concept of reconciliation by his employing the concepts of 'healing wounds', 'catching a new vision', 'a new way of seeing', 'liberation', 'love', 'peace', 'forgiveness', 'repentance', 'demonstration', 'greetings and welcome'. They display him embodying the message of reconciliation by reconciling during his preaching, and bridging the gap between him and his audience' while preaching. He deliberately repeated earlier concepts of reconciliation that we have already examined in chapter 5 and had a vision of a world reached with the gospel of reconciliation so that the Christians may live in peace.

The fact of his recognition as a speaker, to being invited to strategic evangelical mission conferences around the world to preach the message of reconciliation, shows Kivengere acting as a Revival leader. He was a preacher who gained the trust and confidence of international leaders of his generation, and who therefore had the opportunities to influence and shape the world with the message of reconciliation. He was a preacher with a clear and urgent message that he used to mobilize the world for evangelism and influence the life and ministry of pastors in America and elsewhere. His preaching reconciliation to 133 nations at Amsterdam provided a grand-scale opportunity for his message to make a large impact on the world. This was at a time when he was at his fullest potential as a world-class evangelical preacher out of Africa in the twentieth century. Within the next five years he fell sick and died from leukaemia. His sermons had great potential to influence the life of his audiences in Africa, America and the world. He accomplished all this with his preaching of reconciliation.

In chapter 5 we noted that Kivengere preached reconciliation strongly when he preached from Pauline passages making explicit references to the doctrine. But in a sense, this may not show us anything about his own relationship to this doctrine, for, as any preacher true to the text in front of them, he may preach it simply because the text demands he do so. The catalogue of sermons assembled for this thesis acts as some kind of control, however, for it shows from the titles, texts, and year that for the most part his preaching consistently turned to reconciliation and for a long period of time he had been reflecting over this doctrine. A more careful control, chapter 6, therefore examined some addresses based on non-explicit reconciliation passages. This chapter has demonstrated that he preached the message of reconciliation from non-explicit texts and, this in turn, shows without a doubt that reconciliation was central to Kivengere's heart.

CHAPTER SEVEN

Analysis and Conclusions— The Role of the Doctrine of Reconciliation in Kivengere's Preaching

7.1 Collection of Kivengere's Sermons

The role of the doctrine of reconciliation in Kivengere's preaching in the period 1971–1988 in Uganda and beyond could not be analyzed unless his sermons that were scattered in different archives around the world—Africa, United States of America, Europe, Australia, Asia, and New Zealand— were not first collected and catalogued. So the first contribution this study made towards analyzing reconciliation in Kivengere's preaching was to assemble a collection of over 500 transcriptions of Kivengere's unpublished sermons and catalogue them. Besides the transcripts already in existence, fourteen audio sermons were transcribed in preparation for this research.[1] Sometimes transcripts were corrected and clarified by listening to the audio tapes, thus improving the quality of the collection.

With this wealth of primary material, this study undoubtedly is in a better position than those of previous scholars to examine the content of Kivengere's preaching in general, and the doctrine of reconciliation in particular, engaging with the primary sources enabled the author to

---

1. All these unpublished sermon transcriptions we have now deposited in the Moore Theological College Library.

get very close to what historically Kivengere was doing in his preaching of reconciliation.

Since these collected sermons form another primary source for the biography of Kivengere, the history of Uganda and Ugandan Christianity, one contribution of this thesis has been to illuminate further, and sometimes to correct, what has been previously written in these areas.[2]

7.2 Evaluation of Method

The method we employed in this study examined Kivengere's sermons with the social context in view. The sermons were therefore gleaned for what they expressed of Kivengere's circumstances, history, thinking and beliefs. In particular, this study focused on the content of his preaching of reconciliation. It asked the more fundamental questions of *whether reconciliation represents a coherent 'biblical-theological' theme in Kivengere's preaching; what if any, is its role; and, in turn how through the preaching of this theme Kivengere sought to make an impact upon the social context into which he preached.*

As the sermons were examined, we noted the emergence of a distinctive focus on reconciliation and several sub-themes that link with reconciliation, such as the cross of Christ, atonement, the love of God, time, and the change Christ has made, the importance of the 'heart', the mission to the Gentiles, creation, Covenant of Grace, promise-fulfilment. Kivengere asserts reconciliation as the answer to the biblical theology debate about what is 'the centre' of the Bible, or the centre of Paul's theology, which then affects his method, which can be described as 'Theological Exegesis'.

My method examined each sermon for elements of Kivengere's biblical theology, both in terms of his content and the exegetical expository approach that is evident in it. This was applied to Kivengere's preaching of reconciliation from two types of sermons, labelled here 'explicit' and 'non-explicit', depending upon whether or not they were preached on passages

---

2. See Chapters One, Two, and Five where corrections are made in the appropriate place in the footnotes.

explicitly mentioning reconciliation. The sample of twenty-six sermons gave close attention to both his reconciliation language and his theological exegesis. The non-explicit sermons (chapter 6) acted as a 'control' for the explicit reconciliation sermons (chapter 5), demonstrating the centrality of reconciliation as a subject that clearly mattered to him. Reconciliation was never an arbitrary thought, but was very close to his heart and he reflected deeply on it for a long period of time.

As well as the Pauline doctrine of reconciliation itself, the study proposed five angles of influences to be applied to analyzing Kivengere's preaching of reconciliation, namely, the early Keswick Movement, the East African Revival, Karl Barth, Markus Barth and Pauline Theology. Applied to Kivengere's preaching of reconciliation, our analysis found evidence that each of these angles, to varying degrees, influenced Kivengere's preaching in both style and content.

7.3 Towards Kivengere's Homiletics

Investigating *whether reconciliation represents a coherent 'biblical-theological' theme in Kivengere's preaching, and in turn how his preaching sought to make an impact upon those circumstances* has involved provisional findings about Kivengere's homiletics, even though this study did not set out to examine the preaching style of Kivengere. However, in the process of our investigation of Kivengere's preaching of reconciliation, we have made attempts to understand it at points where it is relevant to Kivengere's use of the Christian doctrine of reconciliation.

7.3.1 Content Determines Style

Analyzing the Christian doctrine of reconciliation and the examination of the content of Kivengere's preaching cannot bypass his style of preaching. The focus on the content of his preaching has nevertheless yielded some fruit in regard to style. For example, in most of the sermons, Kivengere bridges the gap between the preacher and his audience. Frequently he is using deferential expressions that close the gap between him and his audience: expressions like, 'including myself', 'God paid for my sin and yours', 'us', 'you', etc. This stylistic feature bringing preacher and audience together can be seen as a direct outworking of his reconciliation message proclaimed by the sermons' content.

As Barth's 'Theological Exegesis' centres on reconciliation in Christ so that the event of Christ then yields an approach to Scripture, the same order is true for Kivengere: content determines style. The reconciliation content also determined the style of illustrations chosen. As was common in the Revival preaching, these drew upon biographical and autobiographical accounts of individuals being reconciled to each other.

On the basis of this research, future discussions of the role of the doctrine of reconciliation in Kivengere's preaching in the period 1971–1988 must give greater attention to its content, rather than its style. This is necessary because, as our analysis has shown, the content exerted a profound influence on Kivengere the man and the Revival preacher, and this was what shaped his preaching. The sermons show Kivengere thinking theologically about the world and about how human lives are changed. Because the content of his message is the same across a variety of audiences, this shows that it does not matter where you are, what matters is the message of reconciliation. The *context* is immaterial but *content* is essential. Whatever the context, it showed great brokenness, which he viewed as a demonstration of the need for reconciliation, first with God, then with other human beings. He believed preaching the gospel of reconciliation brought about this reconciling work. The only way to bring the reconstruction of a broken society, like Uganda in this period, was to preach the gospel of God's reconciliation in Christ. This calls for people to be first reconciled with God and then with each other and this is the only way to rebuild the nation.

7.3.2 Kivengere the Preacher of Reconciliation

My examination of the sermons has revealed a more significant and much clearer portrait of Kivengere as a preacher of reconciliation. They reveal him as a preacher not only shaped and gripped by the doctrine of reconciliation, but as a reconciler in the way he looks at the whole of life.[3] He not only

---

3. Scholars from different angles, have noted that Kivengere saw life through the lens of reconciliation. Senyonyi, 'Philosophy of Evangelism', 135. Russell, 'Ministry of Reconciliation', 304–07. Quinn, 'Kivengere, Festo'. Accessed October 4 2011. Watson,

preached reconciliation but also embodied the message of reconciliation. He used experiences from his own life, marriage, and church to illustrate that reconciliation was not simply a philosophy to be talked about, but a practical way of life. He also used biographical material of other people to show the relevance of reconciliation to his audience. The gospel of Jesus Christ, the crucified reconciler, shaped his thought and outlook on life, and also necessarily shaped his sermons. He believed that the world was still redeemable and the message that would bring hope and transformation was reconciliation.

The sermons show Kivengere as an evangelical who believed that the content and source of his message, reconciliation, is God's message to his audiences and he presented the message of reconciliation as such. He took a verse or two, or a group of verses and presented the truths in the text with great care not to make the message his own ideas. However, at moments in paraphrasing the texts, the sermons show he adds his glosses. For example, Kivengere adds his glosses to Romans 5:8: 'still strangers', 'and sinners', 'and rebels', 'Christ at that time, for those who don't love Him' (p. 10, #14). When Jesus said, 'He who loves his life' [John 12:25 NKJV] Kivengere glosses: 'He who loves himself', 'He who makes himself at the centre', 'He who makes his life all there is about it'. Nevertheless, in preaching reconciliation, he declared for his audiences all that God does for mankind and all that God requires in response to his message of reconciliation. His reconciliation message focused on Christ and the cross of Christ; and, in this way his preaching sustained a Christ-centred and cross-focused theme throughout his life and ministry.

Kivengere's preaching shows him as a preacher with a single message: reconciliation. In the sermons, his purpose is clear: he informs, he persuades, and he boldly calls forth a response to God's reconciling love and asks his audiences to reach out into the world as God's ambassadors for reconciliation. He sets forth the example of how his audiences may respond to the message of reconciliation: repentance (Matt 5:23), forgiveness, love, hope, prayers, and mission.

Confidence in the Living God, 9. Shaw, *Global Awakening*, 107. Cassidy, 'Festo Has Died But He Still Speaks', 8.

Kivengere is an engaging preacher: he engages the minds of his audience to see the reason why God requires them to be reconciled with him—that in Jesus Christ they may gain peace from God and with each other. His preaching is openly against long and empty theological words that have no life in them, and against attempts at reconciliation that arise out of church committee meetings. He recommends reconciliation that comes from the love of God and strikes at the heart of a sinner. Only then the sinner can without fear reach out to others and put right their wrongs with each other.

Kivengere's sermons show his preaching is life-centred. His message of reconciliation arises from 'the very heart of God', namely, 'the cross', and the message of the cross addressed directly to the heart of his audiences. His preaching communicates the practical truth about God as it bears on the present existence of humanity. His preaching is clearly concurrently applicatory—there is no section that he designates application—thus, he constantly called upon his audiences to hear the truth of what God is saying.

7.3.3 Kivengere the Preacher of Revival

The present study redresses two negative criticisms reported by Reed and Rwabyoma. According to Reed's report, Kivengere's style of preaching, 'African style', associated with the East African Revival, was contrasted to the 'linear, closely reasoned and often abstract presentations typical of Western Christianity'. Reed claimed that he relied upon 'a "felt", experiential response, rather than a thought or logical response'.[4] This study found out that the content of Kivengere's sermon was Christocentric. Hence, his style of preaching was dictated by the content of his message. Because Jesus Christ is the content of his message, he is also the centre of his message. In this way, his message is authoritative and the Bible whose central message is Christ the reconciler defines it. His style of preaching makes the Bible speak for itself and to the needs of his various audiences.

Rwabyoma's criticism was that Kivengere's preaching lacked a logical structure, and hence to hazy minds was taxing and confusing.[5] This study has demonstrated that Kivengere's method of 'Theological Exegesis', made

---

4. Reed, *Walking in the Light*, 223.
5. See Chapter One, 3.3.3 'Peter R. Rwabyoma 2007'.

him focus on the big theme of the Bible—reconciliation centred in Jesus Christ. As he looks at the brokenness in the world and God's way of addressing it through his reconciling love in Jesus Christ, then he is not interested in a structured point-by-point sermon since he does not preach verse-by-verse. In fact, we argue that because his content dictates his style of preaching, it is logical that his 'Theological Exegesis' does not have to be forced into, for example, a three-point structure.

This study also found that Kivengere redressed wrong teaching on reconciliation, insisting that reconciliation was not to be taught merely with a theological and personal meaning at the expense of the wider social meaning, but that there must be a right balance between the two. Kivengere especially stressed that Jesus must not be sidelined in preaching reconciliation.

7.4 Five Angles of Influences

Having stated the historical and biographical context of Kivengere's preaching of reconciliation in Uganda in chapter two, and observed how it set him up for his preaching, our investigation proceeded to establish in chapter 3 a trajectory of five angles of influences on Kivengere: from the early Keswick Convention to the East African Revival, from Karl Barth to Markus Barth, as well as the Pauline theology of reconciliation itself.

These five angles of influences provided a trajectory that assisted in analyzing the centrality of the role of the doctrine of reconciliation in Kivengere's preaching between 1971–1988. This New Testament theme in Kivengere's preaching and ministry has not previously been investigated by academic research in Kivengere scholarship. This biblical theological investigation has opened up a new window into understanding his thought and preaching, and into the potential impact of his sermons.

7.4.1 Early English Keswick Influence

On the influence of the early English Keswick Movement, Kivengere appears well acquainted with the Keswick teaching and preaching on the following theological issues: sin, repentance, new birth, separation, the Holy Spirit and the victorious life, and gospel service.

Kivengere preached about sin—carefully explaining it. He said that sin is missing the mark of God's standard of righteousness. Sin is when believers live at cross-purposes with the will of the Father. It is a spiritual disease with paralyzing effects in the life of believers and it cannot be eradicated by human efforts. As a solution to the paralyzing effects of sin, Christ offers to us, here and now, the freedom from the power of all known sin by his precious blood that washes believers clean. Although the decisive factor for successful counteraction of sin is the blood of Jesus Christ, the believers ought to accept it by faith, inviting Jesus to come into their life. This allows the Holy Spirit through Christ to counteract their sinful nature.

There is sin in the believer. As such, sin hinders the flow of the Holy Spirit in the life of believers. With sin blocking the flow of the Holy Spirit in the life of believers, it makes the testimony of believers sound dry. This situation of sin leads to brothers keeping each other at a distance from one another. Sin still exists in the new community, the church, which Jesus brought about through his death and resurrection.

He acknowledges that all through the last one hundred years (1875–1975), Keswick teaching was concentrated on sin in the life of a believer and the Keswick Convention always started with a reminder of sin in the heart of the believer. It is not surprising that his sermons also address the hearts of believers. The sermons emphasize repentance and forgiveness of sin from Christ, and the release that comes with it. The sermons show that living in sin is a major problem for believers; however, the ensuing redemptive work of Christ counteracts the sin.

Traces of the Keswick call to a victorious life are clear in Kivengere's sermons. He emphasized the believer's need to live 'the Christ-life' as opposed to the 'self' or 'I'. His four thematic addresses explored in chapter 6: Revival Begins at the Cross, Remove the Masks, Peace and Victory for the Christian, and the Covenant of Love, besides the sermon In Christ: AO: 19790429, [#2], express from many angles what happens when the believer 'yields' to Christ—Christ becomes 'the centre' of the believer's life. Christ gives the believer 'a new dynamic' to life. Christ becomes 'the foundation' of life for the believer. Christ becomes 'the liberator' in the believer's life and Christ becomes 'the healer' of the believer's life, hence, the believer now lives the victorious Christian life.

The final day of the Keswick Convention was given to sending out people in mission. The missionaries like Joe Church, the missionary of Rwanda mission, could only come to Uganda in the first place because of the Keswick Convention teaching of sending out people in mission. The teaching on sending out people in mission helped to provide later influences on Kivengere. For example, Keswick Conventions spread all over the world as a result of its emphasis of mission including Uganda. Here the focus on Mission-Service extended its influence directly on Kivengere's call. His own missionary call to Tanganyika came at the 1945 Kabale Convention. In Australia the off-shoots of the Keswick Conventions such as Katoomba, Belgrave Heights in Victoria, in turn, played a role in recruiting for CMS from Australia, which lead to Kivengere's close friendship with Australian missionaries in Tanganyika and, through this link, to his further ministry in Australia (and beyond). While in Tanzania, as well as forming friendships with missionaries of CMS, Kivengere did so with those of other denominations, giving him life-long ministry friendships with people such as Don Jacobs of the Mennonite missionaries to East Africa and Billy Graham, from the Baptist denomination.

The appeal for believers to go out into mission service shaped Kivengere's life. It also shaped his preaching reconciliation. For example, continually in the sermons Kivengere exhorts his audience to reach out into the world with good news. Even without the convention week, he took the Keswick message of reaching out in mission and made it transportable to many different places. What was done across a week in the convention was now done within a single sermon.

Another Keswick emphasis is seen when Kivengere exhorts his audience to prayer as a means of supporting the people and work of God. He exhorted his audience to practical Bible teaching or living. He published a few of his sermons, as a ministry of literature that he hoped could bring encouragement to the discouraged and transformation to believers. He tells in his 'Preface' to *I Love Idi Amin*, 'It is a book of praise to encourage those who feel discouraged because of the circumstances in which they find themselves'[6] and in the 'Preface' to *Revolutionary Love*: 'I pray that the shared

---

6. See 'Preface' in Kivengere, *I Love Idi Amin*.

messages of this book—by the power of the Holy Spirit—you will open up to this revolutionary love of Christ and experience a radical transformation of the foundations of your entire systems of life'.[7] This publishing work can also, therefore, be understood against his commitment to mission.

Being involved with the modern Keswick movement also contributed to Kivengere's growth. Clear Bible exposition with its emphasis on the centrality of Jesus Christ, no doubt reinforced the strong emphasis on the centrality of Christ in Kivengere's preaching of reconciliation. Although he acknowledges John Stott's influence upon him—and the fact that John Stott set a new pace for modern Keswick Bible exposition with his clear, analytical, and deep biblical exposition, and his unwavering emphasis on the centrality of Jesus Christ—Kivengere does not emulate John Stott's approach of Bible exposition. Indeed, modern Keswick has not influenced him on this area at all. His Bible exposition has more affinity with Karl Barth's 'theological exegesis'. We explain more on this in the section below, exploring the influence from Karl Barth. Here we simply flag it to show the difference between his approach to Bible exposition and John Stott's expository approach.

The East African Revival embraced many denominations and Christian organizations: the Mennonites, which led to his link with Don Jacobs, later Kivengere's Chairman for AEE; Africa Inland Mission, which led to his close friendship and preaching together at conventions such as the 1985 Kabale Convention; and, the Baptists, which led to his link with his long-time friend Billy Graham and with the Billy Graham International Ministries. The ecumenical spirit of modern Keswick, so applauded by Billy Graham at the 1975 Keswick centenary celebrations, was not new for Kivengere. However, his involvement with modern Keswick and his friend Billy Graham would have further reinforced these commitments.

7.4.2 Revival Influence

Kivengere openly acknowledged the influence of the Revival upon him. He was converted under men who cried when they talked about hell, and laughed when they talked about heaven. Although Kivengere's sermons do

---

7. See 'Preface' in Kivengere, *I Love Idi Amin*, 8.

not display a great interest in these eschatological realities, when these men talked about the heart of a sinner they showed deep concern, and their influence in this area is much more apparent. His preaching shows him preaching victorious Christian living with stories and testimonies from the Revival brethren.

His preaching shows how the brethren managed to sustain their Christian testimony in the midst of much evil displayed by the political turmoil and suffering in East Africa. In Uganda, Luwum, a Mulokole from Northern Uganda, faced the wrath of evil from the murderous rule of Idi Amin, for the sake of the love of God and his people. Even though he was living in exile from Amin, whose hit men were feared to be trailing Kivengere in exile, Kivengere still refused to hate Amin. Because of the cross of Christ he learned to love Amin.

Kivengere used stories of the brethren suffering in the Mau Mau uprising and yet still loving their tormentors. He tells similar stories from the Hutu versus Tutsi revolution in Rwanda, and from the 'Simba' rebellion in Eastern Zaire and others from Burundi. In the midst of evil, the Revival did not succumb to living a defeated life. Christ living in the believer, moment by moment, defeated evil, thus making possible victorious Christian living. The influence of the Revival over him enabled him to '"catch the little foxes that spoil the vine" (Song 2:15), always concerned about little things which short-circuit the power of God in his life as a believer, keeping short accounts with God, and living with great integrity before his Lord in all matters of detail in personal life'.[8]

As a child of the Revival, Kivengere encountered the early Keswick teaching that emphasized not what we do for God but what God does for us. His sermons are full of autobiographical illustrations where he struggles with the Lord on some personal crisis in his life but in the end he 'lets go', he surrenders to the Lord and 'lets God', by faith, have his way in his life and situations. In the sermons he expressed total surrender to God.

Kivengere changed the well-honed Keswick emphasis on the Spirit filling the life of a believer to Jesus being the content that fills the believer's life. Kivengere's preaching shows a most significant difference from this major

---

8. Michael, 'Forward', 3.

Revival influence. This shift from 'Spirit-filling' to 'Jesus-filling' is critical in his preaching of reconciliation, because it centred on Christ. For instance, in 1972 at Keswick Convention (9–20 July) on 'Christ the Liberator', he said: 'When the Holy Spirit came down on the day of Pentecost ... He actually came to bring the risen Lord, the one who died, and enthroned him on the heart of a believer and that heart which was in darkness is flooded with light, flooded with liberty: the liberator is inside'.[9] He argued that believers want life but they have 'not yet discovered that when you live for your self you become empty'.[10]

The fundamental reality of an empty life demands filling—and Jesus comes to fill it. In the sermon 'Love's Quick Way',[11] he explained: 'I am not always full of love, not always seeing [Jesus] clearly. Self-indulgence has a way of creeping in. Sometimes I am thoroughly empty and have to say so in public. But what I have discovered is that *Jesus loves to fill empties!* All I need to do is to keep open to him and to admit frankly what's wrong. He does the rest'.[12]

Here we still see the Keswick emphasis on a deficiency of life that needs to move towards cure, but Kivengere quite clearly and explicitly changes 'Spirit-filling' in the life of a believer to Jesus being the *content* that fills the believer's life. However, Kivengere is not so much countering the Revival tradition in which he was brought up in the aspect of 'Spirit-filling', as he is simply being more precise. Throughout his sermons, Jesus is never separated from the Holy Spirit, but the emphasis and focus of attention must always be Jesus Christ himself.

7.4.3 Influences from Karl Barth

Kivengere's preaching of reconciliation was reinforced by Barth's doctrine of reconciliation and 'Theological Exegesis'. First, regarding the doctrine of reconciliation, the content of the doctrine of reconciliation is the knowledge of Jesus Christ who is the reconciling God, who in his freedom crosses

---

9. Kivengere, 'Christ the Liberator', 121.
10. Kivengere, 'Christ the Liberator', 120.
11. Kivengere, *Revolutionary Love*, 33.
12. Kivengere, *Revolutionary Love*, 130. (Emphasis added).

the frontier, becoming man. Kivengere's sermons show the brokenness of humanity concerned God, so he 'crossed frontiers' and came to man, lighting up our darkness and yet not diminishing his deity. Kivengere's sermons emphasize the cross, as the means God used to bring reconciliation between man and God.

Barth links Jesus Christ to man exalted and therefore reconciled by God. The reconciliation of the world with God takes place in the person of a man in whom, because he is also true God, the conversion of all men to God is an actual event. Kivengere's sermons are clear about reconciliation between God and man and man with each other. Kivengere understands reconciliation to have happened at a cosmic level because Jesus died for all on the cross at Calvary.

There is a difference between the two men, however. Whereas Karl Barth understood that reconciliation between God and man took place in Jesus Christ on the cross, Kivengere's sermons show that he emphasizes reconciliation in Jesus Christ from a personal experience. Although he recognized that Christ died on the cross for all, it is the personal experience of Jesus Christ in the life of a believer, which he emphasized in his theology of the cross. His opening and closing prayers in the sermons focus the Holy Spirit as the one who illuminates Jesus Christ and in the sermons in chapter 6, especially the four thematic addresses, the Holy Spirit's role of quickening the church or community and individuals.[13]

Secondly, from the first sermon under our inquiry, Kivengere's method of preaching shows great affinity with Karl Barth's 'Theological Exegesis'. The sermons show him as a preacher who does not expose the biblical text verse-by-verse, but who tends to preach around a central theme. Furthermore, the sermons in our selection show that his expositions focus on only one theme: reconciliation. This is the big theme that he preached, whether he was using explicit reconciliation passages, or non-explicit. His theological exegesis enabled him to deal with what he saw as the heart of

---

13. See the five basic structures of communication between God and humans throughout salvation history: These are (1) Love, (2) Spirit, (3) Word, (4) Deed, and (5) Life. Cf. Piennisch, Markus, *Kommunikation und Gottesdienst. Grundlinien göttlicher Zuwendung in Bibel und Verkündigung*. Neuhausen: Hänssler, 1995, 212–14.

the New Testament, the reconciling love of God gained through the death of Jesus Christ on the cross at Calvary.

The brokenness of humanity broke the Son of God, for reconciliation is costly: there is no reconciliation without the undying love of the Son of God. Jesus' undying love meant that, on behalf of all sinners, he did not avoid death, even the cruel death on the cross, to bring peace through his reconciling death. When Jesus died he became the means by which humanity gains restored friendship with God. For his own part, Kivengere embraced Jesus Christ the reconciler, abandoning the Bahima ancestral spirits that his father introduced into his worship in his early childhood. Kivengere's conversion story shows that he embraced the reconciling love of Christ who died on the cross for sinners, even him. This was the big message that Kivengere preached from large units of Scripture.

His exposition was not an atomistic exposition, which is verse-by-verse. Even when the modern Keswick movement exposed Kivengere to John Stott's systematic expository approach to the biblical text, Kivengere did not follow it. As is unsurprising in evangelical circles, he concurs with John Stott on the centrality of the Lordship of Jesus Christ. Well before entering into seminary, the Revival, with its Keswick Convention influence, had already drummed this into Kivengere. But, this centrality of Christ was, for Kivengere, the point around which his theological exegesis turned, yielding a constant and deep interest in reconciliation.

Whether addressing a Ugandan audience, or an audience from other parts of the world, Kivengere's theological exegesis, led him to identify and articulate reconciliation as the central New Testament theme and the theme through which other biblical themes find a link to the purposes of God revealed in Jesus Christ, whether 'the Lordship of Christ', 'the cross of Christ', 'the Love of God', 'the Grace of God', 'the working of the Holy Spirit', 'healing', 'spiritual gifts', 'repentance and forgiveness', 'mercy and justice', 'eschatology', 'judgment', 'hope', 'peace', 'holiness', 'sin'.

Being convinced that the centre of the New Testament gospel is the ministry of reconciliation, he also spoke of this being God's unfinished task, which he has placed in the hands of all converts to Jesus Christ, who are all his ambassadors. Once converted to Jesus Christ, you are a reconciler, a receiver of 'a precious treasure' from God: the ministry of reconciliation.

Believing this is 'a precious treasure' God has entrusted to us, at the 1983 Amsterdam Congress, for example, Kivengere used this conclusion from his theological exegesis to critique its neglect or its misunderstanding in Christian teaching. He is not critiquing off the top of his head or arbitrarily: he knows what he is talking about this topic and theology. Reconciliation was so deeply embedded in his life and thought that he felt the need to persuade other influential evangelists to join him in preaching from this theological centre.

He acknowledges that reconciliation was at the heart of Paul's theology since the apostle's Damascus road encounter with the Lord Jesus. Once this encounter placed Jesus at the centre of Paul's thought and life, it remained the central theme of his theology. Fascinated with Paul's reconciliation, Kivengere frequently compares his conversion with Paul's encounter with the Lord on the Damascus road. The sermons show Kivengere understands Paul's reconciliation to Christ to be the source of his overwhelming love for Christ. The love of Christ then compelled Paul to share the gospel of Christ's reconciling love for all. Operating with Christ as the subject matter, Kivengere's theological exegesis therefore brought Paul's conversion very close to the centre of his account of reconciliation. However, it is intriguing that the sermons as well as the catalogue shows that Kivengere never for once preached from Acts 9, the story of Paul's conversion. Nevertheless, because the story of Paul's conversion was centred on Christ, Paul's experience of reconciliation shaped Kivengere's understanding and articulation of his own reconciliation.

His sermons show that he understood Paul as a Pharisee, who understood himself to be blameless according to the standards of the ten commandments, and who therefore believed that he was not against God in being against the Christians. Yet, on his conversion, Paul came to realize that he had been 'alienated' or 'estranged' from God, because in persecuting Christians he persecuted Christ, who is himself God.

We have found out that Kivengere consistently used the Revival influence, for every explanations starts with the cross and ends with the cross. So he starts with the cross in explaining reconciliation, then works his explanation through the rest of the Scripture but will end with the cross.

7.4.4 Influences from Markus Barth

The study has established that Kivengere openly confessed his acknowledgement of his New Testament teacher Markus Barth, but across the board of twenty-six sermons analyzed, evidence for Kivengere making much use of Markus Barth's vocabulary has been small. It has confirmed that Kivengere studied New Testament under Markus Barth, that Kivengere was influenced by Markus Barth's encouragement of his student to always be excited at new discoveries of insights in Scripture. It has confirmed his use of Ephesians 2:14–18 language.

Thus, these elements of Markus Barth's influence cannot be ignored from the sermons analyzed. Few as they are, still they help to paint the portrait of Kivengere the preacher and his reading of Scripture. In fact because Kivengere gives Scripture a high place in his preaching, both discovery and excitement into new insights from Scripture go together.

7.4.5 Influences from Pauline Theology

On the angle of Pauline theology, reconciliation referred to the restoration of relationships between God and man. Paul emphasized humanity being reconciled to God: (2 Cor 5:18–21, Rom 5:10–11, Eph 2:14–17, and Col 1:20–22).

Kivengere appears to be well acquainted with the theological dimension of the Pauline doctrine of reconciliation. He states that reconciliation begins with God the initiator of reconciliation. In his love for humanity, God in Christ first moved into the human situation. This is in line with Paul's theology of reconciliation. According to Paul, reconciliation begins with God who reaches out in his grace to humanity. Since reconciliation is an act that begins with God's grace, reconciliation is an act of God's grace. Kivengere defines God's grace as God's undeserved love. Along with scholars such as Ralph P. Martin, Kivengere asserts that reconciliation is the central theme of Paul's theology of salvation.[14]

In the Romans 5:1–11 passage Kivengere does not speak about justification (Rom 5:1) and the Wrath of God (Rom 5:9). Paul speaks about these two important concepts in the text, but Kivengere does not concern

---

14. E.g., Martin, *Reconciliation*.

himself with them. This may be because Kivengere assumes justification and the wrath of God, because in Romans 5:1 the result of reconciliation is peace in God and all the benefits that it brings, then this peace is based on grace and therefore there is no need to explain justification. Since Paul states that God has justified believers, believers will be delivered from the wrath of God on the day of judgment. Although this may explain Kivengere's neglect of justification and the wrath of God, it is nevertheless intriguing that he would leave out such clear and major points so clearly laid out by Scripture. On the basis that Scripture in his sermons is granted priority over the preacher, Scripture then must be proclaimed in its totality. The fact that he does not speak of these explanations warrant our concern as there is something afoot with his interpretation of Romans 5:1–11. This raises a need for further investigation on his theology of eschatology, justification and the wrath of God.

In Colossians 1:20–22, Paul brings together the crucifixion and reconciliation in Christ: God was pleased 'through him [Christ] to reconcile to himself all things, whether on earth or in heaven, making peace by the blood of his cross. And you who were once alienated and hostile in thought, doing evil deeds, he has now reconciled in his body of flesh by his death'. The Pauline theology of reconciliation notes that what accompanies reconciliation is the unity of two people groups: Jews and Gentiles. The Jews and Gentiles have been united in one body, since the dividing wall between them has been broken down and they are united for the purpose that God might reconcile them 'in one body through the cross, thereby killing the hostility' (Eph 2:16).

In Pauline theology, reconciliation emerges as a counterpart to justification. It marks the end of alienation and hostilities between humanity and God. Reconciliation mends that rupture in the Creator and creature relationship. Reconciliation is gained 'through Christ' or 'in Christ' by his death on the cross at Calvary. God no longer counts sin to sinners, and as a result reconciliation leads to peace from God between the warring parties and peace to individuals.

7.5 Towards Kivengere's Doctrine of Reconciliation

The previous analyzes of Kivengere's sermons show his biblical theology of reconciliation can be summarized as follows.

God created the world with humanity to be in relationship or fellowship with him as partners in managing his world (Gen 1–3). This was a covenantal relationship between God and humanity based on God's trust that man will manage the world with him. In this creation, man was created in the 'image of God' for the purpose of fellowship with God, whose very nature is love. Following the disobedience of man to God, alienation and estrangement and enmity set in, thus cutting off the fellowship. Humanity was cut off from experiencing the love of God, the source of life. This unfortunate situation resulted in our fallen state. As an outcome of the fall, human beings have within them a constant longing for healing and transformation. Had there been no fall, possibly there would be no need for reconciliation!

Moved by his own love for his world, God freely poured his grace on humanity by sending his Son, Jesus Christ, into his created world. 'When all was dark and gloomy',[15] he came in love and redeemed humanity from the grip of sin and its terrible consequence, death. Because he died to redeem humanity, reconciliation is gained through his death and resurrection. This powerful love that loved human beings to the point of dying for them so that they might live for him, links directly to real human experience of life, both in its theological (with respect to God) and social (with respect to other people) dimensions. From this real history of God's salvation of humanity, reconciliation through Jesus Christ leads to a real life to be lived daily. The task and ministry of the church is to do 'the ministry of reconciliation' as its primary calling to enable believers to daily live a reconciled life. The church as a body of believers is called to be involved in the unfinished mission of God: 'the ministry of reconciliation'.

Kivengere placed the doctrine of reconciliation within the framework of God's covenant with creation. This covenant of God was made new in

---

15. See n.37 under relevant section, 2.2.2 'Preliminaries', Chapter Six, in the sermon Kivengere, 'The Triumph of God's Glory'.

Jesus Christ when he came into the gloomy and miserable world which, although created by God, has been so affected by the fall. By this covenant, God is committed to heal and reconcile the world to himself through Jesus Christ dying on the cross at Calvary. Kivengere's sermons show that God intervened in the renewal of his creation by Jesus coming into the situation of human crisis. This covenantal reconciliation cannot be directly applied in the political arena, nor can a church committee create it, because genuine reconciliation begins with God coming into the situation.[16]

Political or church structures are certainly groups of humans seeking to live peacefully together, and Kivengere would encourage this desire. But such groups always have the potential for violence to erupt since they are made up of mere humans. Politicians are committed to their own party's ideals. Church committees are often made of people who also reflect factional or tribal ideals. Thus, as Kivengere's biblical theology of reconciliation is reconstructed from his sermons, they also show him addressing the reconstruction and rehabilitation of Uganda on two fronts. He certainly mobilized physical reconstruction, but his core strategy was one of fundamental spiritual reconstruction. This study has therefore endorsed Senyonyi's conclusion that Kivengere emphasized that the greatest need in Uganda after Amin was 'spiritual reconstruction'.[17]

This conclusion supports Kivengere's statement, made immediately after he returned from exile, that without reconciliation from God, the reconstruction of Uganda was simply waiting for another round of violence. Kivengere's 'prophetic' claim from the theological perspective of 'reconciliation from God' reveals a further aspect of his understanding of this doctrine. Reconciliation with God is the way towards political reconstruction. Without reconciliation, Uganda cannot be reconstructed, and so Uganda needs 'the healing love of Jesus' as the only solution to the poison of Amin's rule.

---

16. For example when he had to repent and forgive Amin, it started with Jesus Christ coming into his situation and convicting him in the middle of a Good Friday service at All Soul Church, London.
17. See Chapter One, 3.2.2 'John M.M Senyonyi 1992'.

7.6 Impact of Kivengere's Preaching

Having analyzed the role of the doctrine of reconciliation in Kivengere's preaching, we now suggest the impact he was trying to achieve with his preaching of reconciliation. This study has opened a new opportunity to understand the impact of Kivengere's preaching. Understanding the doctrine of reconciliation in Kivengere's preaching goes a long way towards exposing how Kivengere's vision of reconciliation shows the impress of the role of reconciliation in his preaching in Uganda and further afield. Specifically, we have observed five areas that Kivengere's preaching of reconciliation had potential impact in the period 1971–1988.

7.6.1 Influence Through his Publications and Recognitions of his Leadership

Two general pieces of evidence for the impact of his preaching are worth mentioning. First, Kivengere influenced many through his published books: *When God Moves* (1973), *Love Unlimited* (1975), *I Love Idi Amin* (1977), *The Spirit is Moving* (1979), *Hope for Uganda and the World* (1980), *Revolutionary Love* (1981). Although it is hard to quantify the impact his books may have had, it indicates something of their influence that his books were reprinted and also translated in languages other than English—Swahili, German, Dutch, and French.

Second, his leadership and preaching gifts were recognized and appreciated by other people. Such recognition includes his membership of the Lausanne Committee on World Evangelization, his role as Vice Chairman of the International Bible Society, and the award to him of the International Freedom Prize (October 1977 in Oslo) for his courageous stand on freedom and human rights in Africa. He also received the Edward Browning award for the ministry of evangelism (1980) awarded by the World Council of Churches; St. Augustine Cross awarded by the Archbishop of Canterbury (1981) for a significant ministry to the Christian community worldwide. He was appointed that Chairman PACLA (1976), to which he invited top African church leaders and theologians (737 delegates).[18] He was invited

---

18. For a list of all African countries, except two that did not attend, see Cassidy, *Together*

to several high profile forums: National Press Club of Australia (1979), American Senate (March 1977), and the US Press Club. Alongside all the above opportunities, he had personal, pastoral and political opportunities that he used to influence and impact the lives of many as he offered the message of reconciliation to his different audiences. In particular, these forums gave him the opportunities to speak of the disease and agonies of Ugandans for whom he points their source of healing to be found in the reconciling love of God.

Few, if any, developments in Kivengere's preaching ministry have been more surprising or controversial than his success in penetrating the world with the gospel of reconciliation, in particular Uganda. It wasn't surprising, of course, that he would want to preach everywhere, and preach nothing but the message of reconciliation.

7.6.2 A Forerunner of the South African Truth and Reconciliation Commission

Kivengere was clear and consistent about his goal in visiting Apartheid South Africa. As always, he sought first to preach the simple gospel message of reconciliation as publicly and to as many people as possible. Second, he sought to encourage believers in these countries, including his friend, Desmond Tutu, with the message of reconciliation. This places Kivengere as one of the forerunners of the Truth and Reconciliation Commission that was later formed in South Africa.

7.6.3 Influence on World Leaders

No other Ugandan Churchman has had anything like the unique access to European and African leadership as Kivengere: the US government, the Commonwealth Heads of government, the African Union (formerly the Organization of African Union). In particular his relationship with Julius Nyerere of Tanzania he was influential to bring about most of the changes on the situation of Ugandans suffering under Amin.

He often made a point of distinguishing himself from being a politician competing with government leaders whenever he challenged the injustices

in One Place, 295.

and oppression on the people of God, in particular during Amin and Obote governments. No clergyman in Uganda faced Idi Amin headlong on the atrocities in Uganda to the extent that Janani Luwum and Kivengere did for the sake of the gospel.

7.6.4 Influence on Evangelical leaders and Preachers

At the Berlin Congress (1969), Lausanne (1974) and Amsterdam (1983), his presentations focussed on the message of reconciliation to the world through the participants, and in this way influenced the evangelical world. In Australia, his message of 1959 modelled for the churches in the Northern Territory a way of conducting fellowship gatherings. Indeed, it is not surprising that he was called 'the Billy Graham of Africa'. It is not any one man has been know of, but Kivengere's example, his hands and mind prepared with his AEE's assistance, set the hearts of Ugandans on the fire of the Spirit of God by his exhortation that became the ringing slogan of Greater Kampala Mission: 'See How God Loves Kampala'.[19]

Undergirding all these achievements, of course, was Kivengere's success—and phenomenal fame in Africa and beyond—as a proclaimer of reconciliation. Simply, but irrefutably put, no one has ever come close to matching him in the physical and spiritual rehabilitation of Uganda. The same is true of evangelism in Africa. For the period 1971–1988, the signature enterprise of his preaching ministry has been and remains the great arena open air crusade, organized by an experienced AE team along lines proven to be effective and involving the cooperation of many other church denominations. And, his preaching ministry culminated in a series of services in which Kivengere calls men and women to reconciliation in Jesus Christ. Thousands, even tens of thousands, come just leaning on the everlasting arms of God. The fact that multitudes of people have made or renewed a commitment to accept Jesus Christ as Lord of their lives, and that additional multitudes have been stirred to greater commitment to reconciliation centred in Jesus Christ has had an immense, if ultimately immeasurable, impact on local churches in Uganda and beyond.

---

19. See *African Enterprise*, Greater Kampala Mission.

A crucial aspect of Kivengere's impact has been his AEE. Though the organization grew out of his vision to evangelize African cities and universities, it has not only helped perpetuate and enlarge upon those successes, but has protected him from the kinds of scandals and problems that have destroyed several other notable independent ministries around the continent. The first of these roles is the more visible; the latter may well have been more important. An all-too-familiar pattern in independent evangelistic ministries has been for the ministry's board of directors to consist of the evangelist, a few relatives, a friendly lawyer, and a smattering of 'yes-men' and 'yes-women'. In such an arrangement, the opportunities for financial and ethical laxity are enormous. Kivengere and the evangelists he chose to help him, built the organization centred on the message of reconciliation.

7.6.5 Hope for Uganda and the World

The Primate of Australia, Marcus Loane, his friend, wrote in his *Memories*: '[Kivengere] saw his country's need second to none'.[20] We have shown that through the preaching of reconciliation he mobilized and rallied the nation of Uganda, offering the story of the peace of God, along with its consequent healing, forgiveness, reconstruction and rehabilitation. This gave *real* hope to the nation and beyond.

In 1971 when the church of Uganda was so divided that the level of its division constituted the possibility of a security threat, Amin feared to let the division which was along tribal lined degenerate into a national catastrophe. We have found out that Kivengere, though not yet a bishop, with his preaching of reconciliation, preached a message from Philippians 2:1–7, bringing the delegates to acknowledge the problem, repent, forgive each other, and enjoy healing and unity. This message changed and shaped the situation and the future of the COU.

In the same year (1972) in Glion, Switzerland, when preaching in the context of South African and East African branches of AEE fellowship, there were currents of racial tensions that disrupted fellowships between members of the two branches, especially Michael Cassidy and Kivengere. Kivengere gave his testimony, walked across the room and embraced

---

20. Loane, 'Memoirs', 100–105.

Michael. Donald Jacobs, chairman of the meeting, recalled that this expression was a turning point in the relationship of African Enterprise and AEE. Still in this same year (July 1972), at the Keswick Convention, England, he addressed the convention, appealed to them to experience a deeper way of doing 'ministry written in the blood of reconciliation' . . . 'A wounded world can never be healed except by a wounded hand'.[21]

In February 1973 he preached before 3,000 people in Kabale town where three fellow Christians had been publicly executed by firing squad. The following Sunday he preached in the area where the three men had lived. In all the sadness, the people burst into a praise song when he told them the story of their sons.

Still in 1973, during the first eighteen months of his time in exile, through his RETURN Programme, Kivengere raised '$300,000 from Australia alone to provide immediate relief aid to Ugandan refugees at the time of their escape, and scholarship assistance for students whose education was interrupted'.[22] He found placement for professional people in employment in African countries. He also sought assistance for the churches in the diocese of Rwanda, Burundi and Zaire, where training and development programmes were interrupted when their funds were frozen in Uganda. He met the emergency and physical needs of 11,000 Ugandan refugees in Nairobi, some with single grants, others on a continuing care programme. Additionally, 344 Ugandan refugees who were professionals were placed in jobs serving many African nations. 'These countries have appreciated the contribution of these refugees have made'.[23] Over two hundred students were placed in universities: 69 in Africa, 65 in the United States of America, 43 in Great Britain, 18 in West Germany and 11 in Australia.

In these ways the long-term impact of RETURN was to preserve and assist in acquiring necessary qualifications for service and leadership in the reconstruction of Uganda.

On an international level, Kivengere impacted the evangelical world through world leaders assembled at the 1974 Lausanne Congress on World

---

21. See Kivengere, 'Christ the Liberator', 122, in *The Keswick Week* 1972.
22. *Southern Cross* (July 1979): 11.
23. *Southern Cross* (July 1979): 11.

Evangelization. He preached during the plenary on the last day of the congress, the message of reconciliation centred in the person and work of Jesus Christ, calling upon evangelicals to unite and use their spiritual gifts well to build the body of Christ. His message of reconciliation, centred in Jesus Christ, impacted the world through the evangelical leaders at the congress. He believed that his message was the hope of Africa with all its conflicting problems.

Back in Uganda in July 1975, Kivengere preached the message of 'Christ's Love Reconciles Us'. Ten years later, in August 1985 Kabale Convention, he preached the message of reconciliation. Before that he went and reconciled with Governor Bashir. The following year, May 1976, together with Billy Graham, they preached to thousands gathered at the Nairobi Nyayo Stadium. They preached a message that brought hope to a broken people. Their theme was 'Jesus Frees and Unites'. In the same year, December 1976, he preached to high profile leaders. The impact of this gathering was that Professor Bosch broke down in the middle of the meeting and asked for forgiveness, opening everybody to reconcile with him. He brought deep healing and unity. He addressed the high profile Australian National Press Club, bringing a fresh understanding of the situation in Uganda to the Australian country and mobilizing the Commonwealth Governments to support the education of Ugandans in exile.

In August 1985 he proposed to the House of Bishops a peace plan for the restoration of peace in Uganda after the military coup (27 July 1985). It was a proposal he had thought over for a long time. It was well received, debated and a position was reached. His colleagues repented for not doing enough to bring peace in the country. In August 1986 held the Kabale Convention with the theme: Christ's Love Reconciles Us.

7.7 Summary

In chapter 1, the period 1971–1988 is identified as crucial for Kivengere's preaching of reconciliation. During these years he was at the centre of the life of the nation of Uganda. Chapter 2 explored the historical and biographical context in which he was preaching the doctrine of reconciliation.

In chapter 3, the potential influences on him from the Keswick Movement, the Revival, Karl Barth and Markus Barth, and a Pauline theology of the doctrine of reconciliation was stated. Chapter 4 mapped a reconciliation time-line of Kivengere's preaching from 1971–1988. In chapter 5, explicit reconciliation passages were then examined. In chapter 6, non-explicit reconciliation passages were examined and the presence of reconciliation in them was explained in terms of the closeness of reconciliation to Kivengere's heart. In chapter 7, his preaching of reconciliation was analyzed and its impact stated.

7.8 Further Research

The study has assembled a catalogue of more than 500 sermons of Kivengere. Without a doubt more research could be done along the following lines:

1. Did Kivengere drop out all of eschatology from his preaching? Where was the place of heaven and hell in his preaching? Why was Kivengere silent on justification by faith alone and the wrath of God in Romans 5:1–11?
2. Transcribing his audio sermons. This would add further readable sermons to the body of primary materials for research on Kivengere's sermons.
3. The thesis has produced a catalogue of Kivengere's transcribed sermons but it has by no means exhausted the list, and improvements are still needed.
4. Given his practice of illustrating reconciliation from human biographical accounts, these sermons may prove useful in extending our understanding of Kivengere's doctrine of reconciliation.
5. Further research can be built on the present work and explore more concretely the influence and impact of Kivengere's preaching.

7.9 Conclusion

The study sought to provide an analysis of the doctrine of reconciliation in Kivengere's sermons from a biblical theological perspective. Brokenness was the order of the day in Uganda and beyond in the period we have examined. Kivengere's message of reconciliation presented Jesus as a missionary of reconciliation, the only hope for Uganda and the world. To Ugandans and the rest of Africa who were bleeding with deep wounds, Jesus the Son of God, was the source of reconciliation and peace that he bought at the cost of his self-sacrificial death, which powers that be like evil behind—the powers of darkness—cannot give. Christians in Uganda (and non-Christians) lived a life in fear of Amin, who murdered Luwum, and after Amin, they lived a life of revenge. But Jesus brought reconciliation. Reconciliation was the message that brought peace and healing to the deep wounds. The message of reconciliation transformed Uganda.

Bibliography

1. Primary Sources

1.1 Works by Festo Kivengere

1.1.1 Books

Kivengere, Festo. *Hope for Uganda and the World: The Secret of Rehabilitation.* Edited by Dorothy Smoker. Nairobi: African Evangelistic Enterprise, 1980.

_____. *Hope for Uganda and the World: The Secret of Rehabilitation.* Rev. ed. Pasadena: African Enterprise, 1981.

_____. *I Love Idi Amin: The Story of Triumph Under Fire in the Midst of Suffering and Persecution in Uganda.* Edited by Dorothy Smoker. Old Tapan, N.J.: Revell, 1973.

_____. *Jesus Our Reality.* Kampala, Uganda: Uganda Church Press, 1973.

_____. *Love Unlimited.* Edited by Dorothy Smoker. Glendale, Ca.: G/L Regal, 1975.

_____. *Revolutionary Love.* Edited by Dorothy Smoker. Fort Washington, PA.: Christian Literature Crusade, 1983.

_____. *The Spirit Is Moving.* Rev. ed. Pasadena, Ca.: African Enterprise, 1979 [1976].

_____. *When God Moves.* Rev. ed. Pasadena: African Enterprise, 1976.

_____. *When God Moves in Revival.* Wheaton, Ill.: Tyndale House Publishers, 1977 [1973].

_____. *When God Moves You Move Too.* Accra: Asempa Publishers, 1973.

1.1.2 Articles

Kivengere, Festo. '25 Years of Ministry: 1962–1987'. *Africa Enterprise (Special Centre Opening Edition)* (September 1987): 1-3.

_____. 'A Challenge In Love'. *Decision* (July 1962): 8-9.

_____. 'Are You Starving?'. *Outlook* 17 (October 1987): 1-2.

_____. 'Awesome Growth in Troubled Uganda'. *Global Church Growth Bulletin* 19/5 (1982): 216-19.

_____. 'Bleeding Africa'. Pages 19-29 in *Proclaiming Christ to His World*. Edited by Hanne-Grete Brommeland and Knud Jørgensen. Oslo: Luther Forlag, 1984.

_____. 'Called to Make Friends'. *Outlook* 20 (Fall 1987): 2.

_____. 'Christ the Dynamic of Life'. Pages 183-194 in *The Keswick Week 1972*. London: Marshall, Morgan & Scott, 1972.

_____. 'Christ the Liberator'. Pages 116-122 in *The Keswick Week 1972*. London: Marshall, Morgan & Scott, 1972.

_____. 'Christ the Renewer'. Pages 66-75 in *The Keswick Week 1972*. London: Marshall, Morgan & Scott, 1972.

_____. 'Citizens of the Kingdom'. *Outlook* 18 (April 1981): 1.

_____. 'Introduction'. *Pastor: A Practical Guide For Church Leaders*. Nairobi, Kenya; Kampala, Uganda: Uzima Press Limited; Centenary Publishing House, 1983.

_____. 'Introduction'. Pages 4-8 in *Golden Jubilee Convention: Behold I Make All Things New: The Fifth Kabale Convention*. Kabale, Uganda: Anglican Diocese of Kigizi, 1985.

_____. 'Love and the Unlovable'. Pages 9-17 in *Revolutionary Love*. Pasadena, USA: African Enterprise, 1983.

_____. 'Love's Quick Way'. Page 82 in *Revolutionary Love*. Port Washington, Pennsylvania: Christian Literature Crusade, 1983.

_____. 'One Antidote Alone'. *Outlook* 16 (June 1979): 1.

_____. 'Only One Option'. *Outlook* 16 (October 1979): 1-2.

_____. 'Practise Christ's Wholeness'. *Outlook* 16 (March 1982): 1.

_____. 'Reflections on a Dynamic Ministry'. *Outlook* 20/3 (1987): 1, 7.

_____. 'Spiritual Indifference'. Pages 333-34 in *World Congress On Evangelism*. Kongresshale, Berlin, 1966.

_____. 'Testimony'. Pages 416-417 in *Let the Earth Hear His Voice: Official Reference Volume, Papers and Responses*. Edited by J. D Douglas. Minneapolis: World Wide Publications, 1975.

_____. 'The Church During and After the Amin Regime'. *Christianity Today* 23/15 (1979): 54-55.

_____. 'The Cross and World Evangelization'. Pages 400-04 in *Let the Earth Hear His Voice: International Congress on World Evangelization, Lausanne, Switzerland: Official Reference Volume: Papers and Responses*. Edited by James Douglas. Minneapolis: World Wide Publications, 1975.

_____. 'The Ministry of Reconciliation'. *Decision* (August 1984): 4.

_____. 'The Release of Forgiveness'. Pages 27-34 in *The Keswick Week 1975: Centenary Year*. London: Marshall, Morgan & Scott, 1975.

_____. 'The Work of the Holy Spirit in Evangelization, Individually and Through the Church'. Pages 277–278 in *Let the Earth Hear His Voice: International Congress on World Evangelization, Lausanne, Switzerland: Official Reference Volume: Papers and Responses*. Edited by James Douglas. Minneapolis: World Wide Publications, 1975.

_____. 'Unshakable Love'. *Outlook* 21/1 (1988).

_____. 'Winners in the New Year'. *Outlook* 17 (1980): 1.

1.1.3 Unpublished Papers

Kivengere, Festo. 'Proposal For Discussion at the House of Bishops Regarding Peace Talks for Uganda Government After the Coup D'état'. Unpublished Proposal, August 1985. Archives of the Church of Uganda, Uganda Christian University. AO:19850823.

1.1.4 Audio and Video Recordings

Kivengere, Festo. *Address to the National Press Club*. Audio Recording from National Library of Australia. Canberra, 1978. ORAL TRC 607. National Library of Australia.

_____. *The Cross and World Evangelization; and Communion Service*. Audio Cassette. International Congress on World Evangelization. Lausanne, 1974. Moore College Library.

_____. *The Spiritual Life of a Pastor*. Videocassette. Sydney: Christian Film Service, 1987. Moore College Library.

_____. *The Triumph of God's Glory (John 17:22)*. Audio Recording. Urbana, 1976. Moore College Library. Corresponds to Sermon Transcript AO: 19761231.

1.1.5 Sermons Analyzed in this Thesis

Kivengere, Festo. 'A New Way of Seeing Jesus'. Sermon Transcript. Preached at Holy Trinity Church, Cambridge, October 12, 1982. AO: 19821012, [#1].

_____. 'Ambassadors For Christ in a Miserable World'. Sermon Transcript, October 16, 1977. AO:19771016.

_____. 'Broken Relationships Restored'. Sermon Transcript. USA, March 1977. AO: 1977[0314?].

_____. 'Christ Has Reconciled the Universe to Himself'. Sermon Transcript. Garden Grove, California., 1979. AO: 1979[est. after May], [#2].

_____. 'Christ Puts All Things Together'. Sermon Transcript, 1972. AO:1972[----]*1.

_____. 'God's Intervening Love'. Sermon Transcript. Preached at Presbyterian Church, Aurora, Illinois, July 29, 1975. AO: 19750729, [#1].

_____. 'His Flooding Love'. Sermon Transcript, July 29, 1975. AO: 19750729, [#2].

_____. 'In Christ'. Sermon Transcript, April 29, 1979. AO: 19790429, [#2].

_____. 'Jesus Came as a Missionary of Reconciliation'. Sermon Transcript, February 21, 1982. AO: 19820221.

_____. 'Life in Jesus'. Sermon Transcript. Sydney, Australia, 1978. AO: 1978 [02--?].

_____. 'No More Distances in the Love of Christ'. Sermon Transcript. Youth Rally, Kansas City, Diocese of Western Missouri, October 14, 1980. AO:19801014, [#1].

_____. 'Peace and Victory for the Christian'. Pages 37-50 in *When God Moves in Revival*. Wheaton, Ill.: Tyndale House Publishers, 1977 [1973].

_____. 'Reconciliation'. Sermon Transcript, April 1982. AO: 198204[--], [#1].

_____. 'Remove the Masks'. Pages 23-36 in *When God Moves in Revival*. Wheaton, Ill.: Tyndale House Publishers, 1977 [1973].

_____. 'Revival Begins at the Cross'. Pages 11-21 in *When God Moves in Revival*. Wheaton, Ill.: Tyndale House Publishers, 1977 [1973].

_____. 'Surprised by Joy'. Sermon Transcript, September 1971. AO:197109[--].

_____. 'The Covenant of Love'. Pages 51-60 in *When God Moves in Revival*. Wheaton, Ill.: Tyndale House Publishers, 1977 [1973].

_____. 'The Cross And World Evangelization'. Sermon Transcript. Given at International Congress on World Evangelization, Lausanne., July 25, 1974. AO:19740725.

_____. 'The Cross Today and Divine Outreach'. Sermon Transcript, April 4, 1980. AO: 19800404.

_____. 'The Evangelist's Ministry of Reconciliation: We Are Christ's Ambassadors'. Pages 157–161 in *The Work of an Evangelist: International Congress for Itinerant Evangelists*. Edited by J. D. Douglas. Minneapolis, Minn.: World Wide Publications, 1984. AO:19830715.

_____. 'The Love of Christ'. Sermon Transcript, July 1977. AO: 197707[--].

_____. 'The Pastor's Joy'. Sermon Transcript. Preached at Mount Hermon, California, January 20, 1977. AO: 19770120.

_____. 'The Reconciling Love of Christ'. Sermon Transcript, October 1981. AO: 198110[--], [#1].

_____. 'The Triumph of God's Glory'. Sermon Transcript. Urbana, December 31, 1976. AO: 19761231.

_____. 'The Unshakable Identity of the Church of Jesus Christ'. Sermon Transcript, October 29, 1977. AO: 19771029, [#1].

_____. 'The Whole Gospel For The Whole World'. Sermon Transcript. Preached at Wheaton Bible Church, Illinois, May 1978. AO:197805[--], [#2].

1.1.6 Other Sermons Referenced in this Thesis

Kivengere, Festo. '20th Anniversary of African Enterprise'. Sermon Transcript. Preached at Pasadena, California, February 16, 1982. AO:19820216.

_____. 'A Special Lecture'. Sermon Transcript. Trinity Episcopal School For Ministry, USA. AO: 1981[----]*1.

_____. 'Abundant, Complete Life'. Sermon Transcript. Preached at Calvary Baptist Church, October 24, 1973. AO:19731024*1.

_____. 'Bishop Festo: On Events in Uganda', February 1977. AO: 197702[--].

_____. 'Broken Relationships Restored'. Sermon Transcript, October 26, 1977. AO:19771026*1.

_____. 'Compassion Harvest'. Sermon Transcript, October 7, 1980. AO: 19801007.

_____. 'Compelling Calvary Love'. Sermon Transcript. Preached at Salvation of Souls Church, Cairo, Egypt, May 5, 1978. AO: 19780505.

_____. 'Costly Breakthrough'. Sermon Transcript. Preached at First United Methodist Church, Carollton, TX, January 12, 1980. AO:19800112.

_____. 'Delivered—Set Free'. Sermon Transcript. Preached at Fuller Seminary, Pasadena, California, October 10, 1973. AO:19731010.

_____. 'Diocesan Tour', July 1979. AO: 197907[--]*1.

_____. 'Divine Sensitivity'. Sermon Transcript. Preached at Santa Barbara, California, April 21, 1980. AO:19800421.

_____. 'Divisions in the Church'. Sermon Transcript, August 15, 1973. AO:19730815.

_____. 'Festo Kivengere's Return'. Sermon Transcript, n.d. AO: [--------]*1.

_____. 'Festo Relates His Escape Story'. Sermon Transcript, March 1977. AO:197703[--].

_____. 'For Me To Live Is Christ'. Sermon Transcript. Evangelical Presbyterian Church, Cairo, Egypt, March 5, 1978. AO: 19780305*1.

_____. 'Forgiveness'. Sermon Transcript. Preached at Sydney, Australia Bridge '78, 1978. AO: 1978[----]*1.

_____. 'From Uganda With Love'. Sermon Transcript. Preached at Kendall, UK, October 1981. AO:198110[--]*1.

_____. 'Glorified in Them'. Sermon Transcript, May 22, 1977. AO:19770522*1.

_____. 'God's Love'. Sermon Transcript, January 6, 1978. AO: 19780106.

_____. 'God's Short-Cut To Humanity'. Sermon Transcript. Preached at Christ Church Greenwich, CT, May 11, 1980. AO:19800511*1.

_____. 'His Excellency the President'. Sermon Transcript, November 28, 1971. AO:19711128.

_____. 'How a Person Can Be Sure of His Right Relationship With God'. Sermon Transcript, October 26, 1980. AO: 19801026.

_____. 'I Am The Light Of The World'. Sermon Transcript. Preached at Pasadena, California, November 2, 1981. AO:19811102.

_____. 'Jesus Came as Light and Life for Men'. Sermon Transcript, December 25, 1980. AO:19801225.

_____. 'Jesus Frees and Unites'. Sermon Transcript, May 24, 1976. AO:19760524.

_____. 'Jesus Is Good News'. Sermon Transcript, October 1981. AO: 198110[--]*2.

_____. 'Jesus is the Fulfilment of the Old Testament'. Sermon Transcript, n.d. AO: [--------]*2.

_____. 'Jesus: The Treasurer'. Sermon Transcript, August 27, 1982. AO: 19820827.

_____. 'Let Your Life And Power Go Out'. Sermon Transcript, June 1977. AO:197706[--].

_____. 'Life in Jesus'. Sermon Transcript. Sydney, Australia, 1978. AO: 1978[----], [#1].

_____. 'Nyaruhanga'. Sermon Transcript, July 1979. AO: 197907[--]*3.

Bibliography

_____. 'Our Bodies: Temples of the Holy Spirit'. Sermon Transcript, 1975. AO:1975[----]*5.

_____. 'Prayer and Praise'. Sermon Transcript, May 10, 1980. AO: 19800510*1.

_____. 'Prodigal Son'. Sermon Transcript. Preached at Pittsburgh, Pennsylvania, November 1973. AO:19731114-18.

_____. 'Sermon on 1 John 3:11'. Sermon Transcript. Preached at Cheltenham, Gloucestershire, November 10, 1982. AO: 19821110.

_____. 'Set Free by Christ'. Sermon Transcript, April 24, 1980. AO: 19800424*1.

_____. 'The Bishop's Charge to the Synod'. Sermon Transcript, 1975. AO:1975[03--?].

_____. 'The Cross at the Centre'. Sermon Transcript. AO: [--------]*71.

_____. 'The Cross of Christ'. Sermon Transcript. Preached at Eugene, Oregon, April 19, 1979. AO: 19790419*2.

_____. 'The Freedom that Jesus Brings for Living'. Sermon Transcript, October 23, 1977. AO: 19771023.

_____. 'The Master Came Down'. Sermon Transcript. Preached at St. Andrew's Presbyterian Church, Newport Beach, CA, October 5, 1980. AO:19801005*1.

_____. 'The Problems Of The New Nations Of Africa'. Sermon Transcript. Preached at Channel City Club, Santa Barbara, California, October 1973. AO:197310[--].

_____. 'The Renewing Presence of Christ in Evangelism'. Sermon Transcript, 1975. AO:1975[----]*6.

_____. 'The Resurrection or Burning Hearts'. Sermon Transcript, May 10, 1980. AO:19800510*2.

_____. 'The Task of Rebuilding'. Sermon Transcript. Muyebe Archdeaconry, July 9, 1979. AO: 19790709.

_____. 'World Vision International: New Briefing', October 4, 1979. AO: 19791004.

_____. 'World Vision: with Festo Kivengere'. Sermon Transcript, May 10, 1979. AO:19790510.

1.2 Other Primary Sources

1.2.1 Archival Sources

African Evangelistic Enterprise. *Return, Relief, Reconstruction and Reconciliation*. Pasadena, Calif.: African Evangelistic Enterprise, n.d. Archives of African Evangelistic Enterprise, Kampala.

Amin, Idi. 'Speech by His Excellency the President, General Idi Amin Dada on the Occasion of Meeting Moslem Leaders'. Unpublished Speech, November 22, 1971. Archives of the Church of Uganda.

Anglican Diocese of Kigizi. 'Golden Jubilee Convention: Behold I Make All Things New: The Fifth Kabale Convention'. Convention Booklet. Kabale, Uganda, August 13, 1985. Archives of Diocese of Kigezi.

Commission on Canon Law, Doctrine and Liturgy of the Church of the Province of Uganda. *The Provincial Canons of the Church of the Province of Uganda*. Uganda: The Church of the Province of Uganda, 1997. Library of Uganda Christian University.

_____. *The Provincial Canons of the Church of Uganda*. Uganda: Centenary Publishing House, 1971. Library of Uganda Christian University.

Diocese of Kigezi. 'Order of Service For the Church and State Funeral of the Late Rt. Rev. Festo Kivengere'. Government Printer, Entebbe, Uganda, May 29, 1988. Archives of the Diocese of Kigezi.

International Congress on World Evangelization. 'Transcript of the Conclusion of the Plenary Session of the International Congress on World Evangelization'. Transcript of Audio Recording. Lausanne, Switzerland, 1974. Collection 53, Subseries A. Billy Graham Center Archives.

Loane, Marcus. 'Memoirs'. Unpublished Manuscript. Sydney, Australia. Library of Moore Theological College.

1.2.2 News Articles

'Amin Admits Eating Humans, Vow to Return'. *Sub-Saharan Africa Report* 2192 (December 21, 1979): 122–23.

'Amin's Death Roll'. *Transition (Accra)* 49/9/6 (September 1975): 17, 21, 27.

'Anglican Fellowship of Prayer to Meet'. *Episcopal News Service*, March 8, 1979. Cited 30 Dec 2010. Online: http://www.episcopalarchives.org/cgi-bin/ENS/ENSpress_release.pl?pr_number=79076.

'Anglican of the Week'. *The Anglican*. Sydney, January 16, 1959.

'Appeal by Bishop: Speak on Uganda'. *Sydney Morning Herald*, February 6, 1978.

'Bishop Muge Faces a Barrage of Attacks'. *The Weekly Review* (September 19, 1986).
'Bishop Omari Arrives for a Six Months Visit'. *The Anglican*. Sydney, December 19, 1958.
Church Scene. 'Appeal for Ugandan Refugees Launched'. *Church Scene*, February 9, 1978.
Episcopal Church. 'African Evangelist Dies in Nairobi'. Press Release, Episcopal News Service, May 26, 1988. Cited 30 Jan 2012. Online: http://www.episcopalarchives.org/cgi-bin/ENS/ENSpress_release.pl?pr_number=88115.
_____. 'Bishop Kivengere Describes Persecuted Ugandan Church'. Press Release, Episcopal News Service, March 11, 1977. Cited 15 Mar 2012. Online: http://www.episcopalarchives.org/cgi-bin/ENS/ENSpress_release.pl?pr_number=77093.
_____. 'Bishop Kivengere Returns To Uganda'. Press Release, Episcopal News Service, May 3, 1979. Cited 22 Nov 2011. Online: http://www.episcopalarchives.org/cgi-bin/ENS/ENSpress_release.pl?pr_number=79146.
'Exiled Bishop Returns to Uganda'. *Southern Cross*, July 1979.
'Help for Uganda Refugees'. *Courier Mail*. Brisbane, February 6, 1978.
'News Makers: Exiled Bishop here to beat freedom drum'. *The Australian*, February 6, 1978.
'Uganda: Amin: The Wild Man of Africa'. *Time* (March 7, 1977). Cited 27 Jan 2012. Online: http://www.time.com/time/magazine/article/0,9171,918762,00.html.
'Ugandan Bishop Visits Brisbane'. *Telegraph*, February 8, 1978.

1.2.3 Unpublished Papers – Festo Kivengere Memorial Lectures

Ekudu-Adoku, John. 'The Extent and Implications of His Spiritual and Social Ministry'. Unpublished Paper, delivered at the Bishop Festo Kivengere Memorial Lecture. Kampala, Uganda, 1994.
Rutayisire, Antoine. 'Forgiveness and Reconciliation'. Unpublished Paper, delivered at the Bishop Festo Kivengere Memorial Lecture. Kampala, Uganda, 2001.
Senyimba, Michael. 'Festo Kivengere: The Man (Who Never Retreated from Challenges) and His Legacy'. Unpublished Paper, delivered at the Bishop Festo Kivengere Memorial Lecture. Kampala, Uganda, May 5, 1991.

1.2.4 Other Unpublished Papers

Kalengyo, Edison M. 'The Place and Role of Bishop Tucker School of Divinity and Theology in Uganda Christian University and the Church of Uganda'. Unpublished Paper, delivered at Archbishop Janani Luwum Memorial Lectures. The Ankrah Foundation, Mukono, Uganda, February 13, 2006.

Ministry of Information and Broadcasting. 'Obote's War Call to Langis and Acholis against Other Ugandans'. Letter. Kampala, Uganda, 1977.

Noll, Stephen. 'Higher Education As Mission: The Role of the University in the Development of the Church's Ministry and Mission'. Unpublished Paper. Uganda Christian University, February 25, 2005.

1.2.5 Audio and Video Recordings

Struck, Duke. 'Former Uganda Attorney General Godfrey Binaisa, Former United States Ambassador to Uganda Thomas Melady, and Journalist Carlos Russell Debate the Response That President Carter Should Make to Idi Amin's Threats Against Americans in Uganda'. Videocassette. *The MacNeil/Lehrer Report*. New York: Educational Broadcasting Corp., 1977.

2. Secondary Sources

2.1 Books and Articles About Festo Kivengere

Bewes, Richard. 'Man of Africa: Bishop Festo Kivengere of Uganda'. *African Enterprise, Sydney* (1979).

'Bishop Kivengere Seriously Ill in Nairobi'. *Outlook* 21/1 (1988).

Briscoe, Jill. *The Man Who Would Not Hate: Festo Kivengere*. Dallas, Texas: Word Publishing, 1991.

Capon, John. 'Exiled Bishop of the Martyred Church'. *Crusade* (May 1977): 18–22.

Cassidy, Michael. 'Festo Has Died But He Still Speaks'. *African Enterprise*/August (1988): 7–9.

Coomes, Anne. *Festo Kivengere: A Biography*. Eastbourne: Monarch, 1990.

'How a Ugandan Bishop Views Africa's Upheaval'. *U.S. News and World Report* 82 (April 4, 1977): 30.

'Interview with Bishop Kivengere on the Nature of the Revival in East Africa'. *African Voice* (February 1987): 3–5.

Kaare, Melhust. 'Festo's Vision'. *African Voice* August (1988): 1–12.

Pirouet, M. Louise. 'Kivengere, Festo, c. 1919 to 1988'. Pages 369–370 in *Biographical Dictionary of Christian Missions*. Edited by Gerald H Anderson. Grand Rapid, Mich.: Eerdmans, 1999.
Quinn, Frederick. 'Kivengere, Festo'. *African Saints: Saints, Martyrs, and Holy People from the Continent of Africa*. New York: Crossroads Publishing, 2002. Cited 15 Mar 2012. Online: http://www.dacb.org/stories/uganda/kivengere_festo.html.
Russell, Jay. 'A Ministry of Reconciliation: Festo Kivengere: 1920–1988'. Pages 304–07 in *Ambassadors for Christ*. Edited by John D Woodbridge. Chicago, Ill.: Moody Press, 1994.
Warwick, Olson. 'Festo Kivengere—The King's Grandson Who Became a Greater King's Servant'. *African Enterprise, Sydney* (May 1988): 1–6.
Wood, William P. 'The Bishop and Idi Amin'. *America* 136/2 (January 15, 1977): 26–28.

2.2 Theses About Festo Kivengere

Rwabyoma, Peter B. 'Bishop Festo Kivengere: An Analysis of His Communication Skills and How He Applied Them in the Mission of the Church in Uganda'. MA Thesis, Cardiff: University of Wales, 2007.
Senyonyi, John M. M. 'Bishop Festo Kivengere's Philosophy of Evangelism'. M.A. Thesis, Deerfield, Ill.: Trinity Evangelical Divinity School, 1992.

2.3 Other Secondary Sources

Achebe, Chinua. *Things Fall Apart*. New York: McDowell, Obolensky, 1959.
Adam, Peter. 'Preaching and Biblical Theology'. Pages 104–112 in *New Dictionary of Biblical Theology*. Edited by Graeme Goldsworthy, T. Desmond Alexander, and Brian S Rosner. Leicester: Inter-Varsity Press, 2000.
Adams, Bert N. 'A Look at Uganda and Expulsion Through Ex-Ugandan Asian Eyes'. *Kroniek van Afrika* 3/6 (1975): 237–49.
Adefuye, Ade. 'The Kakwa of Uganda and the Sudan: The Ethnic Factor in National and International Politics'. Pages 51–69 in *Partitioned Africans: Ethnic Relations Across Africa's International Boundaries, 1884–1984*. Edited by A. I. Asiwaju. London: C. Hurst and Co., 1985.
Adeyemo, Tokunboh. *Africa's Enigma and Leadership Solutions*. Nairobi, Kenya: WordAlive Publishers, 2009.
_____. *Salvation in African Tradition*. 2nd ed [1979] ed. Nairobi, Kenya: Evangel Pub. House, 1997 [1979].

Allen, Gregory J. 'Reconciliation in the Pauline Tradition: Its Occasions, Meanings, and Functions'. ThD Dissertation, Boston University, 1995.

Allen, John. *Rabble-Rouser for Peace: The Authorized Biography of Desmond Tutu*. New York: Simon and Schuster, 2006.

Allen, Peter. *Days of Judgment: A Judge in Idi Amin's Uganda*. England: Kimber, 1987.

Amos, Kasibante. 'The Challenge of the New Pentecostal Churches to the East African Revival: The Confluence of Two Movements in my Life'. *The East African Revival: History and Legacies*. Kampala, Uganda: Fountain Publishers, 2010.

Amstutz, Mark R. 'Human Rights and the Promise of Political Forgiveness'. *Review and Expositor* 105 (2007): 553–577.

———. 'Is Reconciliation Possible After Genocide? The Case of Rwanda'. *Journal of Church and State* 48/3 (2006): 541–65.

Anderson, Gerald H, ed. *Biographical Dictionary of Christian Missions*. Paperback ed. Grand Rapid, Mich.: Eerdmans, 1999.

Andrews, Sally C. 'The Legitimacy of the United States Embargo of Uganda'. *Journal of International Law and Economics* 13/3 (1979): 651–73.

Anguria, Omongole R, ed. *Apollo Milton Obote: What Others Say*. Kampala: Fountain Publishers, 2006.

Apel, William Dale. 'The Understanding of Salvation in the Evangelistic Message of Billy Graham: A Historical-Theological Evaluation'. PhD Thesis, Evanston, Ill.: Northwestern University, 1975.

Apter, David E. *The Political Kingdom in Uganda: A Study in Bureaucratic Nationalism*. 3rd ed. London: Frank Cass, 1997 [1961].

Arndt, William F. *A Greek-English Lexicon of the New Testament and Other Early Christian Literature*. Edited by Frederick W Danker and Walter Bauer. 3rd ed. Chicago: University of Chicago Press, 2000.

Aulen, Gustaf. *Christus Victor: An Historical Study of the Three Main Types of the Idea of Atonement*. 1st ed. New York: Collier, 1986 [1931].

Autrey, C. E. *The Theology of Evangelism*. Nashville: Broadman, 1966.

Avirgan, Tony. *War in Uganda: The Legacy of Idi Amin*. Westport, Conn: L. Hill, 1982.

Ayittey, George B. N. *Africa Betrayed*. New York: St Martin's Press, 1992.

Baker, David L. *Two Testaments, One Bible: A Study of Some Modern Solutions to the Theological Problem of the Relationship Between the Old and New Testaments*. Leicester: Inter-Varsity Press, 1976.

Baker, Mark D, and Joel B Green. *Recovering the Scandal of the Cross: Atonement in New Testament and Contemporary Contexts*. 2nd ed. Downers Grove, Ill.: IVP Academic, 2011 [2000].

Balla, Peter. 'Challenges to Biblical Theology'. Pages 20–26 in *New Dictionary of Biblical Theology*. Edited by Graeme Goldsworthy, T. Desmond Alexander, and Brian S Rosner. Leicester: Inter-Varsity Press, 2000.

_____. *Challenges to New Testament Theology: An Attempt to Justify the Enterprise*. Peabody, Mass.: Hendrickson, 1997.

Barabas, Steven. *So Great Salvation: The History and Message of the Keswick Convention*. Eugene, Or.: Wipf and Stock Publishers, 2005.

Barclay, William. *Many Witnesses One Lord*. London: S.C.M., 1966.

_____. *The Letter to the Romans*. Rev. ed. Daily Study Bible. Edinburgh: Saint Andrew Press, 1975 [1957].

Barkan, Elazar. 'Historical Reconciliation: Redress, Rights and Politics'. *Journal of International Affairs* 60/1 (2006): 1–15.

Barker, G. H. *A Circle of Trees*. Braunton: Merlin, 1989.

Barnett, Paul. *The Message of 2 Corinthians: Power in Weakness*. The Bible Speaks Today. New Testament Series. Leicester, Eng., 1988.

_____. *The Second Epistle to the Corinthians*. The New International Commentary on the New Testament. Grand Rapids, Mich.: W.B. Eerdmans Pub., 1997.

Barr, James. 'Abba Isn't "Daddy"'. *Journal of Theological Studies* n.s. 39 (1988): 28–47.

_____. *Biblical Words for Time*. 2nd ed. London: SCM, 1969.

_____. *The Bible in the Modern World: The Croall Lectures Given in New College, Edinburgh in November 1970*. London: S.C.M. Press, 1973.

_____. *The Semantics of Biblical Language*. Oxford: Oxford University Press, 1961.

Barrett, Charles Kingsley. *A Commentary on the Second Epistle to the Corinthians*. London: Adam & Charles Black, 1976.

_____. *The Second Epistle to the Corinthians*. Black's New Testament Commentaries. Peabody, MA: Hendrickson Publishers, 1973.

Barrett, David B, George Thomas Kurian, and Todd M Johnson, eds. 'Uganda'. *World Christian Encyclopedia: A Comparative Survey of Churches and Religions in the Modern World*. Oxford: Oxford University Press, 2001.

Barrett, David B. 'Blasio Kigozi'. *Biographical Dictionary of Christian Missions*. Edited by Gerald H. Anderson. Grand Rapids, Michigan: Wm. B. Eerdmans Publishing Company, 1998.

Barrett, David B., ed. *African Initiatives in Religion; 21 Studies from Eastern and Central Africa*. Nairobi: East African Publishing House, 1971.

Barth, Karl. *Church Dogmatics*. Edited by G. W. Bromiley and T. F. Torrance. Translated by G. W. Bromiley. Edinburgh: T&T Clark, 1936.

———. *Church Dogmatics IV.4: The Christian Life. Lecture Fragments*. Translated by G. W. Bromiley. London: T. & T. Clark, 2004.

———. *Evangelical Theology: An Introduction*. Grand Rapids, Mich.: Eerdmans, 1992 [1963].

———. *The Epistle to the Philippians*. Translated by James W Leitch. 40th ed. Louisville, KY: Westminster John Knox Press, 2002 [1962].

———. *The Epistle to the Romans*. Translated by Edwyn Clement Hoskyns. Translated from the 6th ed. Oxford: Oxford University Press, 1933.

———. *Theology and Church Shorter Writings 1920–1928*. The Preachers Library. London: SCM Press, 1962.

Barth, Karl, and J. Strathearn McNab. *Credo: A Presentation of the Chief Problems of Dogmatics with Reference to the Apostles' Creed; Sixteen Lectures Delivered at the University of Utrecht in February and March, 1935*. London: Hodder & Stoughton, 1936.

Barth, Karl, and Eduard Thurneysen. *Revolutionary Theology in the Making: Barth-Thurneysen Correspondence 1914–1925*. Louis: John Knox Press, 1964.

Barth, Markus. *Conversation with the Bible*. New York: Holt, 1964.

———. *Ephesians*. The Anchor Bible 34, 34A. Garden City: Doubleday, 1974.

———. *Israel and the Church: Contribution to a Dialogue Vital for Peace*. Research in Theology. Richmond: John Knox Press, 1969.

———. *The Broken Wall: A Study of the Epistle to the Ephesians*. London: Collins, 1959.

Bassler, Jouette M., ed. *Pauline Theology, Volume I: Thessalonians, Philippians, Galatians, Philemon*. Minneapolis: Fortress Press, 1991.

Batholomew, Craig. 'In Front of the Text'. Pages 135–152 in *The Bible in Pastoral Practice: Readings in the Place and Function of Scripture in the Church*. Edited by Paul H Ballard and Stephen R Holmes. Using the Bible in Pastoral Practice Series. Grand Rapids: Eerdmans, 2005.

Bauckham, Richard. *God Crucified: Monotheism and Christology in the New Testament*. Didsbury Lectures. Carlisle: Paternoster, 1998.

Bauer, W. Arndt W. F., Danker and F. W and Gingrich W. F. 'A Greek-English Lexicon of the New Testament and Other Early Christian Literature'. Chicago: University of Chicago Press, 2000.

Baum, Gregory, and Harold Wells. *The Reconciliation of Peoples: Challenge to the Churches*. WCC Publications, 1997.

Baxter, Christina A. 'Barth – a Truly Biblical Theologian'. *Tyndale Bulletin* 38 (1987): 3–27.

_____. 'The Movement from Exegesis to Dogmatics in the Theology of Karl Barth, with Special Reference to Romans, Philippians and Church Dogmatics'. PhD Thesis, University of Durham, 1981.

Bebbington, David William. *Evangelicalism in Modern Britain: A History from the 1730s to the 1980s*. London: Unwin Hyman, 1989.

_____. *The Dominance of Evangelicalism: The Age of Spurgeon and Moody*. Downers Grove: InterVarsity Press, 2005.

_____. 'Towards an Evangelical Identity'. *For Such a Time as This: Perspectives on Evangelicalism, Past, Present and Future*. Edited by Steve Brady and Harold Rowdon. London: Evangelical Alliance, 1996.

Bell, J. Bowyer. *Assassin: Theory and Practice of Political Violence*. New Brunswick: Transaction Publishers, 2005.

Bennett, F. J. 'A Comparison of Health Community in Uganda with Its Two East African Neighbours in the Periods 1970–1979'. Pages 43–52 in *Crisis in Uganda: The Breakdown in Health Services*. Edited by Cole P. Dodge. Oxford, England: Pergamon Pr, 1985.

Berkouwer, G. C. *The Triumph of Grace in the Theology of Karl Barth*. London: Paternoster, 1956.

Berman, Edward H, ed. *African Reactions to Missionary Education*. Publications of the Center for Education in Africa. New York: Teachers College Press, Teachers College, Columbia University, 1975.

Bieringer, Reimund. 'Paul's Understanding of Diakonia in 2 Corinthians 5,18'. Pages 413–28 in *Studies in 2 Corinthians*. Edited by R. Bieringer and J. Lambrecht. Leuven: University Press, 1994.

Bird, Michael F. *A Bird's-Eye View of Paul: The Man, His Mission and His Message*. Nottingham, England: Inter-Varsity Press, 2008.

Birungi, Medad. 'The Glory of the East African Revival in its Characteristics'. Pages 49–64 in *The East African Revival Through Seventy Years (1935–2005): Testimonies and Reflections*. Edited by Manuel J. K. Muranga. Kabale, Uganda: Diocese of Kigezi, 2005.

Blumhofer, Edith Waldvogel, and Randall Herbert Balmer, eds. *Modern Christian Revivals*. Urbana: University of Illinois Press, 1993.

Boers, Hendrikus. *The Theology of Evangelism*. Guides to Biblical Scholarship. New Testament Series. Philadelphia: Fortress, 1979.

_____. *What Is New Testament Theology*. Guides to Biblical Scholarship. New Testament Series. Philadelphia: Fortress, 1979, 1979.

Bolt, Peter G. 'Introduction'. *Christ's Victory Over Evil: Biblical Theology and Pastoral Ministry*. England, Nottingham: Apollos, 2009.

_____. *Jesus' Defeat of Death: Persuading Mark's Early Readers*. First edition. Cambridge: Cambridge University Press, 2003.

_____. *The Cross from a Distance: Atonement in Mark's Gospel*. New Studies in Biblical Theology. Nottingham: Inter-Varsity, 2004.

Bowdish, Callie. 'Santa Barbara County Trails and Mountain Canyons'. Cited 14 Sep 2010. Online: http://www.calliebowdish.com/SBTrailsMountains.html.

Bowen, Roger. *A Guide to Preaching*. Edited by David Lawrence Edwards and Society for Promoting Christian Knowledge. SPCK International Study Guide. London: SPCK, 2005.

Braga, Stuart. *A Century Preaching Christ*. Sydney: Katoomba Christian Convention, Limited, 2003.

Brett, E. A. 'Relations of Production, the State and the Uganda Crisis'. *West African Journal of Sociology and Political Science* 1/3 (1978): 249–84.

Brett, Mark G. *Biblical Criticism in Crisis? The Impact of the Canonical Approach on Old Testament Studies*. Cambridge: Cambridge University Press, 1991.

Breytenbach, Cilliers. 'On Reconciliation: An Exegetical Response'. *Journal of Theology for Southern Africa* 70 (1990): 64–68.

_____. 'Versöhnung: Eine Studie zur Paulinischen Soteriologie'. *Wissenschaftliche Monographien zum AT & NT* 60 (1989): 59–79.

Briggs, Philip, and Andrew Roberts. *Uganda*. 6th ed. Bucks, England: Bradt Travel Guides, 2010.

Briscoe, Jill. *The Man Who Would Not Hate: Festo Kivengere*. Dallas, Texas: Word Publishing, 1991.

Bromiley, Geoffrey W. *An Introduction to the Theology of Karl Barth*. Grand Rapids, Mich.: Eerdmans, 1979.

_____. 'Church and Theology'. Page 286 in *An Introduction to the Theology of Karl Barth*. Grand Rapids: Eerdmans, 1979.

Brooke, Hubert. 'The Message: Its Method of Presentation'. *The Keswick Convention: Its Message, Its Method and Its Men*. London: Marshall Bros., 1907.

Brown, Amy Benson, and Karen Poremski, eds. *Roads to Reconciliation: Conflict and Dialogue in the Twenty-First Century*. Armonk, N.Y: M.E. Sharpe, 2005.

Brown, Colin. *Karl Barth and the Christian Message*. London: Tyndale, 1967.

Brown, Richard Maxwell. *Strain of Violence: Historical Studies of American Violence and Vigilantism*. Oxford; New York: Oxford University Press, 1977.
Bruce, F. F. 'Christ as Conqueror and Reconciler'. *Bibliotheca Sacra* 141/564 (1984): 291–302.
Brummer, Vincent. 'Atonement and Reconciliation'. *Religious Studies* 28 (1992): 435–52.
Brunner, Emil. *The Christian Doctrine of God*. Translated by Olive Wyon. Reprint. J. Clark, 2002 [1950].
Bultmann, Rudolf Karl. 'The Problem of Hermeneutics'. Pages 69–94 in *New Testament and Mythology: And other Basic Writings*. Translated by M. Ogden Schubert. Philadelphia: Fortress, 1984.
———. *The Second Letter to the Corinthians*. Minneapolis: Augsburg Publishing House, 1985.
Burdon, C. J. 'Paul and the Crucified Church'. *Expository Times* 95 (1984): 137–41.
Burkhead, Howell Walker. 'The Development of the Concept of Sin in the Preaching of Billy Graham'. PhD thesis, Southwestern Baptist Theological Seminary, 1998.
Burnett, Richard E. *Karl Barth's Theological Exegesis: The Hermeneutical Principals of the Römerbrief Period*. Wissenschaftliche Untersuchungen Zum Neuen Testament. 2. Reihe. Tübingen: Mohr Siebeck, 2001.
Burrows, Noreen. 'Tanzania's Intervention in Uganda: Some Legal Aspects'. *The World Today* 35/7 (1979): 306–310.
Busch, Eberhard. *Karl Barth: His Life from Letters and Autobiographical Texts*. Grand Rapids, Michagan: W B Eerdmans, 1993.
Byaruhanga, Christopher. *Bishop Alfred Robert Tucker and the Establishment of the African Anglican Church*. Nairobi: Word Alive Publishers, 2008.
Campbell, Douglas A. 'The Story of Jesus in Romans and Galatians'. Pages 97–124 in *Narrative Dynamics in Paul: A Critical Assessment*. Edited by Bruce W. Longenecker. Louisville, Kent.: Westminster John Knox, 2002.
Carson, Donald A. 'Current Issues in Biblical Theology: A New Testament Perspective'. *Bulletin for Biblical Research* 5 (1995): 17–41.
———. *Love in Hard Places*. Wheaton, Ill.: Crossway Books, 2002.
———. *The Gagging of God: Christianity Confronts Pluralism*. Grand Rapids, Mich.: Zondervan, 1995.
———. 'The Role of Exegesis in Systematic Theology'. Pages 39–76 in *Doing Theology in Today's World: Essays in Honor of Kenneth S. Kantzer*. Edited by

John D Woodbridge, Thomas Edward McComiskey, and Kenneth S Kantzer. Grand Rapids, Mich.: Zondervan, 1991.

Casalis, Georges. 'Reconciliation Through Christ as Basis for Living with Others and Living for Others'. *Communio Viatorum* 2 (1961): 103–16.

Cassidy, Michael. *Together in One Place: The Story of PACLA December 9–19, 1976, Nairobi*. Edited by Gottfried Osei-Mensah. Kisumu, Kenya: Evangel Publishing House, 1978.

Charlesworth, James H, Mark Kiley, and Mark Harding, eds. 'A Caveat on Textual Transmission and the Meaning of Abba: A Study of the Lord's Prayer'. Pages 1–14 in *The Lord's Prayer and Other Prayer Texts from the Greco-Roman Era*. Valley Forge, Penn.: Trinity Press International, 1994.

Chick, John D. 'Class Conflict and Military Intervention in Uganda'. *The Journal of Modern African Studies* 10/4 (December 1, 1972): 634–637.

Childs, Brevard S. *Biblical Theology in Crisis*. Philadelphia: Westminster, 1970.

Chilton, Bruce. 'God as "Father" in the Targumim, in Non-Canonical Literatures of Early Judaism and Primitive Christianity, and in Matthew'. Pages 39–73 in *Judaic Approaches to the Gospels*. University of South Florida International Studies in Formative Christianity and Judaism. Atlanta, Ga.: Scholars Press, 1994.

Church, Joseph E. *Awake, Uganda!: The Story of Blasio Kigozi and His Vision of Revival*. Uganda: Uganda Bookshop Press, 1957 [1936].

———. *Quest for the Highest: An Autobiographical Account of the East African Revival*. Exeter: Paternoster, 1981.

Chvála-Smith, Anthony J. 'The Politics of Reconciliation in 2 Corinthians 5'. Pages 210–221 in *Proceedings, Eastern Great Lakes and Midwest Biblical Societies, vol 11, 1991*. Cincinnati: Eastern Great Lakes & Midwest Biblical Societies, 1991.

Clark, Mathew S, and H. I. Lederle, eds. *What Is Distinctive About Pentecostal Theology?* Miscellanea specialia / UNISA. Pretoria: University of South Africa, 1989.

Claydon, David, ed. *A New Vision, a New Heart, a Renewed Call: Lausanne Occasional Papers from the 2004 Forum for World Evangelization*. 3 vols. Lausanne Occasional Papers. Pasadena, Calif.: William Carey Library, 2005.

Conant, Judson Eber. *No Salvation Without Substitution*. Grand Rapids, Mich.: Eerdmans, 1941.

Condie, Keith. '"Of God": Karl Barth and the Coherence of 1 Corinthians'. Pages 32–56 in *The Wisdom of the Cross: Exploring 1 Corinthians*. Edited by Brian S Rosner and Moore Theological College. School of Theology. Nottingham: Apollos, 2011.

Cook, Henry. *The Theology of Evangelism: The Gospel in the World of To-Day*. London: Carey Kingsgate Press, 1951.

Coomes, Anne. *African Harvest: The Captivating Story of Michael Cassidy and African Enterprise*. London: Monarch, 2002.

Cousar, Charles B. 'II Corinthians 5:17–21'. *Interpretation* 35 (1981): 180–183.

Craig, Mary. *Candles in the Dark: Six Modern Martyrs*. London: Hodder and Stoughton, 1984.

Cumming, J. Elder. *Through the Eternal Spirit: A Bible Study on the Holy Ghost*. Stirling, Scotland: Drummond's Tract Depot, n. d.

———. 'What We Teach'. *Keswick's Triumphant Voice: Forty-Eight Outstanding Addresses Delivered at the Keswick Convention, 1882–1962*. Edited by Herbert F Stevenson. London: Marshall, Morgan and Scott, 1963.

Cunningham, Mary Kathleen. *What Is Theological Exegesis?: Interpretation and Use of Scripture in Barth's Doctrine of Election*. Valley Forge, Penn.: Trinity Press International, 1995.

David, Bennett. *The Altar Call: Its Origins and Present Usage*. Lanham, Maryland: University Press of America, 2000.

Dawson, E. C. (Edwin Collas). *James Hannington: First Bishop of Eastern Equatorial Africa: A History of his Life and Work, 1847–1885*, 1849. Cited 21 Feb 2012. Online: http://www.archive.org/details/jameshanningtonf00daws.

Dawson, R. Dale. *The Resurrection in Karl Barth*. Barth Studies. Aldershot: Ashgate, 2006.

Day, Erin. 'Uganda'. Pages 137–141 in *World Minorities: A Second Volume*. Edited by Georgina Ashworth. Sunbury: Quartermaine House, 1978.

Dayton, Donald W. *Theological Roots of Pentecostalism*. Studies in Evangelicalism. Metuchen, NJ: Scarecrow, 1987.

Decalo, Samuel. 'Military Coups and Military Regimes in Africa'. *Journal of Modern African Studies* 11/1: 105–127.

Delton, Franz. 'A Biblical Context for Political Advocacy'. Pages 51–56 in *Christian Political Activism at the Crossroads*. Edited by William R. Stevenson. University Press of America, 1994.

Demarest, Bruce A. *The Cross and Salvation: The Doctrine of Salvation*. Foundations of Evangelical Theology. Wheaton, Ill.: Crossway Books, 1997.

Denoon, Donald, ed. *A History of Kigezi in South-West Uganda*. Kampala, Uganda: The National Trust, 1972.

DeYoung, Curtiss Paul. 'The Power of Reconciliation: From the Apostle Paul to Malcolm X'. *Cross Currents* 57/2 (2007): 203–208.

Dickson, Charles. 'Markus Barth and Biblical Theology: A Personal Re-View'. *Horizons in Biblical Theology* 17/2 (December 1995): 96–116.

Dickson, Kwesi A, and Paul Ellingworth, eds. *Biblical Revelation and African Beliefs*. London: Lutterworth P., 1969.

Dorrien, Gary J. *The Remaking of Evangelical Theology*. Louisville, Ky.: Westminster John Knox Press, 1998.

Douglas, J. D, ed. *Let the Earth Hear His Voice: Official Reference Volume, Papers and Responses*. Minneapolis: World Wide Publications, 1975.

Douglas, James Dixon. *The Work of An Evangelist*. World Wide Publications, 1984.

Doyle, A. D. 'Pilate's Career and the Date of the Crucifixion'. *Journal of Theological Studies* 42 (1941): 190–193.

Dunn, James D. G. 'In Quest of Paul's Theology'. Pages 95–115 in *Pauline Theology: Volume IV: Looking Back, Pressing On*. Atlanta: Scholars, 1997.

———. *The Epistles to the Colossians and to Philemon: A Commentary on the Greek Text*. The New International Greek Testament Commentary. Grand Rapids, MI: William B. Eerdmans Publishing, 1996.

———. *The Partings of the Ways Between Christianity and Judaism and Their Significance for the Character of Christianity*. Vol. 2. London: SCM Press, 2006.

———. 'The Problem of "Biblical Theology"'. *Out of Egypt: Biblical Theology and Biblical Interpretation*. Edited by Craig G Bartholomew and Elaine Botha. The Scripture and Hermeneutics Series. Bletchley, Milton Keynes, UK: Paternoster Press, 2004.

———. *Unity and Diversity in the New Testament: An Inquiry into the Character of Earliest Christianity*. London: S.C.M. Press, 1977.

Dyrness, William A, Veli-Matti Kärkkäinen, and Juan Francisco Martinez, eds. *Global Dictionary of Theology: A Resource for the Worldwide Church*. Downers Grove, Ill.: IVP Academic, 2008.

Earl, Arville, and Sheila Earl. 'Committed to the Ministry of Reconciliation: Moving Beyond Conflict in the Balkans'. *Review & Expositor* 104/3 (Summer 2007): 603–621.

Ebeling, Gerhard. 'Word of God and Hermeneutics'. *Word and Faith*. Philadelphia: Fortress, 1963.

Ellis, Earle E. 'Christ Crucified'. *Reconciliation and Hope: New Testament Essays on Atonement and Eschatology, Presented to L.L. Morris on His 60th Birthday.* Edited by Robert Banks. Exeter: Paternoster, 1974.

Emerson, Michael O, and Christian Smith, eds. *Divided by Faith: Evangelical Religion and the Problem of Race in America.* Oxford: Oxford University Press, 2000.

Enzinga, Nefta. *I Was Kidnapped by Idi Amin.* Los Angeles: Holloway House Pub Co, 1979.

Eric, S. Fife, and F. Glasser Aurthur, eds. *Commission, Conflict, Commitment: Messages from the Sixth International Student Missionary Convention.* IVP Series in Creative Christian Living. Chicago: Inter-Varsity Press, 1962.

Falk, Peter. *A History of the Church in Africa.* Pasadena, Ca.: Fuller Theological Seminary, 1976.

———. *The Growth of the Church in Africa.* Contemporary Evangelical Perspectives. Grand Rapids, Mich.: Zondervan, 1979.

Falke, H. *From Uganda with Love: An Inside Look by Means of Students' Essays and Paintings.* 1st ed. New York: Vantage Press, 1980.

Fauchald, K. 'A Survey of the Benthos of Santa Barbara Following the January 1969 Oil Spill'. *California Marine Research Commission, California Cooperative Oceanic Fisheries Investigations Report* 16 (1972): 125–129.

Faupel, J. F. *African Holocaust: The Story of the Uganda Martyrs.* 2nd ed. Deacon Books Series. London: Chapman, 1965 [1962].

Favazza, Joseph A. 'Reconciliation: On the Border between Theological and Political Praxis'. *Journal for the Study of Religion and Ideologies* 3 (2002): 52–64.

Festo, Kivengere. 'Bishop Festo Kivengere: Press Conference at Trinity Church, USA'. AO: 10771028.

Fields, Bruce L. *Introducing Black Theology: 3 Crucial Questions for the Evangelical Church.* 3 Crucial Questions. Grand Rapids, MI: Baker Academic, 2001.

Figgis, J B. *Keswick from Within.* The Higher Christian Life. New York: Garland, 1985.

Findeis, Hans Jürgen. *Versöhnung - Apostolat - Kirche.* Forschungen zur Bibel. Wurzburg: Echter, 1983.

Finnegan, Ruth H. *Oral Poetry: Its Nature, Significance, and Social Context.* 1st ed. Cambridge, 1977.

First, Ruth. 'Uganda: The Latest Coup d'etat in Africa'. *World Today* 27/3 (March 1971): 131–38.

Fishbane, M. 'Inner Biblical Exegesis: Types and Strategies of Interpretation in Ancient Israel'. Pages 19–37 in *Midrash and Literature*. Edited by Geoffrey H. Hartman and Sanford Budick. New Haven, Connecticut: Yale Univ Pr, 1986.

Fisher, David. *The 21st Century Pastor: A Vision Based on the Ministry of Paul*. Grand Rapids, Mich.: Zondervan, 1996.

Fitzmyer, Joseph A. 'Crucifixion in Ancient Palestine, Qumran and the New Testament'. Pages 125–147 in *To Advance the Gospel: New Testament Studies*. Grand Rapids, Mich.: Eerdmans, 1998.

_____. *Pauline Theology*. Englewood Cliffs, NJ: Prentice-Hall, 1967.

_____. 'Reconciliation in Pauline Theology'. Pages 155–177 in *No famine in the Land*. Missoula, Mont: Scholars, 1975.

Fong, Bruce W. 'Addressing the Issue of Racial Reconciliation According to the Principles of Eph 2:11–22'. *Journal of the Evangelical Theological Society* 38/4 (1995): 565–580.

Ford, Margaret. *Janani: The Making of Martyr*. London: Marshall, Morgan and Scott, 1978.

Forster, F. '"Reconcile": 2 Corinthians 5:18–20'. *Concordia Theological Monthly* 21/4 (1950): 296–298.

Forstman, H Jackson. *Word and Spirit: Calvin's Doctrine of Biblical Authority*. Stanford: Stanford University Press, 1962.

Franzmann, Martin H. 'Reconciliation and Justification'. *Concordia Theological Monthly* 21/2 (1950): 81–93.

Frei, Hans W. *The Eclipse of Biblical Narrative: A Study in Eighteenth and Nineteenth Century Hermeneutics*. New Haven: Yale University Press, 1974.

Fryer, N. S. L. 'Reconciliation in Paul's Epistle to the Romans'. *Neotestamentica* 15 (1981): 34–68.

Funk, Robert W. *Honest to Jesus: Jesus for a New Millennium*. Rydalmere, N.S.W.: Hodder Headline Australia, 1996.

Furnish, Victor Paul. *II Corinthians*. Bible. English. Anchor Bible. 1964. N.Y.: Doubleday, 1984, 1984.

_____. 'Ministry of Reconciliation'. *Currents in Theology and Mission* 4/4 (1977): 204–218.

Garrett, John. *Where Nets Were Cast: Christianity in Oceania Since World War II*. Suva, Fiji: University of the South Pacific, 1997.

Gasparini, A. 'Globalisation, Reconciliation and the Conditions for Conserving Peace'. *Global Society* 22/1 (2008): 27–55.

Gershenberg, Irving. 'A Further Comment on the 1971 Coup'. *Journal of Modern African Studies* 10/4 (December 1972): 638–39.
Gibson, David, and Daniel Strange, eds. *Engaging with Barth: Contemporary Evangelical Critiques*. Nottingham: Apollos, 2008.
Gibson, Jeffry B. 'Paul's Dying Formula: Prolegomena to an Understanding of Its Import and Significance'. Pages 20–41 in *Celebrating Romans, Template for Pauline Theology: Essays in Honor of Robert Jewett*. Edited by Sheila E McGinn. Grand Rapids, Mich.: Eerdmans, 2004.
Gifford, Edwin Hamilton. *The Epistle of St. Paul to the Romans*. London: J. Murray, 1886.
Gifford, Paul. *African Christianity: Its Public Role*. London: Hurst & Company, 1998.
Gilje, Paul A. *Rioting in America*. Interdisciplinary studies in history. Bloomington, Ind: Indiana University Press, 1996.
Gloer, Hulitt. 'Ambassadors of Reconciliation: Paul's Genius in Applying the Gospel in a Multi-Cultural World: 2 Corinthians 5:14–21'. *Review & Expositor* 104/3 (Sum 2007): 589–601.
Goldingay, John. *Theological Diversity and the Authority of the Old Testament*. Grand Rapids: Eerdmans, 1987.
Goldingay, John, ed. *Atonement Today: A Symposium at St John's College, Nottingham*. Gospel & Culture. London: SPCK, 1995.
Goldsworthy, Graeme. *According to Plan: The Unfolding Revelation of God in the Bible*. Sydney: Lancer Press, 1991.
_____. *Gospel and Kingdom: A Christian Interpretation*. Biblical Classics Library. Carlisle, U.K.: Paternoster, 1994 [1981].
_____. *Preaching the Whole Bible as Christian Scripture: The Application of Biblical Theology to Expository Preaching*. Leicester: Inter-Varsity, 2000.
Golooba-Mutebi, F. 'Collapse, War and Reconstruction in Uganda: An Analytical Narrative on State-Making'. *Crisis Studies Research Centre Working Paper* 2/27 (2008): 1–27.
Goodman, Montague. 'The Wondrous Cross'. Pages 38–44 in *The Keswick Week 1947*. London: Marshall, Morgan & Scott, 1947.
Gourevitch, Philip. *We Wish to Inform You That Tomorrow We Will Be Killed With Our Families: Stories from Rwanda*. New York: Picador/Farrar, Straus, and Giroux : Distributed by Holtzbrinck Publishers, 2004 [1998].
Gowan, Donald E. 'In Memory of Markus Barth: A Personal Note'. *Horizons in Biblical Theology* 17/2 (December 1995): 93–95.

Graham, Billy. 'A Hundred Years of Blessing and Glory'. Pages 101–106 in *The Keswick Week 1975: Centenary Year*. London: Marshall, Morgan & Scott, 1975.

———. *Just As I Am: The Autobiography of Billy Graham*. New York: HarperOne, 2007.

———. 'World Congress On Evangelism'. Pages 1–13 in *Why The Berlin Congress?* Kongresshalle, Berlin, 1966.

Grahame, Iain. *Amin and Uganda: A Personal Memoir*. London: Granada, 1980.

Gray, Bennison. 'Repetition in Oral Literature'. *The Journal of American Folklore* 84/333 (1971): 289–303.

Greidanus, Sidney. *Preaching Christ from the Old Testament: A Contemporary Hermeneutical Method*. Grand Rapids, Mich.: Eerdmans, 1999.

Griffiths, Tudor. 'Bishop Alfred Tucker and the Establishment of a British Protectorate in Uganda 1890–94'. *Journal of Religion in Africa* 31/1 (2001): 92–114.

De Gruchy, John W., and Steve De Gruchy. *The Church Struggle in South Africa: 25th Anniversary Edition*. London: SCM, 2005.

Gupta, Anirudha. 'Amin's Fall: Would There Be Other Dominoes?'. *Africa Quarterly* 19/1 (June 1979): 4–13.

Hafemann, Scott J, ed. *Biblical Theology: Retrospect and Prospect*. Downers Grove, Ill.: InterVarsity Press, 2002.

Hakes, Jay E. 'Political Stability in East Africa: An Evaluation'. *Current History* 64/379 (March 1973): 114–117, 132–133.

Hall, David R. *The Unity of the Corinthian Correspondence*. Vol. 251. Journal for the Study of the New Testament Supplement Series. London: T&T Clark International, 2003.

Hall, Joan. 'The East African Revival's Impact on Serving the Lord for Uganda Through 25 Years'. Pages 13–20 in *The East African Revival Through Seventy Years (1935–2005): Testimonies and Reflections*. Edited by Manuel J. K. Muranga. Kabale, Uganda: Diocese of Kigezi, 2005.

Hansen, Holger Bernt. *Ethnicity and Military Rule in Uganda: A Study of Ethnicity as a Political Factor in Uganda, Based on a Discussion of Political Anthropology and the Application of Its Results*. Uppsala: Scandinavian Inst. of African Studies, 1977.

Hansen, Holger Bernt, and Michael Twaddle. *Changing Uganda: Dilemmas Of Structural Adjustment*. 1st ed. Kampala: Fountain Publishers, 1991.

———. *Developing Uganda*. 1st ed. Kampala: Fountain Publishers, 1998.

Hardesty, Nancy. *Faith Cure: Divine Healing in the Holiness and Pentecostal Movements*. Peabody, Mass.: Hendrickson Publishers, 2003.

Harford, Charles Forbes, ed. *The Keswick Convention: Its Message, Its Methods and Its Men*. London: Marshall Brothers, 1907.

Harris, Murray J. '2 Corinthians'. *The Expositor's Bible Commentary: With the New International Version of the Holy Bible*. Edited by Frank E. Gaebelein, J.D. Douglas, and Dick Polcyn. Grand Rapids: Zondervan, 1992.

Harrison. 'Uganda: The Expulsion of the Asians'. Pages 287–315 in *Case Studies on Human Rights And Fundamental Freedoms: A World Survey*. Edited by Ruut Veenhoven. The Hague: Martinus Nijhoff, 1976.

Hart, Max. *A Story of Fire, Continued: Aboriginal Christianity*. 2nd ed. Blackwood, South Australia: New Creation Publications, 1997 [1988].

Hartt, Julian N. *Towards a Theology of Evangelism*. New York: Abingdon Press, 1955.

Hasel, Gerhard F. *New Testament Theology: Basic Issues in the Current Debate*. Grand Rapids: Eerdmans, 1978.

Hastings, Adrian. *Mission and Ministry*. London: Sheed and Ward, 1971.

———. *The Church in Africa, 1450–1950*. Oxford History of the Christian Church. Oxford: Clarendon Press, 1994.

Hay, David M., and E. Elizabeth Johnson, eds. *Pauline Theology, Volume III: Romans*. Atlanta, GA.: Society of Biblical Literature, 1995.

Hay, David M., ed. *Pauline Theology, Volume II: 1 and 2 Corinthians*. Atlanta, GA.: Society of Biblical Literature, 1993.

Hays, Richard B. *Echoes of Scripture in the Letters of Paul*. New Haven: Yale University Press, 1980.

Hellenier, G. K. 'Economic Collapse and Rehabilitation in Uganda'. *Rural Africana* 11 (1981): 27–35.

Hendriksen, William. *Exposition of Colossians and Philemon*. Grand Rapids, Mich.: Baker Book House, 1964.

Hengel, Martin. *Crucifixion: In the Ancient World and the Folly of the Message of the Cross*. London: SCM, 1977.

———. *The Atonement: A Study of the Origins of the Doctrine in the New Testament*. London: SCM, 1981.

Hickling, C J A. 'Centre and Periphery in the Thought of Paul'. Pages 199–214 in *Studia biblica 1978, 3*. Sheffield: JSOT Pr, 1980.

Hills, Denis. *Rebel People*. New York: Africana Publishing, 1978.

———. 'The Jailer as Seen by His Ex-Prisoner'. *New York Times Magazine* (September 7, 1975).

_____. *The White Pumpkin*. New York: Grove Press, 1975.

Hoehner, Harold W. *Chronological Aspects of the Life of Christ*. Grand Rapids: Zondervan, 1977.

Hollon, D. Leslie. 'Reconciliation: Pastoral Reflections and Resources'. *Review & Expositor* 104 (2007): 442–462.

Hopkins, Elizabeth. 'The Nyabingi Cult of Southwestern Uganda'. *Protest and Power in Black Africa*. Edited by Robert I Rotberg and Ali Al'Amin Mazrui. New York: Oxford University Press, 1970.

Hopkins, Evan H. 'Crisis and Progress'. *Keswick's Authentic Voice: Sixty-Five Dynamic Addresses Delivered at the Keswick Convention, 1875–1957*. Edited by Herbert F. Stevenson. London: Marshall, Morgan & Scott, 1959.

_____. 'Deliverance from the Law of Sin'. Pages 157–61 in *Keswick's Authentic Voice: Sixty-Five Dynamic Addresses Delivered at the Keswick Convention, 1875–1957*. Edited by Herbert F. Stevenson. London: Marshall, Morgan & Scott, 1959.

_____. 'Our Old Man Crucified'. Pages 172–175 in *Keswick's Triumphant Voice: Forty-Eight Outstanding Addresses Delivered at the Keswick Convention, 1882–1962*. London: Marshall, Morgan and Scott, 1963.

_____. *The Law of Liberty in the Spiritual Life*. London: Marshall Bros., 1884.

_____. 'The Path and the Power'. Pages 301–07 in *Keswick's Authentic Voice: Sixty-Five Dynamic Addresses Delivered at the Keswick Convention, 1875–1957*. Edited by Herbert F. Stevenson. London: Marshall, Morgan & Scott, 1959.

_____. 'Threefold Deliverance'. Pages 162–67 in *Keswick's Authentic Voice: Sixty-Five Dynamic Addresses Delivered at the Keswick Convention, 1875–1957*. Edited by Herbert F. Stevenson. London: Marshall, Morgan & Scott, 1959.

Hughes, Philip Edgcumbe. *Paul's Second Epistle to the Corinthians: The English Text with Introduction, Exposition and Notes*. Grand Rapids, Mich.: Eerdmans, 1962.

Hunsinger, George. *How to Read Karl Barth: The Shape of His Theology*. New York: Oxford University Press, 1991.

Hurtado, Larry W. *Lord Jesus Christ: Devotion to Jesus in Earliest Christianity*. Grand Rapids, Mich.: Eerdmans, 2003.

Hurtado, Larry W. 'Jesus' Divine Sonship in Paul's Epistle to the Romans'. Pages 217–33 in *Romans and the People of God*. Edited by Sven K. Soderlund and N.T. Wright. Grand Rapids, Mich.: Eerdmans, 1999.

Hyde, Clark. 'The Ministry of Reconciliation'. *Saint Luke's Journal of Theology* 31/2 (Mr 1988): 111–125.

Idowu, E. Bolaji. *African Traditional Religion: A Definition*. Maryknoll, N.Y: Orbis Books, 1973.
Ingham, Kenneth. 'Tanganyika: The Mandate and Cameron'. *The History of East Africa*. Edited by V. T. Harlow and E. M. Chilver. Oxford: Oxford University Press, 1965.
———. *The Making of Modern Uganda*. 2nd ed. Westport, Conn.: Greenwood Press Reprint, 1983 [1958].
Inkelaar-de Mos, Charlotte. 'African Evangelistic Enterprise: Its History, Organization, Context, Message and Activities'. Unpublished PhD thesis, Netherlands: Utrecht University, 1988.
International Commission of Jurists (1952–). *Violations of Human Rights and the Rule of Law in Uganda: a Study*. Geneva: International Commission of Jurists, 1974.
International Congress on World Evangelization. 'Transcript of the Conclusion of the Plenary Session of the International Congress on World Evangelization'. Transcript of Audio Recording. Lausanne, Switzerland, 1974. Collection 53, Subseries A. Billy Graham Center Archives.
Isichei, Elizabeth. *A History of Christianity in Africa: From Antiquity to the Present*. Grand Rapids, Mich.: William B Eerdmans, 1995.
Jackson, Dave, and Neta Jackson. *Heroes in Black History: True Stories from the Lives of Christian Heroes*. Reprinted. Minneapolis: Bethany House, 2008.
Jackson, Robert H., and Carl G. Rosberg. *Personal Rule in Black Africa: Prince, Autocrat, Prophet, Tyrant*. Berkeley: University of California Press, 1982.
Jenkins, Philip. *The Next Christendom: The Coming of Global Christianity*. Rev. and expanded ed. The Future of Christianity Trilogy. Oxford: Oxford University Press, 2007.
Jensen, Michael Peter. *Martyrdom and Identity: The Self on Trial*. London: T & T Clark, 2010.
Jeremias, Joachim. *New Testament Theology*. The New Testament Library. London: SCM Press, 1971.
———. *The Prayers of Jesus*. Philadelphia: Fortress, 1978 [1976].
Jocelyn, Murry. 'A Bibliography of the East African Revival Movement'. *Journal of Religion in Africa* 8/2 (1975): 144–47.
Johnson, Douglas. *Contending for the Christian Faith*. Leicester: Inter-Varsity Press, 1979.
Johnson, E. Elizabeth, and David M. Hay, eds. *Pauline Theology, Volume IV: Looking Back, Pressing On*. Atlanta, GA.: Society of Biblical Literature, 1997.

Johnson, S Lewis. 'Studies in the epistle to the Colossians. IV, From enmity to amity'. *Bibliotheca Sacra* 119/474 (July 1962): 139–149.

Johnston, Thomas Paul. *Examining Billy Graham's Theology of Evangelism*. Eugene, Or.: Wipf and Stock, 2003.

Johnstone, Patrick J. St. G, and Jason Mandryk, eds. *Operation World*. 21st-century ed. Nunawading: Triune, 2001 [1978].

Jørgensen, Jan Jelmert. *Uganda: A Modern History*. London: Taylor & Francis, 1981.

Kabaza, Zabuloni. 'My Life Through Seventy Years of the East African Revival: Some Highlights'. Pages 21–33 in *The East African Revival Through Seventy Years (1935–2005): Testimonies and Reflections*. Edited by Manuel J. K. Muranga. Kabale, Uganda: Diocese of Kigezi, 2005.

Kainerugaba, Muhoozi. *Battles of the Ugandan Resistance: A Tradition of Maneuver*. Oxford: African Books Collective, 2010.

Kantonen, Taito Almar. *The Theology of Evangelism*. Philadelphia: Muhlennerg Press, 1954.

Karugire, S. R. 'The Arrival of European Missionaries'. Pages 1–16 in *A Century of Christianity in Uganda, 1877–1977: A Historical Appraisal of the Development of the Uganda Church Over the Last One Hundred Years*. Edited by A D Tom Tuma and Phares Mutibwa. Nairobi: Uzima Press, 1978.

Karugire, Samwiri Rubaraza. *A Political History of Uganda*. Nairobi: Heinemann Educational Books, 1980.

Käsemann, Ernst. *New Testament Questions of Today*. The New Testament Library. Philadelphia: Fortress, 1969.

Kasfir, Nelson. 'Civilian Participation Under Military Rule in Uganda and Sudan'. *Armed Forces and Society* 1/3 (1975): 344–63.

———. *The Shrinking Political Arena: Participation & Ethnicity in African Politics, With a Case Study of Uganda*. Berkeley: Univ of California Pr, 1976.

Kasozi, Abdu Basajabaka Kawalya, Nakanyike Musisi, and James Mukooza Sejjengo. *The Social Origins of Violence in Uganda, 1964–1985*. Montreal: McGill-Queen's University Press, 1994.

Katarikawe, James W., and John E. Wilson. 'The East African Revival Movement'. Joint MA and MTh Thesis, Pasadena, California: Fuller Theological Seminary, 1975.

Kato, Byang H. *Theological Pitfalls in Africa*. Kisumu, Kenya: Evangel Pub. House, 1975.

Katongole, Emmanuel. *The Sacrifice of Africa: A Political Theology for Africa*. Eerdmans Ekklesia Series. Grand Rapids, Mich.: W.B. Eerdmans Pub., 2011.

Keith, Ferdinando. 'Christian Identity in African Context: Reflections on Kwame Bediako's Theology and Identity'. *Journal of the Evangelical Theological Society* 50/1 (March 2007): 121–43.

Kim, Seyoon. '2 Cor 5:11–21 and the Origin of Paul's Concept of "Reconciliation"'. *Novum Testamentum* 34 (1997): 360–384.

———. *The Origin of Paul's Gospel*. Wissenschaftliche Untersuchungen Zum Neuen Testament. 2. Reihe. Tubingen: Mohr, 1981.

King, A. 'The Yakan Cult and Lugbara Response to Colonial Rule'. *Azania: Journal of the British Institute of History and Archeology in East Africa* 5 (1970): 1–25.

Kittler, Glen D. *The White Fathers*. New York: Image Books, 1961.

Kiwanuka, M. S. M. Semakula. *A History of Buganda: From the Foundation of the Kingdom to 1900*. London: Longman, 1971.

———. *Amin and the Tragedy of Uganda*. Afrika-studien. Munchen: Weltforum Verlag, 1979.

Klooster, Fred H. 'Karl Barth's Doctrine of Reconciliation: A Review Article'. *Westminster Theological Journal* 20/2 (My 1958): 170–184.

Koeberle, Adolf. 'Reconciliation and Justification'. *Concordia Theological Monthly* 21 (1950): 641–658.

Koenig, John. *Charismata: God's Gifts for God's People*. 1st ed. Biblical Perspectives on Current Issues. Philadelphia: Westminster Press, 1978.

Kokole, Omari H. 'The "Nubians" of East Africa: Muslim Club or African "Tribe"? The View From Within'. *Journal of the Institute of Muslim Minority Affairs* 6/2 (July 1985): 420–48.

Kombo, James Henry Owino. *The Doctrine of God in African Christian Thought: The Holy Trinity, Theological Hermeneutics, and the African Intellectual Culture*. Studies in Reformed theology. Leiden; Boston: Brill, 2007.

Kraftchick, Steven J. 'Facing Janus: Reviewing the Biblical Theology Movement'. *Biblical Theology: Problems and Perspectives: in Honor of J Christiaan Beker*. Edited by S. J. Kraftchick, Charles D Myers, and Ben C. Ollenburger. Nashville: Abingdon Pr, 1995.

Kreitzer, L Joseph. *Second Corinthians*. New Testament Guides. Sheffield: Sheffield Academic Pr, 1996.

Kuhn, Thomas S. *The Structure of Scientific Revolutions*. 3rd ed. Chicago, IL: University of Chicago Press, 1996.

Kyemba, Henry. *A State of Blood: The Inside Story of Idi Amin*. New York: Grosset and Dunlap, 1977.

Kymlicka, Will, and Bashir Bashir, eds. *The Politics of Reconciliation in Multicultural Societies*. Oxford; New York: Oxford University Press, 2008.

Ladd, George Eldon, and Robert A Guelich, eds. *Unity and Diversity in New Testament Theology: Essays in Honor of George E. Ladd*. Grand Rapids: Eerdmans, 1978.

Lamb, David. *The Africans*. New York: Random House, 1984.

Lambert, John C. 'Alexander Mackay "The Hero of Uganda"'. *The Romance of Missionary Heroism: True Stories of the Intrepid Bravery and Stirring Adventures of Missionaries with Uncivilised Man, Wild Beasts and the Forces of Nature in all Parts of the World*. London: Seeley & Co., 1907.

Lambrecht, Jan. 'Reconcile Yourselves . . . : A Reading of 2 Corinthians 5:11–21'. Pages 363–412 in *Studies on 2 Corinthians*. Edited by R. Bieringer and Jan Lambrecht. Bibliotheca Ephemeridum Theologicarum Lovaniensium. Louvain: Leuven University Press, 1994.

———. 'The Favorable Time'. Pages 515–529 in *Studies on 2 Corinthians*. Edited by R. Bieringer and Jan Lambrecht. Bibliotheca Ephemeridum Theologicarum Lovaniensium. Louvain: Leuven University Press, 1994.

Langley, Winston E, and Julius Emeka Okolo. 'Uganda: Expulsion of Aliens, and Human Rights'. *Current Bibliography on African Affairs* 7/4 (Fall 1974): 345–59.

Langmead, Ross. 'Transformed Relationships: Reconciliation as the Central Model for Mission'. *Mission Studies* 25 (2008): 5–20.

Leggett, Ian. *Uganda*. Oxford: Oxfam, 2001.

Legum, Colin, and Elizabeth Clements. *Africa Contemporary Record: Annual Survey and Documents, 1975–76, Vol. 8*. New York: Africana Publishing Co., 1976.

Legum, Colin, and Jacqueline Dyck. *Africa Contemporary Record: Annual Survey and Documents, 1978–79, Vol.11*. New York: Africana Publishing Co., 1980.

Lemarchand, René. *Burundi: Ethnic Conflict and Genocide*. 1st ed. Washington, D.C.: Woodrow Wilson Center Press, 1996.

———. *Burundi: Ethnocide as Discourse and Practice*. Woodrow Wilson Center series. Washington: New York, N.Y: Woodrow Wilson Center Press; Cambridge University Press, 1994.

———. 'Le Genocide De 1972 Au Burundi: Les Silences De L'histoire'. *Cahiers d'études Africaines* 167/42.3 (2002): 551–567.

Lewis, C. S. *Mere Christianity*. A revised and amplified edition, with a new introduction, of the three books "Broadcast Talks", "Christian Behaviour" and "Beyond Personality." London: Fontana, 1955.

_____. *Surprised by Joy: The Shape of My Early Life*. London: Geoffrey Bles, 1955.
Lewis, Jack Pearl. *Interpreting 2 Corinthians 5:14–21: An Exercise in Hermeneutics*. Studies in the Bible and Early Christianity. Lewiston, N.Y.: Edwin Mellen Press, 1989.
Library of Congress Federal Research Division. 'Country Studies: Area Handbook Series: Uganda: Bibliography'. Cited 1 Dec 2011. Online: http://lcweb2.loc.gov/frd/cs/uganda/ug_bibl.html.
Lincoln, Andrew T. *Ephesians*. Word Biblical Commentary. Dallas: Word Books, 1990.
Lincoln, Andrew T. 'The Church and Israel in Ephesians 2'. *Catholic Biblical Quarterly* 49/4 (1987): 605–624.
Ling, Timothy J. M. *The Judean Poor and the Fourth Gospel*. Vol. 13. Monograph Series Society for New Testament Studies. Cambridge: Cambridge University Press, 2006.
Lipschutz, Mark R. *Dictionary of African Historical Biography*. Edited by R. Kent Rasmussen. 2nd ed. Berkeley: University of California Press, 1986.
Lloyd-Jones, David Martyn. 'Living the Christian Life—New Development in the 18th and 19th Century Teaching'. *The Puritans: Their Origins and Successors: Addresses Delivered at the Puritan and Westminster Conferences 1959–1978*. Carlisle: Banner of Truth Trust, 1987.
Lofchie, Michael. 'The Political Origins of the Uganda Coup'. *Journal of African Studies* 1/4 (Winter 1974): 464–96.
_____. 'The Uganda Coup – Class Action by the Military'. *Journal of Modern African Studies* 10/1 (May 1972): 19–35.
Lohse, Eduard. *Colossians and Philemon: a Commentary on the Epistles to the Colossians and to Philemon*. Edited by Helmut Koester. Translated by William R. Poehlmann and Robert J. Karris. Philadelphia: Fortress Press, 1971.
Longenecker, Richard N, ed. *The Road from Damascus: The Impact of Paul's Conversion on His Life, Thought, and Ministry*. Grand Rapids, Mich.: W.B. Eerdmans Pub., 1997.
Longman, Timothy Paul. *Christianity and Genocide in Rwanda*. African studies. Cambridge, U.K.; New York: Cambridge University Press, 2010.
Loucks, C. M. 'The Theological Foundation of the Victorious Life'. PhD Thesis, Pasadena, CA.: Fuller Theological Seminary, 1984.
Low, D. A. *Buganda in Modern History*. University of California Press, 1971.
_____. 'Uganda Unhinged'. *International Affairs* 49/2 (April 1973): 219–228.
Luck, Anne. *African Saint: The Story of Apolo Kivebulaya*. London: SCM Press, 1963.

Lukwata, J. M. *The First Hundred Years of the Bugandan Church and Her Worship*. Rome: Ponificium Atheneum S. Anselmi De Urbe, 1991.

Lule, Yusuf K. '"We Stand for Justice": Professor Lule'. *New African*/141 (May 1979): 18–20.

Luwum, Janani. 'Preface'. *A Century of Christianity in Uganda, 1877–1977: A Historical Appraisal of the Development of the Uganda Church Over the Last One Hundred Years*. Edited by A D Tom Tuma and Phares Mutibwa. Nairobi: Uzima Press, 1978.

Lwanga-Lunyiigo, Samwiri, and Kumar Rupesinghe. 'The Colonial Roots of Internal Conflict'. *Conflict Resolution In Uganda*. London: International Peace Research Institute, Oslo & James Currey Ltd, 1989.

MacGorman, J. W. *The Gifts of the Spirit*. Nashville: Broadman Press, 1974.

MacMaster, Richard K, and Donald R Jacobs. *A Gentle Wind of God: The Influence of the East Africa Revival*. Scottdale, Pa: Herald Press, 2006.

MacNeil, John. *The Spirit-Filled Life*. London: Marshall Bros., 1894. Cited 22 Nov 2011. Online: http://hdl.handle.net/2027/[u]: nnc1.cr00285420.

Maddox, M. A. R. 'Jesus Saves Me Now: Sanctification in the Writings of Hannah Whitall Smith'. PhD Thesis, Louisville, Kent.: Southern Baptist Theological Seminary, 2003.

Mamdani, M. 'The Makerere Massacre'. Pages 128–32 in *The Debate: University of Dar es Salaam Debate on Class, State & Imperialism*. Edited by Yash Tandon. Dar es Salaam: Tanzania Publishing House, 1982.

Mamdani, Mahmood. 'Class Struggles in Uganda'. *Review of African Political Economy*/4 (November 1975): 26–61.

_____. *From Citizen to Refugee: Uganda Asians Come to Britain*. London: Frances Printer, 1973.

_____. *Politics and Class Formation in Uganda*. New York: Monthly Review Press, 1978.

Mandryk, Jason, ed. *Operation World*. 7th ed. Colorado Springs, CO: Biblica Publishing, 2010 [1978].

Mangina, Joseph L. *Karl Barth: Theologian of Christian Witness*. Louisville, Ky.: Westminster John Knox Press, 2004.

Marcelion, Komba. 'Amin's Pillage in the Kagera'. *Africa: An International Business, Economic and Political Monthly* 89 (January 1979): 12–17.

Marshall, I. Howard. 'The Meaning of Reconciliation'. *Unity and Diversity in New Testament Theology: Essays in Honor of George E. Ladd*. Edited by George Eldon Ladd and Robert A Guelich. Grand Rapids, Mich.: Eerdmans, 1978.

Martin, David. *General Amin*. London: Sphere, 1978.

Martin, Michel L. 'The Uganda Military Coup of 1971: A Study of Protest'. *Ufahamu* 2/3 (Winter 1972): 80–121.

Martin, Ralph P. *2 Corinthians*. Vol. 40. Word Biblical Commentary. Waco, Tex.: Word Books, 1986.

———. *Ephesians, Colossians and Philemon*. Interpretation, a Bible Commentary for Teaching and Preaching. Louisville: John Knox Press, 1992.

———. 'New Testament Theology: A Proposal; The Theme of Reconciliation'. *Expository Times* 91/12 (1980): 364–368.

———. 'New Testament Theology: Impasse and Exit; The Issues'. *Expository Times* 91/9 (1980): 264–269.

———. 'Reconciliation and Forgiveness in the Letter to the Colossians'. Pages 104–24 in *Reconciliation and Hope: New Testament Essays on Atonement and Eschatology, Presented to L.L. Morris on His 60th Birthday*. Edited by Robert Banks. Exeter: Paternoster, 1974.

———. *Reconciliation: A Study of Paul's Theology*. Revised ed. Grand Rapids: Zondervan, 1989 [1981].

Martin, Ralph P., and N. T. Wright. 'Reconciliation : Romans 5:1–11'. Pages 36–48 in *Romans and the People of God*. Grand Rapids, Mich.: Eerdmans, 1999.

Matthews, Arthur H. 'Terror and death in Uganda'. *Christianity Today* 21/12 (1977): 49–51.

May, John D'Arcy. 'Reconciliation in Religion and Society: A Conference in Honor of Irish Ecumenist Michael Hurley SJ'. *Mid-Stream* 33/3 (1994): 346–349.

Maya, Henry. 'The Imperialist Threat to Africa, 1: Uganda'. *African Communist*/45 (1971): 37–44.

Mazrui, Ali Al'Amin. 'Between Development and Decay: Anarchy, Tyranny and Progress under Idi Amin'. *Third World Quarterly* 2/1 (January 1980): 44–58.

———. 'Casualties of an Underdeveloped Class Structure: The Expulsion of Luo Workers and Asian Bourgeoisie from Uganda'. Pages 261–78 in *Strangers in African Societies*. Edited by William A. Shack and Elliott P. Skinner. Berkeley: University of California Press, 1979.

———. 'Is Africa Decaying? The View from Uganda'. Pages 261–78 in *Uganda Now: Between Decay & Development*. Edited by Holger Bernt Hansen and Michael Twaddle. London: James Curry, 1988.

———. *Is the Nile Valley Emerging as a New Political System? the View from Lake Victoria*. Kampala: Makerere University, 1971.

_____. *The African Condition: A Political Diagnosis*. London; New York: Cambridge University Press, 1980.

_____. *The Africans: A Triple Heritage*. 1st ed. Boston: Little, Brown, 1986.

_____. 'The Lumpen Proletariat and the Lumpen Militariat: African Soldiers as a New Political Class'. *Political Studies* 21/1 (1973): 1–12.

_____. *Towards a Pax Africana: A Study of Ideology and Ambition*. The Nature of human society series. London: Weidenfeld & Nicolson, 1967.

Mazrui, Ali Al'Amin, and Toby Kleban Levine, eds. *The Africans: A Reader*. New York, N.Y.: Praeger, 1986.

Mazrui, Ali Al'Amin, ed. *The Warrior Tradition in Modern Africa*. Vol. 23. International Studies in Sociology and Social Anthropology. Leiden: Brill, 1977.

Mazrui, Ali Al'Amin, and Hasu H Patel, eds. *Africa in World Affairs: The Next Thirty Years*. New York: Third Press, 1973.

Mbiti, John S. *African Religions & Philosophy*. 2nd ed. Oxford; Portsmouth, N.H: Heinemann, 1990 [1969].

_____. *Concepts of God in Africa*. London: SPCK, 1970.

_____. *Introduction to African Religion*. London: Heinemann Educational, 1975.

_____. *New Testament Eschatology in an African Background: A Study of the Encounter Between New Testament Theology and African Traditional Concepts*. London: Oxford University Press, 1971.

_____. *The Crisis of Mission in Africa*. Mukono: Uganda Church Press, 1971.

McCormack, Bruce L. 'The Significance of Karl Barth's Theological Exegesis of Philippians'. Page v–xxv in *The Epistle to the Philippians*. Louisville, KY: Westminster John Knox Press, 2002.

McDonald, J.I.H. 'Paul and the Preaching Ministry. A Reconsideration of 2 Cor 2:14–17 in its Context'. *Journal for the Study of the New Testament* 17 (1983): 35–50.

McGlasson, Paul. *Jesus and Judas: Biblical Exegesis in Barth*. Scholars Press, 1991.

McQuilkin, J. Robertson. 'The Keswick Perspective'. Pages 151–83 in *Five Views on Sanctification*. Edited by Melvin Easterday Dieter and Stanley N. Gundry. Grand Rapids: Zondervan, 1987.

Meierhenrich, Jens. 'Varieties of Reconciliation'. *Law and Social Inquiry* 33/1 (Winter 2008): 195–231.

Meisler, Stanley. 'From Dreams to Brutality'. *Nation* 215/15 (November 13, 1972): 463–466.

Melady, Thomas P., and Margaret Melady. *Uganda: The Asian Exiles*. Maryknoll, N.Y.: Orbis Books, 1978.

Melady, Thomas Patrick, and Margaret Melady. *Idi Amin Dada: Hitler in Africa*. First Edition. Kansas City: Sheed Andrews and McMeel, 1977.
Merrick, James R. A. 'Justice, Forgiveness, and Reconciliation: The Reconciliatory Cross as Forgiving Justice: A Response to Don McLennan'. *Evangelical Review of Theology* 30/3 (2006): 292–308.
Merwe, Hugo Van der, and Audrey R. Chapman. *Truth and Reconciliation in South Africa: Did the TRC Deliver?* University of Pennsylvania Press, 2008.
Meyer, F. B. *Christian Living*. London: Morgan and Scott, 1902.
———. *The Christ-Life for the Self-Life [Formerly "A Castaway"]*. Chicago: Moody Press, 1900.
Michael, Cassidy. 'Foreword to Second Edition'. Pages 3–5 in *Revolutionary Love*. Monrovia, Ca.: African Enterprise, 2001 [1983].
Millar, Norman N. 'Military Coup in Uganda: The Rise of the Second Republic'. *Fieldstaff Reports: East Africa Series* 10/3 (1971): 1–18.
Miller, Jake C. *Prophets of a Just Society*. New York: Nova, 2002.
Miller, Judith. 'When Sanctions Worked'. *Foreign Policy*/39 (Summer 1980): 118–29.
Miller, Keith Graber. *Wise As Serpents, Innocent As Doves: American Mennonites Engage Washington*. 1st ed. Knoxville: University of Tennessee Press, 1996.
Mitchell, Robert Cameron. *African Primal Religions*. Major world religions series. Niles, Ill: Argus Communications, 1977.
Mittelman, James H. 'The Anatomy of a Coup: Uganda, 1971'. *Africa Quarterly* 11/3 (1971): 184–202.
Mmbando, S. I. *The Tanzania-Uganda War in Pictures*. Dar es Salaam: Longman Tanzania, 1980.
Moberg, David O. *The Great Reversal: Evangelism Versus Social Concern*. Rev. ed. Philadelphia: Lippincott, 1977 [1972].
Moo, Douglas J. *The Epistle to the Romans*. The New International Commentary on the New Testament. Grand Rapids, Mich.: W.B. Eerdmans Pub. Co., 1996.
———. *The Letters to the Colossians and to Philemon*. The Pillar New Testament Commentary. Grand Rapids, Mich.: William B. Eerdmans Pub. Co., 2008.
Morgan, Robert. 'New Testament Theology'. Pages 104–130 in *Biblical Theology: Problems and Perspectives: in Honor of J Christiaan Beker*. Edited by S. J. Kraftchick, C. D. Myers Jr., and B. C. Ollenburger. Nashville: Abingdon Press, 1995.

_____. *The Nature of New Testament Theology: The Contribution of William Wrede and Adolf Schlatter*. Vol. 25. Studies in Biblical Theology. London: SCM, 1973.

Moritz, Thorsten. *A Profound Mystery: The Use of the Old Testament in Ephesians*. Vol. 85. Supplements to Novum Testamentum. Leiden: E.J. Brill, 1996.

Morris, Leon. 'Reconciliation'. *Christianity Today* 13/8 (1969): 331–332.

_____. *The Atonement: Its Meaning and Significance*. Leicester: Inter-Varsity Press, 1983.

_____. 'Universalism'. Pages 1–2 in *Hinderances to Evangelism: in the Church*. Kongresshalle, Berlin, 1966.

Mosala, Itumeleng J. 'The Meaning of Reconciliation: A Black Perspective'. *Journal of Theology for Southern Africa* 59 (1987): 19–25.

Moule, H. C. G, and Charles Forbes Harford. 'The Message: It's Scriptual Character'. Pages 65–74 in *The Keswick Convention: Its Message, Its Method and Its Men*. London: Marshall Brothers, 1907.

Moule, H. C. G. *The Epistle of St. Paul to the Romans*. The Expositors Bible. London: Hodder and Stoughton, 1894.

Moyer, B. E. 'The Doctrine of Christian Perfection: A Comparative Study of John Wesley and the Modern American Holiness Movement'. PhD Thesis, Milwaukee, Wis.: Marquette University, 1992.

Muga, Erasto. *African Response to Western Christian Religion: A Sociological Analysis of African Separatist Religious and Political Movements in East Africa*. Kampala: East African Literature Bureau, 1975.

Muhima, Edward Bakaitwako. 'The Fellowship of Christian Suffering: A Theological Interpretation of Christian Suffering under Idi Amin'. PhD thesis, Evanston, Ill.: Northwestern University, 1981.

Mujaju, Akiiki B. 'The Political Crisis of Church Institutions in Uganda'. *African Affairs* 75/298 (1976): 67–85.

Müller, David L. *Foundations of Karl Barth's Doctrine of Reconciliation: Jesus Christ Crucified and Risen*. Mampeter: Edwin Mellen Press, 1990.

Munger, Edwin S., and Anon. *Inside Amin's Uganda: More Africans Murdered*. Vol. 18. Munger Africana Library Notes. Pasadena, Ca.: California Institute of Technology, 1973.

Muranga, Manuel J. K. 'The Revival's Impact on the Naming Traditions of the People of East Africa, with Special Reference to Kigezi and Ankole'. Pages 65–80 in *The East African Revival Through Seventy Years (1935–2005): Testimonies and Reflections*. Edited by Manuel J. K. Muranga. Kabale, Uganda: Diocese of Kigezi, 2005.

Muranga, Manuel J. K., ed. *The East African Revival Through Seventy Years (1935–2005): Testimonies and Reflections*. Kabale, Uganda: Diocese of Kigezi, 2005.

Murray, Andrew. *Abide in Christ: Thoughts on the Blessed Life of Fellowship with the Son of God*. London: Oliphants, 1963 [1895].

———. *The Deeper Christian Life: An Aid to Its Attainment*. Fleming H. Revell, 1895.

———. *The Deeper Christian Life: An Aid to Its Attainment*. Chicago, Ill.: Fleming H. Revell, 1895.

———. *The Full Blessing of Pentecost: The One Thing Needful*. Whitefish, Mont.: Kessinger, 2010 [1908].

———. *The Spirit of Christ: Thoughts on the Indwelling of the Holy Spirit in the Believer and the Church*. London: Nisbet, 1888.

———. *The Two Covenants and the Second Blessing*. London: James Nisbet, 1899.

Murray, John. 'The Reconciliation'. *Westminster Theological Journal* 29 (1966): 1–23.

Museveni, Yoweri. *Sowing the Mustard Seed: The Struggle for Freedom and Democracy in Uganda*. London: Macmillan, 1997.

Mutengesa, Sabiiti, and Dylan Hendrickson. 'Prospects for Addressing Uganda's Small Arms Problem Through Security Reform'. CSDG Papers. Kings College London: Conflict, Security & Development Group, 2007. Online: securityanddevelopment.org.

Mutesa, King of Buganda. *Desecration of My Kingdom*. London: Constable, 1967.

Mutibwa, Phares. *The Buganda Factor in Uganda Politics*. Kampala: Fountain Publishers, 2008.

———. *Uganda Since Independence: A Story of Unfulfilled Hopes*. First Ugandan Edition. Kampala: Fountain Publishers, 1991.

Myers, Ched, and Elaine Enns. *Ambassadors of Reconciliation*. Vol. 1. 2 vols. Maryknoll, N.Y.: Orbis Books, 2009.

Nanjira, Don, and D. C. Daniel. *Status of Aliens in East Africa: Asians and Europeans in Tanzania, Uganda and Kenya*. Praeger Special Studies in International Politics and Government. New York: Praeger Publishers Inc, 1976.

Nanyenya, Peter. 'A Case Study of the Law Relating to the Expulsion of Aliens and Nationalization of Alien Property: The Case of Uganda'. *Uganda Law Focus* 2/2 (September 1974): 100–126.

Naselli, Andrew David. 'Keswick Theology: A Historical and Theological Survey and Analysis of the Doctrine of Sanctification in the Early Keswick

Movement, 1975–1920'. PhD thesis, Greenville, S.C.: Bob Jones University, 2006.

Nets-Zehngut, Rafi. 'Analyzing the Reconciliation Process'. *International Journal on World Peace* 24/3 (2007): 53–81.

New African. 'Uganda's Historical Moshi Conference'. *New African* 141 (May 1979): 14–17.

Newbigin, Lesslie. *A Word in Season: Perspectives on Christian World Missions.* Grand Rapids, Mich.: William B. Eerdmans, 1994.

Nicholls, Bruce J. *In Word and Deed: Evangelism and Social Responsibility.* Grand Rapids, Mich: William B Eerdmans Pub Co, 1986.

Nichols, Alan. *Crusading Down Under : The Story of the Billy Graham Crusades in Australia and New Zealand.* Minneapolis: World Wide Publications, 1970.

Niringiye, D. Z. 'The Church in the World: A Historical – Ecclesiological Study of the Church of Uganda with Particular Reference to Post-Independence Uganda, 1962–1992'. Unpublished PhD thesis, Edinburgh: University of Edinburgh, 1992.

Noll, Mark A. *The New Shape of World Christianity: How American Experience Reflects Global Faith.* Downers Grove, Ill.: IVP Academic, 2009.

———. *The Rise of Evangelicalism: The Age of Edwards Whitefield and the Wesleys.* A History of Evangelicalism. Nottingham: Inter-Varsity, 2004.

Noll, Mark A., and Carolyn Nystrom. *Clouds of Witnesses: Christian Voices from Africa and Asia.* Downers Grove, Ill.: IVP Books, 2011.

Nsibambi, Apolo. 'The Importance of the East African Revival (Obulokole)'. Pages 43–48 in *The East African Revival Through Seventy Years (1935–2005): Testimonies and Reflections.* Edited by Manuel J. K. Muranga. Kabale, Uganda: Diocese of Kigezi, 2005.

Nurnburger, Ralph D. 'The United States and Amin: Congress to the Rescue'. *African Studies Review* 25/1 (March 1982): 49–65.

Nursey-Bray, Paul. 'Uganda: The Resistible Rise of Idi Amin?'. *Flinders Journal of History and Politics* 4 (1974): 95–116.

O'Brien, Peter T. 'Col 1:20 and the Reconciliation of All Things'. *Reformed Theological Review* 33/1 (1974): 45–53.

———. *Colossians, Philemon.* Word Biblical Commentary. Milton Keynes: Word, 1987.

———. *The Letter to the Ephesians.* The Pillar New Testament Commentary. Grand Rapids, Mich.: Eerdmans, 1999.

Obote, Milton. 'Memorandum Outlines Overthrow of Uganda Regime'. *Translations on Sub-Saharan Africa* No. 1717 (March 2, 1977): 127–39.

Okoth, Godfrey P. 'The OAU and the Uganda-Tanzania War, 1978–1979'. *Journal of African Studies* 14/3 (Fall 1987): 152–62.

Okullu, Henry. *Church and Politics in East Africa*. Nairobi, Kenya: Uzima Press, 1974.

Okure, Teresa. 'The Ministry of Reconciliation (2 Cor 5:14–21): Paul's Key to the Problem of "The Other" in Corinth'. *Mission Studies* 23/1 (2006): 105–121.

Old, Hughes Oliphant. *The Reading and Preaching of the Scriptures in the Worship of the Christian Church*. Vol. 7. 7 vols. Grand Rapids, Mich.: W.B. Eerdmans, 2010.

Omara-Otunnu, Amii. *Politics and the Military in Uganda, 1890–1985*. London: Macmillan, 1987.

Opoku, Kofi Asare. *West African Traditional Religion*. Accra, [Ghana]: FEP International Private Limited, 1978.

Osborn, Herbert Henry. *Pioneers in the East African Revival*. Hampshire: Apologia Publications, 2000.

Packer, J. I. '"Keswick" and the Reformed Doctrine of Sanctification'. *Evangelical Quarterly* 27.3 (1955): 153–67.

Padilla, C. René. 'Evangelism and Social Responsibility'. *Transformation* 2/3 (July): 27 –34.

Padilla, Rene C., and Chris Sugden. 'How Evangelicals Endorsed Social Responsibility'. *Texts on Evangelical Social Ethics 1974–83*. Nottingham: Grove Books Ltd, 1985.

Parrinder, Edward Geoffrey. *African Traditional Religion*. 3rd ed. London: Sheldon Press, 1974 [1954].

Parshall, Phil. *Divine Threads Within a Human Tapestry: Memoirs of Phil Parshall*. Pasadena: William Carey Library, 2003.

Pattison, Stephen. *Shame: Theory, Therapy, Theology*. Cambridge: Cambridge University Press, 2000.

Payne, Tony. 'A Short History of Deliverance'. Pages 12–34 in *Christ's Victory Over Evil: Biblical Theology and Pastoral Ministry*. Edited by Peter G. Bolt. Nottingham, England: Inter Varsity Press, 2009.

Penna, Romano. *Paul the Apostle: A Theological and Exegetical Study*. 2 vols. Collegeville, MN: Liturgical Press, 1996.

Perlmutter, Amos, and Valerie Plave Bennett. *The Political Influence of the Military: A Comparative Reader*. New Haven, Connecticut: Yale University Press, 1980.

Peter, Enahoro. 'Whither Uganda'. *Africa: An International Business, Economic and Political Monthly* 16 (December 1972): 13–17.

Pickering, Ernest D. *The Theology of Evangelism*. Clarks Summit, PA: Baptist Bible College Press, 1974.

Piennisch, Markus, *Kommunikation und Gottesdienst. Grundlinien göttlicher Zuwendung in Bibel und Verkündigung*. Neuhausen: Hänssler, 1995, 212–14.

Pierson, A. T. 'Unsubdued Sin'. Pages 100–10 in *Keswick's Triumphant Voice: Forty-Eight Outstanding Addresses Delivered at the Keswick Convention, 1882–1962*. Edited by Herbert F Stevenson. London: Marshall, Morgan and Scott, 1963.

Pierson, Arthur Tappan. *The Keswick Movement in Precept and Practise*. BiblioBazaar, 2009.

_____. *Vital Union with Christ*. Grand Rapids, Mich.: Zondervan Publishing House, 1961.

Pirouet, M. Louise. *Black Evangelists: The Spread of Christianity in Uganda, 1891–1914*. London: Rex Collings, 1978.

_____. *Historical Dictionary of Uganda*. African Historical Dictionaries. Metuchen, N.J.: Scarecrow Press, 1995.

_____. 'Religion in Uganda under Amin'. *Journal of Religion in Africa* 11/1 (1980): 13–29.

Plevnik, Joseph. 'The Center of Pauline Theology'. *Catholic Biblical Quarterly* 51/3 (1989): 461–478.

Plummer, Alfred. *A Critical and Exegetical Commentary on the Second Epistle of St. Paul to the Corinthians*. Vol. 34. The International Critical Commentary. Edinburgh: T. & T. Clark, 2000 [1915].

_____. *The Second Epistle of Paul the Apostle to the Corinthians*. The Cambridge Bible for Schools and Colleges. Cambridge: Cambridge University Press, 1911.

Polman, A. D. R. *Barth*. International Library of Philosophy and Theology. Modern Thinker's Series. Philadelphia: Presbyterian and Reformed, 1960.

Porter, Stanley E. *Idioms of the Greek New Testament*. 2nd ed. Biblical Languages. Greek. Sheffield: JSOT Press, 1994 [1992].

_____. *Katallassō in Ancient Greek Literature, with Reference to the Pauline Writings*. Estudios de filología Neotestamentaria. Cordoba, Spain: Almendro, 1994.

_____. 'Peace, Reconciliation'. Pages 695–99 in *Dictionary of Paul and his Letters*. Edited by G. F. Hawthorn, Ralph P. Martin, and D. G. Reid. Downers Grove, Ill.: InterVarsity, 1993.

_____. 'Reconciliation and 2 Cor 5,18–21'. Pages 693–705 in *Corinthian Correspondence*. Edited by Reimund Bieringer. Bibliotheca Ephemeridum Theologicarum Lovaniensium. Leuven: Leuven University Press, 1996.

Posner, Michael H., Lawyers Committee for International Human Rights, and United States. Congress. Senate. Committee on Foreign Relations. Subcommittee on Foreign Economic Policy. *Violations of Human Rights in Uganda, 1971–1978: Testimony Prepared for the Subcommittee on Foreign Economic Policy of the United States Senate Committee on Foreign Relations*. New York: Lawyers Committee for International Human Rights, 1978.

Potter, Ronald C. 'Race, Theological Discourse and the Continuing American Dilemma'. Pages 27–36 in *The Gospel in Black and White: Theological Resources for Racial Reconciliation*. Edited by Dennis L Okholm. Downers Grove, Ill: InterVarsity Press, 1997.

Price, Charles W. *Transforming Keswick*. Edited by Ian M Randall. Carlisle, Cumbria: OM Pub., 2000.

Pulford, Cedric. *Eating Uganda: From Christianity to Conquest*. Banbury: Ituri, 1999.

Quinn, Frederick. *African Saints: Saints, Martyrs, and Holy People from the Continent of Africa*. New York: Crossroad Publishing Company, 2002.

Räisänen, Heikki. *Beyond New Testament Theology: A Story and a Programme*. 2nd ed. London: SCM Press, 2000 [1990].

Rathe, Mark Steven. 'The Keswick Movement: Its Origins and Teachings'. M. A. Thesis, San Francisco, CA.: Simpson College, 1988.

Ravenhill, Frederick John. 'Military Intervention in the Domestic Political Systems of Black Africa: The Case of Uganda'. Masters Thesis, Halifax, Nova Scotia, Canada: Dalhousie University, 1973.

_____. 'The Military and Politics in Uganda'. *Africa Quarterly* 19/2 (September 1979): 122–47.

Ray, Benjamin C. *African Religions: Symbol, Ritual, and Community*. 2nd ed. Upper Saddle River, N.J: Prentice Hall, 2000 [1976].

Raymond, P. Prigodich. 'A Review of Festo Kivengere: A Biography'. *Missiology: An International Review* XXII/2 (April 1994).

Reed, Colin. *Pastors, Partners and Paternalists: African Church Leaders and Western Missionaries in the Anglican Church in Kenya, 1850–1900*. Brill Academic Pub, 1997.

_____. 'The East African Revival and Australia (1930–1980)'. PhD thesis, Kensington, Australia: Australian College of Theology, 2003.

———. *Walking in the Light: Reflections on the East Africa Revival and Its Link to Australia*. Brunswick East, Vic.: Acorn Press Ltd., 2007.

Reumann, John. *Variety and Unity in New Testament Thought*. Oxford Bible Series. Oxford: Ox. Univ. Press, 1991.

Reumann, John, ed. *The Promise and Practice of Biblical Theology*. Minneapolis: Fortress Press, 1991.

Van Rheenen, Gailyn. *Church Planting in Uganda: A Comparative Study*. South Pasadena, Calif.: William Carey Library, 1976.

Rienecker, Fritz. *A Linguistic Key to the Greek New Testament*. Edited by Cleon L. Rogers. Translated by Cleon L. Rogers. Vol. 2. 2 vols. Grand Rapids, Mich.: Zondervan, 1980.

Rikahuru, S. 'Uganda and Amin'. *African Red Family*/no. 2 (1973): 41–50.

Riss, Richard M. *A Survey of 20th-Century Revival Movements in North America*. Peabody, Mass.: Hendrickson, 1988.

Rittner, Carol, John K Roth, and Wendy Whitworth, eds. *Genocide in Rwanda: Complicity of the Churches?* 1st ed. Newark, Notts., U.K.: St. Paul, Minn: Aegis; Paragon House, 2004.

Roberts, J.H. 'Some Biblical Foundations for Mission of Reconciliation'. *Missionalia* 7 (1979): 3–17.

Robinson, James McConkey. *The New Hermeneutic*. New York: Harper & Row, 1964.

Roels, Edwin D. *God's Mission: The Epistle to the Ephesians in Mission Perspective*. Franeker: T. Wever, 1962.

Roome, William J. W. *Apolo, the Apostle to the Pygmies*. London: Marshall, 1934.

Rosner, Brian S. *Paul, Scripture and Ethics: A Study of 1 Corinthians 5–7*. 1st ed. Biblical Studies Library. Grand Rapids: Baker Books, 1999.

Rosner, Brian S., ed. *The Wisdom of the Cross: Exploring 1 Corinthians*. Nottingham: Apollos, 2011.

Rotberg, Robert I, and Ali Al'Amin Mazrui, eds. *Protest and Power in Black Africa*. New York: Oxford University Press, 1970.

Roth, John D. 'Forgiveness and the Healing of Memories: An Anabaptist–Mennonite Perspective'. *Journal of Ecumenical Studies* 42/4 (Fall 2007): 573–588.

Rothchild, D., and J.W. Harbeson. *The Political Economy of Rehabilitation in Uganda*. African Studies association, 1980.

Rugyendo, Medard. 'How to Keep the Revival Fire Burning'. Pages 81–91 in *The East African Revival Through Seventy Years (1935–2005): Testimonies and*

Reflections. Edited by Manuel J. K. Muranga. Kabale, Uganda: Diocese of Kigezi, 2005.

Rukirande, William. 'The East African Revival and the Church in Kigezi: A Personal Experience'. Pages 1–12 in *The East African Revival Through Seventy Years (1935–2005): Testimonies and Reflections*. Edited by Manuel J. K. Muranga. Kabale, Uganda: Diocese of Kigezi, 2005.

Sampson, Anthony. *Mandela: The Authorised Biography*. New Ed. New York: HarperCollins, 2000.

Sanders, E. P. *Paul and Palestinian Judaism: A Comparison of Patterns of Religion*. London: SCM, 1977.

Sarpong, Peter. *Ghana in Retrospect: Some Aspects of Ghanaian Culture*. Tema: Ghana Pub. Corp, 1975.

Saul, John S. 'The Unsteady State: Uganda, Obote and General Amin'. *Review of African Political Economy* 5 (April 1976): 12–38.

Schmidt, Richard H. *Glorious Companions: Five Centuries of Anglican Spirituality*. Grand Rapids, Mich.: W.B. Eerdmans, 2002.

Schroder, Barbet. *General Idi Amin Dada*. DVD. Criterion Collection. Criterion, 1974.

Seers, Dudley. *The Rehabilitation of the Economy of Uganda: A Report*. London: Commonwealth Fund for Technical Co-operation, Commonwealth Secretariat, 1979.

Segal, Alan F. *Paul the Convert: The Apostolate and Apostasy of Saul the Pharisee*. New Haven: Yale U.P., 1990.

Seiffert, Murray. *Gumbuli of Ngukurr: Aboriginal Elder in Arnhem Land*. Brunswick East, Australia: Acorn Press Ltd, 2011.

Selwyn, Douglas Ryan. 'Uganda: A Balance Sheet of the Revolution'. *Mawazo* 3/1 (June 1971): 37–64.

Sempangi, Kefa F. 'Uganda's Reign of Terror'. *Worldview (New York)* 18/5 (May 1975): 16–21.

Semujju. 'My Life in Exile'. *The Weekly Observer*. Kampala, August 23, 2007. Online: http://www.observer.ug/new/specials/mylife/mylife200708301.php.

Sentamu, John. 'Tribalism, Religion and Despotism in Uganda: Archbishop Janani Luwum'. Pages 144–58 in *The Terrible Alternative: Christian Martyrdom in the Twentieth Century*. Edited by Andrew Chandler. London: Cassell, 1998.

_____. 'Tribalism, Religion and Despotism in Uganda: Archbishop Janani Luwum'. Pages 144–158 in *The Terrible Alternative: Christian Martyrdom in the Twentieth Century*. Edited by Andrew Chandler. London: Cassell, 1998.

Senteza-Kajubi, W. 'Background to War and Violence in Uganda'. Pages 15–52 in *War, Violence, and Children in Uganda*. Edited by Cole P. Dodge and Magne Raundalen. Oslo: Norwegian University Press, 1987.

Sesay, Amadu. 'The OAU and Regime Recognition: Politics of Discord and Collaboration in Africa'. *Scandinavian Journal of Development Alternatives* 4/1 (March 1985): 25–41.

Sharp, Douglas R. *No Partiality: The Idolatry of Race & the New Humanity*. Downers Grove, Ill.: InterVarsity Press, 2002.

Shaw, Mark. *Global Awakening: How 20th-Century Revivals Triggered a Christian Revolution*. Downers Grove, Ill.: IVP Academic, 2010.

Shaw, Timothy M. 'Uganda Under Amin: The Cost of Confronting Independence'. *Africa Today* 20/2 (Spring 1973): 32–45.

Shenk, David W. *Justice, Reconciliation, and Peace in Africa*. Rev. ed. Nairobi: Uzima Press, 1997.

_____. 'The Gospel of Reconciliation Within the Wrath of Nations'. *International Bulletin of Missionary Research* 32/1 (2008): 2–9.

Shore, Megan. 'Christianity and Justice in the South African Truth and Reconciliation Commission: A Case Study in Religious Conflict Resolution'. *Political Theology* 9/2 (Ap 2008): 161–178.

Shorter, Aylward. 'Mukasa Balikuddembe, Joseph'. *Dictionary of African Christian Biography*. Cited 21 Dec 2010. Online: http://www.dacb.org/stories/uganda/mukasa_joseph.html.

Shorter, Aylward, and Eugene Kataza, eds. *Missionaries to Yourselves; African Catechists Today*. Maryknoll, N.Y: Orbis Books, 1972.

Simpson, E. K., and F. F. Bruce. *Commentary on the Epistles to the Ephesians and the Colossians*. London: Marshall, 1957.

Sinclair, Victor. 'The Sovereignty of God in Reconciliation, with Karl Barth as a Guide'. *Irish Biblical Studies* 18 (1996): 156–169.

Smart, James D. *Past, Present and Future of Biblical Theology*. Westminster, U.S.: John Knox Press, 1980.

Smit, D J. 'The Truth and Reconciliation Commission –Tentative Religious and Theological Perspectives'. *Journal of Theology for Southern Africa*/90 (1995): 3–15.

Southhall, Aidan. 'General Amin and the Coup: Great Man or Historical Inevitability?'. *Journal of Modern African Studies* 13/1 (March 1975): 85–105.

_____. 'Social Disorganization in Uganda: Before, During and After Amin'. *Journal of Modern African Studies* 18/no. 4 (1980): 627–56.

Spear, Thomas T., and Isaria N. Kimambo. *East African Expressions of Christianity*. James Currey, 1999.
Spears, Richard A. *McGraw-Hill's Dictionary of American Idioms and Phrasal Verbs*. Chicago: McGraw-Hill, 2005.
St. John, Patricia Mary. *Breath of Life: The Story of the Ruanda Mission*. London: Norfolk Press, 1971.
Stanford, J. Paget. 'Reconciliation in Uganda?'. *Third Way* (April 1981): 13–17.
Stanley, Brian. 'The East African Revival'. *Evangelical Review of Theology* 2/2 (1978): 188–207.
Stanley, Christopher D. '"Neither Jew nor Greek": Ethnic Conflict in Graeco-Roman Society'. *Journal for the Study of the New Testament*/64 (1996): 101–124.
Steinhart, Edward I. *Conflict and Collaboration: The Kingdoms of Western Uganda, 1890–1907*. 1st ed. Princeton: Princeton University Press, 1977.
Stenschke, Christoph W. 'The Death of Jesus and the New Testament Doctrine of Reconciliation in Recent Discussion'. *European Journal of Theology* 9/2 (2000): 131–158.
Stevenson, Herbert F., ed. *Keswick's Authentic Voice: Sixty-Five Dynamic Addresses Delivered at the Keswick Convention, 1875–1957*. London: Marshall, Morgan & Scott, 1959.
_____. *Keswick's Triumphant Voice: Forty-Eight Outstanding Addresses Delivered at the Keswick Convention, 1882–1962*. London: Marshall, Morgan and Scott, 1963.
Stott, John R. W. 'God's New Society (1) New Life (Ephesians 1:1–2:10)'. Pages 43–52 in *The Keswick Week 1975: Centenary Year*. London: Marshall, Morgan & Scott, 1975.
_____. 'God's New Society (2) New Life (Ephesians 2:11–3:21)'. Pages 65–74 in *The Keswick Week 1975: Centenary Year*. London: Marshall, Morgan & Scott, 1975.
_____. 'God's New Society (3) New Life (Ephesians 4:1–5:21)'. Pages 89–100 in *The Keswick Week 1975: Centenary Year*. London: Marshall, Morgan & Scott, 1975.
_____. 'God's New Society (4) New Life (Ephesians 5:22–6:24)'. Pages 123–133 in *The Keswick Week 1975: Centenary Year*. London: Marshall, Morgan & Scott, 1975.
_____. *John Stott at Keswick: A Lifetime of Preaching*. Edited by Keswick Ministries. Milton Keynes, UK: Authentic Media, 2008.

———. *Men Made New: An Exposition of Romans 5–8*. American ed. Grand Rapids: Baker Book House, 1984.

———. *People My Teachers*. London: Candle Books, 2002.

———. *The Cross of Christ*. 20th ed. Nottingham: Inter-Varsity Press, 2006 [1986].

———. *The Message of Ephesians: God's New Society*. 2nd ed. The Bible Speaks Today. New Testament Series. Leicester: Inter-Varsity, 1991 [1979].

———. *The Message of Romans: God's Good News for the World*. The Bible Speaks Today. New Testament Series. Leicester, England: Inter-Varsity Press, 1994.

Stott, John R. W., and Lausanne Committee for World Evangelization, eds. *Making Christ Known: Historic Mission Documents from the Lausanne Movement 1974–1989*. Carlisle: Paternoster Press, 1996.

Stuhlmacher, Peter. 'The Gospel of Reconciliation in Christ: Basic Features and Issues of a Biblical Theology of the New Testament'. *Horizons in Biblical Theology* 1 (1980): 161–190.

Sugden, Chris, and Vinay Samuel. 'Evangelism and Social Responsibility: A Biblical Study on Priorities'. Pages 189–214 in *In Word and Deed: Evangelism and Social Responsibility*. Edited by Bruce J. Nicholls. Grand Rapids, Mich: William B Eerdmans Pub Co, 1986.

Sundkler, Bengt. *A History of the Church in Africa*. Cambridge: Cambridge University Press, 2000.

Taber, Charles R, ed. *The Church in Africa, 1977: Papers Presented at a Symposium at Milligan College, March 31–April 3, 1977*. South Pasadena, Calif: William Carey Library, 1978.

Talbott, Thomas B. 'The New Testament and Universal Reconciliation'. *Christian Scholar's Review* 21/4 (1992): 376–394.

Taylor, J. V. *Processes of Growth in an African Church*. London: SCM Press, 1958.

Tennent, Timothy C. *Christianity at the Religious Roundtable: Evangelicalism in Conversation with Hinduism, Buddhism, and Islam*. Grand Rapids, MI: Baker Academic, 2002.

Theissen, Gunnar. 'Common Past, Divided Truth: The Truth and Reconciliation Commission in South African Public Opinion'. Unpublished Paper presented at the International Institute for the Sociology of Law. Onati, Spain, September 22, 1999. Cited 15 Mar 2012. Online: http://userpage.zedat.fu-berlin.de/~theissen/pdf/IISL-Paper.PDF.

Thielicke, Helmut. *Modern Faith and Thought*. Grand Rapids, Mich.: Eerdmans, 1990.

Thomas, Cal. 'Uganda's New Day gets Big Boost from Christian Leaders'. *Journal Champion* 1/25 (April 20, 1979): 1–8.
Thomas, Caroline. *New States, Sovereignty and Intervention*. New York: St Martin's Press, 1985.
Thomas, Norman E. 'Evangelization and Church Growth: The Case of Africa'. *International Bulletin of Missionary Research* 11/4 (1987): 165–170.
Thomson, Ian H. *Chiasmus in the Pauline Letters*. Vol. 11. Journal for the Study of the New Testament. Supplement Series. Sheffield: Sheffield Academic Press, 1995.
Thoonen, J. P. *Black Martyrs*. London: Sheed and Ward, 1941.
Thrall, Margaret E. 'Salvation Proclaimed, Pt 5: 2 Corinthians 5:18–21: Reconciliation with God'. *Expository Times* 93/8 (My 1982): 227–232.
_____. *The First and Second Letters of Paul to the Corinthians: Commentary*. The Cambridge Bible Commentary. New English Bible. Cambridge: Cambridge University Press, 1965.
Tissington, Tatlow. *The Story of the Student Christian Movement of Great Britain and Ireland*. London: SCM, 1933.
Tobin, Thomas H. *Paul's Rhetoric in Its Contexts: The Argument of Romans*. Peabody, Mass.: Hendrickson Publishers, 2004.
Tolbert, Malcolm. 'Theology and Ministry: 2 Corinthians 5:11–21'. *Faith and Mission* 1/1 (Fall 1983): 63–70.
Tomka, Miklós. 'Religious Identity and the Gospel of Reconciliation'. *Religion in Eastern Europe* 29/1 (2009): 20–28.
Tosh, J. 'Small-Scale Resistance in Uganda: The Lango Rising at Adwari in 1919'. *Azania: Journal of the British Institute of History and Archeology in East Africa* 9 (1974): 51–64.
Tosh, John. *Clan Leaders and Colonial Chiefs in Lango: The Political History of an East African Stateless Society C. 1800–1939*. Oxford University Press, USA, 1979.
Traill, Elizabeth. 'The East African Revival: A School Teacher's Testimony'. Pages 34–42 in *The East African Revival Through Seventy Years (1935–2005): Testimonies and Reflections*. Edited by Manuel J. K. Muranga. Kabale, Uganda: Diocese of Kigezi, 2005.
_____. *Venturesome Love: The Story of Constance Hornby, 1884–1972*. Handsel Press, Limited, 2011.
Treier, Daniel J. *Introducing Theological Interpretation of Scripture: Recovering a Christian Practice*. Nottingham; Grand Rapids, Mich: Apollos; Baker Academic, 2008.

Tribe, M. A. 'Economic Aspects of the Expulsion of Asians From Uganda'. Pages 140–76 in *Expulsion of a Minority: Essays on Ugandan Asians*. Edited by Michael Twaddle. London: Continuum International Publishing Group – Athlone, 1975.

Tripp, Thomas M, Robert J Bies, and Karl Aquino. 'A Vigilante Model of Justice: Revenge, Reconciliation, Forgiveness, and Avoidance'. *Social Justice Research* 20/1 (2007): 3–34.

Trumbull, Charles G. *Victory in Christ*. Fort Washington, Penn.: Christian Literature Crusade, 1980.

Tuma, A. D. Tom. 'Church Expansion in Buganda'. Pages 17–30 in *A Century of Christianity in Uganda, 1877–1977: A Historical Appraisal of the Development of the Uganda Church Over the Last One Hundred Years*. Edited by A. D. Tom Tuma and Phares Mutibwa. Nairobi: Uzima Press, 1978.

Tuma, A. D. Tom, and Phares Mutibwa, eds. *A Century of Christianity in Uganda, 1877–1977: A Historical Appraisal of the Development of the Uganda Church Over the Last One Hundred Years*. Nairobi: Uzima Press, 1978.

Tumusiime, James. *Uganda 30 years, 1962–1992*. Kampala: Fountain Publishers, 1992.

Turner, David L. 'Paul and the Ministry of Reconciliation in 2 Cor 5:11–6:2'. *Criswell Theological Review* 4 (Fall 1989): 77–95.

Turner, Max. 'Human Reconciliation in the New Testament with Special Reference to Philemon, Colossians and Ephesians'. *European Journal of Theology* 16/1 (2007): 37–47.

Tutu, Desmond. *No Future Without Forgiveness*. London: Rider, 2000.

Twaddle, Michael. 'Decentralized Violence and Collaboration in Early Colonial Uganda'. *Journal of Commonwealth Political Studies* 16/3 (1988): 71–85.

_____. 'The Amin Coup'. *Journal of Commonwealth Political Studies* 10/2 (July 1972): 99–112.

_____. 'The Ousting of Idi Amin: Regime's Swift Collapse Took Tanzania By Surprise'. *Round Table: The Commonwealth Journal of International Affairs*/275 (July 1979): 216–21.

Twesigye, Emmanuel K. *Religion, Politics, and Cults in East Africa*. First printing. New York: Peter Lang Publishing, 2010.

Twinamatsiko, David. 'The Church of Uganda and the Amin Regime January 25, 1971 Through April 11, 1979'. MA Thesis, Alexandria: Virginia Theological Seminary, 1994.

Tyle, Laura B, ed. *Encyclopedia of World Biography*. Detroit: UXL, 2003.

U.S. Congress. 'Public Law 95–435'. *United States Statues at Large* 92/1 (95th Congress, 2nd Session 1978): 1051–53.

Ulanov, Ann Belford. 'Practicing Reconciliation: Love and Work'. *Anglican Theological Review* 89/2 (2007): 227–246.

Uzoigwe, G. N. 'The Kyanyangire, 1907: Passive Revolt Against British Overrule'. Pages 179–214 in *War and Society in Africa*. Edited by B. A. Ogot. London: Cass, 1972.

Vadala, Alexander Attilio. 'Famine and Starvation in Ethiopia: Politics, Rights, Entitlements'. M.A. Thesis, Norway: University of Oslo, 2004.

Venter, Al J. 'Amin's Chamber of Horrors'. *South African Journal of African Affairs* 9/2 (1979): 104–10.

Vermès, Géza. *Jesus the Jew: A Historian's Reading of the Gospels*. London: Collins, 1973.

Via, Dan Otto. *What Is New Testament Theology?* Minneapolis: Fortress Press, 2002.

Vickers, Brian. *Jesus' Blood and Righteousness: Paul's Theology of Imputation*. Wheaton, Ill.: Crossway Books, 2006.

Volf, Miroslav. 'A Theology of Embrace in an Age of Exclusion'. Pages 89–100 in *Reconciliation: A Theology of Embrace in an Age of Exclusion: The 1997 Washington Forum*. Federal Way: World Vision, 1997.

_____. *Exclusion and Embrace: A Theological Exploration of Identity, Otherness, and Reconciliation*. Nashville, TN: Abingdon Press, 1996.

_____. 'Forgiveness, Reconciliation, and Justice'. Pages 268–286 in *Stricken by God?: Nonviolent Identification and the Victory of Christ*. Edited by Brad Jersak and Michael Hardin. Grand Rapids, Mich.: Eerdmans, 2007.

_____. 'Forgiveness, Reconciliation, and Justice: A Theological Contribution to a More Peaceful Social Environment'. *Millennium: Journal of International Studies* 29/3 (December 1, 2000): 861 –877. Cited 22 Nov 2011.

_____. *Free of Charge: Giving and Forgiving in a Culture Stripped of Grace: The Archbishop's Official 2006 Lent Book*. Grand Rapids, Mich.: Zondervan, 2005.

_____. 'Love Your Heavenly Enemy: How Are We Going to Live Eternally with Those We Can't Stand Now?'. *Christianity Today* 44/12 (October 23, 2000): 94.

_____. 'Reconciled in the end'. *Christian Century* 116/31 (N 1999): 1098–22.

_____. *The End of Memory: Remembering Rightly in a Violent World*. Grand Rapids, Mich.: Eerdmans, 2006.

_____. 'The Final Reconciliation: Reflections on a Social Dimension of the Eschatological Transition'. *Modern Theology* 16/1 (2000): 91–113.
_____. 'The Social Meaning of Reconciliation'. *Transformation* 16/Jan–Mar (1999): 7–12.
_____. 'The Trinity is our Social Program: The Doctrine of the Trinity and the Shape of Social Engagement'. *Modern Theology* 14/3 (1998): 403–424.
_____. 'When Gospel and Culture Intersect: Notes on the Nature of Christian Difference'. *Evangelical Review of Theology* 22/3 (1998): 196–207.
_____. *Work in the Spirit*. New York: Oxford University Press, 1991.
Vorlander, H. 'Reconciliation'. *New International Dictionary of New Testament Theology*. Exeter: Paternoster, 1978.
Vos, Geerhardus. *Biblical Theology: Old and New Testaments*. Edinburgh: Banner of Truth Trust, 1975.
Wagner, C. Peter. *Your Spiritual Gifts Can Help Your Church Grow*. Glendale, Calif.: GL Regal Books, 1979.
Wall, Robert W. *Colossians and Philemon*. The IVP New Testament Commentary Series. Downers Grove, Ill.: InterVarsity Press, 1993.
Wallace, Daniel B. *Greek Grammar Beyond the Basics: An Exegetical Syntax of the New Testament*. Grand Rapids, Mich.: Zondervan, 1996.
Walther, James Arthur, ed. *Ever a Frontier: The Bicentennial History of the Pittsburgh Theological Seminary*. First Edition. Eerdmans Pub Co, 1994.
Walvoord, John F. 'The Person and Work of Christ, Part XII: Reconciliation'. *Bibliotheca Sacra* 119 (1962): 291–301.
_____. 'The Person and Work of Christ, Part XIII: Reconciliation'. *Bibliotheca Sacra* 120 (1963): 3–12.
Ward, Kevin. 'A History of Christianity in Uganda'. Pages 81–112 in *From Mission to Church*. Edited by Nthamburi Z. Nairobi: Uzima Press.
_____. *A History of Global Anglicanism*. Cambridge: Cambridge University Press, 2006.
_____. 'Archbishop Janani Luwum'. Pages 199–224 in *Christianity and the African Imagination: Essays in Honour of Adrian Hastings*. Edited by David Maxwell, Ingrid Lawrie, and Adrian Hastings. Studies on Religion in Africa. Leiden: Brill, 2002.
_____. *Called To Serve: Bishop Tucker Theological College, Mukono: A History 1913–1989*. Kampala, Uganda: Bishop Tucker Theological College, 1989.
_____. 'Journal of Religion in Africa' 19/3 (October 1989): 194–22.

_____. '"Obedient Rebels": The Relationship between the Early "Balokole" and the Church of Uganda: The Mukono Crisis of 1941'. *Journal of Religion in Africa* 19/3 (October 1, 1989): 194–227.

_____. 'The Balokole Revival in Uganda'. *From Mission to Church: A Handbook of Christianity in East Africa*. Edited by Zablon John Nthamburi. Uzima Press, 1991.

_____. 'Tukutendereza Yesu'. Edited by Mark R Lipschutz and R. Kent Rasmussen. *Dictionary of African Christian Biography*. Berkeley: University of California Press, 1986.

Ward, Kevin, and Emma Wild-Wood. *The East African Revival: History and Legacies*. Farnham: Ashgate, 2012.

Ward, W. Reginald. *The Protestant Evangelical Awakening*. Cambridge: Cambridge University Press, 1992.

Watson, Andrew. *Confidence in the Living God: David and Goliath Revisited*. Abingdon: The Bible Reading Fellowship, 2009.

Watson, Francis B. 'Barth's Philippians as Theological Exegesis'. Page xxvi–li in *The Epistle to the Philippians*. Louisville, KY: Westminster John Knox Press, 2002.

_____. *Text and Truth: Redefining Biblical Theology*. Edinburgh: T&T Clark, 1997.

_____. *Text, Church and World: Biblical Interpretation in Theological Perspective*. Grand Rapids, Mich.: William B. Eerdmans, 1994.

Webb-Peploe, H. 'Dead unto Sin'. *Keswick's Triumphant Voice: Forty-Eight Outstanding Addresses Delivered at the Keswick Convention, 1882–1962*. Edited by Herbert F Stevenson. London: Marshall, Morgan and Scott, 1963.

Webster, J. B. *Barth's Earlier Theology: Four Studies*. London: T. & T. Clark, 2005.

Webster, John D. 'Biblical Theology and the Clarity of Scripture'. Pages 349–382 in *Out of Egypt: Biblical Theology and Biblical Interpretation*. Edited by Craig G Bartholomew and Elaine Botha. The Scripture and Hermeneutics Series. Bletchley, Milton Keynes, UK: Paternoster Press, 2004.

Welch Jr., Claude E. 'The OAU and the International Recognition: Lessons From Uganda'. *The Organization of African Unity After Ten Years: Comparative Perspectives*. Edited by Yassin El-Ayouty. Praeger Special Studies in International Politics and Government. New York: Praeger, 1975.

West, Gerald O. 'Mapping African Biblical Interpretation: A Tentative Sketch'. *The Bible in Africa: Transactions, Trajectories, and Trends*. Boston: Brill Academic Publishers, 2000.

West, Gerald O., and Musa W. Dube Shomanah. *The Bible in Africa: Transactions, Trajectories, and Trends*. Leiden: Brill, 2000.

Wilkins, Michael J, and Terence Paige, eds. *Worship, Theology and Ministry in the Early Church: Essays in Honor of Ralph P. Martin*. Vol. 8. Journal for the Study of the New Testament. Supplement Series. Sheffield: JSOT Press, 1992.

Willard M. Aldrich. 'The Objective Nature of Reconciliation'. *Bibliotheca Sacra* 118 (1961): 18–21.

Williams, E. H. 'The Health Crisis in Uganda as it Affected Kuluva Hospital'. *Crisis in Uganda: The Breakdown in Health Services*. Edited by Cole P. Dodge and Paul D. Wiebe. Oxford: Pergamon Pr, 1985.

Wilson, John. 'Bishop Alfred Stanway – Heroes of the Faith'. *The Melbourne Anglican* (March 2011). Cited 2 Feb 2012. Online: http://melbourne.anglican.com.au/NewsAndViews/TMA/Heroes%20of%20the%20Faith/Bishop%20Alfred%20Stanway%20-%20Heroes%20of%20the%20Faith%20-%20March%202011.pdf.

Winter, Michael. *The Atonement*. Problems in Theology. London: Geoffrey Chapman, 1995.

Wolff, Christian. 'True Apostolic Knowledge of Christ: Exegetical Reflections on 2 Corinthians 5:14ff'. Pages 145–160 in *Paul and Jesus: Collected Essays*. Edited by A. J. M. Wedderburn. JSOT Supp. 37. Sheffield: JSOT Press, 1989.

Wolffe, John. *The Expansion of Evangelicalism: The Age of Wilberforce, More, Chalmers and Finney*. A History of Evangelicalism. Nottingham: Inter-Varsity Press, 2006.

Wolter, Michael. *Rechtfertigung und Zukünftiges Heil: Untersuchungen zu Röm 5, 1–11*. Walter de Gruyter, 1978.

Wood, A. Skevington. *Evangelism: Its Theology and Practice*. Grand Rapids, Mich.: Zondervan, 1966.

Wood, William P. 'A Murder in Uganda'. *America* 136/10 (March 12, 1977): 216–19.

_____. 'The Trial of Idi Amin: It Is a Great Enigma That Something as Universally Abhorrent as Mass Murder Is Not Universally a Crime'. *Christian Century* 97/18 (My 1980): 549–552.

Wooding, Dan, and Ray Barnett. *Uganda Holocaust*. Grand Rapids, Mich.: Zondervan, 1980.

World Council of Churches Executive Committee. 'The Archbishop Has Gone Home to His Lord'. *Ecumenical Review* 29/2 (April 1977): 196–197.

Wright, N. T. *The Climax of the Covenant: Christ and the Law in Pauline Theology.* Edinburgh: T&T Clark, 1991.

_____. *The Epistles of Paul to the Colossians and to Philemon: An Introduction and Commentary.* Tyndale New Testament Commentaries. Leicester: Inter-Varsity Press, 1986.

Wright, N. T., Sven Soderlund, and Gordon D. Fee, eds. *Romans and the People of God: Essays in Honor of Gordon D. Fee on the Occasion of His 65th Birthday.* Grand Rapids, Mich.: Eerdmans, 1999.

Wrigley, Christopher. *Kingship and State: The Buganda Dynasty.* Cambridge University Press, 2002.

Yates, Roy. *The Epistle to the Colossians.* Epworth Commentaries. London: Epworth Press, 1993.

Yoder, John Howard. *For the Nations: Essays Evangelical and Public.* Grand Rapids, Mich.: W.B. Eerdmans, 1997.

_____. *The Priestly Kingdom: Social Ethics as Gospel.* Notre Dame, Ind.: University of Notre Dame Press, 1984.

Young, Richard A. *Intermediate New Testament Greek: A Linguistic and Exegetical Approach.* Nashville, Tenn.: Broadman & Holman, 1994.

Young, Robert. *Untying the Text: A Post-Structuralist Reader.* Routledge, 1981.

Zacharias, Ravi K, and Kevin Johnson. *Jesus Among Other Gods.* Youth ed. Nashville, Tenn: Word Pub, 2000.

Zwemer, Samuel Marinus. *Evangelism Today: Message Not Method.* New York: Flemington H. Revell Company, 1944.

APPENDIX 1

Illustrations

1. Pittsburg Theological Seminary Class of 1966-67

(Source: Pittsbrugh Theological College Library)

2. Festo Kivengere

(Source: AEE, Sydney, Australia)

3. Return of Bishops from Exile, May 1979

(Source: AEE, Sydney, Australia)

L-R: Bishop Melchizedek Otim (Diocese of Lango), Bishop Benoni Ogwal-Abwang (Northern Uganda Diocese), Bishop Festo Kivengere, and Silvanus Wani (Chairman Orgaizing Committee for the welcome of Kivengere from Exile)

APPENDIX 2

Letters

Report of a Very Serious Incident at the Archbishop's House in the Early Hours of Saturday 5th February 1977

At about 1:30 a.m. on Saturday morning I heard the dog barking wildly and the fence been broken down and I know some people had come into the compound. I walked downstairs very quietly without switching any lights on and as usual I stopped at the door. I opened the curtain on the door on one side and I was able to observe one man standing straight in front of the door. He began calling 'Archbishop, Archbishop, open, we have come'. This man was called Ben Ongom. Because he had some cuts on his face and I knew him in the past I thought he was in some kind of danger needing help. So I opened the door and immediately these armed men who had been hiding sprang on me cocking their rifles and shouting 'Archbishop, Archbishop, show us the arms'. I replied 'What arms'. They replied 'there are arms in this house'. I said 'No'. At this point their leader who was speaking in Arabic, wearing a red kaunda suit put his rifle in my stomach on the right hand side while another mar searched me from head to foot. He pushed me with the rifle shouting 'Walk, run, show us the arms, take us to your bedroom'. So we went up to our bedroom where Mary my wife was asleep. We woke her up and they began crawling underneath the bed. They opened the wardrobes climbing right up into the upper decker of the cupboard. They searched the bedroom thoroughly looking in suitcases, boxes, etc. but finding nothing. They proceeded to search the two children's bedrooms upstairs repeating the same exercise of searching everywhere.

Fortunately the younger children slept through it but the bigger children woke up and went round with us.

After that we came downstairs and at this point Mr. Ben Ongom who was handcuffed began to say 'Archbishop, you see sometime back we brought some ammunition and divided it up with Mr. Olobo who works in the Ministry of Labour in Kampala. I kept some and Mr. Olobo kept same. Now mine has been found and certainly because of involving myself in politics I am going to die in any case for it. When we went to Olobo's home with the security people and they searched his house, they found nothing but they arrested him. I thought Mr. Olobo might have transferred his share of the arms to Dr. Lalobo's home (Medical Superintendent of Mango Hospital) since he was also an Acholi and they seem to be related. We have been to Dr. Olobo's home and searched the house but found nothing. The security men have arrested him. Then I suggested to the security men that Dr. Lalobo might have transferred the ammunition to the Arch- bishop's house. This is why we have come to you. Please help us. If the arms are not here, tell us the location of any Acholi or Langi homes on Namirembe so that they may be searched'.

I told Mr. Ongom that I did not come to Namirembe for the Acholi or the Langi but I was the Archbishop of Uganda, Rwanda, Burundi and (Boga- Zaire and there wore no arms in my house. Our house was God's house. We pray for the President. We pray for the security forces—whatever they do. We preach the Gospel and pray for others. That is our work, not keeping arms.

All the same the search continued. They demanded we opened the study. They searched there. We opened the Chapel. They searched there even looking underneath the Holy Table, They searched the food stores putting their hands into sacks of sim-sim, millet, groundnuts trying to feel for hidden objects. We went to the guest wing. They searched through the toilets, bathrooms etc. They searched the cars parked in the compound. Finding nothing we continued to complain that the incident was a serious one for the whole Church since we knew nothing of any arms. I said 'What will the Christians think about this incident when they hear about it since we shall certainly not keep quiet'. I told them I was going to talk to the President immediately.

The Security men thought that since arms had been brought into the country to overthrow the Government and since Ben Ongom suggested our house, they had no alternative but to follow his suggestion. I told them they should have come in a more respectable way. Their leader who was a Nubian remarked that they had to come in a military way since the matter was a serious one. I told him I had done nothing wrong to warrant the treatment of a rifle being put in my stomach.

My neighbours, Bishop home and the Provincial Secretary had rung Old Kampala Police Station when they saw there were men with arms in our compound thinking they were robbers. When the military police came these man sent them away before they entered our compound.

About 3.00 a.m. these men left. They requested that we opened the gate for them to go out but my wife suggested they should go the way they came. I said we were Christians. We have clean hearts and as a witness we should open the gates for them. They left and entered their cars which they had parked down the road. The number plates were covered. Eventually they drove away.

Earlier or Friday evening at 7.00 p.m. I had heard from the hospital that the security men had searched Dr. Lalobo's home and that the doctor was missing. Up to now the doctor is still missing. Since this incident I have done the following:

1. On Saturday morning I telephoned the President using the number 2241 he had given me if I wished to contact him any time of the day or night. I got through about 9.00 a.m. The operator told me the President was busy with visitors and requested that I should ring at 10.00 a.m. When I telephoned at 10.00 a.m. I was told that the President had left with the visitors and he could not be reached by telephone but he had left a message saying that I should leave my message with the operator. If not, I should contact the Vice President. I rang the Vice President's home and was told he was out. Later on I managed to get Col. Maliyamungu. I told him of the incident including the doctor's arrest and other arrests. Ha let me speak to the Vice President. I spoke in Swahili telling him of the incident. He comforted assured and me no that he would call the people

concerned and follow the matter up. Since then we have heard nothing.

2. On Sunday morning the Bishop of Northern Uganda rang to say that Bishop Okoth had been arrested in Tororo. Later on, about 8.00 a.m. Bishop Okoth's children arrived looking very tired and weary. They had obviously been searching for their Father for a long time. About the same time Bishop Ogwal telephoned again to say that Bishop Okoth had been released and was back home In Tororo. Since that time we have heard nothing from Tororo or the Bishop.

3. Yesterday, Monday 7th February someone told us that they had seen the hospital car, No. 099 942 at Naguru. At 2.30 p.m. Sam Willis, the Acting Hospital Manager and I went to Naguru in search of the doctor and the car. We were told that the car was not there and the doctor was not present either. After that we went to the Police HQ in Kampala and requested an appointment with the Commissioner of Police. We were told he was busy but we managed to one his assistant who recorded everything and reported back to the Commissioner while we were there. Both of them suggested we should try and follow the contact already made through the Vice President's Office.

A Statement Made by the Archbishop of Uganda, Rwanda, Burundi and Bola-Zaire the Most Rev. Janani Luwum in Answer to the President's Allegations about 'Arms Found Near Archbishop's House' (*Voice of Uganda*, Tuesday 15th February, 1977)

Your Excellency,

After our meeting with you at the State House on Monday 14th February 1977 at about 9.00 a.m. where the Minister of Public Service and Cabinet Affairs Mr. Raphael Nshekanabo and my wife Mary were present. The statement that followed on all public mass media that evening and the Voice of Uganda of Tuesday 15th February 1977 left me speechless to say the least.

For one thing the statement is completely silent about what I said which left the general public wondering. Sir, since I am still present, it is only fair to the International world, the people of Uganda and myself that I be allowed to speak. For the sake of easy reference I should like to number my points:

1. I have already made my Report to the House of Bishops, copies of which were circulated with the Bishop's memo to Your Excellency, copied to high ranking officials both in the Government and Churches, which I told nothing but the truth. It is quite clear from that Report that Mr. Ben Ongom who took 8 of the Security men to our house was acting under duress and torture that if he did not find the arms, he was going to die that right so he suggested that they should search any house that belong to Lapel or Acholies. If he knew for certain, why did he take the Security men to Mr. Olobo's house, Dr. Lolobo's house, our house and many others in Longo some of whom like myself were innocent.

2. Your Excellency said that the arms 'were found (to quote the Voice of Uganda statement) near Archbishop Janani Luwum's residence'. This is not clear enough, might I ask where exactly? If so who brought them there? When these were found, since it was near our residence and I was searched at gunpoint for them, why was I not brought to witness this discovery in order that the general public may also witness it?

3. When Your Excellency called me at Entebbe, I did not know

that it was to smear me and to almost assassinate my character. I am sorry to say I am not as dirty as that For the sake of myself and the Church that I lead, I would like more concrete evidence about these serious and far reaching allegations.

4. There is a very revealing statement in the Voice of Uganda's Report and I quote The searching team left Archbishop Limn in his house intact and took the anus to the place where interrogations were held. Life President Amin told the Archbishop that the people who directed the Security Forces to his house were school children. Ben Ongom . . .' I did not see any school children at that time 1.30 a.m. on Saturday 5th February 1977 who searched the house and found nothing. If the school children came to our house with the Security men and found the arms, I was not present on that day but still, none of our family including the servants told us any further searching team with children anywhere near our place.

5. If the statement in four above is given to Your Excellency by the Security men or the searching team or school children, it is most confusing and misleading to say nothing of its sound basis.

6. The other statement that arms were transported to me via Bishop Okoth in Tororo is completely baseless whoever saw this must show evidence as to prove this.

7. Your Excellency in conclusion, may I beg that you leave me alone on this matter of arms which I am sure you may by now begin to question the integrity of whoever fed Your Excellency with these false allegations against me and the Church that I am its leader. I would like the whole world to know that I am innocent on this serious matter of State Security.

On a more serious concern Your Excellency, many of our people in Uganda have either fled the country or have been liquidated on baseless allegations such as this one. I hope Sir, you will read my feelings and that of the Church.

I am Your Excellency Your servant in the Lord's Vineyard

Janani Luwum, Archbishop of Uganda, Rwanda, Burundi & Boga-Zaire

A REPORT OF THE RT. REV. YONA BOTH'S ARREST ON SATURDAY, 5TH FEBRUARY, 1977

Bishop Okoth reported in detail the nature of his arrest on Saturday evening, 5th February 1977:

On Saturday night, 5th February I retired to bed early after prayers since I was not feeling welt. At about 10.00 p.m. my aunt reported two cars full of people near my home. They seemed agitated and were carrying sticks (guns). I got up and welcomed them. They asked 'Bishop, why are you sleeping in the village?' I replied 'This is my home'. Their leader told on he respected me as Father and the man in chains (Ben Ongom) repeated the same story as he told the Archbishop about the missing arms which they suspected were hidden in my home. 'Do you think I am having arms. Is that my work? Are you mentally disturbed? I do not know what you are talking about'. Their leader asked 'How many men do you have here?' I replied 'A watchman and my driver but they are both away delivering milk to my wife'. They continued 'How many arms do you have?' 'I have a shotgun and a rifle which I use for shotting animals and birds. I possess the necessary legal documents'.

At once they scattered over the house, searching everywhere, but finding nothing. They went into the sitting room, the food store, the bedrooms. At one point they found a large package. My new water pump had arrived and was still unpacked. They tore it open but found nothing.

They searched and searched—every corner of the house. Then they heard notice. One of the men shouted 'There are many people here'. I said 'Take a lamp, go and see'. They came back and reported they had found only cows: Their leader said 'We are sorry we have to do this, but we have been given a directive from our boss. We are sorry but we shall have to take you'. I replied 'I'm not afraid. If it is death for me it is the gate way to the Lord. If life, I will continue preaching the Gospel.

I was taken by car to Iowa. I asked if they would like to search my house in Tororo but they declined. We drove as far as Jinja and crossed the river Nile. At this point petrol was running out. They called at a number of petrol stations but found no petrol so they returned to certain house in

Jinja. They woke up the house bay and ordered him to make tea. I was to go and wait in the kitchen. There were about 12 men and they began their conference. After a long discussion they told me that their boss had ordered my release since they had found nothing. They explained they were security people who must fulfill their duty. If they heard something. they had to check. They cautioned me to tell no one of the incident but I told them that when such a thing happens to a leader, news is bound to spread. While we waited for petrol to arrive from Kampala I was given breakfast. Finally a black car UVS 297 arrived. The two cars then proceeded to Tororo. The black car in the lead. We reached Tororo at 6.30 a.m. in the morning. Ben Ongom was left in the car. The others came into my house and began to search everywhere--the bedroom. They read through all my correspondence. When they found a game mentioning the ward weapon they were elated until I explained it was only a game. They searched the sitting room, the stares, everywhere but found nothing.

They shook my hand and said I was a free man. They returned my shotgun and a rifle which they had taken from the village. They cautioned no again not to spread the news. 'Go on working normally' they said. I replied 'These are not normal times, if you suspect me, a man dealing in spiritual matters, what of others'.

As they left people were already beginning to go on their way to Church and they wondered what was happening at the Bishop's house.

The Rt. Rev. Y. Okoth

LETTER FROM THE HOUSE OF BISHOPS TO PRESIDENT AMIN

The House of Bishops of the Church of Uganda, Rwanda, Burundi and Boga-Zaire sent the following letter to President Idi Amin on February 10, 1977, following the attack by Uganda Security Forces on the Archbishop, Most Reverend Janani Luwum, and the Bishop of Bukedi, Rt. Rev. Yona Okoth:

Church of Uganda, Rwanda, Burundi and Boga-Zaire,
P.O. Box 14123, Kampala, Uganda.

His Excellency Al-Haji Field Marshall Dr. Idi Amin Dada,
V.C., D.S.O., M.C.

Life President's Office, Kampala, Uganda.

Your Excellency,
Field Marshall Dr. Idi Amin Dade, V.C., D,S.O,, H.C.

We the Archbishop and the Bishops of the Province of Uganda, Rwanda, Burundi and Boga-Zaire meeting at Namirembe on Tuesday, 8th February 1977 humbly beg to submit our most deeply felt concern for the Church and the welfare of the people whom we serve under your care.

In presenting this statement, we are in no way questioning the right of the Government in administering justice, to search and arrest offenders. We believe that the Government has established structures and procedures for carrying out this kind of exercise. It is these established structures and procedures that give the citizens a sense of what to expect of their Government. These structures and procedures give the police, the intelligence and the security forces a framework within which to work. When these procedures are followed in carrying cut their day to day duties this gives the ordinary citizen a sense of security. It creates mutual friendship and trust between such officers and the general public irrespective of uniform. But when the police and security officers deviate from these established structures and procedures in carrying out their day to day duties, citizens become insecure, afraid and disturbed. They begin to distrust these officers.

We are deeply disturbed to learn of the incident which occurred at the Archbishop's official residence in the early hours of Saturday morning, 5th February 1977. In the history of our country such an incident in the Church has never before occurred. Security officers broke through the fence and forced their way into the Archbishop's compound. They used a man they had arrested and tortured as a decoy to entice the Archbishop to open his door to help a man seemingly in distress. Using a man under duress and torture as a source of information can lead to unnecessary suffering of innocent individuals. The Archbishop opened his door. At that point armed men who had been hiding sprung to attack cocking their rifles demanding 'arms'. When the Archbishop asked 'What arms?', the answer was the muzzle of a rifle pressed against his stomach and immediately he was pushed forcefully into his house with the demand 'Archbishop show us the arms, run to the bedroom'. The full story of that incident as told by the Archbishop is appended.

First we want to register our shock and protest at this kind of treatment to the top leader of the Church of Uganda, Rwanda, Burundi and Boga-Zaire. Than we shall draw out the implications of this incident for the rest of the Bishops and all the Christians of the Church of Uganda. Your Excellency, you have said publicly on many occasions that Religious Leaders have a special place in this country and that you treat them with respect for what they stand for and represent. You have on many occasions publicly demonstrated this and we are always grateful. But what happened to the Archbishop in his house on the night we have referred to is a direct contradiction to what you yourself, Your Excellency have said in public and to the established structures and procedures in dealing with security matters. That is why we are very disturbed and with us the whale of the Church of Uganda. We feel that if it was necessary to search the Archbishop's house he should have been approached in broad day light by responsible senior officers fully identified in conformity with his position in society, but to search him and his house at gun point deep in the night leaves us without words.

Now that the security of the Archbishop is at stake, the security of the Bishops is even more in jeopardy. Indeed we have a case in point. The night following the search of the Archbishop's house, one of us, the Bishop of Bukedi was both searched and arrested. It was only when nothing could be found at his personal and official residences that he was later released on the Sunday morning. This left the people in his diocese wondering and the wondering is spreading quickly. The Christians are asking if this is what is happening to our Bishops then where are we? The gun whose muzzle has been pressed against the Archbishop's stomach, the gun which has been used to search the Bishop of Bukedi's houses is a gun which is being pointed at every Christian in the Church, unless Your Excellency can give on something new to change this situation.

The security of the ordinary Christian has been in jeopardy for quite a long time. It may be that what has happened to the Archbishop and the Bishop of Bukedi is a climax of what is consistently happening to our Christians. We have buried many who have died as a result of being shot and there are many more whose bodies have not been found, yet their disappearance is connected with the activities of some members of the Security Forces. Your Excellency, if it is required we can give concrete evidence of what is happening because widows and orphans are members of our Church.

Furthermore we are made sad by the increasing forces that are setting Ugandans one against another. While it is common in Uganda for members of one family to be members of different religious organizations there is an increasing feeling that one particular religious organization is being favoured more than any other. Se much so that in some parts of Uganda members of Islam who are in leading positions are using these positions to coerce Christians into becoming Muslims. Secondly members of the Security Forces are sons of civilians and they have civilian brothers and sisters. When they begin to use the gun in their hands to destroy instead of protecting the civilian, then the relationship of mutual trust and respect is destroyed. Instead of that relationship you have suspicion, fear and hidden hatred. There is also a war against the educated which is forcing many of our people to run away from this country in spite of what the country has paid to educate them. This brain drainage of our country, the fear and the mistrust make development, progress and stability of our country almost impossible. The gun which was meant to protect Uganda as a nation, the Ugandan as a citizen and his property is increasingly being used against the Ugandan to take away his life and his property. For instance, many cars, almost daily are being taken at gun point and their owners killed. And most of the culprits never brought to justice. If required we can enumerate many cases. Too much power has been given to members of State Research who arrest and kill at will innocent individuals. Therefore that which was meant to provide the Ugandan citizen with security is increasingly becoming the means of his insecurity.

We are also concerned about the developing gap between the leaders of the Christian Churches, Archbishops in particular and Your Excellency. We had been assured by you of your ready availability to Religious Leaders whenever they had serious matters to discuss with you. You had even gone to the extent of giving His Grace, the Archbishop the surest means of contacting you in this country wherever you may he. But a situation has developed now where you have become more and more inaccessible to the Archbishop and even when he tried to write he has not received any reply. This gap has brought a sad feeling of estrangement and alienation not only to the Archbishop and the Bishops but also it is reaching down to the ordinary citizens.

While you, Your Excellency, has stated on the national radio that your government is not under any foreign influence, and that your decisions are guided by your Defence Council and Cabinet, the general trend of things in Uganda has created a feeling that the affairs of our nation are being directed by outsiders who do not have the welfare of this country and the value of the lives and properties of Ugandans at their heart. A situation like this breeds unnecessary misunderstanding and mistrust. Indeed we were shocked to hear over the radio on Christmas Day, Your Excellency saying that some Bishops had preached bloodshed. We waited anxiously to be called by Your Excellency to clarify such a serious situation, but all in vain. Your Excellency, we want to say here again that we are ready to come to you whenever there are serious matters that concern the Church and the nation, you've only got to call us. This used not to be so Your Excellency, when you freely moved among us and we freely came to you.

The Archbishop is not only the Archbishop of the Church of Uganda but he is the Archbishop of the Church of Rwanda, Burundi and Boga-Zaire. So what happens to him here is also the concern of the Christians in Rwanda, the concern of the Christians in Burundi and the concern of the Christians in Zaire. In fact, it goes further than that because he is an Archbishop in the Anglican Communion which is a world wide community, so are the Bishops. An action such as this one damages the good image of our nation. It also threatens our preparations for the Centenary Celebrations. Christians everywhere have become very cautious about taking part in the fund raising activities of the Church for fear of being misrepresented and misinterpreted. The ban on sales of things donated for fund raising in aid of the Church is a case in point. This too, could have been cleared if only Your Excellency had given the Archbishop an opportunity to brief you on the matter.

In addition to the concern of the Christians in the Anglican Communion there is also the concern of the Christians of other denominations in Uganda and all over the world with whom we are in fellowship.

In conclusion, Your Excellency, we are very grateful that you have kindly given us this opportunity to express our grievances and concerns to you.

'For God and Our Country'.

Signed:

The Most Rev. Janani Luwum, Archbishop of Uganda, Rwanda, Burundi and Boga-Zaire and Bishop of Uganda.
The Rt. Rev. Silvanus G. Wani, Bishop of Madi and West Nile and Dean of the Province.
The Rt. Rev. Amos Betungura, Bishop of East Ankole.
The Rt. Rev. Yona Okoth, Bishop of Bukedi.
The Rt. Rev. Dr. Yustasi Ruhindi, Bishop of Bunyoro-Kitara.
The Rt. Rev. Cyprian Bamwoze, Bishop of Busoga.
The Rt. Rev. Brian Herd, Bishop of Karamoja.
The Rt. Rev. Festo Kivengere, Bishop of Kigezi.
The Rt. Rev. Melchizedek Otim, Bishop of Lango.
The Rt. Rev. John Wasikye, Bishop of Mbale.
The Rt. Rev. Dr. Dunstan Nsubuga, Bishop of Namirembe.

The Rt. Rev. Dr. B.Y. Ogwal, Bishop of Northern Uganda.
The Rt. Rev. Y. Rwakaikara, Bishop of Ruwenzori.
The Rt. Rev. E. Ilukor, Bishop of Soroti.
The Rt. Rev. C.D. Senyonjo, Bishop of West Buganda.
The Rt. Rev. Y.K. Bamunoba, Bishop of West Ankole.
The Rt. Rev. William Rukirande, Assistant Bishop of Kigezi.
The Rt. Rev. R. Ringtho, Assistant Bishop of Madi and West Nile.
The Rt. Rev. M. Kauma, Assistant Bishop of Namirembe.

Distributed to:

His Excellency Al-Haji Field Marshall Dr. Idi Amin Dada, V.C., D.S.O., M.C. Life President of Uganda.
His Excellency, the Vice President of Uganda and Minister of Defence, General Mustafa Adrisi.
His Eminence Emmanuel, Cardinal Nsubuga, Archbishop of Kampala.
His Eminence Sheikh Mufti of Uganda, Muslim Supreme Council.
The Rt. Rev. Theodorous of Novoratis, Uganda Orthodox Church.
All Cabinet Ministers.
Secretary to the Defence Council.
The Acting Permanent Secretary for Religious Affairs.
All Bishops of the Province of the Church of Uganda, Rwanda, Burundi and Boga-Zaire.

A Prepared Response of the House of Bishops of the C.O.U.—Rwanda—Burundi and Bola-Zaire to His Excellency on Wednesday 16Th February 1977, at the Conference Centre in Kampala

Church of Uganda

The victimization of the Church through false accusations and misinterpretations as well as distorted reporting.

1. We have often been attacked on the U.B.C. by Your Excellency as those who use religious meetings for 'subversive activities'. This has often been picked up by your Provincial Governors and Chiefs, and used against Church activities such as collecting money for the Church buildings and other good works in the Christian ministry. Christian men have often been intimidated by such false accusations. It has been said in public meetings that Christians are collecting money to over- throw the Government.

2. We, the Bishops of the Church of Uganda, with all our spiritual authority and personal conviction, categorically refute such false accusations and insinuations that we have any connection whatever with the said arms and ammunitions. We regard the report in the Voice News Paper and on U.T.V. that arms were found near the Archbishop's house, and near Bishop Okoth's house as dangerous fabrications intended to damage the name of our Church by smearing its leaders. It has been proved beyond any shadow of a doubt by the surprise attack on the Archbishop in his residence on the 5th February 1977 after midnight when after the roughest manhandling of His Grace at gun-point nothing was found on his premises nor anywhere near his house as it has falsely been reported. This was doubly proved when another surprise search by the Security men was carried on at the residences of the Bishop of Bukedi late on Saturday night the same day 5th February 1977. Again, after the party had searched everywhere and found nothing took the Bishop with them and later released him on Sunday morning - no arms were found in or anywhere near his houses as it has again been falsely reported.

3. Your Excellency, our Church does not believe nor does it teach its members the use of destructive weapons. We believe in the Life-living love of Christ, we proclaim that love to all without fear—as Your Excellency

knows. We speak publicly and in private against all evil, all corruption, all misuse of power, all maltreatment of human beings. We rejoice in the truth, because truth builds up a nation, but we are determined to refuse all falsehood, all false accusations which damage the lives of our people and spoil the image of our country. We there- fore reject as completely unfounded the insinuation that our Church is involved in any way with arms supply, or with the activities of the ousted Dr. Obote—as it has been reported.

While individual Christians were members of the former parties before the Military take-over, none was in any party as a representative of the Church. We are made sad by the unlimited use of force by your intelligence officers, who not only go out to investigate and arrest, but carry out death sentences and executions without trial.

This has made these officers such a terror in the Country that a mere mention of the word 'intelligence' sends people into hiding. False reports which are not investigated, death sentences without trial, use of farce, the rule of a gun replacing the law, these have, Your Excellency, damaged the image of Uganda. If you can take steps to bring these under control, you have no reason to fear for the good some of Uganda.

4. We feel that we Church leaders have been under suspicion by the Government for a while. For instance, our freedom to go out of our country to fulfill our international responsibilities has been restricted and our work made unnecessarily difficult. As spiritual fathers in the community we are grieved by the demoralizing effect these false accusations against an are having among those we serve as shepherds. This singling out of as—leaders in the Church and labeling us 'arms suppliers' far the purpose of overthrowing the Government can only be understood as a deliberate act to put the whole Church in disfavor and ultimately under persecution. This, Your Excellency, is a very serious matter indeed. We trust that you will take steps in your power to remedy this situation.

5. We are proud of what our Church has done through its Bishops and Clergy end Laity, to better the image of our country outside. Our Church carries no guilt for the damage of the name of Uganda. In spite of all we have done for our country we are often told that we are the ones who drag Uganda dawn. We want it to be recorded that we have no part in that damaging campaign.

Our advice, Your Excellency, is that you put your Intelligence under strict laws in their work, restore authority to the Police, and let the law replace the gun - then the image will he restored.

'For God and our Country'

APPENDIX 3

Kivengere's Sermons Analyzed By Previous Scholars

Source Sermon Title	Analyzed by Charlotte Inkelaar de-Mos	Analyzed by John M.M Senyonyi	Analyzed by Peter Rwabyoma	Analyzed by Hughes Oliphant Old
The Spirit is Moving[1]				
Christ and the Holy Spirit		Yes		
Christ the Renewer		Yes		
Christ the Liberator		Yes		
God is Alive				
Christ the Giver of Life				
All Things are Yours		Yes		
Jesus Our Reality[2]				
Jesus Our Reality				
Jesus Our Access				
Jesus Our Forgiveness				
Jesus Our Anchor				
Jesus Our Goal				
Love Unlimited[3]				
Repentance Love—The Prodigal Son: Welcome Home, Wanderer!		Yes		

Source Sermon Title	Analyzed by Charlotte Inkelaar de-Mos	Analyzed by John M.M Senyonyi	Analyzed by Peter Rwabyoma	Analyzed by Hughes Oliphant Old
Compassionate Love—The Adulterous woman: Case Dismissed!		Yes		
Healing Love—The Leper: Forever Clean!		Yes		
Deliverance Love—Joshua: The Embarrassed Priest		Yes		
Reconcil[ing] Love—Jacob and Esau: What is your Name?		Yes		
Forgiving Love: Joseph and His Brothers—I am Your Brother		Yes		
Liberating Love—The Samaritan Woman: Surprise at the Well		Yes		
Restoration Love—Zacchaeus: The Big Little Man		Yes		
Empowering Love—David and Jonathan: Robes of the Prince		Yes		
Understanding Love—Martha: Recipe for Peace		Yes		
Trusting Love—Lazarus: Smog in Bethan				

Source Sermon Title	Analyzed by Charlotte Inkelaar de-Mos	Analyzed by John M.M Senyonyi	Analyzed by Peter Rwabyoma	Analyzed by Hughes Oliphant Old
Extravagant Love—Mary: Price Is No Object				
Ministering Love—Jesus and His Disciples: Your Feet, Please!				
Atoning Love—The Soldiers and the Thieves: The Victim from the Cross	Yes			
Immutable Love—Peter: Breakfast on the Beach				
***Revolutionary Love*[4]**				
Love and the Unlovable	Yes	Yes		
Love Unto Joy	Yes			
Love Reconciles		Yes		
Love's Quick Way		Yes	Yes	
Love's Togetherness		Yes		
Love and the Throne				
Love Comes Home		Yes		
Love Enables				
Love in Suffering				
***When God Moves in Revival*[5]**				
Revival begins at the Cross		Yes		
Remove the Masks		Yes		
Peace and Victory for the Christian		Yes		

Source Sermon Title	Analyzed by Charlotte Inkelaar de-Mos	Analyzed by John M.M Senyonyi	Analyzed by Peter Rwabyoma	Analyzed by Hughes Oliphant Old
The Covenant of Love		Yes		
Hope for Uganda and the World[6]				
Sense out of Nonsense	Yes	Yes		
Discover Yourself and Your Brother				
Make Enemies Into Friends		Yes		
Enter a New Community				
Spread the Word		Yes		
Other				
My God Why? Matthew 27:46b	Yes			
The Cross and World Evangelization	Yes	Yes		
Love Triumphs in Suffering		Yes		
The Work of the Holy Spirit in Evangelization, Yes Individually and Through the Church		Yes		
How to Express Unity (Billy Graham Crusade in Brussels, 1975)		Yes		
Billy Graham Western Carolina Crusade, 1977		Yes		
Transcendence and Creativity'[7]		Yes		

Source Sermon Title	Analyzed by Charlotte Inkelaar de-Mos	Analyzed by John M.M Senyonyi	Analyzed by Peter Rwabyoma	Analyzed by Hughes Oliphant Old
Walking in the Light & Godliness[8]		Yes		
The Cross in the World: The Victory in Christ Jesus	Yes			
If Jesus is Lifted up He Will Draw All Men to Himself	Yes			
Released to Bless (Light out of Chaos)	Yes			
Extravagant Love	Yes			
The Unshakeable Identity of the Church	Yes			
The Church's Unfinished Task	Yes			
Revival: Freedom On the Way	Yes			
The Outcome of Having Christ in You	Yes			
The Cost of Renewal or Discipleship	Yes			
The Master Moved down	Yes			
Jesus on the Waves	Yes			
Love God—Love Neighbour and Live	Yes			
Love God—Love Neighbour and Tell the Good News	Yes			
AE shares the message of Hope	Yes			

Source Sermon Title	Analyzed by Charlotte Inkelaar de-Mos	Analyzed by John M.M Senyonyi	Analyzed by Peter Rwabyoma	Analyzed by Hughes Oliphant Old
Zac[chae]us Finds his Identity	Yes			
I am the Light of the World	Yes			
[Not stated] [Feb 1982, USA]	Yes			
Renewal is Recovering Freshness in Living	Yes			
The Liberated Man: A Personal Testimony	Yes			
'Personal Revival'[9]				Yes

---

1. Kivengere, *The Spirit Is Moving*.
2. Festo Kivengere, *Jesus Our Reality* (Kampala, Uganda: Uganda Church Press, 1973).
3. Kivengere, *Love Unlimited*.
4. Kivengere, *Revolutionary Love*.
5. Kivengere, *When God Moves in Revival*.
6. Kivengere, *Hope for Uganda and the World*.
7. Senyonyi, 'Philosophy of Evangelism', 116–117. Kivengere, Transcendence and Creativity, address to the Congress of Laity, San Francisco, April 7, 1984. Cassette CA-85:2:5B. Focus. This may be accessed at TEDs library.
8. See Kivengere, Walking in the Light & Godliness, EXPLO '85, Nairobi, Kenya (December 1995). *Life Ministry*. Videocassette.
9. See Old, *Reading and Preaching*, 198–203. This sermon was preached in 1961 at the Urbana, Illinois, InterVarsity Conference. For the text of the sermon see Festo Kivengere, 'Personal Revival (1961)', http://www.urbana.org/_articles.cfm?RecordId=976. Accessed 13 December 2011.

APPENDIX 4

Some of Kivengere's Sermons Preached in Tandem with Cassidy[1]

Tape (& Side)	Title	Passage	Archive Code
116 (A)	Help! My Unbelief!	John 20	
116 (B)	Cancelled Accusations	Col 2:12–14	
117	Rule My Home, Lord!		
118 (A)	The Great Classifier	Eph 2:12–24	
118 (B)	The Phenomenon of Success	Josh 1:7–9	
119	Four Messages on the Prodigal Son	Luke 15:11–24	
120	Two Messages on the Samaritan Woman	John 4	AO: [--------]*92
121 (A)	Little Foxes	Song of Sol 2:15	
121 (B)	Drawn to the Place of Healing	Mark 14:32–33	
122 (A)	The Cross at the Centre		AO: [--------]*71
122 (A)	The Love of God	2 Cor 5:14–17	
122 (B)	The Lamb of God		AO: [--------]*75

---

1. African Enterprise Cassette tapes and books now located in the African Enterprise office, Pasadena, California, give the numbers 116 to 123. Some of the transcribed versions of these sermons (those preached by Kivengere) appear in the catalogue of our collected sermons in Appendix 5; the originals are to be found in the African Enterprise Office, Pasadena.

123 (A)	First Be Reconciled!	Isa 43:18–19; Matt 5:23	
123 (B)	You Qualify!	John 12:20–24	

APPENDIX 5

Catalogue of Kivengere's Sermons

Since no catalogue of Kivengere's sermons is yet in existence, one was developed as part of the preparation for this research. Because it is my own catalogue, each sermon is identified firstly by my initials: AO. This is then followed by the date the sermon was preached, as recorded on the transcript (year, month and day). Thus a sermon preached on the 29th January 1964 is assigned the catalogue number AO:19640129. If the sermon was preached in multiple services, an additional number indicates the repetition (#1—first time preached, #2—second time preached, etc). Thus the full title: AO:19640129, #1. If the year is known but the month or day is unknown, we use square brackets with dashes to indicate the missing data (for example, AO:196401[--]; AO:1964[--]29; AO:1964[----]). If two sermons still have duplicate codes (e.g. multiple sermons on the same day, but the order in which they were preached is not known), we add an asterisk and an ascending sequence number to ensure each sermon has a unique identifying code.

Sermons with their title in **bold** are mentioned in the body of this thesis.

Archive Code	Title	Place	Occasion	Text
AO: 1965[----]*1	Isaac and Rebecca	Lake Ave Congregational Church, Pasadena, California	Week of meetings	Gen 24; Rom 13
AO: 1965[----]*2	Peace Be With You	Lake Ave Congregational Church, Pasadena, California	Special Meetings	Luke 24:36ff
AO: 197?11[--]		Quito, Ecuador	HCJB Annual Conference	2 Cor 3:17-18
AO: 19710127		Haven of Rest, California	Radio Message	2 Cor 5:17
AO: 197109[--]	**Surprised by Joy**	**California, All Saints Santa Barbara**	**Mission**	**Rom 5:1-11**
AO: 19711128	**His Excellency The President**			
AO: 19711207	The Goal of Life	Gayaza, Uganda	Gayaza School Conference	Heb 12:2ff
AO: 1972[----]*1	**Christ Puts All Things Together**			Col 1
AO: 1972[----]*2	He Is Our Suffering	All Saints Church, Uganda	Uganda Keswick	1 Cor 1
AO: 1972[----]*3	I am a Debtor	All Saints		Rom 1:13
AO: 1972[----]*4	The Women in Jesus' Team	All Saints Episcopal Church, California		Luke 8:1-3
AO: 1972[----]*5		Rotary Club	Message to Rotarians	Gen 11
AO: 197205[--]	Captain of the Lord of Hosts	Salinas, California	Ministers' Conference	Josh 5:13-15
AO: 19720525	Freedom: Woman Taken in Adultery		Bible Study	John 8:1-10
AO: 19721124		Tucker Theological College, Namutamba, Uganda	Mission	Gen 1-3
AO: 19721124-25	Accepted by God	Namutamba, Uganda	Mission	John 15:1-7

Catalogue of Kivengere's Sermons 495

Archive Code	Title	Place	Occasion	Text
AO: 197212[--]	Forgiveness Which Liberates			Col 2
AO: 1973[----]*1	Peace and Victory for the Christian	Published in 'When God Moves in Revival'		
AO: 1973[----]*2	Remove the Masks	Published in 'When God Moves in Revival'		
AO: 1973[----]*3	Revival Begins at the Cross	Published in 'When God Moves in Revival'		
AO: 1973[----]*4	The Covenant of Love	Published in 'When God Moves in Revival'		
AO: 1973[----]*5		Keswick, UK	Keswick Convention	1 Sam 18
AO: 19730815	Divisions in the Church			
AO: 197310[--]	The Problems of the New Nations of Africa	Channel City Club, Santa Barbara, California		Gen 4
AO: 19731010	Delivered—Set Free	Fuller Seminary, Pasadena, California	Chapel Service	Heb 13:11ff
AO: 19731024*1	Abundant, Complete Life	Calvary Baptist Church	Revival	John 10
AO: 19731024*2		Calvary Baptist Church, Santa Barbara, California		John 1:11-14
AO: 19731114-18	Prodigal Son	Pittsburgh, Pennsylvania	Mission: Abundant Life	Luke
AO: 1974[----]	Personal Testimonies	Lausanne, Switzerland	International Congress on World Evangelization	
AO: 19740725	The Cross and World Evangelization	Lausanne, Switzerland	International Congress on World Evangelization	

Archive Code	Title	Place	Occasion	Text
AO: 19741128*1	Keeping the Blessing	Germany	Bishop Festo Mission	Eph 3:6-8, 13
AO: 19741128*2	The Sufficiency of the Grace of God	Germany		Eph 1:6-12
AO: 1975[----]*1	Christ the Liberator	Keswick, England		1 Cor 5:14
AO: 1975[----]*2	Eternal Life is a Quality of Life	Stuttgart, Germany		1 John 5:11ff
AO: 1975[----]*3	God's Time Bomb	New York	Episcopal Renewal Conference	2 Cor 5:21
AO: 1975[----]*4	He Who Has the Son Has Life	Germany		1 John 3:5
AO: 1975[----]*5	Our Bodies: Temples of the Holy Spirit			
AO: 1975[----]*6	The Renewing Presence of Christ in Evangelism			
AO: 1975[----]*7	The Vertical Relationship with God	Keswick, UK	Keswick Convention	2 Cor 5:16-17
AO: 1975[----]*8		Keswick, UK	English Keswick	Rom 1:14; Col 1:17
AO: 1975[03--?]	The Bishop's Charge to the Synod	Uganda		
AO: 19750728*1	How to Express Unity	Brussels, Belgium	Eurofest	Eph 4:1-16
AO: 19750728*2	Unity	Brussels, Belgium	Eurofest	Eph 4:1-16
AO: 19750728*3		Brussels, Belgium	Eurofest	Eph 5
AO: 19750729	God's Intervening Love	Presbyterian Church, Aurora, Illinois		Rom 5:1-10
AO: 19750729, [#2]	His Flooding Love	Westmont Presbyterian Church		Rom 5:1-11

Catalogue of Kivengere's Sermons

Archive Code	Title	Place	Occasion	Text
AO: 19750802	Judgment is Coming	Europe	Eurofest	Matt 25:1-13
AO: 19751012	Tendency to Drift		Bible Study	Heb 2
AO: 19751019		First Presbyterian Church, Seattle		Acts 3:1-8
AO: 19751024	Jesus Makes People Feel At Home		Address to WWP Staff	Phil 2
AO: 19751102	Your Body - A Temple	Calvary Baptist Church, New York		2 Cor 6:19
AO: 1976[----]		Urbana, Illinois	IVF Missionary Convention	John 17:22; Isa 6; Eph 2
AO: 197601[--]		La Canada Stadium, California	Bishop Festo Mission	Col 2:6-13
AO: 19760113		*La Canada*, California	Bible Study	Phil 3
AO: 19760203	Searching and Finding Life's Meaning		Bishop Festo's Mission	Luke 15:11ff
AO: 19760524	**Jesus Frees and Unites**			
AO: 19761007*1		Fuller Theological Seminary, Pasadena	Chapel	
AO: 19761007*2		Fuller Theological Seminary, Pasadena	Chapel	Luke 24: 13-33
AO: 19761021	Grain of Wheat Dies - Bring Forth Fruit	Trinity Parish, New York	Special Festo Mission	John 12:20
AO: 19761024	David and Jonathan	Trinity Parish, New York		1 Sam
AO: 197612[--]*1	Growing In All Things Into Christ	Nairobi, Kenya	PACLA	Eph 4:16
AO: 197612[--]*2	Growing Into Him	Nairobi, Kenya	PACLA	Eph 4:16
AO: 19761231	**The Triumph of God's Glory**	Urbana, USA	Mission	

Archive Code	Title	Place	Occasion	Text
AO: 1977[----]*1	The Holy Spirit and Evangelization	Ghana	Ghana Pastors Seminar	John 7:4
AO: 1977[----]*2		Quito, Ecuador	HCJB Annual Conference	Rom 15:5
AO: 1977[----]*3		Finland	Finland Congress on Missions	Gen 21
AO: 19770115		Presbyterian Church, Arcadia, California	Saturday PM Seminar	Mark 10:30
AO: 19770118		Mt Hermon, California	Mt Hermon Conference	Exod 33:12
AO: 19770120	**The Pastor's Joy**	**Mount Hermon, California**	**Pastors' Conference**	**John 20; Ezek 37**
AO: 197702[--]	On Events in Uganda			
AO: 197703[--]	Festo Relates His Escape Story			
AO: 19770313	At Midnight on the Waves	Presbyterian Church, *La Canada*, California	Sunday Afternoon Rally	Mark 6:45-48
AO: 1977[0314?]	**Broken Relationships Restored**	**USA**	**Mission Night**	**Rom 5:1-11**
AO: 19770317	It's the 700 Club		CBN Broadcast	
AO: 19770320		First Presbyterian Church, Pittsburgh, Pennsylvania	Special Meetings	Mark 6:45
AO: 197705[--]*1		Trimont Conference Centre, Virginia	Clergy Conference	Josh 5:13
AO: 197705[--]*2		World Vision Chapel, Monrovia, California	Chapel Service	Luke 9:51
AO: 19770522*1	**Glorified in Them**	**Cathedral of St Philip, Atlanta, Georgia**	**Interim Eucharistic Fellowship**	**John 17**

Catalogue of Kivengere's Sermons 499

Archive Code	Title	Place	Occasion	Text
AO: 19770522*2		Cathedral of St Philip, Atlanta, Georgia	Special Meetings	John 17
AO: 19770523	Peace with God	Cathedral of St. Philip, Atlanta, Georgia	Charismatic Eucharist	Rom 5:1
AO: 197706[--]	Let Your Life and Power Go Out		Robert Schuller Presents	Luke 6
AO: 197707[--]	The Love of Christ	New York City	Missionary Gathering	Rom 5:1-11
AO: 19770712		Ghana	Pastors' Conference, Congress on Evangelization	1 John 1
AO: 19770712-22		Ghana	Ghana Congress on Evangelization	1 John 1:1-8
AO: 19770727		Finland	Finland Congressional Mission	Luke 19:10
AO: 19770728		Finland	Finland Congress on Mission	2 Cor 3:17, 5:15
AO: 197708[--]	Released to Bless	Toronto, Canada - Christian Church on a Hill	Missionary Service	2 Cor 4:5-6
AO: 19770802		Kaiser-Wilhelm Memorial Church, Berlin, Germany	Mission Berlin 77	Gen 3
AO: 1977082-7		Kaiser-Wilhelm Memorial Church, Berlin, Germany	Mission Berlin 77	Gen 3:9
AO: 19770903	Abiding in the Lord	Greystone United Presbyterian Church, Pennsylvania		John 15
AO: 19770904	Love in Action	Greystone United Presbyterian Church, Pennsylvania		John 12:1-6

Archive Code	Title	Place	Occasion	Text
AO: 19771008			Student Conference on World Evangelism	Acts 4:29; 5:4; 7:?
AO: 19771009*1	Global Mission	Berkeley, California		2 Cor 8:9
AO: 19771009*2	The Church's Unfinished Task	Berkeley, California	Global Mission	2 Cor 8:9
AO: 19771009*3	The Church's Unfinished Task	Berkeley, California		2 Cor 8:9
AO: 19771010	Compassion	First Presbyterian Church, Seattle, Washington	World Concern Rally	Matt 9:3ff
AO: 19771013	Renewal and Reconciliation; Fresh and living Way; Discover the Fresh Way; Fresh and Alive	Fremont Presbyterian Church, Sacramento, CA	Harvest of Hope Festival	Rom 7:24-25
AO: 19771015		Fremont Presbyterian Church, Sacramento, California	Youth Rally	Acts 3
AO: 19771016	Ambassadors For Christ in a Miserable World	Fremont Presbyterian Church, Sacramento, California	Sunday Morning Worship	2 Cor 5:13
AO: 19771023	The Freedom that Jesus Brings for Living	All Saints Episcopal Church, Carmel, California	Youth Rally	John 8
AO: 19771025	The Way	Salinas, California	Luncheon	John 14:16
AO: 19771025	Distance and Misery or Brought Near	Grace Cathedral, San Francisco	Bishop Festo Mission	Eph 2:11 ff
AO: 19771026*1	**Broken Relationships Restored**	**Saratoga, California**	**Bishop Festo Mission**	**Eph 2:14-18**

Archive Code	Title	Place	Occasion	Text
AO: 19771026*2	Evangelism	Bay Area, California	Ministry to the laity	2 Kings 7
AO: 19771026*3		Saratoga, California	Evensong	Eph 2:14-18; Gen 45
AO: 19771027	There is hope in Christ	Grace Cathedral, San Francisco, California	Address to the women of the Cathedral	Phil 4:11
AO: 19771028*1		Stanford University, California	C.S. Lewis Lecture	Matt 26
AO: 19771028*2	Bishop Festo Kivengere - Press Conference	Trinity Church, San Francisco, California	Press Conference	
AO: 19771029*1		Grace Cathedral, San Francisco, California	Bishop Festo Mission	Col 1,2
AO: 19771029*2		St Pauls Cathedral, Oakland, California	Youth Night	Matt 19:22-23
AO: 19771030*1	Jesus the Satisfier	Grace Cathedral, San Francisco, California	Sunday Afternoon Special Mission	John 7
AO: 19771030*2	The Good News: The Power of the Gospel	California	Sunday Night Service	Rom 1
AO: 19771030*3	The Good News: the Power of the Gospel	Standford, California		Rom 1:16-21; Phil 1:21
AO: 197711[--]*1	Drawing Near	Quito, Ecuador		Heb 10:9
AO: 197711[--]*2	God of Again and Again	Quito, Ecuador	HCJB Annual Conference	Heb 10:19
AO: 197711[--]*3	Leadership and Reconciliation	Rhodesian C.L.C		Heb 12:1
AO: 197711[--]*4	The Secret of Christian Fellowship	Quito, Ecuador	HCJB Annual Conference	2 Cor 3:17
AO: 19771108*1	The Church of Uganda: Freedom on the Way	Lake Land, Florida	Clergy Conference	

Archive Code	Title	Place	Occasion	Text
AO: 19771108*2		Lake Land, Florida	Diocesan Mission	Heb 12:2ff
AO: 19771120*1		Quito, Ecuador	HCJB Annual Conference	Eph 4:15, 2:11
AO: 19771120*2		Quito, Ecuador	HCJB Annual Conference	2 Cor 2:14-16
AO: 19771129		Quito, Ecuador	HCJB Annual Conference	Heb 12:1-3
AO: 19772910, [#1]	The Unshakable Identity of the Church of Jesus Christ	Grace Cathedral, San Francisco, California	Convention	Col 1:19-22
AO: 1978[02--?]	Life in Jesus	Sydney, Australia	Australia, Bridge '78	Rom 5:1-11
AO: 1978[----], [#1]	Life in Jesus	Sydney, Australia	Australia, Bridge '78	Rom 5:1-11
AO: 1978[----]*1	Forgiveness	Sydney, Australia	Australia Bridge '78	Col 2:12-14
AO: 1978[----]*2	Jesus Makes All the Difference in Life	Sydney, Australia	Australia, Bridge '78	Eph 2:12-14
AO: 1978[----]*3	Kivengere on Christian Directions	Trinity Memorial, Montreal		Rom 15:5
AO: 1978[----]*4	Kivengere on Christian Directions	Trinity Memorial, Montreal		Rom 15:5-7
AO: 1978[----]*5	Mission Service - Zachaeus	Montreal		Luke 16:19-30
AO: 1978[----]*6	Oh My Dirty Feet	All Saints Episcopal Church, Santa Barbara		Luke 22
AO: 1978[----]*7	Zacchaeus	Montreal	Mission Service	Luke 16:19-30
AO: 19780106	God's Love			
AO: 197802[--]*1	Creativity and transcendence	California	North American Congress of the Laity	Col 1:10ff

Catalogue of Kivengere's Sermons 503

Archive Code	Title	Place	Occasion	Text
AO: 197802[--]*2		Wheaton, Illinois	National Association of Evangelicals Meetings	2 Cor 2:14-17
AO: 19780305*1	For Me To Live Is Christ	Evangelical Presbyterian Church, Cairo, Egypt	Egypt Mission	Phil 1
AO: 19780305*2		Salvation of Souls Church, Cairo, Egypt	Egypt Mission	Luke 24:1
AO: 19780306*1		Assuit, Egypt	AE Mission to Egypt	Acts 2
AO: 19780306*2		Assuit, Egypt	Egypt Mission	1 John 3:16
AO: 19780308*1	Forgiven Priest, The Embarrassed Priest	Egypt	Mission in Egypt	Zech, 2-3
AO: 19780308*2		Egypt	Egypt Mission	Zech 2,3
AO: 19780310		Cairo, Egypt	Evangelistic Mission	Gal 5:1; John 8:36
AO: 1978036-7		Assuit, Egypt	Egypt Mission	Zech 3:1-10
AO: 197805[--]	Broken Barriers Down: Brought Near	Wheaton, USA	Wheaton Bible church Missionary Conference	Eph 2:14
AO: 197805[--], [#2]	The Whole Gospel for the Whole World	Wheaton Bible Church, Illinois		Luke 8:46
AO: 19780501	The Centre That Revolutionises	Wheaton College, Illinois		2 Cor 5:19
AO: 19780503	The Revived Church: Its Effectiveness	Wheaton Bible Church		Acts 4:41
AO: 19780505	Compelling Calvary Love	Salvation of Souls Church, Cairo, Egypt	Egypt Mission	Luke 24:13ff
AO: 19780730*1	My God Why?	Lower Hutt, New Zealand		Matt 27:46

Archive Code	Title	Place	Occasion	Text
AO: 19780730*2	My God Why?	Lower Hutt, New Zealand		Matt 27:46
AO: 19780917*1	The Beauty of Renewed Life in Christ	Notre Dame Church, Canda	Festo Mission	Ezek 37
AO: 19780917*2		Notre Dame Church, Canada	Festo Mission	Ezek 37
AO: 19781204		Pasadena AE Office	Pasadena AE Staff Sharing	
AO: 1979[est. After May], [#2]	Christ Has Reconciled the Universe to Himself	Garden Grove, California		Col 1:19-22
AO: 1979[----]	How Barriers Are Broken Through in Evangelism		NRB 36th Annual Convention	Acts 2:5ff
AO: 19790112*1	An Invasion of Freshness	Carrollton, Texas		Heb 10:19-20
AO: 19790112*2	Evangelism	1st United Methodist Church, Carrollton, Dallas, TX	Evangelism Explosion Banquet	John 4
AO: 19790112*3	Living in Harmony	Carrollton, Dallas, Texas	Bible Study	Rom 15
AO: 19790112*4		First United Methodist Church, Carrollton, Dallas, Texas	Special Meeting	Luke 24:13
AO: 19790115	The Joy of Sharing	Carrollton, Dallas, Texas	Clergy Conference	2 Kings 6
AO: 19790116	The Victory Procession, or Fungus or Fragrance	Carrollton, Dallas, Texas	Bible Study	2 Cor 2:12
AO: 19790123	Community Evangelism	Christian Episcopal Church, Hamilton, Wenham, Massachusetts	Easter Special Service	Luke 24:11-36

Catalogue of Kivengere's Sermons 505

Archive Code	Title	Place	Occasion	Text
AO: 19790219	Uganda's Cry - The Challenge of a Suffering Church			Matt 5:10-13
AO: 19790402	I Am the Way	Grace Church, Lawrence, Massachusetts	7:30pm Service	John 14:6
AO: 19790403		Emmanuel Church, West Roxbury, Massachusetts	7:30pm Church	John 14:25
AO: 19790404	The Friendship Which Restores	St Andrews, Framingham, Massachusetts	Church Service	John 15:15
AO: 19790406	The Love that Restores . . .	St Barnabus, Falmouth, Massachusetts	7:30 Church Service	
AO: 19790407		Trinity Church, Copley Square, Boston, Massachusetts	Saturday Conference	
AO: 19790419*1	Renewal in the Spirit and Evangelism is the Outcome.	Eugene, Oregon	Rally at St. Mary's	2 Cor 5:17-18
AO: 19790419*2	The Cross of Christ	Eugene, Oregon	Thursday Morning ECW	1 Cor 1:23-29
AO: 19790429	God Makes All Mankind His Friend Through Christ	Presbyterian Church, *La Canada*, California		2 Cor 5:15
AO: 19790429, [#2]	In Christ	Presbyterian Church, *La Canada*, California		2 Cor 5:18-20
AO: 19790510	World Vision: with Festo Kivengere			
AO: 197906[--]		Dar es Salaam, Tanzania		Phil
AO: 197907[--]*1	Diocesan Tour			

Archive Code	Title	Place	Occasion	Text
AO: 197907[--]*2	Kivengere's Return to Uganda	Nyaruhanga, Uganda		Rev 21:1-8
AO: 197907[--]*3	Nyaruhanga			
AO: 19790704	God's Life-Fulfilling Love	Trinity Church, Copley Sq., Boston, MA	Saturday Conference	Eph 3:14
AO: 19790709	The Task of Rebuilding			
AO: 19790729	FK Returns to Uganda	All Saints Episcopal Church, Kampala, Uganda		2 Cor 4
AO: 19790904	Love in Action	Greystone United Presbyterian Church		John 12
AO: 19790912	God in company with His people #2	First United Methodist Church, Glendale		Col 1:28-29
AO: 19790912	God in Company with His People	1st United Methodist Church, Glendale	RETURN Banquet	Col 1:28-29
AO: 19790930	Jesus' Encounter with Nathaniel	St Michaels and All Angels, Dallas, Texas	Morning Service	John 2
AO: 19791004	World Vision International: New Briefing			
AO: 19791112	Take Your Cross	East Orange, New Jersey		Mark 8:34
AO: 19791231		St Andrews Presbyterian Church, Newport Beach, California		Luke 2:1-23
AO: 198?0503	Christianity Takes Root in East Africa			
AO: 198?0524	Living for Jesus			Acts 2; John 12

Catalogue of Kivengere's Sermons

Archive Code	Title	Place	Occasion	Text
AO: 19800112	Costly Breakthrough	First United Methodist Church, Carollton, Texas		Heb 10:19
AO: 198003[--]*1		Bishop Tucker Theological College, Mukono, Uganda	Pastors' Conference/ Mission	John 13:1-15
AO: 198003[--]*2		Mukono, Uganda	Holy Week Mission	2 Cor 5:14-15
AO: 19800404	The Cross Today and Divine Outreach	Bishop Tucker Theological College, Mukono, Uganda	Good Friday	2 Cor 5:18-20
AO: 19800419*1	Call to Friendship	Church of our saviour, St. Gabriel	Edward Wilson's Priesthood	1 John 1:1-4
AO: 19800419*2	Call to Friendship	St. Gabriel, Church of our Saviour	Edward's Ordination	1 John 1:1-4
AO: 19800421	Divine Sensitivity	Santa Barbara, California		Luke 8:43-48
AO: 19800422		All Saints Episcopal Church, Pasadena, California	Clergy Day Celebration	Matt 9:35-38
AO: 19800424*1	Set Free by Christ	Colorado	Youth Night, Diocese of Colorado	John 8:36
AO: 19800424*2	The Centrality of the Glory of Christ	Colorado	Clergy Conference	Col 1:24-27
AO: 19800424*3	The Outcome of Having Christ in you	Diocese of Colorado	Diocesan Mission	Col 1:28-29; Luke 24
AO: 19800426		Diocese of Colorado	Message to Seminarians	2 Cor 5:13-20
AO: 19800430*1	Rehabilitation, Reconstruction, Reconciliation	St Peters Episcopal Church, California		2 Cor 4:1-6

Archive Code	Title	Place	Occasion	Text
AO: 19800430*2		St. Peter's Episcopal Church, CA	Rehabilitation, Reconstruction, Reconciliation	2 Cor 4:1-6
AO: 19800501		New Haven, Connetticut	AFP Conference	Col 1:16-20
AO: 19800502*1	Freed in Christ	Greenwich, Connecticut	Mission	Gal, Rom 8:1-3, Luke 15, John 8:32
AO: 19800502*2	The Cost of Renewal or Discipleship	New Haven, CT	AFP Conference	John 15:1-16, 2 Cor 4:6-10
AO: 19800503	Unity Among Christians	New Haven, Connecticut	AFP Conference Eucharist Address	Rom 15:3-7
AO: 19800510*1	Prayer and Praise			
AO: 19800510*2	The Resurrection or Burning Hearts	Long Island, New York	Diocesan Conference	Luke 24:30-35
AO: 19800510*3		Christchurch, Diocese of Long Island	Special Mission	Luke 1:39ff
AO: 19800511*1	God's Short-Cut to Humanity	Christ Church Greenwich, CT	Diocesan Mission	Heb 10:19-22
AO: 19800511*2	Jesus Opens the Living Way for Humanity	Christchurch, Greenwich, CT	Diocesan Mission	Heb 10:19-22
AO: 19800511*3	Put Your Confidence in God	Diocese of Long Island, NY	Diocesan Mission	John 14:6
AO: 19800511*4	Put Your Confidence in God	Diocese of Long Island, NY	Diocesan Mission	John 14:6
AO: 19800511*5	Put your confidence in God	Diocese of Long Island	Diocesan Mission	John 14:6, Rom 7:14
AO: 19800511*6		Long Island	Diocesan Mission	John 14:6; Rom 7:19

Catalogue of Kivengere's Sermons 509

Archive Code	Title	Place	Occasion	Text
AO: 19801005*1	The Master Came Down	St. Andrew's Presbyterian Church, Newport Beach, CA	World Communion Sunday	Luke 22:14-20
AO: 19801005*2		St Andrews Presbyterian Church, Newport Beach, California		Luke 22:19
AO: 19801007	Compassion Harvest	University Club, Pasadena		Matt 9:35-36
AO: 19801010*1	Evangelism	Buffalo, Western New York	Diocesan Mission	John 1:4-5 (Acts 19)
AO: 19801010*2	That I May Become	St James Episcopal Church, Buffalo, New York	Evensong	John 1:2
AO: 19801010*3		Buffalo, New York	Diocesan Mission	John 1:4-5
AO: 19801010*4		Buffalo, New York	Diocesan Mission - Clergy Meeting	2 Cor 4:6
AO: 19801011*1	Finding the Real Me	St. James Episcopal Church, New York	Diocese of Western New York, Youth Day	Luke 19:1-10
AO: 19801011*2	Finding the Real Me	St. James Episcopal Church, New York, Diocese of Western New York	Youth Day	Luke 19:1-10
AO: 19801011*3	Homily on the Eucharist	Buffalo, New York	Diocese of Western New York	Luke 24:36ff
AO: 19801012*1	God Offers His Friendship	St. Luke's Episcopal Church, Jamestown, New York	Diocesan Mission	2 Cor 5:14-17
AO: 19801012*2	God offers His friendship	St. Luke's Episcopal Church, Jamestown, New York	Diocesan Mission	2 Cor 5:14-17

Archive Code	Title	Place	Occasion	Text
AO: 19801012*3		St Paul's Episcopal Cathedral, Buffalo, New York	Diocesan Mission	2 Cor 5:19-21
AO: 19801014	No Longer Strangers or No More Distance	Diocese of West Missouri, Kansas City	Youth Rally	Eph 2:13
AO: 19801014, [#1]	**No More Distances in the Love of Christ**	**Kansas, Missouri**	**Youth Rally, Diocese of Western Missouri**	**Eph 2:13**
AO: 19801015	The Essence of Christian Faith in a Person (Christ in Action)	St. Michael and All Angels' Episcopal Church, Kansas City, Western Missouri	Episcopal Church women's service	John 5:1-18
AO: 19801021	Vitality, Focus and Harmony	St. George's Church, Fredericksburg, Virginia	Diocesan Conference - Morning Address	Rom 15:1-7, Acts 2:1-11
AO: 19801024*1	The Ministry and Evangelism	Diocese of Western Kansas	Clergy Conference	Luke 24:13-39
AO: 19801024*2		Salina, Kansas	Diocesan Convention Morning Banquet	Luke 10:25-37
AO: 19801024*3		Kansas	Friday Morning Service, Clergy Conference, Diocese of Western Kansas	Luke 24:13-30
AO: 19801024*4		Western Kansas	Diocesan Mission	Luke 24:13-39
AO: 19801026*1	**The Basis of Right Relationship with God**	**Christ Church Overland Park, Kansas City**	**Diocesan Mission**	**2 Cor 8:9**
AO: 19801026*2	The Basis of Right Relationship with God	Christchurch, Overland Park, Kansas City	Diocesan Mission	2 Cor 8:9

Catalogue of Kivengere's Sermons 511

Archive Code	Title	Place	Occasion	Text
AO: 19801026*3		Christ Church, Overland Park, Kansas City, Missouri	Diocesan Mission	2 Cor 8
AO: 19801026*4		Christ Church Overland Park, Kansas	Diocesan Mission	2 Cor 8:8-9
AO: 19801225	Jesus Came As Light and Life for Men			
AO: 1981[----]*1	A Special Lecture	Trinity Episcopal School For Ministry, USA		
AO: 1981[----]*2		Kenya	Team Meeting Talk	2 Cor 4:1-6
AO: 198101[--]*1	The Crew of the Good Ship Grace	Hollywood, California		Matt 9
AO: 198101[--]*2		Mission to UK		2 Cor 5:14
AO: 198101[--]*3		Norwich, UK	UK Mission	Acts 3:1-16
AO: 198101[--]*4		UK	UK Mission	Luke 10:25-37
AO: 198102[--]	Love God - Love Neighbour and Share	Conejo Valley, Thousand Oaks, California	Festival of Faith	2 Cor 8:9
AO: 19810201	Love God - Love Neighbour and Move	Conejo Valley, Thousand Oaks, California	Festival of Faith	John 11:33-40, John 12
AO: 19810208	Love God: Love Neighbour and Live	Conejo Valley, Thousand Oaks, California	Festival of Faith	Luke 10:25-37
AO: 19810209	Love God: Love Neighbour and Move	Thousand Oaks, California	Conejo Valley, Festival of Faith	John 11:33-40 and John 12
AO: 19810210*1	Love God - Neighbour and Become	Conejo Valley, Thousand Oaks, California	Festival of Faith	Luke 10:25-37

Archive Code	Title	Place	Occasion	Text
AO: 19810210*2	Love god: Love neighbour and Become	Conejo Valley, Thousand Oaks, California	Festival of Faith	Luke 10:25-37
AO: 19810211	Love God-Love Neighbour and Share	Conejo Valley, Thousand Oaks, California	Festival of Faith	2 Cor 8:9; John 10:17; 1 John 3
AO: 19810212*1	Love God - Love Neighbour and tell the good news	Conejo Valley, Thousand Oaks, California	Festival of Faith	2 Kings 7:1-9
AO: 19810212*2	Love God: Love Neighbour and Tell the Good news	Conejo Valley, Thousand Oaks, California	Festival of Faith	2 Kings 7: 1-9
AO: 19810212*3	The Life-giving Fragrance	St. Patrick's Episcopal Church, Conejo Valley, Thousand Oaks, California	Festival of Faith	2 Cor 12-14, John 12
AO: 19810215	We Are in Partnership	Tennessee	Diocesan Mission	Luke 6
AO: 19810216*1	Come Down Where the Master Stood	Central Presbyterian Church, Chattanooga, Tennessee	Clergy Luncheon	Luke 6:12
AO: 19810216*2		Central Presbyterian Church, Chattanooga, Tennessee	Clergy Luncheon	Luke 6:12
AO: 19810217		Grace Episcopal Church, Chattanooga, Tennessee		2 Cor 8:9
AO: 198110[--]*1	From Uganda With Love	Kendall, UK	Mission	2 Cor 4:5
AO: 198110[--]*2	Jesus Is Good News			
AO: 198110[--], [#1]	The Reconciling Love of Christ	Sheffield, UK		2 Cor 5:18-20

Catalogue of Kivengere's Sermons 513

Archive Code	Title	Place	Occasion	Text
AO: 19811020-21			Mission to UK	2 Cor 5:14
AO: 19811101		Trinity Presbyterian Church, Santa Ana, California		Luke 7:36
AO: 19811102	I am the Light of the World	Pasadena, California	AE Staff	John 8
AO: 19811108		First Presbyterian Church, Bradendon, Florida		Gal 2:20
AO: 19811111		Hope Presbyterian Church, Minneapolis, Minnesota	Missions Conference	1 Peter 2?
AO: 19811114	Zacchaeus	Christian Episcopal Church, Pittsburgh	Youth Service	Luke 16
AO: 19811115*1		Immanuel Church, Pittsburgh, Pennsylvania		John 1:14
AO: 19811115*2		Trinity Cathedral, Pittsburgh, Pennsylvania		John 1:14
AO: 19811116	Bread of Life	Christ Episcopal Church, Pittsburgh, Pennsylvania		Acts 2
AO: 19811117		Ascension Church, Pittsburgh, Pennsylvania	Episcopal Clergy	Exod 33:18,19
AO: 19811118*1		Trinity Episcopal Church for Ministry	Lecture to seminary students	
AO: 19811118*2		Trinity Episcopal School for Ministry, Ambridge, Pennsylvania		

Archive Code	Title	Place	Occasion	Text
AO: 19811122*1	Shares about Africa and Work of PB Fund	Holy Trinity Episcopal Church, Diocese of Pennsylvania	Rally. Festo Shari	Eph 2
AO: 19811122*2	Shares about Africa and Work of PB Fund	Holy Trinity Episcopal Church, Diocese of Pennsylvania	Rally. Festo Shari	Eph 2
AO: 19811122		Diocese of Pennsylvania - St. David's		Eph 2:11
AO: 19820123*1	Devotions	Nairobi	International Council Meeting	Gen 4
AO: 19820123*2		International Council Meeting, Nairobi	Devotions	Gen 4
AO: 19820131	Salt and Light	Nyeri, Kenya	ICT - Devotions before Communion	Matt 5
AO: 19820208		St Christopher		Matt 28:16
AO: 19820214	The Tower of Babel	All Saints By The Sea Church, Santa Barbara, California		Gen 11
AO: 19820215	God's Flooding Love			
AO: 19820216	20th Anniversary of African Enterprise	Pasadena, California	20th Anniversary of AE	2 Kings 4
AO: 19820218		St. Christopher		Matt 28:16
AO: 19820219		Truro Episcopal Church, Fairfax, Virginia	Prayer and praise service	Rev 7
AO: 19820220		Truro Episcopal Church		2 Cor 8:9

Catalogue of Kivengere's Sermons 515

Archive Code	Title	Place	Occasion	Text
AO: 19820221	Jesus Came as a Missionary of Reconciliation	Livonin, MI (Ward Presbyterian Church)	Missionary Commitment	2 Cor 5:14-19
AO: 19820222		Cathedral, Detroit		Matt 7:28
AO: 19820226		Burbank, California	World Wide Pictures	Rev 5:5ff
AO: 19820228*1	Lent	First Presbyterian Church, Pittsburgh, Pennsylvania	Evening Service	Matt 25:3
AO: 19820228*2	Lent	First Presbyterian Church, Pittsburgh, Pennsylvania	Morning Service	Matt 4
AO: 19820301	Relief, Reconciliation, Reconstruction	Pittsburgh, Pennsylvania		Matt 25:40
AO: 19820312*1		Pasadena, California	AE Staff Chapel	2 Cor 3:12-18
AO: 19820312*2			Interview with Bishop Festo, Dick White	
AO: 198204[--], [#1]	Reconciliation	Israel	Celebration of Evangelism	2 Cor 5:18-20
AO: 19820504	Hearts Aflame with God's Love			2 Cor 5:13-20
AO: 19820505	The Debt I Owe			2 Cor 5:13-20
AO: 19820510	The Secret of Fellowship			Col 3:9-15
AO: 19820511	The Secret of Working Together			Col 3:9-15
AO: 19820512	Walking in the Light With the Brethren			John 8:1-12

Archive Code	Title	Place	Occasion	Text
AO: 19820514	We Preach Christ, the Only Message of Hope			Col 1:25-29
AO: 19820527	A Shared Life			John 12:22-24
AO: 19820528	Rediscover the Meaning of Service to Humanity			John 12:22
AO: 19820601	The Church's Unfinished Task			2 Cor 8:9
AO: 19820602	Evangelism Begins in a Crisis			Luke 24:11; John 20:19
AO: 19820603	Exciting Evangelism			Luke 24:11-36
AO: 19820604	Participating in the Mission of Evangelism			John 20:19; Luke 24:11-36
AO: 19820607	The Good News - The Power of the Gospel			Rom 1:16ff; Phil 1:21
AO: 19820608	I am not afraid of the good news			Rom 1:16-21
AO: 19820610	Winsome Witnessing			John 4
AO: 19820611	Share the good news			John 4
AO: 19820615	I am a Universal Debtor			Rom 1:14
AO: 19820616	Announcers of the Good News		Laity Evangelism	2 Kings 7
AO: 19820617	Announcers in Action		Laity Evangelism	2 Kings 7
AO: 19820628	Unity Through Fellowship in Prayer			Col 1
AO: 19820630*1	Being Transformed Into His Image			2 Cor 3:12-18

Catalogue of Kivengere's Sermons 517

Archive Code	Title	Place	Occasion	Text
AO: 19820630*2	Being Transformed Into his Image			2 Cor 3:12-18
AO: 19820703*1	The Blindness that Can Be Cured	Carmel Presbeteryan Church	Church Service	Mark 10
AO: 19820703*2	The Blindness that Can be Cured	Carmel Presbyterian Church		Mark 10
AO: 19820827	Jesus: The Treasurer			
AO: 19821012, [#1]	A New Way of Seeing Jesus	Holy Trinity Church, Cambridge		Eph 2
AO: 19821110		Cheltenham, Gloucestershire		1 John 3:11
AO: 19821113		Pittsburgh, Pennsylvania	Talk to the clergy	
AO: 19830715	The Evangelist's Ministry of Reconciliation: We Are Christ's Ambassador's	Amsterdam	Address to Evangelists	
AO: 19850506	Ambassadors for Christ			2 Cor 5:13-20
AO: 1987[----]	The Spiritual Life of a Pastor	Sydney		
AO: [----]05[--]	The World We Are In	Santa Barbara, All Saints Episcopal Church	Mother's Day	Eph 3
AO: [----]0522	Candidate of Grace	Blue fields, Nicaragua		2 Cor 3:6
AO: [--------]*1	Festo Kivengere's Return			
AO: [--------]*2	Jesus is the Fulfilment of the Old Testament			
AO: [--------]*3	All Things Are Yours			1 Cor 3; Eph 3

Archive Code	Title	Place	Occasion	Text
AO: [--------]*4	All Things are Yours	All Saints Church, Santa Barbara, California		1 Cor 3
AO: [--------]*5	Bankrupt			Phil 4:12
AO: [--------]*6	Calvary Love			2 Cor 5:13
AO: [--------]*7	Christ, the Liberator	Keswick, UK	Keswick Convention	2 Cor 5:14
AO: [--------]*8	Come Near to Me (Grace and Guilt)			John 8:1ff
AO: [--------]*9	Come near to me (Grace and Guilt)			John 8:1ff
AO: [--------]*10	Darkness to Light			1 Peter 1:22
AO: [--------]*11	Darkness to Light			Col 1:13
AO: [--------]*12	Entangled Spiritual Life			Heb 12:1-17
AO: [--------]*13	Entering Christ's Kingdom			
AO: [--------]*14	Entering Christ's Kingdom			John 17
AO: [--------]*15	Entering Christ's Kingdom			John 17
AO: [--------]*16	Expose Your Life to the Touch of Calvary			Luke 4:16
AO: [--------]*17	Extravagant Love			John 12:1-8
AO: [--------]*18	Extravagant Love			John 12:1-8
AO: [--------]*19	Feet, Please			Luke 22:24
AO: [--------]*20	Fellowship and Harmony	Melody Land, California		Phil 2
AO: [--------]*21	Force and Power			1 Cor ?:23-24

Catalogue of Kivengere's Sermons

Archive Code	Title	Place	Occasion	Text
AO: [--------]*22	Forgiveness			Col 2:13
AO: [--------]*23	Fragments of Life			Rom 7:1; 2 Cor 5:17
AO: [--------]*24	From Quarrelling to Singing			Luke 22:24
AO: [--------]*25	Fumes of Fragrance			2 Cor 2:12-14
AO: [--------]*26	God's Flooding Love	Westmont College, Santa Barbara, CA	Chapel Service	Col 1:14-19; 1 John 5: 6-7; Rom 5:1-5
AO: [--------]*27	God's Flooding Love	Westmont College, Santa Barbara, CA	Chapel Service	Col 1:14-19, John 5:6-7, Rom 5:1-5
AO: [--------]*28	God's Intervening Love			Rom 5:1-10; 7:12-25
AO: [--------]*29	Grace of Jesus			2 Cor 8:9
AO: [--------]*30	His Flooding Love	Santa Barbara, California		Rom 5:1-8
AO: [--------]*31	How Does it Work?	All Saints Church, Santa Barbara		Eph 3
AO: [--------]*32	I Am Your Brother			Gen 21:2-30
AO: [--------]*33	In His Fellowship			
AO: [--------]*34	Irrepressible			Rom 5:1-5
AO: [--------]*35	Is Race Prejudice Soluble?	UCLA, California		Phil 3
AO: [--------]*36	Jacob, Seeker After Blessings			Gen 27
AO: [--------]*37	Jacob's Ladder			Gen 28
AO: [--------]*38	Jesus Came All The Way: Jesus Says "Come"			Matt 11:28
AO: [--------]*39	Jesus Himself Draws Near: The Appearance		Easter	John 20; Luke 24:13-30

Archive Code	Title	Place	Occasion	Text
AO: [--------]*40	Laity Evangelism	Saratoga, California	Laity Evangelism Mission	2 Kings 7
AO: [--------]*41	Liberated to Live			Lev 25:10
AO: [--------]*42	Liberated to Live in Right Relationship	Lausanne, Switzerland	Preaching in the Lausanne R.C. Cathedral	Eph 1:6
AO: [--------]*43	Life Running Over			Luke 24:13ff
AO: [--------]*44	Life Set Free			2 Cor 3:12
AO: [--------]*45	Love Embracing, Peace be with you, Prodigal Son			Luke 24:36
AO: [--------]*46	Love Providing (the Prodigal Son comes home)			Luke 15:21-32
AO: [--------]*47	Love Providing: The Prodigal Son Comes Home			Luke 15:21-32
AO: [--------]*48	Love That Breaks Barriers: The Power of the Gospel			Rom 1:12
AO: [--------]*49	Martha and Mary and Lazarus			Luke 10; John 11
AO: [--------]*50	Ministering Women	All Saints		
AO: [--------]*51	Moses on the Mount			Exod 34
AO: [--------]*52	My Cup Overflows			Psalm 23
AO: [--------]*53	New Life in Christ			
AO: [--------]*54	Pentecost		Outlook	Acts 2

Catalogue of Kivengere's Sermons

Archive Code	Title	Place	Occasion	Text
AO: [--------]*55	Pentecost		Outlook	Acts 2
AO: [--------]*56	Personal Encounter with a Mighty Saviour			Rom 7:14-15; Phil 3
AO: [--------]*57	Personal revival		Discipleship Series	Gen 27:14
AO: [--------]*58	Preach Forgiveness			John 8:1-11; Acts 8:35
AO: [--------]*59	Preach Forgiveness			
AO: [--------]*60	Preach Forgiveness	Ethiopia	Radio Voice of the Gospel Conference	John 8:1-11 (Acts 8:35)
AO: [--------]*61	Preach Jesus			Acts 8:35; John 8:1-11
AO: [--------]*62	Preach Jesus			Acts 8:35 (John 8:1-11)
AO: [--------]*63	Release for Captives: Why He Came			John 10:10; Isa 61
AO: [--------]*64	Revival in East Africa: Fullness of the Spirit	Melody land, California		Rom 5:1-5
AO: [--------]*65	Saints in Hiding			2 Cor 3:12
AO: [--------]*66	Sharing the Bread of Life and Sharing a loaf of Bread to the hungry			Acts 2; John 12
AO: [--------]*67	Speak The Truth in Love		Bible Study with lay men	Eph 4:15
AO: [--------]*68	Stooping Down			John 13
AO: [--------]*69	Talking to Young People	Trinity, Pennsylvania		Rom 7
AO: [--------]*70	The Balanced Life	Westmont College, Santa Barbara, California	College Chapel	1 John 1:5

Archive Code	Title	Place	Occasion	Text
AO: [--------]*71	The Cross at the Centre			2 Cor 5:1-21
AO: [--------]*72	The Family	Australia	Gospel Extension Mission	Gen 2:18
AO: [--------]*73	The Holy Spirit's Miracle			Rom 8
AO: [--------]*74	The Key to the Fullness of Life			2 Kings 4:1-7
AO: [--------]*75	The Lamb of God			2 Cor 16
AO: [--------]*76	The Leper Cleansed			Lev 13:45-46; 2 Kings 7
AO: [--------]*77	The Liberating Christ	Santa Barbara, California		Rom 5:1-8
AO: [--------]*78	The Lordship of Christ			
AO: [--------]*79	The Love of Christ Leaves Us No Choice		Message to South Africans	2 Cor 5:14; John 12:24
AO: [--------]*80	The Love that Breaks Barriers	Pasadena (?)		Eph 2:1-2; 14
AO: [--------]*81	The Loving Hand	England (?)		Eph 2
AO: [--------]*82	The Power of the Gospel			Rom 1:13
AO: [--------]*83	The Prodigal Son, or Seeking Fulfilment			Luke 15:11-16; Gal 1:11ff
AO: [--------]*84	The Redeeming love			Col 1:13
AO: [--------]*85	The Released Life			Luke 7:36-50; Rom 7:12-25
AO: [--------]*86	The Samaritan Woman			John 4; Isa 53; 2 Cor 3
AO: [--------]*87	The Samaritan Woman			John 4, Isa 53, 2 Cor 3:17
AO: [--------]*88	The Two-Edged Sword	St Louis, Missouri	St Louis School of Evangelism	Heb 4

Archive Code	Title	Place	Occasion	Text
AO: [--------]*89	The War is Over			Eph 2:7
AO: [--------]*90	The Woman caught in Adultery - Released Life			John 8:1
AO: [--------]*91	The Woman Caught in Adultery: Released Life			John 8:1
AO: [--------]*92	Two Messages on the Samaritan Woman			
AO: [--------]*93	Two Messages on the Samaritan Woman			
AO: [--------]*94	What is Your Name?			Gen 27-33
AO: [--------]*95	'What is Your name?'			Gen 27-33
AO: [--------]*96	Where Are You?			Gen 1-3
AO: [--------]*97	Woman Taken in Adultery - Loved Much Because Forgiven Much	Ethiopia	Radio voice of the Gospel Conference	John 8:1
AO: [--------]*98	Zacchaeus Found the Centre For His Life			Luke 19:2ff
AO: [--------]*99		Garden Grove, California		Col 1
AO: [--------]*100		Ethiopia	Radio Voice of the Gospel Conference	John 8:1
AO: [--------]*101		Keswick, UK	Keswick Convention	John 8:1-11
AO: [--------]*102		Keswick, UK	Jesus International	John 7:37-38
AO: [--------]*103		Switzerland	Crusade	Rom 12-13

Archive Code	Title	Place	Occasion	Text
AO: [--------]*104		Westmont College, Santa Barbara, California	Chapel Service	Col 1:14-19; 1 John 5:6
AO: [--------]*105		Norwich, New York?		Acts 20:22; Rom 5:4-5
AO: [--------]*106		London, UK	Conference	Song of Sol 2:4
AO: [--------]*107		Dr Schuller's Church, Garden Grove, California		Col 1
AO: [--------]*108		Westmont College, Santa Barbara, California	Chapel	Col 1:14-19
AO: [--------]*109		Cathedral Detroi		Matt 7:28
AO: [--------]*110		Garden Grove, CA - Dr. Schuller's Church		Col 1

Langham Literature and its imprints are a ministry of Langham Partnership.

Langham Partnership is a global fellowship working in pursuit of the vision God entrusted to its founder John Stott -

to facilitate the growth of the church in maturity and Christ-likeness through raising the standards of biblical preaching and teaching.

Our vision is to see churches equipped for mission and growing to maturity in Christ through the ministry of pastors and leaders who believe, teach and live by the Word of God.

Our mission is to strengthen the ministry of the Word of God through:
- nurturing national movements for training in biblical preaching
- multiplying the creation and distribution of evangelical literature
- strengthening the theological training of pastors and leaders by qualified evangelical teachers

Our ministry
Langham Preaching partners with national leaders to nurture indigenous biblical preaching movements for pastors and lay preachers all around the world. With the support of a team of trainers from many countries, a multi-level programme of seminars provides practical training, and is followed by a programme for training local facilitators. Local preachers' groups and national and regional networks ensure continuity and ongoing development, seeking to build vigorous movements committed to Bible exposition.

Langham Literature provides majority world pastors, scholars and seminary libraries with evangelical books and electronic resources through grants, discounts and distribution. The programme also fosters the creation of indigenous evangelical books for pastors in many languages, through training workshops for writers and editors, sponsored writing, translation, strengthening local evangelical publishing houses, and investment in major regional literature projects, such as one volume Bible commentaries like *The Africa Bible Commentary*.

Langham Scholars provides financial support for evangelical doctoral students from the majority world so that, when they return home, they may train pastors and other Christian leaders with sound, biblical and theological teaching. This programme equips those who equip others. Langham Scholars also works in partnership with majority world seminaries in strengthening evangelical theological education. A growing number of Langham Scholars study in high quality doctoral programmes in the majority world itself. As well as teaching the next generation of pastors, graduated Langham Scholars exercise significant influence through their writing and leadership.

To learn more about Langham Partnership and the work we do visit **langham.org**

www.ingramcontent.com/pod-product-compliance
Lightning Source LLC
Chambersburg PA
CBHW050300010526
44108CB00040B/1903